STRATEGIC MARKETING FOR NONPROFIT ORGANIZATIONS

Seventh
Edition

STRATEGIC MARKETING FOR NONPROFIT ORGANIZATIONS

Alan R. Andreasen

Georgetown University

Philip Kotler

Northwestern University

UPPER SADDLE RIVER, NJ 07458

Library of Congress Cataloging-in-Publication Data

Andreasen, Alan R.
  Strategic marketing for nonprofit organizations/Alan R. Andreasen, Philip Kotler. —7th ed.
    p. cm.
  Includes bibliographical references and index.
  ISBN 978-0-13-175372-3 (hardcover : alk. paper)
  1. Nonprofit organizations—Marketing. I. Kotler, Philip. II. Title.
  HF5415.K6312 2007
  658.8'02—dc22

                                                                        2007032487

Editor in Chief: David Parker
Product Development Manager: Ashley Santora
Editorial Assistant: Christine Ietto
Senior Managing Editor: Judy Leale
Permissions Coordinator: Charles Morris
Manufacturing Buyer: Arnold Vila
Cover Design: Kiwi Design
Cover Photo: Guggenheim Museum, Bilboa, Cantabria, Spain/Gavin Hellier/Nature Picture Photography
Manager, Cover Visual Research & Permissions: Karen Sanatar
Composition: Integra Software Services
Full-Service Project Management: BookMasters, Inc.
Printer/Binder: Courier/Westford
Typeface: 10/12 Times Ten

Credits and acknowledgments borrowed from other sources and reproduced, with permission, in this textbook appear on appropriate page within text.

Pearson Education LTD.
Pearson Education Singapore, Pte. Ltd
Pearson Education, Canada, Ltd
Pearson Education–Japan

Pearson Education Australia PTY, Limited
Pearson Education North Asia Ltd
Pearson Educación de Mexico, S.A. de C.V.
Pearson Education Malaysia, Pte. Ltd.

10 9 8 7 6 5 4 3 2 1
ISBN-13: 978-0-13-175372-3
ISBN-10: 0-13-175372-X

To Jean Manning, an unending source of great ideas, insightful interpretations, and encouragement.
—*Alan Andreasen*

To Neil Kotler for his deep expertise on the museum world and to Milton Kotler for his deep expertise on nonprofit organizations and China.
—*Philip Kotler*

Brief Contents

SECTION V   ORGANIZING AND CONTROLLING MARKETING
             STRATEGIES   439

Contents

Preface

In the preface to the previous edition of this book, we stated that "nonprofit marketing is poised to have a much greater impact on the field of nonprofit management and on the growing intersection between that sector and the business world." This seventh edition reflects the fact that this impact is now a reality. A number of developments have caused this to happen. First, nonprofit organizations and government agencies are increasingly being pressured to adopt business models and frameworks to guide their operations. Second, the social sector is increasingly populated at the top and at middle-management levels by individuals with business backgrounds and appreciation for what business concepts and tools can do for their new environments.

Third, the concept of "social enterprise" has become much more prominent as a way of thinking about ventures that both social and commercial entities are undertaking. Major scholarship is being devoted to it. Think tanks and training centers are emerging or strengthening at places like Stanford, Duke, and other universities. Payoffs to business have been recognized since at least the 1980s, but a new driver has been the corporate scandals of the twenty-first century. The prominence of the Enron and WorldCom tragedies has led many corporations to invest more heavily—or at least give the appearance of investing—in efforts to make society better.

Finally, a number of major events have cast a brighter light on the social sector and its need for top management. First, natural disasters such as the Southeast Asia tsunami, Pakistan earthquake, and Hurricane Katrina have brought into vivid relief the important role of nonprofit organizations and government agencies in providing rapid responses to natural and manmade calamities. The second set of major events is the dramatic increase in scale of giving by prominent businesspeople like Bill and Melinda Gates, Warren Buffet, Richard Branson, and companies like Google and Yahoo! to address huge world problems like HIV/AIDS.

We have argued that marketing is among the most critical—if not *the* most critical—discipline needed for nonprofit success. Just as in the private sector, success ultimately requires that nonprofits influence behavior in a wide range of key target markets—clients, funders, policy makers, volunteers, and the media, as well as the nonprofit's own staff. This is the province of marketing because marketing is basically the "behavioral influence function." The book positions marketing as central to top management's achievement of the organization's mission. We believe that everyone in nonprofit management—including the CEO—ought to have a thorough grounding in marketing and what it does and can do.

CHANGES TO THIS EDITION

This seventh edition significantly increases the emphasis on key managerial issues. For example, in Chapter 1, we spend much more time focusing on the challenges of marketers and marketing to influence multiple audiences. In the private sector, marketers focus on one audience—target customers—and are evaluated by their ability to drive up sales and market share, thereby pleasing shareholders. In the nonprofit world, marketers have three key publics to influence if their organizations are to grow and prosper. First, there are clients who may or may not provide sales revenues but whose patronage is a key indicator of success. Second, there are various funding agencies and individuals who have to see progress and social value in order to keep providing resources. Finally, there are the volunteers who are often the major resource that organizations like Habitat for Humanity International find essential for achieving their goals. In the private sector, one focus can guide action. In the nonprofit world, many balls must be kept rolling forward—and sometimes success with one audience does not lead to success with another.

Two additional major changes in this edition are the elimination of the chapter on social marketing, incorporating its material throughout other chapters, and the addition of a new chapter on branding. In Chapter 3 on strategy, we make clear that there are two major classes of marketing challenges facing nonprofits. First, there are organizational-level challenges that impact funding and volunteering and broad choices about client missions. Second, there are what we call campaign challenges. These are the efforts to focus on specific behavioral outcomes, including campaigns to obtain legislation and media attention, as well as more responsible behavior by citizens. Social marketing is really a way of looking at campaign efforts, so the material that was once in a dedicated chapter is now salted throughout the new edition. The distinction between organizational and campaign efforts is carried through many revised chapters, particularly that on public relations which has a new section on public advocacy.

Branding is an increasingly "hot" topic in the nonprofit world. Nonprofits are recognizing that branding is critical at the organizational level and have even made efforts to determine the value of their organizational branding. Branding is also critical for specific campaigns as in the truth® campaign of the American Legacy Foundation, and more and more nonprofits are seeking ways to replicate their branding success. In Chapter 7, we focus both on the challenges of implementing a branding focus and on how in practice it ought to be carried out.

A final major change is in wording throughout the manuscript. A difficult problem in discussing nonprofit marketing is that it often does not involve any products and services. So one must ask: In such cases, what is it that a nonprofit really offers? We have drawn on recent thinking in the private sector about the essence of organizational offerings and used the term "value proposition" to encapsulate what a marketer offers. Sometimes this proposition can include physical goods or service delivery, but when you are seeking to get someone to lose weight or get off drugs, you must present them with a value proposition that will get them to take—or begin to take—the appropriate actions. We elaborate on this conceptualization throughout the text, for example referring to "offer" rather than "product" management in Chapters 8 and 9.

There are other important changes and additions in this edition:

1. We have reorganized the chapter sequence, setting out broad concepts and tools in Sections I and II and then following through on major elements of campaigns in Section III. Section IV then turns to the challenges of raising resources from other sources, funders, volunteers, and the private sector. Section V then concludes by considering the problems of organizing and controlling marketing efforts.

2. Entirely new vignettes drawn from the popular press have been added to every chapter. These include stories about the KaBOOM! executive who discovered a new control tool while sitting in a Home Depot office, nude calendars, why voters are perhaps best understood by the stores they patronize, how the Special Olympics cracked into Hollywood, why the Salvation Army worries about getting too big a donation, and why Mohammed Yunis and the Grameen Bank won the 2006 Nobel Peace Prize.

3. Of course, all of the basic data about the nonprofit sector has been updated including the latest findings on the extent of the nonprofit sector in 35 countries worldwide from the Johns Hopkins Center for Civil Society Studies.

4. New, thought-provoking questions to engage students at both undergraduate and graduate levels are now found at the end of every chapter.

5. Hundreds of new endnotes have been added including books, articles, and websites, many from 2005 and 2006.

6. References to marketing research and related topics have been subsumed under the broader term "knowledge management." When one thinks of organizations that are not prized for their concrete offerings, what sets them apart is their ability to accumulate and interpret relevant data—particularly about various target audiences. "Knowledge management" is a useful rubric to emphasize the core competencies that set really great nonprofit organizations like AARP apart.

7. We continue to include new thought-provoking reflections from those on the cutting edge of nonprofit marketing such as Cynthia Currence, Vice President of International Marketing at the American Red Cross, and Bill Smith, Senior Vice President at the Academy for Educational Development.

8. Communications discussions have been extended in many chapters to include the new phenomena of blogging, video sharing, gaming, and related new channels for influence.

SUPPLEMENTS

Instructor's Manual with Test Item File

The Instructor's Manual with Test Item File has been updated to reflect the changes to this edition. This supplement is available online only and can be downloaded by instructors from **www.prenhall.com**.

SafariX eTextbooks Online

Developed for students looking to save money on required or recommended textbooks, SafariX eTextbooks Online saves students money compared to the suggested list price of the print text. Students simply select their eText by title or author and purchase immediate access to the content for the duration of the course using any major credit card. With a SafariX eText, students can search for specific keywords or page numbers, make notes online, print out reading assignments that incorporate lecture notes, and bookmark important passages for later review. For more information, or to purchase a SafariX eTextbook, visit **www.safarix.com**.

ACKNOWLEDGMENTS

The first two editions of this book were the result of a happy association between Philip Kotler and extremely creative and valued colleagues and students in the marketing department of the J. L. Kellogg Graduate School of Management at Northwestern University, including Bobby J. Calder, Richard M. Clewett, Jehoshua Eliashberg, Trudy Kehret, Lakshmanan Krishnamurthi, Stephen A. LaTour, Sidney J. Levy, Api Ruzdic, Louis W. Stern, Brian Sternthal, Alice M. Tybout, and Andris A. Zoltners, as well as reviews by Paul Bloom (University of North Carolina), Roberta N. Clarke (Boston University), and Karen F. A. Fox (University of Santa Clara).

The next four editions, in which Alan Andreasen participated, reflected the input of many additional academics and nonprofit practitioners. Particularly valuable were—and continue to be—the insights of Jean Manning, Bill Smith, Michael Ramah, Rob Gould, Bill Novelli, Robert Hornik, Ed Maibach, Cynthia Currence, Susan Kirby, Tom Reis, Sharyn Sutton, Kurt Aschermann, Jim Austin, Christine Letts, Jim Mintz, Carol Bryant, Bob Denniston, Michael Rothschild, and Paul Bloom. This seventh edition adds many people to the cast of influential colleagues, including Adrian Sargeant, Les Silverman, Joe Fay, Gerard Hastings, Jeff French, Clive Blair-Stevens, Cynthia Round, Nancy Lee, and Kash Rangan. Georgetown University research assistant Meenal Balar provided international material, arranged for many of the illustrations, and provided some of the end-of-chapter questions. Research assistant Michelle Clark provided tables, secondary sources, and an evaluation example.

SECTION I

DEVELOPING A TARGET AUDIENCE ORIENTATION

1

THE GROWTH AND DEVELOPMENT OF NONPROFIT MARKETING

POLITICS AND WAL-MART

The bottom line for any political candidate is to get people to vote for him or her. To get to that point, word of mouth about the candidate needs to be positive and the media need to offer extensive and positive coverage and, ultimately, their endorsement. All of these involve getting someone to do something and that is what marketing is all about! It is what Wal-Mart or Target seeks—getting people into their stores to buy a lot of merchandise and then tell their friends how great the experience was.

Many critics of political campaigning have said in the past that there is too much marketing—that candidates tout shallow differences and focus too much on image. While there is much truth to the charges, what political campaign managers have realized in the twenty-first century is that organizations like Wal-Mart and Target are now using highly sophisticated market targeting techniques that can radically improve the efficiency and effectiveness of political marketing. A case in point is data mining. This is a technique whereby organizations like Wal-Mart take all of the internal and external data they can gather on potential target customers—past purchase behavior, hobbies, media habits—and find ways statistically to group them that tells the store—and potentially the candidate—whom to target and how to speak to them.

Business Week recently reported that candidates in California in 2006, including Governor Schwarzenegger, were using data mining as a superior approach to targeting voters. They have learned that "Applebee's restaurant patrons tend to be middle class residents of the heartland who value family, community, and consistency. A Wal-Mart Stores shopper is likely to be socially conservative, pro-gun and exurban or rural, while a Bloomingdale's or Neiman Marcus customer is probably upscale, urban, and socially liberal." Customers of Target are particularly important politically because they are more often found in so-called "swing states."

Matthew Dowd, the chief strategist for George W. Bush's 2004 election campaign, claims that this lifestyle data mining "allows campaigns to identify supporters with 90% reliability, compared with under 60% for old-style targeting based on factors such as geography or ethnicity."

Lloyd L. Hill, board chairman of Applebee's, puts it in terms repeated throughout this textbook: "It's much the same thing, whether you're looking to influence a person to come to Applebee's or to vote."

Source: Richard S. Dunham, "Shop at Target? You're a Swing Voter," *Business Week,* September 25, 2006, pp. 84, 86.

THE NONPROFIT WORLD

Nonprofit organizations are pervasive institutions affecting our lives and the world around us in numerous ways. They provide soup kitchens for the poor and opera for the affluent. They try to get us to stop smoking and lose weight. They advocate for causes and champion neglected populations. They support political candidates and offer us opportunities to practice a religious faith. Internationally, they tackle critical challenges like HIV/AIDS in Asia and Africa and genocide in Darfur. They offer opportunities for individuals who want to help others and for corporate executives to apply their skills to social challenges.

Why do nonprofits exist? There are three major explanations for their role in civil society. *Public goods theory* argues that they exist to provide services that government does not offer. The government provides services up to a level that satisfies the median voter; the nonprofit sector provides the rest. *Contract failure theory* focuses on the private sector arguing that for-profits cannot be trusted to provide some goods and services such as day care. These services are then provided by a nonprofit based on either what donors choose to support or individuals are willing to pay for. Finally, there is *subsidy theory* that says that, in the main, the government determines what nonprofits offer by their tax breaks, grants, and other subsidies.

Of course, each of these theories provides partial explanations for the existence of some institutions and for some activities. It is also the case that both the scope and character of the nonprofit sector reflects historical developments and the agendas of the public and politicians. In the United States, we rarely worry about influenza but do worry a lot about HIV/AIDS or SIDS. In Europe, they worry a lot about historical buildings; this is of lesser concern in the United States.

SOME MYTHS

Despite the pervasiveness of the sector, it is not uncommon to find otherwise knowledgeable individuals dismissing the nonprofit sector as a rather minor, not very serious corner of society. Among the canards one hears are the following:

- While nonprofits address important problems in nooks and crannies, the sector is not a significant component of the overall output of society.

- While nonprofits may have some importance in North America, in the global economy they are minor players.
- With a few rare exceptions, nonprofit organizations are relatively small, local enterprises specializing in narrow domains.
- Nonprofits tend to be populated with—and run by—"do-gooders" who have limited interest in efficient management and a dismissive attitude toward those who do.
- While the missions of nonprofits may be socially important, the management challenges they face are relatively mundane in comparison to the really hard problems that businesses address routinely.
- Working in the nonprofit sector is a poor career move for those who wish to make "Big Money" and be major players in the national and international scenes.
- Businesses need to have only token involvement in the nonprofit world in order to maintain good public relations or to produce short-term marketing gains.

In this and succeeding chapters of this book, we shall demonstrate that all of the previous statements are myths and, indeed, that the nonprofit sector is a large, growing, important, challenging sector that is relevant to our daily lives and to business and businesspeople in ways they may not have appreciated. Consider the following:

- Nonprofits comprise about 8 percent of the entire paid labor force based on 1998 data.
- Volunteering is a major activity for 28.8 percent of American adults. They add an estimated 8.2 billion hours annually to the nonprofit workforce, equating to $147.6 billion in economic and social contributions.[1]
- The nonprofit sector employs more civilians than the federal and state governments combined.[2]
- The nonprofit sector has been growing faster than most sectors of business (excepting technology).
- Internationally, the nonprofit sector in parts of the world such as Central and Eastern Europe is growing at an extremely rapid pace.[3]
- The sector is now populated with a number of very large, very sophisticated organizations. The top five nonprofits took in over $4 *billion* each in 2005.[4]
- Huge donations by the likes of Bill and Melinda Gates, Warren Buffet, and George Soros and the participation of celebrities like Bono and Michael J. Fox in nonprofit causes have raised the profile of the sector in dramatic ways.
- While most nonprofits are small and often controlled by charismatic founders with limited management experience, the sector is increasingly populated with well-trained MBAs and ex-businesspeople.
- Very few corporate chieftains—when they thought about it—would consider it easier to increase their market share 2 percent than to reduce the number of AIDS cases in an African country with volunteer workers, an antagonistic government, countervailing religious and cultural norms, rampant customer illiteracy, and a crumbling public infrastructure.[5] These are the kinds of challenges nonprofit organizations face daily.

- While nonprofit managers clearly earn less than equivalent for-profit managers (who can get dramatic stock bonuses in addition to salaries), there is still "real" money to be made. A recent survey by *The Chronicle of Philanthropy* listed 16 leaders of major nonprofit organizations (exclusive of hospital and educational organizations) and 21 leaders of foundations with salaries over $500,000 and several over $750,000.[6]

WHY STUDY NONPROFIT MARKETING?

Nonprofit organizations are created and funded because individuals, corporations, and sometimes the government believe that some social challenge needs to be addressed. Nonprofits seek to get addicts off drugs, prevent men from beating their wives or girlfriends, influence votes by legislators, attract people to ballet, teach poor kids basic reading skills and provide them with computers, and lead people to find God. They need others to give them money to do this and must attract volunteers to help them implement their programs. When one thinks about it, their basic challenge is *to influence people to be successful*—volunteers, donors, legislators, people with socially undesirable behaviors, and so on! But this is also what for-profit marketers have to do. They have to get people to buy their products and patronize their services. Both sectors are in the *behavioral influence business* and that is precisely what marketing is all about.

In the private sector, marketers are in charge of getting customers to eat at Wendy's fast-food chain and not at rival eateries or at home. They get retailers to stock their brand of clothing and attract customers to their stores. They get people to fly American Airlines and not Lufthansa, and to stay at a Marriott hotel not a Westin. They get Japan to buy Boeing jets not those of Airbus, and government agencies to use Oracle servers and not those of Sun Microsystems. Private sector managers at all levels, right up to the CEO and COO, know that marketing and a customer-centered marketing mindset are crucial to their success.

The same is true—or ought to be true—in the nonprofit world and in many parts of the public sector. Managers all the way up to the CEO need to know how to get people to do things or, in cases like drug abuse, NOT to do something. It's all about influencing behavior. Fortunately, the private sector has vast experience in carrying out effective marketing programs and the challenge is to apply these insights to the nonprofit sector.

This is the central challenge of this book.

There is also a reason to study nonprofit marketing even if one is not planning a career in this sector. The three main sectors of society—business, government, and nonprofits—increasingly interact with each other.[7] Government agencies such as the National Cancer Institute or the Centers for Disease Control and Prevention partner with organizations like the American Cancer Society or the Boys & Girls Clubs of America to achieve mutual objectives. As we will discuss in a later chapter, joint ventures between corporations and nonprofits are becoming increasingly common. Cause-related marketing is a multi-billion sector, with corporations like Nike and Coca-Cola actively engaged with nonprofits like Boys & Girls Clubs of America in achieving each organization's objectives as well as the objectives they have in common. A further reason to study nonprofit marketing even if one is pursuing a business career is the fact that a great many corporate managers at some time in their careers volunteer for nonprofit organizations and/or serve on their boards.

Thus managers in all three sectors need to understand marketing and how marketing is—and ought to be—used in the nonprofit environment. Nonprofit managers need to know how to be better at influencing all of the different publics whose behaviors determine their success. Government managers need to know about marketing techniques in the nonprofit world because they might be useful in their own environments and because they need to know how nonprofit marketers think and act so that they can work effectively with them. Finally, corporate marketers need to understand nonprofit marketers and the special world in which they operate if they are going to partner successfully with them.

A final reason why managers in many environments (and future managers) need to study nonprofit marketing is that it can be a very "stretching" exercise. How does one adapt basic marketing concepts and tools that are used to sell burgers and airplane seats to obstinate problems like getting New Zealand fathers not to slap their children as a "natural" form of discipline? One of the great personal rewards that have come to commercial marketers who have carried their skills into the nonprofit environment is that they have come away invigorated with new insights and a more profound appreciation for the robustness of their own armamentarium.[8]

Management guru Peter Drucker knew this a long time back. In the *Harvard Business Review* in the summer of 1989, Drucker argued that nonprofit organizations are becoming America's management leaders, especially in the areas of strategy and the effective use of boards of directors. Drucker claimed, "They are practicing what most American businesses only preach." Drucker continued:

> Twenty years ago, management was a dirty word for those involved in nonprofit organizations. It meant business, and nonprofits prided themselves on being free of the taint of commercialism and above such sordid considerations as the bottom line. Now most of them have learned that nonprofits need management even more than business does, precisely because they lack the discipline of the bottom line. The nonprofits are, of course, still dedicated to "doing good." But they also realize that good intentions are no substitute for organization and leadership, for accountability, performance, and results. Those require management and that, in turn, begins with the organization's mission.[9]

More recently, Rosabeth Moss Kanter has argued that nonprofits may be the "beta site" for new management innovations in the twenty-first century.[10]

Fortunately, future prospects for the nonprofit sector look promising. A 2006 Cone Inc./AMP Insights study reported in *Business Week* revealed that 61 percent of young people 13–25 years old said that they "personally felt responsible for making a difference in the world." Further, 89 percent said they were likely to switch brands—if price and quality are equal—to support a cause, 69 percent consider a company's social involvement when choosing where to shop, and 66 percent consider a company's social commitment when recommending products.[11]

SOME HISTORY OF NONPROFIT MARKETING
AS AN ACADEMIC DISCIPLINE

The idea of studying how to apply marketing concepts and tools to nonprofit organizations had its "birth" in a series of articles by Kotler and Levy,[12] Kotler and Zaltman,[13] and Shapiro[14] between 1969 and 1973. These articles argued that

> Marketing is a pervasive societal activity that goes considerably beyond the selling of toothpaste, soap, and steel. Political contests remind us that candidates are marketed as well as soap; student recruitment in colleges reminds us that higher education is marketed; and fundraising reminds us that "causes" are marketed. . . . [Yet no] attempt is made to examine whether the principles of "good" marketing in traditional product areas are transferable to the marketing of services, persons, and ideas.[15]

The 1970s and 1980s saw the growth period of this philosophy and a dramatically steep rise in its acceptance. As Andreasen has noted, adoption of marketing concepts and tools occurred initially and most rapidly in those areas that were most like the private sector in terms of the organizational environment and the kinds of transactions involved.[16] Early applications were in service marketing areas like education, health care, recreation, transportation, libraries, and the arts, as well as in product sales like contraceptive social marketing.[17] These were environments in which one had clear "customers" and sought their patronage to succeed. The 1970s and 1980s also saw the appearance of initial articles and books by the present authors and such people as Christopher Lovelock,[18] Charles Weinberg,[19] Michael Rothschild,[20] Paul Bloom,[21] Gerald Zaltman,[22] and numerous others, as well as others outside the traditional field, such as Robin MacStravic in health care[23] and John Crompton in leisure and recreation.[24]

In the late 1980s, the nonprofit marketing idea extended itself into new organizational environments such as government agencies and new kinds of transactions where, for example, no products or services were involved (child abuse) and no money changed hands. The excitement inherent in this widening of the purview of the field was reflected in several general textbooks that became available,[25] as well as trade books and textbooks in specific subcategories such as the marketing of health care,[26] education,[27] religion,[28] places,[29] countries,[30] and social issues.[31] Specialized readers, conference proceedings, collections,[32] and casebooks[33] abounded. The period also saw the beginnings of *social marketing,* with texts by Manoff appearing in 1985[34] and by Kotler and Roberto in 1989.[35]

The 1980s also saw a number of nonacademic publications appearing that summarized experiences from practicing nonprofit marketers. Prominent among these was a series of reports on contraceptive social marketing from the Population Information Program at Johns Hopkins University,[36] a marketing planning workbook from the United Way of America,[37] handbooks for conducting focus group research[38] and carrying out communications programs for child survival[39] from the Academy for Educational Development, and a planner's guide on health communications from the Office of Cancer Communications in the U.S. Department of Health and Human Services.[40] These were supplemented by speeches and articles from a wide array of thoughtful practitioners, such as William Novelli,

Mary Debus, and William Smith, writing and lecturing about their experiences in applying marketing in the nonprofit sector.[41]

In addition to a growing array of articles on nonprofits in traditional and not-so-traditional journals, several new journals appeared, including the *Journal of Health Care Marketing,* the *Health Marketing Quarterly,* the *Praeger Series in Public and Nonprofit Sector Marketing,* the *Journal of Public Policy and Marketing, Health Marketing, Hospital Public Relations,* the *Journal of Marketing for Higher Education,* the *Journal of Marketing for Mental Health, Nonprofit and Voluntary Sector Marketing,* and the *Journal of Marketing Management for Professionals.* Journals in such diverse fields as library science, art history, leisure studies, occupational therapy, and hospital management joined the marketing bandwagon. In 2002, over 240 universities were offering courses in nonprofit management, a tripling of the number found in 1995.[42]

In the field, marketing specialists in nonprofit organizations were no longer a rarity. Although the content of their jobs still varies widely, they no longer have to hide behind deceptive job titles like director of development, education coordinator, or patient liaison officer. A wide range of consulting organizations sprang up in major centers, especially around Washington, D.C., to offer their services as marketing specialists in the nonprofit sector. To meet this new competition, the major traditional consulting, advertising, and public relations firms found that they had to have special divisions or individuals dedicated to providing nonprofit marketing assistance. The growth of cause-marketing in the 1990s accelerated this pace.

The Twenty-First Century

The beginning of the twenty-first century saw a number of important developments in the field. First, there was a significant acceleration in the growth of social marketing.[43] Once a tiny subset of the field of nonprofit marketing that focused on the applications of private sector marketing to improve social welfare, social marketing has grown dramatically in the last 20 years. Major international and domestic behavior change programs now routinely have social marketing components.[44] In 2006, the British Health Service established the National Centre for Social Marketing Excellence to spur the use of social marketing concepts and tools throughout the health system.[45] Individuals with titles such as "manager of social marketing" can now be found in private advertising/public relations and consulting organizations. Social marketing centers have also been established at the University of South Florida in Tampa, the University of Sterling in Scotland, and in Warsaw, Poland. In addition to pioneering books, new offerings by Andreasen,[46] Donovan and Henley,[47] and Kotler, Roberto, and Lee[48] continue to deepen and broaden the conceptual base of the field. Relevant articles are now routinely published in a range of mainstream journals and the *Social Marketing Quarterly.* A range of new books has also emerged, including textbooks by Wymer, Knowles, and Gomes[49] and by Kotler and Lee,[50] and a number of trade books from various presses.[51]

The second major change begun in the 1990s is the growing attention being paid to the international dimensions of nonprofit marketing.[52] Although non-governmental organizations (NGOs) have been involved in poverty and health programs for many years, their reputation was not great. "Many development economists working for national governments or international organizations like the World Bank looked down on the NGOs as unimportant, under-resourced, utopian, and often obstructionist."[53] However, interest in nonprofit enterprises outside the United States has grown dramatically in recent years and, surprisingly, the four brands in which Europeans trust the most are nonprofit organizations—Amnesty International, World Wildlife Fund, Greenpeace, and Oxfam.[54] This growth is the result of three forces. First, many governments that were once the primary source of social support for their citizens are now cutting back and leaving private nonprofit organizations to shoulder the burden.[55] Second, many international social agencies, such as the World Bank and the U.S. Agency for International Development, have found they must rely on local and international nonprofits to carry out, and then sustain, major social interventions. Finally, the emergence of many new countries, first from "behind the Iron Curtain" and more recently from within the former Soviet Union, has dramatically increased the interest in nonprofit organizations and what they might do to replace programs of defunct socialist states.[56] Many U.S. nonprofits now have major international operations including Goodwill Industries International, Inc.; Habitat for Humanity International; and Gifts in Kind International.[57] It is estimated that the number of nonprofit organizations with international programs exceeds 2,500.

A third major change was the growth in importance of corporate involvement in the nonprofit sector. As described in Chapter 17, corporations have discovered major strategic advantages from partnerships with nonprofit organizations.[58] Involvement in the nonprofit world has provided sales benefits, volunteering opportunities, and chances for executive growth.

The twenty-first century continues to see a focus on the ethics of the nonprofit field. There have always been scams in the charity field, from the individual drunk asking for money for "food" to Jim Bakker asking for donations for the ministry he grossly mismanaged. More recently, concerns have grown in a number of other areas. First, as business organizations have become more involved in social and charitable activities, a number of observers have become particularly concerned about the ethics of both the corporations and the nonprofits that participate with these ventures.[59] Second, as marketing techniques are increasingly employed in trying to bring about changes with regard to highly volatile social issues such as AIDS, abortion, abuse, and so on, marketers have been forced to ask themselves questions about when and how they should be using their powerful technologies.[60] Finally, marketers have recognized that many approaches that they have used in the for-profit world might not be justifiable in other contexts.[61] They have asked whether political advertising should be held to higher standards than corporate advertising, whether market research techniques should probe subjects that are taboo in certain ethnic and religious cultures, or whether the importance of certain ends might justify means that we might ordinarily not condone.[62]

Finally, perhaps the most dramatic symbolic recognition is that nonprofit marketing has finally been embraced by the American Marketing Association, the largest organization of marketers worldwide with 38,000 members. After years of focusing primarily on the private sector, in 2002 the AMA recognized both the importance of the nonprofit sector and the potential for new membership growth by sponsoring its first national conference for nonprofit marketing managers. The conference has found attendance growing substantially in each successive year.

THIS BOOK

We shall revisit all of these issues throughout this book; however, the book has more fundamental objectives. It is targeted to both students and practitioners and offers them the latest concepts, techniques, and illustrations needed to make them first-rate nonprofit marketing managers. The book assumes that the reader is *already* motivated and knows a little about marketing and what it might do but wants to know how to actually carry out marketing programs more extensively and more effectively.

As will be demonstrated repeatedly in the chapters to follow, the book is rooted in two basic premises. First, it posits that marketing goes on everywhere in a nonprofit environment (and the private and government sectors, too) and everyone needs to be good at marketing because he or she must *influence behavior* of many different target audiences to achieve success. Second, we believe that a first-rate marketer (whether a "marketing manager" or a CEO or an HR director) is one who has acquired three things: (1) an ingrained appreciation of the right *mindset*, (2) a comprehensive and practical *process* for developing marketing strategy and tactics, and (3) an awareness and understanding of the latest *tools and techniques* that can be used to make effective marketing decisions in specific areas. The book is organized around these premises.

It is also a book specifically designed for the unique nonprofit environment. The "nonprofit" distinction is not just an academic exercise. If there were not characteristics that were unique to the nonprofit context, there would be no point to a book like this; any of the many excellent general marketing texts would be perfectly satisfactory. But nonprofit marketing is not the same as for-profit marketing. The student and practitioner must appreciate the differences because they have major effects on what one can and cannot do as a marketer. The chapters to follow will constantly remind readers of these distinctions.

Before proceeding, one caveat must be stated. Although the book focuses primarily on "nonprofits," an organizational form that has a relatively strict and clear definition, we will from time to time employ examples and lessons involving organizations in the public sector, such as the Office of Cancer Communications of the National Cancer Institute, or the Centers for Disease Control and Prevention. It is our view that the missions and environments of such entities are not significantly different from those found in the nonprofit sector.

EVOLUTION OF NONPROFIT ORGANIZATIONS

Nelson Rosenbaum has proposed that since the American Revolution, the role of nonprofit organizations in society has evolved through four stages. The earliest stage conforms to what he terms a *voluntary/civic model*.[63] In Pilgrim times through the beginning of the twentieth century, services that were not available from the government and were beyond the means of individual citizens were often provided for each other by neighbors. Thus, in those times—and in some suburban and rural areas and some fundamentalist religious communities today—citizens would band together to operate the volunteer fire department or to help a needy family build a barn. Such a model was (and in some cases, still is) appropriate to a world with homogeneous interests, personal philosophies based on sharing, and a generally low level of economic welfare.

As the country prospered, the industrial revolution concentrated great wealth in the hands of a few families. Whether out of a sense of social responsibility or plain guilt, extremely rich families like the Morgans, Rockefellers, and Carnegies developed a pattern of what Rosenbaum calls *philanthropic patronage*. This patronage significantly benefited major U.S. educational and cultural institutions during the early part of the twentieth century. It finds its remnants today in the large foundations that play a prominent role in funding many nonprofits and also in shaping the national agenda in the areas of education, health care, political reform, and the environment. This role is not without its critics.[64]

Following the onset of the Great Depression and the rapid growth of government-supported social institutions and programs, America in the 1940s and 1950s turned to a nonprofit model based on *rights and entitlements*. Many groups argued that they were entitled to at least some share of public taxation funds for their work, their institutions, or both, in part because they served the general social interest.

The final stage that Rosenbaum describes is the *competitive/market* stage. In the earlier three stages, nonprofits relied for support on (1) individual willingness to share; (2) the generosity of the wealthy; or (3) the largess of federal, state, and municipal governments and the major foundations. Today, nonprofits cannot rely on automatic continuation of traditional sources of support. Further, as they turn increasingly to the marketplace for this support, they find other nonprofits there searching for the same subsistence. The consequence in the twenty-first century is that the greatest challenges facing nonprofit managers are *competitive* challenges. In an important recent volume called *To Profit or Not to Profit: The Commercial Transformation of the Nonprofit Sector*, economist Burton Weisbrod notes:

> Massive change is occurring in the nonprofit sector. Seemingly isolated events touching the lives of virtually everyone are, in fact, parts of a pattern that is little recognized but has enormous impact; it is a pattern of growing commercialization of nonprofit organizations.[65]

He points to the hospitals that are getting into the fitness business,[66] museums generating vast incomes from shops and catalogues,[67] and universities entering profitable research alliances with business[68] and forming for-profit subsidiaries to generate major levels of revenue.[69]

It is likely that this increased use of business concepts and tools in the nonprofit sector will accelerate in the next decade as the result of what might be described as a return to what Rosenbaum calls "philanthropic patronage." In the last five years, several very wealthy businesspeople—typically with computer backgrounds—have amassed great wealth and decided to use at least part of it to address social problems.

- Bill and Melinda Gates have pledged $31.9 billion to their Gates Foundation, which focuses on world health issues and education. Bill Gates has said that he plans to relinquish his management role at Microsoft and devote full time to the foundation.
- Warren Buffett of Berkshire Hathaway has pledged to give away the majority of his fortune, estimated at $40 billion to philanthropic efforts. The majority will go to the Gates Foundation because he believes that the foundation's

leadership has "applied truly unusual intelligence, energy and heart to improving the lives of millions of fellow humans who have not been as lucky as the three of us. . . . I am delighted to add to the resources with which you carry on this work."[70]

- Google has pledged 1 percent of the company's stock (roughly $1 billion) to support charitable causes. Significantly, it has decided to divide this support between a traditional foundation and a for-profit social enterprise.[71]
- Michael Bloomberg, Mayor of New York City, has donated $125 million to the Worldwide Stop Smoking Initiative.[72]
- Pam and Omidyar of eBay have similarly set up the Omidyar Foundation and for-profit network, thus creating two "checkbooks" beginning with $200 million in each fund.[73]
- Steve Case and his wife, Jean, are using AOL proceeds to invest in nonprofits which potentially may pay dividends back to the Case Foundation.

These high-profile investors have joined prominent individuals to fight world problems. Bono has long focused on world poverty and HIV/AIDS. Bill Clinton has emphasized poverty, climate change, obesity, and HIV/AIDS. And in September 2006, British billionaire Richard Branson pledged to invest all of the profits from his Virgin Group airline and train businesses over the next 10 years to fight climate change and global warming. Branson's contributions could be as high as $3 billion.[74]

Some Dissenters

This shift toward using concepts and tools from the commercial world is not without its critics. Peter Dobkin Hall, for example, argues that, except for some faith-based entities, nonprofits are no longer the kinds of voluntary associations that De Toqueville noted were among the new colony's greatest strengths.[75] Authors like Robert Putnam mourn the loss of social capital and argues that we have become a nation of individuals "bowling alone."[76] Hall believes that the so-called independent sector is at a moral crisis point and needs to rethink its place and purpose.

In a similar vein, Eikenberry and Kluver believe that the "marketization" of the nonprofit sector is not healthy for civil society. They conclude: "The nonprofit sector in the United States has increasingly adopted the values and methods of the market to guide management and service delivery. The outcome is the potential deterioration of the distinctive contributions that nonprofit organizations make to creating and maintaining a strong civil society."[77]

There are many reasons why nonprofits have been subject to criticism. As Hall implies, many citizens feel that nonprofits have become too large and too bureaucratic. There have been a number of major scandals implicating poor nonprofit management, ranging from scandals at the United Way involving its former president, William Aramony, to the recent embezzlement of $7 million from a Midwest chapter of the American Cancer Society. Criticism over the American Red Cross's handling of donations around the September 11, 2001, attack on the World Trade Center and Pentagon has led many organizations to rethink what they do and how they do it. Paul Light points to the increased call for a "watchful eye" to keep the sector in line and meet society's needs.[78] Further, some recent studies have concluded that nonprofit organizations are experiencing "disappointing results" from the earned income ventures.[79]

The Need for Better Management

Despite these criticisms, there are numerous and growing pressures on nonprofit organizations to become more "business-like." First, as mentioned briefly at the outset, many nonprofits are now extremely large. For example, excluding universities and health care systems, Table 1-1 shows that the annual revenues in 2005 of the 20 largest nonprofits exceeded $830 million, with the largest, Lutheran Services, generating over $9.5 *billion,* which would put it around 251 in the 2006 Fortune 500, above such private sector giants as Lucent Technologies and Clear Channel Communications.

Such large organizations are under significant internal pressure to introduce much better, more sophisticated management. That is also the case for the largest individual U.S. universities. Income for each of the top five universities reporting total income to the *The Chronicle of Philanthropy* (Stanford University did not) exceeded $3 billion in 2005:[80]

Harvard University	$4,994,068,570
University of Illinois	$3,806,431,000
University of Pennsylvania	$3,785,955,216
Yale University	$3,448,898,026
Columbia University	$3,109,691,000

TABLE 1-1	Total Revenues of the Largest Nonacademic, Non-hospital Nonprofits, 2005	
		Revenues (000)
1	Lutheran Services of America	$9,500,000
2	YMCA of the USA	5,130,857
3	Salvation Army	4,559,292
4	United Way of America	4,175,545
5	American Red Cross	3,888,173
6	Catholic Charities USA	3,385,094
7	Goodwill Industries International	2,592,560
8	Boys & Girls Club of America	1,335,383
9	AmeriCares Foundation	1,316,498
10	Tulsa Community Fund	1,052,762
11	Fidelity Charitable Gift Fund	989,277
12	American Cancer Society	977,851
13	Habitat for Humanity International	940,509
14	The Nature Conservancy	919,113
15	World Vision	905,130
16	Feed the Children	851,964
17	Gifts in Kind International	842,849
18	Volunteers of America	839,435
19	Boy Scouts of America	836,012
20	Easter Seals	833,706

Source: The Chronicle of Philanthropy, October 26, 2006, pp. 8–21. Reprinted with permission of *The Chronicle of Philanthropy,* http://philanthropy.com.

And then there are the nonprofit hospitals and medical centers. The top five are:[81]

Partners Healthcare System (Boston)	$5,586,641,000
Catholic HealthCare West	$4,765,622,000
Rush University Medical Center	$2,166,678,384
University of Texas M. D. Anderson Cancer Center	$1,951,542,626
Memorial Sloan Kettering Cancer Center	$1,951,542,626

For these large organizations, and many others, pressure to improve management is also increasing from external sources. A major influence is the new breed of "venture philanthropists" like Mario Marino. These entrepreneurs have made fortunes in the expanding high-tech environment and want to apply their management and financial skills to their charitable giving. They are forming venture capital funds for nonprofits but are demanding great attention to sound management on the part of their grantees.[82]

Paul Light sees these pressures as leading to three "tides," pressures for (1) scientific management, based on best practices; (2) war on waste, based on increasing efficiencies; and (3) liberation management, based on superior outcomes no matter how they are achieved.[83] Clearly, increased attention to effective marketing can advance all three tides. However, a future major role for marketing thinking in nonprofit organizations would be problematic if many nonprofit observers, managers, and board members feel that "managerial professionalization" is not desirable. It is our view that a marketing perspective is *essential* to effective nonprofit management no matter whether the organization focuses heavily on a mission of voluntary association or focuses more closely on effective management. In any case, the empirical evidence suggests that the problem may not be as serious as Hall believes. A recently published study by Galaskiewicz and Bielefeld traced the extent to which 229 nonprofit organizations in the Minneapolis–St. Paul area shifted in the use of their "business" or "charitable" model between 1980 and 1994. They found for many organizations that "The application of business techniques by nonprofits were essential in order to compete for clients and donations." However, they did not find "wholesale application of business and commercial practices." More importantly, they concluded that "nonprofits experienced no obvious detrimental organizational effects if they adopted business-like tactics or relied on commercial income."[84]

IMPORTANCE OF THE NONPROFIT SECTOR

The United States

An important reason to study the nonprofit sector is that it is surprisingly large and, in many years and in many countries, it has grown faster than the private sector. As reported in Table 1-2, according to the National Center for Nonprofit Statistics, in the United States in 2004 there were 1,367,817 nonprofit organizations registered with the IRS as 501(c) charities. In addition, the National Center estimates that there are also 377,640 congregations, about half of which are believed to be not registered with the IRS. This suggests that the sector in 2004 totaled almost 1.56 million nonprofit organizations.[85] The sector has grown between 1996 and 2004 in numbers by 28.8 percent overall, but public charities grew over 50 percent.

TABLE 1-2	Number of Nonprofit Organizations in the United States, 1996–2004			
	1996		**2004**	
	Number of Orgs.	*Percent of All Orgs.*	*Number of Orgs.*	*Percent of All Orgs.*
All Nonprofit Organizations	1,084,897	100.00%	1,397,263	100.00%
501(c)(3) Public Charities	535,888	49.40%	822,817	58.90%
501(c)(3) Private Foundations	58,774	5.40%	102,881	7.40%
Other 501(c) Nonprofit Organizations	490,235	45.20%	471,565	33.70%
501(c)(3) Public Charities	535,888	49.40%	822,817	58.90%
Reporting Public Charities	297,691	27.40%	317,689	22.70%
Operating Public Charities	261,640	24.10%	272,236	19.50%
Supporting Public Charities	36,051	3.30%	45,453	3.30%
Non-Reporting, or with less than $25,000 in Gross Receipts	238,197	22.00%	505,128	36.20%
*Congregations (about half are registered with IRS)**	-	0.00%	385,874	27.60%
501(c)(3) Private Foundations	58,774	5.40%	102,881	7.40%
Private Grantmaking (Non-Operating) Foundations	56,377	5.20%	98,529	7.10%
Private Operating Foundations	2,397	0.20%	4,35	0.30%
Other 501(c) Nonprofit Organizations	490,235	45.20%	471,565	33.70%
Civic leagues, social welfare orgs, etc.	127,567	11.80%	119,515	8.60%
Fraternal beneficiary societies	102,592	9.50%	87,833	6.30%
Business leagues, chambers of commerce, etc.	68,575	6.30%	71,470	5.10%
Labor, agricultural, horticultural orgs	61,729	5.70%	58,362	4.20%
Social and recreational clubs	57,090	5.30%	56,494	4.00%
Post or organization of war veterans	30,578	2.80%	35,097	2.50%
All Other Nonprofit Organizations	42,104	3.90%	42,794	3.10%

Source: Urban Institute. Reprinted with permission of the Urban Institute.

An alternative method of estimating the size of the nonprofit sector—one that we shall see is more useful internationally—is in terms of employment. The sector is highly labor-intensive, but a significant portion of its labor force is volunteer and therefore difficult to count. The Bureau of Labor Statistics estimates that 28.8 percent of Americans over the age of 16 volunteered through or for a nonprofit organization in 2005. In 1998, Salamon estimates that 501(c)(3) and 501(c)(4) organizations had just below 11 million workers, which is over 7 percent of the U.S. labor force. If one adds 5.7 million unpaid volunteers to this total, the nonprofit workforce of 16.6 million well exceeds that of finance, insurance, and real estate (8.6 million) and construction (8.5 million), and 81 percent of the total for the entire manufacturing sector (20.5 million).[86]

As measured by employment for "membership associations and organizations," the sector is growing faster than other parts of the job market. Over the 15 years from 1990 through 2004, sector employment was growing at an average rate of 2.4 percent per year, which is almost double the 1.3 percent growth rate for total employment.[87]

Despite the overall growth, some nonprofits face significant challenges. For example, data on religious institutions from the University of Indiana suggest that baby boomers are less likely to both attend and give to such institutions.[88] And, giving to churches has stayed constant while church members' incomes have grown. Protestants donated 0.68 percent of income in 1968 but only 0.38 percent in 2004.[89]

THE NONPROFIT SECTOR AROUND THE WORLD

Of course, the United States is not unique in having a thriving nonprofit sector. Nonprofit organizations and voluntary participation have a long history in several other parts of the world and is slowly growing in additional countries, including the former communist countries of Eastern Europe and China.

The most comprehensive portraits of the nonprofit sector outside the United States are being developed by Lester Salamon and his colleagues at the Center for Civil Society Studies (CCSS) at Johns Hopkins University's Institute for Policy Studies (www.jhu.edu/~cnp). Their 2003 overview of the nonprofit landscape (i.e., "civil society") sector covers 35 countries around the world, including 16 advanced industrial nations, 14 developing countries, and 5 transitional countries of Central and Eastern Europe.[90]

They define "civil society organizations" as essentially private, that is, outside the institutional structures of government; that are not primarily commercial and do not exist primarily to distribute profits to their directors or "owners"; that are self-governing; and that people are free to join or support voluntarily. According to Salamon, Sokolowski, and List, an immense upsurge in the civil society sector is occurring on an international scale, which they have termed the "global associational revolution." The authors attribute this upsurge to several key factors:

- *Technology advancements and literacy*—Improved information technology and growth in literacy rates around the world have helped drive the notion that change is possible and that better opportunities do exist. Technology has made it easier for citizens to connect and drive social action, and this has motivated citizen activism.
- *Dissatisfaction with market forces and government* solutions to social, economic, and environmental crises.
- *Strategic partnerships*—The civil society sector's combination of private structure and public purpose, small size, flexibility, connections to public, and ability to tap into private sector support explain their attractiveness to foundations, donors, and corporations as strategically important partners in developing new, creative solutions.
- *Development of "social capital"*—Recent research suggests that the civil society sector contributes significantly to creation of individual "social capital," defined as the advantage created by a person's location in a structure of relationships and which the authors consider to be the foundation of democracy and economic growth.
- *Converting demand to supply*—Salamon, Sokolowski, and List also attribute growth of this sector to an expanding pool of educated professionals in the 1960s/1970s working diligently to convert demand for worldwide civil society organizations into actual supply.

- *Increasing role of external actors*—Multi-lateral agents such as the World Bank, the Catholic Church, Western charitable foundations, and multinational corporations are helping fuel the growth of the international civil society sector by providing financial and human resources support.

Despite the advance of its presence and significance, the international civil society sector still often fails to attract substantial attention from policy makers or the press. Lack of statistics and hard data on the "third" sector has contributed to the lack of acknowledgement, and thus drives the Johns Hopkins Global Civil Society study.

Studies in the 35 countries conclude that the global civil society sector comprises a $1.3 trillion industry as of the late 1990s. This amounted to 5.1 percent of combined GDP of 35 countries. The sector equates to the seventh largest world economy. The sector is a major world employer—39.5 million full-time equivalent workers (57 percent paid staff, 43 percent volunteers). They employ, in aggregate, 10 times more people than the utilities and textile industries in these 35 countries, 5 times more than food manufacturers, and 20 percent more than the transportation industry.

Comparisons across the 35 countries suggest that—not surprisingly—the civil society sector is larger in more developed countries than in emerging economies (comprising 7.4 vs. 1.9 percent of economically active populations, respectively). However, limited presence of the sector in many developing countries is not necessarily an indication of an absence of the civil society connectedness. Many of these nations tend to have instead strong traditions of familial, clan, or village networks that perform the same functions as civil society institutions. The importance of civil society in the 35 countries is shown in Table 1-3.

TABLE 1-3 Civil Society Share of Economically Active Workforce, 1995–1998			
Country	%	*Country*	%
The Netherlands	14.4	Egypt	2.8
Belgium	10.9	Peru	2.5
Ireland	10.4	South Korea	2.4
United States	9.8	Colombia	2.4
United Kingdom	8.5	Uganda	2.3
Israel	8.0	Kenya	2.1
France	7.6	Tanzania	2.1
Norway	7.2	Czech Republic	2.0
Sweden	7.1	Philippines	1.9
Australia	6.3	Brazil	1.6
Germany	5.9	Morocco	1.5
Finland	5.3	Hungary	1.1
Austria	4.9	Pakistan	1.0
Argentina	4.8	Slovakia	0.8
Spain	4.3	Poland	0.8
Japan	4.2	Romania	0.8
Italy	3.9	Mexico	0.4
South Africa	3.4	**Average all 35 Countries**	4.4

Source: Lester A. Salamon, S. Wojciech Sokolowski, and Regina List, *Global Civil Society: An Overview.* Baltimore, MD: Center for Civil Society Studies, Institute for Policy Studies, The Johns Hopkins University, 2003. Reproduced with permission.

Civil society organizations deliver a variety of human services, from health care and education to social services and community development. However, the sector is often highly involved in advocacy and building social capital. They label these roles as advocacy, expressiveness, and community building. As advocates, they identify unaddressed problems and bring them to public attention (protect basic human rights; give voice to social, political, environmental, ethnic, and community interests and concerns). In their expressive role, they provide vehicles through which other sentiments/impulses find expression (artistic, religious, cultural, ethnic, social, and recreational). Their community-building role involves simply increasing social capital, establishing connections among individuals; involvement in associations teaches norms of cooperation that carry over into political/economic life.

Philanthropy is not the main revenue stream for global civil society organizations—fees are the dominant source of revenue for most international civil society organizations, including 32 countries where 53 percent of the income is derived from fees/charges for services and commercial income. The government, or public sector, is the second largest source of income for the international sector, with 35 percent of revenue derived from grants/contracts or reimbursement payments. Private philanthropy plays a very limited role in their revenue streams, accounting for approximately 12 percent.

Civil society fields differ in major sources of revenue. Those offering professional services, education, and development assistance secured major funding from fees as do "Other" organizations. Those in the health sector have a more balanced portfolio of sources, with governments being somewhat more important. Philanthropy was most critical to religious, civil/advocacy, international, environmental, cultural, and social service organizations and foundations.

Salamon and his colleagues classify civil society organizations in terms of overall patterns of workforce composition and sources of fees as follows: Anglo-Saxon, Nordic, Asian Industrialized, and Developing and Transitional. They also find distinctions within the latter grouping, separating out a Latin American model, an African model, Central and Eastern Europe, and all others. The sources of funding vary across several of these distinctions as follows:

	Fees	Government	Philanthropy
Anglo-Saxon	54.6	36.1	9.3
Nordic	59.4	33.3	7.3
Asian Industrialized	61.8	34.8	3.5
Latin American	74.4	15.3	10.3
African	55.3	25.3	19.4
Central/Eastern Europe	49.0	31.5	19.5

Explanation of Cross-Country Differences

In an earlier article, Salamon and Sokolowski propose that differences in the size of the nonprofit sector across countries could possibly be explained by three sets of hypotheses.[91] Following a suggestion by Weisbrod,[92] they propose that the size of the nonprofit sector is determined by *market or government failure*. Citizens in all countries have need for and desire a range of goods and services that, for economic reasons, will not be provided by the private sector (market failure). Theoretically, these needs could be met by government (education, old-age security, and so on). However, societies differ in their willingness to support public sector provision of these goods and services. Nonprofits then step in to meet this "government failure." This leads these authors to predict that the size of the nonprofit sector will vary with:

1. The heterogeneity of the population—The greater the ethnic and religious diversity, the more controversy there will be about what the government should do and therefore the greater the role for nonprofits.
2. The size of government—The more the government does, the less the need for a nonprofit sector.
3. The proportion of nonprofit funding that is from charitable donations—The more individuals want what government and the market do not deliver, the more they are likely to be willing to pay for it.

Salamon and Sokolowski tested these hypotheses with data from 22 of their countries and find that heterogeneity does not predict the size of the sector. The exact opposite is true for the other two hypotheses; a larger nonprofit sector was associated with a *larger* government role and a *smaller* funding role for private charity. In search of an explanation, the authors suggest that perhaps it is that the nonprofit sector is not competitive with government but, in fact, is more often cooperative with it to meet needs in which societies believe strongly. This would explain the positive relationship between the size of the government and the nonprofit sectors previously noted. The authors further predict that sector interdependency would predict both higher proportions of nonprofit funding from the government and greater levels of nonprofit activity in areas where government is already active, namely health and social services. Both of the the latter hypotheses are strongly supported by the data.[93]

The results of their analyses allow the authors to categorize countries according to the "regime" in which nonprofits operate. They partition countries on whether their government spending on welfare is low or high and whether the scale of nonprofit activity is small or large. The resulting four categories are as follows:

Government Social Welfare Spending	Nonprofit Scale	
	Small	*Large*
Low	Statist	Liberal
High	Social Democratic	Corporatist

- *Statist regimes* reflect a government role that looks to the needs of elites and not the middle or lower classes as in the social democratic regimes and, perhaps as a consequence, the nonprofit sector is not powerful (e.g., Japan, Brazil).
- *Liberal regimes* are generally hostile to government programs and enthusiastic about private volunteerism (e.g., the United Kingdom to some extent).
- *Social democratic regimes* believe in government provision of public services and not the volunteer sector (e.g., Austria, Finland).
- *Corporatist regimes* involve a strong role for government, but one in partnership with a strong role for nonprofits (e.g., Germany, France, Belgium).

Their data give good support for this model.

An alternative explanation is offered by Alesina and Angelotis in a September 2005 article in the *American Economic Review*.[94] They contrast the European approach of giving considerable support to public welfare programs to the less expansive approach in the United States, and conclude that the source of these differences lies mainly in attitudes toward poverty. In the United States, the broadest belief is that poverty is associated with laziness and anyone not significantly physically or mentally disadvantaged can climb out of poverty by hard work and initiative. In contrast, European culture argues that someone's position in the social hierarchy is determined by birth, social connections, and plain luck. The perverse effect of the European system is to inhibit upward mobility for the poor. They can still earn a decent income through public support but, if they rise socially, a lot of their income will be taxed by the government to pay for welfare programs. Private charity in the United States helps cushion the problems of the poor but does not provide anywhere near the support—and the disincentive to upward mobility—found in Europe.

THE THREE SECTORS

Implicit in the preceding section is a recognition that the size and performance of the nonprofit sector is not independent from the other two sectors of the economy (the public and commercial sectors). These three sectors both compete and cooperate. In the United States, private and nonprofit hospitals battle over patients. Performing arts centers compete with Broadway and the movies. Commercial firms have often criticized these efforts because nonprofits do not pay taxes. On the other hand, commercial firms have from time to time found it profitable to enter domains that were once thought to be the sole province of nonprofits, such as Lockheed Martin's ventures into job training for the unemployed.[95] Corporations have also seen that partnering across sectors can meet important strategic needs of their own through sponsorships, cause marketing, and various forms of volunteering. Nonprofits have found important new streams of revenue and areas of expertise in these commercial partnerships.

Similarly, nonprofit organizations and government agencies often both cooperate and compete. For example, major economic development, poverty, and health programs around the world almost always involve three-way cooperation.[96] The dramatic relief efforts launched after the Asian tsunami in 2004,[97] the Pakistan earthquake,[98] and Hurricane Katrina[99] vividly demonstrated the value of such cooperation.

THE UNIQUENESS OF NONPROFIT MARKETING

The Tax Benefits of Being a Nonprofit Organization

Because of the important role they serve, nonprofit organizations are often given special status. In the United States, Section 501 of the Internal Revenue Code grants tax-exempt status to 24 different categories of organizations. U.S. nonprofits receive the following special treatments or exemptions:

- Exemption from federal, state, and local income taxes
- Exemption from local property taxes in most cases
- Exemption from unemployment insurance payments in some areas
- Lower bulk postage rates

- Exemption from the Robinson-Patman Act
- Possible lower charges or none at all for federal services
- Exemption from tort liability under common law
- Hospitals and some other organizations can issue tax-exempt bonds
- Charitable, educational, scientific, and certain other organizations can receive donations, gifts, and bequests that permit tax deductions for the giver
- Access to donated space and air time from media

In the past, government was relatively generous in granting special benefits to nonprofits. Ironically, however, the recent successes of revenue-generating marketing in the nonprofit sector have caused some shift in federal thinking about nonprofits.[100] The reason nonprofits have "gotten away" with these "business" activities is that the IRS looks at the overall purpose of the organization, not at individual ventures, to define nonprofit status. In 1950, however, Congress determined that nonprofits must pay taxes on proceeds of "unrelated" business activities. Thus even when an organization has been designated a nonprofit, the government still pays close attention to its individual activities. The government's position is that any revenue-generating activity that is *unrelated* to the organization's basic mission must be taxed as it would be for a for-profit enterprise. Thus a marketing manager must clearly understand whether any present or proposed ventures for which marketing plans are to be developed will be officially classified by the IRS as unrelated business activities. In some cases, it may be desirable to spin off an operation into a for-profit subsidiary.[101] Above all, managers should be extremely careful that the amount of unrelated, taxable activity does not grow to comprise too large a percentage of overall revenue. Hopkins has suggested that if this percentage rises above 35 percent, the organization should be concerned that it may lose its overall tax-exempt status.[102] The IRS will permit most kinds of unrelated business but will be very attentive to the *total* quantity of such ventures.

In the chapters to follow, we will be demonstrating how concepts and tools drawn from private sector marketing can have a significant impact on a nonprofit organization's ability to influence its key target audiences. But up front, it is critical to point out that the two worlds are not the same.

The Special Challenges of Nonprofit Marketing

Marketing in the nonprofit sector is, in our view, much harder than it is in the private sector. In a landmark article, Michael Rothschild implicitly raised this question: Why is it so hard to sell brotherhood like soap?[103] Among the answers that he and other authors[104] have developed are the following:

1. The single most important difference is in the nature of the target audience. In the private sector, the target audience is the customer. It is he or she whose behavior will make or break the organization. And, it is the marketing managers whose responsibility it is to drive sales from this population. In the nonprofit world, organizations vary significantly in their ability to generate revenues through sales of products and services. However, no nonprofit organization survives on such revenues alone. Nonprofits must cultivate a second target audience—those who will give the organization funding through donations or grants and contracts. An irony is that success on the traditional metrics by which for-profits are judged—sales and market share—may or may not affect donations and related funding, especially in the short run. The good thing about donors is that they can be very

patient about traditional measures of success and, indeed, often simply trust in the mission of the organization rather than rely on its performance metrics. The two-audience challenge is further complicated for those organizations that rely heavily on volunteers. Many strategies that serve the other two audiences may or may not sit well with this crucial resource. As we will discuss in Chapter 3, the existence of multiple target audiences makes it much harder for nonprofit managers to develop appropriate strategies that satisfy everyone.

2. Nonprofit marketing is also very different because of the kinds of behaviors it has to influence. For example, the sacrifices target audiences are asked to make often involve much more central ego needs as well as attitudes and behaviors than is the case in the private sector. The behaviors often involve controversial, taboo, or embarrassing topics like AIDS or obesity and, in such cases, it is often very difficult to secure reliable research data from target audiences to serve as the basis for sound marketing decisions. As Bloom and Novelli point out, "While people are generally willing to be interviewed about these topics, they are more likely to give inaccurate, self-serving, or socially desirable answers to such questions than to questions about cake mixes, soft drinks, or cereals."[105]

3. Often the benefits resulting from the behavior that the nonprofit marketer seeks are *invisible*. If oral rehydration therapy is used properly and in time—that is, *before* the child becomes dehydrated—the mother will *not see* any benefits due to the action she took. A similar problem is faced by those trying to market high blood pressure control programs. High blood pressure is a health problem with no overt symptoms, and treatment with appropriate therapy does not result in immediately observable effects for its victims (unless one uses a blood pressure gauge). As Rothschild points out, "In order to establish and maintain a behavior, there must be a positive reinforcer. . . . In many non-business cases, neither positive nor negative reinforcements are perceivable."[106]

4. Consumers are often asked to undertake behaviors where they are either indifferent about the issue or for which there are no clear personal benefits. For example, for many years few people cared about water conservation or the effects of speeding on a country's energy consumption—although the recent rise in oil prices may raise consciousness. On the other hand, many people agree that recycling is important but there are no personal benefits—and, in fact, many costs—for complying. Indeed, in many of these cases, the benefits appear to accrue to others and the individual making the sacrifice sees little or no personal benefits. The latter may be how many potential donors see pleas from charities dealing with the poor, obscure diseases, and the like.

5. Target audiences are often asked to make 180-degree shifts in attitudes and/or behaviors. In the private sector, a marketer simply tries to get consumers to value a product or service *more* than they used to or at least more than a competitor's offerings. Seldom does the marketer have a mandate to convert those who are *against* the product to favor it. Yet nonprofit marketers are asked to do this all the time. They must try to entice "macho men" into wearing seat belts, timid souls into giving blood, or men into taking high blood pressure medication around which swirl rumors about negative effects on sexual potency. Aging citizens are reluctant to finally admit they are infirm or otherwise need assistance, and the obese hope some day to find a "magic pill."

6. In the private sector it is often possible to modify an offering to meet consumer needs and wants better, but this is often difficult in the nonprofit sector. There is

only one way to obtain blood, for example. Pills must be taken if one is to control high blood pressure. An entire music score must be played by an organized set of musicians in order to perform Beethoven's Fifth Symphony. This puts much more pressure on marketers to be creative in other elements of the marketing mix.

7. The target audiences for many nonprofit organizations, especially in the developing world, are often illiterate, unfamiliar with basic scientific notions (like the sources of disease or the impacts of obesity), and accustomed to traditional methods of dealing with problems (e.g., traditional healers). This means that large amounts of information must be communicated to consumers and fundamental attitudes changed. For example, to get consumers in developing countries to use oral rehydration therapy (ORT) correctly and regularly to keep their fragile offspring from dying from the loss of fluids and electrolytes during prolonged and severe bouts of diarrhea, they must learn (a) that dehydration is life-threatening for the child, (b) that ORT will solve the problem, (c) that the benefits of use exceed the costs, (d) that they must use it properly or else it will not be effective or, indeed, may cause more problems than it cures, and (e) that there are specific places where the salts can be obtained and that it will cost x units of the local currency. This is a far cry from introducing Kellogg's new Go-Tart Snack bars or even an iPhone.

8. Because many of the changes to be marketed involve intangible social and psychological benefits, it is often difficult to portray the offering in media presentations. Just how does one describe a symphony concert or the benefits of energy conservation? If a physical object is involved, its portrayal (for example, showing an orchestra or an army tank) simply does not capture the real benefits one is trying to communicate. Indeed, the product may simply carry the wrong connotations (for example, an orchestra in white tie and tails may connote an intimidating formal occasion; a tank may connote skill training that may not seem useful outside of an army setting).

VARIATIONS WITHIN THE SECTOR

Of course, not all nonprofit organizations are the same and it is crucial for both observers and managers to recognize the differences. The National Taxonomy of Tax-Exempt Entities–Core Codes categorizes nonprofits under 10 broad headings:

Arts, Culture, and Humanities
Education
Environment and Animals
Health
Human Services
International, Foreign Affairs
Public, Societal Benefit
Religion Related
Mutual/Membership Benefit
Unknown, Unclassified

Nonprofits also vary in other ways, some by their own choosing and some by the nature of their sector.

Among the most important differences are the following:

1. *The extent of use of volunteers.* Some organizations like AARP are staffed primarily by fully paid professionals. While they may have a core of volunteers—often at the local level—they rely extensively on their paid staff. Other organizations such as Habitat for Humanity International rely on volunteers for their building activities. Indeed, for such organizations, a major social value they provide is the opportunity for volunteering and bonding with other like-minded individuals. A problem with volunteers involves day-to-day management. A universal complaint of managers who have to work with volunteers is that they are unreliable. One manager has what he calls a "rule of thirds" for volunteers. According to his experience, one-third of all volunteers will be highly motivated, eager to help out, and highly responsive to superiors' directions. At the other extreme is the third who seem to want little more than to tell their friends that they volunteered. They seldom appear at all for work. Their promises of assistance are rarely kept, and when they do appear, they resist directions to do anything they don't *really* feel like doing. The third in the middle is the group that can make or break the organization. The ability to effectively motivate and direct this group is the true test of a nonprofit managers' interpersonal skills. The simple fact that a manager doesn't have the "carrot" of a salary or the "stick" of potential firing to use to motivate and direct the people needed to make the marketing program successful is often a crucial hindrance in carrying out an effective and fast-moving marketing program.

2. *The extent of for-profit competition.* Some fields such as health care and the arts have major for-profit competition and, to compete, often have to be much more aggressive than nonprofits that merely compete—and cooperate—with other nonprofits. Even the latter need to be vigilant to possible private sector competition. In recent years, a number of for-profit universities have sprung up such as the University of Phoenix and DeVry University.[107]

3. *Sources of funds.* If the proposed activity or the organization as a whole is funded through private philanthropy or government grants, marketing may be affected by restrictions on what can be done. In some cases, the least bothersome problem (but nonetheless an important source of irritation) is procedural restrictions that formally specify the steps to be taken, the forms to be filled out, the individuals with whom one must "touch base," or all three. To cite a typical example, many U.S. government contracts put a substantial hurdle before nonprofit marketers who wish to carry out research by requiring that questionnaires be approved by the Office of Management and Budget before being taken into the field. A more fundamental challenge is when the funder proscribes specific tactics such as target audience contact via the Web, efforts to eliminate some market segments as too challenging or less in need, or certain promotional styles such as the use of erotic themes.

4. *Nature of the behavior the organization is attempting to influence.* The major *organizational* mission of a church or a synagogue involves the promulgation of religious lifestyles, whereas the major organizational mission of museums involves cultural involvement. But some of the specific *activities* of these two institutions could be virtually identical from a marketing standpoint—both, for example, seek members, conduct fundraising lotteries, and sell goods such as Christmas cards or posters. However, the *way* identical marketing activities are carried out may be

affected by the type of organization. A church, for example, might feel it must be relatively dignified in promoting its lottery or its Christmas cards, a museum might feel it should have a relatively "classy" promotion, and a neighborhood youth group might feel that its image requires a more trendy style.

A Typology of Behavioral Challenges

As we will discuss further in Chapter 4, the behavior that the nonprofit marketer is trying to influence can be thought of as the result of an *exchange*. Target audience members are asked to exchange something they value (e.g., giving up smoking) for something beneficial provided by the nonprofit organization (e.g., becoming part of an anti-tobacco industry cohort). As seen from the target consumer's perspective, he or she is being "asked" to incur costs or to make some sacrifices (that is, to give up something valuable) in return for some promised benefits. In the main, the kinds of costs consumers are usually asked to "pay" by nonprofit marketers are any of four types:

1. *Economic costs*—for example, to give up money or goods to a charity, or simply to buy a product or service.
2. *Sacrifices of old ideas, values, or views of the world*—for example, to give up believing that the world is flat, that women are inferior, that one is not getting senile, or that one is not hooked on drugs.
3. *Sacrifices of old patterns of behavior*—for example, to start to wear seat belts or to let someone else meet some of your physical or psychological needs.
4. *Sacrifices of time and energy*—for example, to perform a voluntary service or give blood to a hospital or the Red Cross.

In return for these kinds of sacrifices, consumers in nonprofit enterprises receive benefits of three basic kinds: economic (both goods and services), social, and psychological. The combination of these kinds of sacrifices and benefits yields the matrix outlined in Table 1-4. Here we see that it is only the first two cells in the top left corner of the matrix that we typically identify as the domain of the profit sector—although, as we've noted, some nonprofits such as hospitals and schools also promote these transactions as

TABLE 1-4	Cost/Benefit Matrix for the Profit/Nonprofit Sector			
	BENEFITS			
Costs	*A Product*	*A Service*	*Social*	*Psychological*
Give up economic assets	Buy a poster	Pay for surgery or an education	Donate to alma mater	Donate to charity
Give up old ideas, values, opinions	Receive free Goodwill clothing	Support neighborhood vigilantes	Support Republicans	Oppose abortion
Give up old behaviors, undertake or learn new behaviors	Practice birth control and receive a radio	Undertake drug detoxification treatment	Go to geriatric group once a week	Wear seat belts
Give up time or energy	Participate in a study and receive a coffeemaker	Attend a free concert	Volunteer for Junior League	Give blood

their primary objective. It is the other 14 cells that are truly in the nonprofit domain, since *by definition* they cannot generate a profit. What does it mean to be responsible for transactions in these 14 cells?

ETHICAL CHALLENGES IN THE NONPROFIT SECTOR

A final dimension that makes the nonprofit sector different comprises the ethical challenges it faces. As Salamon and Sokolowski point out, nonprofits are challenged to meet important social service and value-expressive needs of communities and nations that are not met by the other two sectors.[108] To help them meet these challenges, the government gives them special rights, privileges, and financial support while the citizenry contributes its own time and money to further these ends.

However, this special status comes with special obligations. All organizations and all citizens have the responsibility to pursue their missions and goals in a responsible and ethical manner. But in our opinion, nonprofits have a higher standard to meet. Nonprofits do not operate mainly to advance the interests of their own supporters—they use society's resources and goodwill to meet society's needs. Thus they owe that society careful attention to the ends it seeks and the methods it uses.[109] Some of the ethical issues that we can raise are suggested in Exhibit 1-1. We shall return to many of these issues in succeeding chapters.

EXHIBIT 1-1

SOME ETHICAL ISSUES FOR NONPROFIT MARKETERS

1. Is it ethical to use marketing strategies and tactics for *any* social problem? Is the Ku Klux Klan a nonprofit? Can it use nonprofit marketing techniques? Should a nonprofit marketer work for the Klan?

2. Should nonprofit techniques that are successful in one culture be applied to other cultures? For example, should condom advertising be used in Muslim countries?

3. Do the ends of nonprofit marketing justify any means? Is deception acceptable if one is trying to induce a person to give up harmful drugs? Should radios be given out as an incentive for men to get vasectomies in countries with excessive population growth?

4. Should a nonprofit marketer with *proven* strategies overpromise outcomes in order to be allowed to work on a new social problem where he or she *knows* nonprofit marketing can be very effective?

5. Does the involvement of Girl Scouts selling cookies as their major fundraising activity change Girl Scout members into salespeople? Is this good for the girls?

Summary

Marketing involves efforts to influence target audiences. These audiences may be clients or customers, donors, and other funding agencies and volunteers. Although controversial in the 1970s, nonprofit marketing is no longer considered a radical approach to solving the problems of public and nonprofit organizations. In the twenty-first century, dramatic growth is seen in social marketing, the international sector, cause-related marketing, and concern about the ethical implications of nonprofit marketing strategies and tactics.

This seventh edition text focuses on approaches and techniques that can significantly improve the practice of marketing management in the nonprofit sector on the part of existing and future managers. It emphasizes the development of (1) a proper *mindset* for marketing, (2) a *systematic approach* to solving marketing problems, and (3) an awareness and ability to use the very latest *concepts and techniques* from the private sector.

The starting point for consideration of strategic marketing in nonprofit organizations is a clear perception and understanding of the unique environment in which they operate. Nonprofit organizations can be defined legally, but it is more crucial to understand the organization's environment and the specific—and sometimes unusual—marketing activities that constitute its mission. The missions of nonprofit organizations differ depending on the type of demand they seek to influence and the type of activity in which they are engaged. The organization's type of activity can be defined in terms of the key concept of exchange. On the one hand, target customers are asked to "pay" economic costs; sacrifice old ideas, values, and views of the world; sacrifice old patterns of behavior; or sacrifice time and energy. In return, they can expect products, services, social or psychological benefits, or some combination of these. Although some nonprofits seek to influence exchanges of money for goods and services just like for-profit organizations, what makes them unique is their concentration on exchanges involving nonmonetary costs on the one hand and social and psychological benefits on the other. Influencing such exchanges requires different perspectives and modified techniques. Peculiarities of the kinds of transactions sought in the nonprofit world make it hard to "sell brotherhood" like soap. They also raise important ethical issues with which each nonprofit marketer must grapple.

Questions

1. After a career as a private sector marketer, your cousin is thinking of taking a senior marketing position at one of the top 20 nonprofit organizations. What are some of the major differences she should expect to encounter?
2. Many critics think that "political marketing" gives marketing a bad name. In their view, it represents everything that is evil about the discipline. Do you agree or disagree? Why?
3. Name two socially important subjects where you consider marketing to have had little use or effect (for example, global warming). Why is this the case and what would you recommend? (Be careful not to equate advertising with marketing.)
4. Could marketing approaches be useful in confronting Islamic terrorism? Explain.
5. In which foreign countries would you expect to see the most growth in the number and impact of nonprofit organizations in the next 20 years? Which would have the least growth? Why?

Notes

1. "New Federal Report Outlines Economic Benefit of Volunteering in America," Corporation for National and Community Service, June 12, 2006 (at www.nationalservice.gov/about/newsroom/releases_detail.asp?tbl_pr_id=399; retrieved October 30, 2006).
2. Michael O'Neill, "Developmental Contexts of Nonprofit Management Education," *Nonprofit Management and Leadership*, Vol. 16, No. 1 (Fall 2005), pp. 5–17.
3. Lester M. Salamon, et al., *Global Civil Society: Dimension of the Nonprofit Sector* (Baltimore: The Johns Hopkins Center for Civil Society Studies, 1999).
4. *The Chronicle of Philanthropy,* October 26, 2006.

5. Les Silverman and Lynn Taliento, *What You Don't Know About Managing Nonprofits—and Why It Matters* (New York: McKinsey & Company, March 2005).

6. Noelle Barton, Maria Di Mento, and Alvin P. Sanoff, "Nonprofit Executives See Healthy Pay Increases," *The Chronicle of Philanthropy*, September 26, 2006; M. Gibelman, "What's All the Fuss About? Executive Salaries in the Nonprofit Sector," *Administration and Social Work*, Vol. 24, No. 4 (2000), pp. 59–74.

7. Shirley Sagawa and Eli Segal, *Common Interest, Common Good: Creating Value Through Business and Social Sector Partnerships* (Boston: Harvard Business School Press, 2000); Joseph Galaskiewicz and Wolfgang Bielefeld, *Nonprofits in an Age of Uncertainty: A Study in Organizational Change* (Hawthorne, New York: Aldine de Gruyter, 1998), summarized in *The Independent Sector, Facts and Findings*, Vol. 2, No. 1 (Summer 2000), pp. 1–4.

8. Alan R. Andreasen, "Intersector Transfer of Marketing Knowledge" in Paul N. Boom and Gregory T. Gundlach (Eds.), *Handbook of Marketing and Society* (Thousand Oaks, CA: Sage Publications, Ltd., 2001), pp. 80–104.

9. Peter F. Drucker, "What Business Can Learn from Nonprofits," *Harvard Business Review*, July–August 1989, pp. 88–93.

10. Rosabeth Moss Kanter, "From Spare Change to Real Change: The Social Sector as Beta Site for Business Innovation," *Harvard Business Review*, May–June 1999, pp. 122–132; Robin J. B. Ritchie, Sanjeev Swami, and Charles B. Weinberg, "A Brand New World for Nonprofits," *Journal of Nonprofit and Voluntary Sector Marketing*, Vol. 4, No. 1 (1999), pp. 29–42.

11. "The Big Picture," *Business Week*, November 6, 2006, p. 13.

12. Philip Kotler and Sidney J. Levy, "Broadening the Concept of Marketing," *Journal of Marketing*, January 1969, pp. 10–15.

13. Philip Kotler and Gerald Zaltman, "Social Marketing: An Approach to Planned Social Change," *Journal of Marketing*, July 1971, pp. 3–12.

14. Benson Shapiro, "Marketing for Nonprofit Organizations," *Harvard Business Review*, September–October 1973, pp. 223–232.

15. Kotler and Levy, "Broadening the Concept of Marketing."

16. Andreasen, "Intersector Transfer of Marketing Knowledge."

17. Philip D. Harvey, *Let Every Child Be Wanted: How Social Marketing Is Revolutionizing Contraceptive Use Around the World* (Westport, CT: Auburn House, 1999); Christopher H. Lovelock, "A Market Segmentation Approach to Transit Planning, Modeling and Management," in *Proceedings of the Sixteenth Annual Meeting of the Transportation Research Forum*, 1975, pp. 247–258.

18. Ibid.

19. See, for example, Charles Weinberg, "Marketing Mix Decision Rules for Nonprofit Organizations," in Jagdish Sheth (Ed.), *Research in Marketing*, Vol. 3 (Greenwich, CT: JAI Press, 1980), pp. 191–234.

20. See, for example, Michael L. Rothschild, *An Incomplete Bibliography of Works Relating to Marketing for Public Sector and Nonprofit Organizations*, 3rd ed. (Madison: Bureau of Business Research and Services, University of Wisconsin, 1981).

21. See, for example, Paul N. Bloom, "Evaluating Social Marketing Programs: Problems and Prospect," *1980 Educators Conference Proceedings* (Chicago: American Marketing Association).

22. Kotler and Zaltman, "Social Marketing."

23. Robin E. MacStravic, *Marketing Health Care* (Germantown, MD: Aspen Systems Corporation, 1977).

24. See, for example, John L. Compton, "Public Services—To Charge or Not to Charge," *Business*, March–April 1980, pp. 31–38.

25. In addition to the first five editions of the present volume, there are now the following: Christopher H. Lovelock and Charles B. Weinberg, *Marketing for Public and Nonprofit Managers*, 2nd ed. (Redwood City, CA: The Scientific Press, 1989); David Rados, *Marketing for Non-Profit Organizations* (Boston: Auburn House Publishing Company, 1981); Armand Lauffer, *Strategic Marketing*

for Not-for-Profit Organizations (New York: The Free Press, 1984); Larry L. Coffman, *Public Sector Marketing* (New York: John Wiley, 1986); Douglas Herron, *Marketing Nonprofit Programs and Services: Proven and Practical Strategies to Get More Customers, Members, and Donors* (San Francisco: Jossey-Bass, 1997); Janel M. Radtke, *Strategic Communications for Nonprofit Organizations: Seven Steps to Creating a Successful Plan* (San Francisco: Jossey-Bass, 1998); Adrian Sargeant, *Marketing Management for Nonprofit Organizations* (Oxford: Oxford University Press, 1999).

26. Philip Kotler and Roberta N. Clarke, *Marketing for Health Care Organizations* (Englewood Cliffs, NJ: Prentice-Hall, 1986).

27. Philip Kotler and Karen F. A. Fox, *Strategic Marketing for Educational Organizations* (Englewood Cliffs, NJ: Prentice-Hall, 1985).

28. Robert E. Stearns, *Marketing for Churches and Ministries* (New York: The Haworth Press, 1992).

29. Philip Kotler, Donald H. Haider, and Irving Rein, *Marketing Places* (New York: The Free Press, 1993).

30. Philip Kotler, Somkid Jatusripitak, and Suvit Maesincee, *The Marketing of Nations: A Strategic Approach to Building National Wealth* (New York: The Free Press, 1997).

31. Seymour H. Fine, *The Marketing of Ideas and Social Issues* (New York: Praeger, 1981).

32. For example, Ralph M. Gaedeke (Ed.), *Marketing in Private and Public and Nonprofit Organizations: Perspectives and Illustrations* (Santa Monica, CA: Goodyear, 1977); Michael P. Mokwa, William D. Dawson, and E. Arthur Priere (Eds.), *Marketing the Arts* (New York: Praeger, 1980); Michael P. Mokwa and Steven E. Permut, *Government Marketing* (New York: Praeger, 1981); Philip D. Cooper, *Health Care Marketing: Issues and Trends* (Germantown, MD: Aspen Systems Corporation, 1979); Russell W. Belk (Ed.), *Advances in Nonprofit Marketing* (Greenwich, CT: JAI Press, 1985, 1990); Lee W. Frederiksen, Laura J. Solomon, and Kathleen A. Brehony, Eds., *Marketing Health Behavior* (New York: Plenum, 1984).

33. Christopher H. Lovelock and Charles B. Weinberg, *Public & Nonprofit Marketing: Readings & Cases,* 2nd ed. (San Francisco, CA: The Scientific Press, 1990); Philip Kotler, O. C. Ferrell, and Charles Lamb (Eds.), *Strategic Marketing for Nonprofit Organizations: Cases and Readings* (Englewood Cliffs, NJ: Prentice-Hall, 1987).

34. Richard K. Manoff, *Social Marketing* (New York: Praeger, 1985).

35. Philip Kotler and Eduardo L. Roberto, *Social Marketing: Strategies for Changing Public Behavior* (New York: The Free Press, 1989).

36. For example, *Populations Reports, Contraceptive Social Marketing: Lessons from Experience* (Series J, No. 30, July–August 1985); *Operations Research: Lessons for Policy and Programs* (Series J, No. 31, May–June 1986); and *AIDS Education—A Beginning* (Series L, No. 8, September 1989).

37. *The Marketing Planning Workbook* (Alexandria, VA.: United Way of America, 1989).

38. Mary Debus, *Handbook for Excellence in Focus Group Research* (Washington, DC: Academy for Educational Development, n.d.).

39. Mark R. Rasmuson, Renata E. Seidel, William A. Smith, and Elizabeth Mills Booth, *Communications for Child Survival* (Washington, DC: Academy for Educational Development, June 1988).

40. *Making Health Communications Work: A Planner's Guide* (Washington, DC: Office of Cancer Communications, U.S. Department of Health and Human Services, April 1989).

41. For example, William D. Novelli, "Can We Really Market Public Health? Evidence of Efficacy," paper presented to the Third National Conference on Chronic Disease Prevention and Control, Denver, Colorado, October 19–21, 1988; Mary Debus, "Lessons Learned from the Dualima Condom Test Market," SOMARC Occasional Paper, September 1987; and William Smith, "A Consumer Strategy for Health, Nutrition and Population," Academy for Educational Development, 1989.

42. Roseanne Mirabella and Naomi B. Wish, "Nonprofit Management Education: Current

Offerings in University Based Programs" at http://pirate.shu.edu/~mirabero/Kellogg.html; Roseanne Mirabella and Naomi B. Wish, "Educational Impact of Graduate Nonprofit Degree Programs: Perspectives of Multiple Stakeholders," *Nonprofit Management & Leadership,* Vol. 9, No. 3 (2000), pp. 329–340; Dennis R. Young, "Nonprofit Management Studies in the United States: Current Developments and Future Prospects, *Journal of Public Affairs Education,* Vol. 5 (1999), pp. 13–23; Michael O'Neill, "Developmental Contexts of Nonprofit Management Education," *Nonprofit Management and Leadership*, Vol. 16, No. 1 (Fall 2005), pp. 5–17.

43. Alan R. Andreasen, *Social Marketing in the 21st Century* (Thousand Oaks, CA: Sage Publications, 2006).

44. William A. Smith, *Lifestyles for Survival: The Role of Social Marketing in Mass Education.* (Washington, DC: Academy for Educational Development, October 1989); Michael Ramah, "Social Marketing and the Prevention of AIDS," Washington, DC: Academy for Educational Development AIDSCOM Project, 1992.

45. Jeff French and Clive Blair-Stevens, "From Snake Oil Salesmen to Trusted Policy Advisors: The Development of a Strategic Approach to the Application of Social Marketing in England," *Social Marketing Quarterly,* Vol. XII, No. 3 (Fall 2006), pp. 29–40.

46. Alan R. Andreasen, *Marketing Social Change* (San Francisco: Jossey-Bass, 1995).

47. Rob Donovan and Nadine Henley, *Social Marketing: Principles and Practice* (Melbourne, AU: IP Communications, 2003).

48. Philip Kotler, Eduardo Roberto, and Nancy Lee, *Social Marketing: Strategies for Changing Public Behavior* (Thousand Oaks, CA: Sage Publications, 2002).

49. Walter Wymer Jr., Patricia Knowles, and Roger Gomes, *Nonprofit Marketing* (Thousand Oaks, CA: Sage Publications, 2006).

50. Philip Kotler and Nancy Lee, *Marketing in the Public Sector: A Roadmap for Improved Performance* (Upper Saddle River, NJ: Wharton School Publishing, 2007).

51. Kay Lautman, *Direct Marketing for Nonprofits: Essential Techniques for the New Era (Aspen's Fundraising Series for the 21st Century)* (Washington, DC: Aspen Institute Publishers 2001); Ted Hart, James M. Greenfield, and Michael Johnston, *Nonprofit Internet Strategies: Best Practices for Marketing, Communications, and Fundraising Success* (Hoboken, NJ: John Wiley & Sons, 2005); Sandra Beckwith, *Publicity for Nonprofits: Generating Media Exposure That Leads to Awareness, Growth, and Contributions* (Chicago: Kaplan Publishing 2006); John J. Burnett, *Nonprofit Marketing Best Practices* (forthcoming 2007); Katia Andresen, *Robin Hood Marketing: Stealing Corporate Savvy to Sell Just Causes* (Thousand Oaks, CA: Jossey-Bass 2006).

52. Salamon, et al., *Global Civil Society.*

53. John A. Quelch and Nathalie Laidler-Kylander, T*he New Global Brands; Managing Non-governmental Organizations in the 21st Century* (New York: Thomson South-Western, 2005).

54. Ibid.

55. David Osborne and Ted Gaebler, *Reinventing Government* (New York: Plume, 1993).

56. Miklós Marschall, "The Nonprofit Sector in a Centrally Planned Economy," in Helmut K. Anheier and Wolfgang Seibel (Eds.), *The Third Sector: Comparative Studies of Nonprofit Organizations* (Berlin: Walter de Gruyter, 1990), pp. 277–291.

57. "Goodwill Changes Name to Reflect 'Global Influence,'" *The Nonprofit Times* (December 1993), p. 41.

58. Timothy M. Devinney, Patrice Auger, Gianna Eckhart, and Thomas Birtchnell, "The Other CSR," *Stanford Social Innovation Review* Fall 2002, pp. 30–37; Jocelyn Daw, *Cause Marketing for Nonprofits: Partner for Purpose, Passion, and Profits* (Hoboken, NJ: John Wiley & Sons, 2006).

59. Kathleen M. O'Regan and Sharon M. Oster, "Nonprofit and For-Profit Partnerships: Rationale and Challenges of Cross-Sector Contracting," *Nonprofit and Voluntary Sector Quarterly,* Vol. 29, No. 1 (2000),

pp. 120–140; Alan R. Andreasen and Minette E. Drumwright, "Alliances and Ethics in Social Marketing" in Alan R. Andreasen (Ed.), *Ethics in Social Marketing* (Washington, DC: Georgetown University Press, 2001), pp. 95–124.

60. M. Lindenberg, "Are We at the Cutting Edge or the Blunt Edge? Improving NGO Organizational Performance with Private and Public Sector Strategic Management Frameworks," *Nonprofit Management & Leadership*, Vol. 11 (2001), pp. 247–270.

61. Patrick E. Murphy and Paul N. Bloom, "Ethical Issues in Social Marketing," in Seymour Fine (Ed.), *Social Marketing: Promoting the Causes of Public and Nonprofit Agencies* (Boston: Allyn & Bacon, 1990), pp. 68–78.

62. Andreasen (Ed.), *Ethics in Social Marketing.*

63. Nelson Rosenbaum, "The Competitive Market Model: Emerging Strategy for Nonprofits," *The Nonprofit Executive*, July 1984, pp. 4–5.

64. Mark Dowie, *American Foundations* (Cambridge, MA: The MIT Press, 2001).

65. Weisbrod (Ed.), *To Profit or Not to Profit*, p. 1.

66. Brad Stone, "R$_x$ Thirty Minutes of Stairmaster Twice Weekly: Hospitals Court the Sweaty Set with Health Clubs," *Newsweek*, March 17, 1997, p. 46 (cited in Weisbrod (Ed.), *To Profit or Not to Profit*).

67. Judith Dobrzynski, "Art (?) To Go: Museum Shops Broaden Wares at a Profit," *New York Times*, December 10, 1997, pp. A1, A16 (cited in Weisbrod (Ed.), *To Profit or Not to Profit*).

68. Gina Kolata, "Safeguards Urged for Researchers: Aim Is to Keep Vested Interests from Suppressing Discoveries," *New York Times*, April 17, 1997, p. A13 (cited in Weisbrod (Ed.), *To Profit or Not to Profit*).

69. Reed Abelson, "Charities Use For-Profit Units to Avoid Disclosing Finances," *New York Times*, February 9, 1998, pp. A1–A12 (cited in Weisbrod (Ed.), *To Profit or Not to Profit*).

70. Buffett's commitment pledge, June 26, 2006, at www.berkshirehathaway.com/donate/bmgfltr.pdf (retrieved September 23, 2006).

71. Nicole Wallace, "Blending Business and Charity," *The Chronicle of Philanthropy*, September 28, 2006, pp. 14–15.

72. Caroline Preston, "Mayor Bloomberg Donates $125-Million to Fight Smoking Around the World," *The Chronicle of Philanthropy*, August 31, 2006, p. 31.

73. Ibid.

74. Kevin Sullivan and Mary George, "Branson to Invest Billions to Combat Global Warming," *Washington Post*, September 22, 2006, p. D2.

75. Peter Dobkin Hall, "Philanthropy, Public Welfare, and the Politics of Knowledge: Acquiring Knowledge by Taking Risks," in Deborah S. Gardner (Ed.), *Vision and Values: Rethinking the Nonprofit Sector in America* (New York: The Nathan Cummings Foundation, 1998), pp. 11–27.

76. Robert D. Putnam, *Bowling Alone: The Collapse and Revival of American Community* (New York: Simon & Schuster, 2000).

77. Angela M. Eikenberry and Jodie Drapal Kluver, "The Marketization of the Nonprofit Sector: Civil Society at Risk?" *Public Administration Review*, Volume 62, No. 2 (March/April 2004), pp. 132–140.

78. Paul Light, *Making Nonprofits Work* (Washington, DC: The Aspen Institute, 2000).

79. William Foster and Jeffrey Bradach, "Should Nonprofits Seek Profits?" *Harvard Business Review* Vol. 83, No. 2 (February 2005), pp. 92–100.

80. *The Chronicle of Philanthropy*, October 26, 2006.

81. Ibid.

82. Jed Emerson and Fay Twersky (Eds.), *New Social Entrepreneurs: The Success, Challenge and Lessons of Nonprofit Enterprise Creation* (San Francisco: The Roberts Foundation, 1996); C. T. Clotfelter and T. Ehrlich (Eds.), *Philanthropy and the Nonprofit Sector in a Changing America* (Bloomington Indiana University Press, 1999); Christine W. Letts, William P. Ryan, and Allen Grossman, *High Performance Nonprofit Organizations* (New York: John Wiley and Sons, Inc., 1999).

83. Light, *Making Nonprofits Work.*

84. Joseph Galaskiewicz and Wolfgang Bielefeld, *Nonprofits in an Age of Uncertainty.*

85. Downloaded from http://nccsdataweb.urban.org/PubApps/ profile1.php?state=US (retrieved on October 30, 2006).

86. Lester M. Salamon, *The Resilient Sector: The State of Nonprofit America* (Washington, DC: Brookings Institution Press 2003).

87. Trends in Nonprofit Employment, Earnings 1990–2004. OMB Watch, August 19, 2004, from www.ombwatch.org/article/articleview/ 2347/1/2, retrieved August 23, 2006.

88. Mark Wilhelm, Patrick Rooney, and Eugene Temple, "Changes in Religious Giving Reflect Changes in Involvement: Life Cycle and Cross-Cohort Evidence on Religious Giving, Secular Giving and Attendance," Working Paper, Center on Philanthropy at Indiana University, June 2005.

89. Harvy Lipman, "Giving to Church-Led Charities Declines," *The Chronicle of Philanthropy*, November 9, 2006, p. 27.

90. Lester A. Salamon, S. Wojciech Sokolowski, and Regina List, *Global Civil Society: An Overview* (Baltimore, MD: Center for Civil Society Studies, Institute for Policy Studies, The Johns Hopkins University, 2003).

91. Lester A. Salamon and Wojciech Sokolowski, "Volunteering in Cross-National Perspective: Evidence from 26 Countries," Working Paper, The Johns Hopkins Comparative Nonprofit Sector Project, 2001.

92. Burton A. Weisbrod, *The Voluntary Independent Sector* (Lexington, KY: Lexington Books, 1978).

93. Salamon and Sokolowski, "Volunteering in Cross-National Perspective."

94. Alberto Alesina and George-Marios Angeletos, "Fairness and Redistribution," *The American Economic Review*, Vol. 95, No. 4 (September 2005), pp. 960–981.

95. William P. Ryan, "The New Landscape for Nonprofits," *Harvard Business Review*, January–February 1999, pp. 127–136.

96. Harvey, *Let Every Child Be Wanted*.

97. "Tsunami relief seen as model for cooperation," *Catholic World News*, July 15, 2005.

98. "New Figures Put Quake Toll At More Than 79,000," *Associated Press*, October 19, 2005 (retrieved from www. Msnbc.com/id/9626146 on September 21, 2006).

99. William M. Leavitt and John J. Kiefer, "Infrastructure Interdependency and the Creation of a Normal Disaster: The Case of Hurricane Katrina and the City of New Orleans," *Public Works Management & Policy*, Vol. 10, No. 4 (2006), pp. 306–314.

100. *Unfair Competition by Nonprofit Organizations with Small Business: An Issue for the 1980s* (Washington, DC: Office of Advocacy, U.S. Small Business Administration, November 1983); Robert D. Herman and Denise Rendina, "Donor Reaction to Commercial Activities of Nonprofit Organizations: An American Case Study," *Voluntas: International Journal of Voluntary and Nonprofit Organizations*, Vol. 12, No. 2 (June 2001), pp. 157–169.

101. Bruce R. Hopkins, "The Tax Implications of Profit-Making Ventures," *The Grantsmanship Center News*, March–April 1982, pp. 38–41.

102. Bruce R. Hopkins, *The Law of Tax-Exempt Organizations*, 3rd ed. (New York: John Wiley, 1979).

103. Michael L. Rothschild, "Marketing Communications in Nonbusiness Situations or Why It's So Hard to Sell Brotherhood Like Soap," *Journal of Marketing*, Spring 1979, pp. 11–20.

104. Andreasen, *Marketing Social Change.*

105. Bloom and Novelli, "Problems and Challenges."

106. Rothschild, "Marketing Communications."

107. Goldie Blumenstyk, "For-Profit Education: Facing the Challenges of Slower Growth," *Chronicle of Higher Education*, January 6, 2006.

108. Salamon and Sokolowski, "Volunteering in Cross-National Perspective."

109. Andreasen (Ed.), *Ethics in Social Marketing.*

2

DEVELOPING A TARGET AUDIENCE-CENTERED MINDSET

SERMONS, ROCK & ROLL, AND A LATTE

The headline on the front page of the *New York Times* Sunday business section on October 22, 2006, read: "Prepare Thee for Some Serious Marketing." It seems that a range of religious denominations—most of them Protestant—have found significant value in modern marketing approaches for increasing their congregations and more effectively meeting their needs. A main goal has been to reach young people 18 to 30 who more often say that they have no religious affiliation.

Using ideas "from any number of consumer products companies," the United Methodist Church introduced a full array of mainstream marketing approaches in some churches. Advertising messages are delivered primarily over cell phones and the Internet. Churches make services more welcoming to new people—there are signs to the bathrooms and social hours before and after services. It seems to work. Attendance in churches using these approaches has increased 10 to 19 percent and return rates for first-timers—a key marketing indicator—have risen 4 to 7 percent.

Branding has been equally successful as a way to both differentiate a church's value propositions and to appeal more to young people. Willow Creek Church, a nondenominational church in South Barrington, Illinois, has been one of the pioneers in using modern marketing approaches to draw younger audiences. It provides a range of social services and ways for individuals to connect with each other and meet their spiritual needs. A recent innovation is branded as "The Table." The church uses its member database to connect people within particular high school districts to meet at one person's home around "the table" to discuss social and spiritual issues. The concept grew from meetings that one Willow Creek pastor had with a Texas developer who "mentored me in transferable concepts to the church from his world of business."

Main services at Willow Creek have become more attuned to the needs and lifestyles of younger target audience members. The *Times* article describes a fall 2006 service at Willow Creek's home site, a site that "feels more like a corporate campus—with a Starbucks-like coffee shop and a cafeteria featuring pizza—than a church." At the service—held on a Saturday evening, not Sunday—"nearly 3,000 people listened to jazz and Christian rock in a 7,095-seat auditorium outfitted with plasma-screen televisions and a modern sound system. A group of actors performed a skit on a set designed to look like the inside of a home before the pastor took the stage to deliver the main sermon."

Willow Creek will soon roll out "Neighborhood Life," a branded effort to get the membership at Table events to become involved in deserving charity projects in their neighborhoods.

Source: Fara Warner, "Prepare Thee for Some Serious Marketing, *New York Times,* October 22, 2006, pp. 3–1, 3–4. Copyright © 2006 by The New York Times Co. Reprinted with permission.

It is the central tenet of this book that one can be a successful marketer only if one has adopted the proper *marketing mindset.* This means having a clear appreciation for what marketing comprises and what it can do for the organization. More important, it means developing a philosophy of marketing that *puts the target audience at the center of everything one does.* The target audience may be a potential client, a donor, or a volunteer. The same principles apply. We would argue that much of what is unattractive about marketing practice today is the result of a lack of appreciation of the proper way to go about *doing* marketing. Marketing is not intimidation or coercion. It is not "hard selling" and deceptive advertising. It is a sound, effective technology for creating exchanges and influencing behavior that, when properly applied, *must be* socially beneficent because its major premise is responding to target audience needs and wants. In the wrong hands (i.e., in the hands of those without the proper mindset), what is called "marketing" can be manipulative and intrusive, and an embarrassment to those of us who use marketing as it ought to be used.

A major objective of this book is to develop this proper marketing mindset in the reader to the extent that it will become second nature in his or her future day-to-day marketing practice.

THE BOUNDARIES OF MARKETING

One of the reasons for the rapidly growing interest in marketing is that it applies to such a wide range of situations in individuals' professional and personal lives. We would argue that *all* the following represent instances of *marketing:*

- McDonald's says, "You deserve the best today."
- Safeway claims it has "lower prices overall."
- You—or your son or daughter—asks someone for a date to go to the movies.
- A subordinate asks for a raise in pay.
- You ask a coworker to join you as a volunteer in the upcoming United Way fund drive.
- You approach a foundation for a major grant.

- You seek government approval of a new social venture in a developing country.
- You petition a Senator for a new law.
- Your local public TV station holds a pledge drive.
- You try to convince your sister to stop smoking.
- You request that a supplier give you an additional 3 percent discount if you commit to a larger order.
- You send a press release to a local TV station urging coverage of an upcoming workshop on the homeless.

What is common to all of these situations is that someone (a marketer) is attempting to influence the behavior of someone else (a target market). Marketing is not just something that an organization such as Procter & Gamble or Pepsi-Cola does. It is something nonprofits and government agencies do and something we do daily in our individual personal lives. And, given that all these situations involve marketing, they can all benefit from the application of the very best marketing management techniques.

We define marketing management as follows:

Marketing management is the process of planning and executing programs designed to influence the behavior of target audiences by creating and maintaining beneficial exchanges for the purposes of satisfying individual and organizational objectives.

An important feature of this definition is that *it focuses on exchanges.* Marketers are in the profession of creating, building, and maintaining *exchanges.* For example, I give Wal-Mart 79 cents and Wal-Mart gives me a bar of sweet-smelling soap; or I walk two hours to get to the doctor's office, wait there three more hours and worry that my house and children are being neglected, and the doctor gives my baby an immunization that protects her from measles. Because exchanges only take place when a target audience member takes an action, *the ultimate objective of marketing is to influence behavior.*

This definition permits us to distinguish marketing from several things it is *not.* Marketing's objectives are not *ultimately* either to educate or to change values or attitudes. It may seek to do so as *a means* of influencing behavior. However, if someone has a final goal of imparting information or knowledge, that person is in the education profession, not marketing. Further, if someone has a final goal of primarily changing attitudes or values, that person may be described as a propagandist, a lobbyist, or perhaps an artist, but not a marketer. While marketing may use the tools of the educator or the propagandist, marketing's critical distinguishing feature is that its ultimate goal is to influence behavior (either changing it or keeping it the same in the face of other pressures).

Unfortunately, however, many of those who *could* use marketing principles do not do so because they do not see the relevance of marketing to their tasks. But we would argue that, in nonprofit organizations, public relations specialists, fundraisers, volunteer recruiters, and employee supervisors are all marketers at one time or another. And, as such, they can all benefit from understanding the philosophy and approach to marketing outlined in this book.

However, there are many nonprofit organizations (as well as some in the private sector) who *think* they are marketers but who go about it the wrong way because they do not really understand what proper marketing is all about. Consider the following examples:[1]

- The director of an urban art museum describes her marketing strategy as "an educational task. I assemble the best works available and then display them grouped by period and style so that the museum-goer can readily see the similarities and differences between, say, a Braque and a Picasso or between a Brancusi and an Arp. Our catalogues and lecture programs are carefully coordinated with this approach to complete our marketing mix."
- The public relations manager of a social service agency claims, "We are very marketing oriented. We research our target markets extensively and hire top-flight creative people with strong marketing backgrounds to prepare brochures. They tell our story with a sense of style and graphic innovation that has won us several awards."
- A marketing vice president for a charitable foundation ascribes his success to careful, marketing-oriented planning. "Once a year we plan the entire year's series of messages, events, and door-to-door solicitation. We emphasize the fine humanitarian work we do, showing and telling potential donors about the real people who have benefited from donations to us. Hardly a week goes by without some human-interest story appearing in the local press about our work. The donors just love it!"

Each of these executives *thinks* he or she understands what marketing is all about. *They do not.* A recent study by Andreasen, Goodstein, and Wilson showed that a great many nonprofit executives simply "do not get it" and do not invest in marketing infrastructure. The authors concluded that "marketing is often not accorded its own department and the CEOs and colleagues of nonprofit marketers seldom have a marketing perspective. These characteristics are associated with a misunderstanding of marketing's potential role beyond sales and its characterization as a discretionary expense to be reduced in tough times. Further, the simple ability to apply marketing concepts and tools is seen as hampered by greatly restricted budgets."[2]

THE EVOLUTION OF THE MARKETING MINDSET

To understand modern marketing management, it is useful to trace the evolution of different business orientations toward marketing in the private sector over the last hundred years, in part because examples of all of them exist today. Three orientations can be distinguished.

The Product/Service Mindset

When marketing first emerged as a distinct managerial function around the turn of the century, it found itself in an era that venerated industrial innovation in the design of new products. It was a period that saw the development of the radio, the automobile, and the electric light. In this first period, marketing also was decidedly *product oriented.* The belief was that to be an effective marketer, you simply had to "build a better mousetrap," and, in effect, target audiences would beat a pathway to your door.

Even today, many organizations are in love with their product or service. They believe strongly in its value even if their publics are having second thoughts. They strongly resist modifying their value proposition even if this would increase its appeal to others. Thus, in the nonprofit world many colleges continue to require a foreign language even though few ever learn the language and most students report the whole experience as a waste of time and money. Museums continue to feature favorite works of art year after year even though they attract the attention or interest of virtually no one. And many churches present the same dull Sunday morning sermons year after year as a matter of tradition, ignoring the changing interests of churchgoers and the steadily declining attendance. We define a product/service mindset as follows:

A product/service mindset toward nonprofit marketing holds that success will come to those organizations that bring to market goods and services they are convinced will be good for the public.

The Sales Mindset

For innovative offerings, a product/service mindset will often suffice for a time. This was the case in the early days of international family planning, which thrived on pent-up demand by providing condoms and pills. But eventually, an organization exhausts the untapped market and must find new targets. Now the challenge is seen to be to convince target audiences that the marketer's proposal is *really* desirable and certainly better than alternatives. It is much of what comprises soft drink and beer marketing and the battle between Wal-Mart and Target or between Ford and Toyota. This orientation leads to significant increases in the role of advertising and personal selling in the marketing mix. The best marketer is perceived to be the best salesperson or the most creative advertising copywriter.

A sales mindset toward marketing holds that success will come to those organizations that best persuade target audiences to accept their offerings rather than competitors' or rather than no offering at all.

The sales mindset is common in organizations whose mission does not involve products or services. That is, their challenge may involve simply persuading target audiences to engage in a desired behavior or refrain from engaging in an undesirable one. Examples would be smoking, doing drugs, or practicing abuse. A typical approach is (metaphorically) to shout at the target audience to do what *everyone* knows is the right thing!

The Target Audience Mindset

The previous two orientations begin marketing planning with the *organization* and *what it wants to offer*. The product/service mindset expected grateful target audiences to come to the organization that had the best or cheapest offerings. Under the selling mindset, the task was somewhat different. The organization was forced to go out and convince target audiences that it had a really good—perhaps superior—offering. In the 1950s, a number of leading marketers came to a very important realization: They had the marketing equation turned backward. They had been trying to *change target audiences to fit what the organization had to offer*, but truly the target audience was sovereign. Whatever he or she chose to do was what determined the for-profit organization's success. Target audiences ultimately decided what transactions were to be made—not the marketer. And if this was so, then *marketing planning must begin with the target audience, not with the organization. Outside–inside marketing must replace inside–outside marketing.*

This simple idea is the essence of the modern approach to marketing.[3] It is, in fact, the philosophy that will guide this volume. We shall see that, for the organization, a marketing mindset of "target audience-centeredness" requires that the organization systematically study target audiences' needs, wants, perceptions, preferences, and satisfaction through using surveys, focus groups, and other means. The organization must constantly act on this information to improve its offerings to meet its target audiences' needs better. Fortunately, a growing number of nonprofit organizations are adopting this mindset, including libraries,[4] health care systems,[5] and a range of other nonprofits.[6]

A target audience mindset holds that success will come to that organization that best determines the perceptions, needs, and wants of target markets and continually satisfies them through the design, communication, pricing, and delivery of appropriate and competitively viable value propositions.

This proper philosophic orientation has a great many implications for the way a nonprofit marketing program ought to be run. As we shall see, adopting a target audience orientation does not, as many nonprofit managers and scholars fear,[7] mean that the organization must cater to every target audience whim and fancy. It doesn't mean that a symphony conductor or theater manager must give up his or her artistic integrity. Nor does it mean that health care institutions must abandon their professional standards or that college professors must become classroom song-and-dance performers. Those who argue that these consequences will befall the organization if the devil (marketing) is let in the door simply misunderstand what a target audience orientation truly means. To restate: It means that marketing planning must *start* with target audience perceptions, needs, and wants. It means that, even if an organization can't or ought not change certain aspects of the offering, the highest volume of exchange will always be generated if the way the organization's value proposition is described, "priced," "packaged," and delivered is fully responsive to what is referred to in the current jargon as "where the target audience is coming from."

Consider two examples. For years the Buffalo Philharmonic, like many other symphonies, had a serious problem in trying to broaden its audience. It was willing to change its program somewhat, but ultimately it felt that Mozart is Mozart and somehow target audiences must be made to change *their* attitudes and behavior. Then, in the early 1970s, a modest university research project revealed that many target audience members who indicated that they thought they *might* like to attend a concert did not do so because they expected the occasion to be very formal. As these potential target audiences put it, "We can't go because we don't have the proper clothes. We would feel really uncomfortable around all those fancy-dressed people." The orchestra itself was seen as distant, formal, and forbidding. Once the Philharmonic realized that this was where these potential target audiences were "coming from," they took great pains to humanize the orchestra and the concertgoing experience. Orchestra section members began playing shirt-sleeve chamber music programs at neighborhood art fairs and other local outdoor events. Contact was made with local primary and secondary schools. The orchestra even performed at halftime at a Buffalo Bills football game!

A new conductor, Michael Tilson Thomas, began appearing on local television and giving brief informal talks to audiences at specific concerts. Concertgoing never again had the sense of formality that was clearly keeping many potential patrons away, and attendance figures clearly reflected this new target audience-centered orientation.

Another example is national in scope. For years, organizations committed to reducing the incidence of smoking in the United States believed that the major reason individuals did not quit was that they did not realize the consequences of continued smoking or, if they did, they were not frightened enough of these consequences to take action. As a result the marketing programs focused almost exclusively on communicating the very real dangers of smoking to target smokers. In a sense, they were trying to *sell* the stop-smoking idea to what they thought was an ignorant and reluctant audience.

It was only after an extensive review of a large number of target audience studies that organizations like the National Cancer Institute (NCI) realized that the "product" they were trying to sell—that smoking is bad for you—had already been sold. Seven out of eight smokers reported that they either wanted to quit smoking or had tried to quit several times in the past. Further analysis revealed that these target audiences perceived two extremely significant barriers to quitting. First, they felt they did not really know a technique for quitting that would be effective for them. Second, even in cases where they were vaguely aware of a method that might work, they were reluctant to try to quit because they expected to fail. They had either heard of many who had failed, or had failed themselves many times in the past. For these very reasons, they tended to "turn off" most antismoking commercials, since they saw these commercials as, in effect, asking them to fail again.

Once the cancer-fighting organizations finally understood this target audience perspective, the marketing efforts of NCI and its sister nonprofits changed dramatically. Warnings of the dangers of smoking were, of course, continued to deter new, young potential smokers. At the same time, a major new marketing thrust was developed along two fronts. First, efforts were made to develop and get into the field a wide range of quitting techniques. Second, the NCI and the American Cancer Society worked to persuade physicians and other health care workers to help smokers implement the newly available techniques and, just as important, to cope with smokers' often desperate fears of failing. The effects on cigarette consumption of this new target audience-centered campaign have been considerable.

TARGET AUDIENCE-CENTERED ORGANIZATIONS

The Buffalo Philharmonic and NCI cases are dramatic examples of the way individual marketing programs can be developed to respond to target audiences' needs, wants, and perceptions, and not just to the organization's own needs. But why, one must ask, did these organizations not develop these solutions sooner? The answer—and it is a crucial one—is that the organizations had not (and many still have not) developed a true target audience-centered *mindset* that had seeped into the consciousness of every member of the organization who had any managerial responsibility or contact of any kind with potential target audiences. We define a target audience-centered organization as follows:

A target audience-centered organization is one that makes every effort to sense, serve, and satisfy the needs and wants of its multiple publics within the constraints of its budget.

One result of a target audience-centered orientation is that the people who come in contact with such organizations report high personal satisfaction. They make such comments as "This is the best church I ever belonged to"; "I'm so glad I gave money to them: They tell me all about the wonderful things they are doing"; "I think this hospital is fine—the nurses are cheerful, the food is good, and the room is clean"; and "I met so many great people volunteering for them, I can't wait to go back!" These target audiences become the best advertisement for these institutions. Their goodwill and favorable word of mouth reach other ears and make it easy for the organization to attract and serve more people; they become supporters for life! The organizations are effective because they are target audience-centered.

Unfortunately, too many nonprofit organizations are not highly target audience-centered.[8] They fall into one of three groups. The first group would like to be more target audience-centered but lacks the needed resources or power over employees. The organization's budget may be insufficient to hire, train, and motivate good employees and to monitor their performance. Or management may lack the power to require employees to give good service, as when the employees are under civil service regulations or are volunteers and cannot be disciplined or fired for being insensitive to target audiences. One inner-city high school principal complained that his problem was not poor students but poor teachers, many of whom were "burned out" in the classroom and uncooperative but who could not be removed.

A second group of organizations is not target audience-centered simply because it prefers to concentrate on things other than target audience satisfaction. Thus, many museums are more interested in collecting antiquarian material than in making the material relevant or interesting to museumgoers. The U.S. Internal Revenue Service may be more interested in the number of people it processes per hour than in how much help each one really receives. When these organizations are mandated to exist or are without competition, they usually behave bureaucratically toward their clients.

Finally, there are always a few organizations that intentionally act unresponsively to the publics they are supposed to serve. In the 1980s, a local newspaper exposed that one food stamp office chose to be inaccessible in order to minimize the public's use of its service: "There is no sign on the building indicating that the food stamp office is inside ... there also was no sign anywhere in the building directing applicants to the basement, no sign on the door leading to the stairs, and no sign on the door to the office itself. The only indication that a food stamp office is located in the building is a small, handwritten sign on the door at the top of the stairs. Adding to the inconvenience, the food stamp office was closed from March 10 to April 8."[9]

There is, fortunately, growing evidence that a target audience-centered approach is more likely to lead to superior performance. A recent meta-analysis of 11 empirical papers found that "market orientation" in the nonprofit sector was—*in all cases*—positively related to performance. Further, the authors found that the correlation was *higher* than in a comparison set of for-profit studies. An analysis of the pathways between market orientation and performance found there was a stronger pathway to subjective measures of outcomes than to a combination of subjective and objective measures. Two intervening variables that were found significant were "team spirit" and "organizational commitment." The latter findings would suggest that market orientation has some of its power in strengthening the managerial focus of nonprofit staffers themselves.[10]

On the other hand, as we shall discuss further in Chapter 7 on branding, not every observer of the nonprofit sector thinks that having a marketing orientation is necessarily a good thing for the sector as a whole. Eikenberry and Kluver note the trend but say: "The outcome is the potential deterioration of the distinctive contributions that nonprofit organizations make to creating and maintaining civil society." They see the trend as "incompatible with democratic citizenship and its emphasis on accountability and collective action for the public interest. . . . Furthermore, the market model places little or no value on democratic ideals such as fairness and justice."[11]

DETECTING AN ORGANIZATION-CENTERED ORIENTATION[12]

Conversations with nonprofit managers such as those quoted earlier make it abundantly clear that they *wish* to be target audience-centered and, in virtually all cases, truly believe they already are. In most cases, they are not. Fortunately, a number of "clues" exist that tend to give away an organization's *organization-centered* marketing philosophy. These clues, simply stated, are as follows:

1. The organization's value proposition is seen as inherently desirable.
2. Lack of organizational success is attributed to target audience ignorance, absence of motivation, or both.
3. A minor role is afforded target audience research.
4. Marketing is defined primarily as promotion.
5. One "best" marketing strategy is typically employed in approaching the market.
6. Generic competition tends to be ignored.

Understanding and recognizing these clues is essential if a nonprofit organization is to adopt the appropriate target audience-centered mindset and not deceive itself about its true orientation.

Clue No. 1: The Offer Is Seen as Inherently Desirable

The very nature of the value propositions promoted in the nonprofit sector often leads their sponsors to have an extremely high opinion of the value of their offerings. They simply see the behavior they are promoting as inherently desirable. They find it hard to believe that anyone would turn them down!

Committed theater managers find it hard to believe that right-thinking people wouldn't wish to attend a well-acted play; charitable organizations cannot accept a target audience's unwillingness to give; and those who head up nonprofit social issues groups often can't see why people won't vote for, say, cleaner air or prison reform. One organization that overcame the notion that its value propositions were inherently desirable is the NCI. Most women, NCI discovered, agreed that practicing breast self-examination was a good way to ensure early detection of breast cancer, and many knew how to do it. Yet the majority of women were not practicing breast self-examination, or did so at best only rarely. What was the problem? It turned out that among women who practiced self-examination, the discovery that there was no problem led to a sense of relief the first few times, but eventually the women became bored and stopped the procedure. At the same time, the prospect of finding a problem was so frightening to most other women that they never even tried self-examination. It was only when NCI understood the barriers perceived by the target audience to an obviously beneficial practice that it began to develop more user-oriented marketing programs. NCI's new stance, which was based on assuring women that lumps are often nonmalignant and that progress is being made in the fight against breast cancer, resulted in significant increases in breast self-examination practices among American women.

Clue No. 2: Target Audience Ignorance and Lack of Motivation Are Seen as the Barriers to Success

It is, of course, not surprising to find that if a manager believes that wearing seat belts or giving to the United Way is something everyone should do, then if someone does *not* respond to a specific marketing effort, there are really only two explanations. Either potential target audiences do not *truly* understand the value proposition (that is, do not share the organization's inherent belief in it), or they are simply not motivated enough to take action. Managers conclude that they simply haven't yet found the right way to communicate the benefits of the value proposition or they just haven't found the right incentives to get target audiences to overcome their "natural" inertia.

These managers have a relatively benign view of target audiences. There is, however, a very large number of nonprofit managers who feel—often unconsciously—much hostility toward target audiences. Their basic perception is that target audiences are really *enemies*. The managers feel that it is these recalcitrant target audiences who are standing in the way of the organization becoming more successful. Such views manifest themselves in the organization's treatment of target audiences at the box office, on the telephone, in the field, or in any other personal encounter. They are evident in the disapproving look of the health worker confronted by an impoverished family unwilling to get proper immunization for their children. They are apparent in the resentful faces of fundraisers turned down by those who are "uninterested" or "too busy" and in the sarcastic voices of box office people trying to explain ticket availability to confused telephone target audiences.

It is not hard for the consuming public to sense in these encounters the organization's true colors and to perhaps respond in kind. And if they do, of course, they only convince the managers that they were right about the target audiences in the first place.

A key strategic assumption of managers in organizations with this attitude seems to be that the task of marketing is to get the target audience to change to fit the organization rather than the other way around. They do not realize that (1) in a great many nonprofit marketing situations, target audiences are very hard to change, while the organization is not; (2) the organization is under the manager's control and the target audience is not; and (3) changing the organization to accommodate target audiences, if fully carried out, ensures that target audience needs and wants will be carefully monitored and followed.

Clue No. 3: A Minor Role Is Given to Target Audience Research

Target audience ignorance or lack of motivation is not always the key problem in causing an organization's lack of success. This was obvious in the NCI smoking example discussed earlier. However, many organization-centered marketing managers are unlikely to discover this through target audience research. Because they attribute their lack of success to target audiences, their opinions about what research is needed is very straightforward. Since part of the problem is that too many target audiences are ignorant about the organization's value proposition, they believe one kind of study that is needed is research into the nature and extent of target audience ignorance and into the characteristics of who is ignorant. Further, since motivation is a major problem, research may also be needed to try to map the attitudes of those who are knowledgeable to show why they are so negative and unmotivated. Such research, it is hoped, will yield clues as to how to motivate them to take action.

In the main, however, target audience research is too often absent in nonprofit organizations. As we point out in Chapter 5, there are a number of reasons for this. Many nonprofit managers think that research is too expensive, or they think it is needed only for major decisions. Some managers associate research with statistics and computers that can be intimidating. Often these managers argue that research typically tells managers what they already knew. These myths all get in the way of effective use of key target audience information.

Despite the low level of research activity, the potential can be dramatic. As most profit-sector marketers will attest, research can challenge some managers' most fundamental assumptions about their target audiences. The example of the antismoking groups' assumptions about target audience ignorance of the dangers of smoking is a classic case in point.

Clue No. 4: Marketing Is Defined as Promotion

If one seeks the marketing challenge as one of eliminating ignorance and increasing motivation, then it is inevitable that the tool one will focus on is better communication. Managers will see the need for the following:

- A better copywriter and better copywriting
- A better brochure
- A new image
- Better salespeople with better sales presentations
- More posters in more places
- Ads placed in prime time rather than in public service announcement (PSA) "media ghettos"
- More and better press releases
- Better relations with newspapers and TV news departments
- A new advertising agency

Other elements of the marketing mix such as pricing, offer redesign, and better distribution are seen as "not really the problem."

A good example of the consequences of viewing marketing problems as stemming from target audience ignorance and lack of motivation is found in the efforts to secure blood donations. Many blood-collection agency heads believe that the best way to encourage donations is to tell target audiences about the good things that a donor's blood can do or to stress that giving blood is a civic duty. They believe that people hold back from giving because they don't appreciate the "gift's" virtues or because they are afraid. Thus, agency heads reason, the marketing task is to tell target audiences as dramatically and convincingly as possible about the benefits to society of giving blood and to assure them that the costs are trivial; indeed, giving is not really such a "big deal."

While these messages work for some people, important segments respond to very different approaches that are not based on impersonal media. Many donation programs, for example, have become more successful by simply changing the distribution strategy and going to major target audience groups rather than insisting that they come to the agency, or having the hours of service convenient for potential donors, not just for the medical staff. In some cases, men can be motivated by challenges to their masculinity. Contrary to the view of the typical donor, the macho man who can brag to his coworkers that he is a 20-gallon donor is really responding to benefits he sees for himself. He may care relatively little about "society." Even more perversely, it may be that the higher the costs of giving, the greater the pain and suffering in the process of giving, the greater the rewards! Thus campaigns in factories that publicize individuals' giving records (bar charts or 10- and 20-gallon lapel pins) and that (contrary to the usual program) don't downplay the possible psychological and physical costs of giving can be highly effective. In such situations, informal group pressure, rather than persuasion, is the key marketing tool.

However, social, fraternal, and church group members can be motivated to give blood by the let's-all-participate aspects of a bloodmobile visit. They will respond to messages about camaraderie, about "feeling left out if you don't join in," or about letting the group down if you don't go. Messages of this sort have little to say about the occasion for the get-together or its value to society, recognizing that for these potential donors the key distinction is also selfish: the desire to be wanted and loved by other members of a group. Here again, rather than brochures and advertisements, it is within-group word of mouth stimulated by key opinion leaders that does the job.

Clue No. 5: One Really Good Strategy Is Seen to Be All You Need

Since the nonprofit administrator is not often in as close touch with the market as a target audience-oriented marketer would be, he or she may view the market as monolithic or at least as having only a few crudely defined market segments. Subtle distinctions are ignored or played down. As a consequence, most nonprofits tend to see the need for only one or two marketing strategies aimed at the most obvious market segments (e.g., young people, families, and the elderly). This climate of managerial certainty precludes experimentation either with alternative strategies or with variations across a number of subtle market subsegments. In this view, the problem is to inform and motivate, and the challenge is about the same for every target audience.

Also encouraging this approach is the fact that nonprofit managers often come from nonbusiness backgrounds and may fear taking risks. Personal job survival and slow aggrandizement of the budget and staff are often their paramount objectives. And since such administrators are typically responsible only to a volunteer board that meets irregularly and sometimes prefers to know little about day-to-day operations, they do their best to keep a low profile and avoid causing waves. Simple, consistent strategies that imply well-thought-out analysis are the best choice for career safety. Too much change, too much variation, and too much experimentation may seem to imply that one really isn't too sure about what to do. Such a low-profile, risk-averting strategy is, of course, tactically sound if one's organization happens to make up any losses with fundraising or government allocations. In such cases, aggressive marketing strategies are not really necessary.

Clue No. 6: There Is Assumed to Be No Generic Competition

In the private sector, organizations compete at many different levels, from interbrand competition all the way back to competition at the generic or basic desire levels. In the nonprofit sector, many organizations do, in fact, compete—the Heart Fund with the American Cancer Society, the Metropolitan Museum of Art with the Whitney Museum or the Museum of Modern Art. However, many institutions don't have clear competitors because their value propositions are intangible or stress unique behavior changes. The "competitors" for those marketing, say, blood donations or forest-fire prevention are not immediately apparent. Therefore, it's not surprising that such marketers ignore competition at more basic levels. But at one level, blood banks, for example, undoubtedly compete with other charities (who seek dollars, not blood) for donors. Even institutions with easily identifiable organizational competitors often face competition from unlikely quarters. Thus art museums compete with aquariums for family outings, with books and educational TV for art appreciation, and with movies and restaurants as places to socialize.

Probably the most serious competition that nonprofit marketers face is the status quo. Marketing is most often about behavior change. Existing behavior patterns provide target audiences with important rewards, or they wouldn't be doing them. Naïve marketers seem to think that simply promoting the new behavior will be enough. But, in reality, their biggest challenge will be to "unsell" or at least replace the old behavior. A program that simply urges a teenager to stop using drugs because he or she will be healthier, less likely to be imprisoned, and so on is likely to be much less successful than a program that recognizes that "doing drugs" provides important satisfactions to the user: It may contribute to a sense of belonging (to a gang or a group); it may help the person define himself or herself (e.g., as being unique or "not like mom or dad"); it may relieve boredom or dull the pain and anguish of a dreadful home life. In such cases, the motivations to maintain the status quo will be very powerful. To be effective, marketers must clearly find ways to show that the recommended course of action will meet the same needs that the target audience member has. Simply to say that youngsters "shouldn't" do drugs to escape the reality of their painful lives is naïve in the extreme.

CHARACTERISTICS OF TARGET AUDIENCE-CENTERED MARKETING MANAGEMENT

The preceding sections have held up a mirror to the organization-centered nonprofit organization. We have learned what a true marketing organization is *not*. What, then, are the characteristics that one observes in a nonprofit organization that has fully adopted a modern marketing orientation? It will have the following characteristics.

- It will focus on behavior as the "bottom line" of much of what it does.
- It will be target audience-centered.
- It will rely heavily on research.
- It will have a bias toward segmentation.

- It will define competition broadly.
- It will have strategies using all elements of the "marketing mix," not just communication.

Behavioral Bottom Line

Target audience-centered marketers recognize that their success is ultimately achieved when people act. This is why an understanding of people and why and how they behave is the place where they start in thinking about any new marketing challenge. In well-planned marketing approaches, a considerable amount of time is spent just defining the behaviors that will be the focus and that will let the marketer brag about his or her success. An example of such a definition is the set of 16 critical "emphasis behaviors" defined by a coalition of health promoters for worldwide family health programs outlined in Exhibit 2-1.

Target Audience-Centeredness

In a sophisticated marketing organization, all marketing analysis and planning begin and end with the *target audience*. A target audience-centered organization always asks the following:

- To whom are we planning to market?
- Where are they to be found and what are they like?
- What are their current perceptions, needs, and wants?
- Will these perceptions, needs, and wants be different in the future when our strategy is to be implemented?
- How satisfied are our target audiences with our value proposition?

Sometimes the challenge is recognizing that the target audience does not think as the nonprofit organization marketers do. Date rape is a particular problem in colleges and nonprofit managers learned that many young men think that when a girl says "no" she is really just being coy or cute and wants the boy "to work for it." As a consequence, campaigns have focused on getting young men to stop when the girl says stop (see Figure 2-1).

Reliance on Research

Because the target audience is central, management realizes that it must have a profound understanding of target audience perceptions, needs, and wants and must constantly track changes in them so that the organization can respond to subtle shifts as quickly as they occur. Better still, to ensure that it is not merely reactive but *proactive* in its strategic planning, an alert market-oriented management will have in place a forecasting capability that can *anticipate* changes in target audience needs, wants, and perceptions.

This is not to say that a consistent reliance on research need be expensive. As we shall outline in Chapter 5, there are a great many techniques by which high-quality and clearly useful research can be carried out by imaginative managements at relatively modest cost. The critical requirement for achieving these benefits, however, is the proper mindset. The truly target audience-centered manager must continually "think research." The manager should assume that what he or she "believes" is not necessarily what is true. Intuition, casual observation, or "just common sense" do not constitute the ideal bedrock on which to build social marketing strategies and sound tactical decisions.

EXHIBIT 2-1

EMPHASIS BEHAVIORS FOR FAMILY HEALTH PROGRAMS

Reproductive Health Practices: Women of reproductive age need to practice family planning and seek antenatal care when they are pregnant.

1. For all women of reproductive age, delay the first pregnancy, practice birth spacing, and limit family size.

2. For all pregnant women, seek antenatal care at least two times during the pregnancy.

3. For all pregnant women, take iron tablets.

Infant and Child Feeding Practices: Mothers need to give age-appropriate foods and fluids.

4. Breastfeed exclusively for about 6 months.

5. From about 6 months, provide appropriate complementary feeding and continue breastfeeding until 24 months.

Immunization Practices: Infants need to receive a full course of vaccinations; women of childbearing age need to receive an appropriate course of tetanus vaccinations.

6. Take infant for measles immunization as soon as possible after the age of 9 months.

7. Take infant for immunization even when he or she is sick. Allow sick infant to be immunized during visit for curative care.

8. For pregnant women and women of childbearing age, seek tetanus toxoid vaccine at every opportunity.

Home Health Practices: Caretakers need to implement appropriate behaviors to prevent childhood illnesses and to treat them when they occur.

Prevention

9. Use and maintain insecticide-treated bednets.

10. Wash hands with soap at appropriate times.

11. For all infants and children, consume enough vitamin A.

12. For all families, use iodized salt.

Treatment

13. Continue feeding and increase fluids during illness; increase feeding immediately after illness.

14. Mix and administer ORS, or appropriate home-available fluid, correctly.

15. Administer treatment and medications according to instruction (amount and duration).

Care-Seeking Practices: Caretakers need to recognize a sick infant or child and need to know when to take the infant or child to a health worker or health facility.

16. Seek appropriate care when infant or child is recognized as being sick (i.e., looks unwell, not playing, not eating or drinking, lethargic or change in consciousness, vomiting everything, high fever, fast or difficult breathing).

Source: Adapted from: John Murray, Gabriella Newes Adeyi, Judith Graeff, Rebecca Fields, Mark Rasmuson, Rene Salgado, and Tina Sanghi, *Emphasis Behaviors in Maternal and Child Health: Focusing on Caretaker Behaviors to Develop Maternal and Child Health Programs in Communities* (Washington, DC: BASICS Technical Report, 1997).

Take the case of the Midwestern hospital marketer who believed he had a "foreign doctor" problem. The marketer knew that his hospital had more foreign doctors than major competitors in nearby cities. In part, this situation resulted from the fact that there was a major veteran's hospital nearby and many foreign doctors came there to do

FIGURE 2-1 Promoting a New Way of Thinking

Source: Copyright © 2005 Men Can Stop Rape, Inc. Photography by Lotte Hansen. www.MyStrength.org.

their residencies or to carry out a public service obligation. After such service, the doctors, many of whom had begun to develop modest practices in the area, quite naturally decided to stay in the city permanently.

The marketing manager "knew" that their presence in his hospital constituted a serious problem. After all, he knew the hospital was statistically different in its physician profile. And besides, he saw these doctors regularly in the building. He had heard patients and staff both complain about having difficulty understanding their "foreign doctors." Finally, the one major malpractice issue the hospital had recently faced had involved a foreign doctor. Thus the manager *knew* he had a problem.

To cope with this "problem," hospital management began to develop strategies both to change the mix of doctors in the community (and therefore the hospital) and to change patient and staff perceptions about the "foreign doctor problem." Fortunately, at about this time the hospital decided to carry out a field study with about 500 past and potential patients. Among the other valuable insights gained from this study was the information that the marketing manager's presumption about target audience perceptions of his foreign doctors was entirely wrong! Target audiences were indeed aware that there were many foreign doctors at the hospital, and a few acknowledged that communicating with these doctors was sometimes difficult. But on the whole, they did not see this as a serious problem. In fact, many in the patient sample felt that the foreign doctors were more conscientious and more caring for their patients than were some of their golf-playing, blasé U.S. counterparts. Several respondents said that they thought that cultural and language differences simply made the foreign doctors more conscientious about clearly understanding exactly what the patient really meant and what he or she needed. For many patients, then, the foreign doctors were not a problem but a boon to the hospital.

The lesson, of course, is that for a few thousand dollars (much of which was spent for information serving a wide range of other planning needs), the organization saved itself the cost of an extensive communication and recruitment project that could well have boomeranged.[13]

A Predilection for Segmentation

Just as the target audience-centered manager routinely thinks of the target audience and of the possible need for research before planning programs, so, too, should he or she habitually "think segmentation." That is, in designing any particular marketing program, the nonprofit manager should routinely assume, until shown otherwise, that the market ought best be thought of as a combination of a great many smaller subsegments that may deserve separate marketing programs. Certainly, the political marketers described in the vignette that started Chapter 1 saw great opportunities for micro-segmentation.

Of course, many nonprofit marketing managers do think of segmentation from time to time, but in our experience, only in the most general terms. Managers of symphony organizations, for example, are well aware that their prospects are better in high- than in low-income households, among women than among men, among the well educated rather than the less educated, and among the young or old rather than the middle-aged. And this understanding affects where they concentrate their budgets. But all too often these budgets are spent on a single "best" program, usually aimed at upscale households. (This, of course, stems from the familiar ignorance-and-motivation definition of the marketing "problem.")

Yet even within this market, many possibilities for more subtle segmentation exist and are all too often passed by. A study for the National Endowment for the Arts, for example, revealed that, despite wide industry "intuition" to the contrary, the best predictors of likely symphony attendance were not at all the traditional demographic characteristics like income and education but lifestyle factors, attitudes toward actual attendance, past experience, and childhood training.[14] Considering only the lifestyle measure, the study clearly showed that there were not just one but *two* major lifestyle groups interested in symphony attendance. One group was the "traditional" Cultural Lifestyle Group. This group made cultural events the center of their leisure pursuits. They tended to patronize the theater, opera, and museums, as well as the symphony. They were very much interested in the program content and artists at specific performances and tended to be swayed less by atmospherics and prices. They attended largely for the cultural experience it provided. This group is undoubtedly the one that many theater and symphony marketers have in mind when they design their "one best" strategy.

The research, however, identified a very different lifestyle group that also included excellent prospects for the symphony. The members of this Socially Active Group were very outgoing in their lifestyles. They went out a lot, not only to the symphony but to all sorts of nonclassical events. They liked to give parties and dinners and attend those of their friends. For this group, symphony attendance was largely a social experience. It was an opportunity to meet and talk with their friends. It was an occasion to plan a dinner beforehand and, perhaps, dessert or cocktails afterward. *Going out* was the thing. What was actually on the program was of less interest than who among their friends were going, what restaurants might be worth trying before the concert, and so forth.

Clearly, the appropriate strategies to reach these two groups are very different. More importantly, a strategy designed to appeal to one group might very well turn off the other. Suppose, for example, that a symphony manager designed a typical "one best," nonsegmented strategy stressing program elements. Print ads, public relations releases, and interviews by guest artists and the symphony staff would emphasize the works to be performed—perhaps highlighting a first performance locally of a particular composition, the debut of a precocious youngster, the innovativeness or difficulty of a particular program selection, or the conductor's mastery of the works of the composer featured at the concert. All this would be very appealing to those in the Cultural Lifestyle Group. At the same time, it might have just the opposite effect on the Socially Active Group. The latter might see the event as formal and stuffy, a program for the aficionados and definitely not one that they would understand and enjoy. Certainly it would not seem to them to be something that their friends would attend. The group, then, would be very much turned off by this "best" strategy.

Nonetheless, a marketing strategy could be chosen that emphasized the informality of the audience and the event, described the possibilities of making "an evening" of the occasion, talked about the ease of parking, and implied that "just about everyone" would be there. The Socially Active potential attendees might well be very attracted by such a prospect. At the same time, the Cultural Lifestyle Group may find this set of appeals vaguely distasteful. The marketing program might signal to them that the concert program would not be very challenging or, perhaps, even particularly well performed. Even worse, the campaign might suggest to the cultural sophisticates that all those untutored, unsophisticated social types would be in attendance, overdressed, and applauding in all the wrong places.

The lesson from this and similar lifestyle studies[15] is obvious. Markets can usually be segmented much further and in much more sophisticated ways than the naïve marketer usually imagines. However, only if the marketer has a target audience- and segmentation-oriented philosophy clearly in mind is he or she likely to look for these potentials. As this extended example shows, ignoring segmentation possibilities can mean not only missing chances for attracting new target audiences whom one is not now reaching, but driving away important audiences to whom one may have considerable appeal.

A Richer Conceptualization of Competition

An organization-centered marketer naturally defines the competition as "other organizations like us." Yet if one begins with target audiences, the definition of competition can become very different. Competition, in its most basic sense, really becomes whatever the *target audience* thinks it is. Thus, if certain target audience segments are considering treating a particular medical problem *themselves,* then *that* is the competition a hospital or clinic faces. If a potential donor thinks that money given to the American Red Cross is money that could have gone for a "needed" weekend ski vacation, then that vacation is the competition. If going to the symphony competes with working in the garden or having friends over for pizza in front of the TV, then those activities are the competition. If giving up drugs appears to mean giving up "the gang life," this must be addressed (see Figure 2-2).

Using the Full Marketing Mix

In contrast to those who conceive of marketing largely in terms of communications strategies designed to change target audiences to fit the organization's offering, sophisticated marketers view the marketing function as more diverse and the marketing objective as, above all, responding to target audience needs and wants. A diverse marketing program pays attention not only to communication but also to the nature of the value proposition, its cost to target audience members, and the channels through which it is made available. The true marketer's mindset considers that it is the organization that must be willing to adapt its value proposition to the target audience, and not vice versa. This necessarily means not just a willingness to talk about the value proposition in different terms but actually to change it (within the constraints set by artistic and professional standards and the organization's capabilities). The marketer must be willing to change the value proposition *itself* to which it wishes the target audience to respond. For instance, skilled political infighters in any legislature—federal, state, or local—are well schooled in the need to adjust proposed bills or regulations to fit the needs and wants of specific legislators with whom they are trying to make an exchange. It is not usually effective to take the stance that one knows one's position is *right.* Often one must compromise. Compromising may be seen simply as adaptive marketing.

The marketers must also be willing to change the cost of the value proposition or the place of performance. The marketing director of the Mass Transit District in Champaign–Urbana found that by offering free or minimal-cost bus service on the very coldest, snowiest days, he could induce auto owners who were averse to using buses (but who are perhaps *more* averse to driving and parking their own cars in terrible weather) to try using the bus. The director also cleverly put extra emphasis on on-time performance at every stop on these nasty days, with the reasonable expectation that target audiences would believe that punctual performance under such terrible circumstances surely would predict excellent service on normal days. Clearly, this nonprofit marketer had learned well that effective marketing is a lot more than just good advertising. It is the right value propositions in the right place at the right time and at the right price.

At 4:00 my kid will be at

If you can't fill in the blank, you need to start asking. It's a proven way to steer kids clear of drugs. It's not pestering. It's parenting.

ASK: WHO? WHAT? WHEN? WHERE?
QUESTIONS. THE ANTI-DRUG.

For ideas on questions to ask, contact us 1-800-788-2800 www.theantidrug.com www.drugfreeamerica.org

FIGURE 2-2   Competition for the Anti-Drug

Source: Partnership for a Drug Free America. Reproduced with Permission.

INTRODUCING A TARGET AUDIENCE-CENTERED MINDSET

If marketing is to take its rightful place in nonprofit organizations, management must not only understand and accept its function, but also take care to introduce it effectively.[16] Management may find many obstacles to driving marketing concepts and tools throughout the organization. Interviews with marketing executives at major nonprofits identified a range of problems:[17]

> A continuing refrain in respondent comments was the frustration caused by their limited budgets. As one respondent (VP Marketing, Environment) put it, "We're supposed to be consumer-oriented, but we can't adequately reach the

consumer." Budget problems also make it difficult for respondents to engage in organizational branding and image building, which they worried might appear indulgent and wasteful to their non-marketing colleagues or to monitoring agencies and the media. As noted by a Manager of Special Events Planning, Environment, "We can't brand. Our marketing dollars are limited to promoting specific programs or events." . . . The lack of funds also affects the availability of planning information. Many respondents claimed that they did not do a lot of strategic planning because they did not have the data to do so. As one respondent (Manager of Advertising, Arts) noted, "In the for-profit world, it's a quantifiable process to benchmark and track hard costs and revenues. In the nonprofit sector, you just don't have the data." Another respondent (Director of Brand Development President, Other) indicated a major challenge, "It's really difficult to put a monetary value on a lot of programs, products and services that a nonprofit provides." A President, Other, noted, "Nonprofits think of marketing as an 'occasional' activity, so it can't be effective." Still another person (Director Brand Development, Health) reported, "Upper management hasn't been inclined to appropriately fund marketing programs." There are also internal barriers within organizations, observed a GM of Marketing Alliances, Arts, "Departments in nonprofits act as 'silos,' which makes cross-fertilization of ideas a challenge." Some respondents also found resistance to ideas from the commercial sector in general, not just marketing ideas. Some sense that their colleagues think that marketing and other business concepts and tools are not appropriate. A VP Corporate Relations, Health, observed, "Creating expensive, slick collateral would be perceived by donors and our board as a waste of donor money." . . . Some respondents suggest that management style may discourage the use of business and marketing concepts. "[There] is the focus on building and reaching consensus internally across departments that can result in inertia in nonprofits," said a Director of Marketing, Health.

When seeking to introduce marketing formally into an organization, remember the following:

1. It should be granted that the organization is already doing many things that are "marketing." Marketing will be accepted more rapidly if one adopts the existing language, at least initially, rather than trying to change the organization's accustomed language to fit current marketing jargon.
2. Other pressures on the organization should be recognized (for example, the need to maintain artistic or professional integrity, to secure major government subsidies, and so on).
3. Limited understanding of marketing by present organization members should be expected and accommodated.
4. The translation of for-profit marketing concepts and tools to the specific nonprofit context should not be done mechanically.
5. One should recognize that many nonprofit managers have come to their positions from nonbusiness backgrounds and may be defensive about their naïveté (although not necessarily hostile to marketing).

6. There should be a careful selection of early marketing projects. Lovelock and Weinberg suggest that five criteria should be met by such programs:

   - They should be evaluated by explicit performance measures.
   - They should be completed within a short to medium time period.
   - They should use a limited portion of available resources.
   - They should be neither peripheral nor central to the organization.
   - Their results should be obvious to key decision makers within the organization.[18]

7. In the final analysis, getting marketing accepted in an ongoing organization is much more a *political* activity than a simple attempt to market marketing through persuasion. Allies must be sought—most particularly the chief executive officer. "Enemies" whose view of the organization and of their own turf as being threatened by the new approach (e.g., those in public relations or communications) should be assumed to exist, whether visible or not, and dealt with directly.

8. Setbacks will occur and compromises will have to be made.

The issue of achieving organizational change is a subject beyond the scope of this book. Interested readers may wish to read the works of Argyris and Schon,[19] Quinn,[20] or Weick.[21] How the marketing function should eventually be structured in order to be effective in an ongoing, nonprofit organization will be discussed further in Chapter 18.

HOW FAR TO GO IN ADOPTING A TARGET AUDIENCE ORIENTATION

Marketing is a subarea of management, and not necessarily at the top of the organization. Clearly and importantly, top management has a responsibility to decide what role it will allocate to marketing. *Management* must decide which goals marketing can help achieve and how. It is management's prerogative to say that certain decisions will be made with little or no attention to marketing concerns. Thus the management of a theater company may decide that it will choose the season's program on the basis of the interests of its directors who, in turn, will consider both past programming and the availability of acting and production talent in choosing specific plays and performers. Marketing may *then* be assigned the task of maximizing audience revenues for that given program. It is important to realize, however, that this does not mean that marketing should fall back upon a selling mindset. It means that marketing planning must simply start with target audiences in deciding how to describe, package, price, and distribute a given behavior change program. Marketers must merely recognize that the specific program cannot be changed. But, there are many ways to market *Othello*!

At the other extreme, a theater manager may decide to be very target audience-driven. He or she may carefully survey the potential audience, consider past revenues and audience reactions, and consider what artist and plays are available to maximize future attendance. This organization would then establish a value proposition that limits attention to achieving artistic objectives but that maximizes sales. Note that the two approaches were equally target audience-oriented. They simply differ in the management goals they were designed to achieve.

The question of "how far marketing should go" is really a variable always under the control of management. Since marketing is merely a means of influencing behavior to serve organization ends, those who wish to protect those other ends need not fear marketing. This means, in our view, that top managers—indeed many of those in the nonprofit organization—should have a marketing mindset if their ultimate goal is to influence behaviors of various kinds. We would argue that everyone, at minimum, has to work with other people and a marketing mindset can be helpful even in the most mundane situations. The CEO often has the most important constituencies to influence—the board, the government, regulators, donors, and/or foundations. For this reason alone, the CEO should be the organization's best marketer!

Summary

The starting point for an effective marketing strategy is the proper marketing mindset. Marketing can reflect a product/service mindset, a selling mindset, or a target audience mindset. The first two approaches are characterized by management putting the organization's own needs and desires at the center of the strategic process. It is only when management realizes that it is the target audience who truly determines the long-run success of any strategy that the nonprofit firm can join the ranks of the sophisticated target audience-centered marketing strategists typically found in the private sector.

Several clues can be used to identify nonprofits that are still mired in an organization-centered perspective. They see their value propositions as inherently desirable. They see the ignorance or lack of motivation of their target audiences as the major barrier to the organization's success. Research plays a minor role in strategy formulation. Marketing tends to be defined as synonymous with promotion. A "one best" strategy is typically used in approaching the market, and generic competition is typically ignored in the process.

By contrast, target audience-centered strategies begin with the target audience and the target audience's needs and wants. They rely heavily on research findings about their target audiences. They routinely assume—unless shown otherwise—that their markets ought to be segmented. Since they adopt the target audience's perspective, they inevitably define competition as coming from widely diverse sources, not just from similar products or services. Finally, they use all elements of the marketing mix (design of the offering, cost reduction, distribution, and promotion), not just communication.

Indoctrinating a nonprofit organization from top to bottom with the proper marketing mindset is not an easy task. The experience of those who have successfully achieved this objective suggests such strategies as recognizing the limited understanding of others about what marketing really is; allowing for other pressures on the organization that may temporarily mandate non-target audience-oriented approaches; picking visible, short-term projects for the first marketing applications; and recognizing that the introduction of a new mindset is as much a political exercise as a matter of logic and persuasion. Allies must be sought and enemies deflected. Above all, it is essential to secure a top-management commitment to the new way of thinking. Without it, a true marketing orientation will not be achieved and target audience-centered thrusts in one area will inevitably run afoul of organization-mindedness elsewhere.

Questions

1. Identify a nonprofit organization that you feel has a product/service or sales mindset. How would you recommend it shape its marketing strategy to a target audience-centered mindset? How would shifting its mindset improve its operations?
2. How would you go about justfiying investment in market research to a nonprofit organization that is currently not target audience-centered?
3. Explain the competitive landscape of the American Cancer Society. How might an effective marketing strategy prove to be a competitive advantage for it?
4. How can a nonprofit organization ensure its strategic planning is "proactive" rather than "reactive"? What are the defining characteristics of a "proactive" marketing strategy?

Notes

1. Alan R. Andreasen, "Nonprofits: Check Your Attention to Customers," *Harvard Business Review*, May-June 1982, pp. 105–110.
2. Alan R. Andreasen, Ronald C. Goodstein, and Joan W. Wilson, "Transferring Marketing Knowledge to the Nonprofit Sector," *California Management Review*, Vol. 47, No. 4 (Summer 2005), p. 17.
3. George S. Day, *The Market Driven Organization: Understanding, Attracting and Keeping Valuable Customers* (New York: The Free Press, 1999).
4. Jeanette A. Woodward, *Creating the Customer-Driven Library: Building on the Bookstore Model* (American Library Association 2004); Joan C. Durrance, Karen E. Fisher, and Marian Bouch Hinton, *How Libraries and Librarians Help: A Guide to Identifying User-Centered Outcomes* (Chicago: American Library Association, 2005).
5. Edward Chaplin and John Terninko, *Customer-Driven Healthcare: QFD for Process Improvement and Cost Reduction* (ASQ Quality Press 2000).
6. Paulette Padanyi and Brenda Gainer, "Market Orientation in the Nonprofit Sector: Taking Multiple Constituencies into Account," *Journal of Marketing Theory and Practice*, Spring 2004, pp. 43–58.
7. Adrian Sargeant, S. Foreman, and M. Laio, "Operationalizing the Marketing Concept in the Nonprofit Sector," *Journal of Nonprofit and Public Sector Marketing*, Vol. 10, No. 2 (2002), 41–53.
8. Chris T. Allen and Charles D. Schewe, "An Empirical Assessment of the Relative Marketing Orientations of Museum Directors and Marketing Practitioners," Working Paper 81–14, School of Business Administration, University of Massachusetts, Amherst.
9. Bill Gray, "This Food Stamp Office Is Hiding," *Chicago Tribune*, May 22, 1980.
10. Aviv Shoham, Ayalla Ruvio, Eran Vigoda-Gadot, and Nitza Schwabsky, "Market Orientation in the Nonprofit and Voluntary Sector: A Meta-Analysis of Their Relationships with Organizational Performance," *Nonprofit and Voluntary Sector Quarterly*, Vol. 35, No. 3 (September 2006), pp. 453–476.
11. Angela M. Eikenberry and Jodie Drapal Kluver, "The Marketization of the Nonprofit Sector: Civil Society at Risk?" *Public Administration Review*, Vol. 64, No. 2 (March/April 2004), p. 138.
12. Much of the material in this section was first presented in Andreasen, "Nonprofits."
13. For other approaches to health care marketing, see Michael Siegel and Lynne Doner, *Marketing Public Health* (Gaithersburg, MD: Aspen Publishers, Inc., 1998).
14. Alan R. Andreasen and Russell W. Belk, "Predictors of Attendance at the Performing Arts," *Journal of Consumer Research*, September 1980, pp. 112–120.

15. Sarah Todd and Rob Lawson, "Lifestyle Segmentation and Museum/Gallery Visiting Behaviour," *International Journal of Nonprofit and Voluntary Sector Marketing,* Vol. 6, No. 3 (2001), pp. 269–277.

16. See Philip Kotler, "Strategies for Introducing Marketing into Nonprofit Organizations," *Journal of Marketing,* Vol. 43 (January 1979), pp. 37–44; William R. George and Fran Compton, "How to Initiate a Marketing Perspective in a Health Care Organization," *Journal of Health Care Marketing,* Vol. 5, No. 1 (Winter 1985), pp. 29–37.

17. Andreasen, Goodstein, and Wilson, "Transferring Marketing Knowledge," pp. 10–11.

18. Christopher H. Lovelock and Charles B. Weinberg, *Marketing for Public and Nonprofit Managers* (New York: John Wiley, 1984), p. 561.

19. Chris Argyris and Donald A. Schon, *Organizational Learning: A Theory of Action Perspective* (Reading, MA: Addison-Wesley, 1978).

20. James Brian Quinn, *Strategies for Change: Logical Incrementation* (Homewood, IL: Richard D. Irwin, 1980).

21. Karl E. Weick, *The Social Psychology of Organizing* (Reading, MA: Addison-Wesley, 1969).

SECTION II

STRATEGIC PLANNING AND ORGANIZATION

3

STRATEGIC MARKETING PLANNING

LET'S GET IBM TO COVER OUR OPERATING COSTS!

A major challenge for nonprofit organizations is balancing the interests demanded by the various sources of their support. How do you keep individual donors, corporate sponsors, volunteers, and service clients happy at the same time? If, as we recommend, you start with target audience needs and wants, what do you do if one group's needs and wants impacts another's? How do you balance immediate operating needs with the need to grow and build management capacity?

United Ways have just this kind of challenge. When they talk to individual donors, the donors reveal their passions for specific charities. Some want to address community challenges or focus on a specific charitable organization like the Girl Scouts or local museum. But they very often say that they don't want to see their donation "wasted on" administrative costs. Corporations also have community issues they want to see addressed or recipient groups they want to help because these problems or these charities fit with corporate interests. Home Depot gives to Habitat for Humanity International and local restaurants give to Share our Strength's "Taste of the Nation" promotions. But corporate executives do appreciate the need for administrative support.

The United Way of Central New Mexico (UWCNN) came up with a creative solution to the conflicting and complementary needs of the two groups. It asked: Why not have corporations support the United Way's administrative costs so that UWCNN could then promise individual donors that all their money would go to the charities of their choice? Corporations liked the idea but asked: (a) What if all the costs—especially for capacity building—are not met by corporate gifts, and (b) how would the corporations reap any reputational benefits—a major strategic need? In response, UWCNN developed a program in 1998 it called Corporate Cornerstones that had the corporations agree to cover administrative costs while the United Way undertook a significant corporate recognition program.

The approach has been a considerable success. Corporate gifts since 1998 rose 132 percent while declining 4 percent for United Way nationwide in the same period. At the same time, individual gifts were up 112 percent, presumably because of the apparent absence of pass-through costs. Even better, corporate gifts over the years have exceeded administrative costs and the excess has been used for training board members, fundraising, strategic planning, and a management database. Another fringe benefit has been that several company sponsors have also decided that they ought to become more involved in making sure that UWCNN was well run.

UWCNN has also invested efforts in donor education. It recognizes that the Corporate Cornerstones program may not last forever. UWCNN is putting resources into promoting the benefits to individual donors of building capacity and adequate administrative funding.

Source: "Giving Donors Control," *Stanford Social Innovation Review,* Spring 2006, p. 59. Reprinted by permission of the *Stanford Social Innovation Review.*

DOING MARKETING

As we have said repeatedly, marketing's role in the nonprofit organization is to influence behavior. In this chapter, we begin our consideration of how this role gets played out—and ought to be played out—in the very best nonprofits and government agencies. There are two dimensions here, one philosophical and one operational. The first dimension is the *centrality* of marketing *thinking* to the organization's operations. The second is more structural—how should marketing be *organized* and how should marketing be *done*. The philosophical challenge is to ask: Is marketing crucial to success or relatively marginal? At one end of the spectrum will be organizations like the American Legacy Foundation, whose mission is to eliminate smoking in the United States. If it does not influence the behavior of smokers, it has failed! At the other extreme might be the avant garde theater company that simply wants to put on daring plays, the foundation that wants to provide scholarships for needy students, or Habitat for Humanity International that wants to build homes for the homeless worldwide.

The latter organizations may think that they really do not need to pay much attention to marketing thinking to be successful. But, of course, their management would recognize that, to succeed, they need donations or grants, corporate support, and perhaps a bevy of volunteers. This highlights the tripartite nature of the challenge faced by most nonprofit organizations. To succeed, they typically need to influence three constituencies—clients/target audiences, funding sources (including corporations), and volunteers—in varying proportions. The problem is that many managers of nonprofit organizations do not see the latter two target audiences as marketing targets. They employ fundraisers and volunteer managers and, while the latter may have some marketing insights, they typically would not call themselves "marketers" and would not see themselves as having close affinities with those having to influence potential clients/target audiences. Unfortunately, this is often a view shared by top management and, in such cases, the potential for common approaches and synergies is lost.

The broader, more encompassing view of marketing we are advocating here is that influencing behavior is endemic to any organization function that is designed to influence people. So this means that the CEO needs to be well grounded in the concepts and tools in this book and that marketing thinking should be driven to every corner of the organization, including fundraising and staff recruitment and motivation. Let us be clear; we are not advocating that everyone be labeled a marketer—indeed, the use of the term may raise real barriers on the part of human resources people who have to influence workers and finance people who have to influence bankers. Marketing is not central to their roles. But when they have to influence people, the CEO should make sure that they *think like a marketer!*

Obviously, the structural role for marketing will depend on how management and the board see its role—that is, their philosophy of marketing. If marketing is just seen as responsible for influencing clients/target audiences, it may simply be a silo with that goal as their responsibility. But if management's philosophy is a much broader one, then marketing people would be slotted higher in the organizational structure and at least play a consultative (or perhaps training) role for functions that have only minor or tangential marketing-like challenges.

We would be naïve if we did not recognize that this broader, more pervasive role for marketing thinking is likely to produce conflicts when implemented at the structural level. Public relations people and fundraisers are likely to see themselves as different—of not using marketing approaches but of having their own special set of concepts and tools. In all likelihood, they will resent top management's efforts to develop a common approach to behavioral influence. In such cases, structural implementation of broad marketing thinking may take time and considerable top management sensitivity. In this case, one needs internal marketing of marketing!

In this chapter, we shall focus on the broad challenges of organizational strategy—how one actually plans marketing at two levels! First, there are the broadest challenges facing the entire organization, including:

- What target audiences do we wish to address?
  - What potential clients?
  - What potential donors?
  - What potential volunteers?
- How do we position ourselves against competition to be successful with these audiences?
- What broad approaches will we use across marketing initiatives—that is, what kind of marketing do we want to do?

Then there are challenges whenever one plans *specific campaigns*. These challenges often involve the same kinds of questions but also a host of micro issues such as what behavior to focus on, when and how to communicate about the behavior, what value proposition to offer the target audience, how to implement the campaign, and how to measure success.

In the sections to follow, we will consider both organizational and campaign planning approaches. In subsequent chapters (Chapters 4 through 7), we consider some of the key ingredients in both organization and campaign planning, including understanding target audiences, conducting marketing research, segmenting markets, and branding and positioning. The next major section (Chapters 8 through 14) then focuses more narrowly on campaign marketing, including developing and positioning offers to target audiences, managing perceived—and real—costs to them, communicating about the value proposition (especially through advertising and public relations), and making it easy to carry out the desired actions (which can include inaction!).

The next section focuses more specifically on the challenges of marketing to other groups—donors, corporations, and volunteers. The last section considers how one might organize to carry out these marketing efforts and how to measure effectiveness at both the organizational and campaign levels.

ORGANIZATIONAL MARKETING PLANNING

We begin our consideration of strategy at the broadest organizational level, asking what behaviors should the organization plan to influence over the long run—that is, what is its mission—and how do we organize to achieve this? We call this challenge the organizational marketing planning process (OMPP). The OMPP, as outlined in Figure 3-1, assumes an ongoing enterprise but one that is rethinking what it wants to do. The process is organized into three central components typically carried out in sequence. First is an analysis of the internal and external environments in which the organization must operate. This involves looking inside the organization—at its goals, objectives, culture, and at the strengths and weaknesses it brings to its marketing challenges. Analysis also involves looking outside the organization at the market environment it faces, particularly the publics it will target and its competition. Long-range planning will also require analysis of trends in the organization's macroenvironment, including social, political, technical, and economic components.

The next stage of the OMPP is developing the broad *strategy* that will guide the organization's overall marketing effort and its many details. There are two parts to this, first setting marketing goals and objectives and then specifying what we will call *the core marketing strategy*. The latter consists of specific market targets, competitive positioning, and key elements of the marketing mix. This guiding core strategy comprises the framework within which various campaigns will be developed over the years. A key challenge in developing the core marketing strategy will be how to simultaneously satisfy the three main types of target audience—potential and existing clients/target audiences, funders, and volunteers.

The organizational marketing plan is then completed by the specification of an appropriate and effective structure and a measurement and control system put in place.

For simplicity, we will assume that the organization chooses one broad mandate, although it can have multiple approaches to achieving it. For example, the Campaign to Prevent Teen Pregnancy has a "simple" mission embodied in its name. But it works both directly to influence teens and indirectly to influence the media—movies and television. It also has approaches to parents who have important roles to play and, of course, efforts to influence potential donors and government agencies. In each instance, marketing concepts and tools are brought to bear. Other organizations have

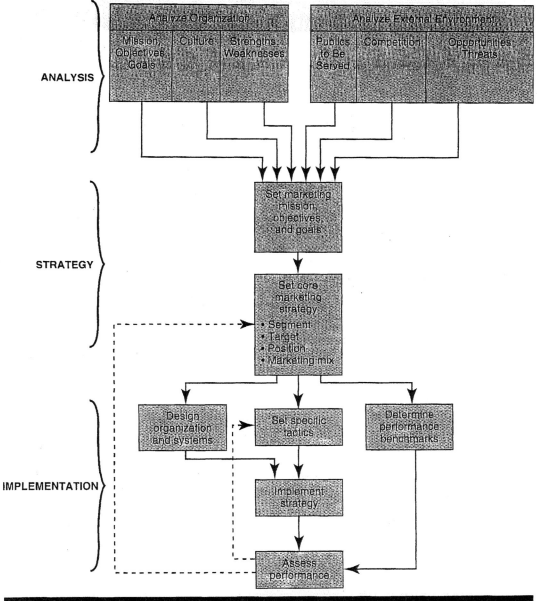

FIGURE 3-1 Strategic Organizational Marketing Planning Process

multiple challenges. For instance, one of many groups within the Academy for Educational Development, the Social Marketing and Behavior Change group, has a very wide range of initiatives and programs in which it was involved, as shown in Table 3-1.

TABLE 3-1 Projects of the Social Marketing and Behavior Change Group at the Academy for Educational Development, September 2006

- AED: Ghana Sustainable Change Project
- AED: Healthy and Ready to Work
- Afghanistan REACH
- Basic Support for Institutionalizing Child Survival (BASICS)
- Best Practices for Parenting Tobacco-Free Youth
- Building Awareness of Mild Traumatic Brain Injury with Physicians and Coaches
- CHANGE Project
- Civic Engagement for Education Reform in Central America (CERCA)
- Communication and Social Marketing Capacity Building to Increase Immunization Rates
- Community Guide Recommendations: Obesity
- Energy Sector Technical Advisory and Assistance Services IQC
- Enhancing Behavioral Change Communication in Border and High Transit Sites of Botswana, Lesotho, Namibia and Swaziland
- Ethiopia Child Survival and Systems Strengthening Project (ESHE)
- From Marketing to Counter-Marketing: Analysis of Strategies for Women
- GreenCOM
- Healthy Weight Initiative
- HIP – Hygiene Improvement Project
- Honduras HIV/AID Program (COMCAVI-Comunicando Cambio para la Vida)
- Improving Reproductive Health in Ukraine
- Improving the Eating and Physical Activity Behaviors of Low-Income Older Adults
- LINKAGES
- Long-Range Planning to Address Overweight and Obesity in the United States
- Making Medical Injections Safer
- Media-Smart Youth
- MIT Dangerous Drinking Campaign
- National Technical Assistance System for Immunization Coalitions
- NetMark
- New Voices National Fellowship Program
- Nicaragua Basic Education Program (BASE II)
- People, Energy and Development IQC
- POUZN
- Preventing Type II Diabetes (STOPP-T2D)
- Promoting Exercise among Older People
- PSN Community Engagement and Media Outreach Technical Assistance Program
- Public Health Alert on Prevention Services for Men Who Have Sex with Men
- Secretariat for Tobacco-Use Cessation Blueprint
- Social Sector Investment Policy Dialogue Program
- Study of Tobacco Industry Documents from Marketing to Counter-Marketing: Analysis of Strategies for Women

- The Social Acceptance Project – Family Planning
- Tuberculosis (TB) Prevention Training Project
- Tween Traffic Safety Initiative
- USAID Development Education Project
- USAID Technical Assistance and Support Contract (TASC 2) – Global Health
- Young Leaders for Peace and Development

Source: Academy for Educational Development web site at www.aed.org/SocialMarketingandBehaviorChange (retrieved September 26, 2006). Reprinted by permission of the Academy for Educational Development.

ANALYZING ORGANIZATIONAL MISSION, OBJECTIVES, AND GOALS

The critical planning reality is where the organization as a whole wishes to go. If the organization is mature and well managed, it should have already completed an organization-wide strategic planning process that will "fill in the blanks" of many of the boxes in Figure 3-1. On the other hand, it may be useful for the board and top management from time to time to rethink its ambitions. These are typically inscribed in three statements:

- *Mission:* the basic purpose of an organization, that is, what it is trying to accomplish.
- *Objectives:* major variables that the organization will emphasize, such as social impact, market share, growth, or reputation.
- *Goals:* the translation of objectives into specific benchmarks with respect to magnitude, time, and responsibility.

Mission

Every organization starts with a mission. To paraphrase Peter Drucker, in setting out its mission an organization needs to answer the following questions: What is our purpose? Who are our target audiences? What value can/should we offer to these target audiences? Although the first question—"What is our purpose?"—sounds simple, it is really the most profound question an organization can ask. Marketers will be particularly concerned about the centrality of behavioral influence to the organization's core mission. Marketers would argue that a majority of nonprofit organizations should define their purpose as accomplishing a specific set of behaviors among a specific set of target audiences. That is, they ought not to be satisfied unless they make specific things happen—or in cases like spousal abuse NOT happen! A mission statement should not outline what these organizations do but what they want to see *happen!* Thus a soup kitchen should not define its purpose by listing the particular services it offers; it should identify the underlying changes it hopes to see. It may be in the "connections business" wanting to get people to come and enjoy companionship and feel better about themselves. Or it may be in the "reform business" getting people first into the soup kitchen but eventually into a job, a better living arrangement, or a stable household situation. Ultimately, the soup kitchen, or any nonprofit organization, has to decide what its mission is so as not to confuse itself with a lot of intermediate goals and services that it might provide.

There are also a number of nonprofit organizations whose central mission is not focused on behavior. Religious organizations might decide that they are in the "feeling good" business, that is, helping people feel better about themselves and the world. Or they might decide that they are in the "hope" business, that is, helping people feel that they will eventually experience joy and fulfillment, either in this life or in the next. A ballet company may have as its mission giving poor children a chance to experience—or observe—modern dance. Or they may have a simpler mission, merely presenting modern dance works by contemporary choreographers. For both kinds of organizations, marketing is a secondary concern—although each would recognize that without the behavior of donors, volunteers, and "audiences" they could not really be successful.

An organization should strive for a mission that is *feasible, motivating to its staff, and distinctive.* In terms of being feasible, the organization should avoid a "mission impossible." The United Way of America set its mission to double its level of volunteers and financial support in the 1990s, but it has discovered this to be infeasible. Staff and volunteers must believe in the feasibility of the organization's mission if they are to lend their support. An institution should always reach high, but not so high as to produce incredulity in its publics.

The mission should also be motivating. Those working for the organization should feel they are worthwhile members of a worthwhile organization. A soup kitchen whose mission includes "changing lives" is likely to inspire more support than one whose mission is "giving homeless people a place to go on cold nights." The mission should be something that enriches people's lives.

A mission works better when it is distinctive. If all soup kitchens resembled each other, there would be little basis for pride in one's particular operation. People take pride in belonging to an institution that "does it differently" or "does it better." A soup kitchen that involves celebrity chefs and waiters is likely to meet more support and have more impact than one that is another storefront in a rundown business district. By cultivating a distinctive mission and personality, an organization stands out more and attracts a more loyal group of members.

It is critical that the organization's mission statement not be vague and platitudinous. Too often, mission statements are like motherhood—"we will improve the lives of America's poor"—or overreaching. The Habitat for Humanity mission statement speaks to providing everyone everywhere with decent housing. But as it acknowledges, over 1.5 billion people worldwide are with substandard housing, and so it must translate its mission into more specific, concrete, doable outcomes.

Following are some mission statements for major nonprofits:

- "The mission of Mothers Against Drunk Driving is to stop drunk driving, support the victims of this violent crime, and prevent underage drinking."—*Mothers Against Drunk Driving* (www.madd.org)
- "The American Red Cross, a humanitarian organization led by volunteers, guided by its Congressional Charter and the Fundamental Principles of the International Red Cross Movement, will provide relief to victims of disasters and help people prevent, prepare for, and respond to emergencies."—*The American Red Cross* (www.redcross.org)
- "The American Marketing Association is an international professional organization for people involved in the practice, study and teaching of marketing. Our principal roles are:
  - Improving – Advancing marketing competencies, practice and thought leadership

- Promoting – Being an advocate for marketing and promoting its importance, efficacy, and ethics
- Supporting – Being an essential resource for marketing information, education/training and relationships."—*The American Marketing Association* (www.marketingpower.com)

- "The YMCA of San Diego County is dedicated to improving the quality of human life and to helping all people realize their fullest potential as children of God through development of the spirit, mind, and body."—*The YMCA of San Diego County (California)* (www.ymca.org)
- "To promote and foster the highest ethical relationship between businesses and the public." "The American Cancer Society is the nationwide community-based voluntary health organization dedicated to eliminating cancer as a major health problem by preventing cancer, saving lives, and diminishing suffering from cancer, through research, education, advocacy, and service." "The American Cancer Society's international mission concentrates on capacity building in developing cancer societies and on collaboration with other cancer-related organizations throughout the world in carrying out shared strategic directions."—*The American Cancer Society* (www.cancer.org)
- "The International Republican Institute (IRI) is a nonprofit, nonpartisan organization committed to advancing freedom and democracy worldwide by developing political parties, civic institutions, open elections, good governance and the rule of law."—*International Republican Institute* (www.iri.org)
- "To promote and foster the highest ethical relationship between businesses and the public through voluntary self-regulation, consumer and business education, and service excellence."—*Better Business Bureau* (www.bbb.org)

Objectives and Goals

An organization's objectives state the broad direction in which the organization will go to achieve its mission. Goals follow from the objectives in that they operationalize what is to be achieved, by what organizational components and by what dates. Objectives are generally statements whereas goals, ideally, are numerical.

For every type of institution there is always a large set of potential objectives relevant to the organization's mission, and top management's task is to make choices among them. For example, the objectives of interest to a college might be increased national reputation, improved classroom teaching, higher enrollment, higher-quality students, increased efficiency, larger endowment, improved student social life, improved physical plant, lower operating deficit, and so on. A college cannot successfully pursue all these objectives simultaneously because of a limited budget and because some of them are incompatible, such as increased cost efficiency and improved classroom teaching. In any given year, therefore, institutions will choose to emphasize certain objectives and either ignore others or treat them as constraints. Thus an institution's major obstacles can vary from year to year depending on the administration's perception of the major problems that the institution must address at that time.

A key feature of *goals* should be that they can be tracked through the organization's evaluation and control system. And goals should have people "attached" to them. It should be clear who is assigned responsibility for goal achievement. Without such goals, it will be impossible for the organization to know how it is progressing, who should be rewarded for progress, and where change is needed. For a school, the objective of "increased enrollment" must be turned into a goal, such as "a 15 percent enrollment increase in next year's fall class." A number of questions may arise: Is a 15 percent enrollment increase feasible? What resources would it take? What activities would have to be carried out? Who would be responsible and accountable? How will we track achievement? All of these critical questions must be answered when deciding whether to adopt a proposed goal.

Depending on the organization's overall attitude toward marketing and its centrality, marketing people may or may not be involved in defining either objectives or goals. However, whenever either goals or objectives involve choices among options and whenever those options depend on the feasibility of a marketing effort, then marketers should be at the table. Because they are the behavior influence specialists and because they operate from a target audience mindset, they can help make choices about what behavioral outcomes are feasible, what a reasonable timetable is, what costs might be involved, who needs to partner to achieve success, and so on. Letting non-marketers set such objectives and goals greatly handicaps the marketer.

Marketing involvement in these choices also helps make an organization's mission statement more operational. We have heard many nonprofit executives say that they are "mission-driven" often as a way of distinguishing themselves from crass marketers. Marketers should not argue with this stance—indeed, it is typically what motivates people to join up at below-market salaries, to donate, or to volunteer. Their role should be—wherever feasible and appropriate—to tie the mission to specific behaviors that ought to occur. The marketers' challenge is then to make these happen.

Philip Harvey and James Snyder point out that clear goal definition is relatively rare in nonprofit organizations for six reasons:

1. Many nonprofit managers fear accountability. They come to the job, in part, because they expect to have limited surveillance.
2. Many projects continue even when they no longer serve an organization's mission and no one wants to look hard at these projects' performance.
3. Nonprofits often undertake projects simply because there is money available for doing them.
4. Some nonprofit managers fear that management science will replace humanitarian concerns.
5. Nonprofit managers often equate busyness with doing something worthwhile.
6. Nonprofits seldom have financial report cards to tell them how they are doing.[1]

ANALYZING ORGANIZATIONAL CULTURE

A number of students of management have pointed out that the "organizational culture"[2] of an institution may be the single most important determinant of what the organization sets as its mission, objectives, and goals and what will be expected of those (such as the marketers) who are challenged to achieve them. Peters and Waterman stress the central contribution of *culture* to the success of "best-run" organizations:

Without exception, the dominance and coherence of culture proved to be an essential quality of the excellent companies. Moreover, the stronger the culture and the more it was directed toward the marketplace, the less need was there for policy manuals, organization charts, or detailed procedures and rules. In these companies, people way down the line know what they are supposed to do in most situations because the handful of guiding values is crystal clear.[3]

The successes of organizations like Ben & Jerry's, Coca-Cola, Ritz-Carlton, and Domino's Pizza reflect the impact of a clear, target audience-centered, pervasive culture. Cultures in many nonprofit organizations are set by charismatic leaders who very much make the institution in their own image. This includes the Boys & Girls Clubs of America under Rick Goings, the Girl Scouts under Frances Hesselbein, and the Metropolitan Museum of Art under Thomas Hoving.[4] And many cultures will change when they get a new CEO.

Consider the Metropolitan Opera. It has been argued that this venerable institution has in recent years languished under the leadership of Joseph Volpe. A new general manager, Peter Gelb, was appointed in the fall of 2006 and he immediately put in place or proposed a range of innovations. Prior to taking over the Met, Gelb worked for Sony for years as a film and television producer and for Creative Artists Management as a talent agent. Soon after his arrival, he announced plans to televise six operas for presentation in movie theaters, offer video of 100 performances over the Internet, invite film directors to stage operas, and offer broadcasts of four performances a week over Sirius Satellite Radio.[5] Gelb's very first production was *Madama Butterfly*, directed by Anthony Minghella, who directed the movies *The English Patient* and *Cold Comfort Farm*. Gelb made sure that the performance was broadcast over satellite radio and onto screens in the plaza outside the opera house and in Times Square.

This is not the "Old Met!"

Of course, the danger of allowing a single individual to dominate an organization is that if the charismatic leader falls from grace, the organization can undergo periods of considerable turmoil. This was the case of the National Association for the Advancement of Colored People after the departure of Ben Chavis in 1994 and the United Way after the departure of William Aramony in 1992.

Culture Conflict

Many organizations in the nonprofit area appear to suffer from a significant, perhaps inherent, *culture conflict*. At a minimum, this conflict can severely inhibit nonprofit marketers' abilities to be effective in the marketplace and, at worst, threatens to tear their organizations apart through internal dissension. The problem is often caused by normal growth dynamics. A significant number of nonprofit programs and institutions were begun by individuals or ad hoc groups committed to doing something positive about an aspect of a society's well-being. Examples include hospitals such as the Mayo Clinic, the "Just Say No" anti-drug campaign of the Reagan era, and many AIDS-prevention and breast cancer organizations.

The early life of most of these organizations is typically dominated by what might be called a *social service culture*. Health care organizations adopting this perspective see their mission as one of maximizing some aspect of the public's health status by "improving health" rather than by "being efficient." The organization is willing to overlook waste and misdirection in the short run as long as the effort is a case of "doing good." Senior managers and most if not all of the staff are recruited from basic health care disciplines such as medicine, social work, or public health. They see themselves as professionals with strict codes of ethics and feel that they should serve everyone possible within the limits of time and economic resources. Camaraderie pervades the organization, in part because it is small, its members share the same training and goals, and there is zeal to "have a real impact." In many respects, the organization and participation in it are ends in themselves to those involved.

A social service culture is ideal for such organizations in their beginning years. Often they lack resources, and employees must endure low salaries, inadequate equipment, limited staff assistance, and so on. Without the vision of significant social service payoffs, such deprivations might be "killing." The vision builds a close sense of camaraderie in the organization and helps members defend themselves from early critics and doomsayers.

The social service culture can survive for years for two reasons. First, the organization is undertaking something the public truly needs at a time of great pent-up demand and little competition. Many wasteful and misdirected approaches are tolerated because most work. Even if they do not, the culture tends to accept any "good-hearted" efforts as long as they are intended to have a social impact. Second, the organization is largely free to "do its own thing" because of a lack of outside supervision. Support is usually from a few individuals or small grants, often with few strings attached. The lack of competition reinforces a sense of freedom to pursue what organizational members personally believe is the right course of action.

Marketers and other managers are often brought in from the business world as such organizations grow and meet challenges. This can produce problems because they come from a *corporate culture*. This culture is significantly different from the social service culture and, to the extent the nonprofit organization is serious about becoming marketing oriented, a severe clash of cultures is inevitable. Much of this kind of conflict is reported in the study by Andreasen, Goodstein, and Wilson mentioned in Chapter 1.[6] In the corporate culture, competitors are not viewed as benign and cooperative. Staff are expected to produce results and are not coddled as long as "their heart is in the right place." Strategic thinking replaces uncoordinated programs, resources are husbanded carefully, and ineffective programs that may be the personal fiefdoms of corporate staff members are routinely called into question. Short-term tactics become equal in importance to long-term programs, and the organization is seen as a means to *achieving* ends, not an end in itself.

When nonprofit organizations bring people from this culture into a nonprofit environment, signs of culture conflict soon appear in subtle and not-so-subtle forms. The marketer is "shocked" by the extent of mismanagement in the organization and suspicious of pet projects lacking clear purposes. Questions are raised about costs and about the "fit" of tactics to general strategies. Concurrently, the founding professionals are equally "shocked" by the marketer's seeming lack of commitment to the organization's "real purposes." The professionals are suspicious of the corporate culture and scrutinize the marketer's every action for signs of the unethical, expedient, and manipulative behavior they are sure this alien culture promotes. The new marketing recruit, in turn, sees professionals as having "their heads in the sand," not recognizing the realities of today's marketplace. The marketer will, indeed, accept the long-run mission of the organization, but will not understand why the specialists fail to realize that unless the organization becomes more effective and uses its resources better in the short run, there will be no long run.

The most serious consequence of culture conflict is that the organization becomes schizophrenic. People are not sure what direction it is taking. Ill feelings and distrust develop among coworkers who have allegiances to different values. The organization vacillates between "giving in" to the marketers for a while and then "coming back to the (mission) basics."

In the private sector, cultural conflict is usually transitional. Stockholders eventually rebel and force some resolution or the company simply fails and goes out of business or is absorbed by others. In contrast, in the nonprofit field, this period of conflict can be prolonged—perhaps interminably. For example, the bottom line is often not clear, no tough-minded board of directors or outside funders intervene, or no clear competitors move into the market vacuum. All these might happen in the private sector.

Part of the problem is that top managers in nonprofit organizations are often part of the conflict. They do not recognize it or see its implications for the organization and those allied with it. The first step in correcting any problem is to recognize its symptoms and face them squarely. The next step is to resolve the problem, which is not an easy task. Several suggestions can be offered.

1. Key members of the organization must learn to recognize the symptoms and then *admit* that, indeed, cultural conflict is present within the organization and that its effects are personally and professionally debilitating.
2. Specific time should be set aside for beginning to resolve the conflict, with the understanding that full resolution will probably (a) take a long time to be effectuated and (b) lead to some resignations.
3. Initial discussions should be guided by the assumption that unless one culture dominates, and those adhering to its rival accommodate themselves to that dominance, the organization is doomed at worst to failure or at best to continuing friction and a generally unpleasant working environment.
4. Because all parties are too close (both perceptually and emotionally) to the crisis, resolution can be achieved only under the guidance of an outside catalyst sensitive to the issues and skillful enough to help the participants face and resolve them.
5. Resolution is most likely if all key organizational members can be brought to articulate for themselves and others (a) what they feel the basic mission of the organization should be, (b) what they feel are the best means of achieving that mission, (c) what they feel are *inappropriate* means for the organization to use (on the grounds of either ethics or efficiency), and, most important, (d) what they *personally* wish to achieve through their participation in the organization.
6. Once these perceptions, wishes, and hopes are "on the table," there should be a mutual exploration, with minimal guidance, of how both the participants and the organization can maximize their goals. In the process, the exploration will inevitably lead to heightened empathy for others' dreams and aspirations and an open consideration of who will have to compromise or resign if the organization is

to survive and grow. The participants also will recognize that, unless the latter goal is achieved, individual dreams are unlikely to be fulfilled.

7. The eventual outcome of this process will be not only a resolution of the cultural conflict but also, through the consideration of the values of participants, a bonding of the remaining coworkers in a more empathetic and productive personal and organizational relationship.

SWOT ANALYSIS

The next major step in the OMPP is a classic planning tool from the private sector, the SWOT analysis. SWOT stands for Strengths, Weaknesses, Opportunities, and Threats. Collectively, they specify what the organization faces externally—both good and bad—and what it brings to these challenges. It is the starting point for organizational and campaign planning.

Analyzing Internal Organizational Strengths and Weaknesses

A cold-blooded review of the organization's strengths and weaknesses, especially as they will impact any marketing programs, is critical to effective strategy development. Clearly, an organization cannot think about tackling a great opportunity if it does not have—and is unlikely to develop—the needed capabilities. On the other hand, an opportunity may be ideal if it fits well with the organization's core competencies.

Weaknesses come in two forms. First, there are weaknesses that are environmental or organizational constraints on what the organization is *allowed* to do. For example, Georgetown University's McDonough School of Business may see a major opportunity to do significant management research on Internet privacy issues. However, a major program of high-quality research would require staffing by doctoral students who carry out much of the work, generate papers, and perhaps help train visiting businesspeople. But the Georgetown School of Business does not offer a Ph.D. in business.

Many nonprofits have externally imposed restrictions. As noted in Chapter 1, the U.S. Internal Revenue Service sets implicit bounds on how much revenue nonprofits can generate from unrelated activities. Similarly, donors may set limits on what may be done with their money. Physicians may effectively limit what a hospital may do in the area of preventive care or holistic health. And governments in developing countries may tell private voluntary organizations (PVOs) that they cannot duplicate activities carried out in the public sector and that they cannot engage in tactics that are offensive to the culture (e.g., advertising on television).

A second form of weakness is more correctable. These are aspects of the organization's structure, strategy, and tactics that are just not very good. Not surprisingly, many managers are often blind to these deficiencies (which is also true in the private sector). For this reason, it is important that management from time to time to require an outside *audit* of the total organization, including the marketing function. A thorough audit typically covers both the external and internal environments.[7]

Analyzing External Threats and Opportunities

A marketer operates in an external environment that is constantly changing. The internal environment tells the planner what is *desired* and what is *permissible*. The external market tells the marketer what is *possible*. The external environment has three components:

1. The *public environment*, consisting of groups and organizations that take an interest in the activities of the focal organization. The public environment consists of local publics, activist publics, the general public, media publics, and regulatory agencies whose actions can affect the welfare of the focal organization.
2. The *competitive environment*, consisting of groups and organizations that compete for attention and loyalty from the audiences of the focal organization. The competitive environment includes desire competitors, generic competitors, form competitors, and enterprise competitors.
3. The *macroenvironment,* consisting of large-scale fundamental forces that shape opportunities and pose threats to the focal organization. The main macroenvironmental forces that have to be watched are the demographic, economic, technological, political, and social forces. These forces largely represent "uncontrollables" in the organization's future situation to which it has to adapt.

We shall consider each of these environmental components in turn.

The Public Environment

All organizations have publics or constituencies to whom they have to pay attention. In the private sector, these include target audiences, suppliers, regulators, stock analysts, employees, and so on. The nonprofit world is no different. Consider an organization like the American Cancer Society. Figure 3-2 shows 16 of the major publics with which such an organization might deal and whose needs it must consider at some level. The importance of various publics is, however, different from the balance in the private sector. In the corporate world, providing superior value to target audiences is the single most important challenge for most corporations. If target audiences are happy and willing to build long-term relationships with the corporation, the stock market will be happy, regulators are likely to be unconcerned, employees will have jobs and a company they can be proud of, and so on. Financial outcomes from target audiences are the key benchmark.

In the nonprofit world—as we have noted—there are three publics that are important sources of resources—target audiences/clients, donors, and volunteers. The relative importance of the three will vary. A nonprofit whose mission is to support needy individuals need pay primary attention to donors. Nonprofits that offer products and services need to focus on both target audiences and donors, since target audiences rarely provide all the income needed. Some nonprofits like Habitat for Humanity International will need to focus on donors and volunteers. Some like AARP will need the support of all three.

The critical implication of this difference between sectors is that the nonprofit will have to balance meeting the needs of more than one public. On some occasions—or even for some period of time—they may need to emphasize the needs of one key audience over another. At others, they may have to give priority to target audiences or to donors. Sometimes, meeting the needs of one group may ignore or even diminish the importance of the needs of another group. Visitors to a museum may have to wait if the

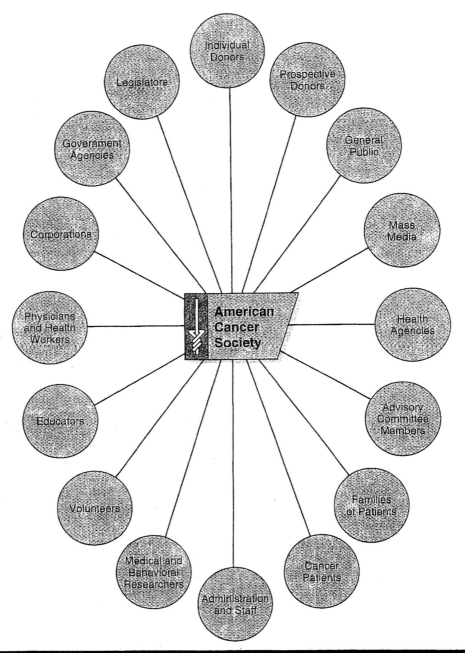

FIGURE 3-2 The American Cancer Society and Its Publics

museum is entertaining donors. Blood donation agency volunteers may have to work odd hours and in less-safe neighborhoods if the goal is to meet the needs of residents who want to give blood at convenient places and times.

The emphasis on multiple publics does not mean that other publics, such as those listed in Figure 3-2, can be neglected. Regulators will be watching that donations are used for the intended purpose. The general public will want the organization to hold high ethical standards and meet broadly defined community needs. The media will want candor whenever they follow a story. Internal publics—employees—will need to understand where the institution is headed and what their own roles are. Partners need to understand their role and receive feedback on values received. Some of these relationships will involve heavy marketing involvement. Others will mainly benefit from the target audience focus emphasized in this volume

The Competitive Environment

As we noted in Chapter 1, an increasingly significant characteristic of the nonprofit marketplace in the twenty-first century is the extent of competition. Unfortunately, many nonprofit organizations still deny the existence of such competition, feeling that this is only characteristic of private sector markets. However, as we will note throughout this book, competition is a reality at two levels. First, there is competition between organizations for resources, target audiences, and volunteers. This kind of competition is most relevant to organizational marketing planning, but it is also critical to recognize that there is competition at what might be called "the behavioral level." This is especially important for campaign marketing planning.

Organization-Level Competition

Hospitals until the 1980s did not like to think of other hospitals as competitors, museums tended to ignore other museums, and the Red Cross saw other blood banks as all seeking the same general public goal. They preferred to think of their sister organizations as simply helping provide social services and not competing. Yet the reality of competition is driven home when one hospital starts attracting doctors and patients from another hospital, blood banks lose donors, or YMCAs see members joining local racquetball clubs and gymnasiums.

By contrast, there are also nonprofits that recognize the existence of potential competitors but seem to think that competing is "not nice." They feel that since all nonprofits, in some sense, are attempting to achieve the same (obviously desirable) social goals, any attention to competition would divert energies from what each competitor should *really* be doing. Sometimes nonprofit marketers are rudely awakened when a competitor doesn't "play fair." A major concern of the American Cancer Society in the 1990s was so-called "look-alike" cancer fundraisers that used similar names and took money that donors intended for the American Cancer Society.

Certainly there are many challenges in which a nonprofit organization recognizes that it is going up against not specific organizations but sometimes an entire industry. That is certainly true of anti-tobacco organizations and campaigns. In the twenty-first century, an industry that is increasingly under attack in the face of growing levels of obesity is the food industry. Sometimes, it is effective if one can carry the campaign directly to this competition.

What many sophisticated nonprofits recognize is that competition may *help* rather than hurt the nonprofit marketers' performance in two important ways. First, the existence of two competitors in the marketplace, clamoring for attention, spending two advertising budgets, and commanding even more target audience attention or media interest can stimulate increases in *the size of the total market.* Thus it is entirely possible that with more competition, an organization might lose market share but discover that, because the entire market grows more than its share loss, total organizational impact on target audiences, donors, and volunteers may be higher.

The second way in which competition can benefit the nonprofit is that it can sharpen the competitive skills of the embattled marketers. It is a serious danger in the nonprofit domain that marketers will become fat and happy by observing growing revenues, increased donations, and swelling volunteer ranks and pretending there is no competition. There is nothing like the effect of new competitive activity to give complacent managers the needed slap to the side of the head. To compete, they have to rethink how their organization is positioned. They have to look to their target audiences more carefully to see if there are better ways to meet their needs and wants. They have to consider the possibility of changing offerings, price, volunteer incentives, partnerships, and advertising. This reevaluation and the continuing close attention to marketing details can only help the marketer's overall performance.

Nonprofit marketers must understand who their competitors are and what strengths and weaknesses each has. Information on competitors can be gained from sources such as those described in Table 3-2. Much of this information is now readily available on the Internet or from syndicated services.

TABLE 3-2	Sources of Intelligence on Competitors
From Competitors Themselves	**From Outside Observers**
Annual reports	Suppliers
Newsletters	Trade associations
Planning documents	Other competitors
Marketing brochures	Newspaper articles
Advertisements	Magazine articles
Speeches and public statements	Stock market analyses (Moody's, D&B)
	Court records
Reports to regulatory agencies	Distribution channels
	Advertising agencies
Want ads	Financial institutions
	Former employees of competitors
From One's Own Organization	**From Competitors' Customers**
Customer contact people	Market research
Personnel department	Interviews
Economic or market researchers	Focus groups
	Surveys

Behavior-Level Competition

Campaigns are focused on getting people to do things—or in some cases, to stop doing them. This means that alternative behaviors or the status quo—for example, not donating or not volunteering—are important competition that must be addressed. At the behavioral level, a marketer can face up to four major types of competitors in trying to serve a target market:

1. *Desire competitors*—other immediate desires that the target audience (donor, target audience, or volunteer) might want to satisfy.
2. *Generic competitors*—other basic ways in which the target audience can satisfy a particular desire.
3. *Service form competitors*—other service forms that can satisfy the target audience's particular desire.
4. *Enterprise competitors*—other enterprises offering the same service form that can satisfy the target audience's particular desire.

Consider the four types of competitors as they were faced by the August Wilson Theater in New York City in the fall of 2006. The theater is offering the musical *Jersey Boys* about Frankie Valli and the Four Seasons. Consider a young professional woman in New York deciding what to do on a particular evening. Suppose her options were evaluated as shown in Figure 3-3. She realizes that she has several *desires* she could satisfy—finishing a project at work, getting some exercise, meeting several household responsibilities, or being entertained. Once she determines that the *desire* she will satisfy is to be entertained, she has to consider various *generic* competitors, including TV at home, a movie, or a live performance. Choosing to be entertained by a live performance, she has to consider various *forms* of live entertainment—a symphony, a nightclub performance, a rock concert, or a Broadway musical. Finally, after settling on

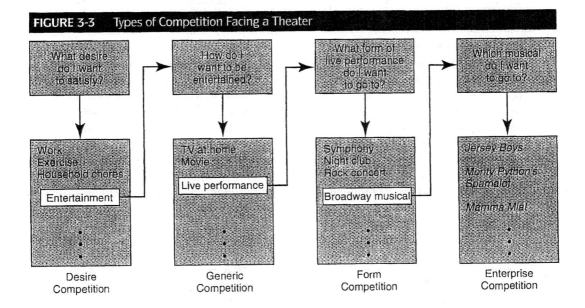

FIGURE 3-3 Types of Competition Facing a Theater

a musical, she has to choose among the offerings of various *enterprises—Jersey Boys* at the August Wilson Theater, *Monty Python's Spamalot* at the Shubert, or *Mamma Mia!* at the Winter Garden.

If the August Wilson Theater is experiencing poor sales, the causes may be a poor marketing campaign strategy at *any or all* of the four levels of competition. The August Wilson Theater may have chosen a poor offering and so loses out to other *enterprise competitors*. Or the musical may be terrific, but too many consumers are choosing to go to other *form competitors* such as nightclubs or rock concerts. In the latter case, the marketing manager's challenge would be to focus on those who like live entertainment and convince them that a Broadway musical is a better alternative. This could involve joint research with other theaters into why the theater is losing out to other forms. It may be that competitors in other forms have discovered better ways to meet consumer needs that the theaters might wish to copy (e.g., reducing prices, selling popcorn or liquor). Or it might be that more people would choose the theater except for certain disincentives ("costs") that the marketer could correct. For instance, potential target audiences could fear for their safety in downtown parking lots (the marketer could build a new structure, put in stronger lights, or hire a bus service to bring fearful people up to the door from a distant, safe lot). Or they could feel their friends might not want to come. In that case, the marketers could offer two-for-one ticket bargains or a "bring-a-friend-free" promotion.

At the next level of behavioral competition, if the manager found that too many promising target audiences were not choosing live entertainment as the preferred generic form of entertainment, the theater manager might consider joint campaigns with its generic comrades (symphony managers, rock concert promoters, nightclub owners) to get people out to "the world of live entertainment." However, if the problem is at the *desire level* of competition, joint promotion by those in the entertainment industry (live performance promoters, movie house owners, TV station managers) could compete with other desires by promoting the theme that "in this stressful, work-conscious world, you need more entertainment to relax, to replenish, to grow."

The Macroenvironment

Managers often forget that organizational marketing planning has its consequences in the future—as does campaign planning. Thus it is crucial that nonprofit marketing managers understand the broad forces creating the future world in which they must operate. These broad forces can be divided into demographic, economic, technological, political–legal, and social–cultural categories. The nature of these forces varies, of course, by the country in which the nonprofit markets, and within a given country their relative impact varies significantly by region, city, and nonprofit sector. Demographic and political–legal trends are very important for strategic planning in social service agencies. Economic trends are important to charities, technological trends to hospitals and libraries, demographic and economic trends to the armed forces, and social–cultural trends to parks, recreation services, and the performing arts.

There are many sources of data on such trends. Many are discussed in Chapter 5 and are available online. Many nonprofits, such as the United Way, consider macroenvironmental forecasting to be so important that the firm creates high-powered committees to carry out this activity on a regular basis.

PORTFOLIO PLANNING

The information from the analysis stage provides a basis for updating the organization's mission, objectives, and goals. Most nonprofits are involved in many offerings and many markets. This means that they must engage in some form of portfolio planning, a systematic "big picture" consideration of the alternatives. They must make strategic decisions about where to grow, where to retrench, and where to change marketing programs. In effect, the marketing manager has a portfolio of options and potential options, not unlike an investor. As Kearns and others have pointed out,[8] a useful framework for thinking about these decisions is the offer/market opportunity matrix outlined in Figure 3-4. Originally a two-by-two matrix proposed by Ansoff,[9] it is here expanded into a three-by-three matrix. Markets are listed at the left and offerings along the top.

Each cell in Figure 3-4 has a name. Potential opportunities—in this case, for a college—are listed in small letters. The choice depends in part on the organization's strengths—its offerings or its market knowledge and experience. The administration

FIGURE 3-4   Offer/Market Opportunity Matrix

		Offerings	
	Existing	Modified	New
Existing	1. Market Penetration	4. Offer Modification • short courses • evening programs • weekend programs • new delivery system	7. Offer Innovation • new courses • new departments • new schools
Geographical	2. Geographical Expansion • new areas of city • new cities • foreign	5. Modification for Dispersed Markets • programs offered on military bases or at U.S.-based firms abroad • web-based offering	8. Geographical Innovation • distance learning
New	3. New Markets A. Individual • senior citizens • homemakers • ethnic minorites B. Institutional • business firms • social agencies	6. Modification for New Markets A. Individual • senior citizens • homemakers • ethnic minorities B. Institutional • business • government	9. Total Innovation • new courses • new departments • new schools

(left axis label: **Markets**)

should first consider Cell 1, *market penetration.* This cell deepens its penetration into its existing markets with its existing offerings.

Cell 2, *geographical expansion,* would involve the college expanding into new geographical markets with its existing offerings. The college could open a branch in another part of the city, or in a new city, or start a new campus in another country and/or seek out donors there. Duke University now offers courses in its M.B.A. program in Asia, South America, and Europe. Northwestern has partners for programs in Israel, Germany, Hong Kong, and Canada.

Another possibility is Cell 3, *new markets,* where one can consider offering a strong portfolio of existing programs to new individual and institutional markets. Colleges are following this approach by increasingly recruiting nontraditional student groups such as senior citizens, homemakers, and ethnic minorities. Iowa State University, for instance, has instituted "College for Seniors," a program for retired and older adults run by its alumni association. In addition, colleges are trying to interest business firms, social service agencies, and other organizations in buying educational and training programs to be delivered on their premises or through distance learning. Many colleges are seeking new sources of donations beyond past graduates, especially new millionaires or residents of foreign countries who would like to be associated with a prestigious university.

Next, the marketing manager can consider whether the organization should engage in *offer modification* to attract more of an existing market that it knows well (Cell 4). Standard courses can be shortened in the evening or on weekends. For example, Alverno College, a private women's school in Milwaukee, instituted a weekend college and drew large numbers of housewives and employed women. Other colleges are beginning to offer courses in the very late evening or very early morning, having discovered a number of working people for whom these hours would be more convenient. The Internet is also being used to grant more options for learning and donating.

Cell 5 is *modification for dispersed markets.* The University of Maryland University College, for example, offers modified programs for members of the armed forces both domestically and abroad.

Modification for new markets (Cell 6) may be a more realistic growth approach for colleges and universities. To penetrate the senior citizens market, for example, may require a modification of standard courses. Specifically, the time period might need to be shorter and less reading might be required, with more comfortable seats and probably books with larger print. *Offer innovation* (Cell 7) involves developing new courses, departments, or schools for existing markets. A business school, for example, might develop a new program in managing nonprofit organizations to offer to its students. New ways of donor giving can be developed—for example, that would spread out payments or tie them to stock performance. New ways of volunteering could be created—say, over the Internet or in other forms of distance mentoring. *Geographical innovation* (Cell 8) involves finding new ways to serve new geographical areas. With the advent of the Internet, home computers, interactive television, and other new media technologies, it is possible to offer courses to national and international audiences through "distance learning."

The final category, *total innovation* (Cell 9), refers to developing new offerings for new markets. The "university without walls" college or UK's Open University, where learning can take place away from a campus, are examples.

The offer/market opportunity matrix helps the administration array new opportunities in a systematic way. These opportunities are evaluated and the better ones are pursued.

CORE MARKETING STRATEGY

The single most important stage in the OMPP is determining the organization's *core marketing strategy.* A core marketing strategy comprises the basic thrust an organization wishes to take over an extended period of time to achieve the marketing objectives it has set for itself. This longer view provides the framework within which detailed tactical elements are created and specific year-to-year programs are formulated. It is the "skeleton" of the entire marketing program. The core marketing strategy has three elements:

- Selection of one or more *specific target markets.*
- A clearly defined *competitive position.*
- A carefully designed and coordinated *marketing mix* to meet the needs of the target markets with a positioning strategy that differentiates the marketer from major competitors, including generic and desire competitors.

An organization's core marketing strategy should flow naturally from the earlier stages of the strategic marketing planning process and will eventually guide specific campaign planning. There will already have been a careful assessment of the organization's mission and goals, trends in the market environment, characteristics of target audiences, and the organization's present strengths and weaknesses. Marketing management will have begun to define marketing's own objectives and goals. The difficult part is translating all this insight and information into a basic strategy that will guide the marketing effort over 3, 5, or 10 years. The core strategy is so important because it is the statement or set of statements that sets out just how the organization will tackle the market challenges.

IBM, Dell, and Apple are all in the personal computer business, but the ways in which they approach target audiences, advertise themselves, position and price their products and services, and work through distributors are very different. It is these elements of substance and style that make the organizations very different. CBS's approach to the news is different from CNN's. The Gap tackles the retail market differently from Nordstrom, and both are different from Macy's. Yale is not MIT, and Carnegie Hall is not Radio City Music Hall. There are many nondescript me-too organizations in every marketplace. What makes successful organizations stand out is that each has a unique view of itself and its role in the marketplace that has the following characteristics:

1. It is *target audience-centered.* It has as its principal focus meeting the needs and wants of its target audiences. It tailors offerings and communications to those it wishes to influence.
2. It is *visionary.* It articulates a future for the organization that offers a clear sense of where the organization is going, what the "new" enterprise will look like, and what it will achieve when it meets with its offerings.

3. It *differentiates* the organization from its key rivals. The marketer stands out; it offers target markets unique reasons to prefer its offerings.
4. It is *sustainable* for the long run and in the face of likely competitors' reactions.
5. It is *easily communicated.* The central elements of the strategy are simple and clear so that both target audiences and the marketer's own staff have an unambiguous understanding of just what the strategy is and why it should be supported.
6. It is *motivating.* A successful strategy has the enthusiastic commitment of those who will carry it out.
7. It is *flexible.* It is sufficiently broad that it allows for diversity in the ways that individual staffers implement it and not so rigid and uncompromising that it is not adaptable to unforeseen contingencies.

In his book *Competitive Strategy,*[10] Michael Porter has proposed three basic core strategies an organization can adopt:

1. *Differentiation.* This approach means offering something that no or few other competitors can offer. Differentiation can be in terms of *real differences* in the products and/or services offered or in donation packages or volunteer programs offered or *perceived differences* created primarily through promotion. Thus a hospital might differentiate itself by:
   a. offering live-in facilities for expecting fathers; gourmet meals, cable television, fax machines, and computers for long-term business patients and visitors; and so on (offer differentiation).
   b. offering "Doc-in-the-box" neighborhood emergency care or physical therapy in the home (place differentiation).
   c. promoting the hospital as the most technologically advanced, the most experimental, or the most patient-friendly hospital (image differentiation).
   d. offering checkout donation options for long term patients or donation options for visitors.
2. *Cost Leadership.* This approach involves marketing the lowest-cost offerings in the marketplace. In an industry where overhead costs often run 50 to 80 percent of donations, the United Way can typically boast that it keeps its administrative costs below 15 percent.
3. *Focus.* This approach involves selecting a limited segment of the market—typically one not served by anyone else—and concentrating on uniquely serving it. Thus a program for the homeless might focus on a particular neighborhood, such as the homeless on the riverfront; a particular target audience group, such as American Samoan homeless; or a particular kind of offering, such as emergency mental care.

Notice that each of these approaches involves a unique combination of the three elements of the core marketing strategy: choice of market segments, positioning, and marketing mix. Porter argues that organizations should not attempt to carry out more than one core strategy at the same time. Furthermore, the choice of core strategy should be based on evaluations of the organization's internal and external environments and should recognize that each type of core strategy will require a different type of organization and often a different organizational culture and leadership style.

CAMPAIGN MARKETING PLANNING

Broad organizational marketing strategies inevitably must be translated into specific campaigns to achieve specific behavioral goals.[11] These goals can target clients, volunteers, commercial partners, donors, or government agencies. For some nonprofit organizations, the targets may be legislators or the media. But, true to the essence of marketing, the bottom line at the campaign level must always be influencing behavior. This fundamental objective reinforces the principle outlined in the previous chapter that the target audience has ultimate control over the success or failure of any campaign efforts. Thus the process of effective campaign marketing planning must constantly keep the target audience as the central focus of this effort.

The structure of the campaign marketing planning process is outlined in Figures 3-5 and 3-6. As 3-6 makes clear, the process begins with the target audience (listening) and constantly returns to that target audience to assess how the campaign is likely to be received (pretesting) and then actually received (monitoring). As shown in Figure 3-6, this amounts to a constant recycling process, going again and again to the people who will govern campaign success.

The six steps are as follows:

1. *Listening.* Campaigns must begin with a thorough understanding of the target audience they seek to influence, whether these are factory workers who might give blood, college students who might volunteer at a soup kitchen once a week, or educated homeowners who might attend the city's symphony concerts during the upcoming season. Effective campaign planning must start with a thorough understanding of "where the audience is coming from"—what do they think of the offer implicit in the campaign, what do they see as the benefits and costs, what do their friends think, and do they think they can actually carry out the behavior that's being recommended? This type of research is often called *formative research.* It has been our experience that one of the most common causes of marketing campaign failures in the nonprofit world is inadequate "listening" to the target audience. We shall outline in Chapter 4 some basic frameworks that will help us

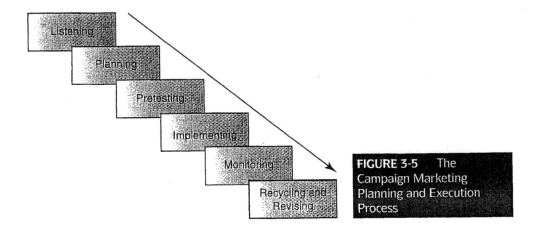

FIGURE 3-5 The Campaign Marketing Planning and Execution Process

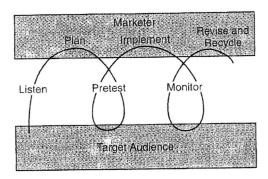

FIGURE 3-6   The Cyclical Process

understand target audiences, and in Chapter 5 show how one can carry out formal research at this "listening" stage.

2. *Planning.* At this stage, campaign planners must translate their learnings about target audiences into concrete programs of action. These programs typically involve crafting a "value proposition" that will contain motivating benefits appealing to the target audience, a sense of minimized costs (both monetary and non-monetary) that could inhibit behavior, communications that "talk" effectively to target audiences about the offer, and a contact system that will make it feasible and easy for the audience to act. Planning will also entail setting goals, timelines, and responsibilities, and making sure that systems are in place and coalitions formed to actually carry out the effort.

3. *Pretesting.* Probably the second biggest mistake in campaign planning and implementation is not pretesting key elements of the plan with the target audience. Planners often think that they have learned enough at the listening stage and are clever enough to translate those insights into an effective program. But target audiences are the ones who will decide a program's fate, and they very often will not have the reactions to program elements that the planners expected. A vivid example of this is the campaign of a major U.S. government agency that sought to increase the number of women getting mammograms by telling them about the factors that heighten a woman's risk of getting breast cancer. The campaign planners neglected the pretesting step and were puzzled when the campaign resulted in increased awareness of the risk factors but a *decrease* in the desired behavior. An evaluation study carried out *after* considerable time and funds had been spent revealed that (a) the target women learned the risk factors well (i.e., the campaign was a great *educational* success) and (b) many women intending to get a mammogram did not have the risk factors and decided not to go ahead even though the risk factors accounted for only 10 percent of all breast cancer cases. Clearly, if the campaign managers had only done a few simple pretest interviews using their campaign materials, they would have quickly learned of the folly of their approach and saved themselves significant amounts of time, money, and embarrassment.

4. *Implementation.* Once adjustments have been made based on the pretest results, the next step is to actually launch the campaign, putting in place all of the influence elements (offer, promotion, availability options) that marketers in the private sector emphasize (they call this the "4Ps"). A key variable here is making sure that

responsibilities are clearly assigned and performance deadlines set. Without such controls, campaigns can wander off target, elements can be neglected or underutilized, and goals can be missed.

5. *Monitoring.* Campaigns (as well as organization-level marketing programs) never turn out as planned. Competition doesn't stand still. Target audiences change, often as a result of early elements of the campaign. The environment has a tendency to toss in unexpected hurdles like an economic downturn or a health scare. For these reasons, it is essential that campaigns have a clear tracking system to monitor program performance along most of the key dimensions. Is the right audience being reached? Are they acting as intended—or at least moving toward action? Are they being reached by the program? How are they responding to elements of the program—is the offer understood and valued? Answers to all of these questions provide the critical clues that tell campaign managers what needs to be done at the next step.

6. *Recycling and revising.* Monitoring data may suggest a return either to the Listening or Planning stages. It may be that the data show that key target audience segments are not "getting" the message—they don't see the benefits that the campaign intended them to value. They think behavior is too costly. Or they are somewhat interested in the behavior but just aren't acting. All of these findings suggest that management has failed to really understand the target audiences and that they must go back to "deep" listening if they are to succeed. However, new listening may not be necessary if the problem is mostly a matter of coordinating campaign elements so they reinforce each other and don't conflict. Or the problem may be a matter of emphasis: Some target audiences are getting too much attention and other target audiences too little. In these cases, management needs to go back to the Planning stage. It is important to note that whether the recycling is back to Listening or Planning, the campaign managers must still remember to *pretest* their new ideas. Once a campaign is well under way, there is a natural tendency for campaign staff to think that they really, really know target audiences and "are sure" how they will react. Too many horror stories from the field have convinced us that such an attitude can effectively sabotage an otherwise well-planned campaign—one that would have benefited considerably from greater attention to mid-campaign program pretesting.

MARKETING EVALUATION AND CONTROL

To ensure that strategic marketing at both the organizational and campaign levels achieves its goals in a timely and efficient manner, the nonprofit manager must develop and put in place effective control systems for these plans. The data from such systems are important for strategic purposes and are also important in providing data for outside evaluators and funders. The latter role is much more important in the twenty-first century due to the increasing involvement of "venture philanthropists" in nonprofit funding.[12] Because of their importance, we shall return to these issues at greater length in the concluding chapter.

Summary

Once the marketer and his or her staff have developed the appropriate marketing mindset, they must determine the basic direction the organization will take over the strategic planning horizon. The means by which this is carried out is called the strategic marketing planning process. This takes place at both the organizational and campaign level. At the organizational level, the first step in this process is to identify the organization's overall mission, objectives, and specific goals and to understand the nature of its basic culture.

The next step is to analyze the strengths and weaknesses that the organization brings to the marketplace. A marketing audit is an effective tool for this purpose. This should be followed by a careful analysis of the organization's external environment. First, management must identify and understand the key publics it must consider in its planning. Depending on the organization, the most important publics will be customers, donors, and volunteers or—typically—some combination.

The second major environmental component is competition. Here, with respect to specific target audience behaviors, the organization must recognize that it has competitors on four levels: desire, generic, service form, and enterprise. It may be required to consider all four of them in its planning. The third component is the macroenvironment. The organization must understand major trends taking place in its social, political, technological, and economic environments. Many nonprofits conduct environmental scanning exercises with private sector assistance for this purpose.

Once the internal and external environments have been analyzed, organizational planners take the information and develop specific objectives and goals for the marketing department. Objectives set out the broad "destinations" for the marketing strategy over the planning horizon. Goals specify numeric milestones for each objective. Goals should give direction to the organization's staff and describe pathways to its future. They should offer benchmarks for measuring progress and provide triggers for contingency plans. Goals should be motivating for staff and provide a basis for assessing future performance. Finally, goals should communicate the organization's direction to the outside world and indicate needs for developing marketing tracking information systems.

Strategic planning at the campaign level involves six steps. First, the organization conducts formative research to deeply understand its target market. This is followed by planning and pretesting. Implementation is the next step, leading to routine performance monitoring and necessary recycling and revision. As with all marketing, the campaign planning process begins and ends with the target audience.

Effective organizations develop formal evaluation systems, which are becoming increasingly important as more formal business tools are brought to the nonprofit sector.

Questions

1. Identify a specific nonprofit's mission statement. What would be your recommendations for improvement? How do you think the mission helps the nonprofit achieve its marketing objectives?
2. Kendra Crowley was a marketing manager at Coca-Cola who decided to pursue an opportunity at a rapidly growing Boys & Girls Club organization in Atlanta. Explain some

of the challenges Ms. Crowley may face as a marketing manager moving from a corporate environment to a nonprofit environment.

3. Conduct an analysis on the external threats and opportunities that may exist for the Smithsonian Insititute in Washington, D.C. Be sure to include public, competitive, and macroenvironment components in your analysis. What are the implications that would be critical in shaping the Smithsonian's organizational marketing planning?

4. The U.S. Department of Health & Human Services recently launched the "Small Step" Campaign to help prevent childhood obesity in America. Evaluate this campaign based on the six steps for campaign marketing planning provided in the chapter.

Notes

1. Philip D. Harvey and James D. Snyder, "Charities Need a Bottom Line Too," *Harvard Business Review,* Vol. 66, No. 1 (January–February 1987), p. 14.

2. The material in this section is drawn from Alan R. Andreasen and Jean M. Manning, "Culture Conflict in Health Care Marketing," *Journal of Health Care Marketing,* Vol. 7, No. 1 (March 1987), pp. 2–8.

3. Thomas J. Peters and Robert H. Waterman, Jr., *In Search of Excellence* (New York: Harper & Row, 1982).

4. See Thomas Hoving, *Making Mummies Dance: Inside the Metropolitan Museum of Art* (New York: Simon & Schuster, 1993).

5. Daniel L. Wakin, "The Multiplex as Opera House: Will They Serve Popcorn?" *New York Times,* September 7, 2006. Retrieved from http://select.nytimes.com/search/restricted/article?res=F30E14F63D550C748CDDA00894DE404482, September 26, 2006.

6. Alan R. Andreasen, Ronald C. Goodstein, and Joan W. Wilson "Transferring Marketing Knowledge to the Nonprofit Sector," *California Management Review,* Vol. 47, No. 4 (Summer 2005), pp. 46–67.

7. For a marketing audit guide for social service organizations, see Douglas B. Herron, "Developing a Marketing Audit for Social Service Organizations," in Charles B. Weinberg and Christopher H. Lovelock (Eds.), *Reading in Public and Nonprofit Marketing* (Palo Alto, CA: Scientific Press, 1978), pp. 269–271. For arts organizations, see Tom Horwitz, *Arts Administration* (Chicago: Review Press, 1978), pp. 81–85. For hospitals, see Eric N. Berkowitz and William A. Flexner, "The Marketing Audit: A Tool for Health Service Organizations," *HCM Review,* Fall 1978, pp. 55–56.

8. Kevin P. Kearns, *Private Sector Strategies for Social Sector Success* (San Francisco: Jossey-Bass Publisher, 2000).

9. H. Igor Ansoff, "Strategies for Diversification," *Harvard Business Review,* September–October 1957, pp. 1,123–1,124.

10. Michael E. Porter, *Competitive Strategy: Techniques for Analyzing Industries and Competitors* (New York: The Free Press, 1980); see also Michael E. Porter, "What Is Strategy?" *Harvard Business Review,* November–December 1996, pp. 61–78.

11. Some of these ideas were developed earlier in Alan R. Andreasen, *Marketing Social Change* (San Francisco: Jossey-Bass Publisher, 1995).

12. Christine W. Letts, William P. Ryan, and Allan Grossman, *High Performance Nonprofit Organizations* (New York: Wiley, 1998).

4

UNDERSTANDING TARGET AUDIENCE BEHAVIOR

MDS: WASH YOUR HANDS AND YOU GET A STARBUCKS GIFT CARD!

A study by the Institute of Medicine in 2000 estimated that between 44,000 and 98,000 Americans die each year due to hospital errors, and one of the leading causes is the spread of bacterial infection due to poor sanitation. Other sectors of the economy have recognized the problem and have done something about it. The cruise industry in the last decade has had a number of disease outbreaks, including Legionnaires' disease, raising concerns among passengers. Partly in response, the Centers for Disease Control and Prevention developed a Vessel Sanitation Program and the industry quickly got behind it. Now, some ships require passengers who have ventured ashore to have their hands squirted with an antiseptic, Purell (a Pfizer product), prior to reboarding. Partly as a result of this diligence, sickness incident rates on cruise ships have gone down significantly.

But what about hospitals? Doctors are a major problem. They are typically very busy and don't feel they have time for "excessive" hand washing. Purell dispensers are often not handy or just unavailable. And some observers think the problem is also "doctor arrogance"—they think that they can't be carrying disease. It must be someone else! Hospitals often have limited authority over doctors' behavior because the latter are free agents simply using the hospital to treat their patients.

Cedars-Sinai Medical Center in Los Angeles decided to do something about the problem—prompted by a staff urologist and former Chief of Staff, Leon Bender, who had firsthand experience with cruise ship sanitation precautions. Cedars-Sinai first tried "education" with posters, faxes, and e-mails with little success. So they decided to adopt key marketing concepts. First, they focused on making it easier to act. They passed out bottles of Purell to doctors when they arrived at the parking lot entrance. They also increased the "value proposition" for target doctors by creating a Hand Hygiene Safety Posse that gave out $10 Starbucks cards as a reward for the right behavior. They also raised the costs of the competitive behavior in dramatic ways. After culturing and photographing the residue on the hands of the doctors at a Chief of Staff's Advisory Committee meeting, the hospital's epidemiologist picked one of the most disgusting images that emerged and had it put up as a "Petri-Dish screen saver" on computers all over the hospital.

Hand-hygiene compliance rose to virtually 100 percent with no decline since the screen saver went up. As Dr. Bender put it: "With people who have been in practice 25 or 30 or 40 years, it's hard to change behavior. But when you present them with good data, they change their behavior very rapidly." That may be debatable unless the data can be made dramatic. As *Freakonomics* authors Stephen J. Dubner and Steven D. Levitt put it: "Some forms of data are more compelling than others, and in this case an image was worth a 1,000 statistical tables."

Source: Stephen J. Dubner and Steven D. Levitt, "Selling Soap. How Do You Get Doctors to Wash Their Hands?" *New York Times*, September 24, 2006, pp. 22–23.

As we have said, the bottom line of all marketing strategy and tactics—commercial and social—is to influence behavior. Sometimes this necessitates changing ideas and thoughts first, but in the end, it is behavior influence we are after. This is an absolutely crucial point. Some nonprofit marketers may think they are in the "business" of changing *ideas,* but it can legitimately be asked why they should bother if such changes do not lead to action. Why bother changing racist whites' attitudes toward blacks or Asians unless it leads to fair treatment socially and in the workplace? If one argues that attitude change alone really does represent success because *eventually* behavior will change, one may be engaging in wishful thinking. In such cases, it is simply reinforcing our fundamental position that the bottom line of nonprofit marketing really ought to be b*ehavior influence,* not something we hope will lead to it.

If the end product of a particular program is *only* a change in a mental state, this should more properly be called *educating* or *propagandizing.* In our view, it is not really marketing. Our definition still leaves a wide area for the application of marketing principles. Of course, there have been scholars like Robert Bartels and David Luck who many years ago said that this view of marketing is entirely too broad.[1] Nonetheless, marketing concepts and principles can be applied to all of the following kinds of behavioral objectives targeting many kinds of audiences:

- Inducing people to buy products and services
- Inducing people to give up undesirable behaviors, such as smoking and drug use
- Inducing others NOT to start smoking or do drugs
- Inducing people to adopt new desirable behaviors, such as exercising or taking high blood pressure medication
- Inducing people to donate time or money
- Inducing staff people or volunteers to carry out specific actions
- Inducing legislators to vote for certain desirable laws or to fund specific programs
- Inducing members of the media to report certain stories

BEHAVIORAL DRIVERS—THE BCOS FACTORS

Why do people behave in ways that a marketer desires? The obvious answer is that behavior is driven by a vast complex of factors both internal and external to the individual actor. In the present volume, we adopt a framework first proposed by Andreasen in 1995[2] that focuses on four key drivers that we call the *BCOS* factors—benefits, costs, others, and self-assurance. These factors reflect the work of Fishbein and Ajzen and incorporate the three key conditions that Macinnis, Moorman, and Jaworski suggest are necessary for behavior to occur. These are motivation, opportunity, and ability (MOA).[3] Target audiences must be motivated to act. But if they lack the opportunity (no health care center nearby) or the ability to act (no understanding of how to get an obese kid to eat healthier), then no action will take place. As Rothschild points out, education may be sufficient if motivation and opportunity are high but ability is low. And in cases where opportunity and ability are high but motivation is low, the needed approach may be the law.[4] In other cases, marketing can have a key role to play.

In the BCOS approach, the first two factors—benefits and costs—are the ones that are the most frequent focus of marketing texts in that they emphasize the role of *exchange* as the relationship with target audiences. Marketers believe that the way to achieve competitive success is to offer superior *value propositions* that will lead (ideally) to lifetime target audience relationships. One way to think of the behaviors that are critical to nonprofit success (and the success of most for-profit firms) is that they involve the buyer making a trade-off—or exchange—between *benefits* and *costs*. Target audiences recognize that they have to give up some costs but in return, get some benefits. In the private sector, the costs are typically money and time, but in the nonprofit world they can include pain (involved in an inoculation, blood donation, or drug withdrawal), embarrassment or loss of self-respect (getting tested for Alzheimer's), guilt (reporting a suspected child abuser), and many other complex decision inputs. The challenge to the nonprofit marketer is to create a compelling package of benefits to overcome these important costs, thereby constructing a compelling value proposition. This can be a daunting challenge.

However, behavior is not driven solely by the benefits and costs that comprise exchanges—although attention to these components alone may be sufficient to bring about considerable success. Behaviors can be—and are—strongly influenced by *others* in the target audience's environment. We all know of occasions when we made our own benefit/cost calculation and came up with the best choice for us and then did something entirely different because someone else—a wife, coworker, or child—wanted us to do so. The force of interpersonal or social pressure can be powerful influences both for and against the nonprofit marketer's campaign. Many large donors give to nonprofits because their peers are giving and have asked them to join them. On the other hand, college freshmen often pressure peers to binge drink, telling them "everyone does it." Therefore, the "other" factor can work for or against a marketer. Clever marketers learn to bring social pressure to bear when it helps and minimize it when it hurts.

Even if the benefits of a particular behavior exceed the costs and even if social pressures are strongly favorable, target audience members may still not act. Considerable experience has shown that the missing factor is what Albert Bandura refers to as *self-efficacy*[5] and what we will call self-assurance. Self-assurance is simply the individual's belief that he or she can actually make the behavior happen. This is easiest to see in the case of smoking and dieting. A significant proportion of all smokers and obese individuals (at least in developing countries) are convinced that the benefits of quitting smoking or dieting well exceed the costs. Further, they know that others who are important to them (e.g., their children) want them to "do the right thing." But they don't act because—sometimes from experience—they think they simply cannot succeed. For the marketer in these cases to add another benefit or to "shout louder" through a clever communications program will simply not succeed. The individual's sense of self-assurance must be addressed if the program is to be successful.

We will return again and again to these BCOS factors throughout this book as we discuss how one researches audiences and how one develops elements of successful programs. In the sections to follow, we will also introduce other factors that impinge on audience behavior. However, we have found that the BCOS framework itself comprises a simple, portable model that is useful in a wide range of behavior influence situations.

THE CENTRAL ROLE OF EXCHANGE AND VALUE PROPOSITIONS

When someone buys a Big Mac, he or she pays $2.09 or 460 Japanese yen and, in exchange, gets a burger. At the simplest level, it is an exchange of money for food. A target audience engages in the transaction because he or she believes that the ratio of benefits to costs is better than alternative actions to meet his or her hunger needs. In the same sense, a reporter for a TV station covers a fundraising event at a nonprofit organization's headquarters because he or she believes the ratio of benefits (either personal or organizational) to the costs in time and equipment is greater than any other alternative at the time of the event.

Similarly, the potential volunteer compares the joys of helping with the time involved; the staffer compares the benefits of working hard on some management directive against the costs in time and stress of doing so; the federal legislator compares the impact on her constituents of a piece of legislation against the costs of time and interpersonal capital in getting it supported and passed; or the man with high blood pressure compares the benefits of better health against the annoyance of having to exercise and take medication. In each case, there is a mental calculation of trade-offs to be made. For the marketer to be successful, the target audience must believe that the exchange that the marketer is promoting is better than any reasonable alternative—including doing nothing. Thus, in the simplest sense, the basic challenge of marketing is, for each target audience, *maximizing the perceived benefits and minimizing the perceived costs* of whatever it is the marketer wants done. This is what we call developing a compelling value proposition.

Further, it should be noted that each of the benefits that a target audience might derive from the transaction represents a cost to the marketer (of providing it), and many of the costs that the target audience pays (e.g., effort expended, money paid, blood given, and so on) represent benefits to the marketer.

Types of Exchanges

Exchanges can vary in whether they are *two party* or *multiple party* and whether they lead to behaviors that are *continuing* or of *fixed duration.* Multiple-party exchanges occur in a number of contexts: The "additional" party can be (1) *allied with the target audience*—for example, other family members, other members of the neighborhood, or other members of a buying group; (2) *allied with the marketer*—for example, an advertising agency or distribution channel member; (3) *independent* of either prime transactor but necessary to *facilitate* the transaction—for example, a credit card company; or (4) *independent* of either party but *seeking to influence* the existence or content of an exchange—for example, a bystander urging a teenager not to take an offered cigarette or a national politician urging citizens to be sure to vote.[6]

"Continuing transactions" are transactions in which one or more parties must perform some continuing behavior as their part of the exchange agreement. "Fixed duration transactions" are, most commonly, specific one-time behaviors like inoculations or sales. Some transactions, such as renting a car or a motel room for several days or weeks, take place over time but are of fixed duration. A great many of the transactions sought in the nonprofit sector, however, require the target audience to change for a long time some behavior or set of behaviors. Examples include campaigns to induce children to brush their teeth regularly, teenagers to avoid drugs, adults to stop smoking, and couples to prevent HIV/AIDS. Implicit in continuing transactions—and therefore crucial to marketers—is the fact that marketing does not stop and *should not stop* with the parties' agreement to the transaction or when the exchange is first performed under the terms of the transaction. Marketers must continue to influence (i.e., reinforce) the desired behavior. In the private sector, this is often called customer relationship management (CRM).[7]

LEVELS OF UNDERSTANDING OF TARGET AUDIENCE BEHAVIOR

As noted in Chapter 3, the marketing manager for a nonprofit organization must begin with an understanding of target audience behavior because the organization's success depends on it. There are four broad classes of management decisions for which an understanding of target audiences is especially crucial. The decisions will determine the following:

1. *How to aggregate target audiences into similar groupings for purposes of marketing planning.*
2. *Which segments to choose as target markets and how many resources to allocate to each.*
3. *How to position the desired behavior or behaviors as a desirable value proposition.*
4. *How to translate the value proposition into specific elements of the offer, its costs, how it will be delivered, and how it will be communicated.*

We take up the first three of these decisions in Chapters 6 and 7 and the last in Section III.

There are also four levels at which a manager can understand target audience behavior so as to make these decisions better:

1. *Descriptive understanding.* At the simplest level, the manager can profile the characteristics of the market at a given point in time. How many buyers of what age, sex, and occupational status are in market A, creating how many exchanges of type B, in month Y, costing X marketing dollars, and so on? At a more sophisticated level, the manager may wish to categorize target audiences in terms of complex indexes such as their social class or family life cycle or their psychographic profile.
2. *Understanding of associations.* At this level, the manager may desire to know what behaviors or characteristics in the profile are associated with what other behaviors or characteristics at a certain point in time. Thus the manager may wish to know

whether museum attendance is associated with occupation, theater attendance with gender, and attendance at both with age and family composition.

3. *Understanding of causation.* If a curvilinear association between family life cycle and arts attendance is found, a manager may wish to know whether getting older and having children *leads* to less performing arts attendance or whether the two sets of factors just happen to occur together for other reasons. This level of understanding moves beyond association to show determinacy. Such information is particularly valuable if the "cause" at issue is a marketing intervention the manager can control.

4. *Ability to explain causation.* Ideally, a manager would like to move beyond knowing that A causes B to know *why* this is so. That is, the manager may "know" that arts attendance has a curvilinear association with age and that the appearance of children *causes* a decline in attendance. However, the manager may only have hypotheses as to why this is so. It is possible, for example, that the explanation is that the appearance of children puts a strain on budgets that precludes former luxuries like arts attendance (an economic explanation). Alternatively, it may be that younger family members put pressure on adult target audiences to *not* attend the performing arts (a sociological explanation). Or, the appearance of children may change the target audience's personal priorities. He or she may decide to devote more time to being with the children or more time working to build a firm economic future for the family, which leaves no room for attending the performing arts (a psychological explanation). Quite obviously, what a performing arts marketer should do to win back families with new children—or whether one should do anything at all—depends on which of these explanations is the most valid.

Developing a sophisticated understanding of various target audience markets is, of course, not easy. It comes with time, experience, and the careful use of the formal and informal research approaches discussed in Chapter 5 to accumulate facts, understand relationships, and slowly form patterns from them. But personal observation and formal research are both likely to be much more effective if they are based on a sound conceptualization or model of target audience behavior. The remainder of this chapter will offer such a conceptualization centered on the BCOS model. We will focus on individual behavior although we recognize that, in some cases, the focus of the marketer may be on groups of individuals (e.g., inducing a corporation or other nonprofit to cooperate in a strategy) or even entire communities. In one sense, one may look at groups as merely aggregations of individuals formally or informally arrayed in groups.

INDIVIDUAL BEHAVIORS

Individual behaviors that a marketer can influence require target audiences to decide to act or not act. Decisions about actions vary in two important dimensions: involvement and complexity.

Involvement and Complexity

While it is obviously a continuum, behavior theorists make a distinction between *low-involvement* and *high-involvement* exchanges. They believe this difference affects the amount of cognition or problem solving a target audience will undertake during and after the exchange process. As defined by Engel and Blackwell, with respect to products and services,

Involvement is the activation of extended problem-solving behavior when the act of purchase or consumption is seen by the decision maker as having high personal importance or relevance.[8]

High personal involvement has been found to occur when one or more of the following conditions are operative:

1. The behavior required of the target audience will reflect upon his or her self-image.
2. The economic and personal costs of behaving "incorrectly" are perceived as high.
3. The personal or social risks of a "wrong" decision are perceived as high.
4. Outside (nonmarketer) reference group pressures to act in a particular way are strong and the target audience's motivation to comply is strong.

Thus exchanges can vary in the extent to which they are personally involving. They can also vary in their complexity for the decision maker. Complexity varies with involvement and the degree of newness of the decision. There are, of course, exchanges made for the first time and exchanges made after years and years of experience. Thus we might expect very complex decision making to occur for exchanges that are highly involving and that are being made for the first time such as finally giving up alcohol. As the target audience gains experience, however, decisions will be simplified to reflect this experience. At some point, given many repeats of the exchange process, the evaluation process may become relatively routine even though the subject of the exchanges is still highly involving, for example, continuing to exercise or refuse offers of drugs. This distinction is indicated in Table 4-1.

It is possible that many other nonprofit exchanges, such as small donations, voting on trivial public issues, signing a simple petition, and so on, are really low-involvement actions. And it is important that the manager not exaggerate the behavior's importance to the target audience. It is our experience that there is the real danger that a myopic organization-centered view of marketing will lead managers to assume that an exchange is highly involving to target audiences *since it is to the marketer.* The marketer then may seek to develop an elaborate level of understanding of an exchange that is basically relatively simple.

Having raised this important caution, we must repeat our position that a much larger number—perhaps the majority—of exchanges with which marketers in nonprofit organizations are involved are in fact considered high involvement and therefore involve what Hoyer and MacInnis call high processing, high elaboration.[9] Decisions about changing health habits, voting for major candidates, choosing a school or a career, giving a significant

TABLE 4-1	A Taxonomy of Consumer Decision-Making Approaches	
	Degree of Personal Involvement	
Experience	*High*	*Low*
None	Extensive decision making	Simplified decision making
Some	Simplified decision making	No observable decision making
Much	Routine decision making	No observable decision making

donation of time or money, attending the arts, changing religious institutions, supporting tax referenda, obeying the laws, and so forth all may be characterized as:

- Involving very elemental aspects of one's self-image
- Involving major personal or economic sacrifices
- Risking major personal or social costs if a wrong choice is made
- Involving considerable peer pressure for or against

HIGHLY COMPLEX DECISIONS

Stages of Change

The typical highly complex decision is one in which the target audience is considering undertaking a behavior for the first time. One of the key conceptual breakthroughs emerging from the nonprofit area called social marketing is the recognition that high-involvement behaviors do not come about quickly; they evolve over time. One does not go from being obese to being a conscientious dieter for a lifetime overnight—or even in a few months. People do not become opera-goers in a month. Villagers in the developing world do not adopt new sanitation practices as the result of a single lecture from a government health worker.

While one may admit that nonprofit marketers have challenges that take a long time to achieve, the breakthrough in the marketing literature (coming originally from social psychology) is that the process over time can be broken up into stages. Further, as research by James Prochaska and his colleagues have made clear,[10] campaigns can be more effective if they tailor interventions to the stage at which the target audience is found.[11] That is, the marketer's challenge ought to be seen not as getting immediate action, but as moving the individual to the next stage. This, of course, is an approach long recognized by fundraisers seeking major donations. One does not go into an executive's office on Day One and ask for a million dollars. The prospect requires a good deal of what the fundraisers call "cultivation." The advantage of the approach offered here is that the stages are given specific labels and their implications for strategy are clearly spelled out.

There are so-called stage models with anywhere from four to six stages. We adopt a four-stage model based on Prochaska and DiClemente's five-stage model, collapsing the Preparation and Action stages into one for simplicity and mental portability. The stages and their brief implications follow.

- *Precontemplation.* There are always a great many members in any given target audience who are not thinking about the behavior in which the nonprofit marketer is interested. This may be a case where they have never heard about the desirability of the behavior (e.g., they don't know there is a vaccine for a particular disease that is killing their neighbors). This would be common when some new idea emerges, such as laying babies on their backs to reduce the risk of Sudden Infant Death Syndrome (SIDS). In other cases, it may be that the individual has heard about the behavior and concluded that he or she is not interested. This may be because social pressures strongly oppose it. It may be because the individual believes it is against his or her religion. He or she may think it is not individually appropriate (e.g., it is a "Western idea" in an Eastern culture). A good example of this is teenagers who think fruity alcoholic drinks

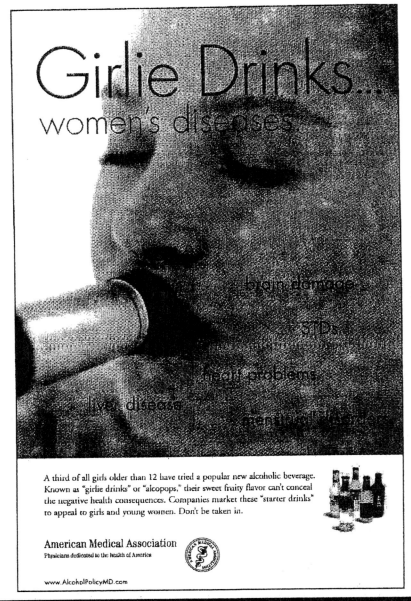

FIGURE 4-1   Long-Term Consequences of Alcoholism

Source: Courtesy of the American Medical Association.

are not a problem. The American Medical Association campaign tries to point out the long-term consequences of alcoholism (see Figure 4-1).

- *Contemplation.* This, of course, is where most marketing is done and it is where most marketers hope to encounter the market. It is where the target audience is thinking about the behavior. The audience is weighing the costs and benefits in the exchange, considering what others who are important do or do not want them to do, and forming a sense of whether they can actually carry out the behavior. Andreasen makes a distinction between early and late contemplation:[12]

- *Early Contemplation.* This is where the target audience is just beginning to think about the behavior. Here, the benefits and costs will be a central focus. Benefits will be especially important because, if the target audience does not see significant benefits, they are unlikely to go further in the process (unless there are very strong social pressures to do so).
- *Late Contemplation.* This is where the target audience is actively considering the option. At this point, the audience is no longer dwelling on the benefits— they pretty much know they are there. They worry more about the costs. This is something we all do when something that once seemed like a really good idea gets closer to hand—the much-anticipated after-work party becomes less appealing as the time draws near, exhaustion sets in, and other obligations grow in importance. Target audiences in Late Contemplation also worry more about what others think and about their own abilities to be successful.

- *Preparation and Action.* As a campaign gains momentum, a great many members of the target audience will be at the stage where they have thought through the behavior and are ready to act. They have just not taken that first step! Sometimes this is a question of a lingering sense of self-doubt. Sometimes, however, it is simply a matter of opportunity and some final push.
- *Maintenance.* Some campaigns are successful if people only act once, but many campaigns need target audience members to continue the behavior. Many smokers quit, but 80 percent or more of them go back to smoking. The National High Blood Pressure Education Program focused much of its early efforts on getting target audience members aware of the problem of high blood pressure, getting them worried about its effects, and taking preventive action. Monitoring research well into the multi-year campaign showed managers that many sufferers were dropping out—in part because prevention offers no personally observable benefits (i.e., one does not feel any different). Subsequent focus in the campaign then had to turn to questions of how to keep people doing the desired behavior.

The stages approach implies different marketing emphases at different stages:

- For Precontemplators, the marketer's principal challenge is creating awareness and knowledge and creating interest (i.e., a sense of personal relevance). Marketers often refer to this as "need arousal." Need arousal can occur spontaneously within the individual. Thus, as Chris Ford graduates from high school, he may recognize that he must pick a college and get further education. This *internal information* is one major source of need arousal. Arousing internal information could also come in the form of physiological drives (e.g., hunger, sex, and so on). Arousing *external information* can come from others (e.g., friends or family who insist that Chris Ford consider college) or from the media (e.g., college advertisements or brochures, posters, magazine articles). These types of information can often be very powerful in getting an individual to look into something that he or she might not otherwise consider.
- For Early Contemplators, the marketer must devise and communicate strong benefits. As noted below, these must be personal benefits, not benefits to others or "society."

- For Late Contemplators, emphasis must shift to reducing costs and bringing social pressure to bear. The marketer must avoid the natural tendency to "push benefits" on a slow-to-act target audience—they will know the benefits; it is the costs and the social issues that are looming large.
- For those in Preparation and Action, the key is to help bolster self-assurance and maximize opportunities to act.
- For those in Maintenance, attention must shift to creating reward systems, making repeat behavior easy, and keeping social pressure bearing down on the good behavior.

The stages concept is one that guides a major campaign of the Consumer Federation of America, called "AmericaSaves." The objective of this campaign, first piloted in Cleveland in 2002 as ClevelandSaves, is to get more people of limited means to start saving—even a little each month. On their home page, the campaign says:

> We find it useful to see individual Americans on a ten mile path to saving. Those that haven't walked a mile don't understand the importance of saving, so don't save. Those at mile three are aware of this value, but don't believe they are capable of saving, so don't do so. Those at mile six see the importance of saving and think they might be able to do so, but haven't started yet. Those at mile seven have begun to save. Those at mile ten are saving as effectively as they can, which also means that they are effectively managing their money and debts.[13]

The Contemplation Process
During the Contemplation stage, the target audience member is seriously considering the campaign's recommended behavior—and, quite probably, other alternatives. The factors and processes that come into play at this stage are outlined in general terms in Figure 4-2, which also reflects factors important at the other three stages.

Information Gathering
Following need arousal, the involved target audience member typically will begin gathering information to help him or her decide what to do. It is important for marketers to understand what this process is because it represents a key *aperture* for marketer influence. As noted in Figure 4-2, one can imagine the target audience seeking information to form a *choice set* and then to evaluate it in terms of costs and benefits in order to decide what he or she is likely to do. "What they are likely to do" is usually conceptualized as their *behavioral intention,* a state that the BCOS model indicates is also influenced by others and self-assurance. Evaluating the choice set in first-time decisions requires that the target audience figure out on what bases the choice will be made, or the *evaluation criteria,* which in turn are influenced by the person's *motives and values* and by the opinions of others.

Forming the Choice Set
Through the process of gathering information, the target audience arrives at an increasingly clear picture of the major available choices. He or she eliminates certain alternatives and moves toward making a choice among the few remaining alternatives. This process of *choice narrowing* can be illustrated for Chris Ford. Ford considered a number of alternatives to college, including working, joining the army, traveling, and

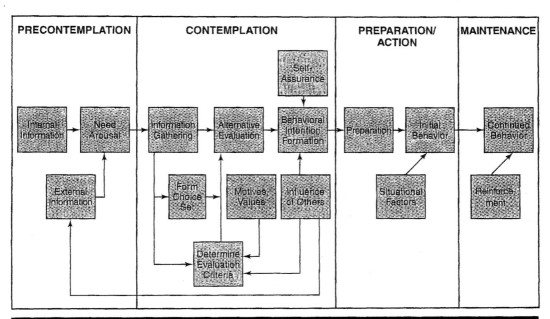

FIGURE 4-2   A Model of Complex Evaluations

loafing. He decided that going to college made the most sense. Should it be a community college, a state university, or a private college? Examining his needs and values, he decided to attend a private college.

We can now examine how Chris narrowed his choice to a specific set of colleges. Figure 4-3 shows a succession of sets involved in this target audience's decision process. The *total set* represents all private colleges that exist, whether or not the target audience knows about them; this list runs into the thousands. The total set can be divided into the target audience's *awareness set* (the colleges he has heard of) and the *unawareness set*. Of those he is aware of, he will only want to consider a limited number; these constitute his *consideration set,* and the others are relegated to an *infeasible set*. As he gathers additional information, a few colleges remain strong candidates, and they constitute his *choice set,* the others being relegated to a *nonchoice set*. (Some research has suggested that choice sets seldom exceed seven alternatives, plus or minus two.) Let us assume that the student sends applications to the four colleges in his choice set and is accepted by all four. In the final step, he carefully evaluates the colleges in the choice set (we shall examine this process shortly) and then makes a final choice, in this case Cornell University.

The implication of this choice-narrowing process is that a nonprofit marketer potentially competes with a large number of other choices for the target audience's interest. Therefore, before making plans to market to a particular segment, the nonprofit marketer must study target audiences to learn (1) whether the recommended behavior is in the segment's awareness, consideration, and choice sets, and (2) if the behavior *is* in the various sets, who the competitors are. If the behavior is not in the choice set, for example, then the desired exchange will not be possible. The first marketing task, then, is to get the alternative into the choice set of the target buyers.

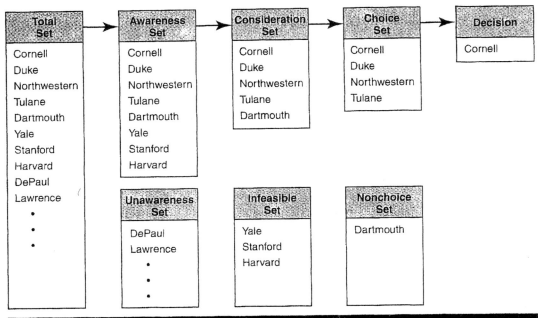

FIGURE 4-3   Successive Sets in Consumer Decision Making

Determining Evaluation Criteria

To make an eventual judgment about which of the alternative behaviors he will select, Chris Ford must develop some basis for forming an overall evaluation of the alternatives in the final choice set. Presumably, developing these criteria is a step he could have taken before or—more likely—during the process of defining his choice set. Clearly, if a college marketer wants to influence Ford, he ought to understand what is important to Ford. And finding what is important to Ford is really finding out two things: (1) what factors Ford considers in judging the various alternatives and (2) the relative value he assigns to each factor. We shall refer to the former as *choice criteria* and the latter as *criteria weights.*

One of the key factors determining Chris Ford's criteria in choosing his college is his own needs. While individuals have many basic needs, the marketer must discover which ones apply in this specific case. One of the most useful typologies of basic needs is Maslow's *Hierarchy of Needs,* shown in Figure 4-4. Maslow held that people act to satisfy the lower needs before satisfying their higher needs.[14] A starving man, for example, first devotes his energy to finding food. If this basic need is satisfied, he can spend more time on his safety needs, such as eating the right foods and breathing good air. When he feels safe, he can take the time to deepen his social affiliations and friendships. Still later, he can develop pursuits that will meet his need for self-esteem and the esteem of others. Once this is satisfied, he is free to actualize his potential in other ways. As each lower-level need is satisfied, it ceases to be a motivator and a higher need starts defining the person's motivational orientation.

We can ask what basic needs are stimulated by the aroused interest in college. Some high school seniors become concerned about whether they can afford college and meet their basic needs for food and adequate housing. Others wonder about how safe they will be away from home. Still others are concerned with whether they can find people they like

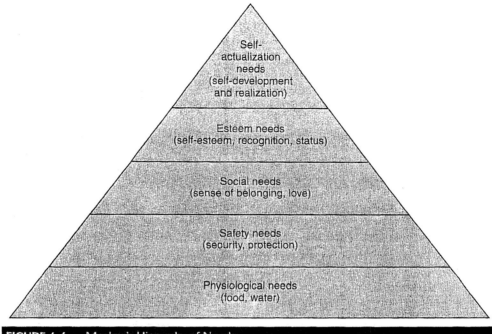

FIGURE 4-4   Maslow's Hierarchy of Needs

and who like them. And others are concerned with self-esteem or self-actualization. A college will not be able to give attention to all these needs. Thus we find colleges that cater primarily to the need for belonging (small schools with small classes, a caring faculty, and a good social life), others to the students' need for esteem (many "name" colleges), and still others to the need for self-actualization (many "arty" schools).

Students often want to satisfy several needs, some of which are in conflict, by the same behavior. Thus a student may have a high need for both achieving and belonging. This can create mental conflict, which can be resolved either by treating one need as more important or by fluctuating between the two needs at different times. Here is where the person's *values* come into play, namely, the principles the person employs to weight the various consequences that might follow a particular choice.

Four different methods for determining evaluation criteria are (1) direct questions, (2) indirect measurements, (3) perceptual mapping, and (4) conjoint analysis.

Benefits and Costs

The BCOS model and work by Fishbein and Ajzen, among others, makes clear that people like Chris Ford who have not yet decided whether to take a particular action, or which of several actions to take, will consider two things:

1. First, they will review their set of perceptions (which are labeled *beliefs*) of the likelihood of specific positive and negative consequences in undertaking each act in the choice set (that is, the benefits and costs).
2. Second, they will think about how important—how valuable—each of the benefits and costs are to them. Some will be very important and many will be trivial. We shall refer to these values as the *criteria weightings*.

Collectively, these perceptions and their importance will comprise what the target audience (Chris) believes is the value proposition being offered. Certainly not being able to hit the beach on a spring break is a valuable consequence for a teen or college kid to avoid. An organization called A Matter of Degree has crafted a powerful message around that very cost.

A useful place to start marketing planning, then, is to attempt to get a sense of these beliefs and their relative importance to the market segment—how they see the value

---

FIGURE 4-5   Portraying Consequences of Behavior Choices

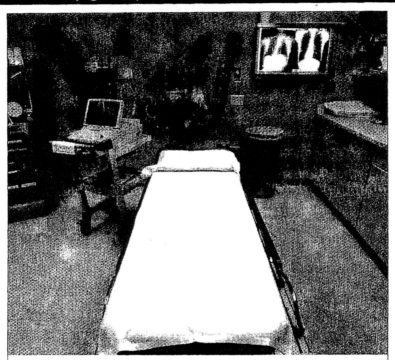

This Bed's For You.

Spring break in the ER, instead of on the beach?

There's no view of the beach and the food is terrible. You don't want your spring break to end in an emergency room.

Yet every year, that's where more and more students are winding up.

Alcohol poisoning. Car wrecks. Falls from balconies. Fistfights. Rape.

Why? Statistics show that half of male students – and 40 percent of females – drink on spring break until they vomit or pass out. The average male student consumes 18 drinks daily. The average female downs 10.

The alcohol and tour industries are urging you on with free beer, all-you-can-drink parties, booze cruises and endless happy hours.

Don't fall for it. Enjoy a fun, safe spring break. And remember. Nobody looks good in a hospital robe.

This message is sponsored by **A Matter of Degree**

The National Effort to Reduce High-Risk Drinking Among College Students

AMOD is a project of the American Medical Association and campus-community partnerships across America • **www.alcoholpolicysolutions.net**

Source: Courtesy of the American Medical Association.

proposition. Ideally, this will be carried out by formal quantitative research, or at least by the informal research approaches described in the next chapter. The combination of beliefs and weightings then should predict what Fishbein and Ajzen refer to as *behavioral intentions*. A history of research has shown that intentions are a good predictor of behavior.

A Note on Beliefs About Objects Versus Behaviors

It is important to realize that the approach we are using here is to model individual attitudes toward an *act*. This is consistent with the entire approach of this book, namely that it emphasizes *behavior*. The predicted consequences of behavior—pro and con— are a central determinant of action. Unfortunately, many marketers and researchers in both the profit and nonprofit sectors believe they ought to study individuals' beliefs about objects involved in an exchange, rather than the consequences of taking an act with respect to the object. In Chris Ford's case, these misguided researchers might try to study Ford's perceptions of Cornell or Duke as an object itself, not his perception of what it would be like to go there. This approach can often yield predictions that are far off the mark. If one were to ask Chris Ford to evaluate colleges, for example, he might indicate as important attributes such features as the reputation of the faculty for research and scholarship, the attractiveness of the campus, the innovativeness of curricula, and so forth. All of these may be very important to Chris Ford's evaluation of these colleges but have little or nothing to do with his evaluation of the opportunity to attend them. Questions about college attributes might never reveal that Ford was very concerned about whom he might meet there who could turn into lifelong friends. It might not occur to him that this is what an interviewer meant when asking about the attributes of a college (an object) rather than about going there (a behavior).

We are firmly of the opinion that in complex high-involvement decisions, it is behavioral intentions that determine behavior, and perceptions of consequences of the behavior are major determinants of those behavioral intentions (along with other interpersonal factors to be noted shortly). This approach will be central to our consideration of strategic planning throughout the rest of the book. And it is research into these beliefs and importances that ought to be critical bases of research prior to carrying out such planning.

Influence of Others

However, as both the BCOS model and Fishbein and Ajzen's extended model point out, whether or not benefits and costs are sufficient to predict *behavioral intention* also depends on *the influence of others*. Albert Bandura then would say that it also depends on the individual's sense of self-assurance. David Reisman pointed out many years ago that there are many individuals who go through life taking their cues about appropriate behavior largely from what are called by sociologists "significant others" or "referents."[15] These referent individuals or groups could be people they know or people they've only seen or read about (for example, movie or rock stars). Further, they can be people they identify with (membership referents), envy, and want to be like someday (aspiration referents), or people they *don't* wish to be like (negative referents). The latter would be exemplified by teenagers who refuse to go to the college where their parents went or to dress or to cut their hair as their parents want them to. These referents can provide input into the criteria individuals use to form their personal attitude toward an act. They can also have *direct* influence on behavioral intentions by exerting pressure on the individual to act in certain ways.[16] "Thermometers" for volunteering and fundraising campaigns can be a subtle way of telling target audiences that others are getting on board.

Some individuals may be directly influenced by several referents at once. Others may not be affected by referents at all. Women in Africa upon marriage often move into their new husband's home. There they come under the influence of the mother-in-law who, especially in developing countries, may be very much opposed to "modern" ideas. This is often complicated when the nonprofit marketer is a western NGO, which—it is feared—is indoctrinating young people into the "wrong" values.

A U.S. example shows similar dynamics. A campaign to get college girls to urge their boyfriends to use condoms discovered that many girls felt that they would be seen as odd or "different" if they did so. Certainly, college is a time when group norms—or perceived group norms—are very important as young people choose new lifestyles. In this case, the college women thought that very few of their peers acted as recommended yet the reality was much more accepting. What then was required as part of the campaign was to broadly communicate the real norms. "Norming" approaches have become relatively common in the last decade as marketers become more sensitive to the potential impacts—pro and con—of people's beliefs about what is the norm.[17]

Self-Assurance

As the BCOS model emphasizes, behavioral intentions are also influenced by self-assurance, which may account for much of the remaining "unexplained" variance in many studies of failed behavioral influence ventures. People need to feel that they can actually accomplish a behavior that will get them outcomes they value. This is a function of two things. First, is there an opportunity to act? Are there playgrounds for exercise or self-help clinics for spousal abusers? Second, do the individuals have the ability to act? Do they have a car to drive to the clinic? Do they own a bicycle to join friends for exercise? All of these factors can sabotage even the best campaigns focused on the first three of the BCOS factors. High-involvement, highly personal behaviors are often the hardest to influence. We all develop life patterns and ritual coping mechanisms for dealing with issues about which marketers seek influence. Challenged target audiences often seek any excuse not to act as recommended. Marketers simply cannot ignore such possibilities if they are to have a fully integrated campaign approach.

Strategy Implications

Suppose a marketer has conducted research into the BCOS factors. What does he or she do next? Take the case of Chris Ford. If one is the marketing director for Duke University, what can be done to improve the university's chances of attracting Ford (besides hope that other colleges turn him down)?

Duke has a number of options depending on what is learned about the BCOS factors:

1. *Change beliefs about alternatives.* Duke could attempt to change Ford's beliefs about Duke University with respect to key benefits and costs on which Duke scores poorly. There are two alternatives here, depending on whether Chris Ford's perceptions are accurate or not.

   a. If Ford's perceptions *are* accurate and there are a great many otherwise highly attractive prospective students like him, Duke might consider taking remedial actions such as reducing its class sizes or improving the quality of its teachers (assuming these are dimensions on which it scores poorly).

b. If Ford's perceptions are *not* accurate and it is clear he and others have a misunderstanding of what Duke is really like, then Duke has a communication problem. By words, pictures, web sites, testimonials, informal research reports, and the like, Duke must tell its story more effectively, being sure that it begins by responding to Chris Ford and his needs and perceptions rather than just telling him what *Duke* thinks he should know.

2. *Change beliefs about competitors.* Similarly, Duke might attempt to change Chris Ford's beliefs about the benefits and costs of attending Duke's competition (which the research has specifically identified as being in his choice set). This would be particularly appropriate if Duke knew that Ford's perceptions were, in fact, wrong. That is, Duke could offer comparative data (if such were available) showing that, for example, Duke had below-average class sizes while major competitors had above-average class sizes.

3. *Change weightings.* A third strategy available to Duke is to attempt to change the importance of weightings assigned to the benefits and costs—admittedly a difficult challenge. One way to look at Duke's problem is not that it is perceived badly but that a cost on which it is rated highly, its lack of financial sacrifice, is not valued highly enough by Chris Ford and his cohorts. Duke would be the *most favored alternative* if it were to convince prospective students like Ford that they ought to pay much more attention to the long-term financial consequences of college choices.

4. *Call attention to neglected favorable consequences.* Attendance at Duke may have consequences that Chris Ford didn't realize. These might include better weather or the chance to visit nearby recreational or cultural centers or lower clothing costs. The college would attempt to have its target audience add these benefits to their salient criteria, especially if they are features that are not offered by competitors.

5. *Add new favorable consequences.* Just as products add new ingredients or new packaging to revive flagging sales, so too could Duke offer new features such as the chance to attend a new study-abroad program or participate in a local work-study option that would meet important basic needs of the target audience that they heretofore had not thought relevant to the college decision.

6. *Bring positive referents to bear.* In addition to these actions, Duke could seek to influence Ford by working through referent groups found to be important to him. Business alumni in Chris's hometown might be contacted to speak to Ford. Letters or phone calls could be directed to his parents. Possibly the applications of Ford and several of his friends could be treated as a "package."

7. Finally, if perceived self-assurance seemed to be holding Ford back—that is, he just feels that he can't handle being that far away from home and the first year curriculum pressures—Duke might promote its many campus programs to assist students having social or academic difficulties.

Duke will need to carefully evaluate these alternative strategies according to their feasibility and cost. The difficulty of implementing each strategy, such as repositioning the college or shifting the importance of criteria, should not be minimized. However, the marketer can take comfort that, at least for these kinds of complex decisions, there are many points at which the decision can be influenced.

Finally, it should be noted that the BCOS factors can be used to segment markets, as can the stages of change. We shall return to these considerations in Chapter 6.

Simplified Behavior

The complex process undergone by Chris Ford in evaluating his college choices is typical of many behaviors that nonprofits wish to influence because these decisions are highly involving. It is also complex because it is a decision Ford is making for the first time and perhaps never making again. If this were a decision that the target audience would be making a second, third, or fourth time, however, we would expect to observe some simplifications of the process as a result of experience. In such cases, we would still expect considerable information seeking and information processing to take place because the decision is an important one. Target audience behavior theory postulates, however, that four kinds of simplification will probably take place when the target audience has experience.

First, little information seeking and thinking will be devoted to defining the evaluative criteria, that is, determining what benefits and costs to consider and what weightings to give each. The first time around, say in evaluating charities, a target audience might have to learn about the various charities to which they might give but also think about how they should go about evaluating their potential behavior. The target audience will take stock of what they really want as benefits from charitable giving and what the costs might be. Friends and coworkers might be asked about how they choose charities. In these circumstances, the marketer has considerable opportunity to influence the criteria since target audiences are still in their formative stage. However, once the first round of charitable choices is completed, the target audience member will have fixed the criteria on which alternatives are assessed. Marketers thus will have very limited opportunity to intervene to change this set. On the other hand, the weightings of some dimensions may change as the target audience's economic and social circumstances change. Indeed, as we note in Chapter 6, marketers often focus on target audiences undergoing status change because this is when the marketer can have a chance of changing behavior patterns.

Second, in repeat behaviors, the choice set may also be relatively well defined. At least a core subset of alternative charities is likely to be constant from occasion to occasion, with marginal alternatives coming and going at the periphery in response to new information or changing criteria or decision rules on the part of the individual target audience.

Thus, at this point, the target audience will be primarily evaluating *given* choices on *given* criteria with relatively *constant* weightings. There is also likely to be limited interpersonal influence and little concern for self-assurance issues. The marketer's first task in such circumstances, therefore, is to learn the contents of the choice set and the set of operative criteria, as well as the target audience's beliefs about the benefits and costs of accepting the marketer's alternative or those of competitors. If the marketer is *not* in the choice set, a kind of Catch-22 sets in. As we shall see in a later chapter, target audiences selectively attend to incoming information (e.g., from marketers). Thus, in the case of behavioral choices, they tend to pay attention to the options they are already considering. Therefore, the poor marketer is in the position of not being able to influence the choice set until his or her option is in the choice set!

However, assuming that the marketer is a part of the choice set, the main option available is to devise marketing strategies to modify *beliefs* about benefits and costs on important dimensions—the value proposition—to secure greater market penetration. This may be the only area in which the marketer can maneuver. Relatively little can be done at this point to influence criteria or their weighting. In general, it may be expected that the more often there is repeat behavior, the faster the target audience will simplify the evaluation process. This makes it much harder for a marketer not chosen to influence the choice and why many marketers dealing with repeated behaviors—like charities and membership organizations—focus almost obsessively on past givers or subscribers. The costs of getting someone new are many, many times the costs of keeping a repeater.

This is shown in a study by Richard Bagozzi of prospective blood donors. Bagozzi found that if one only knew perceptions of benefits and costs, one could explain from 10 to 22 percent of the variance in behavior at a blood drive one week away. However, if one knew how often the respondents had given in the past *and* what they did on the first blood drive, however, one could explain *40 percent of the variance* in behavior in the second drive.[18] Since these study participants had given an average of 13 times in the past five years, they were clearly experienced givers. For many, the behavior may well be described as having become highly simplified, if not routine. This would explain why marketers often believe the best approach to understanding a market is to study *past behavior.* Studying benefits and costs may not be particularly useful either because target audiences cannot really recall what evaluation they went through many years ago or because their attitudes today have been simplified and aligned to support their behavior. Left with behavior only, the marketer can take several approaches.

1. Use past behavior frequencies to segregate the market and concentrate on the "heavy users" (see Chapter 6).
2. Seek to discover behavior modification strategies that "bypass" cognition—for example, use special incentives, free trials, and so on to change behavior (see Chapter 17).
3. Seek to discover persuasion strategies to "shock" habituated target audiences into once again undertaking extensive cognitive activity.

Another approach would be to use what Krugman and others have called *low-involvement* or *incidental learning.*[19] Krugman pointed out that target audiences in developed countries are inundated with hundreds of advertising messages daily. When these messages are about exchanges in which the target audiences are highly involved, they will become perceptually vigilant and process the information vigorously. The question, then, is what happens to the remaining messages that aren't immediately relevant? Krugman suggests that, precisely because the exchange addressed in the message is one of current trivial interest to the target audience, he or she will be neither perceptually vigilant nor perceptually defensive. The message, so the theory goes, bypasses the cognitive evaluation stage and goes directly into long-term memory to be stored in detail or as some vague overall impression. This is what Petty and Cacioppo mean by "the peripheral route." This message then resides in memory until some cue at the time of purchase reactivates it (perhaps subconsciously). It *then* becomes a factor influencing the immediate choice. Since the more often a given message passes the target audience's sensory field (i.e., is repeated), the more likely it is to become lodged in long-term memory, Krugman's postulation of low-involvement learning has led many marketers in repeat behavior categories to emphasize memorable visual images (e.g., cartoon characters, the Energizer Bunny, and so on), jingles or "haunting" melodies (e.g., Coke or McDonald's), or outright repetition (e.g., Sprint long-distance commercials) to increase the probability that a subconscious memory trace will be built. Since most nonprofits cannot afford the budgets necessary to adopt these tactics, it may be expected that where they (reluctantly) conclude that a particular target segment considers the decision to be trivial, imaginative attempts must be developed to build trace recognitions through visual imagery, clever dialogue, or music that someday can be activated when an exchange is contemplated. This is often a task for which branding can be very valuable.

Emotion and Mood

Much of the previous discussion assumes that target audience behavior is more or less the result of rational thinking about alternatives and their relative value propositions. However, one ought not to neglect the role of emotions in behavioral choices—especially in the kind of socially fraught situations that nonprofit marketers are seeking to have influence. In such circumstances—dieting, confronting old age, and the like—many target audience members may be more influenced by their feelings than by rational analyses.[20] The private sector has long made efforts to manipulate emotions through television or magazine advertisements that communicate few "facts" but attempt to create feelings or moods and positive associations with perfumes, cruise vacations, even financial services. Thus Pepsi commercials try to create an emotional response to "the Pepsi Generation" while Coke hopes we will feel "warm and fuzzy" when we hear its commercial refrain "I'd like to teach the world to sing in perfect harmony."

Many nonprofit marketers seek to influence behaviors where emotions could be used effectively as a key strategy component. Hospitals are a good example of where dramatic portrayals of caring nurses and attractive maternity rooms may have a major impact on market share. Drug programs may have more effect by showing the warm, supportive camaraderie of a treatment group rather than emphasizing the facts about the harsh consequences of continuing drug abuse.

Summary

The ultimate objective of all marketing strategy and tactics is to influence target audience behavior. While the short-term focus may be communicating facts or changing attitudes and values, what distinguishes these activities from education or propaganda is that they are not ends but means to other goals. And since the ultimate goal is behavior influence and the proper philosophy is target audience-centered, it is essential that all strategic planning start with understanding target audience behavior.

In this book, we emphasize the fact that target audience behavior is driven by four factors: benefits, costs, others, and self-assurance—the BCOS factors.

The targets of nonprofit marketers' influence strategies can be as diverse as legislators, donors, journalists, or target audiences. In all cases, the marketer's objective is to bring about exchanges wherein target audience members give up some costs in return for some expected positive consequences (benefits). Exchanges may involve two or multiple parties and be of fixed or continuing duration. The starting point for understanding target audience behavior thus must be an understanding of the exchange relationship to be affected. Most importantly, that exchange must be seen from the target audience's perspective.

Exchanges in the nonprofit sector are usually high involvement and often concern target audience behaviors with which audience members have little or no experience. In such highly complex decision situations, once a need has been felt, target audiences move through four stages: Precontemplation, Contemplation, Preparation/Action, and Maintenance. They begin by gathering information to form a choice set of alternative behaviors and to determine the criteria that will eventually be used to choose among them. The criteria, in turn, will be affected by the target audience's own needs and wants and by the influences of significant others.

The next step in the typical process is to evaluate the chosen alternatives on the relevant criteria and to form attitudes and behavioral intentions toward each. These behavioral intentions will again be influenced by others and by perceptions of self-assurance.

Marketers have several options in seeking to influence complex exchanges that are not turning out as a marketer wishes: The marketer can attempt to change the target audience's perceptions of the probable outcomes of choosing the marketer's alternative—that is, its value proposition—and/or the value propositions of competitors; weightings on the criteria can be changed, although this is more difficult; or the target audience can be pointed toward new or neglected favorable consequences.

With experience, target audiences proceed to simplify behavioral patterns. In such cases, criteria are relatively fixed and alternatives are narrowed considerably. Efficacy is no longer a concern. At the routine stage, behavior may appear to occur with little conscious thought or even may appear probabilistic. In such situations, and in even more complex cases, marketers may wish to use emotional appeals, which are found to be highly effective in the private sector.

Questions

1. A marketer for the Smithsonian Institute in Washington, D.C., identifies an association between attendance and family composition. Namely, families with up to three children are much more likely to patronize the Smithsonian than families with four or more children. List possible causes for this association. How might this marketer increase attendance by larger families?

2. Lisa is the president of her company, and is helping her daughter Ella sell Girl Scout cookies at her place of work. Explain how personal involvement will affect Lisa's ability to sell cookies to her subordinates.

3. Apply the BCOS framework to the target audience for a national literacy campaign. Explain how each of the framework elements can contribute to the campaign's success.

4. A marketer for the National Parks System identifies a possible causation association between a decline in visits and changing U.S. demographics, namely the growth of ethnic populations who are not considered traditional parkgoers. How might this marketer create a target audience-centered approach to increase National Park attendance among ethnic populations in the United States?

Notes

1. Robert Bartels, "The Identity Crisis in Marketing," *Journal of Marketing,* October 1974, pp. 73–76; David J. Luck, "Broadening the Concept of Marketing—Too Far," *Journal of Marketing,* January 1969, pp. 53–54.

2. Alan R. Andreasen, *Marketing Social Change* (San Francisco: Jossey-Bass Publisher, 1995).

3. Deborah J. MacInnis, Christine Moorman, and Bernard Jaworski, "Enhancing and Measuring Consumers' Motivation, Opportunity, and Ability to Process Brand Information from Ads," *Journal of Marketing* 55 (October 1991), pp. 32–53.

4. Michael Rothschild, "Carrots, Sticks and Promises: A Conceptual Framework for the Management of Public Health and Social Issue Behaviors," *Journal of Marketing,* Vol. 63, No. 4 (1999), pp. 24–37.

5. Albert Bandura, "Self-assurance: Toward a Unifying Theory of Behavior Influence,"

Psychological Review, Vol. 84 (1977), pp. 191–215.

6. For additional discussion of the concept of exchange in marketing, see Richard P. Bagozzi, "Marketing as an Organized Behavioral System of Exchange," *Journal of Marketing,* October 1974, pp. 77–81; and "Marketing as Exchange," *American Behavioral Scientist,* March–April 1978, pp. 535–556.

7. Jagdish Sheth and Atul Parvatiyar (Eds.), *Handbook of Relationship Marketing* (Thousand Oaks, CA: Sage Publications, 2000); Mary Jo Bitner, "Building Service Relationships: It's All about Promises," *Journal of the Academy of Marketing Science,* Fall 1995, pp. 246–251.

8. James F. Engel and Roger D. Blackwell, *Target Audience Behavior,* 4th ed. (Chicago: Dryden Press, 1982), p. 24. See also Richard L. Celsi and Jerry C. Olson, "The Role of Involvement in Attention and Comprehension Processes," *Journal of Target Audience Research,* Vol. 15 (September 1988), pp. 210–224.

9. Wayne D. Hoyer and Deborah J. MacInnis, *Target Audience Behavior* (Boston: Houghton-Mifflin Company, 2001).

10. James O. Prochaska and Carlo C. DiClemente, "Stages and Processes of Self-Change of Smoking: Toward an Integrative Model of Change," *Journal of Consulting and Clinical Psychology,* 1983, pp. 390–395; James O. Prochaska, and Carlo C. DiClemente, "Self-Change Processes, Self-assurance and Decisional Balance Across Five Stages of Smoking Cessation," in P. F. Anderson, I. E. Mortenson, and L. E. Epstein (Eds.), *Advances in Cancer Control* (New York: Alan R. Liss, Inc., 1984); James O. Prochaska and Carlo C. DiClemente, "Toward a Comprehensive Model of Change," in W. R. Miller and N. Heather (Eds.), *Treating Addictive Behaviors: Processes of Change* (New York: Plenum Press, 1986); James O. Prochaska and Carlo C. DiClemente, *The Transtheoretical Approach: Crossing the Traditional Boundaries of Therapy* (Homewood, IL: Dow Jones-Irwin, 1984).

11. For examples, see their web site at www.uri.edu/research/cprc/.

12. Alan R. Andreasen, *Social Marketing in the 21st Century.* (Thousand Oaks, CA: Sage Publications 2006)

13. www.americasaves.org/about/ (retrieved November 29, 2006).

14. Abraham H. Maslow, *Motivation and Personality* (New York: Harper & Row, 1954), pp. 80–106.

15. David Reisman with Nathan Glazer and Revel Demney, *The Lonely Crowd: A Study of the Changing American Character* (New Haven: Yale University Press, 1961).

16. Robert Burnkrant and Alain Cousineau, "Informational and Normative Social Influence in Buyer Behavior," *Journal of Target Audience Research,* 1975, pp. 206–215.

17. Troy A. Gilbertson, "Alcohol-Related Incident Guardianship And Undergraduate College Parties: Enhancing The Social Norms Marketing Approach," *Journal of Drug Education,* Vol. 36, No. 1 (2006), pp. 73–90.

18. Richard P. Bagozzi, "Attitudes, Intentions and Behavior: A Test of Some Key Hypotheses," *Journal of Personality and Social Psychology,* 1981, pp. 607–627.

19. Herbert E. Krugman, "Low-Involvement Theory in the Light of New Brain Research," in John C. Maloney and Bernard Silverman (Eds.), *Attitude Research Plays for High Stakes* (Chicago: American Marketing Association, 1979), pp. 16–22; and "The Impact of Television Advertising: Learning Without Involvement," *Public Opinion Quarterly,* Fall 1965, pp. 349–356. See also F. Stewart DeBruiker, "An Appraisal of Low-Involvement Target Audience Information Processing," in Maloney and Silverman, *Attitude Research Plays for High Stakes,* pp. 112–132.

20. See, for example, Meryl P. Gardner, "Mood States and Target Audience Behavior: A Critical Review," *Journal of Target Audience Research,* Vol. 12, No. 3 (1985), pp. 281–300; and Gerald Gorn, "The Effects of Music in Advertising on Choice Behavior: A Classical Conditioning Approach," *Journal of Marketing,* Winter 1982, pp. 94–101.

5

ACQUIRING AND USING MARKETING INFORMATION

GIVING YOUR BRAIN A WORKOUT

Many health-focused nonprofit organizations like the American Cancer Society, American Heart Association, and American Lung Association face difficult positioning and communications problems. They typically seek to advance research while at the same time educating target audiences, raising their issue's profile on the public, media, and political agendas and securing donations and grants. In 2004, the Alzheimer's Association addressed such a challenge and sought to rebrand and reposition itself through a campaign developed with the aid of Porter Novelli, a Washington, D.C., advertising and public relations organization. A major concern was getting baby boomers to focus on actions that would reduce their risks and the effects of the disease.

Porter Novelli made sure that research played a critical role in developing and evaluating the campaign. As outlined in Chapter 3, the first step was listening to three key target audiences: individuals with family members affected by Alzheimer's, baby boomers entering the age of risk, and various support groups—including 81 local Alzheimer's Association chapters that would need to support and carry out various elements of the campaign. Research was done through focus groups and a baseline measure was taken of awareness, attitudes, and opinions with respect to the disease and the Association. The main result was a postioning based on hope and research progress and on specific steps baby boomers could take to reduce risk. The campaign was designed to position the Alzheimer's Association as "owning" the issue of "brain health."

The resulting campaign featuring the tag line "Maintain Your Brain" was subject to careful web-based pretesting of the creative concepts. The campaign itself included a number of public relations events featuring celebrities familiar with the disease, release of a report on the impact on Hispanics (with the National Council of La Raza), an international conference on research, and a series of events in Washington, D.C., to advocate more congressional funding for Alzheimer's research. The campaign included paid advertising with dollar-for-dollar match by the media, a video for the 81 Alzheimer's chapters, as well as creation of partnerships focusing on specific racial/ethnic segments.

Project staffer Natalie Adler reported that monitoring and evaluation research revealed web site hits four times the industry average, $81,000 in online donations, and 40 million media impressions for the campaign launch and 350 million for the international conference. Chapter support was also strong. The tag line recognition grew and was tied to both Alzheimer's disease and the Alzheimer's Association.

Source: Based on a Porter Novelli "Platinum PR Awards" application, 2005.

We emphasized in the preceding chapters the centrality of the target audience to planning marketing strategy both at the organization and campaign levels. What those audience members—or segments of them—think and want and how they act determines how a marketer might seek to influence them. This is true whether the target audience is an obese child, a TV news director, a congressperson, or a potential corporate partner. For this reason, marketing research focusing on target audiences is *essential* to effective nonprofit marketing. The research needs to discover what they are like, what they will respond to, and what is keeping them from acting as the marketer wants. These are all essential to effective action.

Marketing research can be very diverse. It can be as simple as analyzing data already in the organization or observing what target audiences do under specific circumstances like visiting a museum on a weekend versus a weekday. It can be more elaborate, involving one-time field research surveys or regular data from a panel recruited over the Internet. It can involve experiments or focus groups. It can be complex and expensive or it can be low-cost and straightforward. What distinguishes it from simple observation and systematic reflection is that it is (1) planned; (2) based on some formal model or understanding of how target audiences respond, or might respond, to marketer inputs; and (3) tied to specific decision-making situations.

MARKETING RESEARCH IN NONPROFIT ORGANIZATIONS

Nonprofit organizations carry out much less marketing research than they can *or ought to*.[1] This is a consequence of their limited budgets, their relative newness in the marketing field, and their limited research expertise. On the other hand, this is rapidly changing as nonprofit organizations become bigger and wealthier, as they hire more and more individuals with private sector marketing experience, and as there are more and more examples published showing how marketing research increased marketing effectiveness.

However, not all nonprofit organizations see the necessity of using research to guide strategy. Sometimes it is because they have only limited—or biased—views of what research is all about. Seven myths keep nonprofit managers from engaging in a more effective marketing research program:

- The "big decision" myth
- The "survey myopia" myth
- The "focus group" myth

- The "big bucks" myth
- The "we can't wait" myth
- The "sophisticated researcher" myth
- The "most-research-is-not-read" myth

If nonprofit managers are to even consider doing more research, these myths must be directly challenged.

The "Big Decision" Myth

Too often marketing research is considered necessary only for decisions involving large financial stakes, and in such cases it should always be carried out. But research should be viewed from a benefit/cost perspective. Its costs are usually of two types—the expenses for the research itself and the amount of impact lost by delaying a decision until the results are in. The potential impact, in turn, is a function of the stakes involved and how certain the manager is about the rightness of the contemplated decision without the research.

It surprises managers that sometimes the benefit/cost ratio comes out against research even when the stakes are high. Take the case of the hospital manager who is thinking of adding an outpatient plastic surgery clinic and investing in a series of advertisements to promote this new service. She calls in a research professional to design a study of consumer interest in plastic surgery that would show how likely acceptance of such a service would be. Although such a study could cost several thousand dollars, in extended discussions with the manager the researcher determines that, unless the survey found virtually *no* interest in outpatient plastic surgery, the manager would go ahead with the decision to add the clinic.

The manager was highly uncertain about the market, but she was certain that her decision to add the clinic was best. The researcher convinced the manager that the research expenditure was unnecessary and that the money could be used more productively to ensure that the new clinic got the advertising send-off needed in order to have the best chances of succeeding.

On the other hand, research can often be justified even when the amount at stake is not very great. This is the case whenever the research can be done inexpensively, will not take very long to complete, and will help clarify which actions to take. Take, for example, advertising or web site copy decisions. While total expenditures are small, managers usually have two or three candidate executions, each of which seems to have potential worth. Showing the options to a small but representative set of prospective target audiences—very modest research—usually reveals one superior candidate, or at least, by pointing out serious defects in one or two candidate ads, allows the choice to be narrowed. This process has the fringe benefit that occasionally it produces extremely good suggestions for entirely different ads.

The "Survey Myopia" Myth

Many managers, when they think of marketing research, think of field surveys. However, any reliable information systematically gathered that improves marketing decisions can be considered good marketing research. If one takes this view, many alternatives to formal survey research come to mind. Consider a social marketing manager thinking of introducing a new low-cost, high-nutrition food product for young children. The manager has no idea whether the target market will accept the product or, once it is accepted, how quickly it can be expected to break even. If successful, the new product would produce profits of only a few thousand dollars in the first few years. The manager could conduct a survey to reduce this uncertainty. However, to make the research 95 percent certain of being within 2 percentage points of the break-even market share figure of 10 percent, the manager must contact a sample of 900 people.

An experienced survey researcher would estimate, assuming the questionnaire and sampling plan are already designed and ignoring analysis and report preparation costs, that simply completing the interviews would cost many thousand of dollars in developed markets. (The amount would depend on the duration and type of interviews done.)[2] Clearly, such research could easily eat up the manager's initial years' contribution profits from product sales. More important is the question of whether the research would yield valid data in any case. One should ask whether it is reasonable to expect respondents to be candid about or even to know their likely behavior with respect to this new food product, especially if many do not want to disappoint the interviewer or the research sponsor by showing little enthusiasm for it.

How else, then, might the research objectives be achieved at lower cost? The company could simply try test marketing the product in representative markets. This approach has the virtue of not only lowering costs but yielding useful data (that is, it shows what people will actually do, not what they say they will do). Testing in a number of markets also allows alternative marketing strategies to be systematically evaluated.

The "Focus Group" Myth

Many nonprofit organizations we come in contact with claim that they regularly conduct marketing research. When asked, they say that they "do focus groups." As we shall later detail, these are groups of 8–12 people who have the time and willingness to get together to talk about some nonprofit marketing issue. They often can be very useful in the initial stages of a campaign or in providing hints about strategic direction. But the myth is that conducting focus groups is all one needs to do to make effective marketing decisions. As we shall point out, the groups are rarely representative of the target audience. Further, they are seldom done in sufficient quantity—maybe two or three—to provide any sense of the potential diversity of target audience reactions. Perhaps most damaging is frequent reliance on a few comments by a few individuals to "prove" something that the marketing manager or CEO wanted to believe all along!

The "Big Bucks" Myth

Managers too often assume that they cannot afford good—that is, useful—marketing research. However, as we shall point out in later sections, there exists a wide range of alternative low-cost research techniques. One needs to use them appropriately but they can be very useful to those with restricted budgets or who must rely extensively on volunteer help.

The "We Can't Wait" Myth

Many managers skip doing research because they believe that it will take much too long and seriously delay getting ahead with the *real* work of the organization—saving lives, improving health, or overhauling communities. Again, this myth follows from the notion that market research involves surveys, sampling, and long periods preparing, implementing, and analyzing research. However, as we shall see, there are many methods that can be carried out in a few days or a couple of weeks that will yield most of the information a manager needs for a particular decision or set of decisions. Telephone interviews can be done overnight—this is done in modern political polling all the time. The Internet now provides vehicles for "instant surveys" that, with the proper software, not only allow collection of data but rapid analysis of it and production of tables of results.

Careful consideration of the question "Just what do I need to know in order to make a good decision?" will often tell a manager that all that is needed is simple, quick, reasonably representative data that can sway a decision one way or another.

The "Sophisticated Researcher" Myth

Just as marketing research need not involve complex sampling and elaborate designs, a high level of sophistication in sampling techniques, statistics, and computer analysis is not essential. Of course, executives of nonprofits planning to undertake research programs should acquaint themselves with at least the rudimentary principles of research validity and reliability. This knowledge will help them evaluate research proposals submitted by contractors and evaluate results. They can often rely on such expertise in the hands of others. Volunteers may have the needed sophistication and experience. Professors at local colleges can sometimes help. We often urge nonprofits contemplating extended research programs to appoint marketing research professionals to their boards of directors.

The "Most-Research-Is-Not-Read" Myth

Executives who would rather not bother with research or who subconsciously fear the results use this last myth to justify not gathering data. Poor research certainly is undertaken, but when it is, it is usually a testimonial to poor planning. In our experience, few pieces of *well-planned* research are rejected as unhelpful, although they may be ignored on other, often political, grounds. The responsibility for making sure that research is useful rests with both the manager requesting the research and the researcher doing it. Research will be most valuable when the following are true:

1. It is undertaken after the manager has made clear to the researcher what the decision alternatives are and what it is about those decisions that necessitate additional information.
2. The relationship between the results and the decision is clearly understood.
3. The results are communicated well.

ORGANIZATIONAL KNOWLEDGE MANAGEMENT

There are two main ways of thinking about marketing research. One is to see it as a set of tools at the campaign level. To develop effective campaigns, one needs specific studies at the formative "listening" stage, then pretest research of specific campaign elements followed by careful monitoring of progress. The other perspective is to think of research—including campaign research—as part of a knowledge management system. This perspective is driven by what is known in the private sector as the resource-based theory of the firm.

The Resource-Based Theory of the Organization

Management scholars in the private sector in the late 1980s and early 1990s recognized a sea change in the nature of corporations and their role in societies. Grant[3] highlights six key changes:

1. An erosion in the importance of land or capital goods as the basis for corporate strength
2. A growing focus on intangibles in businesses processes and business output (services over goods)
3. Networking of communication
4. Digitizing of work and life
5. The rise of virtual work—virtual corporations, transactions, employees
6. Accelerated pace of innovation and compressed life cycles

The response was to rethink what firms were all about and to offer what was called a *resource-based theory of the firm.*[4] Scholars argued that competitive advantage arises from the unique set of resources that the firm has been able to accumulate that are valued by customers, that are unique, and that are costly or difficult to copy. These resources could comprise any one or a combination of physical capital, production processes, patents, specific staff capabilities, well-known brands, unique distribution systems, and the like. To the extent that rivals could not match these resources and to the extent they led to significant customer value, the result would be above average return on investment (economic rents). The challenge for corporate leaders, it was argued, was to marshal as much of the needed resources as possible and then create, promote, and—most importantly—sustain the competitive advantage they provided.

However, as we entered the 1990s, it became increasingly apparent that traditional resources in the nature of physical objects, unique processes, and high-profile brands often were not the most critical factors that set an organization apart for long-term market dominance. What made firms great was not the *things* they amassed but how they used them. Nike does not actually make any shoes itself; it researches and designs them and then develops (with partners) some of the world's most creative advertising campaigns to sell them. Google and Yahoo! produce offerings that only appear when your computer calls them up. Consultants like McKinsey and Bain are important business players; but they provide a service that is mainly people and their brains!

Scholars recognized that in this new environment the only thing that an organization could rely on for its competitive advantage was *its intellectual capital.*[5] That is, the only solid base for long-term market power was one's knowledge. This refinement of the resource-based view of the firm redefined the principal role of corporate leaders from being visionaries or hard-line martinets to being effective *knowledge managers.* This rethinking of the basis for competitive advantage has become what McKinsey & Co. consultants recently described as "one of the trendiest topics in management circles."[6]

As we noted in Chapter 1, nonprofit organizations are becoming increasingly large and complex and are seeking more and different ways to grow. The challenge to growth is, in part, to develop a sustainable competitive advantage. The key to growth and competitive advantage lies in the organization's core competencies. For a great many nonprofit organizations—just as in the private sector—this key resource is found in its *intellectual capital.* This capital comprises the explicit and tacit information that, if properly collected and communicated, can lead to superior performance. It means, therefore, that the principal role of nonprofit leaders in the twenty-first century must shift from being visionaries to being effective *knowledge managers*—just as their private sector counterparts are doing.

Letts, Ryan, and Goodman[7] argue that achieving high performance in the nonprofit sector requires the building of adaptive capacity. Adaptive capacity:

1. Enables organizations to create value for the clients and communities they serve (i.e., deliver effective, scalable programs)
2. Enables organizations to demonstrate their comparative value to funders
3. Enables organizations to motivate staff and volunteers

We would argue that the "adaptive capacity" of which Letts, Ryan, and Grossman speak resides primarily in an organization's *intellectual capital.* Developing this capital comes about through careful *knowledge management.* While the relevant knowledge would include information on personnel issues, financial data, and so forth, a major component of the knowledge management system must be marketing research.

Organization-Level Marketing Knowledge Systems

Nonprofit managers need timely, accurate, and adequate information on the three principal markets as a basis for making sound marketing decisions both long term and short term. We shall use the term *marketing knowledge system* (MKS) to describe the organization's system for routinely gathering, analyzing, storing, and disseminating relevant marketing information. A sophisticated MKS has a number of subsystems, as illustrated in Figure 5-1. At the left is shown the marketing environment that marketing managers must monitor—specifically, target markets (including donors, volunteers, and clients), marketing channels, competitors, publics, and macroenvironmental forces. Developments and trends in the marketing environment are picked up in the company through one of four subsystems making up the marketing information system—the internal reports system, the marketing intelligence system, the marketing research system, and the analytical marketing

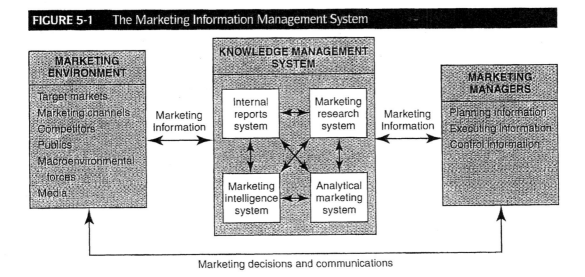

FIGURE 5-1   The Marketing Information Management System

Marketing decisions and communications

system. The information then flows to the appropriate marketing managers to help them in their marketing planning, execution, and control. The resulting decisions and communications then flow back to the marketing environment.

Not all nonprofits will have the resources to include all four elements of the marketing knowledge system. If they do not, they will wish to develop it slowly piece by piece. A good place to begin is with the internal reports system. As we shall note next, an organization's own archives can serve as one of the best low-cost research alternatives available.

Internal Reports System

Every organization accumulates information in the regular course of its operations. A hospital will keep records on its patients, including their names, addresses, ages, illnesses, lengths of stay, supplies and room charges, attending physicians, complaints, and so on. From these patient records the hospital can develop statistics on the number of daily admissions, average length of patients' stay, average patient charge, frequency distribution of different illnesses, and so on. The hospital will also have records on its physicians, nurses, volunteers, donors, costs, billings, assets, and liabilities, all of which is indispensable information for making management decisions.

A museum will keep several record systems. Its contributor file will list the names, addresses, past contributions, and other data on its contributors. Its campaign progress file will show the amounts raised to date from each major source, such as individuals, foundations, corporations, and government grants. Its cost file will show how much money has been spent on direct mail, newspaper advertising, brochures, salaries, consultant fees, and so on.

Internal systems must also be attentive to data that is often ignored. Complaints are an example. Staffers don't like complaints and often do not record them. Yet they can provide valuable feedback knowledge that alerts management to problems and then comprises an informal tracking system that would indicate whether the problem identified has abated.

The Market Intelligence System

As we noted in Chapter 3, marketers need information from both inside and outside the organization to do effective planning. The internal records system is a major source of insight into how the organization is performing. But these data are, by definition, about the past. What marketers also need is information about the future. As outlined in Chapter 3, they need information about the external environment around them that will have a major impact on what they can do and what they ought to do. This is the role of the market intelligence system.

Good marketing managers, of course, have always had an informal market intelligence system in place through their reading of newspapers and trade publications and talking to various people inside and outside the organization, often at national and international conferences. In this way, they are able to spot important developments. However, reliance on this casual approach to gathering marketing intelligence can also result in missing or learning too late of some other important developments, such as a fundraising opportunity with an important donor or a new law that might hurt the organization's nonprofit status. A good market intelligence system needs to be more systematic and more formal.

A simple first step is to improve the collection and transmission of insights gained by everyone in the organization. Often bits and pieces of important intelligence are located in nooks and crannies of the organization but never assembled in one place or transmitted to the people who can really use them. A person working on a commercial alliance might hear about a rival nonprofit's new venture but not tell the organization's strategic planning team, who may be considering something very similar and thinking they will be offering a unique service. To combat this, the organization must "sell" its managers and staff on the importance of gathering marketing intelligence and passing it on to others in the organization. Their intelligence responsibilities can be facilitated by designing information forms that are easy to fill out and circulate. Software can be created for this end and weekly e-mail "surveys" of internal staff can centralize a lot of market wisdom.

Second, the organization should encourage outside parties with whom it deals—advertising agencies, professional associations, lawyers, accountants, and its own board members—to pass on any useful bits of information. A museum's lawyer, for example, may hear about a wealthy donor who is revising his will, and this information can be useful to the development office of the museum.

Third, the organization can designate a person to be specifically responsible for gathering and disseminating marketing intelligence. This person, who is often called the Chief Information Officer, would scan major publications, abstract the relevant news, and disseminate the information to appropriate managers. Much of the information can be obtained from search engines such as Google or Yahoo!. The challenge is to gather information routinely, not just when a problem or challenge arises. The marketing intelligence system can often serve as the organization's early warning system.

In the twenty-first century, a major source of market intelligence is the informal networks set up by web bloggers. These individuals regularly alert their audiences to new ideas, new products, and the latest trends. They voice their own opinions, which can be valuable sources of new ideas or can alert management when campaigns go awry. The so-called "blogosphere" is very quick to spread information about bad offerings—including those of politicians like ex-Senator George Allen making derogatory statements or bad-acting celebrities like Michael Richards or Paris Hilton. David Sifry of Technorati estimated in March 2005 that there were 30,000 to 40,000 new weblogs being created each day and his company was then tracking 7.8 million blog sites having 937 links. He estimates that the number of such weblogs was doubling every five months.[8] Video-sharing has become an increasingly popular means of sharing opinions and ideas through media such as YouTube (recently bought by Google).

The Marketing Research System

As we have emphasized, campaign managers *must* routinely carry out market research studies at the formative, pretesting, and monitoring stages of behavioral influence efforts. Senior management may also occasionally need to commission specific qualitative or quantitative marketing research studies to learn how the organization is positioned in the minds of key publics. A college may want to determine what kind of image it has among high school counselors, or a political organization may want to find out what voters think of its candidates and its competitors. Many major nonprofits and government agencies, such as the Centers for Disease Control and Prevention and the American Cancer Society, currently conduct formal branding studies. We will return to the problem of making these studies valuable next.

The Analytical Marketing System

Data from internal records, marketing intelligence, and specific marketing research studies are only raw data until they are turned into *knowledge* that managers can use. This is the role of the analytical marketing system. The analytical marketing system consists of a set of techniques for analyzing marketing data and marketing problems. These systems are able to produce findings and conclusions often using sophisticated analytical routines. On the other hand, as we shall repeat below, the knowledge must be usable—and this may mean that simple analyses will be more useful than more complex approaches that scare off potential users.

CONDUCTING SPECIFIC STUDIES

For nonprofit organizations with very limited budgets, we would argue forcefully that *no* market research should ever be undertaken unless it can be *applied* directly to a decision. However, where one has a more generous budget, a nonprofit marketer might wish to establish capabilities to undertake one or both of two other kinds of research. One is *basic research*. Basic research has no immediate application to specific management decisions but is generally expected to lay the groundwork for better decisions somewhere down the road. Thus the Association of College, University, and Community Arts Administrators has used part of its members' dues to explore the potential of lifestyle research—specifically, the original VALS approach—to understand consumers' reactions to the performing arts.[9]

The other type of research a nonprofit might undertake alone or jointly with others (including basic academics) is *methodological research*—that is, research designed to improve the organization's ability to do more effective research in the future. Organizations might devise better methods of asking sensitive questions or ways to do field experiments in an unobtrusive fashion.

Managerially useful research is typically of three types, increasing in levels of usefulness—description, explanation, and prediction.

Description

Marketing research can be designed to tell a nonprofit manager what his or her marketing environment is like. It can, for example, tell a hospital manager how many patients were served in each hospital facility each hour of each day of each year and indicate the sex and home address of each patient, his or her attending doctor, any previous admissions to the hospital, and the diagnosis.

While internal reports can often provide these data to hospital management, additional descriptive information could be acquired from a telephone survey to ascertain the patient's family status, occupation, education, media habits, satisfaction with various hospital services, and intentions as to word of mouth and future patronage. At the same time, the manager could acquire from published sources descriptive data on competitors' pricing and advertising expenditures as well as information on national trends in donation behavior, payment methods, wages of specific hospital departments, cost of equipment, and so on. All of these data have in common the fact that they are descriptions at one point in time or descriptions of trends or pattern changes over time. Descriptive data usually serve management decisions in three ways: (1) monitoring performance to indicate whether strategy changes are needed, (2) describing consumers for segmentation decisions, and (3) serving as the basis for more sophisticated analysis.

Explanation

Usually a manager is not satisfied with merely seeing what the market environment looks like. He or she would typically like to know what makes it "tick." In principle, there are three possible levels of explanation: association, causation, and reasons why. Each succeeding level has higher costs and greater resource requirements than the one preceding it, but it also has a higher potential payoff.

1. *Association.* The simplest level of explanation is to discover what seems to be associated with what. Thus the fundraiser might like to know the socioeconomic and demographic characteristics of past donors broken down by levels of giving, number of times donating, and so forth. Such data would be useful in helping the fundraiser decide how to allocate resources across segments and provide insights into the potential lifetime value of a new donor.

2. *Causation.* A nasty feature of association data that is learned by every freshman statistics student is that association is not the same as causation. Thus the fundraiser may believe that a finding that an increasing proportion of donors are women means that the organization has been more effective in promoting to them. However, it may just mean that, over time, more and more women are handling finances in a household!

3. *Reasons why.* The ultimate level of explanation for marketing researchers is to know not only that A caused B, but *why* A caused B. Thus, before making decisions about targeting men versus women, the fundraiser should have a better understanding of the nature of the causation, that is, of the "reasons why." Future research might experiment by offering different appeals to men and women to see which is more effective, thereby yielding more insights into the "reason why" of giving.

Prediction

Of course, descriptions or explanations of what exists or existed in the past are only useful to managers if they tell them about *the future.* Marketing decisions play out in the future. Modeling of findings and the use of longitudinal designs can often give managers more confidence that they are not designing approaches that would work today—or, worse, yesterday!

MAKING RESEARCH USEFUL—THE BACKWARD RESEARCH PROCESS

At both the organizational and campaign levels, marketing managers will want to undertake specific studies to address specific problems or issues.[10] In unsophisticated organizations, the standard approach to the research process—say, conducting a field survey—is to start by defining the problem. The problem is then translated into a research methodology. This leads to the development of research instruments, a sampling plan, coding and interviewing instructions, and other details. The researcher collects data, analyzes it, and writes a report. The executive then steps in to translate the researcher's findings into action. This process often results in management disappointment and leads to the commonly heard view that "most research is unread"—that is, it does not meet the manager's needs.

Part of the problem is that, in the typical case, managers leave the problem vague and general. They say, in effect, "Here are some things I don't know. When the results come in,

I'll know more. And when I know more, then I can figure out what to do." This approach makes it highly likely that the findings will be off target (i.e., not maximally useful).

We advocate instead a procedure that turns the traditional approach to research design on its head. The procedure stresses close collaboration between researchers and decision makers. It markedly raises the odds that the organization will come up with findings that are not only "interesting" but also actionable.

The "backward" approach advocated here rests on the premise that the best way to design usable research is to start where the process usually *ends* and then work backward. Each stage in the design is developed on the basis of what comes after it, not before. The twelve steps in the procedure are outlined in Figure 5-2.

The backward research process may seem time-consuming at first. Indeed, it forces the participants from marketing research and management to spend a considerable number of hours together shaping and refining the goals and structure of the research project. This will be particularly frustrating the first time the approach is used and in the early steps each time thereafter. However, experience has shown that the long-run effects in terms of reduced cost and increased effectiveness can be substantial.

At times, the early discussions will reveal that the research is not needed at all—that management will not act differently unless the results are very far from their expectations. The discussions will also make sure that each element of the design ultimately chosen is necessary for decisions—there are no extraneous questions or "special subsamples" included. Lastly, close up-front collaboration will increase the likelihood that the final product will be one that management can understand, appreciate, and implement with minimum delay. The ultimate test is: Did the research make a real difference in organizational effectiveness? It takes hard work to achieve this goal.

Steps 1 and 2

To most managers, the research "problem" is seen as a lack of important information about their marketing environment. The manager of a social services program might say, "The problem is that I don't know who I am serving and who I am not serving" or "The problem is that I don't know whether my clients are more satisfied with my program than my major competitor's clients are satisfied with hers."

If the problem is defined this way, the "solution" is simply to reduce the manager's ignorance. Research is carried out that simply describes the patient population or that measures the level of satisfaction with alternative programs. These data may be very "interesting" and may give managers a great deal of satisfaction in revealing things they didn't know. But satisfaction can quickly turn to frustration and disappointment when the executive tries to *use* the results—which, of course, is the ultimate test of its value.

Take, for example, a lifestyle study done several years ago on over-the-counter drugs. Some respondents who claimed they were always getting colds and the flu frequently went to doctors, but the doctors were never of much help. The respondents thought that the over-the-counter drugs were often very beneficial, but they weren't sure why. This information, together with other details, caused the researchers to label this group "the hypochondriacs."

What can be done with these results? As is usually the case with segmentation strategies, there are quantity and quality decisions to make. The company has to decide whether to pump more marketing resources into the hypochondriac group than its proportion of the population would justify. The marketing vice president might first say "yes" because the hypochondriacs are heavy drug users.

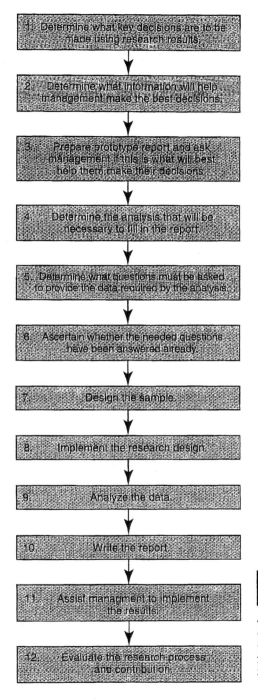

FIGURE 5-2 Backward Marketing Research

Source: Alan R. Andreasen, *Marketing Research that Won't Break the Bank* (San Francisco: Jossey-Bass Publishers, 2003). Reprinted by permission of John Wiley & Sons, Inc.

However, the picture is more complicated than that. Perhaps hypochondriacs are sophisticated buyers, set in their purchase patterns, and very loyal to their favorite brands. If so, money aimed at them would have little impact on the market shares. Light users, however, may have fragile loyalties, and throwing money at them could entice them to switch brands. Of course, just the opposite might be true: The hypochondriacs, being heavy users, might prove to be very impressionable and responsive to compelling ads.

On the qualitative side, lifestyle research could be much more helpful. Since it generates a rich profile describing each group's jobs, families, values, and preferences, this research could tell the company what to say. However, the frustrated manager is not likely to know *where* to say these things. There is no *Hypochondriac's Journal* in which to advertise, and there may be no viewing and reading patterns that apply to heavy users specifically—hypochondriacs or not.

But suppose that the company had first laid out all the action alternatives it might take after the study. If the marketing vice president had made it clear that his problems were (1) whether to allocate marketing dollars differently; (2) whether to develop marketing campaigns aimed at particular, newly discovered segments; and (3) where to aim such campaigns, he would have launched the project in a more appropriate direction.

Step 3

After steps 1 and 2, management should ask, "What should the final report look like so that we'll know exactly what moves to make when the findings are in?" Now the collaboration between the researcher and the manager should intensify and prove both dynamic and exceedingly creative.

Scenarios are a good technique for developing ideas for the contents of the report. The initiative here lies with the researcher, who should generate elements of a hypothetical report and then confront management with tough questions like "If I came up with this cross-tabulation with these numbers in it, what would you do?"

The first payoff from this exercise arises from improvements in the research itself. The exercise can move the project forward by sharpening the decision alternatives and backward by indicating the best design for the questionnaire or how the analysis of the findings should be carried out.

Suppose an arts manager is considering canceling a multiple-purchase discount offer because most of the people taking advantage of it may be loyal customers who are already heavy users, are upscale, and are largely price inelastic. The manager speculates that the discount mainly represents lost revenue. To decide whether to eliminate the discount, one must predict the responses of old and new customers to this step. The researcher should hypothesize tables showing various results.

Suppose the first iteration shows longtime customers to be price inelastic and new customers to be price elastic. This result suggests to the manager that a discount should be offered only to new customers. In considering this alternative, the manager will need to know whether potential new customers can be reached with the special offer in a way that will minimize or eliminate purchases at a discount by longtime customers.

This new formulation of the decision leads to a discussion of results set out in another set of dummy tables showing responsiveness to the proposed one-time discount by past patronage behavior. Other tables would then reveal what television shows various consumer segments watch and what they read or listen to, which will indicate whether they are differentially reachable. And so goes the process of cycling between the decision context and the research design.

The cycling will reveal what research is needed. Sometimes, the researcher will present contrasting tables of regression results only to discover that management would take the same course of action no matter what the results. This is actually a prima facie case for doing away with that part of the research design altogether.

Management participation in the design decision has other advantages. It serves to win managers' support of marketing research and deepens their understanding of research details. That understanding permits the researcher to simplify the report immeasurably. Working with contrasting, hypothetical tables can make the manager eager for the findings and unlikely to be startled by surprising results. Participation will also sensitize management to the study's limitations. Managers are often tempted to go far beyond research "truth" when implementing the results, especially if the reported truth supports the course of action they prefer to take anyway.

Step 4
The form of the report will clearly dictate the nature of the analysis. If management is leery of multivariate analysis, the researchers should design a series of step-by-step cross-tabulations. If management is comfortable with the higher reaches of statistics, the researcher can draw on more advanced analytic procedures. In general, the analysis phase should be straightforward. If the exercise of scenario writing has gone well, the analysis should amount to little more than filling in the blanks.

Steps 5 through 7
The backward approach is also very helpful in designing the data-gathering instruments and the sampling approach. In one study, management wanted to gauge young consumers' knowledge of the preferences for the organization's offering. Not until the researcher had prepared mock tables showing preference data by age groups and sex did the manager's wishes become clear. By "young," the manager meant children as young as 10. The manager also believed that preteens, being a very volatile group, undergo radical changes from year to year, especially as they approach puberty. Design plans to set a low age cutoff for the sample at 13 and to group respondents by age category—such as 13 to 17 and 17 to 20—went out the window. If the researcher had been following the usual design approach, the manager's expectations may not have surfaced until the study was well underway.

Backward design can also help determine the appropriateness of using strict probability techniques. If, for example, management wants to project certain findings to some universe, the research must employ precise probability methods. However, if the manager is chiefly interested in frequency counts (say, of words used by consumers to describe the organization's offerings or of complaints voiced about its staff), sampling restrictions need not be so tight. Researchers often build either too much or too little sampling quality for the uses the organization has in mind. Similarly, scenario writing will often reveal that management wants more breakdowns of the results, requiring larger sample sizes or more precise stratification procedures than initially planned. Through simulating the application of the findings, the final research design is much more likely to meet management's needs with substantially lower field costs.

Steps 8 through 10

Steps 8 through 10 are consistent with a traditional forward approach that implements the research decisions and judgments made earlier. If all parties have collaborated well in the early stages, these steps should merely carry through what has already been decided.

Steps 11 and 12

The traditional research project concludes when the report is dropped on the manager's desk. This, however, is premature and shortsighted. The process began with the researcher and the manager thinking collaboratively about what the research would do to help management decision making. Now that the data are in hand, the researcher should continue to be involved because he or she (1) understands the database and its nuances and (2) has already thought hard about what the results should mean to the manager. Continued teamwork through the application stage will ensure not only good decisions, but that the data are mined as thoroughly as possible and that they are not subject to inadvertent misinterpretations (for example, when the manager *wishes* to believe that a finding is present when it really isn't).

The last step in the process is equally necessary if the research project is not to be a unique event but is to fit into an organization's long-run research strategy. Sometime after the application steps have been inaugurated, the researcher and manager should review the entire research process and ask whether there were any ways in which it could have been carried out better. Only through such careful reflection will the entire research enterprise be perfected and the nonprofit get the most out of the limited resources it allocates to this critical function.

Empirical Research Alternatives

The second requirement for effective implementation of research projects is to choose the right research methodology.[11] As we have noted earlier, when the nonprofit researcher thinks of carrying out research on key issues, the techniques that usually come to mind first are focus groups or the one-time field survey, usually a mail or telephone study using conventionally designed questionnaires. Today, researchers may think of the Internet as a way to reach potential responders. However, these techniques can be very expensive and time-consuming. There are many low-cost alternatives, especially at the formative and pretest phases of campaigns.

Qualitative Research

There are many situations in which management may wish to carry out research that does not require projections to broader populations or the use of sophisticated statistical techniques. In such situations, *qualitative research* techniques are appropriate. Among the uses of qualitative research by nonprofits are the following:

1. Identifying a problem
2. Gathering initial customer insights around the BCOS model (introduced in Chapter 4)
3. Preparing for a subsequent quantitative study:

   a. Generating ideas and hypotheses
   b. Learning appropriate language for questions
   c. Pretesting questionnaires

4. Helping interpret a prior quantitative study
5. Pretesting alternative advertisements, product concepts, packaging, or brochures
6. Generating ideas for new products or services
7. Generating ideas for advertisements or product positioning

Two approaches that are frequently used for qualitative research are *in-depth interviews* and *focus groups.* In-depth interviews involve lengthy questioning of a small number of respondents (rather than brief questioning of large samples) one at a time, often using disguised questions and minimal interviewer prompting. Focus groups involve bringing together groups of 5 to 10 consumers, usually (but not always) a relatively homogeneous group, to discuss a specific set of issues under the guidance of a leader trained to stimulate and focus the discussion. While traditionally both focus groups and in-depth interviews have been conducted in person, more and more researchers are developing approaches using the Internet and the telephone.[12]

Figure 5-3 indicates conditions under which each of these techniques might be used.

The objective of both in-depth interviewing and focus groups is to get beneath the surface of some issue. These approaches are based on the presumption that individuals will reveal more either when they talk at length with a sympathetic and resourceful interviewer or when they are in a relaxed group setting and are stimulated by the camaraderie and comments of others (the "coffee klatsch" model). The trick in both circumstances is to bring out "hidden" or deeper aspects of a subject or issue. Mary Debus, formerly of Porter Novelli, has suggested several techniques that skilled interviewers and group moderators use to achieve this, which are listed in Figure 5-4.

Finally, it is important to have some framework or model to guide the questioning. The BCOS model has been useful in many of the studies in which one of us has been involved. For instance, a study of potential symphony goers in Los Angeles asked subjects in one-on-one interviews to identify "good things that would happen if they attended the symphony next Saturday evening" (i.e., benefits of going and possible social influences) and things that would be unpleasant or troublesome (i.e., perceived costs and self-assurance issues). Management originally thought that they perhaps ought to bring in more "star" performers or reduce ticket prices. But the research guided by the BCOS model revealed that what they ought to do is put more lights in the parking garage (for safety), offer buses from the suburbs and discount restaurant vouchers, and reduce the perceived formality of the concerts. Respondents were not particularly concerned about the ticket costs or who was performing.

Experimentation

A major problem with survey and much qualitative research is that it relies upon what people say. The quality of such data can be biased in all sorts of ways, including by the interviewees or interviewers themselves. An alternative approach is to observe what people actually do. While archival data provide such information, they simply record what happened in the past. Marketers are really interested in "what-if scenarios," and this is the role of experimentation. Experimental opportunities abound. For example:

- A fundraiser could divide a mailing list into three groups and send out solicitations with varying degrees of "personalization."
- A manager of an adolescent drug program could place a television set in the waiting rooms of half the centers and video games in the other half and observe the effects on the return rates of patients.

Issue to Consider	Use focus groups when ...	Use individual depth interviews when ...
Group interaction	Interaction of respondents may stimulate a richer response or new and valuable thoughts.	Group interaction is likely to be limited or nonproductive.
Group/peer pressure	Group/peer pressure will be valuable in challenging the thinking of respondents and illuminating conflicting opinions	Group/peer pressure would inhibit responses and cloud the meaning of results.
Subjectivity of subject matter	Subject matter is not so sensitive that respondents will temper responses or withhold information.	Subject matter is so sensitive that respondents would be unwilling to talk openly in a group.
Depth of individual responses	The topic is such that most respondents can say all that is relevant or all that they know in less than 10 minutes	The topic is such that a greater depth of response per individual is desirable, as with complex subject matter and very knowledgeable respondents.
Interviewer fatigue	It is desirable to have one interviewer conduct the research; several groups will not create interviewer fatigue or boredom.	It is desirable to have numerous interviewers on the project. One interviewer would become fatigued or bored conducting the interviews.
Stimulus materials	The volume of stimulus material is not extensive.	A large amount of stimulus material must be evaluated.
Continuity of information	A single subject area is being examined in depth and strings of behaviors are less relevant.	It is necessary to understand how attitudes and behaviors link together on an individual pattern basis.
Experimentation with interview guide	Enough is known to establish a meaningful topic guide.	It may be necessary to develop the interview guide by altering it after each of the initial interviews.
Observation	It is possible and desirable for key decision makers to observe "firsthand" consumer information.	"Firsthand" consumer information is not critical or observation is not logistically possible.
Logistics	An acceptable number of target respondents can be assembled in one location.	Respondents are geographically dispersed or not easily assembled for other reasons.
Cost and timing	Quick turnaround is critical, and funds are limited.	Quick turnaround is not critical, andthe budget will permit higher cost.

FIGURE 5-3 Which to Use: Focus Groups or Individual Depth Interviews?

Source: Mary Debus, *Handbook for Excellence in Focus Group Research* (Washington, D.C.: Academy for Educational Development, n.d.), p. 10. Reprinted by permission of the Academy for Educational Development.

1. ***Build the relevant context information***—What are the experiences or issues that surround a product or a practice that influence how it/he/she is viewed?

2. ***Top-of-mind associations***—What's the first thing that comes to mind when I say "family planning"?

3. ***Constructing images***—Who are the people who buy Panther condoms? What do they look like? What are their lives about? (Or) Where are you when you buy condoms? Describe the place. What do you see? What do you feel? What do you do?

4. ***Querying the meaning of the obvious***—What does "soft" mean to you? What does the phrase "It's homemade" mean to you?

5. ***Establishing conceptual maps of a product category***—How would you group these different family planning methods? How do they go together for you? How are groups similar/different? What would you call these groups?

6. ***Metaphors***—If this birth control pill were a flower, what kind would it be and who would pick it? If this group of products were a family, who would the different members be and how do they relate to each other?

7. ***Image matching***—Here are pictures of ten different situations/people. Which go with this wine and, which do not? Why?

8. ***"Man from the moon" routine***—I'm from the moon; I've never heard of Fritos. Describe them to me. Why would I want to try one? Convince me.

9. ***Conditions that give permission and create barriers***—Tell me about two or three situations in which you would decide to buy this chocolate and two to three situations in which you would decide to buy something else.

10. ***Chain of questions***—Why do you buy "X"? Why is that important? Why does that make a difference to you? Would it ever not be important? (Ask until the respondent is ready to kill the interviewer!)

11. ***Benefit chain***—This cake mix has more egg whites; what's the benefit of that? (Answer: "It's moister.") What is the benefit of a moister cake? (Answer: "It tastes homemade.") And why is homemade better? (Answer: "It's more effort.") And what's the benefit of that? (Answer: "My family will appreciate it.") And? (Answer: "They will know I love them.") And? (Answer: "I'll feel better; they'll love me back.")

12. ***Laddering (chains of association)***—What do you think of when you think of Maxwell House coffee? (Answer: "Morning.") And when you think of morning, what comes to mind? (Answer: "A new day.") And when you think of a new day? (Answer: "I feel optimistic.")

13. ***Pointing out contradictions***—Wait a minute, you just told me you would like it to be less greasy and now you're telling me it works because it's greasy and oily—how do you explain that?

14. ***Sentence completions and extensions***—The ideal ORS product is one that. . . . The best thing about this new product is. . . . It makes me feel. . . .

15. ***Role playing***—Okay, now you're the chairman of the board, or the mayor of this city. What would you do? (Or) I'm the mayor, talk to me, tell me what you want.

16. ***Best-of-all-possible-worlds scenario***—Forget about reality for a minute. If you could design your own diaper that has everything you ever wanted in a diaper and more, what would it be like? Use your imagination. There are no limits. Don't worry about whether it's possible or not.

17. ***Script writing***—If you were able to tell a story or write a movie about this company or city (or whatever), what would it be about? Who are the heroines and heroes? Does the movie have a message? Would you go see it? Who would?

FIGURE 5-4   Suggestions for Soliciting Responses in Focus Groups

Source: Mary Debus, Handbook for Excellence in Focus Group Research (Washington, D.C.: Academy for Educational Development, n.d.), p. 10. Reprinted by permission of the Academy for Educational Development.

- A museum's cafeteria manager could systematically change prices on the assorted cheesecakes every day over a three-month period and estimate the price–volume relationship.
- Hospital rooms could be decorated in different colors or nurses' uniforms changed on different floors to assess their effects on patients' satisfaction with the quality of care.

These experimental manipulations often require little effort on the part of managers. They can be done as simple "variations" in marketing projects that would be undertaken anyway. In contrast to surveys and many qualitative techniques, they usually can be carried out *unobtrusively*—that is, without the target audience knowing they are part of a study. Researchers, however, should avoid thinking that "just trying something" makes for good experimentation. Careful attention must be paid to random assignment of experimental treatments across subjects, use of control groups wherever possible, and monitoring the surrounding circumstances for possible confounding effects.[13]

Snowball Sampling

A problem for many research studies is that it is relatively easy to contact past users of a service, past donors, and past volunteers. But aggressive marketers will ideally like information on future prospects—that is, those they are not currently serving. One approach is snowball sampling. This is where participants in a study are asked to suggest the names of others "like them" who could be contacted. This would add a group that (1) did not have the familiarity biases of the first group, (2) would be likely to cooperate in the study (especially if the initial respondents allowed their names to be used as references), and (3) would closely *match* the first sample in all other socioeconomic characteristics but that which characterized the initial sample (for example, people already coming to the hospital). Snowball sampling is a particularly good technique for finding rare populations. A hospital trying to broaden its appeal to hemophiliacs, for example, might ask those hemophiliacs already attending the hospital to identify others. Conducting a full-scale random sample to find rare populations, such as paraplegics or bus riders with disabilities or the deaf, would be prohibitively expensive. Yet members of such rare groups may well be known to many others like themselves.

Piggybacking

Nonprofit organizations may be able to add questions onto studies undertaken by others. Several national research organizations regularly conduct omnibus surveys that combine questions from a number of sponsors. Nonprofits could add questions for close to the incremental cost of the question or questions. Board members may be willing to add such questions to planned studies at their companies at no charge or at reduced rates.

Volunteer Researchers

Nonprofits such as hospitals or charities may enlist volunteers to conduct telephone, mail, or "convenience" interviews, or to tabulate questionnaires. Students in business schools, and sometimes in psychology and sociology departments, are also frequently looking for outside, real-world term projects. They can be an excellent source of thought and legwork for nonprofit organizations. However, certain caveats in these cases should be observed. First, student interviewers are not the same as trained professional interviewers. The nonprofit manager must give them guidance or be sure that a professor is overseeing the research process. Second, plenty of lead time is necessary. Student projects must fit within semester or quarter academic systems. Third, the nonprofit manager should set time aside to consult with the students—they are doing this to learn. Finally, the nonprofit manager should be sensitive to the university's research norms. The students cannot be ordered to do the research in a particular way, the professor cannot be treated as a paid consultant or a field supervisor, and the professor may request that the results be made public (although possibly in disguised form).

Secondary Sources

There are a great many studies already completed that can provide marketers with much of what they need to make important decisions. Or, when not exactly on point, they can provide comparative data or suggestions for question wording, sample design, and data analysis. The Internet can be a great source of such secondary information. Trade articles, marketing journals, and government reports can all prove very valuable, especially at the beginning stages of a project. Researchers, however, always need to be careful to investigate the validity of other people's research, especially if the source is non-governmental. Oftentimes a careful reading of footnotes and appendices can reveal serious biases or deficiencies that require caution in the use of the findings.

Among the valuable sources of secondary marketing data are these:[14]

1. **Factiva** (www.factiva.com) Formerly Dow Jones Interactive, Factiva provides full-text access to a wide range of newspapers, trade publications, and other business and company data.
2. **Lexis-Nexis Database** (www.lexis-nexis.com) Provides full-text information on legal, business, and general news.
3. **Reference USA** (www.referenceusa.com) Directory of U.S. businesses.
4. **Gartner Group Research** (www.gartner.com) Data on information technology, news, and product reviews.
5. **ABI/Inform** (Proquest) (www.proquest.com) Current and historic abstracts and articles from a variety of business journals.
6. **MarketResearch.com** (www.marketresearch.com) Full-text market research reports on various topics.
7. **Source OECD** (www.sourceoecd.org) Online international publications from the Organization for Economic Co-operation and Development.
8. **Foundation Directory** (fconline.fdncenter.org) Online directory of foundations and grants.
9. **Catalog of Nonprofit Literature** (lnps.fdncenter.org) Database of literature on philanthropy.
10. **Polling the Nations** (poll.orspub.com) Results from poll and survey data gathered from various national, state, and local surveys.

Summary

Most nonprofit organizations carry out much less marketing research than they should. This is because they have accepted certain myths. They assume that marketing research should only be used for major decisions, that it involves big surveys and takes a long time, that it is always expensive, that a few focus groups are all one needs, that it requires sophisticated researchers, and, when it is finished, that it is usually not read or used. But research using a diversity of techniques, many at low cost, can be extremely valuable to a wide range of decisions.

Sophisticated modern nonprofit organizations recognize that their most important resource is the knowledge they possess. Such knowledge must systematically be developed at the organization level—as well as for specific campaigns. A marketing knowledge system has four major subsystems: an internal records system, a market intelligence system, a marketing research system, and an analytical marketing system.

Research can help managers by describing, explaining, or predicting market characteristics. Most nonprofit research is applied, although some could be basic or methodological research. The applied nature of the research provides a good framework for decisions about budgets and for designing specific research projects.

An applied orientation also recommends a "backward" research design process. Here the research manager first looks to the decisions to be made using the research results and then works backward to design a study that would best inform such decisions. An important step would be determining what report format would provide the most managerially useful information. The report form would then suggest the type of analysis needed, which in turn would specify how the data are to be collected and processed.

Research can be quantitative or qualitative, high cost or low cost. Qualitative research, such as in-depth interviewing or focus groups, can be useful in identifying a problem; gathering background for later quantitative studies; interpreting past studies; pretesting advertisements; offering concepts, packaging, and brochures; and generating ideas for new offerings, services, and advertisements. Other techniques for keeping research costs low are experimentation, low-cost sampling designs, and the use of secondary data and volunteer assistance.

Questions

1. You are a new member of a student-led organization that aims to increase volunteerism among fellow students at Georgetown University. The president of the organization claims to know for a fact that Georgetown students do not volunteer their time or contribute back to society, and is thus prepared to use her limited funds to advertise its slogan, "Hoyas Volunteer!" across campus right before summer break. What research questions would you ask before launching your campaign?
2. Pick a nonprofit organization you know well and outline its key resource-based advantages. How does the organization use them and are they sustainable? How has the organization leveraged these competitive advantages to ensure its success in achieving its mission?

3. You are appointed as the marketing director for a new AIDS awareness organization. Your boss has given you a limited budget for marketing research over the next year and wants to hear your plans for research by the end of the week. What types of research are you likely to undertake? What are the strengths and weaknesses of the research methods you identified?

4. You are an anti-violence counselor for teen youths. Prepare a guide for a focus group discussion that will include 10- to 15-year-old underprivileged boys from inner cities. The objective of the study is to develop a strategy to keep young boys from joining street gangs and engaging in violence.

5. A trust has just provided your community organization with $1 million and the direction to improve the well-being of local orphaned children. The board of the trust wants you to develop a budget proposal in one week before they release the funds. How much money will you spend on market research? How will you justify this decision?

Notes

1. This section draws upon Alan R. Andreasen, "Cost-Conscious Marketing Research," *Harvard Business Review,* July–August 1983, pp. 74–77.

2. For further information on research costs, see Seymour Sudman, *Reducing the Costs of Surveys* (Chicago: Aldine, 1967).

3. R. M. Grant, *Contemporary Strategy Analysis: Concepts, Techniques, Applications,* Second Edition (Cambridge, MA: Blackwell Publishers Inc, 1995).

4. Robert Grant, "Toward a Knowledge-Based Theory of the Firm," *Strategic Management,* Vol. 17 (1991), pp. 109–122; Morten T. Hansen, Nitin Hohria, and Thomas Tierney, "What's Your Strategy for Managing Knowledge?" *Harvard Business Review,* March–April 1999); Rohit Deshpandé (Ed.), *Using Market Knowledge* (Thousand Oaks, CA: Sage Publications, Inc., 2001); R. M. Grant, "The Knowledge-Based View of the Firm: Implications for Management Practice," *Long Range Planning.* Vol. 30, No. 3 (1997), pp. 450–454.

5. Thomas A. Stewart, *The Wealth of Knowledge : Intellectual Capital and the Twenty-first Century Organization* (New York: Currency, 2001).

6. Susanne Hauschild, Thomas Licht, and Wolfram Stein, *Creating a Knowledge Culture* (McKinsey & Company, 2001).

7. Christine W. Letts, William P. Ryan, and Allen S. Grossman, *High Performance Nonprofit Organizations: Managing Upstream for Greater Impact* (New York: John Wiley & Sons, 1999).

8. www.sifry.com/alerts/archives/000298.html (retrieved December 5, 2006).

9. *The Professional Performing Arts: Attendance, Preferences and Motives* (Madison, WI: Association of College, University and Community Arts Administrators, 1977).

10. This section is drawn from Alan R. Andreasen, "'Backward' Marketing Research," *Harvard Business Review,* May–June 1985, pp. 176–182.

11. For more information on low-cost methods, see Alan R. Andreasen, *Marketing Research That Won't Break the Bank* (San Francisco: Jossey-Bass Publishers, 2002).

12. J. A. Smith (Ed.), *Qualitative Psychology: A Practical Guide to Research Methods* (London: Sage, 2003); P. M. Camic, J. E. Rhodes, and L. Yardley (Eds.), 2003, *Qualitative Research in Psychology: Expanding Perspectives in Methodology and Design* (Washington, DC: American Psychological Association, 2003).

13. A good introduction to alternative field experimental designs is found in Donald T. Campbell and Julian C. Stanley, *Experimental and Quasi-Experimental Designs for Research* (Chicago: Rand McNally, 1966). For a good example of a nonprofit experiment, see Richard A. Winett, Ingrid N. Lecklite, Donna E. Chinn, and Brian Stahl, "Reducing Energy Consumption: The Long-Term Effects of a Single TV Program," *Journal of Communications,* Summer 1984, pp. 37–51.

14. This list was prepared by Michelle Clarke of Georgetown University, October 2006.

6

SEGMENTATION, TARGETING, AND POSITIONING

POSITIONING AN OFFERING CALLED "YOU"!

Looking for the ideal job is a major challenge for any undergrad, MBA, junior executive, or seasoned professional. Where do you look for a job and how do you position yourself? Should you be a different prospect for different potential employers? Should you be outgoing and creative for that advertising agency and more serious and meticulous for a software developer? How about banking? Should you dress differently than you would for the advertising firm?

All of these are really questions about "Brand You." Getting a job—or a date—is a matter of choosing which target markets to approach and how you should position yourself for each. In a recent article in *Time*, writer Jeninne Lee-St. John said: "Treating our personalities as products reflects an increasingly competitive society in which the best way to stand out is to develop an engaging—and easily defined—image." But what is the ideal positioning if one wants to work for the American Cancer Society or for the Boy Scouts or Girls Inc.? How should one come across on MySpace and does it matter what your goal is?

Not surprisingly, there are now "personal branding" consultants to help prospects with segmentation and positioning challenges. One of the first things they tell clients is that it is important to understand your strengths and consider ways of positioning your weaknesses as positives. The *Time* article describes a 66-year-old woman seeking a mate whose original statement about herself was that she needed to be taught things and was looking for someone with the patience to help her. A consultant from PersonalsTrainer suggested describing herself as: "Learning new things is a passion."

Personal branding consultants have an array of techniques to help clients understand themselves and to think about optimal positioning. One trick is to ask yourself—and your friends—what kind of a car you would be if you were a car. The *Time* author admits: "Turns out I'm a Mini Cooper . . . people see me as small but bold and stylish and full of energy."

Taped practice interviews also provide great insight into how one comes across as a package and a "performer." What do others see and hear? Consultants can help with this—and the resulting videotape is often a shocker as we see how often we mumble and get off the topic. But the substance still has to be there. You cannot come across as "the real thing" if the thing you have created is not really you. It would be like a nonprofit touting its careful management when it is regularly blindsided by accounting irregularities, employee misstatements, and performance goofs.

The *Time* article tells of a Texas investment advisor who was overwhelmed trying to keep up with the broad field of investment strategies and opportunities for diverse clients. A personal consultant identified his core values as family, church, and hard work and his hobbies as fishing, golf, and travel. The consultant repositioned him as "a wealth planner for active retirees." The result was a 30 percent increase in revenues and a career working with fewer—but more profitable—clients.

Source: Jeninne Lee-St. John, "You World," *Time*, November 6, 2006, p. 61.

A central theme of this text is that, whether a nonprofit marketer is undertaking organization-level or campaign planning, the central issue is—or ought to be—how to induce desired behavior from target audiences. Thus we argue that the three most fundamental challenges of nonprofit marketers is deciding (1) who should be their target audiences, (2) what sort of behavior or behaviors do they want them to take, and (3) what sort of value proposition should they propose to secure their behavioral goals?

With respect to audiences and behaviors, nonprofit organizations with huge challenges and limited budgets cannot be all things to all people (even though their mission statement may grandly imply such ambitions). They must choose audiences, choose behaviors, and then figure out compelling value propositions. We refer to the first as the segmentation and targeting problem, and the second as the positioning problem. In the private sector, the acronym is "STP," and it drives any marketer's thinking and strategizing about how to achieve market success.

In this chapter we consider these challenges; in the next we will specifically focus on the role of branding.

SEGMENTATION

Good marketing starts with the target audience that ultimately determines success. Thus the first element to be set out in any marketing strategy is the organization's approach toward market targets. This can be a challenge for the overall organization when it decides on target audiences that will comprise its mission and basic objectives. A pregnancy prevention organization can decide to emphasize teens, all women, or African-Americans. It can ignore men or incorporate them in their approach. Much depends on organizational strengths and what other organizations are doing. But a primary concern is with the target audience: Who is in need of help, do we know how to influence them, and do we have the resources and knowledge base—or can we acquire them—in order to have an impact? The latter issues raise questions about the organization's ability to raise funds and volunteers. The latter may well be influenced by the target audiences chosen.

Of course, the segmentation question is always a challenge when one is developing a specific campaign. But at both the organizational and campaign level, the marketing manager will constantly keep in mind that target audiences come in many different shapes and sizes and a fundamental problem is how to deal with this complexity. Treating all target audiences the same may achieve economies of scale, but it ignores the diversity that is typically present in most markets, and it probably means that what is offered never really meets any one target audience member's needs very well.

On the other hand, treating everyone as a unique individual deserving customized attention has been—or seemed—too expensive and impractical for most nonprofit situations (except in fundraising, where individualized approaches to foundations, corporations, and major donors are certainly merited). Today, however, treating audience members individually—as markets of one—is becoming ever more practical. Computers and information technology have made individualized approaches through direct mail much more cost-effective. For example, direct mail technology allows a political fundraiser to send letters to Lexus and Hyundai owners living next to each other and to ask for $500 from the Lexus owner and $100 from the Hyundai owner.[1] Even more promising are developments on the Internet where sophisticated software allows marketers to address individuals by name and respond to inquiries with custom-tailored reactions. As the work of Williams and Flora and others has demonstrated, such tailored approaches can be especially valuable in health care.[2]

For the marketer seeking to develop a sophisticated segmentation approach, a process is needed to cope with the sheer enormity of the task. There are really *two* stages to this process. First is a conceptualization and research stage to identify and describe the groups the marketer *may* wish to target. We shall refer to this stage as *developing market segments*. As can be seen in the left side of Figure 6-1, market segmentation requires (1) choosing among the different bases for segmenting the market, (2) developing profiles of the resulting market segments, and (3) developing measures of each segment's attractiveness. The second stage is *target marketing*, the

FIGURE 6-1   Steps in Market Segmentation, Targeting, and Positioning

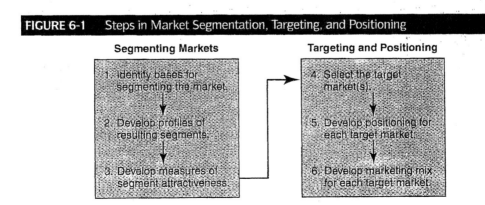

act of selecting one or more of the market segments, deciding how many resources and of what kind to apply to each, and developing a positioning and marketing mix strategy for each.

Dividing Up Markets

There are a great many ways in which a given market can be divided for purposes of marketing strategy. In determining which way one ought to proceed, the manager should first consider *why* segmentation is to be carried out. That is, segmenting the market is fundamentally a research task and, as we noted in Chapter 5, good "backward" research design starts with an understanding of how the data will be used to help managers make decisions. There are three types of decisions for which segmentation information is valuable:

1. *Quantity decisions.* How much of the organization's financial, human, and mental resources are to be devoted to various groups in the target population? Which groups merit zero attention, if any?
2. *Quality decisions.* Among the chosen segments, how should each segment be approached in terms of specific propositions, communications, place of offering, "prices," and the like?
3. *Timing decisions.* Should some segments be targeted earlier and some later with a specific marketing effort?

How, then, to divide up the market? In theory, the criteria are well-defined. A segmentation base is optimal if it yields segments possessing the following characteristics:

1. *Mutual exclusivity.* Is each segment conceptually separable from all other segments? Breaking donors into present givers and past givers, for example, would be confusing for a respondent who could be both a past and a present giver.
2. *Exhaustiveness.* Is every potential target member included in some segment? Thus if there is to be segmentation according to household status, one should have categories to cover relationships like unmarried couples and religious communes where the notion of "household head" does not apply.
3. *Measurability.* Can you measure the size, motivation, ability to act, and so on of the resulting segments? Certain segments are hard to measure, such as the segment of white upper-income teenage female drug addicts engaged in secretive behavior.
4. *Reachability.* Can the resulting segments be effectively reached and served? It would be hard for a drug treatment center to develop efficient media to locate and communicate with white female drug addicts.
5. *Substantiality.* Are the resulting segments large enough to be worth pursuing? The drug treatment center is likely to decide that white affluent female drug addicts are too few in number to be worth the development of a special marketing program. Size is a combination of both the number of audience units and the amount of consumption.
6. *Differential responsiveness.* This is perhaps the most crucial criterion. A segmentation scheme may meet all of the previous criteria but several or all segments may respond exactly alike to different amounts, types, and timings of strategy. In such cases, although it may be *conceptually* useful to develop separate segments in this way, *managerially* it is not useful.

It is typically difficult to address all of these issues when considering a particular segmentation scheme. Responsiveness and reachability are often impossible to measure and, as a result, managers typically use surrogates for what they ideally would like to measure. Segmentation is often based on demographics, for example, because managers assume that such characteristics will be related to likely responsiveness and reachability. Thus one might choose to segment potential symphony target audiences on the basis of gender because it is believed (or past research has shown) that women respond more to communications focusing on the performance itself, whereas men respond more to communications about the networking aspects of attending the symphony *event*. At the same time, it may be believed that ads placed in the sports section of a newspaper would reach a predominantly male audience and ads in the metropolitan news section would be an excellent way to reach females. Symphony marketers may initially conclude—with or without past research evidence—that the added costs of placing two such ads in a given paper may be justified by the better *total* responses achieved over a less costly, single ad that tried a middle approach or tried to combine the two approaches into one (possibly confusing) message. As we will emphasize throughout this chapter, if cost is a constraint, it is often better to focus on only part of the market rather than try to craft an approach that somehow fits everyone!

Alternative Segmentation Bases

Variables that, in the past, have been used to segment markets in particular cases vary according to whether they were *primarily* chosen to reflect expected differences in responsiveness or differences in reachability. Frank, Massy, and Wind developed a two-by-two matrix that serves as a useful vehicle for categorizing segmentation approaches that may be used to achieve these ends.[3] These authors noted that two important ways in which segmentation variables differ are in the extent to which they are (1) objective or psychological and (2) general or behavior-specific. These alternatives are set out in Figure 6-2.

Objective measures are those that can be verified fairly accurately by an independent observer or about which individuals seldom lie (much)—for example, age, income, sex, and the like. *Psychological measures* are mental states peculiar to each respondent

---

FIGURE 6-2   Bases for Market Segmentation

	General	**Behavior-Specific**
Objective Measures	Age, income, sex Place of residence Status change Family life cycle Social class	Past behavior • Purchase quantity • Outlet/brand preference • Loyalty
Psychological Measures	Personality Psychographics/lifestyles (e.g., Personicx) Values (e.g., VALS 2)	Beliefs, perceptions BCOS drivers Stage in decision

that have to be deduced (inferred) from what people tell us; included here are such cognitive factors as perceptions, beliefs, benefits sought, and so forth. The value of psychological variables depends on the candor and cooperation of a target audience and the sophistication of analysts in teasing out "real" meanings from their responses.

General variables are those that might apply to any exchange, whereas *behavior-specific* variables are those that are unique to one type or class of behaviors (for example, voting for particular bills or visiting art museums). Thus the extent to which an individual audience possesses an "aggressive" or "risk-averse" personality would be an example of a general psychological variable, whereas beliefs about the likelihood of getting friendly nursing service or the latest diagnostic procedures at Good Samaritan Hospital would be a behavior-specific psychological variable.

In some respects, marketers would prefer to use objective rather than psychological measures as the basis for segmentation. There are several reasons for this. First, there is the *ease* of identifying target audiences. As noted, most objective general measures such as sex and geographic location are instantly observable. Others, such as education level, occupation, household size, and family composition are relatively easily determined and verifiable. Unlike psychological measures, objective indicators do not always require audience cooperation, nor is there a strong likelihood that an error in measurement would be made either because the wrong wording was used for a question or because respondents did not know the answer or consciously or unconsciously distorted their responses. Second, target audiences can be fairly easily allocated to specific, nonarbitrary categories. Third, the measures can be adapted easily by different researchers to different contexts, permitting extensive comparison of segmentation findings across studies. This is typically not possible with psychological characteristics, where subtle changes in wording can yield major differences in results. Thus how one measures "liberal" or "conservative" in one study may not be the same as in another study.

Objective data are also important because, even when the target market is described in nondemographic terms (say, a personality or lifestyle type), the marketer will need to link these characteristics back to demographic characteristics in order to know the size of the target market and how to reach it efficiently.

Finally, objective measures are often preferred because they are available in a wide range of secondary sources, including Census Bureau data, Simmons reports, Nielsen audience measures, and so on. For example, if one believes that households with young children are the best prospects for a charity drive, then publicly available census data can be used to discover cities or census tracts within cities that have above-average proportions of households with that characteristic. Thus socioeconomic characteristics were the principal criteria used by the National Center for Charitable Statistics to segment the target markets for exempt nonprofit agencies in the 1980s. Their taxonomy of beneficiaries is reproduced in Exhibit 6-1.

Objective General Measures

Among the most commonly used objective general measures are the following:

Demographic Segmentation

As noted, demographic variables have been applied creatively to nonprofit market segmentation for many decades.

EXHIBIT 6-1

A TAXONOMY OF BENEFICIARIES OF NONPROFIT ORGANIZATION PROGRAMS

I. *General*
1. All, general public, no specific beneficiary

II. *Age related*
1. Infants, babies
2. Children and youth
3. Aging, elderly, senior citizens, and retired

III. *Sex*
1. Boys 5 to 19
2. Boys and men (i.e., males 5 and older)
3. Girls 5 to 19
4. Girls and women (i.e., females 5 and older)
5. Men 19 and older
6. Women 19 and older

IV. *Race*
1. Asian, Pacific Islander
2. Blacks
3. Hispanics
4. Native Americans, American Indians
5. Other Minorities
6. Minorities, general, unspecified

V. *Other beneficiaries*
1. Disabled, general, unspecified
2. Disabled, physically
3. Disabled, mentally, emotionally
4. Immigrants, newcomers, refugees, stateless
5. Member or affiliates (organizations)
6. Member (individual)
7. Military, veterans
8. Offenders, ex-offenders
9. Poor, economically disadvantaged

Source: National Center for Charitable Statistics, *National Taxonomy of Exempt Entities* (Washington, D.C.: The Independent Sector, 1987). Used with permission, Independent Sector, www.independentsector.org.

Age   Audience wants and capacities change with age. Thus religious organizations have found it effective to develop different programs for children, youths, singles, married adults, and senior citizens. The organizations try to "customize" the religious and social experiences to the interests of these different groups. Some are even subsegmenting the senior citizens into those between 55 and 70 ("the young old") and 70 and up ("the old old"). The "young old" still feel vigorous and want challenge and variety in their lives, and the "old old" want to settle into a comfortable and routine existence.[4] The American Cancer Society makes extensive use of age to target audiences (see Figure 6-3).

Generation   Many scholars believe that age should not be looked at as simply an issue of maturation but as an indicator of the distinctive norms, values, and goals that one has acquired growing up in a particular generation. Neil Howe and William Strauss have produced a series of extremely complex and thoughtful studies of generational patterns in U.S. and British populations since 1433.[5] They conclude that there are four basic patterns that always follow each other (what they call "turnings") that have repeated over 24 generations of Anglo-American history. They call these the Awakening, Unraveling, Crisis, and High periods that, depending on the period into which one is born, produce archetypal individuals they call Prophets, Nomads, Heroes, and Artists. It is prescient that these authors predicted that the early twenty-first century would be a Crisis turning—a prophesy borne out in the significant impact that the world has felt in the wake of the September 11, 2001, terrorist attacks.

FIGURE 6-3   American Cancer Society Advertisement Targeting Seniors

Source: Used with permission of the American Cancer Society, Inc.

Gender   Segmentation by gender is common in many nonprofit sectors, such as male and female colleges, service and social clubs, prisons, and military services. Within a single sex, further segmentation can be applied. The continuing education department of a large university segments the female adult learners into "at homes" and "working outside the homes." The "at homes" are subdivided into homemakers and displaced homemakers. Homemakers are attracted to courses for self-enrichment and improved homemaking skills, whereas displaced homemakers are more interested in career preparation. The "working outside the home" segment breaks into two subsegments, clerical–technical businesswomen and management businesswomen. Each segment has a different set of motivations for attending college, and different programs are appropriate for each. Furthermore, each segment faces certain efficacy problems in attending college. By addressing the specific problems of each segment, the college is in a better position to attract more women to its campus.

Sexual Orientation   A major shift in marketing segmentation practice in the last decade is the willingness of mainstream marketers like General Motors to target gay markets—both men and women. Certainly, many social challenges—parenting behavior, issues around HIV/AIDS—have differential impacts and complexities depending on one's sexual orientation.

Income   Income segmentation is another long-standing practice in the nonprofit sector. In the medical field, the standard health insurance policy pays for semi-private rooms. Many hospitals, however, offer patients the option of a private room at an additional cost in order to cater to the preferences of higher income groups. Some hospitals have designed entire wings and even whole buildings to serve more affluent patients. Hospitals that establish outreach ambulatory centers vary the decor and service to match different income groups.

Race and Ethnicity Two variables that are often used to segment nonprofit marketing programs are race and ethnicity. There are many reasons for this. One is that different issues impact different racial and ethnic groups. Hispanics and Southeast Asians are particularly concerned with immigration issues, and African-Americans are especially concerned with sickle-cell anemia. However, problems of drugs, poverty, education, and homelessness affect all groups.

Second, racial and ethnic groups differ in their media habits, organizational ties, and shopping preferences. In the United States, most major minority groups have their own newspapers, magazines, and, in some cases, radio and television programming. These permit very precise targeting of marketing messages.

Finally, the way one appeals to different races and ethnic groups is different. It is often essential to use different models and settings in ads for different audiences. Language and colloquialisms often should differ in communications to each segment as well as the basic appeals. Spokespeople will differ. For example, religious leaders can often be extremely effective in transmitting important social messages in Hispanic and African-American markets where preachers and priests are highly respected leaders. The Census Bureau has been especially effective in using race/ethnic segmentation.[6]

Geographic Location In geographical segmentation, the market is divided into different geographical entities, such as nations, states, regions, counties, cities, zip code areas, or neighborhoods, based on the notion that audience needs or responses vary geographically. Many nonprofits focus on specific cities or regions and are able to cater to local interests and concerns. Geographical segmentation is often used as the basis for direct mail or billboard campaigns. It is also combined with other data in the "lifestyle" approaches discused later in this chapter.

Objective Behavior-Specific Measures

For many target audience behaviors, the best predictor of future responsiveness may simply be past behavior in the exchange category or closely related exchanges. Among measures of past behavior often used in marketing are the following:

Occasion Buyers can be distinguished by the occasions when they engage in the behavior. Commuters using public transportation, for example, include those who are traveling to work, those who are shopping, those who are going to entertainment, and those who are visiting friends. Some public transit companies have launched campaigns to encourage the shopping segment to travel in off-peak hours and have even charged lower fares as an incentive.[7]

Doer/Non-Doer Status In many social marketing programs, useful insights can be gained from studying and understanding those who have and have not done a crucial social behavior. For example, a number of HIV/AIDS programs have gained significant insights by understanding more about the differences between those who use condoms and those who do not. Similar approaches can be taken to studies of those who diet or don't, exercise or don't, stop abusing their wives or don't, and so on.

Usage Rate Many markets can be segmented into light-, medium-, and heavy-user groups for the offer (called volume segmentation). Heavy users may constitute only a small percentage of the numerical size of the market but a major percentage of the unit activity. This is often true of both donor and volunteer markets. Marketers make a great effort to determine the demographic characteristics and media habits of the heavy users and aim their marketing programs at them. An anti-smoking campaign, for example, might be aimed at the heaviest smokers, a safe driving campaign at those having the most accidents, and a family planning campaign at those likely to have the most children. Unfortunately, the heaviest users are often the most resistant to change. Fertile families are the most resistant to birth control messages, and unsafe drivers are the most resistant to safe driving messages. The agencies must consider whether to use their limited budget to go after a few heavy users who are highly resistant or many light users who are less resistant.

Semenik and Young segmented the audience attending opera into three attendance-level segments—subscribers, frequent attenders, and infrequent attenders—and found significant differences.[8] Subscribers tended to be longtime patrons, attended as a married couple, and considered themselves to be opera fans. Frequent attenders had similar characteristics but were younger and lower in income and often attended with a friend rather than a spouse. Infrequent attenders did not consider themselves opera fans but attended because of a featured star or well-known opera. The identification of segment characteristics enables the development of separate market strategies designed to maximize attendance and loyalty.

Loyalty Status   One of the hallmarks of twenty-first century marketing is the private sector's focus on building "customers for life."[9] Today's marketers recognize that it is much less costly to keep a customer than to find new ones. They find target audiences who are deeply loyal to a brand (Livestrong), an organization (Harvard University, the Republican Party), a place (New England, Southern California), a person (Bono), and so on. Fundraisers pay a great deal of attention to developing loyal donors and have invested heavily in determining lifetime value as a guide to marketing investment strategies.[10]

Complex General Objective Measures

As nonprofit marketers grew more sophisticated in their use of objective segmentation variables, two developments occurred. First, marketers learned that traditional ways of measuring a given demographic may not be the best approach. Miller found that donation behavior in various zip code areas in Oklahoma was often more closely associated with the *source* of income than the amount of income.[11] He found, for example, that the number of households in a zip code area receiving some form of interest income was a better predictor of total donations than was total adjusted gross income. Predictions of the percentage who would donate were better with measures of the percentage of households receiving dividends, or of the percentage receiving interest, than with average household income. Clearly, routinely using total income in studies may miss insights that more careful measures might yield.

The other development was the creation of complex measures that combined objective measures in a single index. Two such combined measures, social class and family life cycle, have been used extensively in marketing.

Social Class   Social classes are relatively homogeneous and enduring divisions in a society that is hierarchically ordered and whose members share similar values, interests, and behavior. Social scientists have distinguished six social classes—(1) upper uppers, (2) lower uppers, (3) upper middles, (4) lower middles, (5) upper lowers, and

(6) lower lowers—using objective variables such as income, occupation, education, and type of residence. Social classes show distinct consumption preferences in the nonprofit area. Operas, plays, the ballet, symphonies, and lectures attract the upper classes most heavily. Cultural institutions that wish to overcome their elitist image and attract lower-class audiences to appreciate their art forms will have to develop separate marketing programs and strategies for them.

Family Life Cycle   The family life cycle concept is based on the notion that over one's lifetime there are critical transition points when major changes in audience behavior (and other behaviors) take place. These transition points are generally defined in terms of objective variables such as marital status, workforce status, and the presence and age of children. Eight stages are typically specified as the model family life cycle pattern:

1. Young single (under 40, not married, no children at home)
2. Newly married (young, married, no children)
3. Full nest I (young, married, youngest child less than 6)
4. Full nest II (young, married, youngest child 6 to 13)
5. Full nest III (older married, dependent children 14 or older)
6. Empty nest I (older married, no children at home, head working)
7. Empty nest II (older married, no children at home, head retired)
8. Solitary survivor (older single, working or retired)

In an analysis of performing arts attendance data, Andreasen found that family life cycle appeared to have an important effect on attendance at six different types of performing arts. The proportions of households attending multiple events were as follows:

Young, single	17.9%
Young, married, no children	10.7%
Infants at home	8.7%
Children 6 or older	12.4%
Older, no children	15.4%
Elderly	8.8%

The elderly represent a poor market. Among the remaining lifestyle categories, the relationship is clearly curvilinear: Multiple attendance is high at each end of these life cycle categories but low in the middle. It would appear that the presence of children has a dampening effect on arts involvement. Undoubtedly, this is due to several factors, including reductions in leisure time and discretionary income, changes in household priorities, and increased costs for "going out."[12]

It should be noted that while the family life cycle concept can prove to be a useful segmentation variable, it is far from *exhaustive* in that it omits important groups of households. For example, older never-marrieds, and divorced or single parents with spouses absent, are often not included. Further, the high divorce rate in some countries means that the traditional linear life stage progression is far from the norm for as much as half the population.

Status Change   One of the reasons that the family life cycle concept is valuable is that it identifies transition points which lead to behavior changes. Andreasen and others have generalized this notion to explore the broader category of status change—the moment when individuals undergo events that may signal behavior changes or at least increased vulnerability to marketing interventions.[13] Such changes include the life cycle transitions, divorce, a geographic move, the loss of a job, a death in the family, and so on. Such events can often trigger important behavior changes and can open target audiences to possible marketer influences. It was found that life status changes are important predictors of elderly risks of fractures.[14]

Lifestyles Lifestyle segmentation is based on the notion that "We do what we do because it fits into the kind of life we are living or want to live." Lifestyle is seen as more transient, something that can change even from one year to the next. However, what one does or likes to do very much affects what marketing approaches they will find appealing.

There are several different approaches to identifying lifestyle groups in the population. Many, however, are based on measures of target audiences' *activities, interests, and opinions* (AIOs). When lifestyle measures are combined with demographic measurements, they are often called *psychographics*.

Lifestyle approaches can also be customized for specific research needs. For example, Andreasen and Belk used information on the leisure-time activities of respondents in four Southern cities to group potential attenders at symphonies and the theater in six broad categories.[15] The six groups were labeled Passive Homebodies, Active Sports Enthusiasts, Inner-Directed Self-Sufficients, Active Homebodies, Culture Patrons, and Social Actives. The researchers found that membership in the Culture Patron lifestyle group was a very good predictor of attendance at the theater or symphony, presumably because the aesthetic benefits of these performances fit their lifestyles. In contrast, membership in the Socially Active group predicted symphony attendance only, suggesting that it is the symphony performance *event* that meets the lifestyle needs of this group. Lifestyle was found to be a better explanatory variable than any of the traditional socioeconomic characteristics, such as income and education, that are normally used to explain performing arts attendance. Andreasen and Belk suggest that these socioeconomic indicators may simply be masking what are really the more profound explanations—lifestyle compatibility.

Lifestyle information is valuable in many ways. One advantage is that it can give communications specialists rich portraits of their various target market segments.[16]

Geoclustering In recent years, an increasing number of nonprofit organizations have used information on geographical location combined imaginatively with lifestyle information to yield descriptions of neighborhoods that are richer portraits than is possible from traditional demographics. This lifestyle approach is called *geoclustering*. It is based on the notion that people who live near each other are likely to have similar interests and behaviors.[17] As noted in *Business Week,* these systems are founded on the notion that "Birds of a feather flock together."

There are a great many systems for developing these clusters. One of the earliest was PRIZM, developed by the Claritas Corporation. Other approaches are now available. These include ACORN (A Classification of Residential Neighborhoods) from C.A.C.I. in Arlington, Virginia; ClusterPlus 2000 from Strategic Mapping, Inc.; and Personicx® from Acxiom Corporation.

Much of the data for the clusters comes from the decennial Census and so the clusters are updated infrequently. Data about geographic clusters also comes from a wide variety of other sources where the information is tied to specific addresses. These data would include car registrations, magazine subscriptions and various product and service purchases. Personicx draws extensively on Acxiom's extensive internal database of information on consumer spending which is, itself, updated frequently. Such data are used to group individual households into lifestage clusters with similar characteristics. Personicx's latest analysis suggests that the U. S. population can be divided up into 70 geoclusters. And, as with most consumer segmentation systems, Acxiom attaches clever names to each cluster such as "Summit Estates" and "The Great Outdoors" both for marketing purposes but also to give a quick sense of what the cluster is like. Table 6-1 shows 10 of the 70 Personicx clusters with information on their demographic characteristics.

A nonprofit marketer can use the information in the Personicx system to locate new markets or learn what would be appealing to existing markets. For a predetermined fee, the organization can acquire a list of all the clusters in a selected area with lifestyles that would suggest they are good targets for fundraising or for services the organization offers. Personicx can also help define markets, telling the organization which geographic areas are the best prospects for the organization's offering. Personicx can "tell you more than you probably ever wanted to know about [an] area's typical residents: what they like to eat, which cars they like to drive, whether they prefer scotch or sangria, tuna extender or yogurt, hunting or tennis ... which magazines they read, which TV shows they watch, whether they are more likely to buy calculators or laxatives, and whether they're single or potential target audiences for a diaper service."[18]

Here is a more detailed description of the "Tots & Toys" group:

> These professional working couples are consumed by work and family. They're putting their college degrees to work, establishing lucrative careers. At the same time, the joys of home ownership and early parenthood combine to ensure that money made is quickly spent. When not carpooling to the zoo or the beach and making videos of their kids, they are busy clothing their toddlers, buying baby accessories and toys with regular purchases over the Internet and at retailers like Toys 'R' Us. In addition, any spare time is consumed by jogging, aerobics, and softball. Even with time at a premium, they tend to exercise at fitness clubs and rely on the Internet and radio more than other forms of media for sports news. TV viewing tends to weigh toward children-oriented shows like Disney and Nickelodeon, as well as sitcoms.

The group is 1.25 percent of the U.S population and is a subcategory of the broader grouping "Jumbo Families."

Psychological Measures—Getting Inside the Target Audience's Head

Objective methods for segmentation are helpful in that it is often relatively easy to get relevant data from secondary sources. Objective measures are commonly found in field research studies in part because they are easy to measure and relatively unambiguous. And they permit comparisons across studies. Unless one uses some form of geoclustering, the problem is that they really do not tell researchers and marketing managers

TABLE 6-1 Sample Personicx Lifestyle Geoclusters

Group	Nickname	Size	Age	Marital Status	Ownership	Children	Income	Urbanicity	Net Worth
Beginnings	**First Digs**	0.87%	24–29	Single	Renter/Owner	No Kids	Low Middle	City & Surrounds	<$100K
	Young Workboots	0.70%	18–23	Single	Renter	No Kids	Low Middle	City & Surrounds	<$100K
Transition Blues	**Home Cooking**	1.03%	30–45	Married	Owner	No Kids	Low Middle	City & Surrounds	<$100K
Gen X Parents	**Cartoons & Carpools**	1.79%	30–45	Married	Owner	Married	Middle	Kids; Age Mix	<$100K
Cash & Careers	**Shooting Stars**	0.81%	30–45	Married/Single	Owner/Renter	Married/Single	Affluent	No Kids	<$250K
Jumbo Families	**Tots & Toys**	1.26%	30–45	Married	Owner	Married	Affluent	Toddlers/Preschool	<$100K
Flush Families	**Apple Pie Families**	3.01%	46–65	Married	Owner	Married	Upper Middle	School-age Kids	<$500K
Modest Means	**Single City Struggle**	1.94%	46–65	Single	Renter	Single	Low	No Kids	<$250K
Active Elders	**Raisin' Grandkids**	1.85%	66+	Married/Single Parents	Owner	Married/Single Parents	Middle	School-age Kids	<$500K
Leisure Buffs	**Rural Antiques**	1.23%	76+	Single	Owner/Renter	Single	Low	No Kids	<$100K

Source: Acxiom, Inc. Reproduced with permission.

150

much about what the target audience is *really* like, particularly what sort of value propositions might appeal to them.

To provide deeper insight, researchers have attempted to develop psychological measures. These are usually of two basic types. First, there are measures that yield personal typologies that can be applied across a broad range of behaviors. The most widely used approaches are those that segment target audiences by personality and by values. Second, there are measures that gather data on specific behaviors such as knowledge, attitudes, intentions, and the like.

Personality   It has long been believed that variations in audience personality would be reflected in their marketplace behavior. However, in the main, general personality traits have not been useful in past studies, in part because they are very difficult to measure (i.e., they are highly subjective and unreliable across studies) and therefore very hard to link to specific marketplace actions. In contrast, past studies have focused on relatively trivial behavior, such as beer preferences and car choices. It may be that in the future personality measures may finally prove to be helpful in segmenting markets for the more highly involving exchanges that are of interest to nonprofit marketers.

Values   As noted in Chapter 4, a number of disciplines argue that individuals organize and evaluate their behavioral choices in terms of the values they hold. The best-known scholar in this area, Milton Rokeach, distinguishes between *instrumental values* and *terminal values*.[19] Instrumental values guide our ongoing behavior to achieve certain end states. Terminal values guide our choices among those end states. Research has shown that values of both types are closely related to other segmentation variables such as age, family structure and life cycle, race and ethnicity, and geographical location. They are also closely related to attitudes and predispositions, behavioral choices (e.g., exercising, smoking), allocations of time between work and leisure, and the use of various media.

Values are much less permanent than personality traits. Individuals slowly change some of the values they use to guide their lives as they age. Values can also be influenced by life status changes. For example, rural people moving to a competitive big city may come to value prudence over openness in their interpersonal relations. Values also change as societies change. Americans in the twenty-first century approve of many conservative programs (e.g., privatization of prisons) that would have been considered highly reactionary 25 years earlier.

Stages of Change   As noted in Chapter 4, an extremely powerful approach to segmenting markets in high-involvement situations is where they are in the change process. As described there, the marketer's challenge is significantly different if an audience member is discovered to be mentally in the Precontemplation, Early or Late Contemplation, Preparation/Action, or Maintenance stage. Prochaska and his colleagues have used this form of segmentation to successfully influence target audiences to quit smoking, use condoms, lose weight, and exercise.[20] Sometimes researchers and managers use "intentions" as a proxy for stages.

Benefit Segmentation   Research suggests that some target audiences look for one dominant benefit from the offering, and others seek a particular *benefit bundle*.[21] In one application, Bonaguro and Miaoulis developed eight benefit segments for a multiservice family planning agency. These segments are outlined in Table 6-2.

TABLE 6-2 Benefit Segments for a Family Planning Agency	
Immediate solutions to a problem (pregnancy, breast lump, etc.), shoulder to lean on	1. Firefighters
Relief from feeling of desperation, financial stability, marital harmony	2. Desperates
Security about good health, relief from worry	3. Worriers
Conception, birth, children	4. Infertiles
Freedom of choice, control, financial stability, marital harmony	5. Married Rationals
Freedom of choice, financial stability	6. Married—No Children
Pregnancy prevention, financial stability, avoid social stigma	7. Married—With Children
Pregnancy prevention to avoid social stigma, retain independence, financial stability	8. Singles—Without Children

Source: John A. Bonaguro and George Miaoulis, "Marketing: A Tool for Health Education Planning," *Health Education,* January–February 1983, p. 9. Reprinted by permission of SAGE Publications, Inc.

The eight segments were then combined into more manageable subsets. The Firefighters and Desperates were joined into a group that had in common a sense of urgency about health needs. They only seek information and take action in an emergency, at which point they are likely to be agitated, confused, and perhaps irrational. It was decided to ignore the Worriers and Infertile benefit segments because of the agency's limited budget and to group the four remaining original segments as Rationals. This combined group was likely to seek information on their own as a means of improving their families' health and future prospects. Print media, lectures, pamphlets, and posters, all with longer messages, were emphasized within the strategy destined for this group under the theme: "A brighter future—plan it now." Note that in this example, the marketer segmented the market by benefits and then decided to concentrate on only those segments where the organization could have the best impact for its limited resources.

Sacrifice Segmentation   In Chapter 4, we noted that target audiences are likely to undertake exchanges if the benefits outweigh the costs. We further noted that in many cases there is wide appreciation of the *benefits* of a particular action, while it is the *costs* that are the major inhibitors to action. In Chapter 4, we noted that Bagozzi, in his study of blood donors, found little difference among target audiences in the perceived positive consequences that would follow from their behavior. However, Bagozzi found considerable variation in the perceptions of *negative* consequences and learned that they were good predictors of behavioral intentions. These results give rise to the speculation that some markets could be usefully segmented in terms of the relative weight individuals attach to the various *barriers* to action rather than to the benefits. Thus in the blood donation case, target audiences could be subdivided into those who are highly sensitive to physiological risks (infections, AIDS, physical pain), social risks (not being "brave" in the eyes of others), and psychological fears (fears of needles, blood, and "hospitals").[22]

Knowledge and Attitudes   It is fairly common in studies designed to inform health care interventions to conduct formative research into knowledge, attitudes, and practices. These are referred to as KAP studies. They are useful as baseline data in that they can tell nonprofit marketers where knowledge gaps exist and where attitudes toward the desired behaviors lie as well as identifying "doers and non-doers." All of these data—alone or in combination—can then be used to segment audiences for possible interventions.

TARGETING

The previous step in marketing planning ideally will carve up the potential market into an array of segments undoubtedly ranging in size and attractiveness. The next stage is to decide what to do with them all. There are four broad strategic choices:

1. *Undifferentiated (mass) marketing.* The organization can decide to go after the whole market with one offer and marketing mix, trying to attract as many target audience members as possible (this is another name for mass marketing). This is the approach that too many nonprofit organizations think is ideal, arguing that they need to reach everyone—and (therefore) they don't have the budget to do anything more elaborate and nuanced.
2. *Differentiated marketing.* The organization can decide to go after several market segments, perhaps all of them if the budget permits, developing an effective offer and marketing mix for each. The American Legacy Foundation has different approaches to teens and pregnant women.
3. *Concentrated marketing.* The organization can decide to go after one market segment and develop the ideal offer and marketing mix. The Campaign to Prevent Teen Pregnancy says that all teens are their targets—although they do make distinctions within this segment.
4. *Mass customization.* This is the most recent development in segmentation and targeting. It is the case where a marketer seeks to customize the offering to the individual. The Internet makes this option much more feasible in the twenty-first century. Dell Computers and Levi Jeans both practice this approach.

The logic and merits of each of these strategies follows.

Undifferentiated Marketing

In undifferentiated—or mass—marketing,[23] the organization chooses not to recognize the different market segments making up the market. It treats the audience as an aggregate, focusing on what is common among the target audiences rather than on what is different. It tries to design an offer and a marketing program that appeals to the broadest number of potential responders. It would be exemplified by a church that runs only one religious service for everyone, a politician who gives the same speech to everyone, and a museum that highlights the same exhibits to everyone. Mass fundraising mailings often follow this approach.

Undifferentiated marketing is "the marketing counterpart to standardization and mass production in manufacturing."[24] It is typically defended on three grounds. First, many naïve nonprofit marketers think of per-contact costs and argue that economies of scale in mass marketing will yield such an outcome. Production costs, research costs, media costs, and training costs are all kept low through promoting only one offering.

The second argument is one often set forth by government agencies who say that they are mandated to reach everyone. It is an argument that is echoed by many nonprofit organizations that say that their mission requires reaching everyone. The third argument is that it ensures that the approach "speaks with one voice," that there are not different signals and mixed messages that confuse target audiences.

What all of these arguments neglect is the fact that a single, mass market campaign typically needs to appeal to everyone and therefore never really speaks effectively to any segment. In our experience, nonprofit organizations end up making their approaches so bland and general that they don't speak to anyone. The alternative approach is to cram in so much information and motivations that target audiences are likely to be confused and intimidated.

Differentiated Marketing

Under differentiated marketing, an organization decides to operate in multiple segments of the market but designs separate offerings or marketing programs for each. There are two basic options here. One involves creating fundamentally different offerings for each chosen segment. For example, an art museum could develop a children's wing as a differentiated addition to its regular collection, or put on "singles nights" for unattached urban workers who want to avoid the "bar scene." The alternative option is to take an existing offering and not change it but position it differently to different segments. For example, the art museum could show how its basic art collection meets the needs of educators eager to teach their students about the history of various cultures. At the same time, it could position the collection to seniors in the general public who might be interested in a self-taught art-appreciation experience. Similarly, a hospital could take its basic set of services and emphasize (1) the "tender loving care" of its nurses to an elderly market, (2) the national reputations of its leading physicians to a young professional market, and (3) the cost efficiency of its entire operation to business HR officers.

Of course, many nonprofit marketing strategies require this approach. That is, if one is pushing a piece of legislation, one can't tailor the bill to each congressperson. But one can tailor the value proposition around the bill to each target audience member's interests and needs. Similarly, strategies aimed at media outlets typically must find angles in a given story or event that appeal uniquely to each TV station or magazine.

While the net effect of differentiated marketing is to create greater responsiveness, it can lead to higher costs of doing business since the organization has to spend more in offer management, marketing research, communication materials, advertising, and staff training for the given segments. However, a principal advantage of a differentiated strategy is that it allows the marketing manager to vary the amount of resources applied to each of the segments—*including zero!* Thus the manager can trade off the higher costs of differentiation by reducing the number of segments treated. The net effect is often that of achieving significantly higher returns for a given budget or a lower budget for given returns.

A good example of a differentiated strategy is found in the Office of the National Drug Control Policy campaign for "the Anti-Drug." It and one of its agencies, Fleishman Hillard, recognized that the Web is an important vehicle for reaching various market segments but that the "look and feel" of each web site should be

FIGURE 6-4 Focusing on Diverse Markets

Source: Center for School Safety. MN Institute of Public Health/Avert Center, 2006. www.miph.org/avert.

appropriate to each segment. Another approach is simply to target different demographic groups with essentially similar messages as demonstrated in Figures 6-4 and Figure 6-5.

Concentrated Marketing
Concentrated marketing occurs when an organization decides to divide the market into meaningful segments and devote its major marketing effort to only one or two segments. This is often referred to as *"niche marketing."* Instead of spreading itself thin in many parts of the market, it concentrates on serving a particular market segment very well. It can afford to develop greater knowledge of the market segment's needs

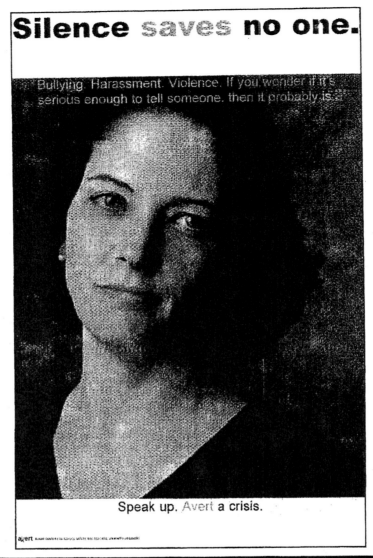

FIGURE 6-5   Focusing on Diverse Markets

Source: Center for School Safety. MN Institute of Public Health/Avert Center, 2006. www.miph.org/avert.

and behavior and it can achieve operating economies through specialization in production, distribution, and promotion. This type of marketing is done, for example, by a private museum that decides to concentrate only on African art, an environmental group like RARE that concentrates only on ecological issues in specific areas, or a private foundation that awards grants only to transportation researchers.

Concentrated marketing involves a higher than normal risk, in that the chosen segment may suddenly decline or disappear. The March of Dimes focused on polio for many years until the arrival of the Salk vaccine. It then shifted to birth defects and, eventually, to a broader focus on well babies.

Mass Customization

Technology—in particular the Internet—has allowed many marketers to adopt their strategies to individuals who seek out their offerings. Thus behavior change programs, such as smoking clinics, can promise to "tailor a program to your individual needs and lifestyles," whereas a marketer of a nicotine patch must use either a mass or differentiated approach. A significant benefit of this approach—besides its unique ability to respond to target audiences' data about themselves—is that it allows the "production" of the offering only "on demand." The latter obviously can produce significant scheduling and cost savings.[25]

Choosing Among Market Segmentation Strategies

The actual choice of a marketing strategy depends on specific factors facing the organization. If the organization has limited resources, it will probably choose concentrated marketing because it does not have enough talent and money to relate to the whole market and/or to tailor special services for each segment. If the market is fairly homogeneous in its needs and desires, the organization will probably choose undifferentiated marketing because little would be gained by differentiated offerings. If the organization aspires to be a leader in several segments of the market, it will choose differentiated marketing. If competitors have already established dominance in all but a few segments of the market, the organization might try to concentrate its marketing in one of the remaining segments. Many organizations start out with a strategy of undifferentiated or concentrated marketing and, if they are successful, evolve into a strategy of differentiated marketing. Some are able to evolve to mass customization.

If the organization elects to use a concentrated or differentiated strategy, it has to evaluate the best segment(s) to serve. Each should be evaluated in terms of the following:

- Its relative attractiveness
- The requirements for success within it
- The organization's strengths and weaknesses in competing effectively

The organization should focus on market segments that have intrinsic attractiveness and that it has a differential advantage in serving. A detailed example of a step-by-step approach for allocating resources across a hypothetical AIDS program is outlined in Andreasen's 1995 book, *Marketing Social Change.*

POSITIONING

As we made very clear in Chapter 3, nonprofit organizations are in competition. At the organization level, this may be competition with rival nonprofits for funds, volunteers, corporate support, or federal grants. At the campaign level, it might be competition with the status quo or other behaviors that are higher on the public agenda.[26] Many nonprofit managers would like to believe otherwise or think it is "not nice to compete," but it is a reality. Nonprofit marketing objectives *always* involve influencing the behavior of target audiences, and target audiences *always* have something else they can do including doing nothing. Potential donors can give money to a different charity, give their time to the charity instead of money, or not give at all. High schoolers can attend a different university or not go to college at all. Mothers in Zimbabwe can feed oral rehydration solution to their children when they have diarrhea, apply herbal potions, or do nothing at all.

In each case, there are alternatives *in the mind* of the target audience, and therefore it is in the mind where the marketer must compete.[27] This is the essential idea of positioning. Once segmentation and targeting steps are completed, one must understand where the nonprofit organization's proposed behaviors stand in the minds of target audiences. This set of perceptions is collectively referred to as the offering's *position.* For target audiences at the Precontemplation stage, the marketer's challenge may be to have *any* position at all—the audience here is simply not thinking about the option. For audiences at the Contemplation stage and beyond, marketers must position their offerings as a superior value proposition to those of their competition—which may simply be inaction or the status quo.

If done correctly, positioning research will tell marketers what the dimensions are on the alternative behaviors considered. For donors, they might be the personal relevance of a nonprofit's mission and its cost-effectiveness. For families dealing with childhood obesity, it may be the financial costs of actions and the likely intrafamily battling over courses of action. These dimensions can then give clues of what the nonprofit ought to do to increase "market share." Frequently research will tell marketers that they need to *reposition* themselves and/or their offerings.[28] In many cases, repositioning first requires that the organization itself and/or its proposed behaviors *become* different. In other cases, the reality is fine—it is the target audience's perception that is the problem. Many nonprofit service organizations fail to succeed at fundraising because they are not seen as different from their competitors. How do the following hypothetical nonprofits differ?

- The Reilly Smith Women's Center
- The Caring Woman
- Abused Wives Recovery Program
- Alice Torrance Women's Refuge
- Western Memorial Hospital's Women-Together Program

They all seem to have something vaguely to do with women. But why should someone become involved with—or give money to—one over another? What services do they offer? How are they staffed (do they need volunteers)? How are they funded (do they need contributions)? Whom do they serve? Who works there? Who supports them? Are they licensed? And so on. If any one of these organizations is to be successful in getting clients and getting volunteer and financial support, it must differentiate itself in the eyes of the target audience—that is, it must develop a more effective positioning. Similarly, in the developing world, an organization seeking to get mothers to use oral rehydration therapy must distinguish this approach to child survival from other means of achieving the target audience's ends, such as options from "traditional healers," and show that it provides superior value in terms of the target audience's own needs and wants.

It is also frequently the case that, as noted in earlier sections, the nonprofit marketer must position itself differently for different segments. Oral rehydration therapy may be positioned as a "modern" approach to urban women, as a way to please mothers-in-law to new wives, and as a means of quick recovery for village mothers with many other children and multiple household duties.

Measuring the Present Position

We all carry around with us a range of perceptions about products (iPods, Porsches, Macintosh computers), institutions (Harvard, McDonald's, the United Way, IBM), individuals (Britney Spears, Bill Clinton), our parents, our friends, and places (San Francisco, Thailand, Brooklyn).[29] However, in all of these cases, the term is used to apply to an *object*. Bill Clinton is smart, San Francisco is expensive, and Porsches are for rich people! It is certainly the case that those simple perceptions of objects can influence behavior. We may want to talk to very smart people, avoid expensive cities, and buy a Porsche to seem richer! The perception target audiences hold of "The Caring Woman," an organization that helps abused women, will affect whether they volunteer, donate, or even go there if they are a victim. But remember, the *perception of objects* should not be our ultimate concern. Our real interest is *what people think about the behaviors we are seeking to induce* relative to the object (e.g., donating, volunteering, voting legislation, writing about or using an organization's services).

Indeed, a narrow focus on the perceptions of objects may lead the marketer to erroneous conclusions and misdirected responses. An organization may be rated very high on a number of objective dimensions, such as size, success, or world impact. But individual volunteers may not want to go there because it is too intimidating! It is the latter that affects behavior.

As we noted in Chapter 4, it is likely that what we really need to know is information about the BCOS factors: how the target audience perceives the benefits and costs of the action or actions we are promoting—the value proposition, what they think others want them to do, and whether they think they can actually do the behavior(s)—their sense of self-assurance.

It is not unusual for target audiences to have serious misperceptions of the proposed behaviors. These misperceptions may be based on erroneous information or from stereotypes. A stereotype suggests a widely held perception that is highly distorted and simplistic and that leads to a favorable or unfavorable attitude toward the object or behavior (e.g., what will happen if you join a Boys & Girls Club that is heavily populated by "street kids?"). If a positioning is based on a stereotype, the marketer's challenge will be especially difficult (because logic or information may not help much). Such stereotypes are likely to keep target audience members in the Precontemplation stage for a very long time.[30]

Finally, we should note that a person's perception of an object or behavior does not incorporate his or her feelings toward it. Feelings may be driven by perceptions but they are different. One can believe that joining a YMCA will help one lose weight, but one may feel negatively about the atmosphere when one drops by, or "uncomfortable" about the kind of participants one finds there. Often feelings are more determinative than perceptions, especially when the behavior involves other human beings.[31]

Measuring the Positioning of Behaviors

Many methods have been proposed for measuring the perceptions of organizations and behaviors. Many of these were developed in the private sector and focus on objects. One of the places where they have found great value is in political campaigning. Local and national pollings typically try to understand how potential voters see particular candidates.[32] Ironically, one of the common approaches to political campaigns in the twenty-first century is to reposition the *competitor* through what is called negative advertising.[33] Fortunately, most of the approaches to measuring positions can readily be adapted to studying the perception of behaviors—voting for the candidate and not the candidate-as-object, volunteering for the charity and not the charity itself.

A fairly common approach to positioning research is the semantic differential. The semantic differential approach[34] offers respondents a set of bipolar adjectives and involves the following steps:

1. *Develop a set of relevant dimensions.* The researcher first asks people to identify the dimensions they would use in thinking about the behavior. People could be asked: "What things do you think of when you consider checking into a hospital for surgery?" If someone suggests "quality of medical care I would get," this would be turned into a bipolar adjective scale—say, "inferior medical care" at one end and "superior medical care" at the other. The scale could be rendered as a five- or seven-point scale. A set of relevant dimensions for checking into one of three hospitals is shown in Figure 6-6.

2. *Reduce the set of relevant dimensions.* The number of dimensions and the number of behaviors to be rated (going to hospital A, hospital B, etc.) should be kept small to avoid respondent fatigue. The typical procedure is for the researcher to conduct a pilot study and then employ a technique called *factor analysis* to remove redundant scales that fail to add much information.

3. *Administer the instrument to a sample of respondents in the Contemplation stage.* The respondents are asked to rate one behavior at a time. The bipolar adjectives should be arranged so as not to load all of the poor adjectives on one side.

4. *Average the results.* Figure 6-6 shows the results of averaging the respondents' pictures of going to Hospitals A, B, and C. Each hospital's perception with respect to the behavior is represented by a vertical "line of means" that summarizes how

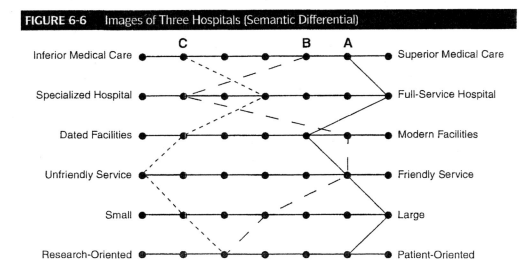

FIGURE 6-6   Images of Three Hospitals (Semantic Differential)

the average respondent sees going to that institution. Thus going to Hospital A is seen as encountering modern equipment, friendly staff, and superior doctors. Hospital C, however, is seen as subjecting one to dated equipment, impersonal staff, and inferior doctors.

5. *Check on the variance in perceptions.* A perception profile that portrays a series of mean values does not reveal how variable the perception actually is—the variance. If there were 100 respondents, did they all see going to Hospital B, for example, exactly as shown, or was there considerable variation? If there is low variance, we would say that the perception is highly *specific* and well-defined, and in the second case that the perception is highly *diffused* or *fuzzy*. The organization will want to analyze whether a highly variable perception is really the result of different subgroups rating the organization's offering differently but each with a highly specific perception or whether the offering is very ill-defined.

Positioning Alternatives

Once the organization analyzes the perceptions that target audiences hold about a specific behavior and perceptions of its major alternatives, the next step is developing a positioning strategy. To repeat: Effective positioning involves (1) understanding your present position, (2) understanding the position of your principal competition, (3) deciding on whether and how to differentiate your offerings from those of competition, and (4) making this positioning known to others. Al Reis and Jack Trout, in their book *Positioning: The Battle for Your Mind,*[35] argue that differentiation is largely a creative exercise carried out to achieve one of three strategies:

1. *Building upon your present strengths.* Avis capitalized creatively on what would appear to be a weak second-place status with its "We Try Harder" positioning. In a similar manner, a hospital with only limited facilities could emphasize its concern with delivering great care in a concentrated number of very important practice areas.

2. *Searching for a niche.* If every hospital in an area understaffs its emergency room and uses interns and residents to treat most patients there, an innovative hospital could position itself as having an emergency room that treats everyone quickly and personally, and with the highest-quality medical staff.

3. *Repositioning the competition.* As noted, political campaigns do this all the time with negative advertising. Wendy's hamburger chain challenged the opposition by asking "Where's the beef?" A hospital that emphasizes high-touch personal treatment could develop a positioning strategy that portrays competitors as high-tech but sterile environments treating patients as serial numbers.

If the organization decides that it does not like its present position, it needs to decide whether the problem is a matter of reality or of the *perception* of reality. If it is the former, then it must make fundamental changes before broadcasting to the world its new position. If it is a perception problem, then much more can be done with creative communications. Indeed, the entire nonprofit sector has something of a perception problem—there are too many look-alike organizations and campaigns. In addition, there is increased blurring between the sectors. For example, many people believe that Newman's Own is a charitable organization; it is not, although the company gives all of

FIGURE 6-7   Newman's Own

Source: Newman's Own. Used with permission of Newman's Own, Inc.

its profits to charity (see Figure 6-7). Similarly, many "social responsibility" mutual funds are not charitable operations but potential moneymaking ventures in the private sector. The former director of the Internal Revenue Service's Exempt Organizations Division, Mark Owens, once noted, "There is a danger of the charities starting to lose their special place and sense of purpose and becoming just part of the way business is done." He feels that the shift of many nonprofits toward generating more revenue from the marketing of products and services has contributed to this blurring of sector positions.[36]

One of the ways organizations effectively position themselves is through branding, a topic we will take up in Chapter 7.

Summary

The first steps in developing a marketing strategy designed to influence target audiences are segmenting the audience, choosing targets, and then developing a positioning strategy for the offering—what is called in the private sector the "STP challenge." Segmentation can help make quality, quantity, and timing decisions with regard to marketing strategies.

Segmenting the market requires partitioning the market into subgroups that are mutually exclusive, exhaustive, measurable, accessible, substantial, and possessing differential responsiveness. Bases for segmentation are general or behavior-specific, objective or psychological. Many nonprofit marketers think first of simple objective general measures such as age, income, geographical location, and marital status. Over the years, more complex general objective measures (such as social class, lifestyles, and family life cycle) and psychological general measures (such as values) have become more popular. Behavior-specific bases for segmentation include objective measures such as user status, usage rate, and loyalty. Psychological specific measures include beliefs about the benefits, and perceived sacrifices of the proposed behavior. Once markets are divided up, one of four approaches to targeting can be chosen: mass marketing, differentiated marketing, niche marketing, and mass customization.

The next step is positioning the organization and/or its offering. This requires research on target audience perceptions of relevant behaviors and the key dimensions on which the perceptions are based. The semantic differential is a useful research tool here. Marketers then need to look for potential positions that will achieve the maximum impact. Reis and Trout suggest three possibilities: Building upon your present strengths, searching for a niche, and repositioning the competition.

Questions

1. You are a marketing manager at the American Red Cross focused on increasing blood donations in the Chicago metro area. Explain how you would go about effectively segmenting the market. Define at least four segments and explain which one(s) you should target and why.
2. Provide an example of a nonprofit organization that segments according to the following complex general objective measures:
   a. Social Class
   b. Family Life Cycle
   c. Lifestyles
3. Explain the competitive landscape of a nonprofit organization focused on promoting healthy eating habits of young children in elementary schools. In other words, what are the alternatives in the mind of the target audience in this case? If you were the marketing manager, how would you position your organization and its mission against these alternatives?
4. Identify the four long-term market positions that an organization might strive for. If you were establishing a new graduate business school at a public university known for its public policy curriculum, which of these market positions might you pursue? Why?
5. How often should an organization consider its market positioning? What are some key events that might trigger an evaluation of one's market positioning? Explain the relationship between an organization's strengths and weaknesses and its market positioning.

Notes

1. "Devising Mailing Lists for Every Market," *Wall Street Journal,* May 7, 1991, p. B1; Stephen W. Colford, "Direct Mail Sophistication Aids Political Campaigns," *Advertising Age,* October 10, 1994, p. 15.

2. J. E. Williams and J. A. Flora, "Health Behavior Segmentation and Campaign Planning to Reduce Cardiovascular Disease Risk Among Hispanics," *Health Education Quarterly,* Vol. 22 (1995), pp. 36–48.

3. A basic review of the segmentation literature is found in Ronald E. Frank, William F. Massy, and Yoram Wind, *Market Segmentation* (Upper Saddle River, NJ: Prentice Hall, 1972). See also Yoram Wind, "Issues and Advances in Segmentation Research," *Journal of Marketing Research,* August 1978, pp. 317–337.

4. Pam Weisz, "The New Boom Is Colored Gray," *Brandweek,* January 22, 1996, p. 28; Paula Fitzgerald Bone, "Identifying Mature Segments," *Journal of Services Marketing,* Vol. 5, No. 1 (Winter 1991), pp. 47–60.

5. William Strauss and Neil Howe, *Generations: The History of America's Future* (New York: William Morrow/Quill, 1991). See also William Strauss and Neil Howe, *The Fourth Turning: An American Prophesy* (New York: Broadway Books, 1997) and Neil Howe and William Strauss, *Millennials Rising: The Next Generation* (New York: Vintage Books, 2000).

6. Dana James, "Census Says: Multiculti Works," *Marketing News,* July 30, 2001, pp. 1, 9–10.

7. Christopher H. Lovelock, "A Market Segmentation Approach to Transit Planning, Modeling, and Management," *Proceedings, Sixteenth Annual Meeting Transportation Research Forum* (1975), pp. 247–258.

8. Richard J. Semenik and Clifford E. Young, "Market Segmentation in Arts Organizations," in N. Beckwith, M. Houston, R. Mittelstaedt, K. Monroe, and S. Ward, (Eds.), *1979 American Marketing Association Educators' Conference,* (Chicago: American Marketing Association) pp. 474–478.

9. Carl Sewall and Paul B. Brown, *Customers for Life: How to Turn That One-Time Buyer into a Lifetime Customer* (New York: Doubleday, 2002); Rex Du and Donald R. Lehmann, "Customers as Assets," *Journal of Interactive Marketing,* Vol. 17, No. 1 (2003), pp. 9–24; Sunil Gupta, Donald R. Lehmann, and Jennifer A. Stuart, "Valuing Customers,: *Journal of Marketing Research,* Vol. 41 (February 2004), pp. 7–18.

10. Adrian Sargeant, "Using Donor Lifetime Value to Inform Fundraising Strategy," *Nonprofit Management and Leadership,* Vol. 12, No. 1 (2001) pp. 25–38.

11. Stephen J. Miller, "Source of Income as a Market Descriptor," *Journal of Marketing Research,* February 1978, pp. 129–131.

12. Alan R. Andreasen, "Acquiring a Lifestyle: An Innovation Adoption Approach," Working Paper, Department of Marketing, California State University, Long Beach, 1988.

13. Alan R. Andreasen, "Life Status Changes and Changes in Consumer Preferences and Satisfaction," *Journal of Consumer Research,* Vol. 11 (December 1984), pp. 784–794.

14. H. Luukinen, K. Koski, S-L Kivela, and P. Laippala, "Social Status, Life Changes, Housing Conditions, Health, Functional Abilities, and Life-Style as Risk Factors for Recurrent Falls Among the Home-Dwelling Elderly," *Public Health,* Vol. 110 (1996), pp. 115–118.

15. Alan R. Andreasen and Russell W. Belk, "Predictors of Attendance at the Performing Arts," *Journal of Audience Research,* Vol. 7, No. 2 (September 1980), pp. 112–120.

16. E. W. Maibach, A. Maxfield, K. Ladin, and M. Slater, "Translating Health Psychology into Effective Health Communication: The American Healthstyles Audience Segmentation Project," *Journal of Health Psychology,* Vol. 1 (1996), pp. 261–77.

17. Bob Minzesheimer, "You Are What You ZIP!" *Los Angeles,* November 1984, pp. 175–192.

18. Christina Del Valle, "They Know Where You Live—And How You Buy," *Business Week,* February 7, 1994, p. 89.

19. Milton J. Rokeach, *The Nature of Human Values* (New York: The Free Press, 1973).

See also Donald E. Vinson, J. Michael Munson, and Masao Nakanishi, "An Investigation of the Rokeach Value Survey for Audience Research Applications," in W. D. Perrault (Ed.), *Advances in Audience Research,* Vol. 4 (Atlanta, GA: Association for Audience Research, 1977), pp. 247–252; and Robert E. Pitts Jr. and Arch G. Woodside (Eds.), *Personal Values and Audience Psychology* (Lexington, MA: Lexington Books, 1984).

20. James O. Prochaska and Carlo C. DiClemente, "Stages and Processes of Self-Change of Smoking: Toward an Integrative Model of Change," *Journal of Consulting and Clinical Psychology,* 1983, pp. 51, 390–395.

21. Martha Farnsworth Riche, "Psychographics for the 1990s," *American Demographics,* July 1989, pp. 24–31, 53–54.

22. Richard P. Bagozzi, "Marketing as an Organized Behavioral System of Exchange," *Journal of Marketing,* October 1974, pp. 77–81; "Marketing as Exchange," *American Behavioral Scientist,* March–April 1978, pp. 535–556.

23. Wendell R. Smith, "Product Differentiation and Market Segmentation," *Business Horizons,* Fall 1961, pp. 65–72; Theodore Levitt, "Marketing Success Through Differentiation—Of Anything," *Harvard Business Review,* May–June 1980, pp. 83–91.

24. Smith, "Product Differentiation."

25. B. Joseph Pine III, Bart Victor, and Andrew C. Boynton, "Making Mass Customization Work," *Harvard Business Review,* September/October 1993, pp. 108–119.

26. J. J. Macionis, *Social Problems* (Upper Saddle River, NJ: Prentice Hall, 2002); M. McCombs, and D. Shaw, "The Agenda Setting Function of Mass Media," in D. L. Protess & M. McCombs (Eds.), *Agenda Setting: Readings on Media, Public Opinion, and Policymaking* (Hillsdale, NJ: Lawrence Erlbaum Associates, 1991), pp. 17–26.

27. Al Reis and Jack Trout, *Positioning: The Battle for Your Mind* (New York: Warner Books, 1982); Jack Trout and Steve Rivkin, *The New Positioning: The Latest on the World's #1 Business Strategy* (New York: McGraw-Hill Professional Publishing, 1997).

28. Glen L. Urban and Steven H. Star, *Advanced Marketing Strategy: Phenomena, Analysis, Decisions* (Upper Saddle River, NJ: Prentice Hall, 1991).

29. Philip Kotler, Donald H. Haider, and Irving Rein, *Marketing Places* (New York: The Free Press, 1993).

30. P. G. Devine, "Stereotypes and Prejudice: Their Automatic and Controlled Components," *Journal of Personality and Social Psychology,* Vol. 56 (1989), pp. 680–690.

31. Julie Edell and Marian Burke, "The Power of Feelings in Understanding Advertising Effects," *Journal of Audience Research,* Vol. 14 (December 1987), pp. 421–433; Meryl Gardner, "Effects of Mood States on Audience Information Processing," *Research in Audience Behavior,* Vol. 2 (1987), pp. 113–135.

32. M. P. Wattenberg, *The Rise of Candidate-Centered Politics.* (Cambridge: Harvard University Press, 1991); J. A. Krosnick, "Americans' Perceptions of Presidential Candidates: A Test of the Projection Hypothesis," *Journal of Social Issues,* Vol. 46 (1990), pp. 159–182.

33. S. Iyengar and S. Ansolabehere, *Going Negative* (New York: Free Press, 1995).

34. C. E. Osgood, G. J. Suci, and P. H. Tannenbaum, *The Measurement of Meaning* (Urbana: University of Illinois Press, 1957). Other image-measuring tools exist, such as *object sorting* [see W. A. Scott, "A Structure of Natural Cognitions," *Journal of Personality and Social Psychology,* Vol. 12, No. 4 (1969), pp. 261–278], *multidimensional scaling* [see Paul E. Green and Vithala R. Rao, *Applied Multidimensional Scaling* (New York: Holt, Rinehart and Winston, 1972)], and *item lists* [see John W. Riley, Jr. (Ed.), *The Corporation and Its Public* (New York: John Wiley, 1963), pp. 51–62].

35. Reis and Trout, *Positioning.*

36. "Reflections of a Top Regulator," *The Chronicle of Philanthropy,* February 24, 2000, pp. 35–37.

7 | BRANDING

THE SPECIAL OLYMPICS GOES HOLLYWOOD!

Building a brand sometimes requires taking risks. Consider the Special Olympics, an organization that gets disabled kids to undertake intense athletic competition. The idea for the Special Olympics event got its start with backyard competitions in 1962 at "Camp Shriver," the home of Eunice Kennedy Shriver. After expanding the idea to over 300 such camps nationally in the next few years, the Kennedy Foundation sponsored the first-ever Special Olympics in Chicago in the summer of 1968. Today, Special Olympics events are held every two years all around the world. In 2005 they were held in Nagano, Japan, at many of the 1998 Olympics venues. Over 1,800 athletes from 84 countries participated.

Despite wider and wider awareness, the Special Olympics as a brand was not particularly well defined, especially to younger people. Management believed that, by making a broader youth audience aware of the impressive feats of Special Olympics athletes, they would gain greater awareness and, by extension, greater acceptance of the handicapped in schools, the workplace, and even the mall.

How to reach young people? Obviously a major source of teens' information and opinions is the movies—especially scary or raunchy or otherwise outrageous movies. One of the best known creators of these kinds of films is the Farrelly brothers, Peter and Bobby, who were the writer/directors responsible for *Dumb & Dumber* and *There's Something About Mary*. By coincidence, it turned out that the Farrellys wanted to make a movie about a sleazy non-handicapped character who wanted to pretend to be disabled and win the Special Olympics pentathlon.

This seemed like a great opportunity to build the Special Olympics brand and to carry forward its key themes. But could the Farrellys be trusted? They were known for outrageous, cliché-challenging humor. Would they be respectful, while not necessarily sugarcoating the athletes and their accomplishments? Special Olympics agreed to go along provided that they had script approval and a technical advisor on the set. Although they did not get final approval of the movie, they decided to risk it anyway.

The result was *The Ringer*, starring Johnny Knoxville, released at Christmastime in 2005. The movie contained scenes filmed at the 2003 Special

Olympics in Dublin. It employed 150 handicapped athletes as extras and showed several events during the course of the movie.

The movie premiere generated $60,000 in revenues for Special Olympics and the film spawned over 1,000 newspaper articles. In January 2006, after the movie opened, the Special Olympics web site received 150,000 more hits than normal. MySpace had a special location where 400,000 people discussed the film.

Kristen Seckler, director of media and public relations at Special Olympics, concluded: "This was a great step in reaching a broad audience of people. In today's mass-media world, it's so hard to reach people, who are being inundated with many messages. We think this has given us the most broad awareness that we've ever gotten."

Source: Allison Stein Wellner, "Reel Appeal," *The Chronicle of Philanthropy,* April 6, 2006, pp. F-4–F-5.

Private sector marketers are fanatical about branding. They recognize that much of what they want to say about their offerings can be attached by consumers to a well-defined brand. The brand can symbolize a product, a service, or the organization itself. General Motors markets car brands like Pontiac and Corvette and service brands like Mr. Goodwrench. And "General Motors" itself constitutes a brand with specific connotations. Similarly, the nonprofit American Legacy Foundation is a brand (although not very well known) that also has the better-known truth® campaign. Brands are really shorthand in the target audience's mind for what the brand—and its sponsor—might offer. Thus a Volvo connotes safety, a BMW is a "driver's machine," and a Corvette is a "hot" car for mid-life males! Private sector marketers spend enormous amounts building and defending their brand. Nonprofit organizations are coming to realize that they have much to learn from their experiences.

James Twitchell likens branding to storytelling and argues that much of what we know about ourselves comes through brands.[1] Two-year-olds are more familiar with Tony the Tiger and Count Chocula than landmarks in their neighborhood. Teens wear must-have brands like Diesel or Juicy Couture. Adults identify themselves by the brand of cars they drive, the jeans they wear, and the beers or colas they drink. Brands send signals. We are an Apple computer person, communicate with our BlackBerry, drink Budweiser, wear Nikes, or are a Pepsi person.

Politicians are brands as are countries. The "United States" is a brand with both favorable and unfavorable connotations around the world. Twitchell argues that colleges like Stanford and Harvard are "megabrands," as are the Metropolitan Museum and some churches with huge congregations.

Not everyone thinks that branding is a good thing. Naomi Klein thinks of brands as bullies, homogenizing products and services.[2] Timothy Burke decries the attempts to get poor people in Zimbabwe to want Lifebouy soap,[3] and George Ritzer thinks that societies are becoming "McDonaldized!"[4] Twitchell talks of the "Nikefication of such social constructs as faith, history, art, place, politics, justice and culture and making them . . . analogous to blue jeans."[5]

But branding is here to stay. Our lives are simply too complex and brands provide great shorthand for products, services, and organizations.

To date, nonprofit organizations have used branding concepts and tools primarily to promote the organization itself. They have had less experience with branding at the campaign level but are recognizing the potential. They see their positioning challenge at the organization level to be one of differentiating their brand so as to get more donations, more volunteers, and more support from business organizations and politicians. They see the brand as potentially offering instant awareness and credibility. A brand like the American Cancer Society is valuable shorthand for a wide range of characteristics and outcomes. A brand can imply certain information (the American Red Cross is there in disasters). It can convey certain emotions (the Boys & Girls Clubs of America provide a safe place for kids). The organization can even have its own personality (the Salvation Army with its Christmas kettles and bell ringers).

Many other marketing challenges can be helped by thinking of them as branding issues. Clearly, political candidates are really brands.[6] Campaign managers seek to have the candidate represent a clear, recognizable "commodity" and spend a lot of effort of keeping the candidate "on message"—by which they mean "keep the brand image clear." In the 2006 mid-term U.S. elections, the brand "George W. Bush" evoked perceptions and feelings that clearly influenced the outcomes of many races. And, of course, the Bush brand connoted different things to different target audiences just as Corvettes connote different things to 40-year-olds and to today's teenagers.

Countries seeking to penetrate the travel market can be thought of as "destination brands."[7] Indeed, the majority of vacation advertising and much business development advertising treats destination countries or a specific region as brands with specific qualities. Bermuda says "Feel the Love." Orange County, California, says it has "Real People, Making a Real Difference."

Some authors have suggested that job applicants think of themselves as brands to be positioned and marketed.[8] Well-known marketing consultant Tom Peters says "Today, in the Age of the Individual, you have to be your own brand." He then goes on to outline: "Here's what it takes to be the CEO of Me Inc."[9] The homepages on FaceBook and MySpace are really examples of branding and brand positioning.

Developing, nourishing, and maintaining a brand is a challenging task. For many organizations that place great emphasis on their brand, it must be a continuing focus. For example, the Make-a-Wish Foundation is well-known and has a name that "says it all." Yet, in 1998–1999, it reconsidered its identity and brand positioning and launched a new brand strategy with PSAs, a new logo, and a revised web site to reposition itself. Similar efforts were recently undertaken by Goodwill Industries.[10]

Another example is Volunteers of America (VOA). The VOA is a very large organization with over 10,000 full-time professional staff and 40,000 volunteers reporting total income of over three-quarters of a billion dollars in 2005. Yet although it offers 300 different services and is one of the largest providers of affordable housing to the poor, few people know about it and what it stands for. As a consequence, VOA also undertook a branding campaign in 2000.

IS BRANDING A GOOD THING?

This is not to say that everyone in the nonprofit sector thinks that an emphasis on organizational branding and positioning is a good idea for nonprofits. In an editorial commentary in the June 14, 2001, edition of *The Chronicle of Philanthropy*, Vikki Spruill, executive director of SeaWeb, said the approach is misdirected:

> [T]he nonprofit world—especially advocacy groups working in fields such as health, education, and the environment—can ill afford to wage corporate-style branding battles. Instead of helping charitable groups work together to build a broad base of support from donors, volunteers and activists, branding becomes a barrier. It fosters unhealthy competition among nonprofit groups for visibility, promotes the hoarding of proprietary information, and leaves donors confused about how their support is making a difference.[11]

Spruill goes on to argue that branding, per se, is acceptable but it ought to be applied to causes, not individual organizations. Her position was countered by Kurt Aschermann, then senior vice president of the Boys & Girls Clubs of America. Aschermann's response in *The Chronicle of Philanthropy* is reported in Exhibit 7-1.

EXHIBIT 7-1

KURT ASCHERMANN, FORMER SENIOR VICE PRESIDENT FOR MARKETING AND COMMUNICATIONS OF THE BOYS & GIRLS CLUBS OF AMERICA, ON THE VALUE OF NONPROFIT BRANDING

Vikki Spruill's column . . . did a wonderful job explaining exactly why her premise is flawed. Ms. Spruill's comments, surprising as they may be coming from a former public-relations executive, nevertheless are prominent in nonprofit circles.

The idea that a nonprofit would perform like a for-profit in order to differentiate itself (create its own unique selling or service proposition, if you will) seems dangerous to Ms. Spruill because, she says, it will cause competition and perhaps result in questionable practices by nonprofit leaders. Yet in the end she asks nonprofits to consider three important questions that are at the heart of branding: Where does the soul of the organization

lie? What was the impetus behind its formation? What need did it fill then, and does that need still exist?

Sorry, Ms. Spruill, you just asked the three fundamental questions of branding. You are asking the nonprofit to simply determine what makes it unique, why it exists, and why someone should support it—all questions that need to be asked in order to create a brand, protect a brand, and enhance a brand's position in the marketplace.

In the for-profit world the questions might be, Why should this company exist? Why was the company formed? And why would the consumer buy the product the company makes or service it offers?

(continued)

EXHIBIT 7-1 (cont.)

The nonprofit-branding naysayers, in my experience, don't understand marketing or branding and see it as some kind of violation of charitable purity. In reality it is an exercise designed to help the nonprofit serve its constituents better by establishing its uniqueness in a very cluttered nonprofit world.

A decade ago Boys & Girls Clubs of America was a $180-million organization, with about 1,000 Clubs nationwide. In the early 90's, with the help of some very savvy board members who were CEO's of Fortune 500 companies, we created and implemented a very aggressive brand strategy.

The strategy required us first to determine who and what we were, second to focus messaging on a limited number of issues that describe what we do for kids, and third to seek corporate, government, and private partners to support our strategy and support our public-relations and information campaign on that strategy.

Result: In 2001 our combined budgets are more than $1 billion, and we are going to open our 3,000th Club this year. In a little more than 10 years we have increased our budgets by more than $800 million and we have opened over 2,000 new Clubs. In the past few years we have opened a new Boys & Girls Club every other day. Two years ago we opened 337 Clubs in one calendar year.

Now, there is no way I will say the brand strategy was single-handedly responsible for this unbelievable growth. But I sure can tell you the American donor knows who we are, what we stand for, and what we do to serve American children well. In short, they know what this brand stands for, and they're "buying."

Source: The Chronicle of Philanthropy, July 26, 2001. Reproduced with permission.

There is now very strong pressure to use branding and positioning concepts in a wide range of settings. Government agencies such as the Bureau of the Census and the Centers for Disease Control and Prevention have developed branding programs.[12] Universities are adopting the approach. Rensselaer Polytechnic Institute in Troy, New York, hired Media Logic, Inc., and launched a branding campaign in 1999 to raise the university's stature around a tag line—"Why not change the world?"[13]

Perhaps the most unusual branding initiative emerged when former U.S. Secretary of State Colin Powell said in 2001 that he wanted to "brand the State Department."

I am going to bring people into the public diplomacy function of the department who are going to change from just selling us in an old [U.S. Information Agency] way to really branding foreign policy. [His goal is] branding the department, marketing the department, marketing American values to the world, and not just putting out pamphlets."[14]

To further this agenda, Secretary Powell appointed Charlotte Beers, former chair of the J. Walter Thompson advertising agency, to the position of Assistant Secretary for Public Diplomacy. She was succeeded in 2005 by President Bush's confidant Karen Hughes, who holds the title of Under Secretary, Public Diplomacy and Public Affairs.

BRANDING FOR NONPROFITS[15]

Kevin Lane Keller, a leading authority on branding, and others have made it clear[16] that an organization's branded offerings can serve several roles:

1. Reflect a unique social contribution
2. Comprise a promise to target audiences and stakeholders
3. Reflect the organization's mission and values

In this sense, a brand is simply *shorthand* for the organization and its various offerings. It implies the value propositions inherent in "doing business" with them. Brands have equity and a smart marketing organization constantly builds and manages that equity. This effort has paid off for many nonprofit organizations. Interbrand carried out research for Habitat for Humanity International in 2002 and concluded that the brand was worth $1.8 billion—equal at the time to Starbucks! The United Way of America has an even more prominent brand, valued at $34.7 billion. This would put it ahead of Intel and Disney. PBS has a brand worth $5.4 billion.[17]

One might ask: Why calculate the value of a brand—except perhaps to allow the organization to pat itself on the back? Two answers are clear. First, identifying a nonprofit brand as having high value can motivate various stakeholders to contribute more—work harder, volunteer more, donate more—and reap personal pleasure from involvement with such a powerful and highly valued institution. The second answer is a commercial one. One of the authors witnessed during a conference in the late 1990s the fact that a great many major nonprofit organizations then had little idea of what they should charge a corporation for presence on the nonprofit's web site. This provoked a lengthy discussion and undoubtedly led to a number of formal assessments of brand value such as that for Habitat for Humanity International.

Nonprofit organizations have increasingly found that their brands can generate revenue *by themselves*! As we will discuss in Chapter 17, corporations have learned in the last 25 years the considerable value of being associated with leading nonprofit organizations. They want to be seen at their events, appear on their web pages, and send workers to volunteer and executives to serve on boards. And they are willing to pay for this opportunity just as they pay for other partnerships or find other profitable economic relationships in co-branding in the private sector (think of Oreos in Breyers Ice Cream!).

One advantage to Habitat for Humanity International of its impressive brand valuation is that it found that it could double the amount companies have to pay to be affiliated with it. Rather than discouraging partnerships, the income from such partnerships went from $16.4 million in 2002 to $40.9 million in fiscal 2004. United Way cites a major benefit of its high valuation to be reinforcement of present partnerships. The high value also motivates chapters to cooperate more closely with the parent organization whenever it conducts brand-related efforts. PBS has used its valuation for the same purpose.[18]

Worldwide, nonprofit brands are quite powerful. A study of consumer trust in brands in Europe and the United States by Edelman Public Relations found that the top four most trusted brands in Europe were actually *nonprofits*: Amnesty International, World Wildlife Fund, Greenpeace, and Oxfam. These organizations were more trusted than the top four corporate brands, Microsoft, Bayer, Ford, and

Coca-Cola. A parallel study in the United States found nonprofits farther down the list—World Wildlife Fund (#8), Amnesty International (#10), Greenpeace (#11), and Oxfam (#21). Quelch and Laidler-Kylander point out that nonprofit brands "have been gaining ground in the last three years."[19] They argue that the reasons leading nonprofit brands do so well on the trust dimension is attributable to five factors:

1. Target audiences are less suspicious of the motives of nonprofit organizations. (This is true, one assumes, even for organizations with which one does not agree.)
2. The organizations' missions are of high social value. Those who work for them believe in their causes and typically take under-market salaries because of it.
3. The leading organizations operate with one brand for all their activities. This provides opportunities for consistency in strategy and execution and less target audience confusion than, say, with all the sub-brands of Toyota or Nissan.
4. There is little ambiguity in the top nonprofit organizations' objectives and consistency over time. One knows what Greenpeace's goals are whereas it may be less clear what Samsung or Deutsche Bank are all about.
5. Because they deal with highly emotional issues—global warming, famine relief, and the like—nonprofit organizations can command significant media coverage that compensates for limited promotional budgets.

On the other hand, branding for nonprofit organizations can be more difficult than for corporations. One challenge is the budget limitation most face. Second, their missions are often so general as to sometimes occasion frequent changes in direction and interest, which makes the brand seem inconsistent. Third, as we have emphasized in this book, nonprofit organizations have to address multiple stakeholders. Some publics may think that efforts to build a brand are wasting scarce resources. Further, it may not be clear what would be the ideal brand position to impress corporate sponsors *and* volunteers *and* those who are being directly served. Fourth, the norms in the nonprofit world are that nonprofits should not compete—although, as we note, they really compete in the minds of donors, volunteers, and the like. Many conservative nonprofit executives believe that the opportunities to overtly compare oneself to a rival are "not good form."

Finally, when nonprofit organizations try to attach their organizational brand to specific campaigns, they are often invisible. Does a starving victim of the Asian tsunami know that her family got help from CARE and not Oxfam or medical help from the International Red Cross and not Medecins Sans Frontiers? Does someone whose behavior is changed by a dramatic ad to prevent SIDS or a call to a diabetes hotline know who sponsored the message? In such contexts, building a brand becomes especially hard. In such cases, how does one measure impacts that the nonprofit has so that one can justify a particular brand valuation?

BUILDING A BRAND

A critical problem that Keller and, in a recent paper, Sargeant and Ford make clear is that branding for a social enterprise is not enough. Too many nonprofits have brands that are very much like others. To be successful, a brand must have distinctiveness. According to Sargeant and Ford, this means a "unique selling proposition" (a term with a long history in marketing) and a personality.[20] The latter should flow from the organization's mission, its offerings, and its values. Most nonprofits share a number of traits that mark the sector—caring, compassionate, and committed to "making a difference." Thus basing a branding strategy on these traits is not differentiating. Research on nine UK nonprofit organizations suggested that strong brands will:

- Stimulate a variety of emotions in their donors
- Have a distinctive media voice
- Offer a different type of service
- Evoke a sense of tradition

There are clear steps one ought to take to create—or in some cases reposition—a nonprofit organizational or campaign brand.[21]

Step 1: Decide on what you want the brand to do and who the key target audiences are for whom branding is important—donors, corporations, volunteers, staff, and/or the general public. Specify your major competitors, whose brand image you also want to understand.

Step 2: Conduct qualitative research among small samples of the key target audiences to understand how the various competitive brands—including yours—are now perceived. In particular, learn what the key dimensions for evaluation would be.

Step 3: Conduct quantitative research among the same target audiences. Analyze the results to reveal the most important dimensions and where each competitor "stands" in various target audiences' perception of the competitive space. (Remember: You want to learn about the "map" in their heads.)

Step 4: Determine whether you are satisfied with your current position and, if not, where change is necessary. Define the desirable position in which you want to be. This should include the "brand promise" and how you want the various target audiences to think and feel about the brand. Make sure that the positioning is robust enough for multiple uses—for example, fundraising and corporate partnering.

Step 5: Get consensus from staff and board about the future direction.

Step 6: Develop and pretest an integrated strategy.

Step 7: Monitor the impact of the branding strategy. (This should be a never-ending task.)

According to Keller,[22] there are nine important concerns on which one must focus:

1. Does the brand have sufficient salience? The brand may be well-positioned among those familiar with it. But if salience is at a very low level, it will be of little value in achieving organization objectives.
2. Does the brand have a fuzzy image? As noted in the previous chapter, the modal brand position may be exactly what the organization wants, but research may show that perceptions are widely varied across key audiences. The corporate world may see it one way, women another, Asians a third, and so on. One measure of fuzziness would be the amount of variation in quantitative judgments in a systematic field study.

3. Does the brand achieve what Keller calls "points of parity?" In many competitive categories, there are traits that all of the competitors must have at some minimum level of delivery simply to be considered for support. Thus relief programs must be able to react within hours of a crisis. A university must offer a basic liberal arts curriculum. A hospital must have a well-staffed 24-hour emergency service. A brand must be free of scandals.

4. Determine whether the brand has a reality problem or a perception problem. If a hospital really has poor people skills, this must be remedied before any kind of communications campaign can be contemplated to heighten awareness of the brand. Dazzling communications cannot fix a fundamental problem.

5. Remember that a brand generates both *perceptions* and *feelings* and one needs to track both. Visiting an art gallery exposes one to great art but surly guards can leave one feeling annoyed and unwelcome. A classy banquet for key donors not only recognizes contributions but also can make benefactors feel proud of their association with the brand.

6. Appoint a "brand champion." A major branding effort can fizzle if no one takes major responsibility for it and is accountable for its results.

7. Make sure everyone is "singing the same song." There needs to be an internal communications plan as well as an external one. This can be a particular challenge for an organization with many separate chapters, especially if some are in other countries. The Boys & Girls Clubs of America faced many branding challenges because each local club is autonomous and has its own board—and sometimes a mind of its own. Getting them all to speak about the brand's core values and even use the same typeface was a long struggle. An even more difficult problem faces the international operations of United Way. It has affiliates in 40+ countries but, in many cases, the local organization doesn't even call itself by the United Way brand name. The operation in Manila is called the Community Chest, in Israel it is Matan, and in Peru it is Caminando Juntos.

   Cynthia Round describes the challenges that United Way faced in building brand support within its U. S. network in Exhibit 7-2.

8. If resources permit, use a branding specialist like Interbrand to help create, strengthen, or reposition the brand. Interbrand guided the Habitat and United Way studies mentioned earlier and has worked with other nonprofit organizations like the American Cancer Society. Besides offering expertise, an outside consultant can bring a fresh perspective to an organization, unencumbered by years spent inside the operation that can lead to stultification and a lack of imagination.

9. Monitor how the branding program is doing. Kurt Aschermann formerly of the Boys & Girls Clubs of America believes strongly that a brand must constantly be defended. This means defense inside the organization from long-timers who have their own agendas and from outside challenges. Certainly potential—or real—scandals can damage a brand if not effectively managed. The American Red Cross from time to time faces such challenges in its handling of donations, receiving criticism for its treatment of the 9/11 donations and praise for its handling of the Katrina catastrophe. Recently, Habitat for Humanity International faced challenges to its brand when its founder, Millard Fuller, was dismissed amid allegations of sexual harassment.

EXHIBIT 7-2

CYNTHIA ROUND, EXECUTIVE VICE PRESIDENT, BRAND LEADERSHIP, UNITED WAY OF AMERICA ON DRIVING BRAND VALUE THROUGHOUT THE ORGANIZATION

United Way is a 120-year old community-based organization dedicated to tackling the underlying causes of the critical human issues facing communities: helping children and youth achieve their potential, improving people's health and promoting financial stability among working families and individuals. United Way's strength is in its relationships and ability to mobilize the whole community—business, faith groups, nonprofits, civic organizations, policy makers, and ordinary citizens—into collective action that creates lasting change.

A recent assessment by Interbrand, Inc, valued the United Way brand at $34.7 billion, placing it among the top 10 most valuable global brands. The key driver of this brand value was identified by Interbrand as "local impact." This local effectiveness is the core strength of the United Way brand, while the diversity of over 1,300 independent community organizations is also the challenge from a brand management perspective. The professional brand valuation by Interbrand, as the recognized authority in the business sector, served to inspire local United Way organizations to think more about the brand as a strategic asset that must be actively and collectively managed. Consistency in brand identity,

messaging, and marketing are important, but United Way is equally focused on consistency of a positive brand experience.

The brand experience starts with making visible the work—the measurable results achieved in the community—and then building a personal, relevant relationship with investors and volunteers that extends year round, beyond an annual pledge in the workplace. Civic engagement and advocacy of public policy are other dimensions of the experience that enable individuals and companies to get involved and make a difference in their local communities.

Local United Ways' commitment to common mission, values, and accountability standards are reinforced by national brand identity and graphics standards, and marketing and message strategies and tools. A brand management intranet is an important channel to align both local United Ways and corporate partners with the latest brand thinking and best practices from around the country. Updated Standards of Excellence for United Way include Relationship Building/Brand Management as one of five core components. This is how brand value is driven throughout the organization to staff and to the more than 1 million volunteers.

A few years back, the American Cancer Society undertook an organization-wide effort to rethink and reposition the brand. Initial research showed that the Society was seen as:

- Respected and trusted
- Committed and dedicated
- Scientific, conservative, and safe
- Philanthropic and unfocused

These traits might seem laudable—and certainly would appeal to insiders—but the Society was concerned, particularly about the last dimension and by the general research finding that it was like a "stodgy old man." After an extensive process following the steps previously outlined, the Society now positions itself as:

- Admired and influential
- Inspiring
- Leading through empathy
- Results-driven and worthy of investment

Adopting an entirely new brand for an ongoing campaign may sometimes be necessary. Robert Denniston, head of the Office of National Drug Control Policy's anti-drug program, describes their need to move away from its "The anti-drug" branding to a new approach based on a new brand "Above the Influence." Sometimes a rebranding effort is necessary to fit an organization or a campaign more clearly into a specific niche. The Fuller Museum of Art in Brockton, Massachusetts, believed that it was not in a unique position to compete in a tough New England art world. So it decided in 2004 to narrow its focus to contemporary crafts and rename itself the Fuller Craft Museum, with a tag line "Let the art touch you." As a result, by 2005, attendance at the openings of exhibits had grown 20 times and attendance revenues had grown 73 percent compared to fiscal 2003. There were also more donations and more people participating in museum tours.[23]

Twitchell suggests that even President George W. Bush could be considered to be someone who undertook a political and personal rebranding. He was born and grew up in New England as part of the Eastern Blue Blood Establishment. He went to Andover, Yale, and Harvard and was inducted into the exclusive Skull & Bones Society while at Yale. Yet he came to the 2000 elections as a born-again Christian, Texas "good ol' boy," and a former oilman and baseball team owner. And he won![24]

Branding Details

The Brand Name

There are a number of choices an organization has to make up front. It has to choose a name for itself or for a campaign it wants to brand. Sometimes the name simply must be changed as when Philip Morris found that it would be better to call itself Altria. It is an issue that faces many nonprofit organizations that have generic names. It is a challenge for the American Cancer Society, American Heart Association, American Lung Association, and American Diabetes Association. For example, just how does the American Diabetes Association differ from these other real organizations:

- The Diabetes Action Research and Education Foundation
- Juvenile Diabetes Foundation International
- International Diabetes Federation
- Defeat Diabetes Foundation, Inc.
- Children with Diabetes Foundation

Some nonprofit organizations have names that are memorable, motivational, and, in some cases, that capture the mission of the organization. Examples include the Make-a-Wish Foundation, the Hole-in-the-Wall Gang (Newman's Own Charity), and Operation Smile.

The Logo

The logo of an organization in many ways represents the "look" of the organization. Elegant typography would be appropriate for the classical arts and a funky logo for a children's group. Again, this is a field in which there are many experts who can be called upon to help. As with many aspects of a branding effort, pretesting of logo alternatives—and other branding elements—should be essential. The "Viva Vitality" logo and character is a way to make exercise something "cool" for young people (see Figure 7-1).

The Slogan

An important challenge for an organization that seeks to get "top of the mind" recall from various target audiences is a compelling slogan. The danger here is using phrases that are generic or that can't be owned by the sponsoring organization. Thus slogans that begin with "leading the way in . . ." or "the nation's leading . . ." are bound to be bland and easily copied. Many examples of generic slogans can be found. For example, the National Highway Transportation and Safety Administration's slogan is "People Helping People." (Think of all the organizations to which this could apply!) Five years ago, AARP, the world's largest membership organization, was eager to change its slogan which at the time was "Creating positive social change." Research found that the slogan represented a need that was being met elsewhere, didn't have any clear connection to AARP or its core competencies, and lacked emotional connection to

---

FIGURE 7-1   Making Exercise Cool

Source: Paliser Health Region.

stakeholders or potential supporters. Considerable research both inside and outside the organization resulted in a new slogan, "The Power to Make it Better," that better reflects AARP capabilities and its mission. And AARP continues to update its mission and focus as described in a new book by CEO Bill Novelli.[25]

Other organizations believe a slogan can help reposition a nonprofit organization and address competition directly. A good example is the Carey School of Business at Arizona State University. Located in Phoenix, it worried about a major competitor, the University of Phoenix. The latter is a commercial venture that delivers much of its content over the Internet. And it is not accredited by the major business school accrediting organization. The Carey school decided to develop a slogan "Get a Real MBA." The slogan was initially seen as strictly confrontational. However, it is being continued and strengthened by messages about what makes a Carey degree real.[26]

The "Look"

It is critical that all of the visual elements surrounding the brand look the same. Many corporations patent or copyright their own color or copyright the shape of their buildings (McDonald's). Great branding campaigns make sure that even simple things like posters and stationery have a consistent look. The need for such consistency can often be made clear to CEOs or nonprofit boards by simply showing branding messages today. One of the turning points in one effort to rebrand a major nonprofit organization was when those leading the branding study brought senior managers into a room on whose walls were pasted a frightenly wide range of executions of the organization name, colors used in materials, type fonts, and so on. The upshot was a branding plan that included very careful specification of what each division must do when it creates visual communications, down to the shape of graphics on posters. Policing this consistency has proved to be challenging.

Sometimes a brand has a "look" or graphic that has both clear meaning and wide acceptance but which the organization finds limiting. This is the example of CARE. The organization's logo is the word "CARE" appearing just as it would be when stamped on a shipping package. This look has been consistent for much of the organization's history. Indeed, the success of the brand and its logo is reflected in the popular term for a collection of items given to help someone else. It is called "a care package." Throughout its history, CARE has focused on providing help—care packages—to the needy, especially in famine regions or after catastrophes. However, current leadership has felt constrained by this identity. It has become concerned about the basic conditions underlying the poverty and hunger CARE responds to and would like to do something about these fundamentals. Should it do so, the present logo will be constraining. A solution may require establishing a separate division with a different brand name and look. But, of course, CARE will find it hard to transfer its parent organization's credibility and reputation to the brand sibling without extensive branding effort.

The Brand Promise

One of the things required of a brand, its logo, and its slogan is that they make clear what the brand stands for. In the case of AARP, the organization describes itself as follows: "The 35 million members of AARP are a powerful force for positive social change. Using our collective will, influence, and good intentions, we make things better not just for ourselves but for everyone." This statement provides a canopy for its efforts to provide direct services to members like insurance and travel options; its lobbying efforts at the federal and state levels; and its social change efforts to get seniors to exercise more, get involved with their grandkids, and so forth.

The Spokesperson

Sometimes brands are attached to persons. The Hole-in-the-Wall Gang is attached to Paul Newman; Habitat for Humanity International is associated with former President Jimmy Carter (although he is not a board member or formal spokesperson for the organization); and many charities are associated with their CEOs or sponsors such as Bill Drayton and Ashoka or Bill Gates and his foundation. Cartoon characters have historically been very powerful brand spokespeople in the nonprofit arena—often much better known than the organization that sponsors them. There is McGruff the Crime Fighting Dog (National Crime Prevention Council) Vince and Larry the Crash-test Dummies (National Highway Transportation and Safety Administration), and Smokey Bear (U.S. Forest Service). Finally, there are many foundations associated with corporations that started them and carry the implications this brings. Examples from the Internet field include the Google and Yahoo! Foundations.

Sometimes spokespeople are effective externally but, if they are members of the organization, there may be jealousy and resentment. *Washingtonian* magazine noted that well-known author Bob Woodward nominally works for the *Washington Post* but rarely shows up there. Some staffers wonder why the paper employs him. "An explanation came from David Carr, media critic for the *New York Times*, who described Woodward as 'a hood ornament' for the *Post*."[27]

Symbols

A branding innovation in the nonprofit sector frequently is the use of symbols to identify a campaign. Often, these symbols provide a direct benefit to supporters because the symbols allow them to identify themselves as such. Bumper stickers and now license plates allow someone to signal support of a nonprofit organization, a social issue, or a political candidate or party. Wearable symbols have become very popular and quite successful in recent years. Perhaps the best known is the pink ribbon developed for the Susan G. Komen Foundation—mimicking the AIDS activists' red ribbon concept—to show support for breast cancer research. There are also pink product and country tie-ins. A great many companies have produced pink products. There have been pink cosmetics, a pink George Foreman Grill, a pink Dirt Devil, and a pink package of Tic-Tacs.[28] In Sierra Leone, there is a Pink Charity Fund.

Color has been the basis for other symbolic branding efforts. The American Heart Association has been frustrated that the public thinks that breast cancer is the number one killer of women. But in fact, heart disease kills 12 times as many women. One response has been to attempt to appropriate the color red. There was a Red Dress push as part of the HeartTruth campaign of the National Insitutes of Health. (www.nhlbi.nih.gov/health/hearttruth/).[29] But there is now a potential source of public confusion with the "red" identification with heart health in the recent announcement by Bono and others of the launching of an international campaign featuring red products to support HIV/AIDS work in Africa. The campaign includes products from Converse, the Gap, and Georgio Armani as well as a red American Express card (initially available only in the United Kingdom). Other celebrities including Oprah Winfrey have joined Bono's efforts.[30]

A similar problem exists with the colorful wristbands made famous by the Lance Armstrong Foundation as part of its Livestrong campaign. There are now colored wristbands for The One campaign (global AIDS and poverty), March of Dimes (saving babies), Musicians for Mental Health (Check Your Head), the Autism Society (Awareness), Operation Military Pride, the Children's Hospital of Orange County, and the American Lung Association.[31]

Living the Brand

It is nearsighted to think of the brand and what goes with it as merely a visual communications challenge. In organizations like the American Cancer Society or the American Red Cross, the nonprofit's staff is a major factor representing the brand. If the organization's slogan is "people helping people" but the telephone staff gives the impression that they are impatient to get to the next caller, millions of dollars in brand-building can go down the drain. Unfortunately, the authors have sometimes seen a tendency for long-time nonprofit staffers to assume that branding is a fad that will blow over. They need not worry about "living the brand" and all they need to do is "play along" for the time being. But good branding programs with strong brand champions will see that internal marketing needs to be a key part of a brand repositioning strategy.

Campaign Branding

Of course, not all branding today among nonprofit organizations is at the organizational level. An increasing number of nonprofits—and governmental agencies—have branded individual campaigns. This, of course, in many cases is a challenge since one is trying to brand something that is a behavior. Many nonprofits do have products as part of the behavioral influence campaign and these are branded. UNICEF cards carry their name. Condoms in many international contraceptive social marketing programs are branded. Population Services International has health-related programs in more than 60 developing countries. One country, India, has the following brands in its portfolio:[32]

Rishta female condom since 2005
ACT 1 STI kit since 2004
Preventol emergency contraception since 2004
Key Clinic Network of physicians providing improved STI services since 2004
Safewat safe water system since 2002
Vitalet-Preg iron-folic acid since 2002
New Born clean delivery kits since 2002
Saadhan voluntary counseling and HIV testing centers since 2002
Depo-Provera injectable contraceptives since 2001
KamaSutra condoms since 2000
Neotral Orange oral rehydration solution since 1998
Masti condoms since 1998
Mala-D oral contraceptives since 1997
Neotral oral rehydration solution since 1995
Pearl oral contraceptives since 1991
Deluxe Nirodh condoms since 1988

Some nonprofit brands are brands of services, such as voluntary counseling and HIV testing. In the United States, brands are used to identify and distinguish educational programs, counseling centers, and religious institutions. Indeed, so-called megachurches such as the Willow Creek (nondenominational) Community church have been accused of using too much marketing and offering "religion-lite." Willow Creek offers branded programs such as CARS that provides repaired cars for people without transportation, Eagles Nest for special needs kids, and Healing Hearts for women who have suffered sexual abuse or sexual assault.[33]

Examples of branded programs designed to influence behaviors also abound. We have already noted the truth® campaign of the American Legacy Foundation, which has had a major impact on teen smoking in the last six years.[34] Other branded campaigns of note are state-level *Click It or Ticket* programs. Rothschild and others have found success in an anti-drunk driving program in Wisconsin called *Road Crew*.[35]

HIV/AIDS programs have sometimes been branded. A program in South Africa called loveLife is described as follows:

> The non-profit has an annual budget of approximately 200 million rand (US$26.6M) and is funded by the Kaiser Family Foundation, the Bill and Melinda Gates Foundation, the Nelson Mandela Foundation, the South African government and the Global Fund for HIV/AIDS, TB and Malaria, as well as a range of corporate partnerships. Started in 1999, loveLife began life as an education program but is now referred to as a brand, and applies branding techniques to fight HIV/AIDS.[36]

A great many other campaign branding examples are found on various resource-rich web sites, including the following:

Science Panel on Interactive Communication and Health
www.health.gov/scipich
American Communication Association (Links to many communications sites)
www.uark.edu/~aca/acastudiescenter.html
University of Iowa Department of Communications Studies (Links to communications resources)
www.uiowa.edu/~commstud/resources/
Purdue University (Health Communications programs)
www.sla.purdue.edu/healthcomm/Research.html
Centers for Disease Control and Prevention (Risk info)
www.atsdr.cdc.gov/HEC/primer.html
Centers for Disease Control and Prevention (Health Communication)
www.cdc.gov/od/oc/hcomm
National Cancer Institute (Communications research)
www.dccps.nci.nih.gov/communicationscenters
National Youth Anti-Drug Campaign
www.mediacampaign.org
Health Canada's social marketing web site
www.hc-sc.gc.ca/hppb/socialmarketing/

Social Marketing Manual, Ohio University
   oak.cats.ohiou.edu/~cm130791/social/social.htm
Tools of Change
   www.toolsofchange.org
Resources developed by Weinreich Communications, California
   members.aol.com/weinreich/index.html
Communications Initiative (in Spanish)
   www.commintit.com/la/
Proyecto Acción SIDA de Centroamerica
   www.pasc.org
Centers for Disease Control and Prevention Spanish web site
   www.cdc.gov/spanish/
National Social Marketing Strategy (UK)
   www.nsms.org.uk/public/default.aspx

Summary

Branding is a concept drawn from the private sector that can apply to an organization, a campaign, a country, a person, or a political candidate. The brand can reflect a unique social contribution, comprise a promise to your target audiences and stakeholders, and reflect the organization's mission and values. Steps in creating a brand involve understanding the target audience and how they view you versus your competition. Then one needs to carefully choose a brand name, logo, spokesperson, the brand promise, symbols, slogan, and your brand "look." Staff support is critical because they must "live the brand." Launching—or repositioning—a brand then requires careful monitoring.

A high-value brand can help in securing both many corporate partners and substantial payments from them for the privilege. It is also valuable in motivating staff, volunteers, and donors. Protecting the brand is also very important and requires constant vigilance.

Questions

1. Take a nonprofit brand with which you are familiar, but one that has clear competitors at the brand or fundraising level. What factors would you use in assessing the value of the brand?
2. Suppose you did a brand perception study for your organization as a major brand. However, your volunteers and your donors see the brand very differently. What would you do about this situation? If you say "do nothing," justify this reaction.
3. Pick a major brand—either a campaign or an organization. Suggest three potential spokespeople for the brand and indicate how you would evaluate them.
4. Suppose your organization had a major embarrassing news report about unethical behavior on the part of the organization's chief financial officer. You are the brand manager charged with guarding and advancing your brand. What steps would you take?
5. The Office of National Drug Control Policy is switching branding for its anti-drug campaign. Is this a good idea?
6. Pick a politician or country that does a good job branding itself. Explain why you conclude this.

Notes

1. James Twitchell, *Branded Nation* (New York: Simon & Schuster, 2004).

2. Naomi Klein, *No Logo: Taking Aim at the Brand Bullies* (New York: St. Martin's/Picador, 1999).

3. Timothy Burke, *Lifebouy Men, Lux Women* (Durham, NC: Duke University Press, 1996).

4. George Ritzer, *The McDonaldization of Society* (Thousand Oaks, CA: Sage Publications, 2004).

5. Twitchell, *Branded Nation*, p. 299.

6. See any issue of the *Journal of Political Marketing* (www.haworthpress.com/store/product.asp?sku=J199). Also, "Editorial: Dems now Must Manage Brand," *Advertising Age*, November 13, 2006, p. 18.

7. Nigel J. Morgan and Annette Pritchard, "Destination Branding and the Role of Stakeholders: The Case of New Zealand," *Journal of Vacation Marketing*, Vol. 9, No. 3 (2003), pp. 285–299.

8. Michael Solomon and Liz Harris-Tuck, *Brand You* (Upper Saddle River, NJ: Pearson Education Inc., 2005).

9. Tom Peters, "The Brand Called You," *FastCompany*, Issue 10 (August 1997), p. 83.

10. Tom Pope, "Make-A-Wish Redesign," *The NonProfit Times*, July 15, 2000, pp. 4–6; Tom Pope, "Repositioning Goodwill through TV Ads," *The NonProfit Times*, March 15, 1999, pp. 1, 4.

11. Vikki Spruill, "Build Brand Identity for Causes, Not Groups," *The Chronicle of Philanthropy*, June 14, 2001, pp. 45–46.

12. Susan Kirby, Melissa Kraus Taylor, Vicki S. Friemuth, and Claudia Fishman Parvanta, "Identity Building and Branding at CDC: A Case Study," *Social Marketing Quarterly*, Vol. VII, No. 2 (June 2001), pp. 16–35.

13. Jamie Smith, "Put Out the Word: University Sets Branding Example," *Marketing News*, May 7, 2001, pp. 6–8.

14. Ira Teinowitz, "Affairs of State: Looking for Love through Branding," *Advertising Age*, April 9, 2001, p. 8.

15. Some of the material in this section is derived from presentations made by Kurt Aschermann, then of the Boys & Girls Clubs of America, and Cynthia Currence of the American Cancer Society.

16. Kevin Lane Keller, *Strategic Brand Management*, 2nd ed. (Upper Saddle River, NJ: Prentice-Hall, 2003); David A. Aaker, *Building Strong Brands* (New York: The Free Press, 1996).

17. Holly Hall, "What's in a Charity's Name? *The Chronicle of Philanthropy*, August 5, 2004, pp. 31–32.

18. Ibid.

19. John A. Quelch and Nathalie Laidler-Kylander, *The New Global Brands: Managing Non-Government Organizations in the 21st Century* (Mason, OH: South-Western, 2006), p. 9.

20. Adrian Sargeant and John B. Ford, "The Power of Brands, *Stanford Social Innovation Review*, Winter 2007, pp. 41–47.

21. See also Philip Kotler and Nancy Lee, *Marketing in the Public Sector: A Roadmap for Improved Performance* (Upper Saddle River, NJ: Prentice-Hall, Inc. 2007).

22. Kevin Lane Keller, *Strategic Brand Management*, 2nd ed. (Upper Saddle River, NJ: Prentice-Hall, 2003).

23. Deborah L. Vence, "The Art of the Craft," *Marketing News*, November 15, 2005, pp. 10–11.

24. Twitchell, *Branded Nation*, p. 7.

25. Bill Novelli (with Boe Workman), *50+: Igniting a Revolution to Reinvent America* (New York: St. Martin's Press, 2006).

26. Sharon Shinn, "Attention Grabbers," *BizNet*, March/April 2006, pp. 22–29.

27. Harry Jaffe, "What Do You Call a Star Who Stays at Home?" *Washingtonian*, November 2006, p. 16.

28. Michelle Woo, "Breast Cancer Fight Sees Pink," *The Arizona Republic*, October 1, 2005.

29. Paula Andruss, "'Think Pink' Awareness Much Higher than Threat," *Marketing News*, February 15, 2006; Jesse Hempel, "Selling a Cause? Better Make It Pop," *Business Week*, February 13, 2006.

30. Shamus Toomey and Rummana Hussain, "Oprah, Bono Spree to Support 'Red' HIV Cause," *Chicago Sun Times*, October 13, 2006.

31. "The Bandwagon," *People*, July 4, 2005, p. 100.
32. www.psi.org/where_we_work/india.html (retrieved October 11, 2006).
33. www.willowcreek.org/welcome.asp (retrieved October 11, 2006).
34. M. C. Farrelly, K. C. Davis, M. L. Haviland, et al., "Evidence of a Dose—Response Relationship Between 'truth' Antismoking Ads and Youth Smoking Prevalence," *American Journal of Public Health*, Vol. 95 (2005), pp. 425–431.
35. M. L. Rothschild, B. Mastin, and T. W. Miller, "Reducing Alcohol Related Crashes Through the Use of Social Marketing," *Accident Analysis and Prevention*, Vol. 38, No. 6 (November 2006), pp. 1218–1230.
36. Ron Irwin, "LoveLife: Ground Breaking," *BrandChannel.com*, September 8, 2003. (Retrieved from www.brandchannel.com/features_profile.asp?pr_id=143 on October 11, 2006.)

SECTION III

DESIGNING THE MARKETING MIX

8

VALUE PROPOSITIONS: MANAGING THE ORGANIZATION'S OFFERINGS

CABS FOR SENIORS

The elderly frequently need transportation help. They often have poor eyesight, poor reaction times, or basic mobility problems. But, like all of us, they need to go shopping, get haircuts, and maybe even go out for dinner once in awhile. And, of course, they often need to go to the doctor. In big cities and small towns alike, elderly mobility is an important community challenge.

Traditionally, providing rides for the elderly has involved volunteers, but volunteers have their own lives and their own schedules. They might have time when you need them but the elderly might find that they have to adjust their own lives and transportation needs just so they can get a ride they need or want. Part of the problem is also that the pool of volunteers can ebb and flow, being particularly scarce during holiday periods. In a crunch, an elderly person could sometimes fall back on family but more and more often, the family is in another city or state or even continent. What the elderly really long for are the days when they had their own transportation—when they could go anywhere they wanted whenever they wanted.

What was needed was a system as close to private transportation as possible. Katherine Freund founded the Independent Transportation Network in Portland, Oregon (ITNAmerica), which set out to provide "dignified transportation for seniors." The model she developed melds the private sector concept of a membership service (think of a gym membership) with charitable giving. As its web site (www.itnamerica.org) says: "Older adults who join the ITN® in their community become dues-paying members of a non-profit organization committed to their independence and mobility. When they pick up the telephone to schedule a ride, they are not asking a favor—they are making a reservation with their own transportation service."

Individuals who are members can order a ride any time—24 hours a day, 7 days a week. Trips can be of any kind—presumably including the frivolous or the "just get out of the apartment" kind. The only restriction is the coverage area. Passengers ride in private automobiles with paid or volunteer drivers. The trips are paid for out of the rider's personal account or partially by merchants who are happily bringing a customer to their stores. The account can be created by the elderly recipient—say, from proceeds of the sale of his or her car—or by a church group, by (guilty) family members, or simply by good Samaritans. Members can earn ride credits by volunteering for ITN service. While each ride results in a charge, there are monetary incentives for advanced scheduling and for ride sharing.

In the 11 years it has been operating in Portland, ITNPortland has grown to the point where it now provides 16,000 rides a year to 1,000 members.

Source: Nicole Wallace, "In Exploring New Revenue Opportunities, Charity Leaders Say to Learn from the Past," *The Chronicle of Philanthropy*, March 23, 2006, p. 33.

The single most important element of the organization's marketing mix is *its offer*. Marketing's ultimate objective is no different from the private sector. It is to influence the behavior of target audiences by offering an attractive value proposition—a combination of desirable benefits and minimal costs in exchange for a desired behavior.[1] However, in contrast to the private sector, the nonprofit organization promotes these exchanges largely to benefit the target audience and/or the society at large and only secondarily to meet the organization's own needs for survival and growth. Nonprofits do not have stockholders with paramount claims.

Most organizations, for-profit and nonprofit, cannot survive for long if they do not offer something fundamentally attractive—or, as the current private sector mantra has it: "provide exceptional value." Further, they cannot grow if they cannot distinguish their offerings in significant ways from the competition, even when the "competition" is inaction or the status quo. Even the most creative and dramatic advertising cannot sell a fundamentally weak behavioral offering. The latter is a marketing truth learned the hard way by such diverse marketers as Coca-Cola ("New Coke"), IBM ("PCjr Personal Computer"), and Federal Express ("Zap Electronic Mail").

UNIQUE CHALLENGES

Nonprofit marketers have especially difficult challenges when they mount offers for campaigns that address problematic behaviors.

1. *They often must meet extravagant expectations.* In commercial markets, marketers are often given responsibility for improving market shares a few percentage points or launching a new product or brand that will yield a reasonable return on investment. In nonprofit marketing campaigns, the challenges may be for complete eradication of a problem or the universal adoption of some desirable behavior. Nonprofit marketers must spend at least some of their time *reducing* the expectations of key oversight publics.

2. *They are often asked to influence nonexistent demand.* Many of the attitudes and behaviors nonprofit marketers are attempting to influence may be entirely new to their target audiences. Households who think that children come "naturally" or as "part of God's plan" need to learn that children are not inevitable. Overweight individuals who think it is totally genetic need to realize this is not so. Moving target audiences from Precontemplation to Contemplation must take place long before any behavior change marketing can be done.

3. *They are often asked to influence negative demand.* It is sometimes the case that nonprofit marketers must attempt to promote a behavior for which the target audience has a clear distaste. For example, driving 55 mph or wearing a seat belt is restricting to most people. Exercising is not anticipated positively by those who have never done it. Drug or alcohol addicts are often afraid to quit their habits. Conserving water, turning down the thermostat, and separating garbage for recycling are all "costly" behaviors that most target audiences would rather avoid.

4. *They often target nonliterate audiences.* Many nonprofit marketing campaigns programs take place in developing countries and/or with populations with limited reading skills. This restricts the kind of media and messages that can be used and creates major creative challenges for nonprofit marketers. In some markets, cartoon characters are used to achieve identification among nonliterate audiences. Special problems are presented when complex information must be communicated, such as in the case of HIV/AIDS.

5. *They often address highly sensitive issues.* Many target behaviors are not only highly involving but embarrassing. Asking a rural mother to regularly weigh her child and expose the fact that her family has little food is much more personal than asking someone to buy a Toyota or new furniture. One consequence of this sensitivity is that it often makes it very hard for nonprofit marketers to carry out the target audience research that they stress is essential to their approach.[2]

6. *The behaviors to be influenced often have invisible benefits.* It is usually apparent what benefits one is likely to get with a Hilton Hotel room or a new Xerox machine. Nonprofit marketers are often challenged to encourage behaviors where *nothing happens.* Immunization is supposed to prevent disease "in the future." Individuals with high blood pressure are told it will be lowered only if they take their pills. Mothers are told that oral rehydration solution will prevent dehydration, a relationship many do not comprehend. Because there is no overt evidence (unless, for example, one gets a blood pressure test) that there has been any result of the recommended behavior, the target audience has difficulty knowing whether the behavior worked. Often target audience members who agree to the behavior have the nagging feeling that the same outcome would have occurred if they *hadn't* taken the recommended course of action.

7. *The behaviors to be influenced often have benefits primarily to third parties.* Some behaviors advocated by nonprofit marketers have payoffs for third parties, such as poor people or society in general, and not to the person undertaking the behavior. Sometimes there are benefits to others and personal costs. This would be the case, for example, for energy conservation and obedience to speed laws. In these cases, most individuals consider slowing down or turning down the heat to

be personal inconveniences, but many still do so because they feel it is in the society's best interests. The challenge for marketers is to craft personal benefits to make the action more likely. This is certainly the challenge for volunteer recruitment and many charitable solicitations.

8. *The behaviors are often crafted by the target audience and frequently require self-rewards.* Private sector marketers can manipulate the qualities of their offerings and change the benefit bundles they provide. However, in nonprofit marketing campaigns, managers often must try to encourage behaviors like dieting or exercise where the target audience chooses the behaviors. Further, for actions like exercise, it is the target audience member who must provide his or her own (mental) rewards in the face of sometimes strenuous efforts.

9. *The behaviors often involve intangibles that are difficult to portray.* Because the consequences of social behavior changes are often invisible, long term, self-generated, and/or apply only to others, they are much more difficult to portray in promotional messages. Marketers must be highly creative to develop advertising indicating the benefits to families of something like growth monitoring. Because symbols in communications became highly central to success, there is often the risk of sending the wrong signals, as when rural target audiences in developing countries are alienated by promotions that seem too "Western."

10. *Influence can take a very long time.* Because many of the proposed behavior changes are highly involving and/or entail changing individuals from negative to positive demand, the process for achieving behavior change can take a very long time. This will be because (1) often very large amounts of basic information will have to be communicated, (2) basic values will have to be changed, and (3) a great many outside opinion leaders and/or support agencies will have to be "brought on board." For example, to create widespread use of oral rehydration therapy (ORT), target audiences in developing countries must learn that dehydration per se is life-threatening; that some "modern" remedies are better than some folk remedies and can be trusted; and that packaged, branded products are safe and reliable. Simultaneously, physicians, pharmacists, and public health workers must be educated about the problem and given/sold supplies to distribute. Marketers accustomed to shorter-term objectives of target audience packaged goods markets can find these complications and the length of time involved in nonprofit marketing campaigns very frustrating.

11. *Campaigns frequently face intense public scrutiny.* Since nonprofit organizations are publicly funded by government contracts, foundation support, private donations, and volunteer efforts, the public feels it has the right to transparency in what the nonprofit does. This scrutiny may be by the government, a funding source, and/or the general public as represented by the press or academic researchers/critics. This scrutiny, among other effects, makes risk taking more difficult in nonprofit marketing campaigns and increases the importance of "politics" and "public relations" in the nonprofit marketing campaigns mix.

12. *Influence on social behaviors is often very hard to detect.* If someone is influenced by an anti-smoking campaign, it may not be clear whether the triggering messages came from the American Cancer Society, the American Lung Association, the American Legacy Foundation, or the sponsors of NicoDerm products.

THE VALUE PROPOSITION

Because nonprofits are involved in a wide range of behavioral challenges, a broad definition of an offer is needed. The key to our definition is rooted in our view of the nature of the influence process. As outlined in Chapter 4, we believe that much of the behavior that nonprofit marketers wish to influence is undertaken because the target audience believes, consciously or unconsciously, that the consequences of the proposed action or actions will be positive on balance and will exceed the consequences of taking any other action (or maintaining a no-action status quo). This is a matter of offering compelling value propositions. We therefore define a marketing offer as follows:

A marketing offer is a proposal by a marketer to make available to a target audience a value proposition consisting of a desirable combination of positive and negative consequences if, and only if, the target audience undertakes a desired action.

There are two main levels at which nonprofit marketers want to generate exchanges. First, there are exchanges *with the organization itself* on the part of a number of key publics—donors, foundations, corporations, and volunteers. At a second level are the exchanges sought by various clients or target audiences that are the focus of the organization's mission. These would include exchanges that lead to behaviors such as stopping smoking, putting a baby to sleep on its back, practicing safe sex, attending a concert, choosing a college, and so on.

Positive consequences, or benefits, may flow from the acquisition of a physical product or a set of products from the marketer, as in the case of condoms sold as part of an AIDS prevention program or food or gift items sold in a museum. They may also result from an exchange for a service from a person (social worker, teacher) or a place (museum, zoo). And the benefits may result from the target audience's *own* actions, as when someone donates to a nonprofit organization or a corporation engages in a cause-marketing partnership.

Negative consequences are, of course, the costs the target audience has to pay. These costs will be discussed in Chapter 10 and can comprise monetary, psychological, and social elements.

Products, services, the organization itself, and recommended behaviors are really alternative vehicles for *the delivery of consequences.* Indeed, we would argue that, at bottom, what target audiences are looking for is the set of positive consequences, and they only evaluate the delivery mechanism in terms of its ability to provide those consequences at a reasonable cost to themselves. In many cases, a specific target audience member may have multiple exchanges with a nonprofit. A homeless person in a cold climate seeking to become warmer at night (the consequence) could (1) purchase a product, say a Hibachi, at a swap meet for a few cents and heat scraps of wood in it at night; (2) acquire a service such as a bed in a "rescue mission" (for which "payment" might be attendance at a daily religious service); or (3) provide for his or her own needs by sleeping in an area that provides more shelter (e.g., an abandoned building or storm duct) or more natural heat (e.g., over a grating or in an underground subway station). As the person gets back on his or her feet, he or she might volunteer for the nonprofit or even give a few pennies back for the care received.

A great many nonprofit organizations simultaneously engage in providing offerings in many categories, as the following examples show.

- Population Development Associates in Thailand sells condoms, T-shirts, and aspirins; rents hotel rooms; provides day care services; and lobbies to get legislators to pass laws creating a new form of nonprofit (and nontaxed) private organization.
- Most concert halls sell pastries and espresso along with concert tickets, rent space to corporations for special events, sponsor music appreciation programs for schoolchildren, and regularly solicit donations from individuals and corporations.
- The AARP lobbies Congress, sells travel excursions and insurance policies to members, and tries to get seniors to exercise more.
- The American Marketing Association sells publications, offers members various conferences, provides a professional "credentialing" opportunity, and seeks donations to its foundation.

Different challenges face the marketing manager designing an offer strategy depending on whether the core benefit is delivered by the organization, a product, a service, or the target audience member himself or herself—or some combination. In the previous chapter, we discussed the challenges of branding both an organization and a behavior influence campaign. As we saw, branding principles can apply whenever one wants to develop memorable shorthand for some offering. In this chapter, we consider the challenges of managing product and service offerings and of encouraging behaviors where products and services are not involved. In all of these cases, the problem is to craft impactful value propositions that get the actions one wants whether the target audience is a legislator, news director, PTA chairperson, homeless person, or potential cancer victim.

PRODUCT MARKETING

It is ironic that marketers traditionally speak of the "4Ps" when discussing integrated influence strategies—Product, Price, Place, and Promotion. These are often augmented by others who add Public Relations and/or Politics as critical parts of nonprofit strategy. In many ways the traditional 4Ps are not well suited to nonprofit marketing. As we have noted, there often is no product, no dollar cost, and no clear distribution point. There is usually promotion and, again as we have noted, too many naïve nonprofit marketers think that this is all one really needs.

The first P is Product. Of course, as we noted in the previous chapter, many nonprofit campaigns involve products that are central to their behavior influence strategies: condoms for HIV/AIDS campaigns, oral rehydration solution to prevent deaths from diarrhea, and bednets impregnated with insecticide to ward off malaria. In addition, many nonprofit organizations market products (and services) as fundraising sidelines to their main enterprise. T-shirts are common to many programs and, of course, museums and art galleries derive significant revenue from their gift shops.

There is a danger, however, in overemphasizing products and using the language of "product marketing." There are three reasons for this. First, product marketing is typically not central to the mission of most nonprofits. Organizations in the major nonprofit categories of education, health care, politics, social service, religion, and the arts are all basically service or self-help enterprises. Although there are the exceptions just noted, for most, product marketing either is supplementary to their primary mission (e.g., drugs for hospitals, uniforms for the Girl Scouts) or is part of fundraising (e.g., Girl Scout cookies; WAMU T-shirts, sweatshirts, and tote bags).

Second, excessive focus on products as *things* whose attributes must be promoted ("highest-quality ingredients," "tested by experts") encourages the unwary marketer to practice organization-centered marketing rather than the target audience-centered approach we advocate here. It is tempting to any marketer to want to brag about the fine qualities of his or her products (and services as well) in his or her own terms ("We're great"). The point missed is that, fundamentally, target audiences acquire products *for what these products can do for them*—that is, for the positive value propositions they deliver. Target audiences do not want highest-quality ingredients; they want something that will taste good or perform well, will impress their friends, or will not have to be replaced very often. They do not want a product tested by experts simply because this certifies how great the product is, but because it is an indicator that the product will meet the target audience's high performance standards, will incur low maintenance costs, or will last a long time.

Vargo and Lusch have recently addressed this problem in proposing a "new dominant logic for marketing."[3] They argue that everything is service delivery—that products are really only "value-delivery" objects as far as the target audience is concerned.[4] Services involve *people* delivering value. Products are *things* delivering value.

The third reason for minimizing the focus on products is because we wish to emphasize the role that the target audience plays in creating successful exchanges. It is the target audience that must think about the offer and construe physical objects and marketer communications into potential costs and benefits. That is, it is the target audience that must construct the value proposition in their own head and then take the action (or continue the inaction) to make the exchange happen. In many cases, such as stopping smoking or desisting from child or spousal abuse, acting may be very hard for the target audience to bring themselves to do. Finally, in many situations, it is the target audience members who must deliver the benefits to themselves after the exchange takes place—for example, by mentally rewarding themselves for sticking to an exercise routine or giving an anonymous donation to a charity.

Product marketing decisions by a nonprofit organization involve deciding on what products to offer (and how to position and price them). Marketers can think of products as individual items, product lines, and product mixes. For clarity, we use the following definition:

A product is anything that can be offered in tangible form to a market to offer value.

Product Item Decisions

In developing a product to offer to a market, the product planner has to distinguish three levels of product features: the core, tangible, and augmented levels.

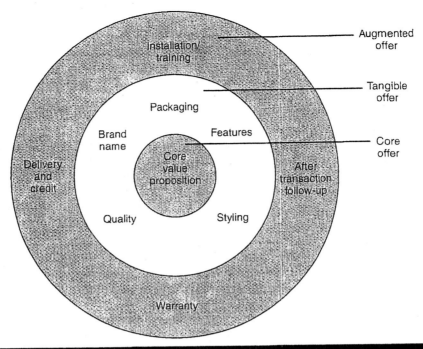

Core Product

At the most fundamental level stands the core product, which answers these questions: What benefits are the target audiences really seeking? What need is the product really satisfying? The Georgetown University bookstore markets textbooks, but students seek future earning power and good grades. The Sierra Club sells calendars, but purchasers are buying an organizing tool, aesthetic pleasure, and a feeling of helping a "good cause." The marketer's job is to uncover the essential needs hiding under every product so that product benefits, not just product features, can be described. The core product stands at the center of the total product, as illustrated in Figure 8-1.

Tangible Product

The core product is always made available to the buyer in some tangible form. A tangible product can be described as having up to five characteristics. First, it has certain *features;* for example, an anti-malaria bednet can come ready-treated or untreated with a supply of insecticide. Second, it has certain *styling;* some T-shirts simply contain a logo or slogan whereas others are highly fashionable and suitable for party wear. The tangible product also has a certain *quality level;* it is made well or badly. Fourth, it has a certain *packaging.* Oral rehydration products come as powders or premixed liquids. Their containers can be gaudy or generic. Fifth, the tangible product can have a unique *brand name.*

Features   Features represent individual components of the tangible product that could be added or subtracted without changing the product's style or quality. Consider a museum marketer seeking to expand sales of calendars to international travelers. He or she might offer the following feature improvements:

1. Reference materials on the back of the calendar (U.S. and international time zones, foreign currency values, useful web sites)
2. Days and months in several languages
3. Dates of major foreign holidays

The use of features has many advantages. Features are a tool for achieving product differentiation vis-à-vis competitors. The organization can go after specific market segments by selecting features that would appeal to these segments. They have the advantage of being easy to add or drop, or they can be made optional at little expense. They are often newsworthy and can attract free media publicity such as the spate of money-raising calendars featuring cleverly concealed naked "models."

Styling   Styling means giving a product (or service) a distinctive look or "feel." Much of the competition in durable goods, such as automobiles, watches, and electronic products, is style competition. The style of a product can be established before or after the target market is identified. Products for Muslim countries need to be more modest and refined than similar products for Europe and the United States markets.

Quality   Quality is the perceived level of performance in a product. Products that have a service component in particular are tremendously variable in quality, depending upon who is providing the service component and how much control the organization exercises over its service providers. Museums typically have higher quality offerings while charitable events have more run-of-the-mill items like T-shirts and trinkets. A basic issue is how response varies with the level of quality in a particular market.

Packaging   Good packaging can add significant value to many core products. It can make the product easier to use, as is the case with single-serving oral rehydration packages containing just the right quantity of chemicals for a suffering child's dehydrated system. It can keep the product safe or fresh for a long time, as is the case for much food aid. It can add psychological value to a product, as is the case of the attractive packages for drug products, differentiating them from products available at government clinics. Many women in developing countries will pay a little more for something that is tastefully packaged and not identified with "poor people's clinics."

It also turns out that packages can affect important behavioral outcomes. Professor Brian Wansink at Cornell University has found that people tend to eat whatever is in a package and this may be a contributor to the obesity problem. Indirectly, this finding has led to Nabisco and others to offer snack products packaged as 100-calorie servings.[5]

Branding   Branding, as noted in the previous chapter, benefits the user by helping the person recognize a product, know its quality in advance, and so on. The seller might also gain. The Family of the Future (FOF) repackaged its basic condom in a new gold-and-white wrapper and branded the new offering as "Golden Tops." Although the tangible product was unchanged, the image of quality permitted FOF to reap a one-third higher price per unit with no loss in sales. (Indeed, the higher price itself probably added to the "quality" image.) The brand name can also help add value by itself. Girl Scout Cookies can command premium prices because of who brands them.

Augmented Product

The marketer can offer to the target market additional services and benefits that go beyond the tangible product, thereby producing an augmented product. Thus a nonprofit that sells used business attire to poor people looking for work could also provide videotape instruction on how to take a job interview and a take-away checklist about workplace etiquette. Organizations augment their tangible products to meet additional target audience wants, to differentiate their products from the competition, or both. Success often depends as much or more on the augmented benefits as on the tangible product. Inducing a news director to run a nonprofit's TV clip may involve hand-delivering it and re-editing the content to permit the insertion of commentary by the local newscaster.

Product Mix Decisions

An organization's product mix can be described in terms of its length, width, and depth. These concepts can be illustrated in a hypothetical example. Figure 8-2 shows a simplified product mix of a museum cafeteria. We see that the product mix, in terms of its length, consists of three product lines: main courses, desserts, and beverages. Each product line has a certain width. Thus the dessert line includes ice cream and pastries. Finally, each product item has a certain depth: Desserts comprise 18 ice cream flavors and 10 pastries.

Suppose the museum's cafeteria operated at a profit and the museum wanted to attract more sales. It could choose any of three alternatives. It could lengthen its product mix by adding a line of appetizers or breakfast combinations. Or it could widen one or more of its product lines, perhaps adding Italian or French entrees to its main course line, fruit or cheese offerings to the dessert line, or mineral water or fruit juices to its beverages. Finally, it could deepen any of its present 10 product items—for example, by adding 10 foreign beer brands, 3 imported wines, another sandwich variety, or 6 new ice cream flavors. The museum would have to assess which of these product mix choices would increase volume, patronage, or profit the most, depending on its objective.

However, the museum may want or need to prune the product mix in order to save money, free management time and energy, or focus its image better. Again it has three alternatives. It could make some product items "shallower." A more serious move would be to cut out an item altogether. Most radical, of course, would be to eliminate an entire line.

In reviewing the product mix, we should recognize that the products differ in their roles and contributions to the enterprise. Some are the enterprise's core products of direct relevance to the nonprofit's mission and others are its ancillary products or fundraising vehicles. Furthermore, certain products play a major role in attracting patrons. They are

---

FIGURE 8-2   Length, Width, and Depth of a Museum Cafeteria's Product Mix

	Main Courses	Desserts	Beverages
	Egg Dishes (4)	Ice Cream (18)	Soft Drinks (4)
Product Line Width	Mexican Dishes (3)	Pastries (10)	Coffee/Tea (2)
	Sandwiches (5)		Beer (3)
	Salads (6)		Wine (3)

← Product Mix Length →

called *product leaders* or *flagship products.* Often an organization seeks to add a star product to its mix. The museum restaurant may offer a Sacher torte from a famous Viennese restaurant for which target audiences save up their calories for weeks. An organization can showcase its flagship product as a symbol in its literature and promotion. The high cost of acquiring one crown jewel is often well repaid by the public relations value it produces.

SERVICES MARKETING

A substantial majority of nonprofit organizations are basically in the services business. People enter into exchanges with them because the nonprofit provides (1) *people* who educate, conduct art museum tours, or perform surgery; (2) *places* where target audiences can play golf in a national park, see exotic animals in the city zoo, sunbathe on county beaches; and/or (3) *the use of objects or equipment* so that target audiences can read a library book, view the distant stars through a high-powered university telescope, or travel across a continent on a government-owned train system. We define a service as follows:

A service is any value proposition offered to a target audience by an individual or an organization that is essentially intangible and does not result in the ownership of anything. Its production may or may not be tied to a physical product.

Services are of a great many types. Christopher Lovelock has pointed out that services have at least nine dimensions that affect how they should be marketed. These dimensions are outlined in Figure 8-3.

Although there is high diversity in the nature of services, they tend to exhibit five important characteristics. A service is typically:

- Intangible
- Inseparable from its producer
- Variable in its characteristics
- Perishable
- Dependent on the involvement of the target audience in its production

Intangibility

Services are intangible; that is, they typically cannot be seen, tasted, felt, heard, or smelled before they are bought. Thus a patient getting plastic surgery cannot see the result before the purchase; a patient walking into a psychiatrist's office cannot know the content or value of the service in advance since there is no tangible product involved. Under the circumstances, one makes a purchase on the basis of secondary cues and one's confidence in the service provider.

Inseparability

A service is inseparable from the source that provides it. The very act of creating the service requires that the source, whether a person or a machine, be present. Thus production and consumption often occur simultaneously with services. This is in contrast to products, which continue to exist whether or not their source is present. Consider going to a U2 concert performance to benefit AIDS programs in Africa. The emotional impact is inseparable from the performer. It is not the same service if an

Services can differ along the following dimensions:

1. Recipient:
   a. Done to people (like health care)
   b. Done to things (like plumbing repair)

2. Tangibility:
   a. Tangible (like a physical examination)
   b. Intangible (like psychotherapy)

3. Length of the service relationship:
   a. One-time (like a tire repair)
   b. Continuing (like telephone service)

4. Connection to customer:
   a. Subscriber (like telephone service)
   b. Nonsubscriber (like a police service)

5. Extent of possible customization:
   a. Low (like movies or public transportation)
   b. Medium (like education)
   c. High (like plumbing or health care services)

6. Stability of demand:
   a. High fluctuation (like hotel or police service)
   b. Low fluctuation (like insurance)

7. Adjustability of supply:
   a. High (like utilities)
   b. Low (like movie theaters)

8. Location of delivery:
   a. Customer comes to the service (like most banking)
   b. Service comes to the customer (like plumbing)
   c. Service is provided at a distance (like TV programming)

9. Role of products versus people:
   a. Mostly products and equipment (like car leasing)
   b. Mostly people (like haircutting)
   c. A mix of products and people (like hospitals)

FIGURE 8-3   Types of Services

Source: Christopher H. Lovelock, "Classifying Services to Gain Marketing Insights," *Journal of Marketing,* Vol. 47 (Summer 1983), pp. 9–20.

announcer tells the audience that U2 is indisposed and that the group's latest videos will be played instead, or that a local rock group will substitute. What this means is that the number of people who can experience a U2 benefit is limited by the amount of time U2 is willing to give to performances.

Variability

Since a service is so closely linked to its source, it can be highly variable, depending on who is providing it and when it is being provided. A pro bono master class by opera star Renée Fleming is likely to be of higher quality than the same class given by a high school chorus master. In addition, Ms. Fleming's quality can vary depending on her energy and mental state at the time of the class. Purchasers of services are aware of this high variability and, when there is a good deal at stake, will engage in extensive risk-reducing behavior such as talking to others and trying to learn who the best provider is.

When demand fluctuates heavily, service firms have especially difficult problems. Public transportation companies, for example, have to use much more equipment during rush hours because of peak demand than they would if public transportation needs were steady during the day.

Perishability

Services cannot be stored. A Goodwill suit can be kept in inventory until it is sold or given away, but the revenue from an unoccupied theater seat is lost forever. This is the reason many theatres give discount tickets on the day of the performance. The perishability of services is not a problem when demand is steady, because it is easy to staff the services in advance.

Target Audience Involvement

Service exchanges are one area of nonprofit marketing that has extensive involvement of the target audience as an integral part in the production of the service itself. The target audience therefore plays a crucial role in the ultimate nature and quality of the experience. At one extreme is client-centered psychological counseling, in which much of the value of the experience depends on the patient. At the other extreme is a makeup service for out-of-work poor people where the provider controls the service. In the middle would be Alcoholics Anonymous's 8-step program in which a leader guides group sessions and individual progress but much of the success lies with the individual.

These characteristics present five major challenges in the design of service offerings.

Making the Intangible Tangible

Services are difficult for target audiences to evaluate because they do not involve products and are not made in advance. Target audiences, therefore, must look to other signs of potential quality. Diplomas can signify the quality of a job training instructor. Plaques and awards are signs that a charity or museum is especially noteworthy. Well-established brand names like the American Red Cross or the YMCA signal high quality and reliability.

Special attention must be paid to "atmospherics."[6] The way a service clerk is dressed, the quality of the brochures used to describe the offerings, and the character of the external architecture and interiors of the marketer's building can all affect the way the target audience expects the service to be delivered. Soup kitchens that are clean and well-maintained are likely to be seen by the homeless as providing healthful meals and by donors as institutions that will use funds wisely. A church or synagogue building that is modern in style will create a different set of expectations from one that is traditional and fitted with antiques and ornate decorations. A college building made of steel and glass will be suitable for an engineering school or an art department, while a granite structure with one or two fireplaces will be ideal for English or philosophy.

Service marketers can also make their offerings tangible through giveaways that are concrete signs of their efforts. Charity races typically offer T-shirts to those completing the event and many breast cancer programs give out pink ribbons. Many target audience–oriented service marketers follow up a service encounter with a handwritten note or a telephone call to check on target audience satisfaction and to demonstrate continuing interest in the target audience member.

Making a Virtue of Inseparability

Services are typically produced by people; therefore, the service is often indistinguishable from the person delivering it. Unfortunately, this can have very negative effects. A pleasant and medically successful hospital stay can be fatally marred by a surly clerk demanding (not asking for) payment or the completion of more forms on the last day of the hospitalization. Initially pleasant museum visits can be sabotaged by the guard who is unresponsive to a simple question or is simply annoyed. The teacher who is always suspicious of student excuses makes job training unpleasant. Also damaging is the social worker who makes clients feel like they are ruining his or her day by mentioning problems, the librarian who makes it clear that interlibrary loans are "difficult," and even the telephone operator at the local chapter who transfers a call and never checks to see that the calling party has reached someone who can help.

The basic cause of these negative experiences is that nonprofit marketers have not trained key target audience contact personnel in the need for a target audience orientation. These personnel do not see their role in protecting—even enhancing—the nonprofit brand. "Problem" service personnel do not see themselves as being there to meet target audience needs and wants—and this is often especially true of volunteers. They put themselves and their organization's needs first and usually give the impression that they would prefer it if the target audiences would just go away so that they could get their jobs done. As an academic colleague once said somewhat facetiously, "This university would run a lot more efficiently and I could get done a lot more of what I am paid to do if only there weren't all these darned students!"

The solution is *internal marketing.* The entire organization must come to realize that every encounter with a target audience is what Jan Carlzon of Scandinavian Airlines calls "a moment of truth."[7] A moment of truth is any occasion in which a target audience comes into contact with some aspect of the organization and has a chance to form an impression. As Albrecht and Zemke note in their book *Service America! Doing Business in the New Economy:*

> The problem and the challenge, from this point of view, are that most moments of truth take place far beyond the immediate line of sight of the management. Since managers cannot be there to influence the quality of so many moments of truth, they must learn to manage them indirectly, that is, by creating a target audience-oriented organization, a target audience-friendly system as well as a work environment that reinforces the idea of putting the target audience first.[8]

The authors then cite a number of what they call "shining moments" when an organization shows that it is truly target audience–oriented in its service delivery. Here are three:

1. A Memphis hospital has a doorman meet surgery patients at curbside and lead them to a special desk for "check-in," and then has a bellman take the "guests" to their rooms. Only then does someone come by to have the guests fill out the necessary admissions records.
2. A policeman in Japan accompanied a tourist back to his motel to inspect the passport the tourist claimed to have forgotten. Having satisfied the legal necessities, the policeman went far out of his way to take the tourist to the restaurant he was

originally seeking, introduced him to the restaurant manager, and only then went back to his business of policing.

3. A college in Florida handles all the registration for enrollees in its professional extension programs, sends them course outlines, and even buys their textbooks for them. It feels that busy executives do not have the time for such busywork and would attend a school that recognized that need.[9]

Going to great lengths to satisfy target audience needs and wants is the secret to success for many organizations in both the private and nonprofit sectors. An obsession with target audiences[10] is being adopted by more forward-looking nonprofit marketers as a critical element for achieving high performance. Such a mindset is especially important in service areas in which target audiences have a great many alternatives and where the real objective of the nonprofit is to build long-term relationships with the target audience and not just one-time exchanges. A good case in point is the plight of classical music. The traditional audience for symphony orchestras is aging rapidly, and symphony and concert hall marketers are trying many approaches to add more target audiences, especially from among infrequent patrons such as young professionals and families. Particularly valuable are efforts to make the events less formal and more social.

"User-friendliness" has become an important ingredient for bringing target audiences to the symphony and for getting them to come back. A case in point is the Dallas Symphony Orchestra (DSO). The story is told of two elderly people who had come to buy season tickets on a Sunday morning. The DSO's marketing director was there to handle their order; however, when the couple returned to their car, they found that the garage had closed. The appropriate action for the marketing manager was crystal clear: He drove them home! The director made the DSO's new marketing mindset transparent: "We abandoned the whole concept of selling tickets and started building relationships with our target audiences instead."[11]

Managing Variability

Quality is the greatest concern of service marketers: how to deliver it and how to keep it consistent. How does one make a second visit to Goodwill or a soup kitchen or to the Ebenezer Baptist Church have much the same look and feel as the first visit? A major asset in achieving this is good personnel selection and a training program that is followed up with consistent internal marketing (including to volunteers). Airlines, banks, and hotels, for example, spend substantial sums of money to train their personnel to provide uniform and friendly service. Far too many nonprofit museums and hospitals rely on untrained volunteers and do very little to train their paid staffs to provide consistently high-quality service. They apparently do not appreciate how a few bad experiences can permanently damage a service provider's position. A second step is to routinize or even automate many parts of the service. A third step for controlling variability is to develop adequate target audience satisfaction monitoring systems. The main tools are complaint systems, target audience surveys, and comparison shopping.[12]

Managing Perishability

Service organizations are, in a sense, associations of individuals, facilities, and/or tangible products brought together to form services as target audiences demand them. Vargo and Lusch in 2004 referred to these capabilities as operant resources—resources that can provide target audience value whether through products or services.[13] They described *all* marketing as follows: "The service-centered view of marketing implies that marketing is a continuous series of social and economic processes that is largely focused on operant resources with which the firm is constantly striving to make better value propositions than its competitors. In a free enterprise system, the firm primarily knows whether it is making better value propositions from the feedback it receives from the marketplace in terms of firm financial performance." In the nonprofit world, "financial performance" can mean client payments, government grants, or corporate and individual donations.

These capacities or "operant resources" can be as simple as a renowned educator sitting at the end of a log awaiting a student or as complex as a grand opera production of *Aïda* complete with elephants and camels awaiting opening night. These capacities are, on the one hand, wasted if demand is too low and, on the other hand, difficult to expand if demand is too high. Service managers must try to bring supply and demand into balance. Sasser has described several strategies for managing demand and supply.[14] On the demand side, the strategies include the following:

1. *Differential pricing* can be used to shift some demand from peak to off-peak periods. An example would be lower fares for riding city buses in off-peak hours.
2. *Nonpeak demand can be developed* through marketing campaigns. The Miami Beach Chamber of Commerce has attempted to convince people to vacation in Miami Beach during the summer months.
3. *Complementary services* can be developed during peak time to provide diversions or alternatives to waiting target audiences. Physician's offices provide magazines for patients to read while waiting.
4. *Reservation systems* are a way to presell service, know how much service is needed, and reduce target audience waiting. Some hospitals, for example, assign patient beds by requiring physicians to make reservations.

On the supply side, these strategies may be used:

1. *Part-time employees* can be used to serve peak demand. Colleges add part-time teachers when enrollment goes up.
2. *Peak-time efficiency routines* can be introduced. Some academic computer centers do not permit large data sets to be loaded during peak periods.
3. *Target audience participation* in the tasks can be increased. New patients may be asked to fill out their own medical histories before seeing a physician during busy periods.
4. *Shared services* can be developed. Several hospitals can agree to shift patients among themselves, depending on load.
5. *Expandable facilities can be planned.* A nursing home can make arrangements with a nearby motel for extra beds during periods of excess demand.

Helping Target Audiences Consume

Many services require the active participation of target audiences. If target audiences misuse the service or do not get as much value from it as they could, then (1) the service is de facto of lower quality than would otherwise be the case and (2) the chance of the target audience being dissatisfied is significantly greater. There are several approaches service marketers may adopt for this problem. They primarily focus on either changing the marketer or changing the target audience.

The most manageable approach is for the marketer to adapt his or her own service as much as possible to the individual target audience's ability to consume and appreciate it. Thus a library designing an online computer-based information retrieval system may wish to design an idiot-proof system with which everyone except the most computer-traumatized or inexperienced user can cope. Art museums could take a number of steps to make the experience that they and the target audience *jointly produce* more meaningful:

- Study the types of visitors coming to the museum and what they are looking for. According to Andreasen, the types include *aesthetes,* those interested in the artistic merits of specific works; *historians,* those interested in where the work fits in the stream of art history; and *romantics,* those who want to know about the artist behind the work.[15] Visitors also differ in other respects. There are those who are willing to read the needed information and those who want to be talked to; those who will visit for a brief period and those who stay longer; and those who are visiting for the first time and those who are familiar with the museum.
- Provide separate suggested itineraries through the museum for each type of visitor.
- Provide guidebooks, wall posters, tape-recorded guides, and docent tours for the different types of visitors.

The alternative route is to try to teach the target audience to be a better target audience. This is routinely done in many nonprofit areas. Museums offer art appreciation classes to potential viewers. Symphonies offer before-concert lectures. Colleges offer how-to-study seminars for new students. There are other steps even these organizations could take. One goal would be to make service users' expectations more realistic. A major source of dissatisfaction on the part of many service target audiences is not inferior service but *exaggerated expectations.* Psychiatric patients often expect instant improvement for serious problems. Playgoers often expect not to be emotionally traumatized or made uncomfortable. Students at many job-training courses expect instant career advancement and high salaries. Nonprofits should routinely ask themselves this: What are potential target audiences being led to expect from this organization and can the organization deliver?

A second goal should be to take every opportunity to make target audiences more discriminating. If the organization is proud of its offer mix and if it has effectively differentiated itself from its competitors, it should have little to fear from teaching target audiences to be more discerning. Thus charities could routinely hand out guides to evaluating charities, or point people to the relevant web sites like the one maintained by the Better Business Bureau. Consultants, museum directors, and psychologists could have booklets available and give introductory "lectures" to new patients on "how to get the most from your consultant/museum/therapy." Nursing homes could teach their residents to hold high (but reasonable) standards. In all cases, a discriminating clientele cannot help but make a caring organization an even better provider of service.

A third approach is to remember that target audience contact should be a continuing activity. Good service organizations do not focus on transactions as individual events—for example, as one-time sales. They see their task to be building long-term *relationships* with their target audience base.[16] A loyal target audience may spend hundreds and thousands of dollars over a decade at a restaurant or performing arts center. Recognizing this, good service marketers are quite willing to take short-term losses and make extra personalized "target audience–training" efforts to build a solid relationship that will have a long-term payoff.

This position is sometimes taken to extremes. Danny Newman, former publicist for the Chicago Lyric Opera, has argued that performing arts organizations ought to *ignore* fickle target audiences who buy tickets for individual events and seek to presell virtually all seats for all performances to subscribers before the start of each season.[17] Newman says that selling all seats in advance would have three benefits:

1. Subscriptions would provide a secure financial platform for all activities.
2. Subscribers would guarantee a basic audience for even the most adventurous productions.
3. Marketing activities could be concentrated in one period of the year and thereby minimize costs.

"PURE" BEHAVIORS

There remain a set of behaviors that nonprofit marketers seek to induce that do not involve products or services that the marketer controls and provides. These are often the focus of what are labeled social marketing campaigns.[18] These are cases--such as a campaign against spousal abuse—where the "value proposition" that the marketer offers is an intellectual proposition. Based on what the marketer has learned from researching how the target audience thinks about the behavioral challenge, the social marketer—employing our fundamental BCOS model—says something like the following:

> If you do behavior X (or refrain from behavior Y), here are the benefits that will fall to you. We know that, if you follow our recommendations, there will be personal costs and here is how you can minimize them. There are others who may argue against this and here is how you can handle them. But there are others who support the behavior (here are examples) and you should pay attention to them. Finally, we know that you may feel that you somehow cannot accomplish this desirable outcome, but here is how you can make it easy.

Backing up this argument may well be products (CDs on anger management) and/or services (anger management workshops) that will make the behavior easier. The campaign may round up spokespeple and endorsers who bring the pressure of "others" to bear. The nonprofit marketers may engage in upstream behavior that changes systems or laws that make the behavior difficult and they may recruit allies to help market their case. All of these require "operant resources" to be effective. Effectiveness then should generate the financial support that allows them to continue their campaigns.

Summary

Its mix of offerings in many ways defines an organization and establishes its position against competition. While traditionally offerings are categorized as products or services, a broader definition focuses on the fact that, from the target audience's standpoint, an offer is simply a set of potential positive and negative consequences that comprise a value proposition. Value can be delivered by products or services or by the target audience's own actions (e.g., dieting or exercising). Many nonprofit organizations promote all three kinds of offerings.

Three levels of the concept of a product offering can be distinguished. The core product defines the needs the product is really meeting. The tangible product is the form in which the product exists. It is comprised of the product's features, styling, quality, packaging, and brand name. The augmented product consists of the tangible product and the additional services and benefits such as installation, after-sale service, delivery, credit, and warranty. As competition increases, organizations must carefully manage the length, width, and depth of their product offerings to compete.

Most nonprofit organizations are primarily in the service business. Services can be delivered by people, places, and objects or equipment. Services are especially difficult to manage because they are typically intangible, inseparable from the producer, variable in characteristics, perishable, and involve the target audience in their production. Service marketers, therefore, must develop ways of making the intangible tangible, such as using brand names and atmospherics.

Inseparability means that services are often synonymous with the people who deliver them. Service marketers must vigorously pursue internal marketing to ensure that key frontline people have a target audience-first attitude and must have internal systems to empower frontline people to take the actions necessary to meet target audience needs and wants.

Variability in service quality can be managed by good personnel selection and careful training along with as much routinization of the service as is possible without diminishing the service itself. Perishability requires attention to service demand and supply, which can be altered to some extent through creative pricing, marketing campaigns, adjustment of personnel and facilities, and sharing services with other organizations during peak periods. Finally, target audience involvement in service delivery can enhance demand and satisfaction if marketers design services so that they are as easy as possible to use and "train" target audiences themselves to be effective and appreciative co-producers.

Social marketing is a term often used for situations where the marketer offers neither a product nor a service but urges the target audience to undertake the desired behavior by offering a compelling value proposition and helping make the recommended behavior easy.

Questions

1. You have been asked to market a line of T-shirts, caps, and other items as a fundraising opportunity. How would you choose what products to offer and why? What would you reject—although they seem reasonable?
2. Describe and evaluate the value proposition of (a) a charity you know and (b) a desirable social behavior (e.g., not littering).
3. You run a soup kitchen and know that your major funder sometimes comes to check out the services posing as a poor homeless person. What negative encounters could she have that would affect future funding? In each case, how would you ensure that frontline staff provide exceptional service?

4. How does a campaign get someone like an overweight friend of yours to exercise? What is the value proposition that would work? How would you figure out how to get your friend to reward himself or herself to keep up the exercise effort?

5. How would you classify a request for a donation? Is it a product or service or a pure behavior? Does it matter and why?

Notes

1. Stephen L. Vargo and Robert F. Lusch, "Evolving to a New Dominant Logic for Marketing," *Journal of Marketing*, Vol. 68 (January 2004), pp. 1–17.

2. N. Ferencic, "Guidelines for Carrying Out In-Depth Interviews about Health in Developing Countries," Working Paper #107, Annenberg School of Communications, University of Pennsylvania, 1989.

3. Vargo and Lusch, "Evolving to a New Dominant Logic for Marketing."

4. Robert F. Lusch and Stephen L Vargo (Eds.), *The Service-Dominant Logic of Marketing: Dialog, Debate, and Directions* (Armonk, NY: M. E. Sharpe, 2006).

5. Kim Severson, "Seduced by Snacks? No, Not You." *New York Times*, October 11, 2006; Brian Wansink, *Mindless Eating: Why We Eat More than We Think* (New York: Bantam Books, 2006).

6. Philip Kotler, "Atmospherics as a Marketing Tool," *Journal of Retailing,* Winter 1973–1974, pp. 48–64.

7. Jan Carlzon, *Moments of Truth* (Boston: Ballinger, 1987).

8. Karl Albrecht and Ron Zemke, *Service America! Doing Business in the New Economy* (Homewood, IL: Dow Jones–Irwin, 1985), p. 27.

9. Ibid., pp. 83–88.

10. James L. Heskett, W. Earl Sasser, Jr., and Christopher W. L. Heart, *Service Breakthroughs* (New York: The Free Press, 1990).

11. Michael Walsh, "Is the Symphony Orchestra Dying?" *Time,* July 22, 1993, pp. 52–53.

12. See, for example, G. M. Hostage, "Quality Control in a Service Business," *Harvard Business Review,* July–August 1975, pp. 98–106; and James L. Heskett, *Managing in the Service Economy* (Boston: Harvard Business School Press, 1986).

13. Vargo and Lusch, "Evolving to a New Dominant Logic for Marketing."

14. W. Earl Sasser, "Match Supply and Demand in Service Industries," *Harvard Business Review,* November–December 1976, pp. 133–180.

15. Alan R. Andreasen, "Non-Profits: Check Your Attention to Target Audiences," *Harvard Business Review,* May–June 1982, pp. 105–110.

16. Sean Mehegan, "Keeping Members: The New Priority," *The NonProfit Times,* April 1993, pp. 21–23.

17. Danny Newman, *Subscribe Now!* (New York: Publishing Center for Cultural Resources, 1977).

18. Alan R. Andreasen, *Marketing Social Change* (San Francisco, CA: Jossey-Bass Publishers, 1995); Alan R. Andreasen, *Social Marketing in the 21st Century* (Thousand Oaks, CA: Sage Publications, 2006).

9

DEVELOPING AND LAUNCHING NEW OFFERINGS

CAN I LOAN YOU $5 TO START YOUR BUSINESS?

In 1976, Muhammad Yunus, a professor of economics at Chittagong University in Bangladesh, visited the nearby village of Jobra and talked to a number of very poor people. He asked what they needed and how might he help. They told him that they needed money for various business ideas and their only option was to go to money lenders who charged unconscionable fees. When Yunus learned that the 42 people he talked to needed just $27 in total, he reached into his own pocket and provided them a loan. They invested the money and repaid him in full.

He thought to himself: "If you can make so many people so happy with such a small amount of money, why shouldn't you do more of it?" Yunus gradually built a small loan network based on the concept of "microcredit" and in 1983 formed the Grameen Bank, an early social enterprise that gave small loans to the poor to invest in farms, shops, and craft-making ventures. He gave loans to groups of five so that each would make sure the others paid back their loans, which were due in manageable weekly amounts. Over the years, Grameen loaned primarily to women because Yunus believes they are more reliable. This was a daring strategy in a Muslim country but it gave women—and the poor in general—much more financial power.

He gives money to beggars and shows them how to make money selling merchandise while they beg. He gives women money for cell phones so they can then charge neighbors who want to make calls in villages with no phone service. In 2005, Grameen Bank had over $5 billion in loans. As of May 2006, it had 6.61 million borrowers, 97 percent of whom were women. Grameen provides microcredit services in 71,371 villages and its impact on the poor has been documented in independent studies by the World Bank, the International Food Research Policy Institute (IFPRI), and the Bangladesh Institute of Development Studies (BIDS). Its model has been replicated in a number of other countries and regions.

On October 13, 2006, Muhammad Yunus and the Grameen Bank were jointly awarded the Nobel Peace Prize.

Source: Grameen Bank web site (www.grameen-info.org) and Celia W. Dugger, "Peace Prize to Pioneer of Loans for Those Too Poor to Borrow," *New York Times*, October 14, 2006, pp. A1, A6.

As we have indicated throughout this text, the market environment facing nonprofits in the twenty-first century is one marked by extremely aggressive competition in a large number of sectors, including health care, charitable contributions, the arts, welfare reform, and education. This increased competition at the organizational level means that nonprofits continually run the risk that their existing offer mix will become obsolete—or at least suboptimal. For a vibrant organization to remain on top of its market, it must produce a continuing stream of new value propositions simply to "stay in place." Producing such new offerings is even more critical if the organization wishes to grow.

This is also true of campaigns. Where one seeks target audiences to engage in difficult or even unattractive behaviors, it is important to constantly reinvent or reposition the fundamental value proposition. Taking high blood pressure medicine, eating foods with less salt, and exercising moderately takes diligence. It is especially challenging because the desired behaviors don't make one feel any different (although the blood pressure numbers will change). Target audiences are constantly at risk of dropping out. Fresh, relevant value propositions are essential for continued success in the Maintenance stage.

New offerings, of course, can come about by chance insight (the "eureka" of discovery). However, a well-managed organization cannot survive merely on chance or insight. New offerings must continually be generated. This requires that a system be put in place for developing and launching new offerings. This is the focus of this chapter. We describe how one systematically generates, evaluates, and brings to market new concepts and then launches and (sometimes) modifies them through the introductory and growth phases of their offer life cycles—just as they do in the private sector.

OFFER DEVELOPMENT—A PROBLEM OF STRATEGIC PLANNING

Developing new and compelling value propositions is one of the most important challenges that any manager faces. What an organization offers very much determines what the organization actually is and how it is seen by its target audiences, competitors, staff, volunteers, donors, and the general public—many of which are the key to basic resources in the future. Choices of new offerings will significantly affect the future of every organization and, therefore, must be carefully thought through and not left to chance or personal preferences.

The nonprofit organization has available to it the nine basic growth strategies described in Table 9-1.[1] These strategies differ by the extent to which the marketer wishes to emphasize development of markets or offerings. First, the organization can decide to focus on its existing offerings and existing markets (cell 1). For this

TABLE 9-1	Offer Strategy Options for Nonprofit Organizations		
	New Offerings:	*New Offerings: Similar*	*Existing Offerings: Dissimilar*
Existing markets	1. a. Market penetration b. Cost reduction c. Share maintenance	4. Offer extension	7. Offer development
New markets: Similar	2. Market extension	5. Continuous diversification	8. Offer diversification
New markets: Dissimilar	3. Market development	6. Market diversification	9. Radical diversification

strategy, it can choose among three substrategies. It can seek to grow by more actively penetrating its existing market either through market expansion or through inducing patronage switching by those already in the market. It can decide not to grow significantly but to become more efficient at marketing to its present clients. Or it can choose to maintain the status quo. While it may seem that neither of the last two strategic postures would appeal to many organizations, there are two situations in which they make sense:

- *Declining markets.* If the market demand is declining, as in the need for funding for polio research and treatment, the marketer might want to treat the program as a "cash cow," pull out resources, or become more efficient, thus producing a surplus to be used elsewhere.
- *New competition.* A market leader always faces possible challenges from new competitors. Thus a major hospital may consider it a great success if it can simply maintain its present level of emergency room volume after a new emergency care center enters the market.

The second posture the organization can take is to seek out new markets for its existing offerings (cells 2 and 3). Firms can add market segments that are similar to their present markets, as when AIDS social marketers seek to take programs that worked in Bangladesh and introduce them in nearby countries like India or Nepal (cell 2, market extension). More daring, and therefore more challenging, would be an attempt to adapt AIDS programs to more dissimilar markets, such as West or East Africa, Tibet, or aboriginal tribes in New Guinea (cell 3, market development).

Carrying out these strategies does not require major changes in the organization's offerings. Rather, it requires more attention to other marketing mix variables like advertising, distribution channels, personal contact, and price and cost management. It can also involve minor changes in the offer, such as packaging changes, redesign of features, and so on.

In this chapter, our attention turns to the six remaining strategies suggested in Table 9-1 that involve new offerings. The nonprofit organization can add new offerings that are relatively similar or relatively dissimilar to their present offerings. In either case, they can focus on existing markets (cells 4 and 7), similar new markets (cells 5 and 8), or dissimilar new markets (cells 6 and 9). Clearly, the riskiest stance of all is cell 9, where entirely new offerings (especially offerings new to the world) are brought to radically different markets. Getting very young children to learn to read by speaking into a voice-reading computer would be an example of such a venture. A system of this type has been explored by Educational Development Associates of Newton, Massachusetts.

One organization that has explored offerings in all six of the new offering cells in Table 9-1 is Mechai Varvaiyadia's Population Development Associates (PDA), Thailand's major social marketing organization:

1. *Offer extension (cell 4).* PDA has added new *types* of contraceptives (that is, new oral pill formulations) to serve its existing target audience markets.
2. *Continuous diversification (cell 5).* PDA has added health care services in its family planning clinics, to which any person can come.
3. *Market diversification (cell 6).* PDA has developed a program for providing health tests in schools and hospitals, using excess capacity among its full-time medical staff.
4. *Offer development (cell 7).* PDA has developed extensive AIDS campaigns in existing markets.
5. *Offer diversification (cell 8).* PDA began helping households in the villages it serves with procedures and funding for building much-needed water tanks for storing rain water.
6. *Radical diversification (cell 9).* PDA has promoted its TBIRD program to entice major businesses into forming community development partnerships.

These new ventures are a common result of the natural enthusiasm of young organizations still in their growth phase. The remainder of this chapter is particularly relevant to the question of how a *mature* nonprofit organization ought to develop new offerings. Every nonprofit sector contains organizations that can be called "innovators." However, a will to innovate is not enough. Many organizations launch new services that fail:

> A 300-bed hospital in southern Illinois got the bright idea of establishing an adult day care program as a solution to its underutilized space. It designed a whole floor to serve senior citizens who required personal care and services in an ambulatory setting during the day, but who would return home each evening. The cost was $16 a day to the patient's family, and transportation was to be provided or paid for by the patient's family. About the only research that was done on this concept was to note that a lot of elderly people lived within a three-mile radius. The Adult Care Center was opened with a capacity to handle 30 patients. Only 2 signed up!

There are many reasons why this and similar value propositions do not yield results:

1. A top administrator pushes the idea through in spite of the lack of supporting research.
2. There are poor organizational systems for evaluating and implementing ideas for new offerings (poor criteria, poor procedures, poor coordination of departments).
3. There is poor market size measurement, forecasting, and market research.

4. There is poor marketing planning—that is, poor positioning, poor segmentation, underbudgeting, and overpricing.
5. The distinctiveness of the offer of target audience benefits is not sufficiently clear.
6. The value proposition is poorly designed.
7. Development costs are unexpectedly high.
8. The competitive response is unexpectedly intense.
9. Promotion is inadequate.

A Warning—Beware of Mission Creep

Of course, a good reason for *not* undertaking new offerings is that they will fail. However, another, more serious problem can stem from offerings that are successful! While it is important for organizations to continually evaluate new ideas to keep the organization growing and employees excited and motivated, there is the real danger that projects will be taken on that are not good fits for organizations. A major source of program innovation for many nonprofits is simply the availability of grant support from government agencies or foundations. Organizations become "grant-chasers" responding to these availabilities without careful thought as to mission fit.[2]

This process can cause a serious distortion of the organization. "Mission creep" can lead the organization into realms and interests that are far removed from its original undertakings. The portrait of the organization begins to look very "lumpy." This has many serious negative consequences. New staff for these new ventures must be acquired and they may be hard to digest organizationally. New skills may be needed that have little synergy with central programs. The organization may be harder to describe to potential donors, and venture philanthropists may shun the enterprise as being ill-focused. Attention may be diverted from remediation needs in the core operations.

Thus it is very important that a prime criterion for every new venture be this: Is it consistent with the mission? This criterion should also be invoked in annual reviews of past undertakings to ascertain whether they have suffered from "program drift" that imperils the mission.

A PROCESS FOR DEVELOPING NEW OFFERINGS

New offerings should not be left to whim or chance. An organization that wishes to be entrepreneurial must set up systems that will develop and launch successful new offerings. There is an effective methodology for introducing new offerings which, while it does not guarantee success, usually raises the probability of success. Figure 9-1 shows the overall steps involved in new product development. These steps are described in the following sections.

Idea Generation

Organizations differ in their need for new ideas. Some organizations are quite busy carrying out their current activities and do not need new things to do. They may be prohibited by their incorporation documents or by their boards from doing certain things. A hospital, for example, is mandated to carry out certain procedures and is not interested in, nor legally able to undertake, new ventures not related to its main business. Other organizations need one or two big new ideas because their main business is

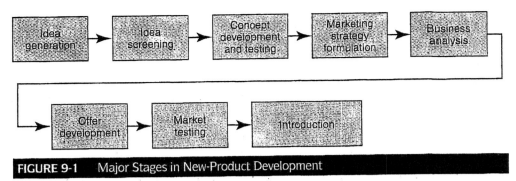

FIGURE 9-1 Major Stages in New-Product Development

taking a turn for the worse. In the early 1970s, the March of Dimes had to come up with an entirely new focus when polio was effectively controlled. Now, after shifting to a focus on birth defects over the succeeding 30 years, the March of Dimes is again thinking through a new redirection. The organization believes that an emphasis on "defects" is too restrictive and negative and it is repositioning its focus as being about "Helping You Have a Healthy Pregnancy and a Healthy Baby" (www.modimes.org). This refocusing throws open the door to all sorts of new enterprises (see Figure 9-2).

The idea generation stage is most relevant to organizations that need one or more ideas to maintain or expand their services. Indeed, it is our position that, given the high failure rate of many new ideas, the *more* ideas an organization generates—and the more diverse they are—the more chance there will be of finding *successful* ideas. Ideas can occur spontaneously from the following "natural" sources:

- Personal inspiration of one or more members of the organization
- Serendipitous stimuli from the environment—for example, learning of a new idea from a competitor or in discussion with nonprofit managers from other parts of the country or the world
- Client or donor requests for new offerings or modification of existing offerings

Such sources have two major shortcomings. First, relying on them requires a chance combination of an idea appearing *and* management's alertness in recognizing it. Reliance on these approaches may be acceptable for a fledgling nonprofit with a limited budget. However, they are definitely not the type of approaches a mature nonprofit organization ought to adopt. These casual approaches have a second problem. As noted by Crompton, "There is a great deal of evidence which suggests that many efforts to produce new programs which meet client needs are incestuous. That is, there is a tendency to reach for prior experiences, prior approaches, or moderate distortions of old answers, as opposed to really searching for new ideas. We become victimized by habit."[3]

If an organization is to be both systematic and creative in its idea generation, four steps must be taken:

1. A *commitment* must be made to seek new ideas routinely and formally.
2. *Responsibility* for this task must be specifically assigned to someone or some group.

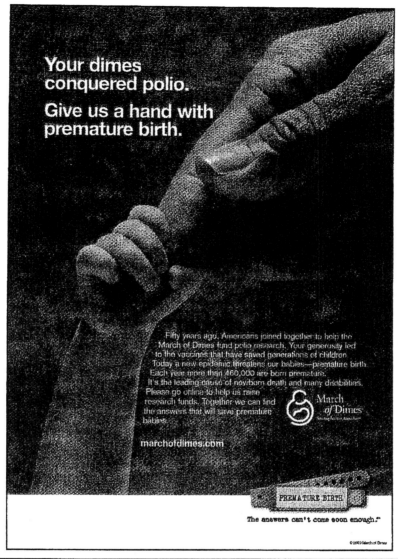

FIGURE 9-2 Refocusing the March of Dimes

Source: March of Dimes.

3. A *procedure* must be put in place for *systematically* seeking new ideas.
4. The procedure must contain a *creative* component if truly new ideas are sought.

Procedures for Gathering New Ideas

Establishing an idea generation *procedure* is part of the organization's knowledge management function as described in Chapter 5. It involves the organization staff outlining all possible sources for new ideas and then a strategy for generating or collecting ideas routinely from each source. Major sources and procedures for mining them are listed here:

1. *Similar organizations*
    a. A jointly funded clearinghouse could be established to share new ideas.
    b. Routine visits or telephone conversations with similar organizations on *specific dates* (for example, the first week of every February and every July) should be scheduled.
    c. Their web sites should be visited regularly.
    d. Particular attention should be given to innovations in other countries.

2. *Competitors*
    a. If the competitor has public meetings, for example, with community leaders, these should be attended to learn their development ideas.
    b. If board meetings are open to the public, someone should be assigned to attend them.
    c. Their web sites should be visited regularly.

3. *Grantmakers*
    a. Foundations and government agency RFPs (request for proposals) should be regularly scanned.
    b. Reports of recent grants should also be scanned in sources like *The Chronicle of Philanthropy*.

4. *Journals, newspapers, magazines*
    a. Potential sources of ideas should be identified, subscriptions should be acquired, and someone (or several people) should be assigned to peruse these sources routinely.
    b. A clipping service can be subscribed to.
    c. A librarian can be hired and assigned these tasks.
    d. Regular Web searches can be conducted on key words.
    e. Internet service providers like AOL can be requested to automatically e-mail relevant articles.

5. *Conferences, trade shows, lectures*
    a. People should be routinely assigned to attend important gatherings to collect ideas and useful literature.

6. *Target audiences and middlemen*
    a. The organization should *solicit* final target audiences and distributors for their ideas rather than wait until they spontaneously offer them. Many organizations obtain most of their best new ideas by actively listening to target audiences.
    b. Setting up a target audience response mechanism on the Internet can be very valuable. Stories from customers have been very helpful in advancing the efforts of the March of Dimes.[4]

7. *Employees and staff*
    a. The organization should *solicit* employees for suggestions and reward them monetarily or in some other way when these ideas are fruitful.

8. *The Internet*

   a. Web sites of competitors or similar profit or nonprofit organizations can be regularly scanned.

   b. General blogs in the broad area of the nonprofit's mission often reveal annoyances and suggestions in many domains.

Specific dates and responsibilities should be set for carrying out each of the previous information-gathering techniques. Further, a formal reporting and assessment mechanism should be developed to ensure that each idea will be formally considered. Finally, the system should be *unblocked*. Lower-level managers should not be able to sabotage the idea generation process by labeling ideas from underlings or outsiders as "too outrageous" or "not really appropriate for us right now." Such judgments must be top management's.

One technique for improving the likelihood that new ideas will emerge is to assign responsibilities to someone who might be called an *idea manager*.[5] The idea manager would serve as a receiving station for the good ideas spotted by others. He or she would do a preliminary analysis and evaluation of the ideas that flow in and make an effort to identify the really good ones—those that help the target audiences and the organization. Finally, the idea manager would shepherd new ideas through the organization and serve as their champion.

The idea manager function should be assigned to someone who has some power and stature in the organization, preferably within a broader "knowledge management" function. Other good candidates are the managers of strategic planning and marketing. Both managers must produce new ideas that will ensure a future for their institution. It is essential, however, that the nonprofit organization's CEO "buy" the idea of assigning idea management to one of these people.

Idea Screening

Once the idea-generating system has accumulated a significant array of ideas, some of them patently outlandish, some attempt must be made to winnow the set to the most promising ideas. The purpose of idea screening is to take a preliminary look at the new ideas and eliminate those that do not warrant further attention. There is some chance that screening might result in an excellent idea being dropped prematurely (a *drop* error). What might be worse, however, is accepting a bad idea for further development (a *go* error) as a result of not screening. Each idea that is developed takes substantial management time and money. The purpose of screening is, therefore, to eliminate all but the most promising ideas.

As an example, assume a university is looking for ideas for new programs to expand its educational services in the greater metropolitan area. Among the new program ideas are (1) a new program of women's studies, (2) a new program of black studies, (3) a school of dentistry, (4) a new adult degree program, and (5) a weekend executive master's degree program in business. The university does not have the resources to launch more than one of these new programs, so it needs a way to identify the most attractive program.

Several steps are necessary to ensure effective idea screening for the organization:

1. A formal screening committee should be established to evaluate new ideas. The committee should include representatives of each key functional department that has expertise that bears on one or more of the proposed undertakings.

2. Regular meetings should be scheduled to evaluate new ideas.
3. Criteria should be developed against which the ideas are to be evaluated. The criteria would be applied consistently over many evaluation sessions. Examples of such criteria include the following:

   a. Size of potential target audience
   b. Size of financial investment necessary
   c. Probable demand on management's time and energy
   d. Newness of the idea to the target audience and organization
   e. Consequences for the organization's desired public image
   f. Extent of probable competition
   g. Likelihood of outside funding assistance
   h. "Downside" consequences if the venture fails.

4. Weights for the criteria should be developed prior to *each* evaluation session. These weights should be set by top management since they will directly affect where the organization wishes to go in the future. Giving a heavy weight to "newness of the idea to the organization" (a negative trait), for example, inevitably means that the organization will accept more ideas nearer to its present offerings. Alternatively, giving a low weight to this factor implies that the organization is more likely to undertake relatively bold innovations.
5. Prior to the committee evaluation meeting, one or more staff members should prepare briefs on each idea as a basis for group discussion. Each brief should present data that are relevant to each of the major criteria.
6. The group should meet and discuss each idea. Afterwards they should rate each idea either individually or collectively on each criterion. (A form should be devised for this purpose.) Each evaluator (or the group as a whole) should also indicate how confident he or she is of the rating on each criterion.
7. A weighted value rating for each new idea should be computed along with a weighted certainty rating.
8. Candidate ideas should then be arranged by value and certainty ratings.
9. The best ideas should be moved on to the next stage. These choices will involve management trade-offs between value and certainty ratings.[6]

Concept Development and Testing

Those ideas that survive screening must undergo further development into full concepts. It is important to distinguish between an idea, a concept, and an image. An *idea* is something the organization can see itself offering to the market. The idea must be developed into a *concept* that is an elaborated version of the idea expressed ultimately as a value proposition in meaningful target audience terms. An *image* is the particular picture that target audiences acquire of an actual or potential innovation.

Concept Development

Suppose that as a result of screening the various new program ideas the university described earlier decides the best one is a new adult degree program. This is an offer *idea*. The university's task is to turn this idea into an appealing concept. Every idea can be turned into several concepts, not all of them equally attractive. Among the concepts that might be created around this idea are:

- *Concept 1.* An evening program with a liberal arts orientation, mostly required courses, and no credit for past experience.
- *Concept 2.* An evening program with a career development orientation, much latitude in the courses that could be taken, and credit for past experience.
- *Concept 3.* An evening program with a general education orientation for people over 50 years of age who want a bachelor's degree.

Concept Testing

Concept testing calls for gathering the reactions of target audiences to each concept. Each concept should be presented in written form in enough detail to allow the respondent to understand it and express his or her level of interest. Here is an example of Concept 2 in a more elaborate form:

> We are proposing to offer an evening program, called the School for New Learning, with a career development orientation and much latitude in the courses that can be taken. The program would be open to persons over 24 years of age, lead to a bachelor's degree, give course credit for past experiences and skills that the individual has acquired, give only pass–fail grades, and involve a "learning contract" between the student and the school.

Target audiences are identified and interviewed about their reactions to this concept. One approach is to use questions like those in Table 9-2. The last question in the table, for example, assesses the target audience's *intention to act* and usually reads, "Would you definitely, probably, probably not, definitely not enroll in this program?" Suppose that 10 percent of the target audience said "definitely will enroll" and another 5 percent said "probably will enroll." The university would apply these percentages (or slightly lower ones) to the corresponding size of the target market to estimate whether the number of enrollees would be sufficient. Even then, the estimate is at best tentative because people often do not carry out their stated intentions. Nevertheless, by ranking the alternative concepts with target audiences in this way, the university would learn which concept has the best market potential.

TABLE 9-2   Major Questions in a Concept Test for a New Educational Program

1. Is the concept of this adult degree evening program with its various features clear to you?
2. What do you see as reasons why you might enroll in this program?
3. What expectations would you have about the program's quality?
4. Does this program meet a real need of yours?
5. What improvements can you suggest in various features of this program?
6. Who would be involved in your decision about whether to enroll in this program?
7. How do you feel about the tuition cost of this program?
8. What competitive programs come to mind and which appeal to you the most?
9. Would you enroll in this program?

It is critical that there be a market for product and service offerings. The *Stanford Social Innovation Review* recently noted that "International development organizations spend lots of money and effort building the capacity of small businesses. Yet they often fail to ask whether people want the businesses' goods and services." Riordan says that "Today, nearly every international development organization claims to be demand-driven, and the term "demand-driven" has become a mantra. But despite the rhetoric, most international development practice remains supply-push, not demand driven." He concludes: "The best way to get a chain reaction of development going is one buyer at a time."[7]

Marketing Strategy Formulation

Once a concept has been chosen, the organization should develop a preliminary outline of the marketing strategy it would use to introduce the new program to the target audience. This is necessary so that the full revenue and cost implications of the new program can be evaluated in the next stage of business analysis.

The core marketing strategy should be spelled out in a statement consisting of three parts. The first part describes the size, structure, and behavior of the target market, the intended positioning of the new offering in this market including any branding options, and the volume and impact goals for the first few years. For the hypothetical university, this might be as follows:

> The target market is adults over age 24 living in the greater metropolitan area who have never attained a bachelor's degree but have the skills and motivation to seek one. This program will be differentiated from other programs by offering course credit for relevant past experience, as well as in its career development emphasis. It will be branded as the "Lived Learning" program. The school will seek a first-year enrollment of 60 students with a net loss not to exceed $300,000. The second year will aim for an enrollment of 200 students and a net profit of at least $100,000.

The second part of the marketing strategy statement outlines the offering's intended price (if any), distribution strategy, and marketing budget for the first year:

> The new program will be offered at the downtown location of the university. All courses will take place once a week in the evening from 6:00 P.M. to 9:00 P.M. Tuition will be $800 per course. The first year's promotion budget will be $100,000, $50,000 of which will be spent on advertising materials and media and the remainder on personal contact activities. Another $20,000 will be spent on marketing research to analyze and monitor the market.

The third part of the marketing strategy statement describes the intended long-run goals and marketing mix strategy over time:

> The university ultimately hopes to achieve a steady enrollment of 400 students in this degree program. When it is built up to this level, a permanent administration will be appointed. Tuition will be raised each year in line with the rate of inflation. The promotion budget will stay at a steady level of $70,000.

Marketing research will be budgeted at $10,000 annually. The long-run target profit level for this program is $200,000 a year, and the money will be used to support other programs that are not self-paying.

Business Analysis

As soon as a satisfactory offer concept and marketing strategy have been developed, the organization is in a position to do a hardheaded business analysis of the attractiveness of the proposal. The university, for example, must estimate the possible revenues and costs of the program for different possible enrollment levels. *Break-even analysis* is the tool most frequently used in this connection. Suppose the university learns that it needs an enrollment of 160 students to break even. If the university manages to attract more than 160 students, this program will produce a net income that could be used to support other programs; if there is a student shortfall, the university will lose money on this new program.

Offer Development

If the organization is satisfied that the concept is financially viable, it can begin giving the value proposition concrete form. The person in charge of the concept can begin to develop brochures, schedules, ads, marketing plans, and other materials to implement the program. Each of the developed materials should be *target audience tested* before being printed and issued. A sample of prospects in the target audience, for example, might be asked to respond to a mock-up of the brochure describing the new program. This usually results in valuable suggestions leading to an improved positioning.

Market Testing

When the organization is satisfied with the initial materials and schedules, it can set up a market test to see if the concept is really going to be successful. Market testing is the stage at which the offer and marketing program are introduced into an authentic target audience setting to learn how many target audiences are really interested in the program. Thus the university might decide to mail 10,000 brochures to strong prospects in the area during the month of November to see whether at least 30 students can be attracted. If more than 30 students sign up, the market test will be regarded as successful and full-scale promotion can be launched. Otherwise, the program can be reformulated or dropped.

Test markets are the ultimate form of testing the target market's reaction to a new product. The organization can use one or more sites to measure the new program's viability without installing it wholesale throughout the system. The market test can serve an important second function—determining which of the several alternative marketing strategies is best. Suppose that the University of Illinois (U of I) was considering the same new program as our hypothetical university. U of I consists of three campuses, not just one campus. It could develop the concept and test it at one of the campuses to see how well it works, or it could test it at all campuses. One campus could emphasize direct mail to alumni, a second could purchase a mailing list of non-alumni who might be interested, and the third could focus on Internet marketing to a broad audience. As a result, U of I could develop valuable insights into the cost-effectiveness of different promotional approaches. If the new program proved successful in one or all of the test markets, it could then be launched at each campus where appropriate.

Introduction to Market

Introduction to market is a set of activities undertaken following the test market's "go" recommendation to actually bring the new offering to market. The first step is to make four crucial decisions about the launch (although not all four will apply in every case):

1. *When* to launch. Factors to consider are (a) whether there is a need to first phase out an old program (for example, use up an existing lease), (b) whether there is a seasonal peak time for introducing the item (for example, a new museum for children at the start of summer or a drunk-driving program just before the Christmas holidays), (c) whether further work on the offer could profitably be carried out, and (d) whether there is any risk that important rivals will reach the market first (or otherwise compromise favorable launch circumstances).

2. *Where* to launch. If the offer is potentially to be marketed in a wide geographic area, the organization must decide whether to tackle the whole market at once or to start slowly, rolling out the offer on a market-by-market basis. A social service program, for example, could be aimed at the entire city or state or tried out neighborhood by neighborhood. The "whole market" approach has the advantages of scale economies, of preempting competitors, and of achieving significant advertising and public relations impact. It does, however, assume that the program has pretty well been finalized and that its chances of ultimate success are excellent. The advantages of the roll-out introduction, which can well compensate for its slower speed and greater total cost, are that (a) one can learn as one goes, and (b) if optimistic projections are not realized, the project can be aborted or "sent back to the drawing boards" at lower economic cost and with less embarrassment to the organization.

3. *To whom* to aim the launch. Even in a local roll-out, the program manager must decide whether to aim at all eventual target audience members or to focus at first on (a) those most likely to respond to the offer, (b) those most likely to have an important leadership role for others, or (c) both of these groups.

4. *How* to launch. Tactical decisions must be made about how to achieve the maximum impact at launch date and thereafter. Included are decisions about teaser ads, degree of secrecy, amount and type of media coverage, and so on.

A second step in this process is to assign responsibility for the launch and introductory period to some individual or group. Here, management must decide whether to have a separate venture management group (or individual) for the new offer, to have a separate new venture *department* to launch *all* new ventures, or to fold the new venture in with the responsibilities of an existing individual or departments.

The last step is to set up a formal scheduling procedure to ensure that all the needed tasks are (1) done in the right order, (2) done on schedule, and (3) done at the least possible cost. There are a number of valuable scheduling tools, such as PERT, CPM, and so on, for this task.[8] Most of them provide (1) directions for individuals who must accomplish each step, (2) a forecast of probable launch dates, (3) the critical series of steps (called *the critical path*) whose delay will mean postponing the launch date, (4) a monitoring tool with checkpoints to ensure that the process is on schedule, and (5) a decision-making capability that would permit the launch manager to decide which activities along the critical path to speed up if the project falls behind schedule.

OFFER LIFE CYCLE

Once an offering has passed through the Introduction to Market stage of the development process previously described, it must be launched and managed carefully. The performance of a new offering launched into the marketplace typically follows an S-shaped pattern known as the *offer life cycle* (OLC) (see Figure 9-3).

The S-shaped curve is marked by the following four stages:

1. *Introduction* is a period of slow growth as the offering is introduced into the market.
2. *Growth* is a period of rapid market acceptance.
3. *Maturity* is a period of slowdown in growth because the offering has achieved acceptance by most of the potential buyers.
4. *Decline* is the period when performance shows a strong downward drift.

The offer life cycle can be defined further according to whether it describes an offer *class* (mental health service), an offer *form* (psychoanalysis), or a *brand* (Menninger Clinic). The OLC concept has a different degree of applicability in each case. Offer classes have the longest life cycles. The performance of many offer classes can be expected to continue in the mature stage for an indefinite duration. For example, "mental health services" began centuries ago with organized religion and can be expected to continue in the mature state for an indefinite duration. Offer forms, however, tend to exhibit more standard OLC histories than offer classes. Thus mental health services are dispensed in such forms as psychoanalysis, bioenergetics, group therapy, and so on, some of which are beginning to show signs of maturity, while others, such as "Rolfing," may well be in their decline stage. As for brands, they are the most likely to have finite histories. Thus the Menninger Clinic is a well-known psychoanalytically oriented clinic that had a period of rapid growth and is now mature. It may pass out of existence or be absorbed by new corners.

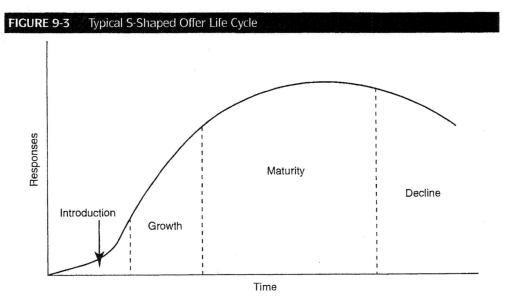

FIGURE 9-3 Typical S-Shaped Offer Life Cycle

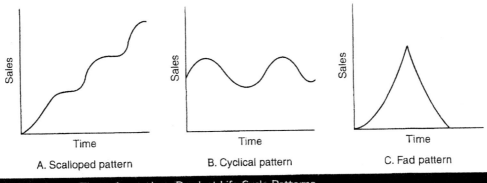

A. Scalloped pattern   B. Cyclical pattern   C. Fad pattern

FIGURE 9-4   Three Anomalous Product Life Cycle Patterns

Not all offerings exhibit an S-shaped life cycle. Three other common patterns shown in Figure 9-4 are as follows:

1. *Scalloped pattern.* (Figure 9-4A) In this case, the offer, during the mature stage, suddenly breaks into a new life cycle. The new life is triggered by modifications, new uses, new users, changing tastes, or other factors. The market for psychotherapy, for example, reached maturity at one point, and then the emergence of group therapy gave it a whole new market. At the brand level, interest in the March of Dimes was waning until the organization shifted its focus to birth defects and later to well babies.

2. *Cyclical pattern.* (Figure 9-4B) The performance of some offerings shows a cyclical pattern. Engineering schools, for example, go through alternating periods of high enrollment and low enrollment, reflecting changes in demand and supply in the marketplace. Preferences for political parties also seem to follow this pattern. The decline stage is not a time to eliminate the offer, but to maintain as much of it as possible, while waiting for the next up cycle.

3. *Fad pattern.* (Figure 9-4C) Here a new offer comes on the market, attracts quick attention, is adopted with great zeal, peaks early, and declines rapidly. The acceptance cycle is short and the offer tends to attract only a limited following of people who are looking for excitement or diversion. Some art and therapy forms exhibit the pattern of a fad.

While the fact that offers have life cycles may at first seem like just common sense, it turns out to be a useful strategic planning device because it alerts management to the fact that they need to adjust the focus of their marketing thinking depending on the OLC stage they are currently in. The next part of this chapter describes marketing strategies for the introduction and growth stages.

INTRODUCTION AND GROWTH STAGES

One way to characterize the changes sought by all marketers is to distinguish between first-time and repeat acceptance of the marketer's offering. Obviously, the strategic problems of getting people to take an action initially are very different from those of getting them to repeat or continue a given behavior. Thus getting someone to give

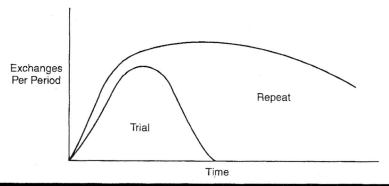

FIGURE 9-5   Trial and Repeat Behavior Over the Offer Life Cycle

blood the first time, begin going to the theater, or even vote Democratic for the first time can be very difficult. Once over this hurdle, the marketing task is infinitely easier, especially if the initial experience is satisfying.

Following this line of reasoning, responses in the offer life cycle can be divided into the two parts shown in Figure 9-5. For some nonprofit offerings, the OLC may *only* involve first-time use (i.e., innovation adoption). Thus a person needs to have only one smallpox shot; there (usually) is no need to repeat the operation. This, however, is relatively rare. Most strategies involve trial followed by repeat exchanges. Repeat exchanges may differ, however, as to whether we mean repeating an action like giving blood or attending an opera or whether we mean continuing a newly adopted behavior pattern like not smoking.

Innovation Adoption

Clearly, a challenge for many nonprofit behavioral interventions is to induce target audiences to try something new. Fortunately, there is a long history of social science disciplines studying the process by which target audiences begin something new.[9] Cultural anthropologists have researched how ancient cultures adopted new metals, new pot-glazing techniques, and new crops. Rural sociologists have studied how farmers have adopted new fertilizing and farm management practices and new types of seeds. Economists have investigated how firms adopt new manufacturing technologies like oxygen lancing in steel making, while educators have studied the dynamics of adopting teaching innovations, such as the "new math" or "new English." Social psychologists have studied the processes by which individuals acquire smoking, drug, and drinking addictions. And marketers, of course, have long studied new product and service adoptions.

The findings from these studies can help nonprofit managers understand how to induce first-time behaviors. First, they provide insights into the characteristics of those who adopt an innovation at different points during its introduction, growth, and maturity phases and into the interactions among these characteristics. Second, they describe the typical stages that individuals go through to adopt a given innovation. Finally, they identify the characteristics of offerings that will be relatively easy to introduce as compared to those that will not.

Finding Potential Innovators

A mass market approach to launching a new innovation typically does not make sense for a new nonprofit venture. It has two drawbacks: (1) It requires heavy marketing expenditures, and (2) it involves a substantial number of wasted exposures to nonpotential and low-potential target audience members. These drawbacks lead to a second approach, target marketing, in which the offer is directed to the groups that are likely to be most interested. It turns out that persons (or organizations) differ in how much interest they show in new ideas and in how fast they will move through the stages of change and try them. These people (or organizations) are early adopters, and the marketer of an innovation ought to direct marketing efforts to them. *Innovation-adoption theory* holds that:

1. Persons within a target market differ in the amount of time that passes between their exposure to a new offering and their trial of it.
2. Early adopters are likely to share some traits that differentiate them from late adopters.
3. There exist efficient media for reaching early adopter types.
4. Early adopter types are likely to be high on opinion leadership and therefore helpful in "advertising" the new offer to potential buyers.

Individual differences in response to new ideas is called their *innovativeness*. Specifically, innovativeness is the degree to which an individual or organization is relatively earlier in adopting new ideas than the other members of the social system. On the basis of their innovativeness, individuals or organizations can be classified into different *adopter categories*. In each product area, there are apt to be "consumption pioneers" and early adopters. Some women are the first to adopt new clothing fashions or new appliances, such as the microwave oven; some doctors are the first to prescribe new medicines;[10] and some farmers are the first to adopt new farming methods.[11]

Other individuals, however, tend to adopt innovations much later. This has led to a classification of people into the adopter categories shown in Figure 9-6.

The adoption process is represented as following a normal (or near-normal) distribution when plotted over time. After a slow start, an increasing number of people

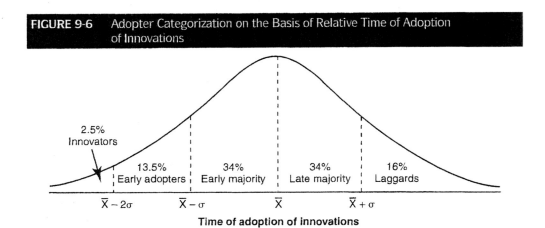

FIGURE 9-6   Adopter Categorization on the Basis of Relative Time of Adoption of Innovations

2.5%
Innovators

13.5%
Early adopters

34%
Early majority

34%
Late majority

16%
Laggards

$\overline{X} - 2\sigma$ $\overline{X} - \sigma$ $\overline{X}$ $\overline{X} + \sigma$

Time of adoption of innovations

adopt the innovation, the number reaches a peak, and then it diminishes as fewer persons remain in the nonadopter category.

Convenient breaks in the distribution are used to establish adopter categories. Thus innovators are defined as the first 2.5 percent of the individuals to adopt a new idea; the early adopters are the next 13.5 percent who adopt the new idea, and so forth.

Rogers has characterized the five adopter groups in terms of their central values.[12] The dominant value of the small group of Innovators who are the very earliest in the process is *venturesomeness;* they like to try new ideas, even at some risk, and are cosmopolitan in orientation. The dominant value of the next group, the Early Adopters, is *respect;* they enjoy a position in the community or in an industry as opinion leaders and adopt new ideas early with an eye to whether the adoption will enhance their status as trendsetters. This group contains a subset called the Opinion Leaders who are often looked to by others for leads on new ideas. The dominant value of the next group, the Early Majority, is *deliberateness;* these people like to adopt new ideas before the average member of the social system, although they are rarely leaders. Indeed, this group more often comprises the followers who pay attention to the advice given or the example set by the opinion leaders who preceded them. The dominant value of the Late Majority is *skepticism;* they do not adopt an innovation until the weight of majority opinion seems to legitimize its utility. They typically pay little attention to the opinion leaders, relying more on market cues of general acceptance. Finally, the dominant value of the Laggards is *tradition;* they are suspicious of any changes, and adopt the innovation only because it has now taken on a measure of tradition itself.

Rogers has characterized the traits of the key Earlier Adopters as follows:

> The relatively earlier adopters in a social system tend to be younger in age, have higher social status, a more favorable financial position, more specialized operations, and a different type of mental ability from later adopters. Earlier adopters utilize information sources that are more impersonal and cosmopolite than later adopters and that are in closer contact with the origin of new ideas. Earlier adopters utilize a greater number of different information sources than do later adopters. The social relationship of earlier adopters are more cosmopolite than for later adopters, and earlier adopters have more opinion leadership.[13]

These findings have obvious implications for the kind of strategy one should adopt as one moves through the introductory and growth phases.

Innovators

This group enters the market during the introductory phase of OLC. The marketer can largely ignore the group, however, for three reasons. First, they are a relatively small group. Second, because of their venturesomeness, they are likely to discover the innovation even without the marketer's help. Finally, they have little or no influence on those who follow later. Since the Early Adopters and Early Majority tend to look upon the Innovators as "try-anything-once" oddballs, the marketer runs a severe risk of cutting off further adoption by identifying too closely with this group.

Early Adopters

Early Adopters are the key to the success of most innovations. If one does not win them over, the introductory period will be prolonged, or the innovation may totally fail. Thus an important first step in any marketing program involving an innovation is to identify the Opinion Leaders. Unfortunately, opinion leadership is not a generalized trait. Particular target audiences or households may be Innovators in one area but not in another. The fraternity or sorority fashion leader may not be the first to give blood or attend the latest movies. Furthermore, the notion that innovations "trickle down" from the upper to the lower classes has been found to have limited application. Past research has shown that Opinion Leaders are not necessarily the elite of a society; they can be found in all social strata. Indeed, in recent years many innovations in fashion, music, sports, and the media have received their early push "on the streets" in poorer and ethnic neighborhoods. However, there is some evidence that the same opinion leaders may be found for *similar* innovations. Thus the Early Adopters of protective car seats for their babies might be good prospects as Opinion Leaders supporting airbag legislation. Yet these assumptions should be tested. Three approaches to identifying opinion leaders are possible:[14]

- *Self-reporting.* Individuals can be asked directly whether they would classify themselves as Opinion Leaders either in general or in ways related to the innovation in question.
- *Reputational.* Individuals may be asked to identify others to whom they might go for information or advice in this particular category. They can be asked to describe the most salient characteristic of these significant others.
- *Sociometric.* The researcher could directly map the interaction among members of a population and use this to determine the most influential members. Thus Coleman, Katz, and Menzel found that by asking physicians in a particular community whom they would contact (a) to refer a patient, (b) to secure advice on a medical problem, and (c) to socialize with, they could rather accurately predict who would be the Early Adopters of a new drug and who would be likely to follow them when they did.[15]

Early Majority

Some time will elapse before the marketer's strategy of attracting Opinion Leaders has its effect. The marketer should then make it clear to the Early Majority that the Opinion Leaders have already adopted—and, therefore, legitimized—the innovation. This can be accomplished by testimonials, editorials, and news and feature items. A good example of the use of opinion leadership has been the role of former First Lady Betty Ford in trying to get others to follow her lead in the detection of breast cancer and in the treatment of drug abuse, Elizabeth Taylor leading the way on HIV/AIDS, or U2's Bono setting an example in speaking out against Third World debt.[16]

The Late Majority and Laggards

Once the Early Majority has been heavily penetrated, tactics should shift from securing trial to emphasizing repeat behavior. This is desirable on two grounds. First, if a good trial rate has been achieved, competitors will enter the market and attention must shift to providing superior offers. Second, the emergence of more suppliers and offers will send a clear signal to the Late Majority that the innovation is accepted. By changing a campaign that says "Try this" to one that says "Try ours, not theirs," the marketer can make the Late Majority realize that the innovation is no longer risky. Whether such tactics will have an effect on the Laggards is unclear.

Stages in the Innovation Adoption Process

Rogers and Shoemaker[17] have identified four steps that individuals typically go through in adopting some new pattern of behavior. These steps exactly parallel the stages of change we have been using throughout the book:

1. *Knowledge* (Precontemplation stage). First, the target audience must (a) become aware of the innovation and (b) learn enough about it to deduce that it has some relevance to his or her needs, wants, and lifestyle.
2. *Persuasion* (Contemplation stage). Next, the target audience must move from simple awareness and vague interest to being motivated to take action. This is primarily a matter of attitude change, although it is also possible that a behavioral response could be achieved through *incentivization* or *coercion* with relatively little attitude change.
3. *Decision* (Preparation/Action stage). At some point, the target audience thinks through the probable consequences of the proposed behavior change and makes a decision to adopt or reject it. This stage might well involve a vicarious or personal trial. Thus a person suffering from hypertension might reduce salt intake for a few days or quiz others who have tried this approach.
4. *Confirmation* (Maintenance stage). After the initial decision, it is hoped that the target target audience will continue the behavior. This can be a major problem for social change agents.

The value of the stages of change model in launching new offerings is threefold. First, it points out that there is a *sequence* of tasks necessary to move a given target segment to adopt. Thus early messages must create awareness and interest, subsequent messages must persuade, and later messages and other marketing interventions must secure and reinforce behaviors.

Second, it provides a monitoring framework to help detect and identify reasons for a slow rate of acceptance. Thus if research on quitting smoking shows that many smokers are blocked at the Preparation/Action stage, persuasion attempts are no longer necessary and effort should focus on inducing a decision and action.

Finally, the model can be used to develop a segmentation strategy. Suppose that research has identified three target segments for a new health program: males working in blue-collar jobs, pregnant women, and senior citizens. Suppose that various proportions of the target audience members have reached the stages of the adoption process as listed in Table 9-3. Obviously, strategies aimed at the blue-collar male sample (Contemplators) should seek to produce decisions and action. As for pregnant women, some messages should create greater interest in the health program (for Precontemplators); other messages should reinforce the behavior of those who have already acted and are in the Maintenance stage. (Further research differentiating these two subpopulations could lead to finer tuning of strategy.) Finally, the majority of senior citizens are not being reached by current messages (Precontemplators). New messages, better execution, or better media are warranted.

TABLE 9-3	Hypothetical Distribution of Target Audience Members Across Adoption Categories		
Stage of Change	**Blue-Collar Male**	**Pregnant Women**	**Senior Citizens**
Precontemplation (No awareness)	4%	12%	53%
Precontemplation (No knowledge)	26	51	35
Contemplation	61	14	6
Preparation/Action	2	23	4
Maintenance	7	0	2
	100%	100%	100%

Innovation Characteristics

The innovation's characteristics will affect the rate of adoption.[18] Five characteristics have an especially important influence on the adoption rate. The first is the innovation's *relative advantage,* the degree to which it is perceived to be superior to previous ideas and behaviors. The greater the perceived relative advantage (higher quality, better lifestyle, lower cost, and so on), the more quickly the innovation will be adopted. Thus a five-day smoking cessation program that has a 35 percent initial success rate will be adopted faster than a three-month program that has a 20 percent initial success rate—even though both programs may have the same long-term effectiveness.

The second characteristic is the innovation's *compatibility,* the degree to which it is consistent with the values and experiences of the individuals in the target social system. Thus persuading Muslim women to practice birth control when they believe that their number of children is "in God's hands" will take more time than persuading them to boil water before drinking it, because the latter has no religious significance.

In the first year it attempted to establish opera in Los Angeles, the Los Angeles Music Center Opera organization portrayed a popular movie star, Dudley Moore, dressed in a modern suit on its promotional materials rather than traditional scenes from older operas. This strategy made opera attendance more compatible with Los Angeles's contemporary lifestyles and its identification with the movie industry.

The third characteristic is the innovation's *complexity,* the degree to which it is relatively difficult to understand or use. More complex innovations take a longer time to diffuse, other things being equal. Introducing dietary changes is much more difficult than introducing carpooling. Recycling has often been a challenge. Howard County has tried to make the behavior as simple as possible (see Figure 9-7).

The fourth characteristic is the innovation's *trialability,* the degree to which it may be tried on a limited basis. The evidence of many studies indicates that divisibility helps increase adoption. Thus a severely hypertensive person will be more ready to adopt a self-restricted diet than corrective heart surgery, since the latter is an all-or-nothing proposition.

The fifth characteristic is the innovation's *communicability,* the degree to which the intended results are observable or describable to others. Innovations whose advantages are more observable will diffuse faster in the social system. Thus obese people will adopt new eating and exercise habits faster than hypertensives because the former

FIGURE 9-7 Making Behavior Easy

Source: Howard County.

will observe their weight loss, whereas hypertensives will not observe any changes unless they use a blood pressure gauge.

The marketing strategist should research how any proposed innovation is perceived by the target market in terms of these five characteristics before developing the marketing plan. Preliminary studies of the potential for injectable, longer-term contraceptives in developing countries, for example, have brought to light the following characteristics:

1. *Relative advantage.* Three advantages are clear. First, the technique puts less of a burden on the woman in terms of memory and possible interferences with sex (real or perceived). Second, it is a technique that can be adopted easily and in

private. Thus it permits women to secure protection without their parents, friends, and sometimes their husbands or boyfriends knowing about it. Third, depending on the formulation, protection from one injection lasts one to three months.

2. *Compatibility.* Women are accustomed to taking injections for other purposes so that the concept is not as "strange" as some alternatives.

3. *Complexity.* There is an understandable problem for women in that the physical side effects are diverse and sometimes quite pronounced in early months. The problem is also complex for physicians because the U.S. Food and Drug Administration has banned the product because of a very, very small risk that it might produce breast cancer. Doctors face a tough ethical choice between endangering the mother due to the product and endangering her health from too frequent pregnancies.

4. *Divisibility.* Divisibility exists because the product can be stopped and another technique substituted. Several months have to elapse, however, before the women can become pregnant again.

5. *Communicability.* The product's effectiveness in preventing pregnancies can be easily communicated. However, there are problems at the confirmation stage in convincing women that the strong side effects are not serious and will disappear soon.

After learning how the innovation is perceived by the target audience, the marketer can then proceed to make the innovation relatively more advantageous, more compatible, less complex, more divisible, and more communicable.

Summary

To be successful in today's nonprofit environment, organizations must learn to effectively and efficiently develop and launch new offerings. These may involve new or existing offerings in combination with new or existing markets. Extensions into new offerings or markets may involve undertakings that are similar or dissimilar to present marketing programs. Often the challenge is in inducing target audiences to adopt behaviors that are new to them.

To be successful in developing new offerings, the organization must be both creative and systematic. The first stage of the process is to generate ideas for new offerings. This can involve careful searching of available information or attempts to create new ideas through artificial idea-generating techniques. Once the ideas have been produced, it becomes necessary to screen them to eliminate those that do not meet established organization goals.

The next stage involves elaborating the idea into a concrete concept that can be subjected to formal testing. The concept, if successful, must then generate a specific marketing strategy which, in turn, must survive a rigorous business analysis. The final stages of the development process then involve specific offer development and market testing, followed by a carefully orchestrated and timed commercialization process.

New offerings follow an S-shaped pattern over their life cycle. They move through introductory, growth, maturity, and decline stages. The strategic issues facing the nonprofit marketing manager differ across these stages.

In the introductory and growth stages, the manager must first be concerned with securing trials of the new offering. Five target audience groups may be identified on the basis of when they are likely to enter the innovation adoption process. First are the Innovators, who will try almost anything that is new and who are often considered odd by the rest of the population. They can usually be ignored by the new offer manager. The second group, the Early Adopters, cannot be ignored because they are the opinion leaders who influence the next large group, the Early Majority. The Late Majority, which enters next, pays less attention to others in making their decisions to adopt and must be convinced that the new offering is not a fad. The last group, the Laggards, can typically also be ignored because they are very tradition oriented and very slow to try anything new.

There is a clear set of stages through which anyone goes in adopting an innovation, from knowledge to persuasion to decision and confirmation. Innovations that have significant relative advantages over old approaches, that are compatible with the culture, and that are not complex and can be communicated easily and tried out before full adoption will diffuse faster than other innovations.

Questions

1. Suggest a fundraising event that has never been tried before but holds great promise. What would be your goals and how would you market it for maximum impact?
2. Is it reasonable to think of Innovators and Early Adopters among poor people in Africa? If so, how would you use the ideas for a microcredit enterprise?
3. How would you go about selecting villages in a specific African country where your limited staff should go to launch a microcredit program?
4. Think of a museum with which you are familiar. Assume that it has been offered a very large donation for a new wing if the donor can be assured that the wing will house something that will generate greatly increased attendance. What are the options and how should your team evaluate them?
5. You run a successful after-school mentoring program that emphasizes teaching and advancement in education. You would like to double the size and impact of your program. What are the kinds of new offerings that should be considered and how should they be evaluated?

Notes

1. A slightly different framework is provided in Chapter 3.
2. Mark R. Kramer, "Donors Too Often Support Visionaries Who Don't Have Management Skills," *The Chronicle of Philanthropy,* January 11, 2001, p. 48.
3. John Crompton, "Developing New Recreation and Park Programs," *Recreation Canada,* July 1983, p. 29.
4. www.shareyourstory.org
5. Philip Kotler, "Idea Management: A Way to Increase Health Services' Marketing Effectiveness," Presentation to Academy of Health Services Marketing, Las Vegas, Nevada, March 11, 1985.
6. See also Barry M. Richman, "A Rating Scale for Product Innovation," *Business Horizons,* Summer 1962, pp. 37–44; and John T. O'Meara, Jr., "Selecting Profitable Products," *Harvard Business Review,* January–February 1961, pp. 83–89.
7. James T. Riordan, "One Buyer at a Time," *Stanford Social Innovation Review,* Winter 2007, pp. 48–55.
8. For example, see Yoram J. Wind, *Product Policy: Concepts, Methods and Strategy*

(Reading, MA: Addison-Wesley, 1982), pp. 237–239; and Glenn L. Urban and John Hauser, *Design and Marketing of New Products* (Upper Saddle River, NJ: Prentice-Hall, 1980), p. 469.

9. Everett M. Rogers, *Diffusion of Innovations*, 5th ed. (New York: The Free Press, 2003).

10. See James Coleman, Elihu Katz, and Herbert Menzel, "The Diffusion of an Innovation Among Physicians," *Sociometry*, December 1957, pp. 253–270.

11. See J. Bohlen and G. Beal, *How Farm People Accept New Ideas,* Special Report No. 15 (Ames: Iowa State College Agricultural Extension Services, November 1955).

12. Everett M. Rogers, *Diffusion of Innovations,* 4th ed. (New York: The Free Press, 1995).

13. Ibid., p. 192.

14. Everett M. Rogers and David G. Cartano, "Methods of Measuring Opinion Leadership," *Public Opinion Quarterly,* Fall 1962, pp. 43–45; and George Booker and Michael J. Houston, "An Evaluation of Measures of Opinion Leadership," in Kenneth L. Bernhardt (Ed.), *Marketing 1776–1976 and Beyond* (Chicago: American Marketing Association, 1976), pp. 562–564.

15. Coleman, Katz, and Menzel, "The Diffusion of Innovation."

16. Barron H. Lerner, *When Illness Goes Public: Celebrity Patients and How They Look at Medicine* (Baltimore: The Johns Hopkins University Press, 2006).

17. Everett M. Rogers with F. Floyd Shoemaker, *Communication of Innovations* (New York: The Free Press, 1971).

18. Ibid.

10

MANAGING PERCEIVED COSTS

HOW DARE THEY CHARGE FOR THAT!

Jeffrey Sachs is a professor at Columbia University and was a Special Advisor to the UN's Kofi Annan. In recent years, he has become an active voice on strategies for fighting poverty and disease around the world. In many speeches and his latest book, *The End of Poverty,* Sachs has railed against the use of business approaches to social problems, particularly efforts by the International Monetary Fund and the World Bank to promote water and sanitation improvements towards which the poor would be expected to contribute.

He strongly argues against charging prices for products and services aimed at the dire problems of the poor. Here is what he said in his 2005 book: "In some cases, donors [for example, the US Agency for International Development] have supported a compromise formula called social marketing. . . . Social marketing has been applied, for example, to the sale of contraceptives and antimalarial bed nets. These recommendations have failed repeatedly. They have been unrealistic about what the poor can actually afford to pay, which is usually little or nothing. . . . The history of user fees imposed on the poor is a history of the poor being excluded from basic services."

Social marketers counter that very small prices can add value to a product or service designed for the poor. Organizations such as Population Services International have evidence that the poor value contraceptives more if they carry a small charge—often the cost of a single cigarette. Equivalent free public health products are often perceived as "not so good if they are free." Free items tend to sit on the shelves if they are free, whereas if one pays for something one is more likely to consume it. Indeed, an MBA student of one of the authors told of visiting a poor family in an impoverished African country and discovering several bednets in a back room that were described as "probably not very good. They were free!"

Source: Jeffrey Sachs, *The End of Poverty,* London, England: Penguin Books, 2005, especially p. 276.

Our view of the marketing task is that it starts with target audience members and their perceptions of the value proposition that the nonprofit marketer is offering. In the preceding three chapters, we considered some of the tactics a manager might use to increase the real and perceived benefits that flow from undertaking the desired behavior. In the present chapter, we look at the other side of the exchange equation: its costs. The reader will note that we said "costs," not "cost." This distinction is crucial to the manager's understanding of this component of the marketing task.

THE NATURE AND ROLE OF COSTS

In the Contemplation stage, target audience members mentally balance the expected benefits from an action against the expected costs. Money payment might be only one of these costs or sacrifices—a price in the traditional economic sense. Sometimes currency transactions might be absent altogether. Consider the case of a woman who is deciding whether to go to a doctor's office to have a breast examination because she has a history of breast cancer in her family. She has been exposed to social behavior marketing urging her to have regular examinations and to learn self-examination techniques. The visit to the doctor will cost her money. She will have to pay the doctor (or make a co-payment along with her insurance company). If she is an hourly worker and has no automobile, she will have to pay money for transportation and lose perhaps three hours of wages. If she is at home with a young child and drives, she may have to pay for a baby-sitter, an expressway toll, gasoline, and a parking fee.

Getting to and from the doctor involves nonmonetary costs in terms of physical energy or effort. For many, this may not be an important cost. For an elderly person, however, such a cost can be very dramatic. There are also a number of psychic costs, including:

- Awkwardness at having to ask for time off from work.
- Embarrassment at having to explain to coworkers where you are going (or lying to them).
- Aggravation at having to find a taxi and find one quickly so as not to wait long (or if she drives, aggravation at traffic delays and wasting time looking for a parking space).
- Worry that the doctor will be late in seeing her.
- Potential embarrassment that she will be criticized for delaying the examination.
- Embarrassment at having her breasts examined.
- Fear that the examination might hurt (for example, if a biopsy has to be done).
- Fear that something will be found.
- Worries that, if something is found, treatment will be costly, consume even more time, and be painful.
- Worries that treatment might involve breast removal, which can cause "disfigurement" problems, and embarrassment with her husband, children, and friends.

All of these perceived costs will run through the target audience's mind. A mistake that many marketers make when they expect mental resistance is to focus on restating again and again the *benefits* of having a periodic breast examination. Simply shouting about the good things that will result ignores what is really on the target audience's mind. It will probably fail to motivate many women. In fact, many women already know the benefits. *It is the vast array of perceived costs that keep them from completing the action the marketer wants.* This is particularly true in the latter part of the Contemplation stage. In a great many of the exchanges a nonprofit marketer seeks, managing the perceived costs is often much more important than managing the benefits. Furthermore, the nominal *money* price tag on the exchange may be the least important of the perceived costs the target audience member is concerned about; in social behavior exchanges, there usually is no monetary price tag at all. We define perceived costs as follows:

A *perceived cost is any expected negative consequence of a proposed behavior considered by a target audience member.*

It may be the case that many of the perceived costs are real and reasonable to think about. But there may be others—for example, fears of injury in the breast exam itself—that are unfounded. Rumors are a bane to many social marketing programs, especially in developing countries. Fears that high blood pressure medicine will affect a man's potency have caused some men not to carry out needed recommendations. It is important that rumors and unfounded beliefs about costs of behaviors be discovered and addressed if major progress is ever to be made.

The Duality of Costs

In an exchange, what is a benefit for one side of the exchange is typically a cost for the other. Thus a health care marketer who provides benefits to the target audience in the form of high-quality service, nice surroundings, and a satisfaction guarantee does so at a cost to the marketer's own organization. These are the economic costs *the marketer* has to pay. On the other hand, a target audience member paying money in exchange for these benefits provides a benefit for the marketer. Therefore, where an exchange involves a money price tag, the marketer is faced with an odd dilemma. While the marketer will work hard to *minimize* the various nonmoney costs target audiences might consider, the marketer would like to *maximize* the monetary costs to the target audience so the organization can stay in business and grow. To complicate matters even further, there may be occasions when the marketer may not want to minimize nonmoney costs and, indeed, may want to *increase* them. This is because the marketer will enjoy economic savings, which in turn will mean more profits from the exchange that could be used to reduce costs elsewhere or permit lower prices overall. Thus a transit authority may reduce the frequency of its service in a high-income area (thus increasing waiting time and frustration for this market) so as to provide more service in a low-income area, add more access for the disabled, or reduce the subsidy required from city or county revenues. Or a hospital may require a patient to walk in for simple outpatient surgery and bear some of the physical, economic, and psychic costs of managing his or her own convalescence in order to keep all patients' out-of-pocket costs as low as possible.

COST MANAGEMENT

This dual nature of cost management presents a delicate problem for the nonprofit marketer. An optimal cost management strategy from the marketer's standpoint is one that maximizes the number of exchanges (or revenues) for a given cost to the marketer. How can such a strategy be developed? As is always the case, the marketer must begin by researching audience perceptions of the costs they think they must pay. Otherwise, marketers may miss crucial but subtle barriers affecting particular audience segments. Consider the following examples:

- The National Cancer Institute only realized within the last 30 years that a perceived cost keeping many people from trying to quit smoking was the fear of failure.
- In rural villages in many countries, women who personally want to practice contraception do not do so because all the methods they know require that someone (or many people) become aware of their behavior.
- Some potential attenders of symphony concerts won't go because they believe they have to "dress up."
- Many elderly people do not attend theater in downtown areas because they believe they will be mugged or robbed.
- Many elderly people will not accept nursing home care because this involves admitting that they are old.
- Many alcoholics avoid treatment because they don't want to admit to themselves that they are alcoholics.
- Some males do not take medication for high blood pressure because they believe it will make them sterile or impotent.
- Some organizations won't hire consultants because to do so would be an admission that they lack certain competencies.
- Sanitary water systems are resisted in some villages because they disrupt established social intercourse systems (for example, the twice-daily congregation at the village well).
- Many potential theater, ballet, opera, and symphony attenders avoid going because they don't want to feel ignorant about what's being presented.

Once target audience perceived costs are understood, the marketer can consider the following questions: Are there strategies that can be used to reduce the perceived costs? What is the cost to the marketer of reducing a perceived cost to the target audience? What is the probable responsiveness of the audience to given levels of perceived cost reduction expenditure by the marketer?

While there are many factors to the cost challenge, we shall adopt a practical perspective.

Practical Management of the Cost Bundle

The difficulty of precisely estimating the likely audience response to a cost reduction should not discourage the marketer. If there is a single clearly important cost that drives audience demand (for example, money price), then a formal analysis of a single response curve may well be justified. As noted in Chapter 4, audience responses to value propositions are usually a reaction to a *bundle* of costs (and, of course, a bundle of benefits). The problem in managing *costs* rather than *a cost* (singular) is to figure out which of many costs to reduce and how much to reduce them. For these decisions, the marketing manager needs to know relative responses. That is, for a given amount of the marketer's expenditure, which cost or costs should be reduced to yield the largest net gain in the number of exchanges?

Suppose a nonprofit clinic is considering reducing one of several target audience costs. Suppose further that preliminary research indicates that four nonmoney costs keep potential patients from coming in more often (for example, for checkups) or drives them to other clinics or doctors. These costs are parking costs and the accompanying frustrations, waiting time in the office, inconvenience in filling out forms (for example, for insurance), and the generally unpleasant experience of waiting in unattractive facilities.

The marketer should first determine ways to reduce each cost. Assume that the marketer can spend increments of $5,000 to bring about improvements in each area. For $5,000, the clinic could improve its appearance (for example, the waiting and other rooms could be painted and new curtains installed). For $10,000, the clinic could also acquire new waiting room furniture. For $15,000, new carpeting could be installed, and so on. What the marketer now needs is a set of response functions for each of the four areas where costs can be reduced, as suggested in Figure 10-1.

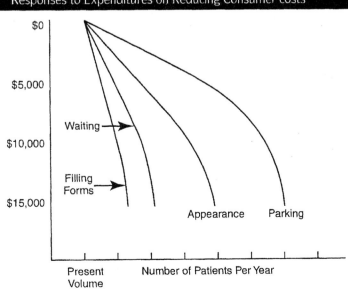

FIGURE 10-1   Responses to Expenditures on Reducing Consumer costs

As we can see, the best place to put the first $5,000 is toward improving parking. This yields the largest gain in exchanges. The next $5,000 should also go for parking. At that point, assuming that the cost functions are independent, a further $5,000 should be spent on appearance. Given that the marketer can estimate the economic value of the extra exchanges generated by each expenditure increment beyond those indicated in Figure 10-1, he or she can expend $5,000 amounts until the gain in value from the added number of patients is no greater than the last expenditure.

The level of precision the marketer needs for this task is not great. It may be adequate simply to secure intentions data from a representative sample of current and past clinic target audiences.

SETTING MONEY PRICES

A major determinant of the demand for many of the offerings of nonprofit organizations such as in the performing arts or at museum stores is money price. Further, more and more nonprofit organizations are seeking controllable revenues to reduce their reliance on grants, donations, and government contracts. These revenues come about from products and services for which prices have to be set.

In handling the complex issues in money pricing, an organization should proceed through two stages. First, it should determine the *pricing objective*, whether it is to maximize profit, usage, fairness, or some other objective. Second, it should determine the *pricing strategy*, whether it should be cost based, demand based, or competition based. Marketers may also wish to use promotional pricing on a short-term basis.

Setting the Pricing Objectives

The first thing an organization must decide in developing a price or pricing policy is the objectives that it wants to achieve. Often the objectives are in conflict, and a choice must be made. Consider the following statement made by a camp director: "I want to keep my camp tuition fees as low as possible to enable more people to enjoy a summer camping experience, but I also must keep the price high enough to ensure that the camp will not lose money in the long run."[1] In this case, the camp director is in conflict over the two opposing goals of *audience size maximization* and *cost recovery maximization*.

However, these are only two of several possibilities. Five different pricing objectives can be distinguished: surplus maximization, cost recovery, market size maximization, social equity, and market disincentivization. Returning to the camp illustration, the camp may aim for surplus maximization on conferences, full cost recovery on weekend retreats, market size maximization for its summer camp program, and lower prices for all events for low-income families to increase social equity.

Surplus Maximization

One would think that nonprofit organizations never use the principle of profit or surplus maximization. This is not so. There are many situations in which a nonprofit organization will want to set its price to yield the largest possible surplus. Thus a charity organization will set the price for attending a major benefit dinner with the objective of maximizing its receipts over its costs. A university whose faculty has developed patented inventions will price these inventions to maximize its profits. And, of course, the myriad nonprofits with extensive catalog and retail operations will clearly seek surplus maximization.

Surplus-maximizing pricing requires the organization to estimate two functions, the response (demand) function and the cost function. These two functions are sufficient for deriving the theoretical best price. The demand function describes the expected quantity demanded per period (Q) at various prices (P) that might be charged. Suppose the organization is a local opera company with many amateur performers and is able to determine through demand analysis that its demand equation is

$$Q = 10,000 - 100P \tag{10-1}$$

This says that attendance is forecasted to be at most 10,000 people (over multiple performances) if the price is 0, and for every $1 increase in price, there will be 100 fewer seats sold. Thus the number of seats sold at a price of, say, $40 would be 6,000 units [$Q = 10,000 - 100(40)$] for total revenues of $240,000.

The marketer then would need to figure out what the costs would be of generating each level of demand. For theatres, there will be a high fixed cost of putting on a production and opening the doors for each performance. There are then the marketing costs—advertising, public relations—involved in generating excitement plus staffing, playbills, and other costs that vary per person attending. These components yield total costs at various levels of demand. Suppose the fixed cost of all productions is $100,000, the cost of each performance (X) is $10,000, and the cost for attracting and servicing each person attending (Y) is $10. The cost equation is as follows:

$$C = \$100,000 + \$10,000X + \$10Y$$

If there are six performances and if tickets are sold for $40, then total costs are $220,000 and the surplus is $20,000.

The surplus maximizing price can be found in theory or in practice. Assumptions could be made or the researcher could use trial and error, trying out different prices over time to determine the shape of the surplus function and the location of the optimal price. However, the objective of seeking the surplus maximizing price, in spite of its theoretical elegance, is subject to five practical limitations:

1. The approach shows how to find the price that maximizes short-run surplus rather than long-run surplus. There may be a trade-off between short-run and long-run surplus maximization, as when clients get angry at high prices they must pay in the short run (e.g., for a special opera or a star performer) and eventually switch to other sellers (e.g., go to the theater instead).
2. There are other parties to consider in setting a price. The approach only considers the ultimate audience's response to alternative prices. Other groups that may respond are competitors, suppliers, intermediaries, and the general public. A high price might lead competitors to raise their prices, in which case the demand would be different from that suggested by the demand function if it assumed no competitive reaction. Various suppliers, employees, banks, and

producers of costumes and sets may take the price to reflect the organization's ability to pay and may raise their prices accordingly, in which case the cost function would be different from that assumed with no supplier reaction. Ticket brokers who handle the production may have some strong feelings about the proper price. Finally, the general public might complain about the organization if its price appears to be too high.

3. The local government, acting in the interests of the public, might establish a price ceiling, and this may exclude the surplus maximizing price.

4. This pricing approach assumes that price can be set independently of the other elements in the marketing mix. But the other elements of the marketing mix affect demand and must be part of the demand function in searching for the optimal price. Thus an opera company may be able to charge a higher price (i.e., shift the demand function) if it advertises extensively and builds up audience interest.

5. This pricing approach assumes that the demand and cost functions can be accurately estimated. In the case of a new opera company, there will be no experience upon which to base these estimates. Unless data are available on a similar company, estimates are likely to be highly subjective. Because the demand and cost equations are estimated with an unknown degree of error, the criterion of maximizing surplus may have to be replaced with the criterion of maximizing *expected* surplus where various demand levels for each price are weighted by their likelihood of occurrence. In any situation of risk and uncertainty, the pricing decision maker will want to see how sensitive the theoretically calculated optimal price is to alternative estimates of the demand and cost functions.

Cost Recovery

Many nonprofit organizations seek a price that would help them recover a "reasonable" part of their costs. The expectation is that taxpayers, donors, and corporate sponsors will pick up the rest. This is the idea behind the pricing of Metropolitan Opera productions, postal services, and public mass transit services. Although some of these organizations could conceivably charge higher prices and increase their revenue (for example, if they have a monopolistic position), they do not want to incite an adverse reaction from the public or legislature.

How much cost should the organization try to recover through its pricing? Some organizations—such as universities and public mass transit organizations—aim at recovery of their operating costs. This would not provide money for expansion for the development of capacity but is sometimes seen as "fair." Many nonprofit organizations brag about their low overhead yet such a condition may mean that the organization is ill-prepared for environmental shocks or is postponing maintenance (a problem at Smithsonian Institution museums) or development of state-of-the-art knowledge management systems.

Market Size Maximization

Some nonprofit organizations (public libraries and museums, for example) and social marketers dealing with the poor and needy want to maximize the total number of people who carry out sought behaviors—reading, attending the arts, or exercising. In these cases, a zero price will attract the greatest number of users. Even here there can be exceptions. Consider the following situation:[2]

Health marketers in India initially believed the distribution of free oral rehydration solution for the control of diarrhea would lead to the greatest level of usage. However, they discovered two flaws in the reasoning. Some potential target audience members interpreted the zero price to signify low quality and avoided the free brand. In addition, many retailers would not carry it or display it prominently because it did not yield them profit, with the result that fewer units were ultimately available to target audience members.

In most situations, a low price normally stimulates higher usage *and* may produce more revenue in the long run. Weinberg advocates that theaters should set low ticket prices because this attracts a larger audience, many of whom would eventually make donations to the theaters that would more than make up for the lower ticket prices.[3]

Social Equity

Organizations may wish to price their services in a way that contributes to social equity. In a study of who pays for library services, Weaver and Weaver concluded that "public libraries actually distribute income from the poorest to the more affluent strata of the community."[4] One of the principal arguments leading to this conclusion is that because the poor rarely use the public library and because public libraries are typically supported out of general tax revenues, the working poor are paying for the nonpoor's libraries. Admittedly, there are other situations, such as city parks and welfare services, where the reverse is true. Our concepts of social equity hold that, wherever possible, public (and by extension, nonprofit) services should not operate to transfer wealth from the poor to the rich. In the public library case, the goal of social equity might be achieved by charging users for library services, perhaps charging even more for services (such as DVD rentals) that the upper classes use relatively more often.

Market Disincentivization

Pricing might be undertaken for the objective of discouraging as many people as possible from engaging in a particular behavior. There are many reasons an organization might want to do this. It might want to discourage people from overtaxing a facility; it might be trying to ration anti-flu drugs to solve a temporary shortage; or it might want to discourage certain classes of buyers—for example, those getting pleasure from various self-help groups without actually needing much help.

The purpose of the high government tax on cigarettes and liquor is to drive up the price and thereby discourage the use of these products. It is considered one of the best tools for reducing teen smoking. But the price is never raised high enough to have a huge impact because the government has come to rely on the substantial revenue produced by these taxes. A tax that is truly disincentivizing would yield the government no revenue and possibly create a large black market.

In this regard, the Chinese government faces a particular dilemma.[5] The cigarette industry is controlled by a government monopoly. It sells about one-third of all of the world's cigarettes, in part because 60 percent of Chinese men smoke and ads from the tobacco industry proclaim health and social benefits from consumption. Most significant to both pricing and anti-smoking decisions is the fact that cigarette taxes bring in about 10 percent of government revenues. Outside attempts to get the government to face the health consequences of smoking—for example, by raising taxes and therefore prices significantly—have found little support.

Public mass transit companies frequently use disincentive pricing to smooth demand and not overburden their systems. The Metro system of Washington, D.C., raises fares during morning and evening rush hours.

A final example is the city of London, England, which imposed a price on a previously free good—driving in the city.[6] Faced with increasing congestion and growing air pollution, London Mayor Ken Livingston decided in 2003 to create "congestion charging zones" in the city to cut traffic on major streets at busy times. If a motorist wants to come into the city, he or she must pay a fee to do so. Livingston claimed that in the first two years of the program carbon monoxide levels were down, 50,000 fewer cars were entering the city daily (a drop of 30 percent), and more people were taking the bus.

These strategies have the effect of creating potential costs for one behavior because the nonprofit organization really wants the alternative behavior. Target audiences change their behavior in order to *not* pay a fee or to pay a lower fee. This means that it is especially important for nonprofit marketing managers to carefully understand what the target audience considers as competition for the behavior. Sometimes the marketer—as in the case of Ken Livingston—can control aspects of the value propositions for both the desired behavior (not driving into the city) and its competition (driving into the city). States that raise tobacco taxes while simultaneously promoting non-smoking behavior and supporting just-quit clinics are similarly affecting both the desired behavior and its competition.

CHOOSING A PRICING STRATEGY

After the organization has defined its pricing objective, it can consider the appropriate strategy for setting a specific monetary price. Pricing strategies tend to be cost oriented, value based, or competition oriented.

Cost-Oriented Pricing

Cost-oriented pricing refers to setting prices largely on the basis of costs, either marginal costs or total costs including overhead. Two examples are markup pricing and cost-plus pricing. They are similar in that the price is determined by adding some fixed percentage to the unit cost. *Markup pricing* is commonly found in the retail trades where the retailer adds predetermined but different markups to various goods. Museum gift shops use markup pricing in pricing their various items. *Cost-plus pricing* is used to describe the pricing of jobs that are nonroutine and difficult to "cost" in advance, such as some kinds of marketing research and many services.

Nonprofit organizations vary in where they peg their prices relative to their costs. The American Red Cross charges a price for its blood that covers the "irreducible cost of recruiting, processing, collecting, and distributing the blood to the hospitals." However, as previously noted, several nonprofit organizations in the arts have historically charged less than their costs (called cost-minus pricing). Tuitions at private colleges and ticket prices for symphony orchestras often cover less than 50 percent of the total cost of these services; the remaining costs are covered by donations, grants, and interest on endowment funds.

A popular form of cost-oriented pricing uses *break-even analysis*. The purpose of break-even analysis is to determine, for any proposed price, how many units of an item would have to be sold to cover fully the costs; this is known as the *break-even volume*. To illustrate, the director of a summer camp wants to set tuition for an eight-week summer session that would cover the total costs of operating the camp. Suppose the annual fixed costs of the camp—real estate taxes, interest charges, physical property, insurance, building maintenance, vehicle expense, and so on—are $200,000. This is shown on the break-even chart in Figure 10-2 as a horizontal line at the level of $200,000.

The variable cost for serving each camper—food, handicraft supplies, camper insurance, and so on—is $500 per camper. This is shown on the total cost line, starting at $200,000 and rising $500 for each camper. Finally, the camp director initially considers charging $1,000 tuition per camper. This is shown on the total revenue line, which begins at $0 and rises $1,000 per camper. The number of campers needed to break even is determined by the intersection of the total revenue and the total cost lines, here 400 campers. If the camp fails to attract at least 400 campers at $1,000 each, it will suffer a loss varying with the number of campers attracted. If the camp attracts more than 400 campers at $1,000 each, it will generate profits. The camp director's task is to estimate whether it will be easy or difficult to attract 400 campers at a tuition of $1,000.

FIGURE 10-2   Break-Even Analysis

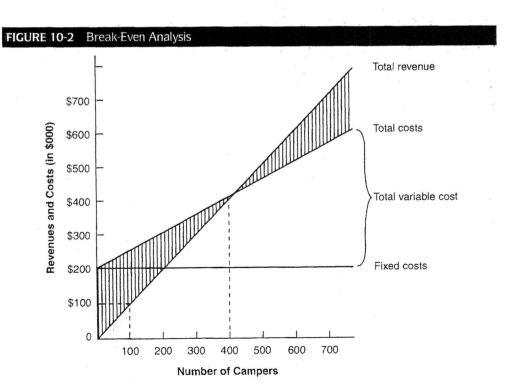

The break-even volume can be readily calculated for any proposed price by using the following formula:

$$\text{Break-even volume} = \frac{\text{Fixed cost}}{\text{Price} - \text{Variable cost}} \qquad \textbf{(10-2)}$$

Using the numbers in the previous example, we get

$$\text{Break-even volume} = \frac{\$200,000}{\$1,000 - \$500} = 400$$

However, if the camp director thought of charging $700 tuition, he would have to attract 1,000 campers to break even (Equation 10-2).

Cost-oriented pricing is popular for a number of reasons. First, there is generally less uncertainty about costs than about demand. By basing the price on cost, the seller simplifies the pricing task considerably; there is no need to make frequent adjustments as demand conditions change. Cost-plus pricing is also easier to implement for organizations that have a great many items to price, such as museum bookstores or Boy Scout equipment centers. Second, when all organizations in the industry use this pricing approach, their prices are similar if their costs and markups are similar. Price competition is therefore minimized, which would not be the case if competitors paid attention to demand variations. Third, there is the feeling that cost-plus pricing is socially fairer to buyers and sellers. Sellers do not take advantage of buyers when the demand becomes acute, yet sellers earn a fair return on their investment. It is also seen as socially fair when different prices must be charged to different users (i.e., everyone pays 20 percent over costs). Thus the popularity of cost-oriented pricing rests on its administrative simplicity, competitive harmony, and social fairness.

Value-Based Pricing

The problem with cost-oriented pricing is that it ignores how valuable the offering is to target audiences. Value-based pricing looks at the strength and nature of demand rather than the level of costs to set the price. Value-based approaches estimate how much value buyers see in the offer, and then price accordingly. Thus a fine arts organization might set a ticket price of $150 for a Yo-Yo Ma concert and $45 for a cello concert by a less well-known performer. The premise is that price should reflect the *perceived value* in the audience's head. A corollary is that an organization should invest in building up the perceived value of the offer if it wants to charge a higher price. Thus a private college that builds a reputation for excellence in teaching and research can charge a higher tuition than can an average private college.

There are two difficulties in employing value-based pricing. As mentioned earlier, it is often difficult to learn what target audience members would pay for a given product or service. This is especially true if the offering is one that is very new to the world or the target market and if it involves outcomes that are hard to describe or predict. If a nonprofit in Latin America decides to offer a weight reduction program based on hypnotism to overweight rural men as a way of improving their longevity, establishing a price may be very difficult because (1) it may be hard for the target audience to envision what benefits they might get from participating—and, indeed, what participating itself might actually involve, and (2) it may be hard for the nonprofit to be very confident about the success rates it claims for the service. Nevertheless, presenting target audiences with the concept and seeking their reactions to different pricing strategies may reveal the most acceptable price and perhaps the upper limit.

The other difficulty for the nonprofit is an ethical one. Many nonprofit offerings are very valuable to target audiences. Pills to reduce hypertension can be *extremely* desirable to persons who have lost relatives to high blood pressure. AIDS "cocktails" are critical to the long-term survival of those with the disease. And sugar/salt solutions can be *extremely* valuable to families who have lost children to diarrhea. In such cases, it is possible for the nonprofit to secure very high prices if it were to look only at the perceived value to the audience. However, it will typically choose a price that will be substantially less than what the traffic will bear because of the organization's broader ethical responsibilities to its society.

Competition-Oriented Pricing

Competition on which pricing may be based on alternative organizations, such as a rival museum. On the other hand, the museum marketer may consider competition to include movies or dining out for audiences who see museum-going as a relaxing break from routine. In such cases, the nonprofit marketer may choose to charge the same as the competition, a higher price, or a lower price. The distinguishing characteristic is that the organization does *not* seek to maintain a rigid relation between its price and its own costs or demand. Its own costs or demand may change, but the organization maintains its price because competitors maintain their prices. Conversely, the same organization will change its prices when competitors change theirs, even if its own costs or demand have not altered.

Ethical Challenges in Pricing

Nonprofit organizations have some difficult challenges in setting prices because the public—or specific segments—may have strong feelings about what is "fair" or whether there should be any charge at all. Should there be lower prices—or no charge—for the poor for condoms or anti-malarial bednets? What about cultural facilities? Museums owned by the government in Washington, D.C., are free, but the Corcoran Gallery of Art lists an "Admission" of $8 for adults but says "visitors are invited to make a donation in an amount of their choosing."

Views are mixed. The director of the Museum of Modern Art in New York says that "it's almost a moral duty that museums should be free." In the other corner is the director of the Metropolitan Museum of Art who says that prices are extremely high for rock concerts and sports events and "What is it about art that it *shouldn't* be paid for?" Ironically, the $20 fee at MoMA is mandatory (as is the $12 fee at the Art Institute of Chicago), while at the Met the policy is like the Corcoran—pay as you wish but $20 is *suggested*. Are these organizations really entertainment centers or educational and research institutions? Public libraries are free—but should they have a "suggested charge?"[7]

One of the reasons that museums have become more aggressive about pricing may be that the revenues from their growing gift shop and related product sales have fallen short of expectations and even declined.[8] On the other hand, many museums have recently gotten subsididies from city governments or local corporations and so have eliminated fees. But what if they do not? One might argue that donor gifts adequately support arts institutions (unlike libraries). But donors usually pay only for art and not operations. Are museums let off the moral hook if they charge but allow free or pay-what-you-wish hours or days for the general public? These are not trivial issues as museums can derive as much as 15 percent of total revenues from admissions fees.

VARYING COSTS ACROSS SEGMENTS

Price discrimination goes on in nonprofit organizations all the time. For example, theaters and concert halls discriminate very often on the basis of (1) time of purchase (early ticket purchasers pay less than those who pay at the door), (2) location (seats close to the stage cost more than seats in the rear balcony), (3) method of payment (purchasers through Ticketmaster will pay a premium over those who come to the box office to purchase), (4) time of performance (those wanting to go on a Saturday night will pay more than those going to a Sunday matinee), and (5) quantity and timing of purchase (those who buy season tickets will pay less than those who buy at the door).

Each of these tactics represents an attempt by a nonprofit marketing manager to achieve one of the following goals:

- Match the price to the cost of providing the product or service: Ticketmaster charges premiums to help pay for extra paperwork, credit card processing fees, and so forth.
- Match the price to the value received: Closer seats are more valuable.
- Regulate demand: Lower prices for matinees are, in part, an attempt to shift demand to "off-peak" hours of service.
- Capture the most a target audience will pay.

The latter is an important point. Target audiences who pay a premium to a ticket broker or to attend on a Saturday night are doing so because this is what they really want. They are willing to pay more in order to get what they really want. A Rolls Royce Silver Cloud does not cost 10 to 15 times more than a Honda Civic to build, but target audiences are willing to pay that much more because that is what they want, and they can afford to pay it. Much so-called discriminatory pricing is designed to capture that "target audience surplus" (i.e., what some potential target audiences would be willing to pay over and above a simple cost-plus price).

PROMOTIONAL PRICING

Often a nonprofit organization will maintain its list price but introduce "price specials" in order to stimulate increased buying. This, of course, happens in the private sector all the time. Promotional pricing can take many forms. Consider a theater performance group that wants to attract a larger audience to its performances. Here are some promotional pricing options:

1. The theater group can promote a series subscription that represents a savings over buying individual tickets to all of the performances. A popular way to express the savings is "See five plays for the price of four." Newman strongly favors discounts for subscription series on the grounds that the savings are a prime motivator for buying a subscription.[9] But Ryans and Weinberg, in a survey of subscription buyers for the American Conservatory Theater (ACT) in San Francisco, found that subscribers reported that the main reason for buying subscription series was not the savings but to make sure they went to the theater more often and were assured a good seat. ACT abandoned the discount in the next season with no palpable impact on subscription sales.[10]

2. The theater group can offer an "early bird" discount on the series subscription to those subscribing up to two months in advance of the first performance.

3. The theater group can offer second tickets at half price. Andreasen and Belk found potential theatergoers reacting extremely favorably to this proposal, reacting even more positively than to percentage discounts ("40 percent off") that were better bargains.[11] It apparently taps into the notion of bringing a friend or a date to the theater.

4. The theater group can offer unsold tickets at half price on the day of the performance. This method is used successfully by the ticket kiosks in New York City, Boston, London, San Francisco, and Washington, D.C. The theater gets not only the extra seat revenue it would have lost, but also the revenue from the sale of drinks and candy during intermission.[12]

Summary

Nonprofit marketers seek to influence exchanges through attractive value propositions. From the target audience's perspective, these exchanges involve trading bundles of benefits for bundles of costs. Costs are the prices the target audiences perceive they must pay to participate. They can be monetary, nonmonetary, or mixed. Nonmonetary costs include psychic pain, the need to change old habits or ideas, expenditures of time and energy, and dislocations of social arrangements.

The nonprofit manager has a dual task in managing these costs. Some costs must be kept reasonably high if they are needed to ensure continuing revenues to the organization. Other costs must be reduced as much as possible to lower barriers to target audience action. Since it will cost the organization to reduce each of these costs, it needs to know the relative responsiveness of target audiences to each of these reductions.

In developing a strategy for monetary prices, the organization must first establish objectives. It could seek surplus maximization, cost recovery, market size maximization, social equity, or market disincentivization. Its specific strategy to meet these objectives may be primarily cost oriented, demand oriented, or competition oriented. On some occasions, the imposition of a fee on undesirable behavior, when this is under the marketer's control, in effect adds a value to the desired behavior—a cost saving.

Questions

1. What forms of price discrimination could a YMCA manager utilize if her goal is to maximize revenues? Explain your reasoning for each form you identified.
2. Do all people over 75 perceive the same costs of moving from their home to an assisted-living location? Identify the cost differences for various segments and explain how you would seek to reduce these costs.
3. You are the board chairperon for your local children's museum. The museum is high on intereactivity and education and historically has been supported by the state's education department and three local coporations. In the last two years, two corporations have shifted their support to other charities and the state has cut back on subsidies. The museum director has come to the board with a proposal to begin charging admission for the first time. How would you organize the discussion of this proposal? What would be your position?
4. You want to use costs as a way to allocate the usage of the equipment and play areas of your after-school facility. One suggestion is to charge annual—but low—fees based on income. Another idea is to make it harder to use the Playstation games and the craft materials. What is your reaction to these ideas?
5. What position would you take on Jeffrey Sachs' argument that it is immoral to charge poor, starving people anything for something that could save their lives or the lives of their children?

Notes

1. Quoted from an article by Ben F. Doddridge, "Toward the Development of a Practical Approach for a Solution of the Pricing Dilemma," *Christian Camping International*, January–February 1978, pp. 19–22.
2. See T. R. L. Black and John Farley, "Retailers in Social Program Strategy: The Case of Family Planning," *Columbia Journal of World Business*, Winter 1977, pp. 33–43.
3. Charles Weinberg, "Marketing Mix Decision Rules for Nonprofit Organizations," in Jagdish Sheth (Ed.), *Research in Marketing*, Vol. 3 (Greenwich, CT: JAI Press, 1980), pp. 191–234.
4. Frederick S. Weaver and Serena A. Weaver, "For Public Libraries the Poor Pay More," *Library Journal*, February 1, 1979, pp. 325–355.
5. Geoffrey York, "In China, Cigarettes Are a Kind of Miracle Drug," *Globe & Mail*, June 11, 2005, p. A14.
6. Rachel Gordon, "London's Traffic Tactic Piques Interest in S.F. Congestion Eased by Making Drivers Pay to Traverse Busiest Areas at Peak Times," *San Francisco Chronicle*, June 4, 2005.
7. Roberta Smith, "Should Museums Always Be Free?" *New York Times*, July 22, 2006, pp. A13, A19.
8. Stefan Toepler, "*Caveat Venditor?* Museum Merchandising, Nonprofit Commercialization, and the Case of the Metropolitan Museum in New York," *Voluntas*, Vol. 17 (2006), pp. 99–113.
9. Danny Newman, *Subscribe Now!* (New York: Publishing Center for Cultural Resources, 1977).
10. Adrian B. Ryans and Charles B. Weinberg, "Target Audience Dynamics in Nonprofit Organizations," *Journal of Target Audience Research*, September 1978, pp. 89–95.
11. Alan R. Andreasen and Russell W. Belk, "Target Audience Response to Arts Offerings: A Study of Theater and Symphony in Four Southern Cities," in Edward McCracken (Ed.), *Research in the Arts* (Baltimore: Walters Art Gallery, 1979), pp. 13–19.
12. "New York City Opera Rolls Back Prices," *The Cultural Post*, Vol. 7 (March–April 1982), p. 9.

11

FACILITATING
MARKETING BEHAVIORS

PERRY ELLIS DRESSES KATRINA VICTIMS!

Suppose you are Fanny Hanono, Secretary-Treasurer of Perry Ellis International, a major clothing manufacturer. This is how your company describes itself: "Perry Ellis International is a leading designer, distributor and licensor of apparel and accessories for men and women. The company, through its wholly owned subsidiaries, owns or licenses a portfolio of brands that includes 27 of the leading names in fashion such as Perry Ellis®, Axis®, Savane®, Farah®, Original Penguin®, Cubavera®, Ping® Collection, Nike® Swim, Jantzen®, Tricots St. Raphael®, and Grand Slam®."

It is August 30, 2005, and you have been inundated with vivid images of Hurricane Katrina and the damage its 125-mph winds have done—and are doing—to Louisiana and Mississippi, especially to the city of New Orleans. You hear about the number of nonprofits rushing to help residents. Donations are pouring in to the American Red Cross, the Salvation Army, and other relief agencies. You want to help not with money but with the merchandise for which you are famous. People are homeless and thousands have lost most of their possessions. You can help.

But companies like Hanono's have a number of concerns. First, how do they actually get the merchandise to where it is needed? Who should be the recipients at the disaster sites? How does one make sure that the clothing goes to the needy and not find its way onto the black market?

Fortunately, there exist a number of nonprofit organizations expressly focused on helping with distribution problems for firms like Perry Ellis which have merchandise they want to give to social causes. A great many corporations have charitable giving programs that go beyond giving money and volunteering staff—the donation of goods and services. The organization that Perry Ellis turned to for help was Gifts in Kind International, in 2006 the seventh largest nonprofit organization in terms of donations received.

It turns out that Gifts in Kind International maintains a carefully selected—and vetted—set of charity partners in each of the affected areas (as it does in hundreds of other areas, including international sites). Further, it has in place an efficient warehouse and distribution system to take delivery of the merchandise and make sure it gets in the right hands. And, finally, it has strong agreements with its recipient agencies to make sure they do not misuse the goods. In connection with Katrina, Gifts in Kind established over 30 donation and relief centers throughout the gulf region. They then passed on merchandise like Perry Ellis's $450,000 worth of goods to frontline organizations for distribution.

The CEO of Gifts in Kind International was able to say: "Hurricane Katrina has devastated the lives of thousands of people and we hope that our collaborative efforts will give Katrina victims a sense of relief and support during this difficult and challenging time."

Source: "Perry Ellis International Aids Victims of Hurricanes Rita and Katrina," 2005 press release, www.pery.com. Retrieved November 6, 2006.

In this chapter, we focus primarily on the challenges involved in getting target audience members through the Preparation/Action stage. As we have said repeatedly, the bottom line of nonprofit marketing is influencing behaviors. And behaviors take place on specific occasions at specific times and places. Making behavior easy to accomplish—even pleasant to accomplish—is a key component of the marketing mix. In the case of products, this means that the goods must be made available and physically delivered to target audiences through Internet connections, retail outlets, or shops on the nonprofit's premises. For services, it means making the services available when and where the consumer can use them and, preferably, in an attractive, welcoming environment that encourages repeat visits and/or strong word-of-mouth promotion. For social behaviors where a product or service is not involved, it means arranging stress-free, convenient means for target audience members to do what the marketer hopes that he or she will do.

In the private sector, this is often referred to as the "place" component of the marketing mix. Here, we refer to it as "Facilitation."[1]

Consider the challenge of getting a TV news director to cover a nonprofit event. Assume she has become aware of the event through past communications or some memo and has thought about it enough to be inclined toward covering it. However, she is still reluctant. It is at this point that the nonprofit marketer needs to think very hard about what can be done to make the event feasible, easy, and (hopefully) pleasant and rewarding for the news director and her staff. The marketing director should also be thinking of ways to use the occasion to build an enduring relationship that will lead to future transactions (i.e., future coverage). Among the facilitation options the marketer may employ are these:

- Scheduling the event when it is best for the director's news cycle
- Providing convenient VIP parking and easy access for the film crew and their equipment
- Having attractive, articulate interviewees ready for the TV crew when they arrive
- Making sure that the event itself has a lot of visual elements that would look good on TV

- Making sure the event (or the interview) is completed in time for the news director to get the tape edited and onto the evening newscast

In this situation, the creation of the "event strategy" may be a highly interactive process whereby the marketer and the target audience member (the news director) work together to complete the transaction and presumably build a pleasant and mutually rewarding long-term relationship. The marketer's task is to create *time and place utility* for the target audience member.

THE NATURE AND ROLE OF FACILITATION PLANNING

Creating time and place utilities is *facilitation*. There are two principal dimensions to the facilitation process. One involves the set of activities that need to take place on the marketer's side to bring the exchange opportunity to the target audience member. We refer to this component as the *channel strategy*. The second dimension is the content of the behavioral event itself, its characteristics and choreography. We refer to this component as the *occasion strategy*.

Channel Strategy
We define a channel as follows:

A channel is a conduit for bringing together a marketer and a target audience member at some place and time for the purpose of facilitating behavioral opportunities.

Among the channels a marketer can use are specific buildings (i.e., stores, offices, clinics, and showrooms); human beings such as paid or volunteer staffers; independent organizations such as transportation companies, wholesalers, and retailers; telephones; direct mail; and the Internet. In the future, there may also be interactive television.

A host of other organizations face the problem of locating a set of facilities to serve optimally a spatially distributed population. Hospitals have to build branches to reach a dispersed population. Schools need to be local as do fire stations and voting booths.[2]

An example of the set of channels in the health care industry is given in Exhibit 11-1.

Careful planning of channel strategy can have important positive payoffs, but there are also important resource challenges. Nonprofit organizations are typically deficient in resources, both financial and personnel. They often cannot put in place all elements of the channel strategy and will need the help of other individuals and organizations to bring their offerings to the public. The careful use of independent channels can make marketing programs more *efficient* by sharing costs, achieving economies of scale, and so on, and make them more *effective* by leveraging meager resources, small staffs, cramped facilities, and so on. The National Cancer Institute's (NCI) anti-smoking program, for example, was able to have a significant impact with a relatively small budget by enlisting the help of physicians to distribute how-to-quit materials and to carry out "personal selling" with patients who had a history of smoking. NCI was able to obtain the same kind of leveraging for its breast self-examination program by securing the help of major corporations to serve as intermediaries for its awareness and training programs.

EXHIBIT 11-1

HEALTH CARE DELIVERY SYSTEMS IN THE UNITED STATES

Health care delivery systems are institutions that deliver preventative and curative health services to the public. In the past, Americans obtained health care services in two ways: by visiting a private physician or an emergency room of a local hospital. Some target audience members sought out their pharmacists for advice on minor problems such as the common cold.

Today's health care services are available through several channels.

1. *Health maintenance organizations.* A growing number of people obtain their medical care through health maintenance organizations. By joining and paying a monthly fee, they can see staff doctors at any time and also get their hospitalization costs covered.

2. *Neighborhood health clinics.* Target audience members in poorer neighborhoods often go to neighborhood health clinics for help. The clinic charges no fee or a low fee and has doctors ready to examine sick patients. The clinic is supported by public money, private money, or both.

3. *Hospital-based ambulatory care units.* Many hospitals have opened clinics in shopping areas or apartment buildings where people pay a fee for service. Since some of these patients need hospital care, these clinics serve as feeder operations to the hospital.

4. *Group practices.* The vast majority of physicians now belong to private group practices, which give them the opportunity to structure their hours better and gain the advantages of having expert colleagues. Patients pay a fee for service every time they visit their physicians.

5. *Freestanding specialized service units.* Target audience members can directly obtain specific services such as X-rays, blood tests, and minor surgery in specialized units set up for these purposes. They pay fees that in most cases are reimbursed by their health insurance plans.

6. *The Internet.* The Internet is a great source of information and advice about health matters. Highly useful Web sites are managed by government agencies like the Centers for Disease Control and Prevention, nonprofits like the American Cancer Society, and for-profits like DrKoop.com. Sites like Medscape exist for finding the latest medical news and research.

Today the Internet is a major channel to deliver information on how to carry out socially desirable behaviors. There are sites on how to quit smoking or drugs, what diets seem to work, how to craft exercise options, and where to go for in-person help. Web sites typically provide methods for asking questions and some provide opportunities for contacting other individuals facing similar challenges. Blogs and YouTube provide opportunities for individuals to help each other directly.

Another growing method of facilitation is though partnerships with the private sector (discussed in a later chapter). Many corporations find that giving their employees access to health care options, quit-smoking programs, chances to give blood or money, and so on all contribute to improved employee satisfaction and lower turnover.

Some nonprofit organizations do not think of channel problems and possibilities. But it has been suggested that organized religion, for example, can be thought of as operating a religion distribution system. Consider the following example of the Evangelical Covenant Church of America.

The central church office can be seen as the *manufacturer* or originator of the church's product; the regional offices throughout the country can be viewed as the *wholesaler;* and the individual churches, such as Faith Evangelical Covenant Church in Wheaton, might be viewed as the *retail outlets* for the church's services and products. Faith Covenant Church is the part of the organization that comes face to face with the target audience member or members of the church and potential members. It is the individual "outlet" that can perform many of the critical functions needed to maintain members of the church and in fact, to increase its membership rolls.[3]

COMPONENTS OF A CHANNEL STRATEGY

All marketers need conduits to their target audience members, and target audience members need access to the marketer's offerings. The kinds of channels a marketer might use will vary depending on whether goods, services, or communications are the major flows within the channel. There are a number of strategic problems, however, that apply to all channel decisions:

1. *Direct versus indirect marketing.* The nonprofit must decide whether to carry out channel services within its own organization or with outsiders and, if so, which ones. An example of using an outside but critical delivery system to promote the 2000 U.S. Census is described by Richard Delano and David Lange in Exhibit 11-2.

EXHIBIT 11-2

RICHARD K. DELANO OF SOCIAL MARKETING SERVICES AND DAVID LANGE OF SCHOLASTIC MARKETING PARTNERS ON MOBILIZING CHILDREN AND TEENS FOR CENSUS 2000 THROUGH THE "SCHOOL MARKETING CHANNEL"

Census bureau staff had observed a steady decline in the mail response to the 1970, 1980, and 1990 decennial mail outs (78% in '70 to 65% in '90). Prior to the 2000 Census, the National Academy of Sciences projected a mail response rate below 60 percent. The Census bureau estimates that each percentage point decline in mail response translates into about a $25 million cost increase due largely to the follow-up activity that must take place to gather information not provided on the first mail out. Advertising and publicity were traditionally accomplished through the Advertising Council on a pro bono basis. Bureau staff made the case to Congress that a paid advertising (social marketing) campaign was needed to boost participation. Congress agreed. Incremental funds were allocated to the "dress rehearsal"

(continued)

EXHIBIT 11-2   (cont.)

process in April 1998 so all Census advertising and promotional materials could be evaluated. Dress rehearsals are "live" tests held two years prior to each decennial.

Bureau staff were also concerned about the net "undercount" of approximately 4.7 million in the 1990 Census. They estimated that children accounted for about half of the undercounted population. This undercount of children in 2000 would mean that programs that serve children and their families were less likely to be adequately funded throughout the 2000 to 2010 decade.

Recognizing that an undercount in a decennial census can have a long-term impact on the well-being of children, the Census Bureau decided to implement the *Census in Schools* program for Census 2000. The short-term goal of the *Census in Schools* program was to help students understand the Census and its importance to them, their families, and their community. The program was designed to increase participation in Census 2000 by engaging parents through schools and through the active involvement of children and teens. (Adult voting rates are known to rise in communities where schoolchildren hold "mock elections".) In the longer term, Census staff believe adults who learned about the Census as children are more likely to participate in future decennials.

To engage the education community, the *Census in Schools* project would provide educators with teaching tools to bring the Census to life for students and to explain to them and to their parents the importance of Census participation. The U.S. Census Bureau and Young & Rubicam (Y&R) contracted with Scholastic Inc. who helped to develop the messages, packaging, and distribution strategy that would be most effective in reaching U.S. educators, motivating them to involve their students

and the parents of those students. All Y&R design, slogan, and strategic targeting decisions were integrated into the *Census in Schools* materials.

Census in Schools was tested, along with advertising from Young & Rubicam, in the three "dress rehearsal" communities in April 1998. The post–dress rehearsal research helped Census 2000 planners determine how best to deploy their communication budget to reach targeted audiences, including parents. Modifications were made as necessary for the rollout of Census 2000.

Scholastic's Social Marketing Solutions, part of the company's custom publishing unit, helped the Census Bureau and Y&R design this part of the larger program. Scholastic Inc. generates over $2 billion in sales annually through book clubs, book fairs, and classroom magazines because of its unique understanding of how to market through what is sometimes referred to as the "school marketing channel." This commercial "know-how" on how to motivate teachers, parents, and students through schools is significant and desirable from a social marketing perspective.

Scholastic recommended to Census staff that all education materials and their distribution should be modeled on successful commercial marketing strategies and commercially viable products. For instance, elementary school teachers in targeted low-response Census tracks (correlated to percentage of students receiving free or reduced school meals) received take-home materials similar in design to book club "kits." Over 1 million (out of 3 million total) U.S. teachers are Scholastic agents for book clubs. By modeling this part of the *Census in Schools* program on this familiar product (a four-page teacher wraparound and 32 identical four-page parent take-home fliers), we believe the performance of this communication activity was enhanced.

Similarly, a pre–K program called *Everybody Counts* was modeled on a best-selling Scholastic Early Childhood product. Head Start centers receive a "Big Book" that the instructor uses before the assembled class and 30 identical but smaller individual "Little Books" that each child could take home to read with a parent. Scholastic's research suggested that the process of first reading the big book in class stimulates a "nag" factor compelling parents to read the lap book at home.

Similar modeling provided the formative design of many other materials and the distribution of those materials including *Making Sense of Census 2000* teaching kits, principal materials, American Indian maps, materials for Puerto Rico and the Island Areas, as well as special materials for Adult Literacy programs.

Census in Schools partners included 23 national education associations and government agencies that helped spread Census 2000 messages and information about the *Census in Schools* materials.

The Census Bureau promoted *Teach Census Week* (March 13–17, 2000) as a prime time to teach about Census 2000.

It coincided with the week when the questionnaires were delivered to most homes. Other school activities were organized by other partner organizations throughout the country.

By April 2000 nearly 2 million *Making Sense of Census 2000* kits had been distributed to educators in public, private, and parochial schools in the United States, Puerto Rico, and the Island Areas. These kits were offered to all schools and were available on the Internet. About 35,000 sets of *Everybody Counts* were sent to Head Start Centers and 200,000 Adult ESL/Literacy teaching kits were mailed to instructors of adult education nationwide. In addition, 45 million copies of the take-home activities were distributed for K–8 students to share with their families. Of the $167 million Census 2000 advertising and publicity budget, approximately $20 million was provided for the *Census in Schools* promotion.

The Census Bureau has funded extensive research designed to determine, among other things, how adults across the country learned about Census 2000. We expect that the results of this research will help us better understand the role that the "school marketing channel" can play in large-scale social marketing programs.

2. *Length and breadth of the channel structure.* The nonprofit must decide on (a) the number of levels to be interposed between the production of the offer and its eventual exchange with target audience members (length decisions) and (b) the total number of different channels or the number of elements to be included at each level of the channel (breadth decisions).

3. *Allocation of functions.* The nonprofit needs to decide who will handle the several channel flows (for example, information, goods, and money) in the channel.

4. *Recruiting channel members.* The nonprofit needs to know how to recruit and motivate channel members.

5. *Coordination and control.* The nonprofit must develop systems for coordinating and controlling various channel members in the system.[4]

In considering these issues, we use efficiency and effectiveness as our principal criteria. *Efficiency* is the extent to which a system achieves a given level of performance at the least possible cost in financial, time, and personnel resources. *Effectiveness* is the extent to which a system achieves the maximum performance for a given level of resources.

Direct versus Indirect Channels

Other things being equal, organizations normally prefer to deal with their target audience members directly and not use intermediaries. There are a number of advantages to such an approach which can often be carried out over the Internet:

1. Any organizational benefits (e.g., revenue, brand building, media attention) from the transaction do not have to be shared with other organizations or individuals.
2. All channel activities are controlled by the marketer.
3. Direct contact with target audience members provides the marketer with a better understanding of their needs and wants. Feedback channels can be built into the system.
4. Direct contact with target audience members means quicker awareness of any problems with programs and products.
5. Responses to changes in the marketplace (e.g., to new competitor initiatives) can be more rapid.
6. Opportunities for experimentation with alternative ways of reaching target audience members are available.
7. More attention can be given to the marketer's offering than would be possible if it were only one of many carried by an intermediary.
8. Strategies aimed at various target audience segments can be precisely tailored.

Given all of these advantages, why would an organization give up control at all? One reason we have already noted is that many organizations lack the financial resources to carry out a full program of direct marketing themselves.

Even if an organization has the funds to build its own channel to the target audiences, it might not be able to do so as cheaply as through using an existing system. The cost of distributing nonprofit health care products throughout India is low when commercial intermediaries agree to carry the items and share in the cost of the distribution network. The same reasoning applies to services. In the developing world, child-care services are provided through existing community organizations (private clinics, schools, community centers) rather than through new duplicative facilities. And, as noted, in the developed world, corporations and civic agencies often provide market access for various social services.

The nonprofit organization should not build its own distribution system if it can put its funds to better use. Thus the number of infant deaths averted might be higher if Indonesian nonprofit organizations spent their funds to advertise the advantages of oral rehydration or Vitamin A nationwide rather than using all their money to set up their own distribution systems or their own health care clinics.

The case for using intermediaries often rests on their superior efficiency and effectiveness in the performance of basic marketing tasks and functions. Marketing intermediaries, through their experience, specialization, contacts, and scale, offer the producing organization more than it can usually achieve on its own. This is very much the role Gifts in Kind International plays in facilitating product giving by corporations as in the Perry Ellis example above.

Length versus Breadth

Whether or not a nonprofit decides that it would be efficient to use intermediaries, decisions must be made as to how many levels of distribution to have and how many units to have at each level. These are often referred to as length and breadth decisions, and they usually are not independent decisions. Consider first the breadth decision.

The most economical decision is to work with a single outlet or a single web site. By having one large library in a major city, duplication of books, staff, and building costs are avoided. Citizens gain in that they will find an extensive collection of reading material. They pay the price, however, of having to travel a longer distance. A system consisting of many smaller libraries would attract more users. Most major cities compromise by building a central library and several branch libraries for the convenience of target audience members. Some go further and operate bookmobiles, which are mobile libraries that park in different neighborhoods on different days and make books available to target audience members. The same problem applies in health care where a non-profit could create one large central clinic or operate though many, many local centers and mobile health units.

At the local level, breadth decisions are often dictated by target audience members. Certain offerings must be mass distributed because target audience members will not go out of their way to come in contact with them. In commercial marketing, these offerings are called *convenience goods and services*. In retailing, they usually involve offerings that are not particularly distinctive. For example, men will normally not go far out of their way to acquire condoms for the prevention of AIDS. As a consequence, many AIDS prevention strategies feature the installation of condom vending machines in men's rooms and the provision of goblets of free condoms near the exits in gay bars.

Not all behavior opportunities must be made maximally convenient for target audience members. There are some offerings for which target audience members will undertake some effort to find and evaluate—they need not be exceptionally convenient. In retailing, these are referred to as *shopping goods and services,* since target audience members believe they would gain something by looking around and finding the best option. Thus target audience members will go a moderate distance to secure the best emergency care service or smoking-cessation clinic. They will go some distance to see a good museum or watch a good play. In such cases, channel breadth becomes less important.

The final class of offerings is usually referred to as *specialty goods and services.* These are offers that target audience members find so special that they will make a strong effort to seek them out, often at considerable cost. Further, these offerings are perceived to be sufficiently unique that target audience members will typically not accept substitutes. This status of being a specialty offering is one that many nonprofit marketers covet. The Mayo Clinic, for example, is clearly a "specialty institution" for well-off target audience members with unusual afflictions. Art museums have found that a number of high-profile traveling art exhibits have proved to be "specialty goods" that target audience members would go long distances and endure long lines to see.

If a nonprofit organization determines that its target audience members require a broad distribution system, the next channel strategy question is "How long should

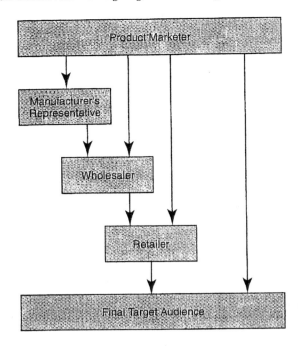

FIGURE 11-1 Alternative Channel Structures for a Hypothetical Nonprofit Product Marketer

the channel be?" For nonprofits that market a product (like the Sierra Club or the U.S. Treasury), two-, three-, and four-level channels are possible, as suggested in Figure 11-1.

In general, the *broader* the distribution at the local level, the *longer* the channel has to be. That is, if a nonprofit marketer wanted only *exclusive distribution* in a few major locations, a two-step channel (manufacturer to supplier to consumer) would be perfectly adequate. However, if a *selective distribution* system is chosen, with, say, half a dozen outlets handling the nonprofit's line in each of the 50 largest metropolitan areas in the United States, then several regional wholesalers may be needed to provide coverage. In addition, if the nonprofit wishes to have *mass distribution* in every nook and cranny of the country, then a manufacturer's representative may be needed to contact the hundreds of wholesalers required to service such a broad market.

Finally, note that strategic decisions about the length and breadth of a channel and whether the channel should be owned by the nonprofit marketer are independent decisions. That is, a marketer could choose a three-tiered system but set up its own wholesaling functions. This tactic would be known as *forward integration*. An environmental lobbying organization that produced its own books and calendars, for example, initially could use wholesalers to market them to recreation areas, book chains, university bookstores, and the like. But later, it could decide that recreation areas were underserved and that it could do better by handling its own product lines and even those of other manufacturers seeking better representation in recreation areas.

Nonprofit organizations can also undertake *backward integration*. A growing number of nonprofit organizations such as museums and hospitals have active retail operations for which they contract with one or more wholesalers for merchandise. Many service-based nonprofits, such as nursing homes and religious institutions, acquire substantial amounts of supplies from wholesalers to carry out their operations. Some of these organizations could use available investment capital to integrate backward in their channel by buying out or setting up a wholesale operation of their own, possibly serving other outlets as well. Again, the prime consideration in such a move should be whether it would result in important efficiencies, better service, or new revenues.

Finally, many nonprofit organizations will want to have multiple channels for target audiences to reach them and be served. This can include physical distribution options, the Internet, and telephone call centers. While marketers often want to force target audiences to use the cheapest (for the marketer) channel, it is now accepted wisdom that the system must provide what target audiences want by way of contact points.

ACHIEVING COORDINATION AND CONTROL

Whether a nonprofit marketer is the "captain" of a channel system or a member of someone else's system, a crucial set of issues involves day-to-day management. In a mature marketing system, it is usually extremely important not only to have the right intermediaries performing the right function, but to make sure that they are carrying out those functions *when* and exactly in the *form* that is in the best interests of the overall system (e.g., maximizing customer "delight").

For many reasons, coordination and cooperation are difficult to achieve in nonprofit organizations. Among the impediments are the following:

- Competition among nonprofits for limited funds from either federal sources or third-sector agencies like the United Way may make some nonprofits reluctant to help out present or future rivals. Cooperation may be viewed as helping another agency grow, possibly at the expense of one's own operations.
- Nonprofit leaders or staff may perceive cooperation as potential meddling, a waste of time, or a distraction from a job with low security.
- Territoriality can be a problem if one agency is unwilling to be subservient to another in an area in which the first agency believes it should be in charge.
- Differences in goals and values can often raise problems when marketing "rears its ugly head." Those who have a social service orientation (Chapter 3) may feel that involvement with another agency that is an aggressive marketer will be "unprofessional" or will otherwise taint the potential channel member.
- Excessive time and energy costs may occur. If the channel is not well managed, much time may be spent in meeting, planning, and "coordinating." Besides delaying action, this can drive away more action-oriented participants. It has discouraged more than one private sector marketer from cooperating in a nonprofit program.
- Personality clashes are not unusual. Early in their organizational life cycle, many nonprofits are small and dominated by strong-willed, charismatic executives. In the struggling years of the enterprise, rivalries with other equally strong-willed leaders may develop. These can be very acrimonious and for many years stand in the way of needed cooperation.

The Basic Problem in Coordination and Control

The fundamental difficulty in achieving coordination and control is that another, separate organization with different perceptions, goals, and skills must undertake tasks that will help your organization achieve its goals.[5] Yet the "channel cooperation problem" is not really different from the problem involved in marketing to final target audience members. The problem is still one of *influencing the behavior of target markets,* in this case, key independent intermediaries. As such, the steps involved in developing an effective intermediary marketing strategy are clear.

1. Identify all potential intermediary segments.
2. Evaluate potential segments and select the best subset for detailed investigation.
3. Identify the basic BCOS factors that are likely to influence these target intermediaries; for example:
   a. What benefits are they likely to see?
   b. What costs are likely to hold them back?
   c. What groups of others might influence them positively or negatively?
   d. What barriers do they see that would cause them to believe that they cannot make the partnership work?
4. Develop strategies to increase the perceived benefits and reduce the perceived costs of participation, bring the pressure of "important others" to bear, and remove any important barriers that diminish the intermediary's sense of self-assurance.
5. Evaluate the probable costs and payoffs of each strategy and select, for the given planning period, those that will best achieve the organization's objectives.
6. Determine optimal strategies for maintaining the desired relationships.

Implicit in this approach are a number of marketing principles that we have already emphasized:

- The best marketing strategy begins with the target audience member (the intermediary) rather than the nonprofit organization.
- It is the target audience member's needs, wants, and perceptions that are crucial to success, not those of the nonprofit organization.
- Since these needs, wants, and perceptions are subjective phenomena, the marketer cannot know them and so must resort to formal or informal research to ascertain them.
- The number of exchanges increases if and only if the cost/benefit ratios perceived by selected target audiences are changed in a favorable direction.
- Since change in cost/benefit ratios is crucial, the key research issue is how will target audience perceptions change as a result of alternative marketing strategy choices?
- Strategies must be developed not only to create first-time trials, but also to ensure continued usage by trial participants, to increase usage by present or trial participants, or both. That is, the Maintenance stage is particularly important here.
- Finally, the selection of optimum short- and long-run strategies is not merely a matter of increasing effectiveness in creating exchanges; the selection must also take into account the costs to the organization of creating exchanges (the efficiency issue).

Developing Intermediary Coordination Strategies

The nonprofit marketer must choose influence strategies that will secure intermediary participation and cooperation in particular programs. The choice should be based on an analysis of the marketer's power bases. While the choice often yields a mixed strategy, the options can be grouped into three broad strategic categories. These categories can be described as follows:

1. *Requiring* intermediary cooperation through the use of coercive or legal power, often in the framework of specific contracts.
2. *Rewarding* intermediary cooperation through the manipulation of rewards.
3. *Persuading* intermediaries to cooperate through the use of experts and information (although persuasion, in a sense, is implicit in *all* of these alternatives).

Requiring Cooperation

Requiring cooperation is a common form of channel control in both the private and public sectors. It is carried out through the use of formal contracts, which specify in greater or lesser degree the rights and duties of each party. These contracts can cover specific functions, as when an advertising agency agrees to provide copy and execution for a series of ads, place the ads in media, and perhaps evaluate the advertising's effects.

Such contracts can be beneficial to the nonprofit because it benefits from the skills and economies of others while maintaining the contract power to insist on performance. An issue here is how tightly to word the contract. In the private sector, contracts sometimes involve voluntary assistance by the contractee at or below market prices. In such cases, the temptation is to write the contract loosely so that the pro bono subcontractor (e.g., a research or advertising agency or broadcasting medium) is not "offended" by "meddling" in its delegated area of responsibility. This loose wording is generally unsatisfactory to both sides. Subcontractors may not know what is expected of them. They may exaggerate their independence and feel abused when the contractor tries to impose its will upon them. Ethical issues may arise. The contractor, however, may feel that it has no clear grounds for making criticisms, and that it has lost control of the subcontracted operation. And, of course, if legitimate disputes do arise, the ensuing bickering can destroy a channel relationship that may be the *only* way for a nonprofit contractor to get its job done.

A channel control technique that has become increasingly common in the private sector is *franchising*. For years, there have been territorial agreements in the automobile and beverage industries whereby the number of dealers in an area is regulated. In return for this local partial monopoly, the franchisee is expected to meet certain performance standards (e.g., quotas) and to carry on the enterprise in a particular fashion (e.g., use certain signs, charge certain prices, engage in so much cooperative advertising, and so on). Recent growth, however, has been in franchise systems with much stronger central control. In chain franchises like McDonald's, Burger King, and Midas Muffler, among others, virtually the entire operation of the franchise may be specified by the franchisor down to the size of the dollop of catsup to go on a hamburger or the number of straws in a soft drink. Usually, the franchise is based upon some distinctive trade name or style such that the franchisee is willing to pay for both the expertise and the extra marketplace competitive edge.

One way to visualize the Boys & Girls Clubs of America is as a franchise system. All of the 4,000-plus individual clubs that collectively serve over 4.8 million boys and girls are independent organizations. They have their own boards of directors and respond to local needs. They can reject what the Atlanta head office recommends. The challenges of crafting nationwide strategies and tactics become much more difficult in such a system. On the other hand, there are important advantages of having the local communities feel that they have ownership of what goes on in their clubs.

The contractual approach ultimately relies on legal authority and the potential imposition of penalties as a means of achieving the nonprofit marketer's ends. As long as the terms are carefully described, are fair to both sides, and there is a sense of shared responsibility for desired social outcomes, a contractual approach can work well, and the use of formal power by the contractor need only be a subtle background issue. However, if the contractual relationship is unclear and the interaction between the parties is discordant, power may be used by the contractor to coerce the contractee into performing the needed channel functions. To the extent that such formal coercive power has to be used, the long-term potential for the channel relationship is not promising.

Rewarding and Persuading Cooperation

Rather than base channel cooperation on negative incentives, many organizations simply make it *worthwhile* for others to help them out. They follow their basic marketing principles—learning what benefits might be valuable to the target audience, and what costs and barriers they might see of cooperating. Headquarters then can offer specific rewards such as commissions or noneconomic rewards such as increased prestige through cooperating with a major social program. In both cases, extensive persuasion may still be needed to convince potential target intermediaries that cooperation will benefit both parties. Oftentimes, the pressure of others can help a channel leader achieve widespread cooperation.

As we suggested in Chapter 7, the building of strong nonprofit brands can significantly increase the reward potential for a potential partner. It is a strong incentive for the cause-related marketing partnerships described elsewhere. It can be equally strong when inducing cooperation by organizations that are needed to deliver the organization's offerings.

OCCASION STRATEGIES

A component of nonprofit marketing mixes that has seen limited attention is the management of behavioral occasions. The behaviors that a marketer wants will take place in a specific time and place—or, for a behavior like exercising that is continuing, in several places over time. Getting kids to exercise more means that streets have to be safer, parks have to be opened, schools have to schedule phys ed classes, and so on. If an organization is going to maximize the number of behaviors, it needs to consciously plan and implement attractive, convenient occasions to ensure that the behavior is:

- Easy to accomplish in a physical sense
- An emotionally positive experience
- Rewarding and reinforcing

Making Behavior Easy

There are many factors that can have major effects on the ease in which a behavior can be performed that the marketer can potentially control—or at least influence:

- *Convenience in time*—for example, making blood donations possible after midnight for shift workers; holding job training at night; offering instructions for various health behaviors on the Web or on videotapes, DVDs, or CD-ROMs (and loaning VCR or DVD players if necessary); and minimizing paperwork.
- *Convenience in location*—for example, bringing the product or service to the community or to someone's home through mobile vans, videos, or traveling trainers; providing transportation to remote sites; offering opportunities in the workplace or at airport terminals or train stations; and allowing behavior (e.g., donations or volunteering) through the Web or by telephone.
- *Offering minimal distractions*—for example, providing play areas or child care for accompanying kids.
- *Having complete availability of any tools, equipment, or advice that might be needed*—for example, having multiple sets of necessary gear, and providing instructions in simple terms and in multiple languages.

However, providing maximum ease is not without cost. The marketer must determine the level and quality of service to offer to the target market. Each organization can visualize a maximum level of service that could be offered. Following are some examples:

- A public welfare department must distribute thousands of checks a year to people on public relief. The maximum level of service would be to mail checks daily to their homes or even to deliver the checks personally to avoid mail theft.
- A public library could render the maximum amount of service if it stood ready to receive calls for books and deliver them within a few hours to the person's home.
- A city health department could dispatch doctors to the homes of sick patients upon call.
- A university could send a lecturer to any home or dorm room upon request.

These solutions are oriented toward maximum consumer convenience. But they are not practical because target audience members would probably not pay for the extra convenience and the supplying organization could not afford the cost. Organizations have to find solutions that offer less consumer convenience in order to keep down the cost of distribution. Libraries and health departments, for example, can bring down their costs by offering services in only a few locations and leaving the cost of travel to the target audience members. They can cut their costs further by running an efficient organization in which waiting time is borne mainly by target audience members instead of becoming idle time borne by the staff. If a health clinic had five doctors instead of ten, the doctors would be continually busy while the patients would absorb the cost of waiting. Finally, organizations could reduce their costs by using other media for delivery, such as when a university offers interactive TV lectures over the Web or on pay cable for those who wish to pay for it.

One way to make behavior easy is the use of 800 numbers. The Massachusetts Department of Public Health mounted a campaign to give individuals cues as to when they should act should they suspect someone of having had a stroke and then provided an 800 number so that action was easy. They backed this with a carefully designed message campaign (see Figure 11-2).

FIGURE 11-2   Teaching Clues of a Stroke Attack

Source: Massachussets Department of Public Health.

Making the Behavior Occasion an Emotional "High"

Behavioral occasions can be mundane or they can be charged with very positive emotions. Opportunities abound:

- 10K races or walk-a-thons can be made exciting occasions to donate. Celebrities and TV cameras can add to the excitement. T-shirts can be rewards. Events can feature music and secondary information sites.
- Walking up stairs (for exercise) at work can be made fun by providing videos or office-related cartoons on the landings.
- Exercise classes can be enlivened by upbeat music (think "Jazzercise").
- Scary or painful health procedures like blood donations can be made positive experiences by warm, enthusiastic staff members.

One of the important contributors to an emotionally satisfying encounter is what private sector marketers call "atmospherics."[6] *Atmospherics* describes the conscious designing of the place of delivery to create or reinforce specific effects on buyers, such as feelings of well-being, safety, intimacy, or awe. Where the nonprofit organization provides the service in some location, the marketing manager needs to make decisions on the "look" of the facilities, because the look can affect target audience members' attitudes, behavior, and level of satisfaction. Consider how the "atmosphere" of a hospital can affect patients. Many older hospitals have an institutional look, with long narrow corridors, drab wall colors, and badly worn furniture, all of which contribute a depressed feeling to patients who are already depressed about their own conditions. Newer hospitals are designed with colors, textures, furnishings, and layouts that reinforce positive patient feelings. They have circular or rectangular layouts with the nursing station in the center, permitting nurses to monitor patients better. Single-care units are replacing the traditional semi-private rooms, based on the overwhelming preference of both patients and physicians. Waiting areas are like hotel lobbies.

An organization that is designing a service facility for the first time faces four major design decisions that will affect the atmospherics. Suppose a city wishes to build a public art museum. The four decisions are as follows:

1. *What should the building look like on the outside?* The building can look like a Greek temple (as many museums have looked in the past), a villa, or a glass skyscraper (Frank Gehry's Bilbao museum). It can look awe inspiring, ordinary, or intimate. The decision will be influenced by the type of art collection and the message that the museum wants to convey about art in general. It says things about how inviting the facility is.

2. *What should be the functional and flow characteristics of the building?* The planners have to consider whether the museum should consist of a few large rooms or many small ones. (Many museums compromise by having large rooms with many movable walls.) They also have to consider whether the major exhibits and best-known artworks should be located near the entrance or at the other end of the building. The rooms and corridors must be designed in a way to handle capacity crowds so that people do not have to wait in long lines and experience congestion.

3. *What should the structure feel like on the inside?* Every building conveys a feeling, whether intended or unplanned. The planners have to consider whether the museum

should feel awesome and somber, bright and modern, or warm and intimate. Each feeling will have a different effect on the visitors and their overall satisfaction with the museum.

4. *What materials would best support the desired feeling of the building?* The feeling of a building is conveyed by visual cues (color, brightness, size, shapes), aural cues (volume, pitch), olfactory cues (scent, freshness), and tactile cues (softness, smoothness, temperature). The museum's planners have to choose colors, fabrics, and furnishings that create or reinforce the desired feeling.

Making the Behavior Occasion Rewarding and Reinforcing

Target audience members are likely to repeat an important behavior and to spread positive word of mouth if they come away from the experience feeling that their expectations were met and that they received the kind and level of benefits—and minimal costs—they anticipated. A critical factor here is *expectations management.* Research has shown that individuals rate their experiences (e.g., the purchase of a product or an encounter with a service provider) by comparing their experience with their expectations. A given level of experience may lead to satisfaction if expectations are met or exceeded or dissatisfaction if expectations are not met. (Sometimes the latter can be mitigated if the target audience members are given a chance to complain and/or receive some remediation.[7])

Thus it is important to keep expectations at or below what the nonprofit can deliver. If waiting time can be as high as an hour, do not promise "quick service." If there is high turnover of staff, do not promise exceptional levels of personal care and a client-centered mentality. On the other hand, whenever possible, the nonprofit should consider an approach many commercial marketers have adopted, which is to plan not just to *satisfy* target audience members but to *delight* them! These cutting-edge marketers ask what they can do to make the behavior occasion significantly better than people expected. Premier service providers are especially good at this. The Ritz-Carlton knows that a request by a guest for some missing item can be remedied by having a replacement item delivered, but that the guest may be delighted if the manager leaves a phone message offering regrets or a letter is sent later to his or her home apologizing for the oversight and offering an upgrade on the next visit.

Many of these tactics do not cost very much, but they do require planning and training on the part of nonprofit marketers. Their payoff in repeat behaviors can be significant—and therefore highly cost-effective.

Reinforcing behavior is, of course, a standard principle of behavioral psychology. It is well known that people will repeat behaviors when they are rewarded.[8] Hotels give "frequent guest rewards." There is no reason that a nonprofit clinic could not offer the same reinforcement. T-shirts are clearly one way of bringing people back to rock concerts or walk-a-thons. "Goodies" at fundraisers frequently make the event memorable for the year until the next such event.

Marketers often use unexpected material rewards as reinforcers. Nonprofit marketers can offer these, also. Indeed, fundraising organizations are masters at this. However, we emphasize that it is the *unexpected* reward that can have the most reinforcing effect. Personal letters from the CEO (or maybe a celebrity board member) to a donor who just increased his or her giving or to a volunteer who performed extra services can be powerful reinforcers. Sometimes such rewards can be social as well as psychological, as when high-volume blood donors are portrayed in a poster on a factory wall or a great volunteer or donor is praised at an annual banquet or in the organization newsletter.

Finally, we must recognize that, while rewards can be administered by the nonprofit in many instances, oftentimes the only—or perhaps major—rewards and reinforcements will come from the target audience members *rewarding themselves*. Thus nonprofit marketers need to think about tactics that could help audiences reinforce themselves. For example, dieters or blood donors could be provided with score sheets that allow them to tell how well they are doing. Alternatively, if means can be found to have them record progress through the Web, then their progress can be given direct praise from the unseen Web correspondent—and, where relevant, the progress can be posted (perhaps in disguised form) for others to see and admire. This can be very reinforcing.

Summary

Making behaviors happen requires facilitation. Marketers must find ways to make behavioral opportunities convenient and personally pleasant and rewarding. This involves developing channel strategies to bring behavioral opportunities to the target audience and "occasion strategies" to make the actual encounter entirely reinforcing.

Channel strategies ensure that offers are made available at a particular time and in a particular place. Often, this requires the services of other agencies (who can provide warehouse and transportation facilities) and careful coordination of complex interacting systems. Although channels may simply be a means to facilitate target audience members' time and place utilities, they have the potential to either significantly augment or effectively sabotage carefully designed marketing programs.

To achieve an effective and efficient channel strategy, the nonprofit marketer must decide what quality of service to offer and whether marketing will be direct or indirect. Often marketers will want to offer multiple channels including the Internet and telephone answering systems. Then the marketer must determine the length and breadth of the channel, recruit channel members, and assign functions. Finally, the marketer should put systems in place for effective coordination and control among the channel members.

The other major facilitation challenge is making occasions easy, emotionally satisfying, and rewarding. This requires attention to atmospherics and to customer reinforcement. Often target audiences need to be taught how to reward themselves.

Questions

1. You are the Art Museum marketer in Cranston, Mississippi. You have a unique set of 1832 antique dolls and the retailer Pier 1 has agreed to market them across the United States. What conditions would you set for this arrangement? How could it go wrong?

2. You run a soup kitchen in Washington, D.C., which has been successful in getting many homeless people employed. You think that your approach could be franchised as a way to help other nonprofit organizations with similar missions and to bring in additional revenue. Briefly describe a business plan for this venture.

3. You have an idea that your web site could provide a "place" where teens with eating disorders could congregate and help each other to straighten out their lives. How would you set this up?

4. What would the U.S. Mint have to do to successfully reintroduce the $2 bill? Earlier attempts were met with indifference by the public, lethargy by the banks, and resistance by retailers with limited-capacity cash registers.
5. The superintendent of schools in Toledo, Ohio, has noticed that more and more of her teachers and parents are becoming obese. She has the idea of using each school's gym and other exercise equipment after hours for these target audiences. How should she proceed?

Notes

1. Early intimations of this approach are found in Sidney J. Levy and Philip Kotler, "Beyond Marketing: The Furthering Concept," *California Management Review*, Vol. 12 (Winter 1969), pp. 67–73.
2. Ronald Abler, John S. Adams, and Peter Gould, *Spatial Organization* (Upper Saddle River, NJ: Prentice-Hall, 1971), pp. 531–532.
3. Quoted from an unpublished term paper on the Faith Covenant Church of Wheaton written by Mark F. Pufundt at Northwestern University, 1980.
4. An excellent introduction to these issues is found in Louis W. Stern and Adel I. Ansary, *Marketing Channels*, 2nd ed. (Upper Saddle River, NJ: Prentice-Hall, 1982).
5. The material in the following section is adapted from Alan R. Andreasen, "A Power Potential Approach to Middlemen Strategies in Social Marketing," *European Journal of Marketing*, Vol. 18, No. 4 (1984), pp. 56–71. See also John R. French and Bertram Raven, "The Bases of Social Power," in D. Cartwright (Ed.), *Studies in Social Power* (Ann Arbor: University of Michigan Press, 1959); Jack Kasulis and Robert Spekman, "A Framework for the Use of Power," *European Journal of Marketing*, October 1980, pp. 70–78.
6. For more details, see Philip Kotler, "Atmospherics as a Marketing Tool," *Journal of Retailing*, Winter 1973–1974, pp. 48–64.
7. Arthur Best and Alan R. Andreasen, "Consumer Response to Unsatisfactory Purchases: A Survey of Perceiving Defects, Voicing Complaints, and Obtaining Redress," *Law and Society Review*, Vol. 2, No. 4 (1977), pp. 701–742.
8. Michael Rothschild and William C. Gaidis, "Behavioral Learning Theory: Its Relevance to Marketing and Promotions," *Journal of Marketing*, Spring 1981, pp. 70–78.

12

FORMULATING COMMUNICATION STRATEGIES

BLOGGING FOR CHARITY!

Consumer-generated media (CGM) represent a new opportunity for nonprofit organizations to contact supporters and potential supporters. It is based upon the idea of the nonprofit providing options for target audiences to "talk" to each other electronically and to the organization. As Thomas Abrahamson of Lipman Hearne Inc. notes, "It's not just about pushing messages one way, but creating forums and conversations and facilitating word-of-mouth for people to share experiences." The concept got its start, many think, with the 2004 political campaigns where young people used the Internet to talk about candidates, set up meetings, raise funds, and promote turnout and specific choices.

The March of Dimes uses the concept to promote its own work on preventing birth complications by having families share their experiences with neonatal intensive care units in hospitals (www.shareyourstory.org). Families with babies with birth defects "talk" with others and collectively focus attention on the March of Dimes' work in combating birth traumas. Moderators track input to the site to make sure shared information is medically correct. If not, the moderators enter their own messages setting the record straight. In June 2006 there were 12,000 registrants on the site, a 50 percent increase in six months. The site registers on average 270 posts each day.

The Sierra Club has used blogs and e-mail to generate concern and activism around environmental issues. Executive Director Carl Pope regularly posts his thoughts on issues of the day (www.sierraclub.org/carlpope/), and there is an opportunity for others around the world to comment on what he says. The blog is often a vehicle for rallying support for specific legislative initiatives of interest to the club.

Political nonprofits like MoveOn.org have a longer tradition of effectively using the Internet to rally supporters around an issue—for example, to get signatures on a petition. Representative John Conyers in June 2005 was able

---

> to deliver a petition to the White House about the Iraq war with 560,000 signatures, almost two-thirds of which were generated by MoveOn.org through the Internet. In the 2005 election cycle, MoveOn was able to add 450,000 new members and raise $9 million for candidates and campaigns it cared about.
>
> Chris Wolz of Forum One Communications points out that these online communities can be very effective in building organizational visibility and affinity. "Doing this online can be, for many organizations, more cost-effective than offline. But, more interesting, online community approaches can also let them build new kinds of client relations that they really could not do offline."
>
> *Source:* Deborah L. Vence, "Smart Organizations Use Technology to Spark Dialogue, Cement Relationships," *Marketing News*, July 15, 2006, pp. 15–16.

In Chapter 1, we defined marketing as a philosophy, process, and set of concepts and theories for influencing behavior—either changing behavior or preventing it from changing (e.g., keeping teenagers from taking up smoking). In the immediately preceding chapters, we considered the offer, price, and facilitation components of the marketing mix and saw that these components must be put in place before any program can be successful. We have also seen that these components can influence behaviors directly by providing incentives for action (benefits) or reducing disincentives (costs) that we collectively call the value proposition. Once these elements are thought through, in the vast majority of nonprofit marketing strategies, influencing behavior then involves significant amounts of *communication*. It is a matter of:

1. *Informing* target audiences in the Precontemplation stage about the alternatives for action and getting them interested.
2. Telling those in the Contemplation stage of the positive consequences of choosing a particular option and of the positive approval of role models.
3. Providing motivations for acting at a particular time and place and teaching any needed skills for acting to those in the Preparation/Action stage.
4. Offering rewards for *continuing* to act for those in the Maintenance stage.

On the other hand, we want to make very clear that advertising—or communications in general—is NOT marketing. Too many nonprofits overemphasize communication in their marketing mix and outside observers often think that communication is *all* marketing is about. It is often the most visible sign of what a nonprofit does. But one should not mistake it for the sum of what the nonprofit marketer does. Communication is just part of an integrated marketing strategy, not a substitute!

On the other hand, communication is not something that nonprofits can ignore. Everything about an organization—its products, employees, facilities, and actions—communicates something. Each organization must examine its communication style, needs, and opportunities and develop a communication program that is influential and cost-effective. The organization's communication responsibilities go beyond communicating to target audiences. The organization must communicate effectively with all of its external publics such as the press, government agencies, and potential donors, especially if its mission is reliant upon changes in the legal and regulatory environment. It also must communicate effectively with its internal publics, particularly its board members, middle management, and professional clerical employees, as well as any volunteers it uses.

An organization may use a great many communication vehicles to inform and motivate target publics. These include:

TV and radio advertising	Word of mouth; viral marketing	Packaging
Print ads		Books and articles
Web site messages	Posters and show cards	Endorsements
Web banner ads	Point-of-sales materials	Special events
Mailings	E-mails	Giveaways
Speeches; community meetings	Catalogs	Public service announcements
	Demonstrations	
Logos and other design features	Soap operas or movie scripts	Blogs
		Videologs
Brochures and annual reports	Conference exhibits	

These are only the more conventional vehicles. Nonprofit marketers in Thailand have painted logos on water buffalo. Buses and Volkswagens have been painted with prevention messages. And celebrities have appeared at congressional hearings to support their favorite causes (and gain some personal publicity).

Decisions on which of these vehicles to use, when to use them, and how to use them must follow from a clear understanding of the communication process.

THE COMMUNICATION PROCESS

Any communication process involves a message *sender* and a message *receiver* (a target audience).[1] The sender has an *intended message,* but whether the *received message* is in most respects identical with what is intended is determined by the extent to which the communication process is relatively noise free and the sender and receiver share the same *cultural codes.* This process is outlined in Figure 12-1.

A *sender* (Gifts in Kind International, for example) formulates an *intended message* ("Gifts in Kind helps the world's corporations donate valuable products to needy people everywhere"). The *encoder* (an advertising agency) translates this intended message into an *encoded message* (a picture of a group of families affected by Hurricane Katrina receiving clothes provided by Perry Ellis International, and several paragraphs describing: "Gifts In Kind International is a nonprofit organization that provides products donated by many Fortune 500 companies to assist those in need and manages a collaborative emergency relief plan that directly connects

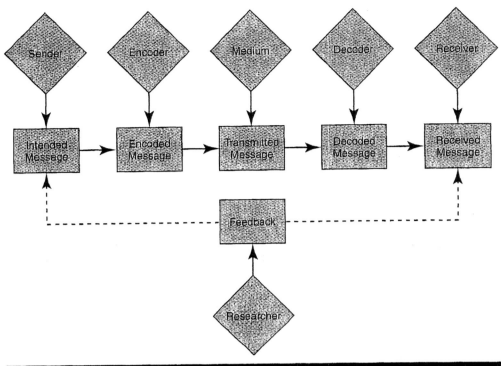

FIGURE 12-1 Elements in the Communication Process

community needs with corporate product giving." The paragraphs also offer quotes from both the Gifts in Kind International CEO and a Perry Ellis representative on the value of the relief program.)

This message is transmitted through such *media* as major regional newspapers that the ad agency believes will add an aura of "seriousness" to the encoded message. The *decoders* may be a young couple in Biloxi glancing at a magazine in a doctor's office, discussing between themselves the direct and implied content of the ad ("I thought charity just involved money and not product giving"). Finally, each *receiver* in the couple retains traces of the memorable parts of the message and associations (e.g., the emotional connotations of Hurricane Katrina and a first-time awareness of Gifts in Kind International), which can be assessed by a market *researcher* checking for *feedback* in a post-campaign telephone survey.

In many actual situations, the roles portrayed in Figure 12-1 may be combined. For example, there can be two-party communication involving (1) the sender–encoder–medium–researcher and (2) the decoder–receiver. This would be the case in many kinds of personal influence situations, such as a fundraising presentation to a potential major donor. The fundraiser would decide what message to get across, encode it into a "prospect pitch," transmit it verbally, and watch for or inquire about the potential donor's response. The donor would decode the fundraiser's pitch and store whatever was personally meaningful in it.

Even in this relatively simple two-party situation, a number of kinds of "noise" can creep in:

1. *Encoding.* The fundraiser may choose the wrong wording to convey key concepts. For example, he or she may intend to make it clear that the donor can be anonymous, but by making frequent references to *possible* forms of recognition leave the overall impression that the donor cannot escape publicity.

2. *Transmitting.* Vocal inflections or body language in the delivery of the message can change its meaning. For example, if a person seeking a donation for a hospital adopts too "serious" a tone of voice when speaking about the scientific quality of the research work being done at the hospital, he or she may unintentionally convey the impression that the scientists are pessimistic about possible breakthroughs. In another example, if a flip chart is used to outline the possible types of funding sought and possible uses of those funds, the speed with which pages of the chart are physically flipped may unintentionally tell a potential donor which areas the hospital *really* thinks are important.

3. *Decoding.* The target audience can mishear what is said. A 70 percent success rate for a health care facility may be heard as 17 percent. A distracted decoder may miss important benefits. The meaning given to statements heard orally can also vary greatly, depending on what experiences the decoder brings to the message. A potential donor with queasy personal reactions to the sight of blood may not really "see" flip chart pictures or slides showing or implying "bloody" events. A biased potential donor may "decide" that an agency is not well run if "too many" female or 20-something staff members are portrayed. The target audience member may not like the fundraiser and so tend to discount his or her opinions or assertions.

4. *Researching.* Individuals vary greatly in their ability to read the responses of target audiences. Thus noise is added to the communication process if the fundraiser interprets a potential donor's silence as signaling a lack of interest when it actually means that the donor is reflecting carefully on the merits of a proposal. Alternatively, the fundraiser might decide that the cause of a potential donor's indifference is stinginess when in fact it is caused by the donor's irritation at the fundraiser's manner of presentation. Finally, it is possible that a target audience member may encode his or her own feelings with some distortion. Indeed, feedback is really another communication process with the target audience as the sender and the marketing organization as the receiver.

Of course, in a great many communication situations, the process involves several agencies or individuals acting in one or more of the roles indicated in Figure 12-1. In these cases, the potential for "noise" is enhanced:

1. *Encoding.* Celebrity spokespeople may be designated as agents for communicating top management's sense of mission for the nonprofit organization, and they can get the message wrong or distort it. Alternatively, an advertising agency or public relations firm may be given the task of encoding the organization's *intended* message but may produce words or images that distort or inflate management's intentions. For example, too-slick graphics or a "cool" ad layout for a

symphony orchestra may suggest that the orchestra is not a solid, well-trained ensemble or that its repertoire is too avant-garde for most tastes. Every time another participant is added to the communication process, he or she brings to it his or her own interests, values, goals, and perceptions. Some advertising or public relations agencies working pro bono or for reduced fees may direct their messages at least partly toward their fellow advertising or PR colleagues whom they want to impress. Sometimes their main goal seems to be to attempt to dazzle their peers with the style and drama of a message's "encoding." The advertising community is replete with stories of campaigns that secured very high recall scores but did not "move the product." Early Pepsi ads featuring Shaquille O'Neal scored very high in ad tests while actual Pepsi sales declined 1.6 percent.

2. *Transmitting.* The vehicle through which you say something can enhance or distort a message. Many advertisers believe that putting an ad in a particular medium (e.g., *The New Yorker* or *Vanity Fair*) can add a sense of "class" to their presentation. Or they may choose a spokesperson (e.g., Denzel Washington, Julia Roberts, or Martin Sheen) who will bring his or her own prestige or charisma to the nonprofit agency's message.[2] Sometimes, however, the spokesperson can be inappropriate, "doing it for the money;" or have little in common with the target audience. Celebrities like Mel Gibson can prove toxic to a campaign because of their personal conduct.

   Certain media can be inappropriate. Radio ads on a rock station may be wrong for a "serious" hospital, and a classical music station may be wrong for a hospital trying to position itself as being "for everyone." Print ads in *Maxim* may get high readership but convey the wrong impression about a clinic's exercise therapy program. A college that wants to seem less elite should avoid *The New Yorker,* whereas a political candidate might find this magazine an appropriate vehicle for an interview adding to his or her "stature."

3. *Decoding.* Depending on how they are viewed by potential target audiences, channel members and their agents may serve as decoders for target audiences. Thus a physician may be asked by a patient to interpret the latest publicity release on smoking or high blood pressure, or by an older woman to explain what a new calcium pill will do for osteoporosis. In a similar fashion, newspaper or TV critics may "decode" a symphony or theater's offering. The *Consumers Union* may evaluate products, services, and even advertising themes. Reporters and political analysts play the same role for voters. In all of these cases, what the marketer wants to say may take on very different meaning once it is filtered through these "helpful" role players.

4. *Researching.* Outside agencies can be hired by the marketer to assess directly the target audience's present moods, opinions, or specific responses to the marketer's messages. To the extent that this intervention involves the perceptions, judgments, empathy, *and* communication skills of these other agents, there is significant potential for distortion.

   Most problematic is the case where "independent" third parties take on the role of providing feedback to the marketer. Examples include the self-appointed spokesperson for the oppressed who tells marketers "the truth" about how the group has been mistreated and the opinion polls from trade associations or politically connected "foundations" that purport to tell the government how the public is reacting to particular ongoing programs or new proposals. Nonetheless, there are also many respected associations that offer accurate feedback about what their members think and feel as well as thoughtful newspaper, magazine, and television commentators who are well attuned to the public opinions of special subgroups.

Strategic Implications

The major implication of this complex view of the communication process is that in any given situation the probability is very high that the *received message* will be different from the *intended message*. Two corollaries of this conclusion are as follows:

1. The more role players there are in the communication process, the greater the chance for distortion.
2. The less control the marketer has over the role players in the communication process, the greater the chance for distortion.

These concerns have several implications for marketing strategy:

1. The nonprofit communicator should *never* assume that the target audience will "receive" what the communicator thinks is being "sent."
2. If communication strategy is to be improved, it is essential that the marketer know what is likely to be received (through pretesting) and actually received (through posttesting monitoring).
3. If knowing what is received is crucial, careful attention must be paid to the quality of the *feedback* link in the system (i.e., the research).
4. If formal feedback research is carried out before the launch of the message or a message campaign, pretesting should simulate the *entire* communication process. For example, if a program of patient hypertension education is to be conducted with PowerPoint presentations and through brochures that physicians pass along to patients, simply testing physicians' responses or patients' responses to the materials alone would be inadequate. The marketer must test *both* steps in either a laboratory or a test market setting to see (a) how the physicians perceive the materials, (b) how often and with what advice they pass them on to the patients, and (c) how patients decode and store what the physicians tell them.
5. If communications are distorted at the receiving end, it is important to trace the source of the distortion to its roots. In the preceding example, the hypertension message could be inaccurately received for a variety of reasons, including these:

   a. It was poorly encoded by the marketer in the first place (that is, the brochures and slides were poorly designed).
   b. It was well encoded, but physicians often added their own embellishments, verbal cues, or body language that changed the content.
   c. The typical receiver was sufficiently misinformed about the disease *before* hearing the message such that parts which seemed frightening were simply not "heard" at any important level.

The changes needed in the communication program would vary significantly depending on which of these problems was the primary source of message noise.

1. If a message *must* be received undistorted (for example, instructions about what a mother should do when her child is in a life-threatening situation), and it must be the same for all target audiences, perfectly clear written communications directly delivered to the target audience are obviously superior.
2. However, if a message must be carefully adjusted to individual target audiences (e.g., how a person should change personal diet and exercise patterns), then a flexible, personally delivered message strategy is preferable because of its potential for ongoing feedback. (The one proviso here is that the personal spokesperson be one who is naturally empathetic or carefully trained in *undistorted listening* techniques.)

MAJOR STEPS IN DEVELOPING EFFECTIVE COMMUNICATIONS

There are six steps in developing communications strategies: (1) setting communication objectives, (2) generating possible messages, (3) overcoming selective attention, (4) overcoming perceptual distortion, (5) choosing a medium, and (6) evaluating and selecting messages. We turn later to the possibilities of modifying behavior directly.

Setting Communication Objectives

The first step calls for the marketer to define carefully the objective or objectives of the communication program. For a specific campaign, one useful way to think about possible objectives is to organize them by the stages of change in which one finds the audience. Possible objectives are:

1. Precontemplation stage
    a. Making target audiences aware of social behavior that should be addressed
    b. Increasing the perceived social importance of the behavior (social norming)
    c. Creating awareness of products, services, organizations, and behaviors that can yield solutions
    d. Influencing the media to cover the issue and possible solutions
    e. Changing perceptions about the sponsoring organization
    f. Influencing funding agencies
2. Contemplation stage
    a. Educating target audiences about the details of a specific action
    b. Changing beliefs about the negative and positive consequences of taking a particular action
    c. Changing the relative importance of particular consequences
    d. Communicating wide social support for an action
3. Preparation and Action stage
    a. Teaching skills needed to carry out the behavior
    b. Enlisting the support of intermediary agencies (e.g., securing shelf space)

   c. Recruiting, motivating, or rewarding employees or volunteers who can help make behavior happen

   d. Influencing governing agencies, review boards, commissions, and the like who can make the behavior easier

4. Maintenance stage

   a. Telling stories of successes

   b. Praising continuation of behaviors

   c. Combating injurious rumors

There are, of course, many other communications objectives that a nonprofit organization might have. For example, it may speak to potential employees, attempt to reposition an organization or its brand, brag about accomplishments, make announcements of landmark events, and so on. Many of these will be considered in Chapter 14 on public relations.

Generating Possible Messages

Once the nonprofit marketer has determined a broad objective or set of objectives for a communication campaign, the next step is to encode it in *specific* messages. Message generation involves developing a number of alternative appeals, themes, motifs, and ideas from which the best one can be chosen.

Messages can be generated in a number of ways. One approach is to talk with members of the target audience and other influential parties (for example, in focus groups) to determine how they see the product or service or behavior, talk about it, and express their desires about it. A second approach is to hold a brainstorming meeting with key personnel in the organization to generate several ideas. A third method is to use some formal deductive framework to tease out possible communication messages. We discuss two of the many possible deductive frameworks next.

Rational, Emotional, and Moral Framework

One framework identifies three types of messages that can be generated: rational, emotional, and moral.

1. *Rational messages* aim at passing on information, serving the audience's self-interest, or both. They attempt to show that the service will yield the expected functional benefits. Examples are messages discussing a service's quality, economy, value, or performance or messages spelling out the long-term health consequences of exercise or increasing calcium intake.

2. *Emotional messages* are designed to stir up some negative or positive emotion that will motivate the desired behavior. Communicators have worked with fear, guilt, and shame appeals, especially in connection with getting people to start doing things they should do (e.g., brush their teeth, have an annual health checkup) or stop doing things they shouldn't do (e.g., smoke, drink and drive, abuse drugs, overeat, or bring illegal fruit across the border). Advertisers have found that fear appeals work up to a point, but if there is too much fear the audience may ignore the message. Communicators have also used positive emotional appeals such as love, humor, pride, and joy. Evidence has not, however, established that a humorous message, for example, is necessarily more effective than a straight version of the same message.

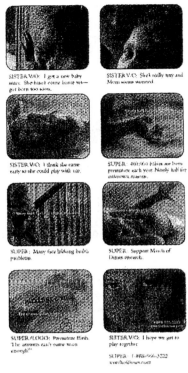

MARCH OF DIMES

objective | Build awareness and concern for the growing problem of premature births.

FIGURE 12-2 Emotional Television Advertising

Source: March of Dimes.

Positive emotions can also be very powerful The March of Dimes has been very effective in creating television advertising that tugs at the heartstrings of parents who might be worried about premature births (see Figure 12-2).

3. *Moral messages* are directed to the audience's sense of what is right and proper. They are often used in messages exhorting people to support such social causes as a cleaner environment, better race relations, equal rights for women, and aiding the disadvantaged. An example is this March of Dimes appeal: "God made you whole. Give to help those He didn't." The truth® campaign makes effective use of a moral theme aimed partly at its competition by pointing out the real negative effects of the tobacco industry's campaigns (see Figure 12-3).

The BCOS Theory Framework

A second way to generate possible messages is to work through the BCOS framework, particularly if the target audience is in the Contemplation or the Preparation/Action stage. Here, one would use audience research to ascertain the potential impact of messages around perceived benefits, costs, the wishes of others, and sense of self-efficacy.

Consider the communication problem of the marketing director of St. Anthony's Hospital, Axel Arneson, who is seeking to persuade a specific physician, Dr. Laura

FIGURE 12-3 Confronting the Competition

Source: American Legacy Foundation.

Goldman, to admit more of her patients to the hospital's oncology ward instead of to a competitor, the Downtown Medical Center (DMC). Suppose that from conversations with Dr. Goldman, Mr. Arneson has determined that there are four key potentially positive consequences (benefits) that Dr. Goldman considers when deciding where to admit a patient—the behavior that is the bottom line of this potential influence process. These are the consequences:

1. The extent to which the nursing staff is well trained enough to competently administer Dr. Goldman's treatment plan and to make sensible judgments on occasions when the plan doesn't apply and Dr. Goldman is unavailable for consultation.
2. The extent to which other physicians affiliated with the hospital (especially those in oncology) can provide good advice and share in patient treatment.
3. The extent to which Dr. Goldman will have access to the latest testing and treatment equipment and other patient care facilities.
4. The extent to which Dr. Goldman will have her wishes respected and carried out regarding admissions, treatment, office space, fees, and billing.

Mr. Arneson has estimated Dr. Goldman's beliefs about the likelihood of achieving these positive consequences if she takes the behavior of affiliating with each of the rival hospitals on a scale of 0 to 1 as follows:

	St. Anthony's	Downtown Medical Center	Importance
Good nursing care	.8	.7	20%
Access to knowledgeable colleagues	.9	.6	30
Access to best facilities	.5	.7	30
Have my wishes respected	.4	.8	20

Note that Mr. Arneson is not interested in Dr. Goldman's perceptions of the alternative organization but of her perceptions of the consequences of a behavior toward them. It is the behavior that Mr. Arneson knows he has to influence and so he is resolutely focused on this.

From his conversation, Mr. Arneson also judges that Dr. Goldman gives weightings of 20, 30, 30, and 20 percent, respectively, to the four benefits of the alternative behaviors. Mr. Arneson further believes that Dr. Goldman's perceptions of the likely outcomes are very similar to those of a sizable contingent of other physicians in the area. Finally, Mr. Arneson believes that his hospital's low ratings on the "facilities" and "respect" consequences stem from the relative age and overcrowded appearance of his physical facilities.

There are three ways that the overall evaluation of the benefits of taking action can be changed: (1) changing the importance of one or more consequences, (2) changing beliefs about one or more consequences, or (3) adding new (presumably positive) consequences.

Changing Importance Weights The first possibility open to Mr. Arneson is to attempt to change the importance weightings that Dr. Goldman and those like her attach to the four behavioral consequences. Thus he might attempt to increase the weighting given to "access to knowledgeable colleagues" (on which his hospital scores well) and reduce that given to "access to best facilities" by arguing as follows:

> Many physicians think that the kind of hospital they want to work in is the one with the very best equipment and testing facilities. We know that's important. But the best equipment is only as good as the people who make it work and who help draw the most from its results. It is one thing to have the latest CT scanner, quite another to be around colleagues who know just when to use it and how to wring the last ounce of meaning from its readouts. We think that is *really* the kind of institution you want to be affiliated with, one that has the most up-to-date facilities but, even more, that has the staff and colleagues who are on the leading edge of research and diagnoses using these new technical wonders.

Notice that this attempt at changes in perspectives made no mention of St. Anthony's or its rivals. Mr. Arneson knew that St. Anthony's scored well on "knowledgeable colleagues" and not so well on "facilities." He knows that if he can switch the weightings from 30 to 40 percent on "colleagues" and 30 to 20 percent on "facilities," St. Anthony's would be the favored institution, not Downtown Medical Center.

Changing Beliefs Should Arneson decide that changing the weightings is too difficult or too risky to attempt, he has another option, trying to change beliefs. Here he can make use of suggestive social science frameworks, such as dissonance theory.[3] One characteristic of human beings is that we prefer order and meaning. We like things to fit well together. We don't take kindly to messages that run counter to our present cognitions. When we encounter such dissonant messages, if the issue is involving, we will attempt to reassert order in our cognitive structure (our view of the world). That is, we will attempt to restore consonance.[4] We adopt several strategies to cope with dissonance.

Suppose that Dr. Goldman heard a rumor that two Downtown Medical Center laboratory technicians had drug abuse problems. This would be dissonant with her view that Downtown had reasonably good colleagues for her to work with (and, of course, with any interest in sending her patients there). Dr. Goldman could restore consonance in several ways:

1. *Denial.* She could convince herself that the rumors "couldn't be true" (e.g., that they were the work of "enemies" of DMC).
2. *Search for disconfirmation.* She could seek information from administrators at DMC that would counter the rumors.
3. *Reduce the importance of the issue.* We can all live with some amount of dissonance provided it isn't perceived to be related to an issue in which we are highly involved. Thus Dr. Goldman might decide that although the rumor may be true, it isn't really a very serious matter because (a) the people in question probably don't work in highly technical areas like hers, (b) even if they did, she could personally spot them and avoid them, (c) hospital administrators would certainly take care of the problem, or (d) even if the problem can't be entirely dealt with, it would be no better anywhere else (e.g., at St. Anthony's).
4. *Change prior beliefs.* Dr. Goldman may judge the rumors to be true and change her belief about DMC's staff and her own decision to send patients there.

The last mentioned is, of course, an instance of *changed beliefs.* It is a case in which new information caused a negative result from DMC's standpoint but a positive one where St. Anthony's is concerned. While one would not expect Mr. Arneson to resort to spreading unsubstantiated rumors about a rival institution, one can see that the introduction of dissonant information can change beliefs. Thus Mr. Arneson could seek to offer facts about St. Anthony's or about Downtown Medical Center that he believed Dr. Goldman would find dissonant. It is crucial that the facts chosen (1) be so convincing that they cannot easily be denied, (2) concern some highly involving area not likely to be minimized by Dr. Goldman, and (3) be difficult to counter by other facts.

Adding Consequences   A third alternative available to Mr. Arneson is to add one or more new, positive beliefs to the value proposition. Indeed, this is a common strategy in the commercial sector for differentiating a brand in a highly competitive market environment or resuscitating a brand in the decline phase of its life cycle. Potential target audiences are told about a new consequence of using the product or service or engaging in a behavior. Sometimes, these new consequences only require imagination and not a fundamental change in the offering. Thus a marketer may point out to those not swayed by arguments about the positive health consequences of participating in a stop-smoking clinic that participation may also lead to making new friends. Or new parents may be encouraged to use a library not only for information about parenting, but also to learn about library services that their child could appreciate or learn to use later in life, such as weekly storytelling hours or children's CD rentals.

In Mr. Arneson's case, he may discover additional "perks" that might appeal to Dr. Goldman. This could be an augmentation to the basic value proposition such as a special parking location, an advanced real-time computer system for patient reports, or first perusal of the library's copies of key journals in her field. Alternatively (or in addition), Mr. Arneson may simply point out additional existing features of

St. Anthony's and its staff, such as the publication record of attending physicians, which would indicate that both secretarial facilities and knowledgeable colleagues would be available for whatever writing ambitions Dr. Goldman might harbor.

Introducing Other Components of the BCOS Model

Mr. Arneson must recognize that perceived benefits and costs are not the only factors likely to drive Dr. Goldman's value perceptions and ultimate behavior. She may be influenced by important groups of "others." For example, she may perceive a strong positive benefit/cost ratio for St. Anthony's in terms of consequences important to her but still not choose to affiliate because some important patients of hers object or because her clinic partners think it is a mistake. Arneson's challenge then may be to mount a mini-campaign aimed to change the views of these *other* voices that can influence Dr. Goldman. Alternatively, he can add additional voices that he knows Dr. Goldman respects (for example, having a prestigious doctor make a personal telephone call urging her to affiliate).

Finally, there may be matters of self-assurance that could "kill" the campaign even if the other BCOS elements are positive. If for some reason Dr. Goldman thinks that it is just not *possible* to affiliate with St. Anthony's, she will not do so. Subtle probing may lead Mr. Arneson to discover that Dr. Goldman views the prospect of switching her records over to the sophisticated info-tech system at St. Anthony's to be too complicated and challenging, especially since her long-time assistant just went on a six-month maternity leave. Arneson may raise her sense of personal self-assurance by offering to loan her a part-time staffer knowledgeable in info-tech systems for the six-month transition period.

Overcoming Selective Attention

Change in beliefs about a value proposition is only possible if the audience member perceives the message. Mr. Arneson must recognize that people are constantly bombarded with promotional messages—perhaps thousands daily. But, of course, we perceive far fewer. We selectively attend to the information environment around us. This is often called "the cocktail party effect."[5] It helps us simplify and manage our lives. We attend to subjects, themes, or images that interest us and ignore others that don't. Thus older people will notice ads for extended vacations, hypochondriacs catch ads for over-the-counter drugs, teens pay attention to rock stars, and businesspeople seldom ignore computer ads.

In contrast, we tend to avoid messages that don't interest us or that in some way frighten us. This is a particular problem with fear appeals. Many nonprofit organizations involved in social or health issues find it tempting to use fear appeals. For example, the Metropolitan Energy Council, a group of New York fuel dealers, tried to compete with gas suppliers with an ad in the *New York Times* that depicted a young mother saying, "Gas comes from a big utility. They don't know my family. If you need prompt service from them, you have to say, 'I smell gas.' That's what scares me most. I think gas heat is dangerous—too dangerous for my home, my kids."[6]

The use of emotional appeals will continue to be a controversial topic in nonprofit marketing.[7] Experimental research by Bagozzi and Moore demonstrated that emotional anti–child-abuse ads were more effective than rational ads in generating negative emotions, empathy for victims, and the decision to help.[8] The researchers recognized that nonprofit marketers have to create powerful impacts with limited budgets. They conclude that "high-impact ads that evoke strong emotions and stimulate empathy

FIGURE 12-4 Truth Cuts Your Blinders

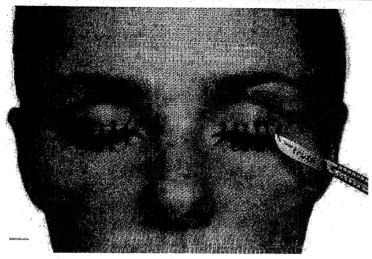

Source: America Legacy Foundation.

could require fewer exposures, yet be successful in influencing attitude formation and decision making." They note, however, that ads that evoke strong negative emotions could have rapid wear-out with repeated exposure. They think that, in situations such as those they studied involving the stopping of child abuse, nonprofit marketers will have more effect than private sector marketers because target audience members will not mentally counterargue the message as they might with a commercial sector ad.

In many cases, a shocking and unusual image will get attention of a target audience. The truth® campaign used such an approach in pointing out how many teens are blinded to the tobacco industry's propaganda (see Figure 12-4).

Message Execution

Overcoming the selective attention problem is the responsibility of the creative specialists on the nonprofit communication team (in-house or at the advertising or public relations agency). These specialists have several variables at their command in designing an effective message. They need to find a *style, tone, wording, order,* and *format* to make the message effective.

Any message can be put across in different *execution styles.* Suppose the YMCAs around the country are planning to launch an early morning jogging program (6:00 A.M.) and want to develop a 30-second television commercial to motivate people to sign up for this program. Here are some major advertising execution styles they can consider:

1. *Slice-of-life.* A husband says to his tired wife that she might enjoy jogging at the Y in the early morning. She agrees, and the next frame shows her coming home at 7:45 A.M. feeling refreshed and invigorated.
2. *Lifestyle.* A 30-year-old man pops out of bed when his alarm rings at 6:00 A.M., races to the bathroom, races to the closet, races to his car, races to the Y, and then starts racing with his companions with a "big kid" look on his face.

3. *Fantasy.* A jogger with a YMCA T-shirt runs along a path and suddenly imagines seeing her friends on the sidelines cheering her on.

4. *Mood.* A jogger runs in a residential neighborhood on a beautiful spring day, passing nice homes, noticing flowers beginning to bloom and neighbors waving to her. This ad creates a mood of beauty and harmony between the jogger and her world.

5. *Musical.* Four young joggers run side by side wearing YMCA T-shirts. Specially written pulsating rock music fills the background.

6. *Personality symbol.* A well-known sports hero is shown jogging at the Y with a smile on her face.

7. *Technical expertise.* Several Y athletic directors are shown discussing the best time, place, and running style that will give the greatest benefit to joggers.

8. *Scientific evidence.* A physician tells about a study of two matched groups of men, one following a jogging program and the other not, and the greater health and energy felt by the jogging group after a few weeks.

9. *Testimonial evidence.* The ad shows three members of the Y jogging group telling how beneficial the program has been to them.

The communicator must also choose a *tone* for the message. The message could be deadly serious (as in an anti-smoking ad), chatty (as in a message on weight control), humorous (a Panda in a zoo ad), and so on. The tone must be appropriate to the target audience and target response desired. Sites for young kids should have cartoon characters and preferably a cute name like the "Scrub Club" web site (see Figure 12-5).

Teenagers are accustomed to more off-the-wall communications images, high levels of intensity, and fast cutting. Setting a tone of "cool" for young people is a

FIGURE 12-5 A Web Site Aimed at Kids

Source: NSF International.

challenge for many web sites devoted to youth issues such as FreeVibe, the web site for the Office of National Drug Control Policy of the U.S. federal government (www.freevibe.com).

Words that are memorable and elicit attention must be found. This is nowhere more apparent than in the development of headlines and slogans to lead the reader into the message. There are six basic types of headlines:

- *news* ("United Way Offers New Giving Options")
- *questions* ("How Many Calories in This Health Shake?")
- *narrative* ("In the September 11 Terrorist Attack in New York, the Middle Classes Became the American Red Cross's Newest Victims")
- *command* ("Save Water—Shower with a Friend")
- *1–2–3 Ways* ("12 Ways to Enjoy the High Cs at the Long Beach Opera")
- *how—what—why* ("You Can't Get AIDS from a Door Knob, a Public Swimming Pool, or a Handshake")

Once the headline and the themes are determined, the communicator must consider the ordering of the ideas to be communicated. There are three issues: does one draw conclusions, offer one- or two-sided arguments, and put one's case at the start or end of a message?

The first is the question of *conclusion drawing,* the extent to which the message should draw a definite conclusion for the audience, such as telling them to give five hours a week to volunteering. Experimental research seems to indicate that explicit conclusion drawing is more persuasive than leaving it to the audience to draw their own conclusions. There are exceptions, however, such as when the communicator is seen as untrustworthy or the audience is highly intelligent and annoyed at the attempt to influence them.

The second issue is the question of using *one-* or *two-sided arguments*—that is, whether the message will be more effective if one side or both sides of the argument are presented. Two-sided arguments are of two types. First, there is the approach that admits that the offering has some costs. Thus a blood donation campaign might recognize that there is a needle involved but it is like a pin prick and one is providing potential life-saving help to a sick child. Other costs that ought to be recognized in communications strategies include:

- Alcoholics, smokers, and drug addicts *know* that quitting or cutting down will be agonizing and require very strong willpower.
- Older persons *know* that investigating a retirement home means admitting negative things about their own competence.
- Young people *know* that not drinking or smoking in some cases may subject them to the teasing of friends and classmates.
- Symphony, theater, and museum goers *know* that a great many of the events they could attend will have elements they don't understand.

A two-sided message would recognize these counterarguments or perceived costs and, where possible, directly address them.

The other kind of two-sided argument recognizes the fact that there are other alternatives. The burger and cola "wars" are message campaigns fully recognizing that there are tough competitors "out there." In the nonprofit sector, there are many parallel situations:

- Going to the theater or symphony means not going to a movie or nightclub or just staying home to watch TV.
- Having a medical checkup or practicing breast self-examination means giving up the "bliss of ignorance."
- Giving to the United Way may mean not giving to the American Cancer Society or a university's alumni fund.
- Choosing UCLA means not choosing Stanford, Northwestern, and Georgetown.
- Choosing politician X means not choosing politician Y.
- Choosing to vacation in Jamaica or Southeast Asia means not vacationing in Sun Valley or Paris.
- Practicing birth control means not having the potential long-run economic benefits of another income producer and immediate psychic pleasures of an additional child.

One-sided presentations are common in the nonprofit sector often for the wrong reasons. In part this is because of the "mindset problem" described in Chapter 2. Nonprofit staffers see the target audience as "the problem" and their ignorance as a barrier to their undertaking an obviously desirable behavior. The tendency is to want to harangue the audience with virtues of the behavior. In the private sector, this is called a "hard-sell" approach. Sometimes, as social science research suggests, one-sided approaches may be relatively more effective in three situations: (1) when the audience is less educated, (2) when the audience already favors the message's central proposition, and (3) when the audience is not likely to be exposed later to counterpropaganda. Two-sided messages are said to be more effective when the opposite is true.

There is another, perhaps more compelling, factor that should influence whether two-sided messages are used: It is the degree of the audience's involvement in the behavior that the marketer is attempting to influence. In general, we believe that the higher the audience's involvement in the behavior, the more frequently the nonprofit marketer should use two-sided messages.

There are several reasons for this. As the BCOS model emphasizes, in high-involvement situations, target audience members are more likely to be very concerned about the *costs* of the behavior, be opposed to the action advocated if it means important changes, and be aware of very attractive alternatives. In high-involvement situations, the target audience will engage in extensive internal cognitive activity, which will include considering costs and alternatives. They will engage in an extensive external search that will make available to them the "other side" of the argument. The marketer should seize the initiative and deal with the other side of the issue rather than leave it to the individual or to competitors. A useful concept in this regard is what is called *inoculation theory*. If a communicator knows that a target audience member will *later* be exposed to counterpropaganda (the "other side"), a more favorable outcome will be achieved if the marketer deals with the counterarguments in advance (in effect "inoculating" the target audience against the later influence attempts).

Finally, it must be reemphasized that in situations in which a two-sided strategy would be appropriate, the nonprofit communicator must go to great lengths to understand what *the target audience* perceives to be the key costs of the behavior and what *they* consider to be the reasonable alternatives. Only with a solid research base can an effective two-sided strategy be developed.

In the case of St. Anthony's Hospital, Mr. Arneson should recognize that Dr. Goldman will be exposed to counterpropaganda from DMC at some later point. Thus the two-sided inoculation concept indicates that Arneson must say things like "I know you'll hear people say that St. Anthony's is overcrowded. Let me set the record straight right now." If at all possible, Arneson should seek to have Dr. Goldman agree with St. Anthony's arguments. Internalizing a position makes it more likely that an individual will adhere to it even after other information is received.

A third issue for the marketer in cases where several ideas are to be conveyed is the best *order of presentation.* Social scientists have found that, other things being equal, people tend to remember the items in a message stream presented first (the primacy effect) and last (the recency effect). Thus many web sites make sure that their key promotional points are on the front page. There are arguments for Mr. Arneson putting his strongest statements in either position.

Format elements can also make a difference in a message's impact, as well as in its cost. If the message is to be carried in a print ad, the communicator must choose among the elements of headline, copy, illustration, and color. Attention-getting devices such as *novelty, contrast, arresting pictures,* and *movement* can be helpful. If the message is to be carried over the radio, the communicator carefully has to choose words and voice qualities. If the message is to be carried on television or given in person, then all of these elements plus body language (nonverbal cues) have to be planned.

Overcoming Perceptual Distortion

As we have already noted, individuals have a substantial background of experiences, categorization schemes, prejudices, associations, needs, wants, and fears that can markedly affect what they "see" or "hear" in the message. Thus poor children will imagine foreign coins that they have seen larger than will children who are economically better off. Pessimists will see half-empty glasses, optimists half-full ones.

This potential for distortion can work to the communicator's advantage. Messages can be relatively economical in what they say by using associations that they know people will bring to a symbol, a word, or an example. For example, readers need to see only *one* of the following symbols depicted in an ad to know that a restaurant is *not* a fast-food outlet: a tablecloth, flowers on the table, silverware, a waiter taking an order, candles, subdued lighting, upholstered chairs, wine glasses, or china. Someone sipping wine is assumed to be of a higher social class than someone holding a beer mug. Someone wearing eyeglasses is supposed to be smarter than someone without them. Colors have symbolism. In the United States, white is pure, gold is rich, blue is soothing, pastels are "modern," and so on.[9]

Symbolism, however, varies significantly both within and across cultures. In Norway, an advertisement showing a female flight attendant fluffing a pillow and offering a brandy to a tired businessman was considered offensive as depicting women as merely servants to men.[10] The airline company, Singapore Airlines, viewed the scene very differently, of course, since its cultural norms were very different. Similarly, showing wives making the decisions about the couple's social life would be perfectly appropriate in upper-class white American social settings but less appropriate for many immigrant groups.

Symbols can help or hurt communicators. The problem, of course, is to choose the right symbols and to be assured that your audience sees them as you do. Mr. Arneson may make an important mistake by assuming, for example, that Dr. Goldman would associate stainless steel furnishings with high-quality office décor, whereas she sees it as always needing cleaning! While Mr. Arneson should carefully plan his choice of associations, one advantage of personal communication is that a sensitive communicator can secure feedback on how the message is actually perceived and fine-tune it so that it is perceived as intended.

Even if a message is perceived in an appropriate fashion, this does not guarantee that it will be retained or, more importantly, recalled at the moment it is "needed" to influence a particular behavior. One technique to reduce this possibility is, of course, *repetition*. Krugman and others have suggested that up to three repetitions will improve the probability of retention under high-involvement conditions.[11] Thus Mr. Arneson might mention the hospital's superior accounting and scheduling services several times in a conversation or over a series of conversations to increase the likelihood that the information will be permanently retained. Another technique is to link the new information to existing cognitions. Individuals are more likely to recall things that they can assimilate well.

Choosing a Medium

The message the marketer decides to use will be transmitted to the target audience through some medium or a combination of media. The medium chosen can be *personal,* as with a blog from an organization's own spokesperson, or *impersonal,* as when a poster, a brochure, a magazine or newpaper advertisement, a product container, a shopping bag, a web site, or a banner ad on the side of a truck is used. The medium can be perceived by the target audience as an *advocate* for the offering or as *independent*. Thus there are four possibilities, as suggested in Table 12-1.

In the twenty-first century, an important new medium for reaching audiences is the Web. The Web is particularly powerful with young audiences, especially teenagers. A study commissioned by Craver, Matthews, Smith, and Company suggests that the Web may also be a preferred vehicle for reaching "social activists."[12] Web sites accommodate a wide range of information that can be tailored to the audience's interests by various homepage options. Thus an anti-drug site can have pages for parents devoted to "detecting drug use," for potential donors on "what your money can do," for potential volunteers on "getting involved in solutions" or, perhaps, for teachers on "classroom materials on drug issues." The tone and appearance of these sub-pages will differ by audience—cool, dynamic, and noisy for teens; serious and formal for parents; full of upbeat pictures and movie vignettes for potential donors; and how-to-do-it sub-pages for teachers.

Web sites and weblogs are extremely promising vehicles for allowing use of all sorts of content, tone, and modalities.[13] They can offer videos for those who want them,

TABLE 12-1 Alternative Media		
	Personal	*Impersonal*
Advocate	Salesperson	Brochure
	Political supporter	Advertisement
	"Friend of the Arts"	Billboard
Independent	Newscaster	*Wall Street Journal*
	Independent researcher	Government study
	Noted physician	Target audience reports

interactive quizzes and games for others, celebrity testimonials (written, spoken or videotaped), chances to have instant-messaging contact with others with the same issues (e.g., cancer sufferers or their family members), or access to lots of research data and related web sites for those who like "the facts."[14]

The Office of National Drug Control Policy has used this medium very effectively in its teen anti-drug campaign (www.freevibe.com). In Exhibit 12-1, Beverly Schwartz, now at Ashoka, and Ann Hardison of Fleishman Hillard describe their approach using a conceptual framework employing four stages parallel to those described through this book.

EXHIBIT 12-1

BEVERLY SCHWARTZ, ANN HARDISON, FLEISHMAN HILLARD INTERNATIONAL COMMUNICATIONS, ON USING THE WEB TO "ENGAGE" AUDIENCES

As the power and reach of the Internet have evolved, social marketers have gained an invaluable new tool for use in behavior change campaigns. While social marketers may sometimes envy product marketers for their ability to implement large-scale marketing programs to finely segment, reach and influence audience groups, the Web offers us a new tool to achieve these objectives.

The Online Integration Model to Promote Behavior Change was developed by Fleishman Hillard to generate a paradigm for online activities—something that could be used as a guide to develop a Web-based program that delivered four elements. It needed to be as strategic as it was sustainable; as informative as it was behavioral; as cohesive as it was dynamic; and could transport the individual user from being a

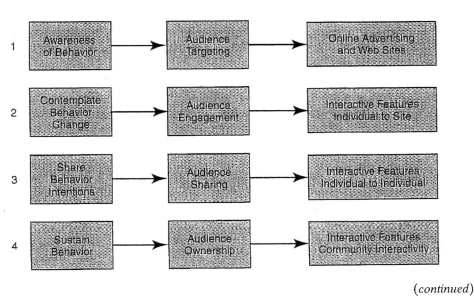

(continued)

EXHIBIT 12-1   (cont.)

lone entity facing an inanimate computer screen—to being a part of a community. We realized that it was imperative to not only "know" our audience, but to critically examine the nexus of the audience, the market, and the technology and to understand how the interplay of those dynamics determine our approach to the development of Web components. Our objective was to create an online communication strategy that went beyond building well designed and attractive Web sites to building sites that encouraged the development of online communities with individuals personally adopting and advocating a campaign's messages.

The model was developed and tested as part of the Office of National Drug Control Policy's National Youth Anti-Drug Media Campaign targeting both adolescents and parents. Since Internet-based components were determined to be vital to integrating the advertising and non-advertising activities within this campaign, we needed to extend and support the active involvement of youth and adults to the Web components, thereby ensuring a more balanced and behaviorally oriented integrated approach.

To achieve behavior change, at some point along the behavioral continuum, passivity—e.g., uni-directional intake—must be transformed into multi-directional activity. Therefore, as our interactive strategy evolved, two behavioral models—the transtheoretical model and the diffusion of innovation model—were utilized as the foundational underpinnings for the model.

The initial results of this application indicate a high degree of success in using the Internet to encourage adolescents along the behavior change continuum and, although more challenging, a real potential for success with parent audiences. Engaging partners—online and offline—has also emerged as critical to the success of the interactive strategy.

The continually evolving interactive programs in this campaign have clearly moved this social marketing campaign from a traditional "information out" approach to a revolving door where the target audiences have first become partners and then advocates for the campaign's message within their own social networks.

Choosing a Spokesperson

Choosing a spokesperson is also an important challenge. In many situations involving either paid or unpaid advocacy of a nonprofit organization—its product, service, or cause—the marketing manager will wish to use some person to deliver the message. Whom to choose and what to have the person say are crucial questions.

Spokespersons typically will be viewed positively for one of two reasons.[15] First, they may be respected as *credible experts* on a particular topic. This would be the case where a teenage former drug user or a noted medical expert is the spokesperson for an anti-drug program. The other case is where the person is not an expert but is considered by the target audience to be highly *trustworthy*. Thus the nonprofit might use Tom Hanks or Oprah Winfrey to advocate a drug-free life. The target audience may reason that although the spokesperson doesn't necessarily know anything about the subject, he or she can be counted on to tell the truth or advise one wisely. Laura Bush, when speaking about drugs, is presumably both a credible and a trustworthy person. The same can be said of Denzel Washington or baseball's Alex Rodriguez when they speak for the Boys & Girls Clubs of America (to which they once belonged). In all cases, it is important that the nonprofit marketer research the credibility and trustworthiness of the proposed spokespersons with the target audience.

Pretesting is always valuable. And, of course, the wise nonprofit organization marketer has a contingency plan should the spokesperson be found to have a recent or past experience that sullies the nonprofit image—for example, unfortunate choices of words that turn off key audiences. In the run-up to the 2006 U.S. elections, Senator George Allen got himself in considerable "image trouble" when he called a reporter a "Macaca," which turned out to be a racial slur. Allen later was also less than straightforward about revelations of his Jewish heritage.[16]

Message Evaluation and Selection

The marketer must select the best message from the set of alternatives, preferably with some form of formal pretesting. Twedt suggested that contending messages be rated on three scales: *desirability, exclusiveness,* and *believability.*[17] He believes that the communication potency of a message is the product of these three factors because if any of the three has a low rating, the message's communication potency is greatly reduced.

The message must first say something desirable or interesting about the product, service, or behavior. This is not enough, however, since many competitors may be making the same claim. Therefore the message must also say something exclusive or distinctive that does not apply to every alternative. Finally, the message must be believable or provable. By asking target audiences to rate different messages on desirability, exclusiveness, and believability, these messages can be evaluated for their communication potency.

COMMUNICATION IN THE PREPARATION/ACTION STAGE

Persuading target audience members to become predisposed toward acting is not the same as getting them to actually undertake the act (i.e., to move from the Contemplation stage to the Preparation/Action stage). A set of models around the concept of "shaping" can be useful here. This concept recognizes that there are some behavioral outcomes that a marketer wishes to have repeated that can be approached, not in one step, but by successive approximations. This is known as "shaping" behavior. Shaping can take place directly by the manipulation of the "size" of the requested behavior or indirectly by *modeling* the desired behavior (e.g., sensible eating or exercise) either in person (e.g., in demonstration seminars) or through the media. Marketers using the media, however, lack direct feedback from the people they are trying to influence. Thus they need to conduct research to learn whether they are having the effects they desire. Exhibit 12-2 shows how the Academy for Educational Development learned that it was modeling the wrong immunization behavior.

One of the areas in which shaping is used as a behavior change technique is in securing smoking cessation. The smoker is asked to observe his or her own smoking behavior, noting two things: the occasions on which a cigarette is smoked, and the relative importance of smoking behavior on each occasion. The smoker then determines his or her own schedule of cutting down (shaping) the smoking behavior. In a sense, the smoker slowly increases the psychological "size" of the behavioral challenge. The smoker starts by eliminating the least important smoking occasions and then works up

EXHIBIT 12-2

WILLIAM SMITH OF THE ACADEMY FOR EDUCATIONAL DEVELOPMENT ON MODELING IMMUNIZATION BEHAVIOR IN ECUADOR

The Academy for Educational Development works with governments around the world helping develop social marketing strategies to save infants from diarrhea, protect adults from AIDS, and help couples space their children. Immunization of children is a big priority, and the problem in many developing countries is that mothers just don't realize or believe that more than one shot is needed to protect their child fully from polio, diphtheria, or tetanus.

Working in Ecuador from 1985 to 1988, AED staff helped the government's massive program of immunization draw thousands of women for their child's first shot. But by the end of year 1, most children over one year old were still not fully immunized (three shots plus one for measles were needed).

The campaign had popularized two children, the PREMI kids, as the major theme. Focus groups and intercepts conducted after phases 1 and 2 of the campaign discovered the kids looked two to three years old to most mothers. We'd found the problem! The campaign's biggest visual cue modeled the wrong behavior.

The answer was a birth in the family. The PREMI kids had a baby brother, Carlitos, who became the hook to tie all our messages to "get your Carlitos" immunized by age one. A special gold star was added to a diploma women received if their child was immunized by age one. A "crystal bell" radio and TV campaign was tied into the Carlitos program to remind mothers each week, at the sound of the bell, "ask yourself—does your child need his next shot?"

Research, the right cues, and simple incentives made a difference. Full immunization coverage rose from 14 percent to 32 percent over the course of the program. Carlitos became widely known, and the certificate with a gold star became a prized possession.

Source: William Smith, Senior Vice President, Academy for Educational Development, private correspondence, December 1989.

to the most important. Smokers are trained to either reward themselves directly or to report their successes to a smoking cessation group or an individual therapist for attention, praise, and affectional reinforcement.

Messages to provoke action sometimes are sufficient "behavior starters" if they simply focus on getting a *first step*. That is, they can focus primarily on getting someone from not acting to beginning to act. For example, the Boys & Girls Clubs of America has found it hard to sign up both tough streetwise kids and law-abiding respectful kids. They learned that each group thought that there would be too many of the other group in the clubs. So, to overcome this misperception, many of the clubs hold events in the clubs with no strings attached. There is no mention of membership or anything beyond the event, which might feature a local sports star or musician. Once the kids are inside the door, the challenge is then to get them on to the next step—coming to some regular series of events and then perhaps joining the club.

COMMUNICATION IN THE MAINTENANCE STAGE

The approaches offered to this point for communication strategies have been based on a model of behavior change that assumes that the BCOS factors for a particular target audience and behavior must be understood *before* the behavior change. As a consequence they are appropriate for the Precontemplation, Contemplation, and Preparation/Action stages. In the Maintenance stage, our interest is in securing repeat behavior. Here, another communication approach is needed, known variously as *instrumental conditioning* or *behavioral modification* and most closely associated with the name of B. F. Skinner.[18]

The approach is still grounded in the view of target audience behavior that we have used throughout this text, namely that one of the important sets of reasons why target audience members take particular courses of action is because of the proposed value proposition. The BCOS approach to behavior change seeks to modify target audience's *anticipations* about possible consequences. Behavior modification attempts *to modify the consequences themselves*. By teaching the target individual that a particular action will lead to a desired reward, the probability of the action is increased. Thus if a blood donor gets an *unanticipated* award certificate or a free promotional gift after being dragged by coworkers to give blood, behavior modification theory predicts that the chances are increased that the donor will return. Further, his or her attitudes toward the behavior will become more positive. The rewards after the behavior are referred to as *reinforcers*. Cracker Jack offers little toys as just such reinforcers. Fundraisers are also known for giving tokens for donations and follow-up letters reinforcing the donation behavior. Clever volunteer recruiters also find ways to reward those helping out, especially first-timers.

There are many kinds of reinforcers, including:

- *Economic:* Coupons, trading stamps, prizes, rebates, chances in a contest, free T-shirts, pens
- *Social:* Praise, commendation, affection, conversation, attention
- *Other:* Certificates, feedback on achievement

Social scientists have documented that children who are given more attention and praise after eating unfamiliar foods are more likely to repeat this behavior (and subsequently to "like" the foods) than those who are not so rewarded. Simple feedback on household energy consumption has led to a reduction in energy use. Reductions in home oil use, for example, were induced by rewarding householders with a window sticker saying "We Are Saving Oil."

A great many companies have used economic rewards to get their employees to take better care of their health. At one time at Johnson & Johnson, for example, employees could earn "Live-for-Life Dollars" to be exchanged for sweat suits, socks, or fire extinguishers for attending smoking or stress workshops, exercising for 20 minutes, wearing seat belts, or installing home smoke detectors. Intermatic, Inc., gave employees who quit cigarettes for a year a trip for two to Las Vegas. Hospital Corporation of America paid workers 24 cents for each mile walked or run, each quarter mile swum, or each four miles bicycled. The government of Bellevue, Washington, and firms like Berol Corporation and King Broadcasting in Seattle gave rewards negatively related to the amount of health insurance claims an employee filed. Speedcall Corporation gave a $7 bonus for each week an employee didn't smoke on the job. In four years, the number of smokers in the company fell 65 percent and the number of health insurance claims by those who quit smoking fell 50 percent.[19]

There is some controversy about what patterns of reinforcement should be used. In general, *constant reinforcement* (rewarding every instance of the desired behavior) yields the *fastest* rate of learning but also the fastest extinction of the behavior when the reinforcements are stopped. However, *variable or random reinforcement* yields slower rates of initial learning but also slower extinction. The reasons offered for this finding are that during the reinforcement period, the subject in the Maintenance stage is initially not sure which behavior (if any) is being rewarded. This accounts for the slower rate of initial learning. Then, when rewards *are* linked to the behavior, the subject must interpolate his or her own rewards on those occasions when the externally provided rewards are absent.

In a study, Deslauriers and Everett found that offering 10-cent tokens to bus riders had a positive effect on bus usage. However, they found that variable reinforcement (every third passenger) was just as effective as continuing reinforcement and, of course, much more economical.[20]

For this type of behavioral modification to work, certain simple conditions must be present:

1. The desired behavior must be under the individual's control (thus it is not particularly effective with physical drug dependency).
2. There must be a clear link between the behavior and the reinforcement, although this need not always be apparent to the subject; the closer the reward is in time to the behavior, the greater the effect (thus praising someone two days after a desired behavior—for example, cutting out certain smoking occasions—is less effective than immediate praise).
3. The reinforcer must constitute a reward for the individual (thus praise from a feared autocratic schoolteacher would not be as reinforcing for a schoolchild as praise from a peer).

In our continuing example, once Dr. Goldman begins to send patients to St. Anthony's, Mr. Arneson should not consider his marketing task completed. He should find opportunities to reward Dr. Goldman for her behavior. Options could include taking her to lunch, having other staffers come around to say "Glad you're here," and/or paying especially close attention to the patients she refers and rewarding *them* for their patronage.

Self Rewards

As we noted earlier, many of the socially desirable behaviors that nonprofit marketing managers seek require that target audiences *reward themselves.* That is, those taking preventive medicine must tell themselves that they are doing the right thing for their long-term health or to protect their family. Exercisers need to find ways to convince themselves to go back and sweat some more. Marketers in such cases can be helpful in suggesting to audiences things they should tell themselves to keep going. The Maintenance stage is, in a great many cases, much more in the hands—and minds—of the target audiences than marketers.

Rewards from Allies

Many behaviors that will improve a person's life are visible—or at least known—to others. Thus someone quitting smoking or engaging in exercise or practicing anger management may be strongly influenced by the interpersonal support of friends, family, coworkers, and even bosses. We all have experiences when we tried harder or were pleased with something we did or when grandmother says how strong we've gotten; when the high school coach remarked at how much faster we are now that we quit smoking, and when the teacher praised our research on a paper. These experiences encourage nonprofit marketers to consciously recruit potential allies and offer them incentives and strategies to reward good social behavior.

Again, this is an effort to influence a behavior, and therefore an opportunity once again to use the influence approaches outlined throughout this volume.

INTEGRATION

A common phrase in private sector marketing today that one hears frequently is the need for integrated marketing communications.[21] It is critical that all elements of the communication program be integrated. Themes should be consistent. The "look" should be similar across executions. Spokespeople in one medium should be carried over into others. Where relevant, one communication component (e.g., a web site) should replicate another component (an advertisement or speeches by the CEO) and lead the audience to a third channel (an 800 number or a web site) that permits them to send out a final component (a brochure that repeats the themes and look of the ads and web site). Posters are often very powerful and immediate ways to back up other campaign components, particularly advertisements, or they can stand alone. Posters are particularly useful when one is trying to get a public institution to change, for example, in efforts to get the University of Wyoming to stop selling and condoning "spit tobacco" (see Figure 12-6).

Such integration creates opportunities to build repeat impressions that increase the likelihood of the desired effects on knowledge, perceptions, and behavior. However, in complex, large nonprofit organizations (and even some smaller ones with multiple locations), ensuring an integrated communication strategy across chapters and divisions requires extensive training and constant reinforcement. One of the central roles of central offices in complex nonprofits like the United Way and the YMCA is providing other organizational units with communication templates that can be adapted to local needs but that maintain a carefully crafted integrated campaign.

Summary

Every contact a nonprofit has with its many publics directly or indirectly is an occasion for communication and influence. These contacts may be carried out by many different departments or people using diverse vehicles ranging all the way from standard paid and unpaid media to package designs, corporate publicity releases, personal presentations, and even promotional "gimmicks" like shopping bags and T-shirts. For programs to be effective, however, they must be grounded in a clear understanding of communication processes.

Communication typically involves persuasion. This requires the preparation and transmittal of specific messages. Messages must be encoded by the marketer, communicated through media, and then decoded by the receiver. At each of these stages, considerable noise can be introduced into the communication process such that the accumulated effect of the received message is very different from what was intended.

FIGURE 12-6 Poster to Raise Awareness

Source: Wyoming Department of Health Substance Abuse

In general, the more parties involved in the communication system and the less control the marketer has over them, the greater the chance of miscommunication. Marketers use formal and informal feedback to track these effects. Where communication is face to face, feedback can be easily obtained. Where it is not, as in media campaigns, pre-and posttests of message strategies must always be carried out.

Six steps are involved in developing effective messages. First, the communication objectives must be determined. Second, messages must be generated. These can be rational, emotional, or moral, or they can be generated from the BCOS framework. Third, thought must be given to how these communications can overcome target audiences' tendencies to selectively expose themselves or attend to messages in which they are interested. The style, tone, wording, order, and format of the messages are all critical to getting a message noticed. Fourth, thought must be given to constructing the communications to overcome perceptual distortion, the tendency to add to and reinterpret what is actually in the message based on the audience member's own past experience, motives, and biases. Fifth, a medium must be chosen to convey the message to achieve maximum impact. In the nonprofit sector this often means choosing a spokesperson. If a spokesperson is used, the marketer must ensure that he or she is credible and trustworthy and that the message is so clear that it cannot be distorted by a target audience. Sixth, the marketers must evaluate all the possible messages and select the ones that are most desirable, exclusive, and believable. The BCOS model developed in Chapter 4 is a useful framework guiding this set of decisions.

The marketer must recognize that strategies to influence behavior need not rely only on advanced communication—that is, on first changing cognitions in order to change behavior. Other strategies, such as behavior modification, can simply manipulate rewards in the Maintenance stage. These strategies rely on a different model, in which it is assumed that changing behavior is an adequate goal in itself and that, once behavior is changed, perceptions may also change. However, management of rewards must often be a critical part of a nonprofit marketer's strategy.

Questions

1. You want to use blogs to communicate to young people about smoking and spit-tobacco use. How would this fit into an overall strategy?
2. List five spokespeople who might be considered for an after-school mentoring campaign targeted at suburban professionals. Develop a set of criteria that can be used to evaluate these spokespeople. Rate the candidates on the criteria and select a spokesperson. (The spokesperson can be an actual person or a type of person.)
3. You are responsible for training volunteer fundraisers for a charity devoted to supporting peace between Israelis and Palestinians. Based on the communications process model in this chapter, what are the possible sources of noise that would concern you?
4. You believe that "others" are important influences on teen crime. Suggest three people you would choose to support your anti–teen crime campaign and describe a communications campaign to get each to help.
5. You have learned that some young people are communicating incorrect information on marijuana use over the Internet through blogs. How would you develop a strategy to counter these messages?

Notes

1. See, for example, Peter L. Wright, "The Cognitive Process Mediating Acceptance of Advertising," *Journal of Marketing Research,* February 1973, pp. 53–62.
2. Matthew Thomson, "Human Brands: Investigating Antecedents to Consumers' Strong Attachments to Celebrities," *Journal of Marketing,* Vol. 70 (July 2006), pp. 104–119.
3. Leon Festinger, *A Theory of Cognitive Dissonance* (Stanford, CA: Stanford University Press, 1957). See also A. G. Greenwald and D. L. Ronis, "Twenty Years of Cognitive Dissonance: Case Study of the Evolution of a Theory," *Psychological Review,* Vol. 85 (1978), pp. 53–57.
4. For an example showing target audiences' willingness to live with dissonance in a nonprofit context, see M. T. O'Keefe, "The Anti-Smoking Commercials: A Study of Television's Impact on Behavior," *Public Opinion Quarterly,* 1971, pp. 242–248.
5. See J. T. Bertrand, "Selective Avoidance on Health Topics: A Field Test," *Communications Research,* July 1979, pp. 271–294. See also Wolfgang Schaefer, "Selective Perception in Operation," *Journal of Advertising Research,* February 1979, pp. 59–60.

6. "Death Turns Up the Thermostat," *Newsweek,* October 15, 1984.

7. See Michael L. Ray and William L. Wilkie, "Fear, The Potential of an Appeal Neglected by Marketing," *Journal of Marketing,* January 1970, pp. 55–56; Brian Sternthal and C. Samuel Craig, "Fear Appeals Revisited and Revised," *Journal of Target Audience Research,* December 1974, pp. 22–34; John J. Burnett and Robert E. Wilkes, "Fear Appeals to Segments Only," *Journal of Advertising Research,* Vol. 20, No. 5 (October 1980), pp. 21–24.

8. Richard P. Bagozzi and David J. Moore, "Public Service Advertisements: Emotions and Empathy Guide Prosocial Behavior," *Journal of Marketing,* Vol. 58 (January 1994), pp. 56–70.

9. Edward T. Hall, *The Silent Language* (Garden City, NJ: Doubleday, 1973).

10. John Karevoll, "Singapore Girl Nixed in Norway," *Advertising Age,* March 23, 1981, pp. m-2-m-3.

11. Herbert E. Krugman, "Why Three Exposures May Be Enough," *Journal of Advertising Research,* December 1972, pp. 11–15.

12. *Socially Engaged Internet Users: Prospects for Online Philanthropy and Activism* (Arlington, VA: CMS and The Mellman Group, 1999).

13. Rebecca Blood, 2002. *The Weblog Handbook: Practical Advice on Creating and Maintaining Your Blog* (Cambridge, MA: Perseus Publishing, 2002).

14. P. Klemm, D. Bunnell, M. Cullen, R. Soneji, P. Gibbons and A. Holecek, "Online Cancer Support Groups: a Review of the Research Literature," *Computers Informatics Nursing,* 21 (2003), pp. 136–142; M. White and S. M. Dorman, "Receiving Social Support Online: Implications for Health Education." *Health Education Research* 16 (2001) pp. 693–707

15. See Brian Sternthal, R. R. Dholakia, and Clark Leavitt, "The Persuasive Effect of Source Credibility: Test of Cognitive Response," *Journal of Target Audience Research,* Vol. 4 (1978), pp. 252–250; C. Samuel Craig and John M. McCann, "Assessing Communications Effects on Energy Conservation," *Journal of Target Audience Research,* Vol. 5 (September 1978,) pp. 82–88.

16. Tim Craig and Michael D. Shear, "Allen Quip Provokes Outrage, Apology: Name Insults Webb Volunteer," *Washington Post,* August 15, 2006, p. A1.

17. Dik Warren Twedt, "How to Plan New Products, Improve Old Ones, and Create Better Advertising," *Journal of Marketing,* January 1969, pp. 53–57.

18. Michael Rothschild and William C. Gaidis, "Behavioral Learning Theory: Its Relevance to Marketing and Promotions," *Journal of Marketing,* Spring 1981, pp. 70–78.

19. "Giving Goodies to the Good," *Time,* November 18, 1985, p. 98.

20. Brian C. Deslauriers and Peter B. Everett, "Effects of Intermittent and Continuing Token Reinforcement on Bus Ridership," *Journal of Applied Psychology,* Vol. 62, No. 4 (1977), pp. 369–375.

21. Paul Russel Smith and Jonathan Taylor, *Marketing Communications: An Integrated Approach,* 4th edition, (Sterling, VA: Kogan Page, Limited, 2004); see also Don Schultz, Robert Lauterborn, and Stanley Tannenbaum, *Integrated Marketing Communications,* (Lincolnwood, IL: NTC Business Books, 1993).

13

MANAGING COMMUNICATIONS: ADVERTISING AND PERSONAL PERSUASION

THE LARGEST CIRCULATION MAGAZINE IN THE WORLD!

In the commercial world, the trend in readership and profitability for a great many newspapers and magazines is falling—sometimes dramatically. Advertising revenues have decreased, in part as advertisers have sought new markets in new places such as through the Internet. But one publication that is bucking this trend is the magazine of a major nonprofit organization—AARP.

AARP in 2006 had about 37 million members and every one of these households received a copy of *AARP The Magazine* six times a year. The organization brags that the magazine is the world's largest circulation magazine, and it is increasingly attractive to advertisers. Ad revenue grew 37 percent from 2003 to 2005. Ad pages were up a further 13.6 percent in the first seven months of 2006. The September–October 2006 issue was touted as the biggest ever and featured more and more major advertisers. The back cover had an ad for Michelob Light and cosmetics companies have increasingly seen the magazine as a prime ad vehicle, according to its publisher.

AARP has done this by making the magazine very much a lifestyle magazine for those over 50—the nonprofit's prime target. Its glossy covers feature glamorous celebrities like Sally Field, Paul Newman, and Susan Sarandon. Mixed among the medical, real estate, and insurance information are articles about cruise vacations, exercise opportunities, and marital counseling. There are celebrity profiles such as one might find in *People* and—not surprisingly—tips on living longer.

AARP has found that its audience comprises at least three major segments—those in their 50s, 60s, and 70s. Each of these groups gets a different cover with different articles featured. Eugene Levy is mentioned on the cover of September–October 2006 issue for the 50s segment while Sir Richard Branson is highlighted on the other two issues. What AARP and its advertisers have learned is that Boomers and other "oldsters" are working longer and have more income and spending power. Families are smaller and so discretionary resources are growing. And, after 50 or 60, they no longer have the kid-rearing expenses of college. So seniors can take trips, buy a fancier car, and make other moves that make brand marketers salivate.

No longer is the image of seniors one of retired old folks reading drug ads and tips for shuffleboard. They more often want advice on the best golf courses, the best home gymnasiums and elegant—but not-so-pricey—wine!

Source: Richard Siklos, "At Some Publishers, Nonbusiness is Going Strong," *New York Times*, August 20, 2006, p. BU3.

The role that communications play will vary depending on the nonprofit organization's strategic and tactical needs. Tactical communications are those involved in specific behavioral influence campaigns, and they will be our principal concern in this chapter. Strategic communications are those focused on longer term concerns. Two principal strategic interests are the positioning of the organization and its various brands and advocacy around particular social issues. The latter has a tactical implication in that campaigns really cannot get traction unless the social behavior at issue has achieved enough prominence in the agendas of the media, the public, and the world of politics.[1] Strategic communications issues involving public relations and advocacy will take up the next chapter.

In carrying out either role, the nonprofit marketer has a large number of tools available for carrying a message to a target audience. There are seven main tools, and each differs in the coding and encoding problems (discussed in the previous chapter) that it presents to managers.[2]

- *Paid advertising: Any paid form of nonpersonal presentation and promotion of an offer by an identified sponsor through a formal communication medium.* Paid advertising permits total control over encoded message content and over the nature of the medium, plus substantial control of the scheduling of the message (and therefore its specific environment). However, paid advertising permits no control over message decoding by the audience and little (or, at best, lagged) feedback on the received message.
- *Joint advertising: Any form of advertising where a partner pays for the message placement, often as part of the partner's own advertisement.* Many Internet banner ads for nonprofits are on the web sites of other organizations, often corporations that consider the ads as either good strategy for themselves or as part of their public service. Depending on the partnership agreement, the nonprofit may have great or limited control over the message content. The audience is obviously whomever the partner normally reaches.
- *Direct mail or Internet promotions: Short-term incentives to encourage the performance of a behavior such as the purchase of a product or service.* Marketer control is substantial, although the decoding of specific promotions by the receiver is not controllable.

- *Personal persuasion: Oral presentation of information about an offering in a conversation with one or more prospective target audience members for the purpose of securing a desired transaction.* In personal persuasion, the organization has less control over encoding, that is, what the individual actually says. The individual, however, has excellent opportunities to secure feedback on how the message is being received. The personal persuasion may be by someone paid by the nonprofit marketer or a nonprofit volunteer. On the other hand, it may be by people who are allies, such as physicians, teachers, or employers who are not formally beholden to the marketer and may or may not follow the desired marketing strategy.
- *Unpaid (public service) advertising: Any form of advertising in which space or time for the placement of the advertisement is free.* Marketer control is similar to that with paid advertising except that there is very little control over the scheduling of the message and therefore the audiences reached. Many public service radio or television advertisements appear after midnight or on Sunday mornings when the audience is small and the media have unsold spots. This is a reason that many campaigns like those of the American Legacy Foundation have switched to paid advertisements.
- *Publicity: Nonpersonal stimulation of behavior by securing the reporting of significant news about the offer in a published medium or on radio, television, the Web, or in movies that is not paid for by the sponsor.* Here, the marketer's control over message encoding and the medium varies depending on whether journalists or scriptwriters will use and revise the message. Some feedback is possible from journalists or from selected target audiences.
- *Blogging.* These are informal Internet messages written sometimes by the nonprofit organization and its leaders and staff (controllable) and more often by individual bloggers with their own views and opinions. A subsidiary or parallel category is online videos that may be totally visual but can also contain opinions and commentary.

CAMPAIGN COMMUNICATIONS

It is important at the outset to again urge the nonprofit manager to be judicious in the use of personal persuasion tools, particularly advertising. One of the characteristics of the organization-centered nonprofit organizations described in Chapter 2 is that they rely excessively on advertising and promotion to achieve their campaign objectives. As we noted, this is partly because they have a distorted view of what it takes to influence people's behavior, but it is also partly due to what might be called "client pressure." A great many nonprofit CEOs and general managers equate marketing with advertising. When they want better marketing, they *think* they want more advertising.

Therefore, when considering advertising and promotion, nonprofit marketing specialists must be vigilant to make sure of the following:

1. Advertising and promotion are not relied upon as the only way—or even the primary way—to achieve behavioral objectives. Almost always, advertising can only get target audiences aware and interested in a new behavior. It is much less effective

at achieving final action. That is, it is useful in the first two of the stages of change but not the last two.

2. The objectives for advertising and promotion are within the nonprofit's reach. A great many naïve general managers think that a good dose of advertising is all that is needed to solve performance problems for the organization. They also expect advertising to make dramatic changes when only modest goals are more realistic.

3. There is a careful consideration of the ethical implications of advertising. Because advertising must simply convey messages and because they often use symbols to imply absent traits, there is a significant potential to deceive. As we discussed earlier in this book, those with the public trust that nonprofits and government agencies have should be especially diligent that they do not abuse this trust. Those who want to achieve "good" must *do* good.

ADVERTISING

Advertising is everywhere—often to the consternation of people inundated with it. It is found in such traditional media as magazines and newspapers, radio and television programming, outdoor media, circulars, pop-up and web site ads, and direct mail. Today, advertisers are discovering new media such as the cell phone and video games. Google and Yahoo! are major media. Product placement in movies and TV programs has also dramatically escalated. Blogs have been used by marketers to tout products and services. E-mails for products and services show up in our mail—sometimes from disreputable sellers. Some marketers produce mini-movies on the Internet that feature their products in order to "sell" the items to the general public. Auto manufacturers send DVDs to the homes of potential buyers.

Total media advertising spending in the United States aimed at both consumers and business was estimated to be $271 billion in 2005.[3] Breakdowns for the major categories (in millions of dollars) was as follows:

Direct mail	$ 55,218	20.4%
Newspapers	$ 47,335	17.5%
Broadcast TV	$ 44,293	16.3%
Cable TV	$ 23,654	8.7%
Radio	$ 19,640	7.2%
Yellow Pages	$ 14,229	5.2%
Consumer magazines	$ 12,847	4.7%
Internet	$ 7,764	2.9%
Billboards, posters	$ 6,232	2.3%
Business publications	$ 4,170	1.5%
All others	$ 35,692	13.2%
TOTAL	$271,074	

Paid advertising is coming into increasing use by public agencies and private nonprofit organizations. Political advertising has skyrocketed in recent elections. Total campaign advertising in the 2006 mid-term elections in the U.S. was estimated to be $1.6 billion.[4] This is only slightly down from the $1.9 billion spent two years earlier in a higher profile

Presidential election year. Various government units are now frequent advertisers. Municipalities, states, and counties spend considerable sums to attract new residents, tourists, and industrial developers. Park and recreation departments advertise outdoor recreational facilities. Police departments issue messages to the general public on safety issues. The federal government has used paid advertising to sell products (postage stamps), services (veterans' hospitals and express mail), and behaviors (energy conservation).[5]

A great many nonprofit organizations now pay for their advertising rather than relying on unpaid public service announcements (PSAs). Colleges, museums, symphonies, hospitals, and selected religious organizations all have strong communication programs and develop annual reports, direct mailings, classified ads, broadcast messages, and other forms of advertising. Various professionals whose ethical codes formerly banned advertising (social workers, dermatologists, cosmetic dentists, psychologists, and so on) have been free to advertise ever since the Federal Trade Commission ruled that the American Medical Association could not prevent physician members from advertising.

Professional and trade associations have substantially increased their use of paid advertising. The American Bankers Association, the American Dental Association, and the National Association of Realtors spend several million dollars annually on television and print advertising and on their web sites. Public service advertising programs have recently been undertaken by professional associations representing lawyers, accountants, engineers, and nurses. Issue advertising is also burgeoning—especially in election years.

SETTING ADVERTISING OBJECTIVES

In developing an advertising program, marketing management must make five major decisions (see Figure 13-1). We considered message issues in the preceding chapter and therefore will discuss the remaining four decisions in this and the following sections. We begin with advertising objectives. These objectives must flow from prior decisions about the target market, the basic value proposition, and the marketing mix.

FIGURE 13-1 Major Decisions in Advertising Management

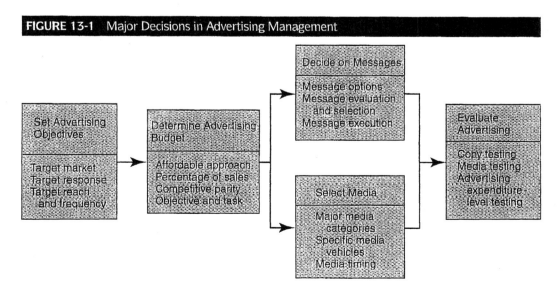

Target Market Selection

A marketing communicator must start with a clear target audience (or, in well-segmented programs, audiences plural) in mind. The audience may be potential future targets, current and potential participants (clients, donors, volunteers, corporate partners, and potential partners), and those who might influence them. The target audience has a crucial influence on the communicator's decisions on *what* to say, *how* to say it, *when* to say it, *where* to say it, and *who* should say it.

Consider this in terms of a (fictitious) small private college in Iowa called Bradford. Suppose it is seeking applicants from Nebraska, and it estimates that there are 22,000 graduating high school seniors in Nebraska who might be interested in Bradford College. The college must decide whether to aim its communications primarily at high school counselors in Nebraska high schools or at the high school students themselves. Beyond this, it may want to develop communications to reach parents and other people who are influential in the college decision process. Each target market would warrant a different advertising campaign.

Target Response

Once the target audience is identified, the marketing communicator must define the target response that is sought. The ultimate response, of course, is behavior—enrolling at Bradford. In highly involving and infrequent decisions, however, behavior is the end result of the target audience going through all of the stages of change. The marketing communicator needs to know the current stage of the decision process of the target audience and which stage it should be moved to next. Two important values of the stages of change model are that it suggests obvious segmentation possibilities and it can be used to track progress. That is, at any point in the academic year, some students will still be in Precontemplation, the majority in Contemplation, and a few ready to take action. Presumably, different messages must be tailored to groups at different stages. And, depending on research, different segments—urban/rural, male/female—undoubtedly merit different approaches.

It is also a framework that can encompass more extensive lists of specific communication objectives for advertising. While there are a great many objectives that could be considered, it is likely that they will be some version of informing (Precontemplation stage), persuading (Contemplation stage), and spurring action (Preparation/Action stage).[6] Particularly in the Precontemplation stage, Bradford will want to make sure it becomes known and part of the *consideration set*. In the Contemplation stage, research should have identified the various BCOS factors each segment considers and emphasize how Bradford scores well on the most important ones. For those in the Preparation/Action stage, Bradford's marketers will want to identify those choosing it and make sure they follow through. The latter objective can relatively efficiently be addressed through direct mail.

Target Reach and Frequency

The third objective a nonprofit manager must set is the optimal *target reach and frequency* of the advertising. Funds for advertising are rarely so abundant that everyone in the target audience can be reached, and reached with great frequency. Marketing management must decide what percentage of the audience to reach (e.g., which segments are most promising) with what exposure frequency per period. Bradford College, for example, might decide to use local newspapers and buy 20,000 advertising exposures aimed at Contemplators. This leaves a wide choice available concerning target reach and frequency. Bradford could place an advertisement in one paper in a large city and reach 20,000 different students one time, or it could place two different ads a week apart in five smaller papers and reach 10,000 students twice, and so on. A key issue is how many exposures are needed to create the desired response, given the market segment's state of readiness. One exposure could be enough to convert students from ranking Bradford low to at least making it part of the consideration set. This level of exposure would not be enough to convert students from awareness to preference.

ADVERTISING BUDGET DETERMINATION

We assume that Bradford College will be using an *objective-and-task* approach to setting advertising budgets. Suppose that Bradford wants to place two ads in five papers (its task) to reach 10,000 students twice (its objective). The gross number of exposures would be 20,000. Supposing the average ad in each paper costs $2,000 and design costs for the two ads are $5,000, Bradford will need a rough advertising budget of $25,000.

In addition to estimating the total size of the required advertising budget, a determination must be made about how the budget should be allocated over different market segments, geographical areas, and time periods. In practice, advertising budgets are allocated to segments according to their respective populations or past response levels or in accordance with some other indicator of market potential. It is common to spend twice as much advertising money in segment B as in segment A if segment B has twice the level of response potential. In principle, the budget should be allocated to different segments according to their expected marginal response to advertising. A budget is well allocated when it is not possible to shift dollars from one segment to another and increase total market response.

PAID MEDIA SELECTION

Once the advertising budget is set for a given market segment, region, and time period, the next step is to allocate this budget across paid media categories and vehicles. Presumably some thought will already have been given to this problem, since the selection of a target segment inevitably leads to research questions about the media to which the segment is most frequently exposed. Also, the media considered will affect the size of the overall budget; a television campaign is obviously much more costly than a radio campaign. Finally, the choice of media will affect the kind of messages one can use.

There are three basic steps in the media selection process: choosing among major media categories, choosing among specific media vehicles, and timing. An important consideration here is finding the *aperture* (opening) when the target audience is likely to be most receptive to a campaign's message. If the target audience is in the Precontemplation stage, the marketer wants an opening where the target audience would not ignore the message or be defensive or dismissive of it. For targets that are at the Contemplation stage, the marketer would want to know where the target audience expects to see useful information or where he or she goes to look for it. A viewer of the network evening news is more likely to see a lot of ads for prescription drugs and investment services. This is in part because the audience is proven to be upscale but is also likely to be in a thoughtful, concerned mood—and therefore receptive to messages about their health and finances. Bradford may conclude that expenditures on Internet promotions—banner ads, for example, with links to its own web site—would well serve many markets.

Choosing Among Major Media Categories

The first step calls for allocating the advertising budget to the major *media categories*. These categories must be examined for their capacity to deliver reach, frequency, and impact. In order of their advertising volume, they are newspapers, television, radio, magazines, cinema, and outdoor advertising, although Internet expenditures are catching up.

Marketers choose among media categories by considering the following variables:

1. *Target audience media habits.* For example, radio, television, and the Internet are the most effective media for reaching teenagers.
2. *Product, service, or behavior to be marketed.* Media categories have different potentialities for demonstration, visualization, explanation, believability, and color. Television, for example, is the most effective medium for demonstrating how a product or service works or for creating an emotional effect, while magazines are ideal for accurately reproducing the appearance of a social scene or the victim of some crime. The Internet serves as a vehicle for those audiences wanting more control over what they see and a chance to interact with the marketer.
3. *Message.* A message announcing an emergency blood drive tomorrow requires radio, the Internet, newspapers, or posters. A message containing a great deal of technical data might require specialized magazines, direct mailings, or a complex web site. Messages that would benefit from target audiences adding their own images and fantasies might be most effective on the radio.
4. *Cost.* Television is very expensive, and newspaper advertising, the Internet, and billboards are relatively inexpensive. What counts, of course, is the cost per thousand exposures rather than the total cost. In developing countries, posters are often highly cost-effective.

On the basis of these characteristics, the marketer has to decide how to allocate the given budget to the major media categories. The U.S. Army Recruiting Command, for example, might decide to allocate $140 million to evening television spots, $40 million to male-oriented magazines, and $20 million to daily newspapers. The advantages of various means of communication including both paid and unpaid media and various personal transmission vehicles are indicated in Exhibit 13-1.

In the United States, many nonprofit organizations would love to afford television advertising—especially network television. However, in developing countries, the preferred medium is often radio, because it is ubiquitous and does not require literacy. Many social marketers there combine advertising on radio with "social" soap operas that are heard by millions.[7] Airtime for the latter is typically provided free, although the scripts must be paid for. Soap opera subjects have included family planning, immunization, and AIDS prevention. Some social marketing programs have even given away radios run by hand-cranked batteries so that poor people in remote areas can have access to social messages as well as the news.

A popular medium long being used by nonprofits, particularly for fundraising and the promotion of events, is direct mail. Robert Coen of McCann-Erickson estimates that direct mail expenditures in 2006 would total $56 billion.[8] Bill Novelli, now CEO of

EXHIBIT 13-1

PROS AND CONS OF ALTERNATIVE COMMUNICATIONS VEHICLES

A. Media	Strengths	Weaknesses
Print	• large reach; can be free or low cost • information can be kept and shared • works well with complex messages	• literacy implications • possibly low emotional appeal • cost barrier
Newsletters	• reaches opinion leaders; low cost • message preservation high; responsive	• labor intensive; requires dedicated people • preaching to the converted • literacy may be an issue
Radio	• large reach; specific • can be low cost/free (e.g., community-based radio) • interactive (e.g., phone-in shows) • timely and repetitive • possible use of celebrities • possible access to creative team • literacy not an issue	• high cost; no guarantees PSAs will be played • staff discomfort with live interviews • no visuals • no control over placement (if free) • can only reach a specific group (station dependent) • limited to reception area of radio
Television	• extensive reach; can be free (cable) • different target groups reached • impact of visuals	• very expensive or limited to cable stations • high level of complexity possible • not everywhere like radios (e.g., in cars, etc.)
Outdoor	• wide reach • can be inexpensive (e.g., posted flyers) • at times, captive audience (e.g., transit) • high message repetition and duration • geographically focused • visuals can have great impact	• can be expensive (e.g., billboards) • low specificity (e.g., may not reach specific audiences) • short, simple messages only

(continued)

EXHIBIT 13-1 (cont.)

A. Media	Strengths	Weaknesses
Telephone	• confidential; personal/private • interactive; can follow up • can direct efforts to specific groups • inexpensive if a pre-taped response	• cost can be high (expensive and labor intensive if staffed) • intrusive • onus on individuals to call (if a hotline)
Mail	• reaches specific area (e.g., postal code) • information can be kept; can follow up • appeals to visual learner • if directed, "named" individuals will read	• cost can be high • can get lost (e.g., junk mail) • misses low literacy groups • can create negative associations
Point of purchase	• timely; immediate reinforcement • can be interactive (e.g., demonstrations) • info where it is needed; effective targeting • good opportunity to partner	• relatively small reach • loses effectiveness over time/ need to change • may discriminate low income • difficult to partner if controversial • depends on others to get message out
Curricula	• requires expert writers • reaches select and captive audience • interactive • higher likelihood of being used	• small reach • often inconsistent implementation (time spent, teacher confidence/importance of issue, etc.) • possible low receptivity
Computer-based communication	• large reach but select audience • interactive • more youth friendly • can control info received (e.g., CD-ROM)	• select audiences; literacy barrier • high cost of equipment • requires skills and training • if on CD-ROM cannot easily update

B. Interpersonal Presentations	Strengths	Weaknesses
Interpersonal presentations	• interactive • specific and captive audience • information can be timely • can provide handouts to retention • can control content • good presenter can provide high motivation	• relatively small reach; attracts the "converted" • costly in terms of time and resources • poor retention • personal bias/beliefs of presenter • inconvenient for people who work, parents, etc.

C. Events	Strengths	Weaknesses
Informal networks	• interactive; specific • comfort of cultural similarities, small group (familiar, safe) • may encourage work at societal levels, etc., or in other areas of life • provides access to other networks	• information can be biased or unreliable • focus on experience may be narrow • requires a certain personality • can be cliquish, exclusive • limited, homogeneous group
Clinical settings	• large reach; captive audience • credible source for many • up-to-date, specific, and in-depth info • presenting for a specific reason	• small reach; audience may be inhibited • client preoccupied, e.g., with pain/fear • difficult to sell idea/message to health professionals • traditional medical model/ treatment oriented
Community-wide	• social support provided • large reach • interactive and fun • high visibility; high level of interest • opportunity for media coverage	• difficult to follow up and evaluate • can't tailor a specific group/public • labor and resource intensive • short lifespan
Specific group	• captive audience; direct/specific • provides immediate feedback • evaluation easier; cost benefit relationship	• narrow focus; reaches only a few • higher cost to reach fewer individuals • labor intensive (time); low visibility • no spillover to other communities • special needs requirements

Source: The Health Communication Unit @ Centre for Health Promotion, Department of Public Health Sciences, University of Toronto. Permission is granted for educational publications. The full workbook, *Overview of Health Communication Campaigns*, is available free of charge at www.thcu.ca.

AARP, has suggested that direct mail has seven important advantages for nonprofit marketers (and these advantages also apply to the Web):[9]

1. It tends to be very focused: It can achieve maximum impact on a specific target market.
2. It can be private and confidential, a major advantage for charities and programs dealing with venereal disease, child abuse, and AIDS.
3. Purchase of direct-mail services is not forbidden to government agencies, whereas purchase of broadcast, newspaper, magazine, outdoor, and other media sometimes is forbidden.

4. Cost per contact and cost per response can often be very low, which is an important appeal to impoverished nonprofits.
5. Results are quite often clearly measurable, and this can help make nonprofit marketing programs more accountable. The American Heart Association may not know its effect on cholesterol levels, but it can calculate how many responded to a specific mail promotion of a low-cholesterol cookbook and what cost it incurred per inquiry.
6. Small-scale tests of proposed strategies are very feasible with direct mail. In fact, direct mail is an ideal field-test vehicle. A number of marketing factors can be varied over several mailings and the results compared to baseline measures. In tests of other media, it is often difficult to link a specific surge in sales to, say, a flight of radio advertisements. By contrast, if more cookbook requests come in from those who receive a mailing with a message about cholesterol involving a medium level of fear than from those who get a high-fear or low-fear treatment, it is hard not to conclude that a medium-fear message works best.
7. The effectiveness of direct mail can be assessed directly in terms of *behavior* (e.g., orders, requests, and inquiries), whereas other media assessments usually require attitude and awareness indicators that are fraught with measurement problems.

In developed countries, a vehicle more and more often considered in the promotional mix is the Internet. Many nonprofits find it a powerful tool for reaching upscale markets and young people. It is also increasingly penetrating the developing world with the help of generous grants and donations from private sector organizations like Microsoft and Google.

The Internet has great potential for interactive "conversations" with those one wishes to influence. The accelerating popularity of personalized web sites such as MyPlace and YouTube indicate the huge potential here. Wikipedia describes MySpace as "a social networking web site which offers an interactive, user-submitted network of friends, personal profiles, blogs, groups, photos, music, and videos. MySpace also features an internal search engine and an internal e-mail system."[10] YouTube allows members to share videos they create with others. Both these innovations—which have attracted the strong interest of Google (which bought YouTube) and Yahoo!—hold great possibilities for custom-tailored behavioral interventions and communications.

Web advertising is also considered potentially very valuable. Its major advantage is that it makes messages available to audiences who *intentionally* come to a site, as opposed to messages that people are exposed to unintentionally as when browsing a magazine or watching television. Indeed, Google and other search engines only charge advertisers when someone actually clicks on the advertiser's site. Web ads have four additional advantages important to nonprofit marketers:

1. It is possible to track performance (web site hits) minute by minute (for example, if an advertisement is changed or a new offer is made available).
2. Messages can be changed more or less whenever the marketer wants. Underperforming ads can be quickly replaced with better options.
3. Messages can potentially be tailored to "segments of one" if the marketer is able to obtain any incoming clues about the person visiting the web site. This, of course, is a prime marketing approach used by innovative commercial marketers like Amazon.com and Netflix. The latter always offer suggestions to returning visitors

to their sites based on what their prior searches—or purchases—indicate in terms of interests.

4. Messages can be inexpensively rotated on a random schedule to keep a campaign fresh and reduce target market fatigue.

Creating powerful web sites is now possible with the availability of web sites that are specifically design to help nonprofit organizations such as TechSoup (www.techsoup.org) and N-Ten, the Nonprofit Technology Transfer Network (www.nten.org).

Another new medium of interest to nonprofit marketers is video games.[11] The so-called "serious games" movement got started in 2002 when the U.S. Army created a game that would give players a sense of what it was like to join up (www.americasarmy.com). Over 5 million players registered for the free download. The Health Media Lab, with funding from the National Institutes for Health, created a game called *Hungry Red Planet* (www.hungryredplanet.com) that teaches kids about healthy eating by having them plan menus for visiting Martians. Other games that have been developed around social issues are:

- *Food Force* (www.food-force.com), from the United Nation's World Food Program, on providing food to poor people isolated in a crisis.
- Tubula Digita has a 3-D game for teaching algebra to kids (www.tabuladigita.com).
- ImpactGames is developing a game for release in 2007 called Peacemaker (www.impactgames.com) that simulates challenges to peace between Israelis and Palestinians.
- Archimage has a game called Nanoswarm (www.archimageonline.com) on preventing obesity and Type 2 diabetes.

Selecting Specific Media Vehicles

The next step is to choose the specific vehicles within each media category that would produce the desired response in the most cost-effective way. Consider the category of male-oriented magazines, which includes *Playboy, GQ, Esquire, Motorcycle*, and so on. A media planner focused on the United States can reference several volumes put out by *Standard Rate and Data* that provide circulation and cost data for different ad sizes, color options, ad positions, and quantities of insertions. The media planner can then use *Simmons Choices 3,* a data set on media and markets that provides rich data on the demographics and psychographics of readers, listeners, and viewers of major media vehicles.[12]

The media planner will next evaluate the different male-oriented magazines on qualitative characteristics such as credibility, prestige, availability of geographical or other submarket editions, reproduction quality, editorial climate, lead time, and psychological impact. The media planner makes a final judgment as to which specific vehicles will deliver the best reach, frequency, and impact for the money.

Of course, media choice in part depends on the nature of the message. For example, when the Partnership for a Drug-Free America creates an anti-drug message featuring Andy MacDonald, one of the world's best skateboarders, for a TV ad aimed at kids, it will seek placement in programming watched by what psychologists call "sensation seekers," a segment found to be particularly prone to experiment with—and use—drugs.

Deciding on Media Timing

The third step in media selection is *timing.* It breaks down into a macro problem and a micro problem. The macro problem is that of *cyclical* or *seasonal timing.* For most products and services, audience size and interest vary at different times of the year.

There is not much interest in Senator X until her reelection comes up or much interest in university affairs during the summer. Most marketers do not advertise when there is little interest, spending the bulk of their advertising budgets or scheduling public service announcements just as natural interest in the product or service class begins to increase and when it peaks. Counter-seasonal or counter-cyclical advertising is still rare in practice. The concept of *aperture* is relevant here. The marketer seeks to reach the target audience members at the moment in which they are most likely to be interested and receptive to the intended messages.

The other challenge is *short-run timing* of advertising. How should advertising be spaced during a short period of, say, one week? Consider three possible patterns. The first is called *burst advertising* and consists of concentrating all the exposures in a very short period of time, say, all in one day. Presumably, this will attract maximum attention and interest, and if recall is good, the effect will last for a while. The second pattern is *continuous advertising,* in which the exposures appear evenly throughout the period. This may be most effective when the audience buys or uses the product frequently and needs to be continuously reminded. The third pattern is *intermittent advertising,* in which intermittent small bursts of advertising appear with no advertising in between. This pattern is able to create a little more attention than continuous advertising, yet it has some of the reminder advantage of continuous advertising.

Timing decisions should take three factors into consideration. *Audience turnover* is the rate at which the target audience changes between two periods. The greater the turnover, the more continuous the advertising should be. *Behavior frequency* is the number of times the target audience takes the action one is trying to influence (e.g., smoking, not wearing seat belts). The more frequent the behavior, the more the advertising should be continuous. The *forgetting rate* is the rate at which a given message will be forgotten or a given behavior change extinguished. Again, the faster the forgetting, the more continuous the advertising should be.

ADVERTISING EVALUATION

The final step in the effective use of advertising is *advertising evaluation,* both before and after execution. The most important components are copy testing, media testing, and expenditure-level testing.

Copy testing can occur both before an ad is put into actual media (pretesting) and after it has been printed, broadcast, or put on the Web (posttesting). The purpose of *ad pretesting* is to make improvements in the advertising copy to the fullest extent prior to its release. There are several methods of ad pretesting:

1. *Comprehension testing.* A critical prerequisite for any advertisement is that it be comprehensible. This can be a major problem when dealing with less-educated or even illiterate audiences. When words are used in a print advertisement, a marketing staff member can apply one or more readability formulas to predict comprehension. These formulas measure the length of sentences and the number of polysyllabic words. One popular measure of comprehensibility called SMOG has been used by the Office of Cancer Communications of the National Cancer Institute to test public and patient education health materials.

2. *Formal questionnaires.* Here a panel of target audiences or advertising experts is given a set of alternative ads and fills out rating questionnaires—possibly through the mail or over the Web. Sometimes a single question is raised, such as "Which of these ads do you think would influence you most?" Or a more elaborate form consisting of several rating scales may be used. Here, the person evaluates the ad's attention strength, read-through strength (i.e., did audiences pay attention all the way through), cognitive strength, affective strength, and behavioral strength, assigning a number of points (up to a maximum) in each case. The underlying theory is that an effective ad must score high on all these properties if it is ultimately to stimulate action. Too often ads are evaluated only for their attention-getting or comprehension-creating abilities. Unfortunately it is also true that direct rating methods are judgmental and less reliable than harder evidence of an ad's actual impact on target audience members. Direct rating scales help primarily to screen out poor ads rather than to identify great ads.

3. *Portfolio recall tests.* Here respondents are exposed to a portfolio of ads—print, web-based, video, or audio. After being exposed to them, the respondents are asked to recall the ads they saw—unaided or aided by the interviewer—and to describe as much as they can about each ad. The results are taken to indicate an ad's ability to stand out and its intended message's ability to be understood.

4. *Physiological tests.* Some researchers assess the potential effect of an ad by measuring physiological reactions—heartbeat, blood pressure, pupil dilation, perspiration—using such equipment as galvanometers, tachistoscopes, and pupil measuring equipment. These physiological tests at best measure the attention-getting and arousing power of an ad rather than any particular cognition or emotion that the ad might produce.

5. *Focus-group interviews.* Since advertisements are often viewed in a group setting, pretests with groups can often indicate both how a message is perceived and how it might be passed along. As noted in Chapter 5, the focus-group technique also has the advantages that (a) synergism within a group can generate more reactions than a one-on-one session, (b) it is more efficient in that it gathers data from 6 to 12 people at once, and (c) it can yield data relatively quickly, especially if the focus group is conducted over the web or by telephone.[13]

There are three popular *ad posttesting methods,* whose purpose it is to assess if the desired impact is achieved after transmission or what the possible ad weaknesses are.

1. *Recall tests.* These involve finding persons who are regular users of the media vehicle and asking them to recall advertisers and products contained in the issue or program or on a web site under study. They are asked to recall or play back everything they can remember. The administrator may or may not aid them in their recall. Recall scores are prepared on the basis of their responses and used to indicate the ad's power to be noted and remembered.

2. *Recognition tests.* Recognition tests call for sampling the audience of a given vehicle, say a magazine, and asking them to point out what they recognize having seen or read before. In one such magazine-rating technique, Starch Readership Services (www.roper.com/products/starch) computes three different readership scores:

   - *Noted.* The percentage of readers of the magazine who say they had previously seen the advertisement in the particular magazine.

- *Seen/associated.* The percentage of readers who say they have seen or read any part of the ad that clearly indicates the names of the product (or service) of the advertiser.
- *Read most.* The percentage of readers who not only looked at the advertisement, but who say that they read more than half of the total written material in the ad.

3. *Direct response.* The preceding techniques measure *cognitive outcomes* of advertising. But favorable cognitive outcomes may not translate into *behavioral outcomes*. Behavioral responses can be solicited by a message, however, and the results directly measured. The effectiveness of alternative messages or media in influencing behavior can be tracked as follows:

- Placing mailback coupons in the advertisement with a code number or P.O. box that varies by message and medium.
- Asking target audience members to mention, send, or bring in an advertisement in order to receive special treatment (e.g., a price discount or free parking).
- Setting up an 800 number and asking individuals to call for further information (on which occasion the marketer can ask where they saw or heard the ad, what they remember, and so on).
- Staggering the placement of ads so that this week's behavior can be attributed to ad A while next week's can be attributed to ad B. This is also an effective method for assessing alternative expenditure levels.
- On the web site, tracking frequency of visits before and after ads are introduced and, where relevant, tracking how visitors move around the site. Web tracking can also be used to learn the source of visitors (i.e., from what other web sites—for example, ones with your banner ad—did they come?).

One of the most elaborate and careful efforts to research the effectiveness of nonprofit advertising was the 1990 study of the American Cancer Society's colon cancer prevention campaign. This is described in Exhibit 13-2.

EXHIBIT 13-2

ASSESSING THE IMPACT OF A PUBLIC SERVICE ADVERTISING CAMPAIGN

One of the most difficult challenges in nonprofit marketing is assessing the effectiveness of specific marketing activities. Typically, too many things are going on in a competitive, complicated real world environment to be able to "see" what a specific effort has done. This is especially problematic with advertising, because the intended effects are often not directly observable, but are cognitive and personal. Without measures of effectiveness, however, nonprofit marketers do not know how to spend their limited resources.

To remedy many of these problems, a unique study was carried out by the Advertising Research Foundation and the Advertising Council's Advertising Research Committee in 1989 and 1990 to (1) measure the effects of public service advertising (PSA) on the awareness, beliefs, and actions of a target audience; (2) measure the effects of both average and above-average media schedules over time; and (3) create a research model to aid in evaluating future public service advertising campaigns.

The focus was on a PSA campaign developed for the American Cancer Society's Colon Cancer Early Detection campaign entitled "Don't find out too late in life," developed and placed by Calet, Hirsch & Spector, Inc.

The campaign was run in four U.S. test markets that have been used for private sector marketing research by Information Resources, Inc. (IRI). The campaign targeted adults 40 to 69, particularly men. IRI's Behavior Scan research technology split the households in each of the four markets into two cells and directed average levels of advertising to one cell and above-average levels to the other cell. IRI technology allowed monitoring of actual exposure to the ads (i.e., finding out which sets were on) in 40 percent of the households. The campaign consisted of the same 30-second PSA running one year from July 31, 1989, to July 23, 1990, in a media schedule skewed toward dayparts reaching adults 40 to 69, especially men.

The *average* level was the equivalent of $21.3 million in media time, 53 Gross Rating Points, and the *above average* level was the equivalent of $53.3 million in media time, 143 Gross Rating Points. Research on the campaign's impact was conducted on samples of households contacted in each market on three occasions: before the campaign, after 6 months, and after 12 months.

The major findings of the research were the following:

- Above average spending is not cost-effective. There was a relatively limited increase in effect from spending 2.6 times more advertising effort.

- PSAs can have a significant and continuing impact on awareness. Proven/related levels of awareness of the need to prevent colon cancer increased steadily over the campaign, going from 11 percent before the campaign to 29 percent at 6 months and 40 percent at 12 months.

- Targeting media placements can significantly increase effectiveness. Awareness increased faster for men than for women, reflecting the more careful placement of ads in sports, prime-time, and early news programming.

- PSAs can reinforce existing beliefs. Smaller increases were found in beliefs about the curability of colon cancer and the desirability of annual checkups after 40. Both beliefs were already relatively high before the campaign.

- *Actual* exposure should be monitored. Households found to be exposed to 31 or more ads over the year expressed the highest personal concern about colon cancer.

- Advertising wearout can be observed with respect to intentions to act. Peak intention levels occurred with 16 to 30 exposures. After this point, ads appeared to have diminishing returns, although this could be attributable to the fact that there was only one execution of the advertisement.

- Patience and consistency are necessary. It took one year for there to be significant effects on reported behavior; 7 percent of the sample recalled talking about colon cancer with their doctors during their last visits at both the baseline and 6-month points. However, this figure rose to 10 percent after 12 months. The figure for men rose to 15 percent after 12 months, more than double the baseline figure. This could translate into 2.7 million more men over 40 consulting their doctors about colon cancer as a result of this campaign.

Source: Advertising Council, *A Strategic Research Approach to Measuring Advertising Effectiveness,* n.d. Reproduced with permission.

PERSONAL MARKETING

It has been our experience that the marketing tool about which nonprofit marketers are most ambivalent is exerting personal influence. This reticent posture seems to follow from two attitudes. First, as noted in Chapter 2, nonprofit managers typically believe that whatever they are recommending is inherently desirable and needs simply to be brought to the attention of the target audience to be happily embraced by a grateful public. Second, they often believe that planned personal influence strategies are synonymous with manipulation and reflect all the "hard selling" that is evil about private sector marketing. They are comfortable using personal marketing techniques for fundraising and for promoting events or products in a gift shop, web site, or catalog—as long as it is tasteful! However, when it is proposed that the nonprofit's workers should personally persuade people to attend a college or join a political party, library, or church, resistance to using a planned, vigorous approach is not uncommon.

The one dramatic exception is political candidate marketing. Personal persuasion here is often quite aggressive and often reflects the seamier side of marketing. A major problem is that campaigns often follow a *selling* mindset. The best campaigns attempt to learn what might concern—and persuade—potential voters through careful polling. But more often—especially when campaigns cannot afford polling or the seat is considered "safe"—personal influence strategies tend to tell the audience what the campaign thinks it ought to hear. Most egregious are efforts to vilify the competition, a ploy that, unfortunately, has been found to be particularly effective.[14]

On the positive side, there is one area where the right kind of target audience orientation can be very valuable to nonprofit managers. The best-run for-profit service organizations long ago recognized that *every time* a member of the organization interacts with a member of a key public, there is an opportunity to further or weaken progress toward the organization's marketing goals. The right kind of persuasive communications can be very helpful. How often have our favorable feelings about a hospital or museum been tarnished by the perfunctory or surly attitude of a guard or the cashier? What nonprofit marketers have to recognize is that almost everyone in their organizations is at one point or another in the role of a *boundary person*. Their personal communication style will affect the organization's success. Managers can increase their effectiveness if personable persuasion skills are consciously imparted to frontline personnel.

We shall use the term *personal marketing* to refer to *attempts by an organization staff member or volunteer to use personal influence to affect target audience behavior*. Personal marketing can be a very effective tool for certain activities such as lobbying, fundraising, and volunteer recruitment. It can play a role at key points in the stages of change. The strongest role can be at the Contemplation stage where personal marketing skills can argue for the right behavior, pointing out the benefits and minimizing the costs. Contact people can help target audiences move through the Preparation/Action stage by accompanying them while they take the desired action and, if they are around at the Maintenance stage, can play an important role in giving the target audience member a verbal and emotional "pat on the back."

This is because personal marketing has three distinctive qualities in comparison to advertising:

1. *Adjustable interaction.* Personal marketing involves a living, immediate, and interactive relationship between two or more persons. Each party is able to observe the others' needs and characteristics at close hand and make immediate adjustments.
2. *Real-time evaluation.* Persuaders can receive important clues as to how the target audience is responding and can directly solicit feedback so as to change tactics as necessary.
3. *Follow-up can be built in.* Persuaders can determine on the spot when and how follow-up influence opportunities are needed and/or appropriate.

These distinctive qualities come at a cost. Personal marketing is the organization's most expensive target audience contact tool. To be most effective, there must be careful training and constant reinforcement of people who have potential contacts with target audience members, including many who do not think of themselves as key links to the target public.

Establishing Personal Influence Objectives

Personal communication is part of the marketing mix, and as such is capable of achieving certain marketing objectives better than other tools in the marketing mix. Personal contacts can perform as many as five tasks for their organizations:

1. *Prospecting.* Personal representatives can find and cultivate new target audiences.
2. *Communicating.* Personal representatives can communicate useful information about the organization.
3. *Persuading.* Personal representatives can be effective in the art of "salesmanship"— approaching, presenting, answering objections, and inducing action.
4. *Servicing.* Personal representatives can provide various services to target audiences— counseling on their problems, rendering technical assistance, and reducing service times.
5. *Information gathering.* Personal representatives can supply the organization with useful market research and intelligence.

The organization has to decide the relative importance of these different tasks and coach their personal representatives accordingly. College recruiters, for example, spend most of their time prospecting, communicating, and persuading. Lobbyists, in contrast, tend to emphasize communicating, servicing, and information gathering. Each organization normally gets its representatives to set specific goals for each of its activities so that its performance against these goals can be measured.

Selecting Personal Communicators

Most nonprofits have at least some individuals whose primary responsibility is to influence target audiences on a person-to-person basis. These include fundraisers, lobbyists, telemarketers, and gift shop sales clerks. Selecting the individuals to serve in these roles would not be such a problem if one knew the characteristics of an ideal personal communicator. If ideal personal communicators were outgoing, aggressive, and energetic, it would not be too difficult to check for these characteristics in applicants. But a review of the most successful personal communicators in any organization is likely to reveal a good number who are introverted, mild-mannered, and far from energetic. The successful group will also include men and women who are tall and short, articulate and inarticulate, well groomed and slovenly.

Nevertheless, the search for the magic combination of traits that spells surefire persuasion ability continues unabated. The number of lists that have been drawn up is countless. Most of them recite the same qualities. McMurry wrote:

> It is my conviction that the possessor of an *effective* sales personality is *a habitual "wooer," an individual who has a compulsive need to win and hold the affection of others.* . . . His wooing, however, is not based on a sincere desire for love because, in my opinion, he is convinced at heart that no one will ever love him. Therefore, his wooing is primarily exploitative . . . his relationships tend to be transient, superficial and evanescent.[15]

McMurry went on to list five additional traits of the super personal communicator: a high level of energy; abounding self-confidence; a chronic hunger for rewards; a well-established habit of industry; and a state of mind that regards each objection, resistance, or obstacle as a challenge.[16]

Mayer and Greenberg offered one of the shortest lists of traits exhibited by effective personal communicators.[17] Their seven years of fieldwork led them to conclude that the effective personal communicator has at least two basic qualities: (1) *empathy,* the ability to feel as the target audience does, and (2) *ego drive,* a strong personal need to make the sale. Using these two traits, they were able to make fairly good predictions of the subsequent performance of applicants for sales positions in three different industries.

However, each persuasion job is characterized by a unique set of duties and challenges. One only has to think about college recruiting, corporate fundraising, and Congressional lobbying to realize the different educational, intellectual, and personality requirements that would be sought in the respective sales representatives. How can an organization determine the characteristics that its prospective personal communicators should "ideally" possess? The particular duties of the job suggest some of the characteristics to look for in applicants. Is the job mostly order taking, or must a lot of "influencing" be carried out? Is there a lot of paperwork? Does the job call for much travel? Will the personal communicator confront a high proportion of refusals? Is creativity necessary? Will the personal communicator be closely supervised or be expected to use a lot of initiative? In addition, the traits of the company's most successful sales representatives can suggest additional qualities to look for. Some organizations compare the standing of their best versus their poorest sales representatives to see which characteristics differentiate the two groups.

One of the traits that has proved to be particularly valuable in social marketing settings is *empathy* with the target audience. In social marketing, one is often dealing with extremely delicate subjects. Finding personal communicators, or *change agents* as they are sometimes called, from among the population to be influenced is usually very effective. They are most likely to know the audience's concerns, the appropriate language and metaphors for discussing problems and possible solutions, and which motivations can be played upon to bring about needed behavior change. In Ethiopia, for example, as outlined in Exhibit 13-3, the Ministry of Health found that former prostitutes were better at asking difficult intimate questions and communicating information about AIDS to other prostitutes than were traditional social workers.

EXHIBIT 13-3

USING EMPATHETIC (IF UNORTHODOX) SALESPEOPLE IN ETHIOPIA

In a tin-roofed, shanty-like classroom where primary school students usually struggle to learn math, a smartly dressed prostitute posed her problem to a nurse conducting a seminar on AIDS.

"I don't have a baby and I want one," she said, "But if I use a condom, I won't become pregnant."

The nurse, Etaferahu Kebede, replied that the woman could solve her problem by having only one sex partner. "Then you can have safe sex and you don't need a condom," she said.

The classroom session, during school vacation, was part of an unusual program in the government's efforts to gather more accurate information on the spread of AIDS in Ethiopia and warn prostitutes about the dangers of not protecting themselves.

The nurse's briefing to the 10 prostitutes seated on the classroom's benches was a prelude to the program's focus.

The Ministry of Health hired the former prostitutes and trained them in the art of asking delicate questions in the hope that they can succeed where social workers have failed: in persuading prostitutes to talk frankly. As confidential interviewers, the former prostitutes are more persuasive in selling the virtues of condoms, epidemiologists said. At the conclusion of the interviews, prostitutes are asked to donate blood for testing and given condoms.

As in other African countries, AIDS is largely a heterosexual disease in Ethiopia; primary carriers are prostitutes, truck drivers, and soldiers.

Prostitution has become more endemic in Ethiopian cities because of increasing poverty. Sociologists here say that another result of poverty is promiscuity in general, as young people find it too expensive to marry and so tend to have numerous affairs, increasing their risk of AIDS.

A 20-year-old woman waiting to be interviewed in the dirt schoolyard said she turned to prostitution five months ago. "I'm trying to make a living," said the woman, a kerchief over her head. She knew about AIDS, she said, and was grateful for the seminar. "It is going to help us in prevention."

The Ethiopian medical authorities, confronted with some of the worst public health problems in the world—the rate of child immunization is the second-lowest in the world, according to the United Nations—were prompted to further action on AIDS after a blood survey last year showed an alarming spread of the virus. In one town, Dessie, a major transportation hub, 38 percent of prostitutes and drivers of the Ethiopian Freight Transport Corporation tested positive for the virus.

With money from the World Health Organization, the Ministry of Health started its AIDS program two years ago, focusing mainly on education and tracking the disease.

Source: Excerpted from Jane Perlez, "Ethiopia Uses Unlikely Warriors in Anti-AIDS Effort," *New York Times,* October 10, 1989, p. 14. Copyright © 1989 by the New York Times Company. Reprinted by permission.

OTHER COMMUNICATIONS ISSUES

Relationship Marketing

A major recent trend in private sector marketing is the shift in selling approaches from transactional marketing to *relationship marketing*[18]—in our terms, shifting from a focus on target audience members in the Contemplation and Preparation/Action stages to those in the Maintenance stage. In transaction marketing, the emphasis is on the individual exchange, getting the target audience member to act in some desired way one time (e.g., a visit to a clinic or museum or a one-time donation). In relationship marketing, the focus shifts to building long-term relationships where the target audience member is encouraged to continue his or her involvement with the marketer. Thus a Nordstrom department store in the United States will often take seemingly foolish steps like giving credit for returned merchandise it never sold in the first place. The company argues that, while this might not be a way to maximize immediate profits, it is a very good way to make someone a lifetime target audience.

Building strong long-term relationships rather than making transactions is important in many areas of nonprofit marketing and it is one in which personal contact can play a major role. It is critical in fundraising and blood donations. Here, for example, a smart marketer who encounters a reluctant donor will willingly forego securing a direct donation but get the individual to take some small supporting step, like signing a pledge for a future donation or helping stuff envelopes for a half hour. Praise for such help can then make the reluctant target audience member feel like part of the marketer's team.[19] In such circumstances, he or she is much more likely to want to build long-term commitments, to become part of the Volunteers of America or Memorial Hospital family of supporters.

Relationship marketing means focusing on key target audience members and giving them continuous attention. People who have carried out one transaction with the organization are better sources for future transactions than is someone entirely new. Therefore, relationship marketing is easier and more cost-effective. Smart marketers are always thinking about new ways to promote further interactions with their existing target audience base. For example, colleges and universities were once mainly interested in getting students to enroll in their institutions. Now they realize that these students can be lifetime target audiences. In future years, former students can be donors of funds and services. They can nominate future students or can serve as advisors or influencers for those who are uncertain about attending. For many individuals today, learning is a lifelong enterprise. Former students are often the best candidates for the money-making seminars, workshops, and advanced degrees that many colleges and universities are now promoting.

A relationship marketer recognizes that attention to target audience members now (i.e., those in the Maintenance stage)—talking with them from time to time, giving them small rewards for patronage, asking them for new ways they can be of help—may seem costly in the short run; however, these small gestures can have important effects on the target audience member in the long run. This nurturing of target audiences can also have important payoffs in favorable word of mouth. When one of the authors taught on the West Coast, his students were always regaling him with "Nordstrom Stories." These were tales of the extraordinary lengths Nordstrom sometimes went to in order to make its target audiences happy. Of course, these gestures helped build tight relationships with Nordstrom's own target audiences. But they also had impressive ripple effects on the rest of us who heard the tales.

Internal Marketing

As noted earlier, every individual in the nonprofit organization (full-time, part-time, or volunteer) who has contact with target audience members is at that moment a marketer. Thus it is important that the marketing director not neglect these key influencers: They need to be the focus of marketing efforts because they can have a great positive and negative effect on organizational performance. In developing an internal marketing program, the place to begin is with an audit of the organization and its external relations—what are all the points of contact with "the outside world" and who is involved? The next step is to alert the relevant organization members and make clear to them how important their attitudes and behaviors can be to the mission of the organization.

Probably the most difficult challenge is to get telephone operators, security officers, cleaning staff, and the like to (a) see that target audience contact is part of their jobs and (b) have the right target audience mindset when they do pay attention to target audience members. The first problem is relatively easily resolved by carefully crafted job descriptions and initial orientation. The latter is more difficult.

Internal marketing is extremely important at the American Cancer Society. The organization maintains a Cancer Information Service that provides information on community programs and services to cancer patients and their families as well as the public. This is a comprehensive 24-hour resource and referral service that they say includes:

- Information about the nature of your cancer and its treatment
- Facts about your rights as a person with cancer
- Referrals in arranging equipment loans
- Referrals to summer camps, especially for children with cancer
- Help in locating resources to assist with financial problems.
- Direction in locating a second opinion through Illinois hospitals with cancer programs approved by the American College of Surgeons
- Help in locating free or low-cost lodging while receiving treatment away from home
- Information on Reach to Recovery, a breast cancer support and information program
- Information on Man to Man, a prostate cancer support and information program
- Information on Special Friends, a support program for kids with cancer and their siblings
- Information on Look Good, Feel Better, a program that provides self-help information for women undergoing treatment
- Oncology Nurse Specialists available 24 hours a day[20]

The call center builds a database on each caller and seeks to develop long-term relationships with them. E-mail addresses are also solicited as both a way to ship information instantaneously to them and a way to begin a longer-term dialogue. Well-trained operators secure useful information from each caller that goes directly into the American Cancer Society's Atlanta database and is used to craft future communications around the caller's needs and situations. A major payoff has been the number and amount of donations that have resulted. In the 1990s, it collected $4.5 million via this route and found that, without any promotion, the average first-time gift to the call center was $47.25, compared to $25.60 from other forms of fundraising.[21]

Recruiting Allies in Personal Persuasion: The Role of External "Others" in the BCOS Model

Many nonprofit programs can only succeed if others help carry their message to the right audiences. Some potential target audiences can *only* be reached through others. For example, people with eating disorders or depression may not know they need help. Thus any campaign aimed directly at them will have no impact. This is where others can be very influential in bringing the problem up and getting victims in the Precontemplation stage into treatment situations, or at least thinking about treatment.

Others must play a role sometimes because they are part of the problem. Many child abuse or drug abuse programs recognize that the abuser or the user is not the whole problem. The problem may be with a dysfunctional family or a renegade brother or father. Solutions must be at the family level, not at the individual level. Everyone needs to work on solutions.

Other individuals can also play a role in helping someone starting a new behavior to keep it up at the Maintenance stage. Quitting smokers and dieters need a lot of willpower and support to achieve their objectives. The family member or coworker who praises the weight loss of a friend will do wonders to keep him or her going. The ex-smoker who tells the target member how he or she was able to quit may serve as an influential role model, and the in-law who talks to the smoker who keeps failing in his or her attempts to quit (as most do) and urges them to try something else can be more influential than any direct advertising campaign. Advertising messages can stress the important role of others, as in the Ad Council campaign that tells people that "Friends Don't Let Friends Drive Drunk." Other types of communication, such as soap operas and movies, can show desired behaviors (for instance, modeling the farmer talking to his friend about new environmentally friendly land use and fertilization practices).

An analysis of some of the results of nonprofit behavior change programs in Africa suggests the power of "others." It has been noticed that once the rate of adoption of some new practices passes a certain point in terms of percentage of adopting households, then the influence of external nonprofit marketers diminishes significantly. What this suggests is that, although nonprofit programs are very important in promoting behavior change at early stages of a diffusion process, after some time the process becomes self-sustaining. The reason for this is that when many people in a close-knit community are doing a new activity, three things happen: (1) There are many more people to pass along information about the new behavior, (2) there are many more people who are demonstrating the behavior to nonadopters, and, perhaps most important, (3) the new behavior replaces the old as the community norm. This is akin to what private sector marketers call "viral marketing."[22]

These findings again demonstrate the enormous power that the influence of friends, neighbors, coworkers, and relatives can have on the behavior of target audiences—the importance of the "O" component of the BCOS model. Unfortunately, this power can also work against programs. Many social marketing efforts to get young mothers in developing countries to adopt new practices in the preparation of more nutritious meals, the treatment of diarrhea, or the practice of breast-feeding can run afoul of mothers-in-law. Tradition in many such countries requires that new brides move in with the husband's family immediately after the wedding. While in her birth home, the bride was influenced by her own family; after marriage she comes under the not inconsiderable influence of her mother-in-law. Programs aimed directly at the new "more modern" mothers often simply cannot overcome the power of the mother-in-law. The latter must be won over first.

Sometimes, to get the proper social support, entire villages or even countries must be changed. A program to get parents in a Southeast Asian country to allow their daughters to go on to secondary school as the boys did found that it had to work first at convincing the entire country that educating girls was not a waste of valuable resources.[23]

Summary

Advertising, nonpersonal communication conducted through paid media under clear sponsorship, must be planned strategically like any other element of the marketing mix. Objectives must be set, budgets determined, messages defined, media selected, and a system of evaluation established. Marketers should not make grand promises of what advertising can do and should be alert to ethical issues.

Advertising objectives must fit with prior decisions about the target market, offer positioning, and the nature of the remainder of the marketing mix. It must be clear what response is sought from the target audience. Typically, the response is movement forward through the stages of change described in Chapter 4.

There are a number of decisions a marketing manager must make. Budgets must be set and allocated among various media vehicles. Managers must also decide on media timing. Ads should be scheduled seasonally or cyclically to parallel changes in audience interest. Within seasons, decisions must be made on short-run timing. The major options are to advertise continuously, intermittently, or in preplanned bursts. These choices should be based on audience turnover, the frequency of the behavior to be influenced, and forgetting rates.

Evaluation schemes involve pretesting and posttesting advertising. Pretesting can incorporate comprehension studies, mailed questionnaires, portfolio recall tests, physiological tests, focus-group interviews, or self-administered questionnaires. Posttests are usually based on recall, recognition, or some direct behavioral response such as inquiries or sales.

Personal interventions are critical to many behaviors. They are essential in fundraising and volunteer recruitment. Care must be taken in selecting personal persuaders with the right traits. Personal interventions can build long-term relationships. They can be carried out by many people in the organization who might not normally think of themselves in this role. Internal marketing to this group is important as is the involvement of others outside the organization who can help in persuasion campaigns.

Questions

1. You have been given the task of devising a strategy that would create a 5-minute video promoting non-drug use that is to be placed on your web site. How would you create a campaign to attract young people to watching your video?

2. You are the marketing director for an anti-drug campaign. What are the ethical issues you would think about in deciding whether to post blogs on MySpace or other sites pretending that you are a teenager and discussing how you overcame your drug habit?

3. Would you ever use spam as an e-mail strategy to promote a fundraising effort for the American Cancer Society? Why or why not?

4. How would you measure the effectiveness of a radio serial broadcast in several languages in South Africa that is designed to get mothers to inoculate their babies against infectious diseases?

5. How would you vary a campaign over the school year to recruit student volunteers at a university to help at a homeless shelter?

Notes

1. F. Cook, T. Tyler, E. Goetz, M. Gordon, D. Protess, D. Leff, et al., "Media and Agenda-Setting: Effects on the Public, Interest Group Leaders, Policy Makers, and Policy," *Public Opinion Quarterly*, Vol. 47 (1983), pp. 16–35.

2. See Figure 12-1.

3. *Advertising Age*, January 1, 2007, p. 10.

4. AdAge DataCenter, originally published June 23, 2006. Retrieved from adage.com/datacenter/article?article_id=111843 on October 17, 2006.

5. Janet Meyers, "Pentagon to Cut Ad Ammunition?" *Advertising Age*, December 18, 1989, p. 3.

6. See Russell H. Colley, *Defining Advertising Goals for Measured Advertising Results* (New York: Association of National Advertisers, 1961).

7. A great many examples are provided by the Communication Initiative at www.comminit.com/radio/.

8. Retrieved October 17, 2006 from publications.mediapost.com/index.cfm?fuseaction=Articles.showArticle&art_aid=37881.

9. William D. Novelli, "Social Issues and Direct Marketing: What's the Connection?" presentation to the Annual Conference of the Direct Mail/Marketing Association, Los Angeles, CA, March 12, 1981.

10. Retrieved from en.wikipedia.org/wiki/MySpace on October 19, 2006.

11. Jinny Gudmindson, "Movement Aims to Get Serious About Games," *USA Today*, May 15, 2006, available at www.usatoday.com/tech/gaming/2006-05-19-serious-games_x.htm (retrieved October 20, 2006). See also www.seriousgames.org.

12. Simmons has generously provided previous versions of the database to many university libraries.

13. P. M. Camic, J. E. Rhodes, and L. Yardley (Eds.), *Qualitative Research in Psychology: Expanding Perspectives in Methodology and Design* (Washington, DC: American Psychological Association, 2003).

14. David Mark, *Going Negative: The Art of Negative Campaigning* (Lanham, MD: Rowman & Littlefield Publishers, Inc., 2006); Stephen Ansolabehere and Shanto Iyengar, *Going Negative: How Political Advertisements Shrink and Polarize the Electorate* (New York: The Free Press, 1995).

15. Robert N. McMurry, "The Mystique of Super-Salesmanship," *Harvard Business Review*, March–April 1961, p. 117.

16. Ibid., p. 118.

17. David Mayer and Herbert M. Greenberg, "What Makes a Good Salesman?" *Harvard Business Review*, July–August 1964, pp. 119–125.

18. Jagdish Sheth and Atul Parvatiyar (Eds.), *Handbook of Relationship Marketing* (Thousand Oaks, CA: Sage Publications, 2000); Mary Jo Bitner, "Building Service Relationships: It's All about Promises," *Journal of the Academy of Marketing Science*, Fall 1995, pp. 246–251.

19. Carol A. Scott, "Modifying Socially Conscious Behavior: The Foot-in-the-Door Technique," *Journal of Target Audience Research*, 1977, pp. 156–164.

20. www.cancer.org/docroot/COM/content/div_IL/COM_11_2X_patient_services_11935.asp?sitearea=COM (retrieved December 7, 2006).

21. Clint Carpenter, "Call Centers Nearly Double ACS's Average Gift," *Nonprofit Times*, January 15, 2000, pp. 1, 4.

22. Emanuel Rosen, *The Anatomy of Buzz—How to Create Word-of-Mouth Marketing* (New York: Doubleday & Company, 2000).

23. Susan E. Middlestadt, Beverly Schwartz, Jaraid Kaiser, Cecilia Verzosa, and Achintya Das Gupta, "Promoting Secondary Education for Women in Bangladesh: Using a Theory-Based Behavioral Elicitation Technique to Identify Salient Consequences for Enrolling Daughters," *1997 Innovations in Social Marketing Conference Proceedings*, pp. 41–44.

14

MANAGING PUBLIC MEDIA AND PUBLIC ADVOCACY

WHEN IS A GENEROUS GIFT TOO MUCH?

Suppose you are a major charity that prides itself on its humble grassroots approach to fundraising. To your surprise, a wealthy donor just gave you $1.5 billion. Further, she had some very specific ideas about how the money ought to be used. This is just what happened to the Salvation Army in the fall of 2003. Joan Kroc, the wife of Ray Kroc, the founder of McDonald's Corporation, died in 2003. In her will she gave the Salvation Army this significant sum with the specification that it be used to build 30–40 Kroc Centers around the country. The centers would have swimming pools, indoor ice and roller skating rinks, playing fields, and perhaps a theater—all available to low-income families who otherwise would have no access to such facilities.

Commander Israel L. Gaither, the newly installed leader of the Salvation Army, has expressed worries that the creation of the Kroc Centers will change the way people look at the charity and what it does and how the charity looks upon itself. His dilemma is markedly different from that of National Public Radio, which also received from Mrs. Kroc an unexpected $200 million grant. In their case, most of the money went into an Endowment Fund for Excellence, which is consistent with NPR's mission.

But if you are a particular kind of religious organization—which is what the Salvation Army is—your mission is providing help for the poor such as housing for the elderly, transitional homes for struggling families, summer camps, and after-school and drug rehabilitation programs. The public's impression of the Salvation Army is of a bare bones operation that collects money by ringing bells in the cold at Christmas time. The mayor of Salem, Oregon, says "The army's always been there, quietly behind the scenes taking care of what needs to be taken care of without much fanfare or attention."

But the Kroc Centers may leave many with the impression that the Salvation Army is rather well off and doesn't need as much public generosity. The pilot center in San Diego has sleek, modern facilities rarely available in poor areas and a $2.5 million Henry Moore sculpture prominently displayed. But it is costly to run and it—and the future Kroc centers—will require a lot of extra attention to generating revenue. The Kroc grant only provides funding of half the operating costs. Salvation Army staff and volunteers might well ask if finding funds to keep the Kroc Centers running is how they ought to be spending their time.

Still, early experiences seem promising. An August 2006 article in the *New York Times* noted that the location of the San Diego Center was rapidly decaying. The mayor is quoted as saying: "All around here was a two-to-three mile radius where kids didn't have any activities, nothing to do but wander around the streets." Since the center opened, families have bonded together around a water aerobics class and kids are excited about taking up skating and ice hockey. And the center still gives food to the needy, offers parenting classes, and makes referrals to a host of local social programs.

So far, the center seems to be a hit in the neighborhood. It is not yet clear what 30–40 centers mean for the future image and support of this venerable charity.

Source: Stephanie Strom, "New Wealth, and Worries, for the Salvation Army," *New York Times,* August 4, 2006, pp. A1, A14.

Paid promotion through advertising or the personal persuasion of staffers is only one of the ways in which nonprofit organizations seek to achieve their behavior change objectives through communications with target audiences. A second major approach is through media that are not paid for or controlled by the organization, the earned media. We define earned media very broadly as *any form of communication not paid for or under the control of the nonprofit marketing organization through which the organization must earn coverage.*

In the twenty-first century, earned media are extremely important vehicles for promoting the nonprofit organization's objectives.

- Appearances on key talk shows can do more to further a nonprofit marketing cause than can tens of thousands of dollars in media advertising. The President of the United States can often do much more for his legislative agenda by appearing on Larry King Live than he can by individual arm twisting with senators and representatives.
- Articles in major newspapers can sway thousands toward a particular course of action. A former Surgeon General who holds a press conference and is quoted in the *New York Times* or the *Washington Post* can have a great effect on people's awareness of the risks of a particular health problem such as cigarette smoking or AIDS.
- Op-ed pieces are now a major vehicle for trying to influence public opinion. Advocates on both sides of the school voucher issue regularly pen op-ed pieces, hoping to sway citizens to take action for or against school voucher funding.

Thus public media can be an extremely positive force in achieving a nonprofit organization's goals However, they can also be potentially damaging or, at best, a thorn in the side of many organizations. Vigorous investigative reporting by the press and such television newsmagazines as *60 Minutes, 20/20,* and *Dateline*—and informal investigations by online bloggers and web sources like the Smoking Gun (www.theSmokingGun.com)—have uncovered a number of dark corners in the nonprofit world, bringing to light financial scandals involving such prestigious organizations as the American Red Cross and United Way of America, charging that the Girl Scouts were exploiting the cookie-selling capabilities of their girls (and their parents), and reporting child molestation charges against Catholic dioceses.

Because sophisticated nonprofits recognize the power of the public media to influence, or inhibit, their marketing programs, they typically assign specific individuals to the task of working with these media. In many organizations, this person's title is public relations manager. Traditionally, public relations managers have been responsible for protecting and enhancing the *organization's* image. The public relations manager's job was to seek out opportunities to plant positive stories about the organization and its activities in the media. He or she also was the one responsible for extricating the organization or one or more of its staff members when some whiff of impropriety hit the public airwaves and pressrooms or the Web. This traditional approach can be challenged by those who think that the public media have a broader role to play in nonprofit organization strategy.

Recently, the role of public relations has been expanded to encompass strategies and tasks related to nonprofits' basic missions and to specific campaigns. This new role, which we call "public advocacy," involves efforts to change the societal structure of norms and values surrounding controversial individual behaviors (often referred to as "changing social norms" or "norming") and to raise their importance in media, public, and political agendas. It also involves attempting to change the way debates on issues of importance to nonprofits are carried out and to pressure actors in those debates to take particular positions. One kind of public advocacy is lobbying, but there are many others.

In this chapter we briefly consider the traditional role of public relations and then focus on the more modern, expanded conception of public relations in the nonprofit organization.

TRADITIONAL PUBLIC RELATIONS

The traditional *public relations manager* can have one or both of two roles. One is the responsibility for maintaining and enhancing the reputation of the organization among key publics.[1] While the principal focus of this effort is on support publics, it is quite clearly recognized that an organization's image has important effects on its own employees, its donors and volunteers, and its clients. By employing a public relations manager, the organization can gain several advantages: (1) better anticipation of potential problems, (2) better handling of these problems, (3) consistent public-oriented policies and strategies, and (4) more professional written and oral communications.

A second role of the public relations function is at the campaign level. Because budgets for significant social goals are usually inadequate to the task, campaigns often rely heavily on "earned" messages (along with other kinds of material and partner support). This is especially important when trying to raise an issue's public importance.

Positioning Public Relations

The public relations function can be accorded high or low influence in the organization, depending on the board's and chief executive officer's attitude toward the function. In some organizations, the public relations manager is a vice president and sits in on all meetings involving information and actions that might affect public perceptions of the organization. He or she not only puts out fires but also counsels management on actions that will avoid starting fires. In other organizations, public relations is a middle-management function charged with getting out publications and handling news, the annual report and special events. The public relations people are not involved in policy or strategy formulation, only in tactics.

Campaign-level public relations efforts are typically structured in one of two ways. In some organizations, the public relations function or department has staffers who are assigned to particular campaigns and serve to advance their strategies. If the organization believes that campaign managers should have all the tools needed to carry out their objectives, the campaign may hire its own public relations person or a person from the public relations department will be assigned to the campaign on a full-time, possibly long-term, basis.

There is a third approach to structuring the public relations function, that is, to put it *within* the marketing area. A major challenge to chief administrators and boards is, from time to time, is deciding what should be the relationship between marketing and public relations in a nonprofit organization. Clearly, the two functions work well together in commercial firms with marketing focusing on the development of plans to market the company's products and services to consumers, while public relations takes care of relations with other publics. In nonprofit organizations, however, the relationship between the public relations and marketing departments has often been marked by tension and lack of clearly defined areas of responsibility. This is because of the important role of public relations at the campaign level. Many marketing efforts simply cannot succeed without powerful public relations efforts!

The tension is often an historical artifact.[2] In many institutions, the public relations function was already well established when marketing was introduced. Friction between the two areas subsequently arose, first because the marketing department was often assigned functions that were "taken away" from public relations. They did their one media relations and events. Second, public relations directors often felt that *they* should have been given the better paying new position of marketing director when it was created. Third, many public relations executives felt that marketing ought to be a division within *their* departments or that marketing as a separate function was not needed at all.

These frictions were often exacerbated by the lack of clearly specified separate roles for the two functions and a clear understanding of how they were to be coordinated with each other. Our own view is that there is a need for an organization-level public relations function but the campaign-level functions should be under the control of the marketing people because of the crucial role public relations must play in most campaigns. Indeed, when nonprofit organizations hire advertising or public relations organizations to help with campaigns, they often specifically seek organizations like Porter Novelli or Ogilvy Public Relations because the firms have both advertising and public relations capabilities.

PUBLIC RELATIONS AT THE ORGANIZATION LEVEL

We cannot emphasize strongly enough the need for careful long-range planning of organization-level public relations. It has been our experience that in many organizations, public relations is mainly (or only) *reactive*. It gets out press releases as needed, fights "brush fires" as they emerge, and copes with individual and group complaints. This reactive stance has many negative consequences, including:

1. The environment rather than the organization sets the public relations agenda.
2. The organization's image is defined only by its response to special situations rather than by the creation of a set of carefully designed messages over a long period of time.
3. The organization's responses to crises are not guided by a long-term strategy.

The *active* public relations stance at the organization level avoids these problems and ensures that the organization has control over how others see it. There are several steps to this strategic approach as outlined in Figure 14-1.

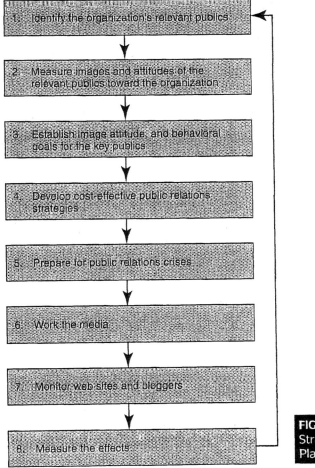

1. Identify the organization's relevant publics

2. Measure images and attitudes of the relevant publics toward the organization

3. Establish image attitude, and behavioral goals for the key publics

4. Develop cost-effective public relations strategies

5. Prepare for public relations crises

6. Work the media

7. Monitor web sites and bloggers

8. Measure the effects

FIGURE 14-1 The Strategic Public Relations Planning Process

1. Identify the Organization's Relevant Publics

An organization would like to have the goodwill of every public that is affected by, or affects, it. Given limited public relations resources, however, the organization will have to concentrate more of its attention on some publics than others. An organization has primary, secondary, and tertiary publics.

An organization's primary publics are those that it relates to actively and continuously, such as clients, employees, directors, and the general community. Secondary publics are those it must monitor and relate to less frequently but on a fairly continuous basis—suppliers, agents, government officials, and competitors. Tertiary groups are those that do not have any present impact on the organization but whose support and goodwill may be helpful in the future. Tertiary publics may also include groups to whom the organization might like to market in the future.

The various publics are related not only to the organization, but also to each other in many important ways. A particular public may have great influence on other publics. Consider a college whose students are highly satisfied. Their enthusiasm will be transmitted to their parents and to friends back home who might be potential students. Their enthusiasm will have a reinforcing effect on the faculty, who will feel that their teaching is effective. Their enthusiasm will affect the future level of support they give to the school as alumni. Finally, the good "buzz" will potentially improve the university's public perceptions and standing, which can have unknown payoffs in future years.

Publics also affect each other in the agenda-setting role of campaigns discussed later in this chapter.

2. Measure the Images and Attitudes of the Relevant Publics

Once the organization has identified its key publics, it needs to find out how each public thinks and feels about the organization. Management will have some ideas of each public's attitude simply through its regular contacts with that public. However, impressions based on casual contact cannot necessarily be trusted. At one time, a particular college wanted to rent its stadium facilities to a professional football team for five Sundays as a way of raising more revenue. The college's administrators thought that most local residents and city council members would approve. When it sought a favorable city council vote, however, a group of local citizens verbally attacked the college, calling it insensitive and arrogant. They complained that football crowds would use up parking spaces, leave litter, walk on lawns, and be rowdy. During the sometimes heated dialogue, large numbers of citizens, including city council members, revealed deep-seated hostile attitudes toward the college that only needed an issue like this to bring out their animosity. Even in this case, the college's administration dismissed the community spokesman as a minority voice. Needless to say, the vote went against the college, to its surprise.

To know a public's attitudes well enough to use them as a solid basis for its strategic planning, the organization needs to undertake the kind of formal "listening" marketing research we discussed in Chapter 5. A good start is to assemble focus groups of publics regularly to probe their knowledge and feelings about the organization. While the observations of these focus groups are not necessarily representative, they normally contribute perspectives and raise interesting questions that the organization will want to explore more systematically. Most importantly, they will alert management to key problems as they emerge. Larger nonprofit organizations consider it essential to their "knowledge management" approach to marketing research to conduct formal field surveys on a regular basis.

3. Establish Image, Attitude, and Behavioral Goals for Key Publics

By periodically researching its key publics, the organization develops hard data on how these publics view the organization. To translate this information into a strategic plan, the organization must evaluate each key public in terms of whether each has a negative, neutral, or positive attitude toward the organization and the degree of impact its members can have on the organization if they act on their attitude.

Suppose the public relations manager for St. Anthony's Hospital rates 20 key publics in terms of these two factors (see Table 14-1). She concludes that there are five groups that are unfavorably disposed toward the hospital (bottom row). However, the competitive nature of the hospital market and the relatively weak position of unions in this particular state have led her to conclude that the negative reactions of two of these publics, competitors and labor unions, will have little impact on the hospital. Local politicians are seen as hostile, but no legislation is presently pending. If politicians do decide to act, however, they can be troublesome, so the hospital must pay some attention to them. Technicians and insurers (lower right corner) are a more serious problem. Technicians are upset about the hospital's recent decision not to buy certain state-of-the-art equipment to replace older equipment. Insurers are rankled by the hospital's antiquated billing procedures and higher-than-average charges for certain exotic surgical procedures. Both groups should receive considerable attention in the upcoming year.

Physicians, patients, and media should also receive close attention. Although the present attitude of these groups is not negative, it is not positive and can have a major impact on the organization. All of these groups are concerned about a recent scandal at the hospital in which two physicians were discovered abusing drugs. The same issue has caused a potential problem for the other groups in the other two "neutral" cells of the matrix. Informal soundings indicate that all four publics in these two cells are concerned about the hospital's medical staff and control systems. Medical schools and

TABLE 14-1	A Portfolio of Publics for St. Anthony's Hospital		
Probability of	*Potential Impact*		
Negative Reaction	*Low*	*Medium*	*High*
Low	Suppliers	Nursing schools Volunteers	Board Nurses Regional health agency Charities
Medium	General public Nonmedical staff	Medical schools Research foundations	Physicians TV/Radio Newspapers Patients
High	Competitors Labor unions	Local politicians	Technicians Insurers

research foundations must be satisfied, since future negative attitudes could have the potential for affecting future recruitment of physicians and winning of research grants.

Those with positive attitudes (top row) would seem not to merit immediate attention. The upper right cell is a discretionary target. Some attention may be devoted to the board, nurses, regional health agencies, and charitable organizations. Their interest and concerns, however, might be met by programs directed at other target publics. However, to the extent that their positive attitude might bleed through to some of the neutral and negative publics, they must not be ignored. They may well be some of the organization's most useful (and one hopes vocal) supporters.

As for the three remaining cells of the matrix, the analysis suggests that the public relations manager with a finite budget can pay relatively little attention to suppliers, nursing schools, volunteers, the general public, and nonmedical staff in the upcoming year. She should continue, however, to monitor their attitudes over the year to make sure that her initial assessment of a favorable attitude is correct and that they do not "migrate" to other, more potentially damaging cells.

Once the public relations manager has determined the amount of effort to direct to each key public in the matrix, specific communication goals must be set for each segment. The manager might set a goal, for example, that "Ninety percent of TV and radio news directors and city newspaper editors within a 50-mile radius of the hospital should know within six months the full details of the hospital's internal policing system. Seventy-five percent should have full confidence in the hospital by the end of that period." These specific goals naturally suggest the means for their achievement and indicate what results should be measured later to evaluate the success of the strategic plan.

4. Develop Cost-Effective Public Relations Strategies

An organization usually has many options in trying to improve the attitudes of a particular public. Its first task is to understand why negative attitudes have arisen so that the causal factors can be appropriately addressed. It is especially important to establish whether the attitudes are problems of perception or reality. Clearly, if the problem is perception, then the challenge is really one of communications and positioning. However, if there are aspects of the organization and its performance that need to be fixed, this must come first. Credibility is probably the single most important attribute that a public relations professional must carry into the field. Nothing will damage that credibility as much as lying. Presumably, a public relations professional would never commit an outright lie, but attempts to put a positive spin on a basically flawed situation is not only hard to do but seriously risks the organization's credibility and the likelihood it will be believed in the future. This means that CEOs for their part must never lie to the public relations professionals as the long-term consequences of this can be disastrous.

In the college football stadium problem previously mentioned, the college learned that it first needed to make real changes in the ways it relates to the community and thus establish stronger ties with that community. It needed to develop a *community relations program* as part of its public relations strategy. Here are some of the steps it might take to build ties once it makes the needed fundamental changes in the way it operates:

1. Identify the local opinion leaders (prominent businesspeople, news editors, city council members, heads of civic organizations, school officials) and build better relationships by inviting them to campus events, consulting with them on college issues that will affect the community, and sponsoring luncheons and dinners.

2. Encourage the college's faculty and staff to join local organizations and participate in community campaigns such as the United Way and American Red Cross Blood Bank programs.

3. Develop a speakers' bureau to provide speakers to local groups such as the Kiwanis, Rotary, and so on.

4. Make the college's facilities and programs more available to the community. Classrooms and halls can be offered to local organizations for meetings.

5. Arrange open houses and campus tours for the local community.

6. Participate in community special events such as parades, holiday observances, and so on.

7. Establish an advisory board of community leaders to act as a sounding board for issues facing the college and the community.

8. Put links to university web sites on the web pages of the Chamber of Commerce and other "booster" organizations.

Each project involves money and time. The organization will need to estimate the amount of expected attitude improvement for each project to arrive at the best mix of cost-effective actions.

5. Prepare for Public Relations Crises

Every nonprofit organization that is more than a few years old has "horror stories" of organizational oversights, executive improprieties, volunteer excesses, and so on that were for many days and weeks the focus of dramatic and potentially damaging stories in the press. A month seldom passes without a story of malfeasance in the popular press or in *The Chronicle of Philanthropy*. A strategically oriented public relations program must manage such crises and not let the crises manage them.

Crises are not always the result of steps an organization takes for which it deserves to be embarrassed. It may be that they are just very controversial. For example, in the first years of the new millennium, the Boy Scouts of America faced a significant amount of negative press as a result of dismissing a former Eagle Scout who was a troop leader because he was gay and, in the Boy Scout organization's view, not of "strong moral character."[3] The troop leader, James Dale, sued and eventually the U.S. Supreme Court ruled that, as a private organization, the Scouts were exempt from state anti-discrimination laws. The Scouts believed they did the right thing. Many gay rights groups and many in the general public criticized the organization and urged schools to stop allowing Boy Scout meetings on their premises and individuals to stop donating. Some regional Boy Scout councils, such as one in New England, responded to the public relations crisis by adopting more tolerant "Don't ask, don't tell" policies.

There are two approaches to crisis management: long term and short term. In the long term, the public relations manager must actively prepare for the inevitable unexpected disaster or controversy. This means, first of all, cultivating strong media relations. If the public relations staff truly has a customer-centered approach to its relationships with the media, it will have established itself as having *the media's interests* at the center of its public relations program. This should lead to key media people giving the organization the benefit of any doubts and a clear opportunity to get its story across.

The other long-term approach is to train key managers in how to deal with the media in crisis situations. This means, first, creating an *attitude* on the managers' part that regards members of the media not as the enemy, but rather as individuals attempting to do their jobs as thoroughly and professionally as possible. Second, it means giving managers role-playing experience in holding press conferences and being part of high-stress interviews with the media.

One of the keys to any response from a marketing standpoint is to remember that the organization ultimately relies on the goodwill of the public. A simple example of the proper response is offered by David Gunn, at the time general manager of the Washington, D.C., Metro system. During a morning rush hour in the second week of May 1993, service on the Metro's Red Line was delayed two hours because a woman was struck by a train. Rather than ignoring the issue or treating it as just an unfortunate random occurrence over which Metro had no control, Gunn issued a *written apology* to Red Line riders. Gunn said, "We're selling a product, and if we don't deliver it—and we didn't big-time that morning—we owe the people an apology."[4]

6. Work the Media

One of the major tasks of a public relations department is to find or create favorable news about the organization and market it to the appropriate media. The appeal of publicity for many organizations is that it is "earned advertising"—that is, it represents exposures at no financial cost. It also may prove to be much more effective than paid organizational advertising about itself. It can have *higher veracity* than advertising because it appears as normal news and not as sponsored information. Second, it tends to catch people off guard who might otherwise avoid sponsored messages. Third, it has high potential for dramatization in that it arouses attention, coming as it does in the guise of a noteworthy event.

Public relations releases traditionally have been in written form. But for broadcast media, video news releases are often prepared. These releases are, in effect, TV news stories created by the nonprofit organization to look like a regular news report. Harried TV stations can then use all or part of the material in their local newscasts. Viewers are unaware of the source. The latter must be treated carefully. Both the media and the nonprofit organization can come in for public criticism if they seem to be deliberately misleading the public.

Getting news items in the local press or on television or radio can benefit from a marketing perspective. This would normally be the case when public relations efforts are part of campaigns and monitored by marketing professionals. However, organizational public relations people may have limited marketing training. Marketers would first urge them to start with the needs and wants of the target audience and NOT the organization's needs and wants. One must understand what *the media* are looking for in a news story and not attempt to push the organization's view on a frequently resistant target audience. The latter would clearly be a selling approach that we argued against in Chapter 2.

Among the factors the media will be looking for are these:

1. How interesting is the subject to *their* audience?
2. Is there a possibility for dramatization through pictures, live interviews, and so forth?

3. How clear and exhaustive is the press release—if there is one (e.g., including supporting materials, statistics, and so on)?
4. How much further "digging" must they do?
5. Will they have exclusive coverage—for either the entire story or for a specific angle?

A nonprofit organization can increase its newsworthiness by creating events that attract the attention of target publics and the media. Thus a hospital seeking more public attention can host major research symposia, feature well-known speakers and celebrities, celebrate anniversaries of important events in the history of the institution, create birthday parties for special patients, and hold news conferences. Each well-run event not only impresses the immediate participants, but also serves as an opportunity to develop a multitude of stories directed to relevant media vehicles and audiences.

7. Monitor Web Sites and Bloggers

In the new millennium, an extremely important source of information and insight about the nonprofit organization is its web site. Web sites that the nonprofit controls can present facts about the organization, recent press releases, and examples of advertisements and programs, all designed to give visitors to the site a sense of the organization and what it does. They are places where people go to volunteer or to donate. If they are well designed, they will have ways for visitors to follow up with personal contacts. There will be links to other sites people might find helpful and perhaps chat rooms where they can "meet" and discuss common concerns, such as the American Cancer Society's web site area, "The Cancer Survivors Network." Web sites of news organizations are places where one can learn about crises and how they are being handled.

It is also important to recognize that there are web sites, homepages, and blogs that are not under the control of the nonprofit organization and that are not populated by trained reporters or investigators. They are just individuals who feel they have something to say. They can be the source of legitimate and valuable information. But they can also spread negative opinions and, worse, falsehoods about the organization or a specific social issue. Webloggers can be inflammatory and vitriolic and pay only limited attention to the facts. Public relations staffers need to monitor such sources routinely and carry out countermeasures whenever they seem appropriate. Fortunately, there are web sites that see their role as countering untruths as does the Annenberg school's FactCheck.org. Wikipedia, a source for much information on nonprofits and specific social challenges, claims that its own contributors are very good at correcting errors—usually very rapidly. Finally, for every negative blog, there are often dozens of other bloggers who will challenge what is being said and voice their own opinion.

When confronted by negative blogging, public relations specialists may be tempted to join the fray by sending out their own blogs. This is a sensible practice but serious ethical challenges arise if nonprofit bloggers do not identify themselves as to their organizational affiliation. PR staffers may think this adds to their credibility in the chaotic blogging world, but there are excellent chances that their "cover" will be blown and this can easily make a modest problem highly toxic.

In the case of the organization's own web site, the "look" of the web site and the ease of interacting with it can affect the public's reaction to the organization. Young publics will appreciate highly visual, fast-moving sites, preferably with moving images and the latest songs and CDs, whereas older groups may prefer more text-based appearances and more sober content. It is extremely important to keep the site fresh and change its content from time to time to keep people coming back. The latter is most likely to happen if the visitor gets the sense the webmaster is someone who is always looking for ways to serve the visitors' needs better. Webmasters can be very important members of the public relations and marketing team.

8. Measure the Effects

Publicity is designed with certain audience-response objectives in mind, and these objectives form the basis of what ought to be measured. The major response measures are exposure, awareness, comprehension, attitude change, and specific behaviors.

The easiest and most common measure of publicity effectiveness is the number of *exposures* created in the media. Most professional publicists supply the client with a "clippings book" or reports of web searches showing all the media that carried news about the organization and a summary statement such as the following:

> Media coverage included 3,500 column inches of news and photographs in 350 publications with a combined circulation of 79.4 million; 2,500 minutes of air time on 290 radio stations and an estimated audience of 65 million; and 660 minutes of air time on 160 television stations with an estimated audience of 91 million. If this time and space had been purchased at advertising rates, it would have amounted to $1,047,000.

The purpose of citing the equivalent advertising cost is to make a case for publicity's cost-effectiveness, since the total publicity effort must have cost less than $1,047,000.

On the other hand, such a measure gives no indication of how many people actually read, saw, or heard the message, and what they thought afterward. Furthermore, there is no information on the net audience reached, since publications have overlapping readership. Indeed, there is the very real danger that the organization will attempt to maximize *what it can measure*. It is easy and satisfying to measure success by brochures passed out, articles written, and so on. Distributing more brochures in 2007 than in 2006 can be considered great progress but it is not clear that this means greater impact.

Better measures call for finding out what change in public *awareness, comprehension,* or *attitudes* occurred as a result of the publicity campaign (after allowing for the impact of other promotional tools). Calls to 800 numbers can provide chances to assess this as can counts—and evaluations—of blog entries. However, formal surveys over the Web or by telephone can provide greater depth of insight and more research credibility.

CAMPAIGN-LEVEL PUBLIC RELATIONS

Public relations is usually a very important part of a nonprofit organization's efforts to bring about some desired social behavior. Because marketing concepts and tools are simply approaches to influencing behavior, they can be directly applied to specific public relations campaigns that involve inducing journalists or news editors to run a story or cover an event.

To illustrate the use of the principles outlined in Chapter 2, let us take the case of a hypothetical public relations specialist for a gun owners' association and consider, first, how an *organization-centered* specialist would approach the problem of getting favorable press coverage of a story of importance to the organization:[5]

1. The organization-centered PR specialist would begin by assuming that he or she has a basically interesting story in which the general public would really be fascinated *if only* the journalist would cover it.
2. If journalists are reluctant to run the story, then it is assumed to be either because they do not fully appreciate how truly interesting it is and how much their audience would like to be exposed to it or because they have the usual liberal bias against gun owners and want to run as little as possible that is positive about them.
3. The PR specialist will reflect on his or her years of experience with journalists and take pride in knowing how they think. There will be little need to explore *in advance* how journalists will react to this kind of story opportunity. The specialist will prepare the necessary press releases and rely on his or her well-tested ability to be persuasive on the telephone or through imaginative direct mailings.
4. Getting coverage will be seen mainly as a matter of convincing journalists of the fact that it is a great story. This means pushing the story hard to make sure that the journalist comes to see the PR specialist's view of its great merit.
5. Different materials will be prepared for print, radio, and television journalists, but one or two treatments for each broad category ought to do it.

What would a *customer-oriented* approach look like? This PR specialist would proceed in a very different way:

1. He or she would not assume that the likely reactions of target journalists are known or that they are likely to be the same as the PR specialist's. Further, he or she will assume that there may be major differences both within as well as among media.
2. If time permits when planning the strategy for securing news coverage, the PR specialist would begin with calls to a few key newspeople to get initial reactions to the proposed story and to learn which features seem to resonate with the interests of which kinds of journalists.
3. The PR specialist would recognize that getting the story covered means that it must meet the journalists' near-term needs and wants. These needs will differ by journalist and may include one or more of the following concerns:
   a. How long will the story need to be?
   b. How well will the story appeal to the journalists' audiences?
   c. How well will the story appeal to the journalists' editors or news directors?
   d. What opportunities are there for a journalist to contribute his or her own "spin" to the story?
   e. Will the journalist have to dig further to cover the story well (some may want a lot of opportunities for digging, others none)?
4. Persuasion is not the heart of the strategy. The PR specialist would recognize that the "product" to be offered has to be right in the first place. The journalists should be presented with not only the facts of the story but a range of peripheral material that may respond to specific needs and wants of theirs. This peripheral material

could include photos or photo opportunities, profiles of key figures in the story, names of follow-up sources both inside and outside the association, lists of reference materials, DVDs with news release materials in each journalist's own word processing language, and so forth.

5. The PR specialist would recognize that the story is only one of many he or she will want to have covered over the years by target journalists. Thus each particular story is to be marketed as a part of a longer-term strategy of building *relationships* with the journalists. This often means sacrificing near-term gain for a long-run benefit. For example, selling-oriented PR specialists are usually reluctant to help journalists dig up critical (or even objective) material about the organization for the particular story. This would be seen as just getting in the way of "making the sale." A customer-oriented PR specialist providing journalists the names of one or more independent outside sources of follow-up information will recognize that this may cause short-run problems but (a) the journalist in all likelihood will find sources anyway (often more hostile ones), (b) providing outside sources will increase the credibility of the present message, and (c) most importantly, the PR specialist will more likely be seen (except by the most cynical journalists) as someone who is basically concerned about meeting the *journalist's* needs—not just selling a story. The customer-oriented news source is someone who tries to help.

PUBLIC ADVOCACY

Many nonprofit organizations have recognized both the potential and the need for efforts to change the institutional and social environment in which undesirable behaviors take place. Thus various groups see the need to bring about such reforms as:

1. Changing tax legislation so that willing donors can give more property to nonprofits.
2. Bringing pressure on manufacturers and retailers to package goods in degradable containers rather than just encourage individuals to recycle.
3. Ending the informal ban that many TV stations in the United States have on advertising of condoms on television.
4. Changing the perception of rape victims from "deserving it" to being true victims.
5. Changing the nutrition issue from one of helping people eat better and lose weight to one of getting food producers to reduce saturated fats in their products and provide better nutrition labeling.[6]
6. Bringing pressure to bear on the U.S. Congress to reduce tobacco farm subsidies and/or increase tobacco taxes so that higher prices will reduce tobacco consumption.
7. Urging more advertisers to include disabled people in their advertisements so that society will consider it normal to make accommodations for them.[7]

Achieving these reforms through public advocacy is increasingly being given a central role in nonprofit marketing strategies. Those who once were called traditional public relations specialists are now being given the challenge, usually in cooperation with many other individuals and organizations, of changing the social and institutional structure surrounding social problems. with a principal goal of influencing social agendas.

Social Agendas

One of the key challenges for many behavioral influence campaigns is simply that the behaviors at issue are not very important to people. They have not risen to a level of public consciousness where individuals and upstream players feel they need to do much about them. As Andreasen points out in his book *Social Marketing in the 21st Century*,[8] the challenge is one of influencing social agendas—and this is a key role for public relations.

Social problems go through a relatively predictable set of stages by which they arise and are eventually dealt with—or fall back into obscurity. The stages that Andreasen proposes are the following:

> *Stage 1: Inattention to the problem.* This is where the social problem exists, often as evidenced by concrete data or dramatic anecdotes. But it is not anyone's concern.
>
> *Stage 2: Discovery of the problem.* The problem comes to the attention of individuals or groups—including the media—who think it needs addressing. Nuances of the problem will emerge, for example, a sense of who is impacted most.
>
> *Stage 3: Climbing the agenda.* For action to take place, funders and activists need to find the issue sufficiently important for attention.
>
> *Stage 4: Outlining the choices.* Analysts and advocates look at the data and consider how the problem might be addressed.
>
> *Stage 5: Choosing courses of action.* This is where debate takes place over costs and the efficacy of various solutions. It is also where opposing forces emerge and solidify their positions.
>
> *Stage 6: Launching initial interventions.* At this stage, foundations and/or the government put money into programs. Organizations mount pioneering efforts and test alternative strategies and tactics.
>
> *Stage 7: Reassessing and possibly redirecting effort.* With most difficult changes, progress will be both slow and exhibit periods of acceleration, deceleration, progression, and regression. At some point, key figures feel that it is time to take stock of where the problem stands. The outcome may be a reorientation and resurgence of interventions. But it may not! The history of HIV/AIDS provides a vivid example of these vicissitudes.
>
> *Stage 8: Achieving success, failure, or neglect.* After a number of years, the problem will have found some major solutions or will have proven basically intractable and, in the absence of dramatic progress or new data, will "drop off the radar screen." The latter may also be the result of new competition from the latest social problem to capture the public's imagination!

Scholars have made clear that there are really three agendas that are important to the advancement of social problems.[9] First, there is the media agenda. The prominence of an issue is very often in the hands of the journalists and editors at the *New York Times* and *USA Today,* the news directors at Channel 4 and WAMU, and writers for the *New Yorker* and *People.* But they only play one role. Cohen has pointed out that the media don't determine what society thinks about an issue, but they do have a large effect on what we think *about.*[10]

The second agenda of importance is, of course, the public agenda. The public agenda very often determines the third agenda, the policy agenda. Unfortunately for policy makers and nonprofit marketers, determining where the public stands on any issue is a very difficult task, yet very important to public relations specialists and nonprofit marketers who want to advance particular solutions. Daniel Yankelovich argues that commonly used public opinion polls are poor measures of where people really stand on any important and personally challenging social issue.[11] He argues that there is a difference between "mass opinion" and "public judgment." The former is relatively shallow, contradictory, and not grounded in any sense of personal accountability. Public judgment results when individuals have thought through the issues, understood the choices, and considered the personal implications of the choices that might be made.

Tools and Tactics

The targets of public advocacy may be legislators, regulators, media gatekeepers, business executives, potential allies, and the general public. When focused on legislators and regulators, their advocacy is typically called lobbying.

There are a great many tools and tactics that a nonprofit public relations advocate can use to achieve a campaign's aims. We outline the major ones.

1. Conducting Public Education Campaigns

This is particularly important in Stage 2 of the agenda-setting process. Before people would consider taking precautions to prevent AIDS, they had to know that there was such a problem and that the problem is one that could affect them personally unless they changed their behavior. One must say to college students, "AIDS is a killer; it is more prevalent than you think; and it is not just a problem for somebody else."[12] One must tell African women that their men may contract AIDS in other relationships and they need to take care of themselves.

2. Framing the Issues

A key challenge in advancing a social problem through Stages 3, 4, and 5 is to influence how the problem is framed. Whichever organization or institution determines the labels and symbols that are used in any important debate has an important advantage in determining the outcome. Early in the abortion debate, one side framed the issue as between those who were pro-abortion and those who were pro-life. Put on the defensive, the pro-abortionists attempted to reframe the debate as *really* between those who were anti-abortion and those who were pro-choice. Being first to frame an issue is always the preferred strategy. But if the advocate is not first, at least the debate should never be argued on the opponent's terms without a challenge.

3. Engaging in Media Advocacy

Michael Pertchuck describes media advocacy as "the strategic use of mass media to advance a public policy initiative"[13] It is particularly important in Stages 4 and 5 when various foundations, government agencies, and social change nonprofits are trying to decide what to do about the problem. Wallack describes the role of media as follows:

Media advocacy promotes a range of strategies to stimulate broad-based media coverage in order to reframe public debate to increase public support for more effective policy-level approaches. . . . It does not attempt to change individual risk behavior directly but focuses attention on changing the way the problem is understood.[14]

Media advocacy can also play an earlier role in Stage 2. If the issue is still being discovered, Wallack suggests using what he calls "creative epidemiology." This approach uses good, hard science to bring the media's attention to an issue that they should cover and to frame the data in such a way that the media cannot afford to ignore it. He cites the example of an American Cancer Society videotape on smoking that says that "1,000 people quit smoking everyday—by dying. That is equivalent to two fully loaded jumbo jets crashing every day, with no survivors."[15] Such vivid use of the facts not only makes the point clear but also gives the media gatekeepers a graphic word-bite they can instantly use in the next edition or next newscast.

4. Creating Pseudo-Events

Often a campaign needs something dramatic to get the attention of the media, policy makers, and the general public. Daniel Boorstin first described an approach he called "the pseudo-event" in 1961 as a "newsworthy" event artificially created by advocates to bring media attention and coverage to an issue of importance to campaign marketers.[16] Examples of pseudo-events are press conferences, ribbon-cutting ceremonies, televised legislative bill signings, and most "photo opportunities" in a political campaign. A classic example of the pseudo-event is the tactic of advocates in the early part of the century to bring the public's attention to the degree to which unregulated food products contained toxic substances. The advocates set up a press conference in which reporters faced a table on which were piled powders in several colors. After the reporters arrived, various people at the head table silently proceeded to spoon the substances into their mouths. The point made to the assembled reporters was that the piles represented the amount of formaldehyde, arsenic, and so on that a typical consumer ingested every year. Such an event got more coverage than any dry report and set of statistics could ever achieve.

A good example of a contemporary pseudo-event is a documentary movie by Morgan Sperling called *Super Size Me* that earned an Oscar nomination in 2004. Spurlock ate only McDonald's hamburgers three times a day for a month and gained both a great deal of weight and some serious health problems. The backlash from the movie caused McDonald's to mount its own public media campaign, including creating its own counter-arguing commercials to be shown in movie theaters. Other potentially important movies include Michael Moore's *Sicko*.

In the twenty-first century environment, it may not always be necessary to motivate attention from the formal media. The participants on YouTube are very good at capturing dramatic events whether real or contrived. Politicians for the next decade are going to have to be very cautious about their "pseudo-events" because home video enthusiasts may be there covering the politician's every move and utterance. Indeed, opposition candidates often hire such video enthusiasts. It was just such a person who captured the event that sunk Senator George Allen's reelection campaign in 2006.

5. Producing Influential Books and Op-Ed Pieces

The debates on a number of major social issues have been dramatically changed by the publication of a landmark book by a committed advocate. Upton Sinclair's *The Jungle* upset the meatpacking industry forever. Betty Friedan's *The Feminine Mystique* changed the way women thought about themselves and gave major impetus to the women's movement. Ralph Nader's *Unsafe at Any Speed* first brought America's attention to serious safety deficiencies in the way most automobiles were designed and resulted in major safety legislation in the 1970s. And Rachel Carson's *Silent Spring* profoundly changed the level of concern about the environment shared by people all over the world.

The subsequent debates around solutions then can be enhanced by book publications and by op-ed pieces in newspapers. Many public relations agencies have specialists in such tactics often ghostwriting books and articles for more prestigious advocates to "author."

In the twenty-first century, Putnam's *Bowling Alone*[17] has called attention to America's decreasing lack of community. Ritzer has alerted us to the "McDonaldization" of the world[18] and Eric Schlosser has written about the negative consequences of becoming a *Fast Food Nation.*[19] Schlosser's book was turned into a movie in 2006 starring Greg Kinnear and Bruce Willis.

6. Enlisting the Help of the Entertainment Media

We have already spoken in several places about the power of celebrity spokespeople who can galvanize attention to an issue by attaching to it their personal charisma and ability to attract the attention of the media and policy makers. Washingtonians are quite accustomed to having celebrities appear on Capitol Hill not so much for what they know about an issue—although some like Michael J. Fox are exceptions—but for their ability to get congresspeople to listen to an issue being raised and to make the evening news. Among the recent sightings were:

- Michael Jackson bringing attention to AIDS in Africa (March 2004)
- Jessica Simpson promoting Operation Smile, which provides free surgery for cleft palette children in poor countries (March 2006)
- Muhammad Ali calling attention to his Parkinson's Disease (May 2002)
- Ashley Judd on the need for HIV vaccines in Africa (2005)
- Bono on the need to forgive the debt burdens of poor countries (October 2005)

The entertainment world has a second role to play in campaigns. Movies and television can have a great deal of influence on what citizens consider normal or acceptable behavior, what goals they seek, who they treat as authorities, and so on. These effects can be negative. Many argue that the casual and sensational attitude of directors, scriptwriters, and producers toward sex, smoking, and drug use has made a major contribution to the problems we have today, especially among young people. Teen smoking patterns often seem to rise and fall depending on what is shown in the movies.

However, as noted earlier television and the movies can also be instruments of positive change. Al Gore's movie *An Inconvenient Truth* has been credited with having a dramatic effect on public attitudes—and attention—to issues of global climate change. Sometimes, it is simply a matter of bringing an issue to the attention of the broadcast or movie industry. In the first years of the twenty-first century, the NBC program *The West*

Wing did a great deal to educate the public about important public policy issues. Many social observers believe that this program has done more to explain the issues of the day (the nature of terrorism, the use of sampling in the Census) than has any other public discussion or media coverage. (Observers have also noted that the program has also done a great deal to counteract the widespread notion that federal government leaders were immoral, self-serving egotists—an unanticipated public relations coup!)

7. Lobbying

Volumes have been written about the importance of lobbyists in the legislative and regulatory process. Many nonprofits hire organizations whose sole responsibility is to get to know legislators, their key aids, committee members, and other major players in any public policy debate that can affect the nonprofit's future and the success of its various missions. The lobbyist's job is to make sure that the nonprofit's position is clear to ultimate decision makers. Often, this means ensuring that nonprofit spokespeople have access to important people in order to present their case.[20] Andreasen suggests that many of the approaches of marketers can be applied to what are traditionally conceived to be lobbying challenges.[21]

8. Working Through the Educational System

The timeline for some campaigns may require generations of influence to move an issue up the various agendas and get solutions proposed and implemented. In such cases, initiatives expressly targeted at school systems are sometimes seen as a way to influence future target audiences and future decision makers and sometimes affect the way an issue is debated.[22] School programs can also have short-run effects. In many developing countries, it has been discovered that one of the best ways to influence parents is to influence their children first in school and have them carry the messages home. Nonprofit marketers often prepare class syllabi, handouts, audiovisual aids, and quizzes to change the way people think about good eating or the value of the union movement.[23]

9. Marshalling the Grassroots

Twenty years ago, the fax machine was a critical communication vehicle for revolutionaries in Eastern Europe who wanted to document what was happening inside their countries for the rest of world, especially foreign media,. Today, viral marketing through the Internet has proven to be similarly powerful (www.viralmarketing.com). For example, Amnesty International has created an advocacy network called FAST (Fast Action Stops Torture), which links a wide range of individuals and organizations who can speak out when a major human rights problem emerges around the world. In October 2000, it urged net members to contact Turkish authorities about Sehmuz Temel, a Kurd in custody who had previously been tortured by authorities. The campaign prompted 2,200 e-mails and Temel was released, quite possibly because of this campaign.[24]

Grassroots advocacy can also be very powerful, especially in Stages 5 and 6—choosing options and launching interventions.[25] A deluge of e-mails can have powerful influences on media and public agendas. AARP, with its 37 million members, prides itself in its ability to marshal powerful direct mail and telephone advocacy for particular approaches through its state offices and volunteers. It regularly produces a Priorities book in PDF form (assets.aarp.org/www.aarp.org_/articles/legpolicy/PrioritiesBook.pdf) to keep its potential advocates informed about what is currently important and where AARP stands.

10. Using the Annual Report

Most nonprofit organizations issue an annual report of some kind. In small organizations, this might be a simple document of several pages. In larger organizations, it is seen as a potentially powerful public relations vehicle aimed at major target audiences (see Figure 14-2). An impressive report can influence future funders and individual donors. It can show stories that encourage volunteers. And it can be motivational for permanent staff who can see themselves as part of a classy organization.

A Reminder: Public Advocacy Must Be Audience-Centered

A reminder is needed here. A danger in the public relations components of many nonprofit campaigns is to become so immersed in seeking a "noble" behavioral goal that the effort is mainly one of *selling* the advocate's position. This would be a major tactical mistake.

The key point is to show the various targets how the recommended action is in *their* interests. We discussed earlier how this approach would apply to reporters and others in the media. When policy becomes critical and legislators must be the focus, a key need is always going to be reelection. As a consequence, the nonprofit public advocate needs to demonstrate how the proposed action will aid reelection or at least not harm it. One of the ways many lobbyists, such as those for the National Rifle Association, seek to demonstrate positive electoral impact is by orchestrating grassroots phone calls and

FIGURE 14-2 Salvation Army Annual Report

Source: The Salvation Army. Printed with Permission of Pinnacle Communications Resource Co., LLC.

letters from constituents telling the senator or representative that a certain position would certainly please the voters. This is just sound marketing that can apply equally to other advocacy targets.

Summary

Public relations is a well-established function in profit and nonprofit organizations. Traditionally, public relations has been responsible for maintaining and enhancing the organization's public image. A second major role is as part of specific behavioral influence campaigns..

Traditionally, the task of public relations is to form, maintain, or change public attitudes toward the nonprofit organization, its programs, and its personnel. The process of public relations consists of eight steps: (1) identifying the organization's relevant publics, (2) measuring the images and attitudes held by these publics, (3) establishing image and attitude goals for the key publics, (4) developing cost-effective public relations strategies, (5) preparing for public relations crises, (6) working the media, (7) monitoring the web site and independent bloggers, and (8) measuring effects.. Just as elsewhere in the organization, a customer orientation is the best philosophy to apply to both long-term and short-term public relations strategies.

In their role in specific campaigns, nonprofit public relations specialists are increasingly being asked to influence the "upstream" social structures and agendas, norms, and values that have profound effects on individual behaviors "downstream." This is referred to as public advocacy. It is important to understand the stages through which social problems become recognized and dealt with. At various stages, there are a number of tools and tactics the public relations team member can use to achieve campaign goals, including reframing the nature of public debate, conducting public education, encouraging media advocacy, creating pseudo-events, writing influential books and op-ed pieces, enlisting the help of the entertainment media, working through the educational system, lobbying, and putting grassroots efforts to work through e-mail, the telephone, and the fax machine.

Questions

1. You are the marketing director for the American Legacy Foundation. Your research shows that the general public is not very concerned about the dangers of chewing tobacco, which is still consumed by a significant—but small—portion of the population. Your challenge is to raise the importance of the issue on the agenda of the public, politicians, and the media. Your ultimate goal is stronger legislation. Describe the major elements of your approach.
2. Muslim charitable foundations in the United States are seen by many Americans as potentially supporting radical groups. How would you mount an approach to convince people that your Muslim Foundation is deserving of trust?
3. The controversy around stem cell research has religious groups opposing it and scientists supporting it. A group of scientists has asked your help in framing the issue so that more people will support their work using stem cells. How would you proceed?
4. Your job used to be fundraising for a charity. You are now reassigned to be the public relations person. You have been given a small budget to take three academic courses. What courses would you choose and why?
5. You think public relations should be restructured so that it is subordinate to marketing. How would you convince the CEO of the American Cancer Society that this is a good idea?

Notes

1. Some of the material is this chapter is adapted from Philip Kotler and William Mindak, "Marketing and Public Relations," *Journal of Marketing,* October 1978, pp. 13–20.

2. Scott M. Cutlip, "The Beginning of PR Counseling," *Editor and Publisher,* November 26, 1950, p. 16.

3. Robert Hanley, "New Jersey Court Overturns Ouster of Gay Boy Scout," *New York Times,* August 5, 1999, p. A–1.

4. Robert F. Howe, "Metro Apologizes for Delays," *Washington Post,* May 14, 1993, p. C4.

5. Material in this section is taken from Alan R. Andreasen, "Communicating by Listening," *Issues & Opportunities,* Vol. 1, No. 5 (August 1989).

6. Brian Wansink, "Environmental Factors that Unknowingly Increase Food Intake and Consumption Volume of Unknowing Consumers," *Annual Review of Nutrition,* Vol. 24 (2004), pp. 455–479.

7. Richard W. Pollay, "The Distorted Mirror: Reflections on the Unintended Consequences of Advertising," *Journal of Marketing,* Vol. 50 (1986), pp. 18–36.

8. Alan R. Andreasen, *Social Marketing in the 21st Century* (Thousand Oaks, CA: Sage Publications, 2006).

9. James W. Dearing and Everett M. Rogers, *Agenda-Setting. Communication Concepts* (Thousand Oaks, CA: Sage, 1996).

10. B. C. Cohen, *The Press and Foreign Policy* (Princeton, NJ: Princeton University Press, 1963).

11. D. Yankelovich, *Coming to Public Judgment: Making Democracy Work in a Complex World* (Syracuse, NY: Syracuse University Press, 1991).

12. Jeffrey D. Fisher and William A. Fisher, "Changing AIDS-Risk Behavior," *Psychological Bulletin,* Vol. 111, No. 3 (1992), pp. 455–474.

13. Advocacy Institute, *Smoking Control Media Advocacy Guidelines* (Bethesda, MD: National Cancer Institute, National Institutes of Health, 1989).

14. Lawrence Wallack, "Media Advocacy: Promoting Health Through Mass Communication," in K. Glanz, F. M. Lewis, and B. K. Rimer (eds.), *Health Behavior and Health Education* (Jossey-Bass Publishers, 1990), p. 376.

15. Ibid., p. 377.

16. Daniel Boorstin, *The Image or What Happened to the American Dream* (New York: Atheneum, 1961).

17. Robert D. Putnam, *Bowling Alone: The Collapse and Revival of American Community* (New York: Simon & Schuster, 2000).

18. Ibid.

19. Eric Schlosser, *Fast Food Nation: The Dark Side All American Meal* (New York: Houghton Mifflin, 2001).

20. Kenneth M. Goldstein, *Interest Groups, Lobbying, and Participation in America* (Cambridge, UK: Cambridge University Press, 1999).

21. Andreasen, *Social Marketing.*

22. M. B. Mittelmark, et al., "Community-wide Prevention of Cardiovascular Disease: Education Strategies of the Minnesota Heart Health Program," *Preventive Medicine,* Vol. 15 (1986), pp. 1–17.

23. Charles T. Salmon, "Campaigns for Social 'Improvement': An Overview of Values, Rationales, and Impacts," in Charles T. Salmon, *Information Campaigns: Balancing Social Values and Social Change* (Newbury Park, CA: Sage Publications, 1989), p. 45.

24. Nicole Wallace, "Activists Use E-Mail to Combat Torture," *The Chronicle of Philanthropy,* November 16, 2000, p. 33.

25. M. Edelman, "Social Movements: Changing Paradigms and Forms of Politics," *Annual Review of Anthropology,* Vol. 30 (2001), pp. 285–317.

SECTION IV

DEVELOPING RESOURCES

15 GENERATING FUNDS

I REALLY, REALLY MEANT TO GIVE!

Have you ever thought about giving money to a charity or relief agency but somehow never got around to it? Or you thought about volunteering but couldn't seem to find the time? And what of that friend who seems to be drinking too much? Did you feel that you probably shouldn't meddle? How often did you intend to be a socially responsible person but passed up the opportunity?

The Advertising Council has chosen to directly address this problem—people not following through when there is a chance to help. The campaign is called "Generous Nation" and the campaign, begun in September 2006, carries the tag line "Don't almost give. Give." The campaign was created with the help of a major advertising agency—as are the majority of Ad Council projects. Six ads are planned. The first ads show hungry kids sleeping in a car and a neglected elderly person and then shows people who could have helped—but didn't. The campaign does not emphasize any particular charity but wants to change attitudes and prompt action.

Peggy Conlon, CEO of the Ad Council, says that the idea for the campaign came about because of the generous outpouring of money and help for the victims of Hurricane Katrina and the Southeast Asian tsunamis. The new campaign is to "Remind people of others in need." The Ad Council believes so strongly in the message that it is putting up $500,000 of its own resources to produce the ads rather than counting on donations from agencies and others as it typically does. The campaign's web site at www.dontalmostgive.org allows someone to see the ads and to receive tips—and reminders—to help children, animals, seniors, disaster victims, the hungry, and the homeless, and to address other challenges in the areas of safety, education, the environment, health, and community. The site provides several links to places to volunteer and donate. The campaign will also accommodate nonprofits that want to provide links for people who no longer want to "almost give."

Source: Web site materials and Brennen Jensen, "Ad Campaign Aims to Reach People Who 'Almost' Gave," *The Chronicle of Philanthropy,* October 12, 2006, p. 11.

BALANCING MISSION AND RESOURCES

The marketing strategies and tactics outlined in the preceding chapters are used to plot the course the nonprofit organization will be undertaking in both the near and longer term. The challenge then is to provide adequate resources to support them and their specific campaigns—and to provide long-term growth in their infrastructure. As Letts, Ryan, and Grossman[1] have pointed out, the last-mentioned—capacity building—is too often neglected in nonprofit organizations. Indeed, one of the values of the rise of so-called venture philanthropy is that venture philanthropists are insistent that attention be paid to both operating and capacity-building needs.

Resources to serve these needs are of three main types and sometimes they are substitutes for each other. First, nonprofit organizations need financial resources. As we have discussed previously, a challenge for nonprofit organizations is that the flow of financial support (other than direct revenues) they seek from foundations and donors is not always tied to overall mission performance. The second resource is personnel and, in the nonprofit world, this often means a significant pool of volunteers. The third—and fastest growing—source of support is from the private sector. Clearly all three sources interact. Fewer financial resources are needed if there are more volunteers or more corporate support. Corporate support may be greater if ways are developed to tie this to corporate volunteering. And, in turn, volunteer recruitment and fundraising may be more successful if corporations cooperate.

We shall devote a chapter to each of these resource challenges focusing on how to maximize them while minimizing the headaches they sometimes present. We begin with fundraising.

FINANCIAL RESOURCES

Mission Creep

Nonprofit organizations are constantly in search of financial support. Some, like Goodwill Industries and the YMCA, can rely on their own sales efforts for much of their income. Others have to find grants, donors, and partnerships to support their efforts. Sometimes the search for funds overwhelms everything else the organization tries to do, distorts its operations, and drives it away from its core mission. Some have accused organizations in the social services sector for behaving like budget maximizers. Excessive pursuit of donors and foundation grants can lead a nonprofit far afield from its motivating ideals and objectives. This phenomenon is what is known as "mission creep." An organization starts out with one set of objectives, but it sees a lucrative grant that is slightly related to its core competencies and goes after it. This gives it new capabilities and so it seeks grants even farther afield. Soon, it is difficult to understand what the organization really is. Branding certainly becomes much more challenging.

In more recent years, "mission creep" has also resulted from many nonprofits venturing into product and service marketing, much like commercial firms. The hope is that this tactic will generate revenues that the nonprofit organization can control itself and that, ideally, can free it from reliance on the whims of grant makers and politicians and the national economy. Such a pursuit can lead to both organizational distortion and bad publicity. Lawrence Small, former head of the Smithsonian

Institution, faced significant criticism for his money-raising corporate partnerships that critics said was "selling America's precious heritage to crass commercialism."

Thus a primary challenge in generating funds is to achieve an appropriate balance. We argue that this criterion is a more important measure of successful fundraising than is revenue growth or the financial success of individual campaigns and events.

Sources of Funds

The four major sources of funds for a nonprofit organization comprise several subcategories:

1. Donations
   a. Major individual cash gifts (e.g., grants, bequests, planned giving)
   b. Small gifts

2. Donations
   a. Corporate and corporate foundation cash donations (e.g., a Google Foundation grant)
   b. Non-corporate foundation cash grants (e.g., a Gates Foundation grant)
   c. Product donations

3. Self-generated revenues
   a. Sales of principal products and services (e.g., hospital charges, university tuitions, sales of oral rehydration solutions, museum gift shop revenues)
   b. Revenues from unrelated enterprises (e.g., catalog sales, Girl Scout cookies, T-shirts)
   c. Membership dues (e.g., payments to American Marketing Association, American Medical Association)
   d. Investment income

4. Partnership proceeds
   a. Cause-marketing shares (e.g., proceeds from the annual Race for the Cure)
   b. Licensing fees
   c. Web site advertising fees

Not surprisingly, different organizations have different balances of support streams. Table 15-1 ranks major charities by the amount of self-generated support as a proportion of total annual income. One of the largest fundraisers, the Salvation Army, raises about 79 percent of its income from donors whereas the YMCA gets only 16 percent of its income from donations. A number of nonprofits rely almost totally on donations. These include United Way of America and AmeriCares, which primarily raise cash donations, and Gifts in Kind International and America's Second Harvest, which rely on product donations to serve their organizational missions.

Funds with "Strings"

A principal challenge for each organization in managing different sources of funds is how to generate optimal support streams in the future while protecting the mission. Balance implies that not all revenues are equally desirable. Revenues can be

| | TABLE 15-1 | Income Sources for Top 20 Fundraisers, 2005 | | |

Rank	Organization	Private Support	Total Income	Private Support %
1.	AmeriCares Foundation	$1,315,086,789	$1,316,498,349	99.89
2.	Gifts in Kind International	$ 838,427,739	$ 842,480,186	99.52
3.	United Way of America	$4,036,163,427	$4,175,545,319	96.66
4.	American Cancer Society	$ 929,587,000	$ 977,851,000	95.06
5.	Feed the Children	$ 803,447,654	$ 851,964,213	94.31
6.	Fidelity Charitable Gift Fund	$ 891,364,989	$ 989,276,886	90.10
7.	Salvation Army	$3,595,515,000	$4,559,292,000	78.86
8.	Tulsa Community Foundation	$ 791,262,100	$1,052,762,000	75.16
9.	World Vision	$ 647,855,000	$ 905,130,000	71.58
10.	Nature Conservancy	$ 475,076,000	$ 919,113,000	51.69
11.	Habitat for Humanity International	$ 449,612,188	$ 940,508,907	47.81
12.	Boys & Girls Clubs of America	$ 630,424,832	$1,335,383,255	47.21
13.	Boy Scouts of America	$ 300,892,000	$ 836,012,000	35.99
14.	American Red Cross	$1,278,772,449	$3,888,172,726	32.89
15.	Catholic Charities	$ 646,191,894	$3,385,093,754	19.09
16.	Easter Seals	$ 151,049,000	$ 833,706,602	18.12
17.	YMCA	$ 826,046,000	$5,130,851,000	16.10
18.	Goodwill Industries	$ 413,748,000	$2,592,560,000	15.96
19.	Volunteers of America	$ 88,580,387	$ 839,435,494	10.55
20.	Lutheran Services	$ 723,253,495	$9,500,000,000	7.61

Source: The Chronicle of Philanthropy, The Philanthropy 400, 2005. Reprinted with permission of *The Chronicle of Philanthropy,* philanthropy.com.

undesirable for one of two reasons: They may distort the mission and they may not be cost-effective. This can happen due to external factors and internal factors.

1. *External causes.* An example of a problematic external influence is when a donor dangles large amounts of money with strings attached. The donor will give funding to a museum, but it must "improve the 'good taste' of its exhibits," which may restrict what a curator thinks is relevant. A donor will endow a chair at a university but insists on having final say on who holds the chair. A drug company will fund university research but states that research results may not be published for five years. In each case, the nonprofit is tempted to move in a direction it did not want or, perhaps more critically, forced to compromise its standards and ethics in order to get the financial support.

2. *Internal causes.* Many nonprofits that rely extensively on foundation grants live a fluctuating and anxiety-prone existence. Staff is assigned to projects funded by grants and risk losing their jobs if the grant is not renewed. Much of foundation funding is short run (one to three years) and may or may not be renewable (and, even if it is renewable, it must be "competed"—that is, it might go to someone else). The organization then has both the pressure to grow and the pressure not to shrink and to have to lay off valued friends and coworkers. The one-year or three-year cycle also means that the nonprofit must focus on short-range

accomplishments to report to the funder rather than long-run impact. As noted earlier, this also leads an organization to "chase grants" where the organization may have some competency, some personal connection, or some small reason to believe a proposal might succeed. Although this may keep staff employed and the organization afloat, like rich desserts, grants that are off-mission may be immensely satisfying in the short run but very damaging in the long run if relied on for continual nourishment.

Funds That Cost Too Much

Some revenue sources may be undesirable because they cost more to generate than they bring in. Again, the causes may be internal and external.

1. *External causes.* Many promoters come to nonprofits with good ideas for fundraising. These can include both fast-talking con artists and legitimate corporations. Many rock concerts that promise to be high-profile moneymakers turn out to have unexpectedly high costs—including fees to the promoter that, when accompanied by negative publicity about fans being ripped off, are not worth the undertaking. Many corporate partnerships turn out to be extremely time-consuming such that if the opportunity cost of the nonprofit's staff time is included, the venture would be clearly unprofitable. (Still, it is not uncommon for nonprofits to put up with such off-book costs in the hopes that the investment in personal corporate connections will yield future, more profitable alliances.)

2. *Internal causes.* A great many nonprofits are tempted to think they can generate great amounts of revenue by selling products largely unrelated to their core businesses.[2] These can range from T-shirts and mugs to extensive lines of clothing, gift items, or products closely related to their main business. They can prove to be good revenue sources but also can be distractions or, at worst, disasters. For example, in the 1980s one of the authors investigated attempts by several nonprofit family planning organizations worldwide to add over-the-counter health products like facial tissues and medications to the distribution systems they had built for their condoms, pills, and other contraceptive products. What they found was that they simply could not compete with the private sector and lost considerable time and money.

With this caveat in mind, we now turn to the marketing challenges involved in generating the two major revenue streams for most nonprofits: fundraising and revenue generation.

FUNDRAISING

It is commonly heard among top executives of nonprofit organizations that they feel they spend too much time on fundraising and not enough time on their main mission. This is, in part, because the two are often only minimally related. One might think that the better that the organization performed on its mission, the more money it would raise. But fundraising levels are often more a function of such things as:

- The performance of the stock market
- The involvement—or absence—of celebrity endorsers

- The scope and excitement—and media coverage—of an annual event, such as a footrace, banquet, and so forth
- The time the nonprofit CEO puts into raising donations
- The whims of major givers

Still, raising funds must be an organization—and CEO—priority.

The total amount of charitable money raised by all organizations in the United States in 2005 according to *Giving USA 2006*[3] was $260.45 billion—a gain of 28 percent since 2000. Seventy-six percent of these contributions came from *individuals* ($199.07 billion), with the remainder coming from *bequests* ($17.44 billion), *foundations* ($30.00 billion), and *corporations* ($13.77 billion). By far, the largest proportion of the money ($93.18 billion or 35.8 percent) was raised by religious organizations; the rest was raised by educational institutions ($38.56 billion), health-related groups ($22.54 billion), human services organizations ($25.36 billion), groups concerned with arts, culture, and the humanities ($13.51 billion), public and societal benefit organizations ($14.03 billion), environment and wildlife organizations ($8.86 billion), international affairs organizations ($6.39 billion), foundations ($21.7 billion), and other groups ($16.15 billion). The international affairs organizations show the greatest growth, doubling in importance. This is undoubtedly attributable to the growing tensions around the world and to greater attention to international issues such as HIV/AIDS and hunger.

A major source of the increase in all gifts in 2005 was the attention of individuals and corporations to disaster relief. The GivingUSA Foundation estimated that $7.37 billion went to meet these challenges. Corporations provided 19 percent of this total, almost four times their overall rate of giving. About one-quarter of proceeds from both sources went to tsunami and earthquake relief and the rest to Katrina aid.

Customer-Centered Fundraising

Nonprofit organizations typically pass through three stages of marketing orientation in their thinking about how to raise funds effectively—similar to the stages described in Chapter 1.

- *Product orientation stage.* Here the prevailing attitude is "We have a good cause; people ought to support us." Many churches and colleges operate on this concept. Money is raised primarily by the top officers through an "old boy network." The organization relies on volunteers to help raise additional funds. A few loyal donors supply most of the funds. Glamorous events are primary tools—simply giving donors a chance to meet a celebrity, participate in a race or banquet, and so on where the nonprofit organization can "tell its story." The mindset is one that says "we have a good offering. There is a real need. We just need to tell people about our work and our plans."
- *Sales orientation stage.* Here the prevailing attitude is "There is a lot of competition out there. People are usually reluctant to give. If we want to grow, we're going to have be much more aggressive!" The institution appoints a "hard-charging" development director who hires a staff that is given specific assignments and target numbers. The staff raises money from all possible sources, typically using a "hard sell" approach or dramatic emotional appeals

featuring emaciated children in Ethiopia, AIDS patients on their deathbeds, hurricane and earthquake victims, and so on. Efforts are put into clever advertising. The fundraisers have little influence on the institution's policies or personality because their job is to raise money, not improve the organization. A majority of large nonprofit organizations are in this stage.

- *Customer orientation stage.* Here the prevailing attitude is "Like all marketers, our challenge is to understand the needs and wants of our target market and then figure out how to meet them." A signal that an organization has shifted from a sales to a customer orientation in its fundraising is when it spends significant time trying to understand donors and potential donors to see what they might be seeking.

One of the authors sought to redirect a regional office of the United Way of America from being organization-centered to being customer-centered in the 1980s. At that point, the United Way marketing approach might be described as "You ought to give to us because we are supporting all these very good charities like the Girl Scouts and your local homeless shelter!" However, they were experiencing difficulties reaching and influencing the rapidly growing class of young professionals who were not part of large old-line corporations where one gave through payroll deduction. Interviews with members of this target market revealed clearly that the United Way did not really understand its needs and wants and was certainly not positioning itself to meet those needs.

What the interviews showed was that these young professionals looked upon charitable giving much like their other investments. In the main, they wanted to give back to their communities and support some of the organizations that they thought were doing meritorious work. However, they were unsure how much they should give and how to distribute it across the various charities they were considering. These individuals were accustomed to investing in the stock market where they could get a lot of data and much advice. They could choose individual stocks that met their portfolio needs or they could choose one or more of hundreds of mutual funds that would spread their risk. To them, charitable "investing" was nothing similar—and so many just made token gifts and tended to repeat patterns established years earlier.

As a result of this investigation and an analysis of the United Way's strengths and weaknesses in influencing this market, the following recommendations were made:

1. The United Way should reposition itself from being a collection agency for its charity partners to being a "Charity Investment Counselor." As part of its fund allocation process, the United Way accumulated a great deal of information about all of the major charities in its communities (i.e., the ones that had asked for funding). It was just the kind of data—and expertise—that the young professionals said they were seeking.

2. It needed to abandon its tradition (at the time) of not giving donors any choice. Consistent with its self-image, the United Way of America believed that it knew best what was needed in its community and therefore donors should just trust it to use donations wisely.

3. Rather than one take-it-or-leave-it portfolio of charities, it should offer distinctive "Charitable Mutual Funds" around themes significant to blocks of donors. Thus it could have a "mutual fund" comprised of charities concerned with the elderly or

FIGURE 15-1   Workplace Giving Poster

Source: Courtesy of United Way of America

with children. There could be "mutual funds" built around the poor or minorities or around education. The funds could be tested; the ones that are desired would then be retained while the "losers" would be disbanded and their charities absorbed elsewhere or into a "general fund."

4. Extensive resources should be put into reporting back to donors. Young professionals were accustomed to tracking their portfolios without delay, but their experience with most charities was that they would hear from them every once in a while and then often with information that did not speak to their interests. Among other advantages, the mutual fund approach would allow the United Way to identify the interests of donors and provide them with personally relevant feedback much more likely to build long-term mutually satisfying relationships.

Of course, change took a very long time to happen. The United Way of America is a very large organization with an elaborate chapter structure with significant local autonomy. It was also handicapped by the fact that campaign leadership turned over each year—and, in fact, was a major plum for local corporate executives. However, some local chapters, such as Southern Pennsylvania, did experiment with the "Mutual Fund" concept. Over time, in part because of new competitive pressures and internal scandals, the United Way began to offer donor choice in most chapters around the country. This is now the organization's approach system-wide.

The United Way is constantly seeking new ways to engage donors. However, its strength continues to be workplace giving, from which it gets the majority of its funds (see Figure 15-1).

FUNDRAISING IN THE TWENTY-FIRST CENTURY

When nonprofit organizations start up, they tend to seek support from one or two sources, often wealthy individuals or friendly foundations. As organizations grow, they (1) diversify their donor bases, (2) shift from periodic fundraising efforts to year-round programs, (3) hire specialists in fundraising, (4) develop extensive databases for tracking donors and donor prospects, and (5) seek increasingly imaginative means to help people and organizations give—including elaborate, tax-friendly estate-planning options.

The fundraising environment has seen a number of significant innovations grow in the twenty-first century. Principal among these are Internet options for individual donors, the emergence of charitable mutual funds from organizations like Fidelity and Charles Schwab, and the rise of so-called "venture philanthropists." The Fidelity Investments Charitable Gift Fund is now one of the largest private fundraisers. And venture philanthropists like Mario Morino and George Roberts, who became millionaires in the high-tech or investment communities, have established organizations like Venture Philanthropy Partners and the Roberts Foundation that "invest" in nonprofits, treating them like entrepreneurial ventures. The venture philanthropists seek to build portfolios of promising organizations and then, rather than stand aside and hope for good outcomes, directly intervene with management assistance and insist on tough reporting standards to monitor performance.[4]

Another trend has been the emergence of very large gifts. Bill Gates's substantial gifts to start his own foundation set the standard here. He has been followed in recent years by wealthy entrepreneurs like Warren Buffet and Richard Branson. Their mammoth gifts have allowed foundations to focus on longer term and programmatic needs. For example, the Gates Foundation gave a massive $150 million grant to the Vaccine Fund in Washington in 2005 to address rampant diseases like polio and measles around the world. Large gifts have also been flowing to universities as executives who prospered in the post-World War II economic boom have retired and sought to leave an academic legacy—including named buildings and prestigious chairs. Harvard University is now the third largest nonprofit organization in terms of total income.

UNDERSTANDING SOURCES OF FUNDS

An organization can tap into a variety of sources for contributions. The four major donor markets are *foundations, corporations, government,* and *individuals.*

Foundations

According to *The Foundation Center,* in 2004 there were 67,736 foundations in the United States, a 29 percent increase over 2000. The foundations controlled $510 billion in assets.[5] They fall into the following groups:

1. *Independent foundations* are set up to support a wide range of activities and are usually run by a professional staff. There were 60,031 of these foundations in 2004 holding $425 billion in assets and giving out $23 billion in grants. Independent foundations include large well-known organizations such as the John D. and Catherine T. MacArthur Foundation and the Ford and Rockefeller Foundations, which support a wide range of causes as well as more specialized foundations that give money in a particular area, such as in health (Robert Wood Johnson Foundation) or education (Carnegie Foundation).

2. *Corporate foundations* are set up by corporations and are allowed to give away up to 5 percent of the corporation's adjusted gross income. There were 2,596 corporate foundations in 2004, holding over $16.6 billion in assets and giving out $3.4 billion in grants.

3. *Community foundations* are set up as vehicles for pooling bequests from many private local sources, including individuals, corporations, foundations, and nonprofit organizations. This is one of the fastest growing areas of giving although the numbers are still small. There were 4,409 community foundations in 2004 holding over $38.8 billion in assets and giving out $2,164 million in grants. The number of community foundations has grown more than eightfold since 2000.

The 10 foundations that gave away the most money in 2005 are listed in Table 15-2. Foundation giving overall has nearly tripled since 1995.

There are two recent trends that nonprofit organizations that seek foundation grants need to follow. The first is increased government scrutiny of foundation and nonprofit governance. Recently, Barry Munitz was forced to resign as executive director of the huge J. Paul Getty Trust after criticism emerged of his $1.2 million salary and perks such as a $72,000 Porsche.[6] To combat such excesses, foundations—and nonprofits generally—are being urged to consider adopting the provisions of the

TABLE 15-2	Ten Largest Foundations in Terms of Awards Paid in 2005
Foundation	*Grants*
Bill & Melinda Gates Foundation	$1,355,279,478
Ford Foundation	$ 532,579,756
Robert Wood Johnson Foundation	$ 372,860,000
William and Flora Hewlitt Foundation	$ 319,012,992
Annenberg Foundation	$ 251,663,628
W. K. Kellogg Foundation	$ 219,862,847
Gordon and Betty Moore Foundation	$ 218,882,706
Andrew W. Mellon Foundation	$ 199,300,000
John D. and Catherine T. MacArthur Foundation	$ 193,000,000
David and Lucille Packard Foundation	$ 176,137,000

Source: *The Chronicle of Philanthropy,* March 23, 2006. Reprinted with permission of *The Chronicle of Philanthropy,* philanthropy.com.

Sarbanes-Oxley legislation for corporations passed by Congress in 2002 after the Enron scandal. This will require nonprofits to be much more transparent as they seek outside support.

Second, there is concern that the Patriot Act may add another factor to the fundraising challenge for some nonprofits. The Patriot Act was passed in the aftermath of the September 11, 2001, terrorist attacks and made it illegal to support individuals and organizations supporting terrorism. This has raised caution among nonprofits and foundations doing charitable work in places like the Middle East and North Korea. Arrests have been made under the act. The Holy Land Foundation for Relief and Development and seven officials were charged in 2004 with providing over $12 million over six years to alleged Palestinian terrorist groups.[7] Organizations such as the Asia Foundation must be particularly careful as they support projects affecting North Korea—a member of the "Axis of Evil" and recent member of the Nuclear Club. Other foundations, like the Ford Foundation, that give money to Palestinian groups have come under fire from Jewish organizations. Subsequently, Ford restructured many grants to support joint efforts by Israeli and Palestinian groups to work towards peace.[8]

Tapping into Foundation Grants

With over 67,000 foundations, it is important for the nonprofit manager in charge of grant-seeking to know how to locate the few that would be the most likely to support a given project or cause. Fortunately, there are many resources available for researching foundations. Most of these can be searched on the Internet. An important resource is the Foundation Center, a nonprofit organization with research centers in New York, Washington, DC, and Chicago, which collects and distributes information on foundations. Similar databases are maintained by *The Chronicle of Philanthropy.*

The first step in seeking foundation grants is finding a match between the foundation's interests and scale of operation and that of the nonprofit. Too often a small nonprofit organization will send a proposal to the Ford Foundation because it would like to get the support of this well-known foundation. However, the Ford Foundation only accepts about 1 out of every 100 proposals and may be less disposed toward helping small nonprofit organizations than more regional or specialized foundations would be. The Gates Foundation makes small grants but it is very focused on programmatic priorities (global development, global health, social inequities in the United States, particularly education) and strengthening the charitable sector. The Gates Foundation—as do others—provides a searchable database for its grants (www.gatesfoundation.org/Search/default.htm).

After identifying a few foundations that might have strong interest in a project, the nonprofit organization should try to estimate more accurately the foundation's likely level of interest before investing a lot of time in grant preparation. Most foundations are willing to respond to a simple, straightforward letter of inquiry, telephone call, or personal visit and indicate how interested they would be in a project. The foundation officer may be very encouraging or discouraging and may suggest ways in which the nonprofit's interests may match those of the foundation. If the foundation appears receptive, the fund-seeking nonprofit can then make an investment in preparing an elaborate proposal for this foundation. However, as we noted earlier, it is extremely important that the nonprofit make sure that, in the course of adapting a proposal to a foundation's interests, the organization not distort its mission.

Writing successful grant proposals is becoming a fine art, with many guides currently available to help the grant seeker, including sources on the World Wide Web.[9] The larger foundations will have clear guidelines and will usually make these available on their web site. Each proposal should contain at least the following elements:

1. *A cover letter* describing the history of the proposal; its title; a one-sentence overview; who has been contacted, if anyone, in the foundation; and the kinds and levels of support being sought
2. *The proposal,* describing the project, its uniqueness, and its importance
3. *The budget* for the project
4. *The personnel* working on the project, along with their resumes

This is, of course, simply another occasion for effective marketing. Each solicitation is a "campaign" as discussed in Chapter 3. Thus it ought to begin with the right mindset and then a thorough "listening" to the target audience (i.e., careful formative research of the foundation). As always, the right mindset is to be customer-driven. Target audiences in this case (i.e., foundations) make grants because it is in *their* interest. A fundamental mistake many grant seekers make is to ask for the grant because the grant seeker needs and wants it. But the foundation knows this—what it will be asking is this: Compared to the many other solicitations we receive, is this a good way for us to invest our limited funds?

The challenge, therefore, is to conduct formative research in order to understand as thoroughly as possible a foundation's interests and "needs." Many foundations describe their broad funding priorities on their web site, and in their annual reports or press releases. A review of recent grants given (available from the Foundation Center or *The Chronicle of Philanthropy*) will indicate preferences and priorities. Conversations with recent grantees can also be instructive.

An important piece of information to learn in this process is the relative importance of typical criteria for projects that are clearly within the foundation's areas of interest. These data have clear implications for the "campaign." Typical criteria include the following:

1. *Track record.* Most foundations prefer to bet on likely winners and, in such cases, the proposal marketer should stress, if possible, his or her organization's longevity and previous successes.
2. *Quality of staff.* In the absence of a track record—and/or in addition to one— foundations may look at the credentials and character of key personnel. This can be a matter of providing impressive resumes (or taking on board consultants with impressive resumes) or promoting a charismatic leader. It is said that many foundations like to give to *people* as much as to good ideas. If this is the case, the organization should send its highest-ranking, most impressive officials to the foundation.
3. *Ability to measure results.* In the twenty-first century, more and more foundations want to see potential grantees indicate clearly how they are going to track performance. Monitoring systems of the type described in Chapter 19 are crucial.
4. *Generalizability.* Many foundations have significant communications staffs whose task it is to disseminate to others findings from the work of their grantees. These can be research findings or data on best practices. The grantee's campaign can anticipate this step by making clear how the results are likely to have relevance far beyond the relatively narrow focus of the specific undertaking.
5. *Governance.* A granting agency these days is going to look carefully at how a nonprofit organization governs itself. It will want to make sure that its support is not used inappropriately or will result in unfavorable publicity.

Marketing to foundations should not be solely a matter of conducting specific grant-seeking campaigns. Nonprofit organizations that plan to have foundation grants as a continuing source of revenue need to develop an overall organization strategy based on long-term relationships with key foundations. They should not contact foundations only on the occasion of a specific proposal. Each organization should cultivate a handful of appropriate foundations in advance of specific proposals. In the private sector, this is called "relationship marketing." One major university sees the Ford Foundation as a "key customer account." The development officer arranges for various people within the university to get to know people at corresponding levels within the foundation. One or more members of the university's board arrange to see corresponding board members of the foundation each year. The university president visits the foundation's president each year for a luncheon or dinner. One or more members of the university's development staff cultivate relations with foundation staff members at their levels. When the university has a proposal, it knows exactly who should present it to the foundation and who to see in the foundation. Furthermore, the foundation is more favorably disposed toward the organization because of the long relationship and special understanding they enjoy. Finally, the organization is able to do a better job of tracking the proposal as it is being reviewed by the foundation.

Corporations

Business organizations represent another distinct source of foundation funds for nonprofit organizations. There are now nearly 2,600 corporate foundations. However, according to the Foundation Center the corporate proportion of total giving has declined since the 1980s, perhaps as a result of their shift to such tactics as cause-related marketing.[10] Drug companies are typically the most active givers, making a major portion of their giving in the form of pharmaceutical products. Microsoft also gives away a good deal of product in the form of software. The 12 corporations with the largest giving of both cash and products in 2005 according to *The Chronicle of Philanthropy* were the following (in $1,000s):[11]

Pfizer	$1,618,100
Merck	$1,039,000
Bristol-Meyers Squibb	$ 758,903
Johnson & Johnson	$ 591,926
Microsoft	$ 334,000
Time-Warner	$ 293,772
Wal-Mart	$ 273,314
Altria	$ 189,761
General Electric	$ 171,149
IBM	$ 148,500
Target	$ 147,649
Safeway	$ 146,000

Some corporations give a significant number of donations outside the United States.

Merck & Company	$450,420,000
Pfizer	$410,000,000
Bristol-Myers Squibb	$103,021,537
Microsoft Corporation	$ 65,600,000
ExxonMobil Corporation	$ 51,696,000
IBM	$ 45,500,000
General Electric Company	$ 43,345,722
Citigroup	$ 37,455,450
Chevron	$ 35,100,000
Altria Group	$ 31,101,499

Education and societal benefits/public affairs are the two largest recipient areas, capturing almost half the total corporate giving.

Corporate giving has changed dramatically in recent years. As Craig Smith points out,[12] at the turn of the century corporate philanthropy was the special province of corporate barons like Morgan and Rockefeller, who decided on their own which favorite charities would benefit from business-generated profits. The corporations themselves did not have giving programs, believing that society did not want them to be involved in social issues. In the 1950s, barriers to such involvement were removed, and corporations began to establish major giving programs. Recently, strong pressures from stockholders and the competitive marketplace forced corporations to become leaner and more efficient. This caused firms to rethink their approach to philanthropy. Smith identified a new paradigm, now labeled "strategic philanthropy," in which companies have come to think of philanthropy as a *competitive weapon*. As Weeden and others have pointed out, corporations have learned that they can "do well by doing good." As we shall discuss further in Chapter 17, strategic philanthropy can meet a number of corporate goals:

- Changing the image of an organization, as when AT&T's sponsorship of the arts changed it from dull and boring to sophisticated and upscale[13]
- Building alliances that give the corporation public support in times of crises such as ecological disasters or product problems
- Creating awareness and interest in the organization for future customers and future employees
- Providing a means of binding together employees and distributors in projects that elevate their job time to working on something "bigger" than merely making money
- Producing increased sales, as when American Express or Coca-Cola engages in cause-related marketing (discussed later in this chapter)

Corporations have also become more active in involving their own workers in community and social projects. Corporations now have significant volunteer programs (as described in Chapter 16). And many also have active "matching gift programs." A study of 1,007 companies by the Council for Advancement and Support of Education in 2000 found that 51 percent matched employee gifts to at least one non-educational organization the previous year. There are usually minimum and maximum levels set. Employee gift matching is particularly strong for educational initiatives.[14]

Philanthropy has also become a tool of international competition. Foreign companies such as Hitachi have established foundations in the United States, and many U.S. companies with international operations are beginning giving programs abroad. Craig Smith argues that in markets such as Brazil and Hungary where philanthropy is weak at present, real opportunities exist for U.S. corporations to obtain differential advantages.

Donor Advised Funds

Corporations often use donor-advised funds. This form grew 20 percent from 2004 to 2005.[15] Charitable giving tax laws require that gifts by individuals and corporations at least give the appearance of being under the control of the charity recipient. However, donors can "advise" how these funds are used. Donor-advised funds are major vehicles for corporations and for securing estate funds in that the donor can get immediate tax benefits and advise their use over a future period. The Fidelity Charitable Gift Fund is just such a vehicle and has grown very large.

Donor-advised funds have proven to be an important vehicle for international donations. Individuals and corporations cannot get tax deductions if they give directly to foreign charities or non-governmental organizations. However, they can give a donor-advised gift to a U.S. charity like United Way International and achieve the desired outcome.

Approaches

Seeking grants from corporations and their foundations is, conceptually, no different from the approach recommended for independent foundations. Of the 2,600 business foundations that might be approached, relatively few are appropriate to any specific nonprofit organization. The best prospects for corporate fundraising will be those where the nonprofit can easily demonstrate that it provides the corporation with strategic payoffs. Such corporations are likely to have one or more of the following characteristics:

1. *Local corporations.* Corporations located in the same area as the nonprofit organization are likely to see direct benefits to it and its staff from grantmaking. A hospital, for example, can base its appeal on the health care it offers to the corporation's employees, and a performing arts group can argue that its cultural offerings improve the local climate and thus help corporations attract and keep top-flight talent. Further, it is logistically easier to build long-term corporate relationships where corporate and nonprofit executives can find time for cultivation off the job.
2. *Kindred activities.* Corporations located in a field kindred to the nonprofit organization's are excellent prospects. Hospitals can effectively solicit funds from pharmaceutical companies, and colleges can attract funds from companies that hire many of their graduates.
3. *Personal relationships or contacts.* Nonprofit organizations should review their personal contacts to obtain clues to which corporations they might solicit. A university's board of trustees consists of influential individuals who can open many doors for corporate solicitations. Corporations tend to respond to peer influence in their giving. It is a maxim of fundraising that people do not give to institutions or causes: *People give to people.* This is especially true in corporate fundraising. As Austin points out, many valuable long-term relationships between corporations like Starbucks and Timberland first began through personal acquaintance.[16]
4. *Structural similarity.* Nonprofits with a national or international scope should seek out corporations that match them structurally. Thus Coca-Cola developed a partnership with Boys & Girls Clubs of America, in part because they both catered to the teen market and in part because they both have an organizational structure comprised of a headquarters and multiple local independent operators (club branches and franchised bottlers).

Nonprofits that rely heavily on corporate support must constantly keep up on changes in corporate philosophy toward philanthropy. In the twenty-first century, there has been a good deal of interest in "wiring the world" through Internet and cell phone technology. Among corporations taking leadership here are Intel, Cisco, and Microsoft.

Community Foundations

As previously noted, community foundations are the fastest growing sector of the foundation world. They have risen as a means for corporations, individuals, and civic groups to pool their gifts to serve local needs.[17] Their assets grew 13.5 percent in 2004 and giving rose 15 percent. They are particularly valuable targets for nonprofit organizations with local or regional focuses such as on health, safety, and the environment.

Government

While not strictly foundations, many government agencies at the federal, state, and local levels can be major sources of funds in that they are able to make grants to worthwhile causes. For example, many years ago, the federal government set up the National Endowment for the Arts (NEA) to make grants to support museums, ballet companies, art groups, and other arts organizations, large and small. Other government agencies make grants to support health care, university teaching and research, social services, and other worthwhile causes. Web sites announcing government requests for proposals (RFPs) are routinely watched by organizations that have projects of likely interest to government agencies.

Government agencies normally require the most detailed paperwork in preparing proposals. They tend to place the main weight on the proposal's probable contribution to the public interest as well as the agency's own agenda. Reputation of the proposing agency is important while personal relations between the agency and grantee are less determinative. Nonprofits with good performance records can often successfully "recompete" for extensions of current grants.

Individual Givers

Individuals are the major source of all charitable giving. Individual gifts accounted for 76.5 percent of the total in 2005 with giving through bequests adding an additional 6.7 percent. Individual giving has doubled since 1980 (adjusted for inflation) Bequests more than tripled through 2000. However, they have dropped significantly in the last five years, in part because of a decline in the number of deaths and because of a decline in household assets.

Characteristics

Robert Sharpe suggests that individual givers can be divided into three groups based on their life cycle stage and giving patterns:[18]

- *The early years.* Up to age 50, potential donors are absorbed in establishing their families and their careers. They have limited discretionary income; when they do give, it is in relatively small amounts. They are regular givers, often to their churches or synagogues. They give cash and sometimes property.
- *The middle years.* Between 50 and 70 years of age, donors are at a stage where they are relatively settled. The children have been through college and most major assets are paid off. Regular giving continues during this period, but middle-year households are beginning to be candidates for making large gifts for the special needs of a nonprofit organization. These households could buy a new van for the YMCA, endow a scholarship at a local college, or underwrite a major fundraising event.
- *The later years.* Households with members over the age of 70 are prime candidates for giving what Sharpe calls "the Ultimate Gift." They are less likely to be regular givers because their incomes are shrinking. They can, however, be approached for bequests and other forms of planned giving.

The distribution of the population across these three categories in the early twenty-first century is affected by the baby boom, which has resulted in relatively fewer households in the middle years category than was the case in earlier periods. This pattern will soon change, however, and fundraising prospects should improve. Other interesting findings about individual giving are these:

- About two-thirds of all families gave to charity in 2002, averaging $1,872. Their major recipients were:
  - Religion, 60 percent
  - The needy, 11 percent

- Combined charitable purposes, 10 percent
- Health and education, 5 percent each[19]
- Female millionaires give more generously than their male counterparts.[20]
- Perceptions that minority groups give less are misplaced. Lower giving rates on their part are more attributable to lower income, education, and wealth.[21]
- "Giving Circles" are becoming more common. These circles involve individuals pooling their charitable gifts and acting like foundations. A study by New Ventures in Philanthropy found that giving circles had different priorities than traditional foundations, focusing more on youth development, women's and girl's issues, and mental health/crisis intervention.
- Community foundations have led to greater giving among rural donors who now have a way to help their local communities.[22]

Motives

There are many lists of motives for giving. And, of course, the relevant motives will vary by the type of organization—for example, programs for the poor versus support for the Kennedy Center. They also will depend on the type of gift—an annual drive, a bequest, an offer of goods or services, and the donor—young/old, male/female, individual/couple, etc. Adrian Sargeant suggests the following as commonly found:[23]

Altruism
Sympathy
Empathy
In memorium
Relief of a negative state
Self esteem/Self interest
Guilt
Pity
Social /Distributive justice
Fear
Prestige
Making a difference
Reciprocation—paying back
Insurance

One of the reasons people give is that they "feel strongly about the cause." However, this reason is even more important for wealthy individuals. Online studies by Harris Interactive also established important differences between men and women in motivations. In the study, women were more likely to give because of a health problem of a family member or friend while men (and wealthy Americans of both sexes) emphasized tax benefits. Women are more likely to give to health charities and women's organizations and men to sports and recreation. The wealthy give more than the general population to educational institutions, health organizations, arts or cultural organizations, and organizations involved in political advocacy. Selected results are reported in Table 15-3.

In health care, a larger part of the differences in giving levels across health problem areas is attributable to interest in specific health problems, particularly about

TABLE 15-3   Reasons for Giving by Gender and Wealth Status

	Women (%)	*Men (%)*	*Wealthy (%)*	*All (%)*
Why People Give				
Feel strongly about the cause	59	59	74	59
Personal experience with the organization	38	41	55	40
Tax benefit	18	36	54	28
Response to specific request	22	28	46	25
Moral imperative—the right thing to do	43	50	42	47
Involvement of family member, friend, coworker	32	35	38	33
Religion, spirituality	36	37	37	36
Charity event	25	27	35	26
Illness of family member, friend, coworker	39	22	30	30
Family tradition	17	14	21	16
Tithing	18	23	17	21
News or media story	20	11	16	15
New wealth	8	3	14	5
Business connection	5	4	13	4
Where People Give				
Educational institutions	28	33	53	30
Children and youth services	41	47	52	44
Health and medical charities	45	35	51	40
Religious and faith-based organizations	47	50	45	49
Homeless or low-income services	37	32	36	35
Disaster relief organizations	21	26	35	24
Arts or cultural organizations	11	16	35	14
Political or advocacy organizations	11	17	32	14
Disability organizations	31	30	31	30
Elderly or aging services	25	17	25	21
Animal-rights groups	28	21	24	24
Environmental groups	12	14	22	13
Sports or recreational groups	13	20	21	16
Women's organizations	20	7	21	14
Civil-rights groups	9	10	16	9
Family planning or child-rearing organizations	12	5	10	8

Source: Elizabeth Greene, "Study Finds Differences in Giving Patterns between Wealthy Men and Women," *The Chronicle of Philanthropy,* May 3, 2001, pp. 12–15. Reprinted with permission of *The Chronicle of Philanthropy,* philanthropy.com.

the disease's *severity, prevalence,* and *remediability.* Thus, heart disease and cancer are severe diseases—they kill—whereas arthritis and most birth defects are considered less serious since they do not kill. Cancer has a higher prevalence than muscular dystrophy and therefore attracts more support. Finally, people believe that cures or preventions are possible for heart disease and less so for birth defects, which leads to more giving to heart disease.

When a nonprofit organization plans a fundraising campaign aimed at individuals, it needs to begin with a clear sense of why people give in general and then why they do—or might—give to them. We argue that most often individuals give in order to get something back. In other words, donations should not be viewed as a *gift* but as a *transaction* where the nonprofit offers significant benefits that the donor wants and the donor "pays" with his or her donation. The question is, what does—or could—the donor *get?*

Is there such a thing as giving without "getting" (i.e., pure altruism)? Some people give and say that they expect nothing back. But, in our view, actually they most likely privately enjoy the self-esteem of being "big enough" to give money without requiring recognition. The *New York Times* recently made the following comment:

> People get several things from acting altruistically. There's the enlightened self-interest: the needy may feel they are more likely to receive help when they themselves are in trouble. Then there is the inner glow that comes from acting according to one's ideals: be it giving to needy children or to church on Sunday. Having a good deed known also has its own glory, as well as avoiding the stigma of not contributing when everyone else in the congregation, alumni association or social club has.[24]

A problem for a great many nonprofit organizations that do *not* have a customer orientation is that they attempt to solicit funds by telling potential donors that *the organization* needs the money. They describe at great length and with enthusiasm all the good work the organization does and then point out how much more could be done if only they had more funds. They have the fundraising transaction exactly backward. They try to motivate giving to meet the organization's needs. But, as the BCOS model introduced in Chapter 4 makes clear, people (i.e., donors) take actions to meet their own needs. Fundraisers need to find out what each target audience wants and then show them how the proposed action (i.e., donating) meets *their* needs.

These motivations reflect the benefits and influence of others specified in the BCOS model. However, that model also points out the importance of the perceived costs of the donation. It is important to also understand what potential donors think might be the negatives of giving—is it giving up some other expenditure, being identified as "an easy mark" for other solicitors, or perhaps feeling that they have given to an organization that will waste their money? If such costs are identified, the fundraiser must address them, not just (as is typical) try to overpower them by emphasizing benefits.

The BCOS model also emphasizes the importance of self-assurance. Many donors may feel that, despite the worthiness of a cause, they cannot give because they just don't know how to manage the expenditure financially. Fundraisers who solicit major gifts have many devices to cope with these concerns. However, financing help may also be important for the low-income person solicited in an annual drive.

TYPES OF INDIVIDUAL FUNDRAISING

Fundraising at the individual level for larger nonprofit organizations is typically divided into annual giving, major giving, and planned giving. We will discuss each of these in turn.

Annual Giving

Although some new nonprofit organizations rely heavily on a few principal donors to keep them going in the early years, eventually most charitable organizations come to rely on annual giving campaigns as the bedrock of their fundraising activities. As pointed out by several authors,[25] a number of basic components must be present for an effective annual giving campaign: (1) strong volunteer leadership and staff support, (2) clear organization structure, (3) ambitious but realistic goals, (4) careful segmentation of donors and prospects, (5) extensive prior research, (6) thorough training of volunteer solicitors, (7) a detailed timetable of activities and mileposts, (8) extensive reports and accountability, (9) donor and volunteer recognition, (10) online giving options, and (11) building of lifetime donors. We address several of these challenges next.

Leadership

Most nonprofits rely on volunteers to lead and staff their annual fund drives. This approach not only provides large numbers of solicitors, but it also is a way of binding those solicitors more closely to the organization. For the campaign to be effective, strong, dedicated leadership among these volunteers is necessary. Annual fund drive leaders typically emerge from the ranks of past volunteers. They are often community leaders or nationally known figures. In many cases, they are senior members of the organization's board of directors. Although the leadership task is very demanding, it is one often sought after by up-and-coming business and professional people for the prestige and networking it affords.

This volunteer leadership must be fully backed by a cadre of professional staffers who will (1) ensure that the volunteers have the information they need to take effective action, (2) maintain continuity between each program stage, and (3) prepare the reports and other materials used to track performance. Senior management must be cautious so that rivalries among professional staff and volunteers do not emerge in the heat of a high-pressure campaign.

Organization

Today, most major annual campaigns use multiple approaches to raising money. There may be direct mail, telephone solicitations, personal contact, fundraising events, telethons, and imaginative use of the Internet and the organization's own web site, as well as web sites of cooperating partners or intermediaries. Under the general guidance of a campaign committee, specific individuals are made responsible for each of these tactical areas. In many sophisticated campaigns, workers within telephone and person-to-person solicitation divisions may be further organized into groups responsible for specific geographic areas or particular professions. Thus one group may be responsible for telephoning every household on the Upper East Side while another group might be responsible for personal solicitation among lawyers. Obviously, there is a careful attempt to match the skills and personalities of volunteer fundraisers to the tasks they are likely to do best. Team captains and subcaptains are often employed to ensure continuity and increase motivation and enthusiasm among the field workers. Captains often rise upward to become campaign CEOs of the future.

Goals

Setting the annual campaign goals, overall and for each segment and tactic, is one of the most important tasks of any annual campaign committee. Goal setting is usually preceded by a careful environmental scan. The committee begins with the previous year's performance: Were goals met? Why or why not? What changes have taken place in the social and economic environment? Have there been plant layoffs, an economic downturn, or wage freezes? What is the competitive situation? Are new charities coming on the horizon? Does the local university or art museum have a special campaign planned this year that will drain funds from major corporate and individual donors? All of these considerations are investigated so that the campaign committee can set goals that have the following characteristics:

- *Realistic.* They must be *attainable* by campaign workers or else the workers will be discouraged at the outset.
- *Motivating.* They should be just beyond the current reach of the workers so that the workers will try especially hard to reach them.
- *Clear.* Specific numeric target amounts should be set for each specific component.
- *Benchmarked.* Goals should be set for various stages of the campaign so that workers will know if they are on target for achieving overall goals or whether extra effort is necessary.
- *Assigned.* Each goal should be assigned to a specific individual so that someone can be held accountable for ultimate success or failure. There should be no room for finger-pointing.

Segmenting Markets

Successful campaigns make extensive use of the segmentation concepts discussed in Chapter 6. The overall target market is subdivided in ways that will help campaign managers decide (1) how much effort to assign to each target member and (2) how specifically to approach him or her. Effort level is typically based on donation potential: The more one is likely to give, the more effort should be devoted. Prospects with small donation potential typically are approached by direct mail, the least cost-per-contact method. Those with larger potential then may be approached by telephone, and the most significant donors may be reached with person-to-person solicitation. Within all three groups, there may be further opportunity for segmentation.

Direct mail and Internet solicitations may differ according to what is known about the likely recipients. For example, the American Cancer Society in the past has based much of its direct-mail fundraising on the PRIZM geodemographic system mentioned in Chapter 6. The American Cancer Society's marketing director obtains detailed lifestyle information about each of the zip code areas to which the society might direct solicitations. He or she can then tailor the type of appeal to the destination zip code. Thus different messages would go to areas best characterized as "Money and Brains" than to areas categorized as "Shotguns and Pickups." Other organizations that do not subscribe to a geodemographic system can make adjustments based on the type of database they use. Most direct solicitations are aimed at members on a list. The best list is the organization's past contributors. However, many organizations seeking *new* donors move beyond present members to new databases that they purchase from other organizations that they know (e.g., the local museum or public television station) or they may buy them from independent suppliers that can supply highly specialized lists of specific types of potential donors. Thus one can buy lists of heating contractors or school superintendents or physicians. Obviously, one can tailor different messages to each audience based on reasonable assumptions about their interests and lifestyles.

The availability of computers enhances careful record keeping and allows the charity's direct solicitation specialists to evaluate the productivity of the various lists they acquire and, over time, to fine-tune the database to include only the very best prospects. These databases can contain detailed information on each prospective donor (interests, children's names, employer, and so on) that is particularly valuable for telephone and personal solicitations. These databases can also be segmented. In the last year, the American Cancer Society has gone to the costly trouble of attaching geographic coordinates to every donor record in its possession. It can now look to see how successful it has been in reaching people in "Shotguns and Pickups" neighborhoods and how this level of success differs in different parts of the country. Such data allow the organization to evaluate present programs and also to identify undertapped markets and to set dollar targets for such neighborhoods in future campaigns.

Distinguishing between repeat donors and new donors is always a sound strategy. It is an old marketing maxim from the private sector that it is always easier to sell to existing customers than it is to find new ones. Yet the drop-out rate for many annual fund drives, especially those that rely on direct mail, can be as high as 40 to 60 percent, often because this key group is neglected. Of course, there are always substantive reasons people drop out of annual drives or give up their memberships, including changes in economic circumstances or social interests or disappointment with the organization itself; however, the most common reason for not renewing is simply forgetting. Mal Warwick suggests that a planned sequence of messages directed to past donors can effectively reduce the drop-out rate. For annual memberships, he proposed that "renew early" messages be sent out 90 days in advance of the expiration date, followed by "time to renew" mailings and substantive appeals. Once the membership has expired, he suggests messages such as "Have you forgotten?" followed by later messages talking about "the last newsletter" or asking "Why forsake us?" He suggests telephone calls to stragglers 120 days after expiration.[26]

In tackling new members, there are many techniques that can be used in annual campaigns to appeal to particular interests. These include walkathons, bike-athons, dance-athons, and so on; bingo nights; fairs; TV or radio marathons; book or craft sales; parties in unusual places; cause-related marketing; on-street solicitation (i.e., the Salvation Army); lotteries and sweepstakes; and commemorative gifts. A particular concern is finding under-40 givers. Several organizations such as Boys & Girls Clubs of America and the Robin Hood Foundation have made particular attempts in recent years to tap this young market.[27] The March of Dimes has also focused on young mothers to advance their cause (see Figure 15-2).

Recognition

Both donors and volunteers should be recognized for their contributions after the campaign is completed. In many campaigns, donors are directly rewarded with some type of premium. This is particularly popular in fundraising for public television.

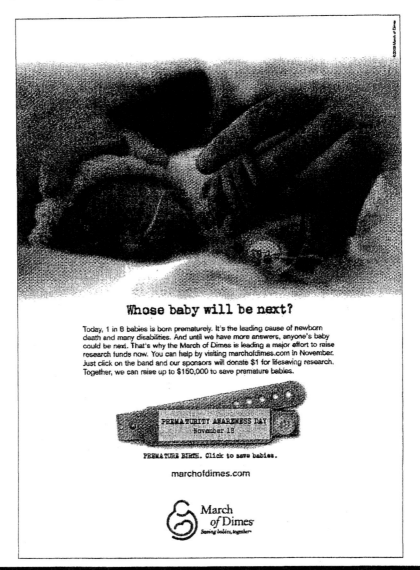

Whose baby will be next?

Today, 1 in 8 babies is born prematurely. It's the leading cause of newborn death and many disabilities. And until we have more answers, anyone's baby could be next. That's why the March of Dimes is leading a major effort to raise research funds now. You can help by visiting marchofdimes.com in November. Just click on the band and our sponsors will donate $1 for lifesaving research. Together, we can raise up to $150,000 to save premature babies.

PREMATURITY AWARENESS DAY
November 18

PREMATURE BIRTH. Click to save babies.

marchofdimes.com

March
of Dimes
Saving babies, together

FIGURE 15-2 Targeting Mothers

Source: Printed with permission of Porter Novelli and the March of Dimes.

Donors giving at different levels can get T-shirts or dinners or membership in some inner circle. But concrete tokens can only go so far. One of the frequent complaints of donors to charities is that they never hear from the organization once they have donated their money. Yet individuals like to know how their money is being used, especially if it is a significant amount. Remember that 60 percent of all donors give to only *one* organization. Typically, they feel close ties to that organization, and careful feedback after the campaign can do much to cement the all-important relationship between donor and charity that can last a lifetime.

Warwick suggests a number of ways to make sure donors are "yours" for a lifetime:[28]

- Thank donors quickly.
- Send new donors a welcome package.
- Telephone every new donor who gives over a given threshold (e.g., $500).
- Set up a donor information hotline.
- Offer donors choices as to how gifts will be used.
- Host special events especially for donors.
- Send unsolicited pins, autographed books, or certificates to top donors.
- Send personal notes and annotated news clippings to the very best donors.

Online Giving

A phenomenon that is growing dramatically in the twenty-first century is the availability and use of online giving. In the dot-com boom years in 2000 and 2001, a number of central "collection" sites sprang up, but many quickly disappeared when the boom deflated and when donors did not rush to the sites. However, most major charities now provide donation opportunities on their web sites. This has proved particularly valuable for organizations that are featured in the evening news, such as those involved with disasters or the homeless.

The annual survey by *The Chronicle of Philanthropy* in 2006 showed dramatic growth in giving over the Internet.[29] Relief organizations that focused on the Asian tsunami and hurricanes Rita and Katrina particularly benefited. However, non-relief agencies in the survey still showed significant growth of 50 percent from 2004 to 2005. Fidelity Charitable Gift Fund does much of its business online. It collected $180,000,000 in 2005, a 53 percent increase. It now finds that 48 percent of all new donor-advised funds it opened in 2005 were set up over the Internet. Among other organizations collecting over $15 million via the Net in 2005 were the following:

American Cancer Society	$ 30,131,986
American Red Cross	$157,700,000
Catholic Relief Services	$ 15,261,321
National Multiple Sclerosis Society	$ 26,200,000
Salvation Army	$ 45,964,040
Save the Children	$ 15,951,997
United Way of America	$140,949,586
World Vision	$ 37,100,000

Jeff Patrick, president of Common Knowledge, a consulting company in San Francisco that helps nonprofit groups use the Internet for fund raising and advocacy, believes that while large nonprofits may now be bringing in 10 to 20 percent of their donations online, smaller and mid-sized nonprofit organizations are still exploring the potential. There is concern that online giving will take away the "personal touch" that is important to smaller organizations and often gives them other opportunities, especially "growing" a modest giver into one making a major contribution. Some also feel that e-mail solicitiations are annoying.

Building Lifetime Donors

Of course, nonprofits are interested not just in individual gifts but in attracting a donor for his or her lifetime. Much thought is put into those donors we would describe as in the Maintenance stage to build high loyalty.[30] The change in focus of many fundraisers has been to be willing to invest more heavily in donor acquisition with the expectation that each donor recruited would yield significant returns over many years, not just the year of the recruitment. It is proposed that fundraisers calculate not just the benefit/cost ratio of a specific donation but the *lifetime value* of a donor against the cost of acquiring him or her. In a recent study in the United Kingdom, Sargeant and McKenzie analyzed databases of four charities to develop statistical models of "lifetime value" (LTV). The procedure uses retention rates to calculate the present value of future donations of all of those recruited through each medium. The LTV of donors is then compared to the cost of the medium to provide recommendations as to the amount that should be invested in each method of donor recruitment.[31]

A Caveat

While we have urged greater use of marketing approaches throughout nonprofit organizations, it is important to remember the downside of *inappropriate* marketing. Fundraisers who think their objective is "selling"—even hard selling—do not have the proper target audience-oriented mindset. Potential donors can be very sensitive to such techniques and do not react favorably to a strictly sales approach. A recent series of focus groups carried out by Public Agenda for the Kettering Foundation and the Independent Sector surfaced a number of complaints about "slick," inappropriate, or what the group members saw as wasteful practices. Specific concerns were "highly polished direct mail campaigns, telemarketing, unsolicited premiums, multiple or duplicated appeals" with charities acting too often "like businesses." Particularly relevant was the study's report that: "Many of the small donors interviewed voiced their disdain for what they saw as the charities 'selling' to people."[32]

Major Giving

Both individuals and corporations are sought out for major gifts, which often generate 80 percent of fundraising dollars with 20 percent of the effort. Major gifts are those designed for a specific purpose, and the tactics used to raise them are much different from those used for annual campaigns. There is a much more intense effort made to identify prospects who might be able to make the major gift to the museum's acquisition fund or the university's scholarship pool or to the YMCA's capital campaign. This is now made easier by the availability of search engines and other services on the Internet such as those from Yahoo!, Google, Northern Light, and Forbes that can track high-potential donors on a regular basis.[33]

As noted earlier, the number of high-potential givers has risen significantly in the last 10 years with the so-called dot-com boom. While the subsequent downturn in this area deflated many portfolios, firms like Microsoft and AOL have created dozens of new millionaires. These newly rich often need help in using their wealth for social contributions, and some firms such as Cisco Systems have provided "philanthropy counseling" services to staff for this purpose.[34]

Business Week lists the most generous philanthropists from 2002 to 2006 in terms of gifts or pledges.[35] Many of these names will be unfamiliar to many people but Gates and Buffet are not. The top 10—with amounts in millions of dollars—are:

Warren Buffet	Berkshire Hathaway CEO	$40,612
Bill and Melinda Gates	Microsoft co-founder	$ 3,350
George Soros	Investor	$ 2,066
Gordon and Betty Moore	Intel co-founder	$ 2,049
Herbert and Marion Sandler	Golden West Financial co-founders	$ 1,379
Eli and Edythe Broad	Sun America, KB Home founder	$ 1,378
Walton Family	Family of Wal-Mart founder	$ 1,250
Donald Bren	Real estate developer	$ 935
Bernard Osher	Banking, investments	$ 805
Alfred Mann	Medical devices	$ 695

If one seeks this kind of support, there are several steps involved: (1) identifying prospects, (2) "qualifying them" (i.e., looking into secondary records or past giving history to see if they would have the *capacity* to donate the required amount), (3) determining appeals that might be used, (4) assigning one or more volunteers or professional staff members to make the personal solicitation (usually over several calls and visits), (5) preparing the presentation and making the solicitation, and (6) following up the gift with full recognition (in public, if the donor is willing; many are not) and involvement of the donor in the organization and activities that relate to the gift area.

As with many kinds of marketing activities, it is extremely important to understand the *benefits* and *costs* that each prospect might see in the giving opportunity. As we noted in Chapter 4, it is these costs and benefits along with social pressure that will be the major determinants of their actions. However, as we have repeatedly said, volunteer solicitors and fund managers, in their enthusiasm about their own organizations and the fundraising activity itself, tend to emphasize the *benefits* when talking to donors. Benefits, of course, are important. However, when outlining benefits, volunteers must be careful to do two things:

1. Emphasize benefits *to the donor,* not benefits to the organization. Thus the volunteer solicitor should learn *not* to say "If you give us this money for a minority scholarship, we can attract more high-quality African American and Hispanic applicants." Rather, the benefit should be stated in the *donor's* terms, saying "If you give us money for a minority scholarship, you can feel that you are helping your alma mater increase the richness of the educational experience it can give future students like you."
2. Tailor the benefits to the individual's own needs, wants, and lifestyle situation. Thus the minority scholarship presentation might be different for a potential donor who is seeking more high-quality minority workers for his or her organization; for a donor who has a son, daughter, niece, or nephew thinking of going to the alma mater; or for a donor who wants to have some influence on the direction that the university will take in the future.

However, as we have said, benefits are only part of the story. As we noted in Chapter 4, individuals undertake difficult behaviors in stages.[36] In the early Contemplation stage of thinking about the action (i.e., giving a major gift), potential donors will be weighing benefits and costs but will be paying most attention to the benefits. Certainly, if they do not see major benefits, they are not likely to act. However, as they get closer to action (Late Contemplation), the potential negative factors will become much more dominant in their minds. As noted earlier, the kinds of costs a major giver might consider would include the following:

- Opportunity costs (other expenditures that would have to be foregone, including donations to other charities)
- Publicity that might lead them to be inundated with solicitations from other organizations
- Worries that the money might be misused or wasted
- Worries that a large payment might temporarily put the family at risk in case an emergency arises

Solicitors should seek to minimize all of these potential costs, especially if they seem significant to the donor. For example, the organization could propose a phased payment plan for the donor who is concerned about having to make a very large single payment.

Tactics

There are a great many techniques that nonprofit organizations use to solicit major gifts. These include auctions, benefit events (theater, sports), invitational dinners (e.g., the $1,000 a plate political "roast"), dances (especially in exotic locales such as a museum or zoo), fairs, fashion shows, small gatherings in a sponsor's home, celebrity meetings, and challenge grants.

An issue in designing solicitations for major gifts is to decide whether potential donors should be "coached" in how much to give or whether this should be left to their own judgment. In fact, there are three possibilities:

1. Don't specify any amount.
2. Suggest a specific dollar amount on the low side.
3. Suggest a specific dollar amount on the high side.

The first approach is the most common. People differ in what they can give, and it is felt that this is best left to their individual judgments. Suggesting a specific amount on the low side is seen as accomplishing two things. It helps prospects know what is considered a minimum proper amount to give. And the "low-amount feature" allows people to get into the habit of giving (the "foot-in-the-door" theory).[37] While there is the problem that many people might have given more, research suggests that the technique can be quite effective. Brockner and others found that in a campaign for a relatively obscure charity, the National Reye's Syndrome Foundation, concluding the sales presentation with the phrase "even a dollar will help" resulted in *twenty times* as much money being raised as when this suggestion was not made.[38] Further, this was more effective than saying "even five dollars will help." The researchers found that the latter yielded more total dollars than the control condition (no request), but *less* than the "even a dollar" condition. This was due to increased frequency of donating under the "dollar" condition, rather than larger amounts being donated. Finally, the research found that the technique applies to both telephone and face-to-face solicitation. Citing earlier research, they also claim that the technique has been shown to work for at least three different charities: Reye's Syndrome, the American Cancer Society, and the Heart Association.[39]

Suggesting a high amount to give works on the theory of the "door-in-the-face." It stretches people's idea of what they should give, and it is hoped that they will give this much or something close to it. Thus the Give Five Program suggests that citizens give 5 percent of their income and/or 5 percent of their time each week to help others. Most people regard these amounts as too high, but end up giving more than they normally would, that is, not shutting the door on the solicitor.

Planned Giving

Of growing importance to many nonprofit organizations is planned giving. Planned giving is a euphemism for charitable gifts that are made at the time of the donor's death. These gifts are often very substantial amounts and, therefore, are of considerable interest for nonprofits with major capital needs (e.g., arts organizations, universities, research-based charities, and hospitals). The approach to securing planned gifts is similar to that for major gifts but often the time period is much longer. It is only after considerable cultivation that many major planned gifts are awarded.[40]

Planned giving can take a wide range of forms, and each vehicle has its own requirements for when and if cash must be turned over and its own tax implications. The two simplest forms of planned giving are through ordinary wills in which the donor pledges a fixed amount or percentage of the estate, and life insurance in which the charity is named as the beneficiary. More complicated forms are also possible.

Charitable Remainder Trusts

Cash and/or property is donated during the donor's lifetime, and the donor and the charity receive income and/or other distributions based on the trust's assets. In a *unitrust,* the income interest is variable, based on each year's appraisal of the assets. In an *annuity trust,* the income interest is a fixed amount based on the assets' fair market value. In both cases, the nonprofit receives the assets upon the death of the donor.

Pooled Income Fund

Donated cash and/or property is pooled by the nonprofit with assets of other donors, and each donor receives income as a proportional share of the earnings of the pool.

Charitable Gift Annuity

Cash or property is donated during the donor's lifetime in return for an annuity to the donor. The nonprofit receives the assets upon the donor's death.

Charitable Lead Trust

Cash or property is donated for a fixed period of at least 10 years, during which time the charity receives all the earnings. Assets revert to the donor at the end of the period.

Life Estate Agreement

A residence is donated to the nonprofit although the donor reserves the right to live in the property for life.

The major benefit of a planned gift to the donor is that he or she can make a major contribution to a favored nonprofit while at the same time reaping significant tax advantages, particularly the avoidance of estate taxes. Because planned gifts represent major investments for donors and because they are subject to tax regulations that change regularly, most nonprofits retain specialists to market and manage these giving opportunities. These specialists can then tailor the planned gift to meet the financial circumstances, age, and number of heirs and dependents of each potential donor.

Nonprofits that receive assets as part of planned giving programs must be especially careful to manage them with the greatest degree of fiduciary responsibility. Nothing can tarnish the credibility of a nonprofit as fast as poor trust management or inappropriate investments. For example, nonprofit CEOs or boards that have authorized loans to officers out of trust funds have quickly found themselves the subject of public scrutiny and early dismissal.

REVENUE FROM SALES AND SERVICES

As we noted at the outset of this chapter, an important growth area for many nonprofit organizations is in the generation of their own revenue. This growth has resulted from two forces. On the one hand, competition for traditional sources of funding has intensified. There has not been strong growth in corporate or individual donations that can sustain the even faster growth in the number of nonprofits competing for such funds. On the other hand, it has long been the dream of many nonprofit managers, especially those involved in international assistance and local development, to make their programs self-sufficient. In this regard, the BRAC organization has been particularly successful (www.brac.net).

The growth has come through expanding three kinds of activities. First, nonprofits that market products and services as their principal mission—universities, hospitals, clinics, museums, the performing arts—have all improved their marketing skills, and many have significantly increased their market share vis-à-vis the private sector.[41] These marketers have also been more effective in their pricing strategies so as to increase returns per customer.

Second, many organizations have added retail operations to their main mission. This has been in two principal forms. Where feasible and appropriate, organizations like the Smithsonian, the Kennedy Center, and many local museums have gift shops that market both goods related to their prime mission (e.g., health products at the Mayo Clinic) and goods that might appeal to their typical clientele (i.e., "artistic" products in museum shops). A few organizations, such as the Metropolitan Museum of Art and some PBS stations, have opened retail outlets in malls. Many have sought a second line of growth by extending these activities through catalog and web site operations. For example, a visit to the Smithsonian Web site (www.smithsonianstore.com) allows anyone anywhere in the world to acquire such exotic items as "Chinese Porcelain Ladies" or a "Piggy Watering Can."

Third, the more imaginative nonprofits have sought to capitalize on their unique skills, marketing them to private sector, government, and other nonprofit organizations. A major promoter of this perspective is Billy Shore, the charismatic co-founder of Share Our Strength, one of the earliest participants in cause-related marketing. Shore has written extensively about his views in *Revolution of the Heart* and *The Cathedral Within*. His central thesis is that nonprofits can "make money—lots of money potentially—by selling things none of them understood they had: their good names, their expertise at solving difficult social problems, their ability to organize and train untapped labor pools, their artistic talents, even their access to inner-city youth markets."[42] Nonprofits like JumpStart can market their know-how about teaching at-risk preschoolers through profitable educational books and software. Other organizations can help corporations by training special populations, such as training former prison inmates to work in the sheet metal industry. Shore has said that 80 percent of Share Our Strength's operations budget is generated from corporate partnerships and licensing arrangements.

This effort is not without its critics. There are those who decry the competitive advantages that tax-free nonprofit product marketers have that allegedly hurt small businesses. Others feel that commercializing nonprofits takes them away from their core missions. The expectation was that they were supposed to be filling in where the private sector and governments have failed instead of becoming just like the private sector in too many ways. Shore and other "social entrepreneurs" have responded that what they recommend is, at bottom, really mission-driven. What they are doing is helping nonprofits to move away from handouts toward responsibility and independence.

There are a number of scholars who think that the move toward increasing revenue from these sources in not a good thing for the nonprofit sector. Weisbrod, a senior Northwestern professor who has studied this phenomenon extensively, argues "forcing nonprofits into either alliances or competition with profit-oriented firms is the root to breaking down the lifeblood of many nonprofits—robbing them of the public trust in their integrity."[43]

Summary

Although nonprofits obtain funds from other sources, fundraising remains essential to their survival and growth. Organizations are gradually shifting from a product or sales orientation to a customer orientation in their approach to fundraising. Greater attention is being paid to establishing relationships with donors rather than merely to raising funds.

Donor markets are of four basic types: foundations, corporations, government, and individual donors. The first three groups are no different from individuals in that fundraisers must understand the potential donor's needs and wants and then show how giving to the nonprofit organization is a way of meeting those needs and wants. Often careful research and preparation will be necessary. In particular, foundations, corporations, and governments will look for indications that the nonprofit has a clear mission, careful controls, experienced staff, and a track record of achievement. Secondary sources can help identify grantmakers, but nonprofits are urged to look at various programs more carefully, especially those of foundations, because their views of their roles are changing.

Individual donors go through three stages over their donation history. The early years involve regular small gifts. The middle years provide opportunities for nonprofits to secure major gifts, and the later years provide opportunities for planned giving. In each case, it is crucial that fundraisers be aware of the demographic characteristics of potential donors and their likely motives for giving.

Every fundraising activity starts with clear goals and a well-thought-out strategy. The approach differs depending on the type of campaign. For annual giving campaigns, strong volunteer leadership must first be established and backed up with thorough staff support. Organizational design should match the types of solicitation to be used, and specific goals and accountability should be established to ensure that someone is responsible for every key outcome.

Major gift campaigns involve the use of tools similar to annual drives. However, major gift solicitations are always in person and they often require very long investments of time. Planned gifts also often require long cultivation and, because of their complexity, usually are turned over to highly trained specialists.

Raising funds from the nonprofits' own activities has become an increasing source of revenue for the sector. However, these initiatives are not without their critics who believe they are taking organizations away from their core missions.

Questions

1. You have been recruited by the actress Julia Roberts to head a new charity that she is funding with $10 million of her own assets and a further $10 million from friends and business associates. How would you set up the charitable foundation to ensure that it secures more funds in the future?
2. Pick a web site of some nonprofit. How should it design the web site to maximize donations? If it already has a mechanism, provide any relevant criticisms and suggestions.
3. Your charity can get funds from small donations, large donations, corporations, foundation grants, and from its own money-making ventures. How would a specific organization decide on the best balance?
4. What would you want to ask of a specific first-time donor to ensure that he or she returns next year and gives more?
5. Imagine that you are a successful businessperson and your old university comes to you describing funding opportunities for a new building that will house classes and faculty in the subject area where you got your degree. How should it pitch to you?

Notes

1. Christine W. Letts, William P. Ryan, and Allen Grossman, *High Performance Nonprofit Organizations* (New York: John Wiley, 1999).
2. Burton A. Weisbrod, "The Nonprofit Mission and Its Financing," *Journal of Policy Analysis and Management*, Vol. 17, No. 2 (Spring 1998), pp. 165–174.
3. *Giving USA 2006: The Annual Report on Philanthropy for the Year 2005* (Glenview, IL: Giving USA Foundation, 2006).
4. Thomas J. Billitteri, "Venturing a Bet on Giving," *The Chronicle of Philanthropy*, June 1, 2000, pp. 1, 7–10.
5. Ian Wilhelm, "A 'Reinvention' to Aid Grant Seekers," *The Chronicle of Philanthropy*, November 9, 2006, pp. 16–17.
6. Noelle Barton, Caroline Preston, and Ian Wilhelm, "Slow Growth at the Biggest Foundations," *The Chronicle of Philanthropy*, March 23, 2006.
7. John Mintz, "Muslim Charity, Officials Indicted," *Washington Post*, July 28, 2004, p. A01.
8. Michael Anft, "Attacks on Ford Foundation Hamper Grant Making to Middle-East Causes," *The Chronicle of Philanthropy*, August 31, 2006, p. 23.
9. *The Foundation Directory Online* at www.fconline.fdncenter.org. See also Sandra A. Glass, *Approaching Foundations: Suggestions and Insights for Fundraisers: New Directions for Philanthropic Fundraising #28* (San Francisco: Jossey-Bass Publisher, 2001).

10. Key Facts of Corporate Foundation, The Foundation Center at foundationcenter.org/gainknowledge/research/pdf/corporatekeyfacts.pdf (retrieved October 23, 2006).

11. *The Chronicle of Philanthropy* web site at philanthropy.com/stats. See also Mark Dowie, *American Foundations: An Investigative History* (Cambridge, MA: The MIT Press, 2001).

12. Craig Smith, "The New Corporate Philanthropy," *Harvard Business Review,* May–June 1994, pp. 105–116. See also Michael Skapinker, "Philanthropy During a Downturn," *Financial Times,* April 27, 2001, p. 12.

13. Robert J. Williams and J. Douglas Barrett, "Corporate Philanthropy, Criminal Activity, and Firm Reputation: Is There a Link?" *Journal of Business Ethics,* Vol. 26, No. 4 (August 2000), pp. 341–350.

14. Erin Peterson, "In Search Of: Fifty Years After Their Debut, Corporate Matching Gift Programs Continue to Evolve," *Currents,* Vol. 31 (January 2005) pp. 32–37.

15. Leah Kerkman, "A Soaring Year: Assets at Donor-Advised Funds Rose by More Than 20%," *The Chronicle of Philanthropy,* May 4, 2006.

16. James E. Austin, *The Collaboration Challenge* (San Francisco: Jossey-Bass Publisher, 2000).

17. Emmett D. Carson, "A Crisis of Identity for Community Foundations," *The State Philanthropy 2002* (Washington, DC: National Center for Responsive Philanthropy, 2002), pp. 7–11.

18. Robert F. Sharpe, Jr., "Successful Fundraising in Challenging Times," presentation to American Cancer Society National Fundraising Leadership Conference, Orlando, FL, September 23, 1994.

19. *Distribution of Household Giving by Type of Recipient, 2002* and *Average and Median Amounts of Household Giving and Volunteering, 2002,* The Center on Philanthropy at Indiana University, released March 2006 (at www.philanthropy.uipui.edu).

20. Thomas J. Stanley, *Millionaire Women Next Door: The Many Journeys of Successful American Businesswomen* (Kansas City, MO: Andrews McMell Publishing, 2004).

21. Richard Steinberg and Mark Wilhelm, "Religion and Secular Giving, by Race and Ethnicity," in Patrick Rooney and Lois Sherman (Eds.), *Exploring Black Philanthropy: New Directions for Philanthropic Fundraising* (San Francisco: Jossey Bass, 2005).

22. Community Strategies Group, Growing Local Philanthropy: The Role and Reach of Community Foundations, 2005. Washington, D.C.: The Aspen Institute, 2005 (at www.aspencsg.org/rdp/resources/surveys.php).

23. Adrian Sargeant, Indiana University, personal correspondence, December 8, 2006. See also R. Bennett, "Factors Underlying the Inclination to Donate to Particular Types of Charity," *International Journal of Nonprofit and Voluntary Sector Marketing,* Vol. 8, No. 1 (2003), pp. 12–29; W. K. Bryant, H. Jeon-Slaughter, H. Kang, and A. Tax, "Participation in Philanthropic Activities: Donating Money and Time," *Journal of Consumer Policy,* Vol. 26, No. 1 (2003), pp. 43–74; J. Harvey, "Benefit Segmentation for Fundraisers," *Journal of Academy of Marketing Science,* Vol. 18, No. 1, (1990), pp. 77–86; A. Sargeant, J. B. Ford, and D. C. West, "Perceptual Determinants of Nonprofit Giving Behavior," *Journal of Business Research,* Vol. 59 (2006), pp. 155–165.

24. Eduardo Porter, "Putting Charity Through the 'What's In It for Me?' Test," *New York Times,* October 2, 2005, p. WK 4.

25. Stanley Weinstein, *The Complete Guide to Fund-Raising Management* (San Francisco: Jossey-Bass Publisher, 1998); Kent E. Dove, Jeffrey A. Lindauer, and Carolyn P. Madvig, *Conducting a Successful Annual Giving Program* (San Francisco: Jossey-Bass Publisher, 2001).

26. Mal Warwick, "How to Boost Your Renewal Rate," *NonProfit Times,* December 1993, p. 40.

27. Jennifer C. Berkshire, "Courting Generation Next," *The Chronicle of Philanthropy,* November 9, 2006, pp. 25–27.

28. Mal Warwick, "Increase Donors' Lifetime Value," *NonProfit Times,* November, 1993, pp. 58–59.

29. Nicole Wallace, "Charities Make Faster Connections," *The Chronicle of Philanthropy,* June 15, 2006.

30. Kenneth Burnet, *Relationship Fundraising* (London: White Lion Press Limited, 1992). See also Alan R. Andreasen, *Marketing Social Change* (San Francisco: Jossey-Bass Publisher, 1995).

31. Adrian Sargeant and Jane McKenzie, "A Lifetime of Giving: An Analysis of Donor Lifetime Value," London: Charities Aid Foundation, Research Report 4, 1998.

32. Ana Maria Arumi, Ruth Wooden, and Jean Johnson with Steve Farkas, Ann Duffet and Amber Ott, *The Charitable Impulse,* (Washington, DC: Public Agenda 2005).

33. Meg Sommerfeld, "Prospecting the Web for Donors," *The Chronicle of Philanthropy,* August 9, 2001, p. 27.

34. Nicole Lewis, "Philanthropy Counseling: The Latest Benefit for High-Tech Workers," *The Chronicle of Philanthropy,* December 14, 2000, p. 10.

35. "The 50 Most Generous Philanthropists," *Business Week,* November 27, 2006, p. 75.

36. James O. Prochaska and Carlo C. DiClemente, "Toward a Comprehensive Model of Change," in W. R. Miller and N. Heather (Eds.), *Treating Addictive Behaviors: Processes of Change* (New York: Plenum Press, 1986).

37. In a study by Freedman and Fraser, the experimenters asked subjects to comply with a small initial request. Two weeks later, they were contacted and asked to comply with a large request. It was found that 76 percent of the experimental participants *agreed* to comply with the large request, compared to a 17 percent compliance rate by those subjects approached with *only* the large request. See J. L. Freedman and S. Fraser, "Compliance Without Pressure: The Foot-in-the-Door Technique," *Journal of Personality and Social Psychology,* Vol. 4 (1996), pp. 195–202. See also Chapter 17 of this text.

38. Joel Brockner, Beth Guzzi, Julie Kane, Ellen Levine, and Kate Shaplen, "Organizational Fundraising: Further Evidence of the Effects of Legitimizing Small Donations," *Journal of Consumer Research,* June 1984, pp. 611–613.

39. Peter H. Reingen, "On Inducing Compliance with Requests," *Journal of Consumer Research,* September 1978, pp. 96–102; Robert B. Cialdini and David A. Schroeder, "Increasing Compliance by Legitimizing Paltry Contributions: When Even a Penny Helps," *Journal of Personality and Social Psychology,* October 1976, pp. 599–604.

40. Douglas E. White, *The Art of Planned Giving: Understanding Donors and the Culture of Giving* (San Francisco: Jossey-Bass Publisher, 1998).

41. Howard P. Tuckman, "Competition, Commercialization, and the Evolution of Nonprofit Organizational Structures," in Burton A. Weisbrod (Ed.), *To Profit or Not to Profit: The Commercialization of the Nonprofit Sector* (Cambridge, MA: Harvard University Press, 1998), pp. 25–45.

42. Tracy Thompson, "Profit with Honor," *Washington Post Magazine,* December 19, 1999, pp. 7–10.

43. Burton A. Weisbrod, "Some Unhealthy Alliances," *Atlanta Constitution,* June 27, 1999.

16

ATTRACTING HUMAN RESOURCES: STAFF, VOLUNTEERS, AND BOARD MEMBERS

NUDE VOLUNTEERING!

One can always volunteer. Nonprofit organizations need people to stuff envelopes, staff soup kitchens, serve as marshals at road races, coach a little league team, solicit their buddies for donations, or even serve on a nonprofit board. One can do all of these activities fully clothed!! But suppose one considered volunteering in the nude!!

Of course, one need not be totally nude—but at least give the appearance of being au naturel! In recent years, many nonprofit organizations have used risqué calendars as a novel fundraising—and brand-building—tactic. For example, the Topeka Civic Theatre in Kansas produced a calendar in which board members, a key donor, and prominent citizens were photographed in various backstage scenes and even a board meeting in what appeared to be no clothing at all. (Of course, the photos are not entirely revealing in that various signs and plants and desks covered the parts that were supposed to be "private!")

The city of Kansas then allowed the theatre to put life-sized cardboard cutouts of these same characters around the city for a whole month—publicizing both the theatre and the individuals. Over $16,000 in sales resulted plus reams of favorable (mostly) publicity and reaction. And some of the models even felt flattered by their depictions.

The boom in nude calendars can be traced partly to the success of the 2003 movie *Calendar Girls* starring Helen Mirren and Julie Waters. The film had as its premise the prospect of local (shy?) women getting naked for charity. In 2005, the San Diego Performing Arts League sold 1,800 calendars of local artists and performers—"Expose Yourself to San Diego's Performing Arts"—netting $18,000 and requests for future calendars .

Nude calendars are not one-time ventures for many organizations. Broadway Cares/Equity Fights AIDS in New York has a long history of producing such calendars. It did its first one in 1999 and, when people complained that there was no calendar in 2000, agreed to do one in 2001 and every year since.

Perhaps not surprisingly, the performing arts are especially good at getting volunteer models for their calendars. But LifeServices, a nonprofit in California, was able to recruit a group of "ordinary" seniors to create a calendar "Old Broads Get Naked for Charity." In 2004, there was a "Vail Undressed" and a "Norwegian Women's Soccer Team Floya" nude calendar. There was "The Men of Rappahannock County," "Women in Waders 2004," and calendars for many rugby and football clubs in the United Kingdom. The UK Cancer Blog signaled that it isn't always easy to get volunteers when in 2006 it advertised: "Naked London traders needed! Strip nude for charity calendar."

Source: Maria de Mento, "Charity Calendars Show More than Date." *The Chronicle of Philanthropy,* April 6, 2006, pp. F-7–F-8.

To be effective, all organizations need planning, management, and operations. In the private sector, more and more of this work is done by systems and not people. However, the nonprofit world is much more dependent on individuals and their contributions—it is very much a "people sector." Human capital represents the second key resource successful nonprofit organizations must command.

The human resource challenges for marketers lie in three areas, each with unique features. First, permanent staff must be recruited at wages that are typically below market. Second, in a great many sectors, the full-time staff must be supplemented by volunteers. And, finally, board members must be attracted. Board members are especially important because of their unique role in the nonprofit sector. In contrast to the private sector, nonprofit boards set the strategy for the organization and approve major initiatives. They have special fiduciary responsibilities and are typically careful critics of the performance of the nonprofit CEO.

There are two major advantages that the nonprofit world has in meeting these challenges. First, as Peter Frumkin has noted, nonprofit organizations have *an expressive character.* They "allow people to demonstrate commitment to social ends and values."[1] In effect, this means that a significant proportion of the population—particularly in developing countries—is willing to accept "psychic rewards" to augment meager (or zero) salaries and modest perks. Second, the corporate sector increasingly sees value in worker volunteer programs and executive participation on nonprofit boards. The Taproot Foundation recently said that there are at least 6 million professionals available in corporations to volunteer for nonprofit organizations.[2] Finally, in the twenty-first century, celebrities like Nicole Kidman, Madonna, Bono, and others see important career advantages in some form of attachment to nonprofit and/or an important cause.

However, marketing to attract human resources is still necessary. It is our position that, while the special status of nonprofit and public service organizations offers a highly positive platform for seeking help, the organization must also explicitly or implicitly have other benefits to offer as well. This is in part due to the fact that all nonprofits have real competition. Doctors who could help with an anti-smoking campaign or contribute to a charitable activity may agree that what you're doing is admirable and ought to be supported. Nonetheless, they may have many demands placed on their time by other organizations and, indeed, make their social contribution by providing free services to impoverished patients. To get their help, the nonprofit marketer must make them see that the benefits exceed the costs of the help and the benefit/cost ratio for this contribution is better than anyone else's.

ATTRACTING STAFF

While employee recruitment is typically not seen as a marketing challenge, nonprofit human relations specialists might benefit from marketing thinking. As readers have noted, our constant reminder is to focus on the needs and perceptions of the target audience as the starting point of any effective effort to influence behavior. This ought to be followed by careful attempts at segmenting markets and clearly positioning the nonprofit organization for potential hires. The value proposition ought to speak to the needs uncovered but special attention must be paid to the expectation of potential hirees that they will have to "take a vow of poverty" by joining the nonprofit world. It turns out that the latter expectation is less and less true for the larger nonprofit organizations.

CEOs of nonprofit organizations are now commanding significant salaries as are their top vice presidents. In 2005, top salaries for various sectors included the following:[3]

- *Museums and Libraries:* Glenn D. Lowry, director of the Museum of Modern Art in New York, earned compensation of $875,301. At 13 museums and libraries in *The Chronicle of Philanthropy* survey, chief executives earned a median average of $464,170; an increase from 2004 of 4.1 percent.
- *Health Charities:* M. Cass Wheeler of the American Heart Association in Dallas earned $656,608, more than any of the other health charity leaders. The median pay for the 18 health charities on the list was $351,366; their median increase was 5.6 percent.
- *Public Affairs:* Edwin Feulner Jr., president of the Heritage Foundation, a think tank in Washington, received compensation totaling $633,849. At the 10 public affairs groups in the survey, leaders made a median of $273,507, with a median increase of 5.7 percent.
- *Social Services:* Marsha J. Evans, who stepped down as president of the American Red Cross in December 2005, made $493,616, more than any other social service leader. Top executives of the 20 social services groups in the survey earned a median salary of $197,208; the median increase was 3.8 percent from 2004.

It is significant that the rates of pay increases well exceeded increases in the cost of living.

Of course, potential hirees see—or hear about—potential costs of working in a nonprofit environment. This is especially a challenge as nonprofit organizations increasingly seek to recruit executives from the commercial sector. A study by Andreasen, Goodstein, and Wilson published in 2005 of nonprofit executives who had made this transition[4] revealed many frustrations that could restrict the hiring pool. They report:

> Marketing is often not accorded its own department and the CEOs and colleagues of nonprofit marketers seldom have a marketing perspective. These characteristics are associated with a misunderstanding of marketing's potential role beyond sales and its characterization as a discretionary expense to be reduced in tough times. Further, the simple ability to apply marketing concepts and tools is seen as hampered by greatly restricted budgets.

Clearly fundamental changes in nonprofit cultures would seem to be needed to incorporate some of the better features of commercial management techniques if cross-sector transitions are to be more common in the future. Fortunately, the trend is in the right direction.

RECRUITING AND MANAGING VOLUNTEERS

According to a 2003 study by The Urban Institute, four out of five charitable organizations in the United States use volunteers.[5] Volunteers staff the fund drives, serve as candy-stripers in hospitals, coach the sports teams, take meals into the homes of the housebound elderly or AIDS victims, and assist in elementary school classrooms. Their ranks include a significant portion of the adult population in the United States and a growing number of individuals in both the developed and developing parts of the rest of the world. Volunteerism helps keep nonprofit organization expenses down while providing a channel for socially conscious people to contribute time to a cause they believe in. Among the organizations that make heavy use of volunteers are hospitals, political parties, trade associations, arts organizations, charitable institutions, churches, and social reform organizations. Also, smaller volunteer units are found in schools and social service organizations.

In one respect, recruitment of volunteers in the future seems quite promising. The students that the authors see in their universities typically seek out nonprofit volunteering opportunities to advance their careers and to provide personal satisfaction. A very large percentage of them enter higher academic programs already having been volunteers in high school. In fact, a number report that volunteering is a *requirement* for high school graduation. A telephone interview study by the Corporation for National and Community Service along with The Independent Sector and the U.S. Bureau of the Census in early 2005[6] reported that 38 percent of the youth population had engaged in a service activity through school and two-thirds of these were required to fold their experiences into the classroom.

Volunteerism is a significant activity in the United States. A survey by the Bureau of Labor Statistics of volunteering in 2005 revealed the following:

- 65.4 million people or 28.8 percent of the population volunteered.
- Their service is valued at $150 billion.
- Women volunteered more often than men (32.4% versus 25%).
- Volunteering was high in age groups 35 to 44 (34.5%), 45 to 54 (32.7%), and among teens (30.4%). Rates were lowest for twenty-somethings and seniors.
- Whites volunteered more (30.4%) than did blacks (22.1%) and Asians (20.7%). Rates were lowest for Hispanics/Latinos (15.4%).

- Volunteers were also more likely to:
  - Be married
  - Have children under 18
  - Be employed—especially as part-timers

The study also revealed that the annual median hours of volunteering was 50, with the number much higher for seniors and much lower for teens.

A distribution of the jobs performed by volunteers in 2005 was as follows:

29.7 percent fundraising
26.3 percent food service
22.5 percent general labor or transportation
21.3 percent tutoring or teaching

The kinds of organizations they joined (many of them multiple organizations) are the following:

34.8 percent religious organizations
26.2 percent education
13.4 percent social and community service
7.7 percent hospital or other health
6.4 percent civic, political, professional, or international
3.3 percent sport, hobby, cultural, or arts
8.4 percent other and not determined

African-Americans were more likely to be involved in religious organizations, and Hispanics/Latinos in education as were—not surprisingly—families with children under 18.

Cross-National Comparisons

The concept of volunteering is well-ingrained in the modern American experience. Early colonists actively supported each other through barn raisings, community socials, and clothing collections for the needy. The rigors of frontier living made community reciprocity essential for survival. Further, the notion that a person ought to be his or her "brother's keeper" is explicit or implicit in many Christian theologies. Indeed, in his analysis of the American "experiment" in democracy, Alexis de Toqueville[7] argued that the willingness of Americans to establish voluntary associations to meet community needs was one of the key sources of democracy itself.

However, the concept of volunteerism is less well-accepted in other parts of the world. In some countries, especially in Scandinavia, the society is governed by a "social democratic" model that tends to let the state carry out many of the charitable activities one finds handled privately in countries such as the United States, the United Kingdom, and Australia, where "welfare capitalism" is the governing norm. In Sweden and Denmark, there is simply less need for volunteerism.[8] There also used to be little need for volunteerism in the Socialist states of the former Soviet Union and the Iron Curtain countries. Today, however, as newly democratic states are less willing, and even less able, to provide social services, countries like Russia and Hungary are turning to private volunteerism and the nonprofit sector to provide needed services and safety nets.[9]

Private voluntary organizations (PVOs) are also becoming more important in Africa, where private sector and state-run efforts at economic and social development have had limited success. Hyden and others[10] have argued that PVOs are to be preferred over corporate and government entities because they (1) have lower overhead costs, (2) are less bureaucratic, (3) are less subject to political influence, (4) are more sensitive to grassroots needs and wants, and (5) are better able to mobilize the poor while at the same time providing services when the public sector fails.

In Asia, the pattern of volunteerism is also ingrained as it is in the United States; however, in countries such as Japan, it is rooted in a different religious culture. Thornhardt notes that the Japanese have an extremely effective voluntary self-help system organized through neighborhood associations, called *jichikai*.[11] She quotes Vogel: "The Japanese have been able to provide for the well-being of their population without requiring many except the very old and infirm to become economically dependent on the state, and they have done it in such a way as to reinforce their communitarian ideals."[12] These ideals are rooted in Confucianism, which promotes the community over the individual. Under Confucianism, the individual is expected to help others and to seek harmony and cooperation in interpersonal relations. Today's *jichikai* not only promote social services but also have adapted to the times by becoming active lobbyists and environmentalists.

Voluntary participation in 35 countries worldwide is reported in the study by Salamon, Sokolowski, and List discussed in Chapter 1.[13] They found the level of volunteering to be equivalent to 12.6 million full-time workers including religious congregations. This represents 22.1 percent of the adult population in the countries studied. However, as suggested in the preceding paragraphs and indicated in Table 16-1, the

TABLE 16-1	Volunteer Share of the Nonprofit Workforce in 35 Countries, 1995–1998		
Country	*%*	*Country*	*%*
Sweden	75.9	U.S.A.	36.9
Tanzania	75.2	Czech. Republic	35.5
Philippines	63.8	Spain	34.8
Norway	63.2	Mexico	33.5
Uganda	55.9	Australia	30.6
Romania	55.5	Slovakia	29.7
Finland	54.3	Japan	24.5
Morocco	52.8	Colombia	24.0
France	51.6	South Korea	22.8
South Africa	47.0	Austria	22.1
U.K.	44.2	Belgium	21.7
Pakistan	40.8	Ireland	21.1
Germany	40.4	Poland	20.8
Italy	40.2	Hungary	18.0
Argentina	40.1	Israel	17.7
Kenya	39.1	Brazil	11.9
Peru	38.2	Egypt	2.8
Netherlands	37.1	**Average All 35 Countries**	38.0

Source: Lester A. Salamon, S. Wojciech Sokolowski, and Regina List, *Global Civil Society: An Overview.* Baltimore, MD: Center for Civil Society Studies, Institute for Policy Studies, The Johns Hopkins University, 2003. Reproduced with permission.

contribution of volunteering to nonprofit workforces varies significantly across the 35 countries, from a high of 75.9 percent for Sweden and 75.2 percent in Tanzania to a low of less than 20 percent in Hungary, Israel, Brazil, and Egypt. The structure of volunteering also varies across the 35 countries.

In an earlier paper, Salamon, Sokolowski, and List proposed that variations in volunteering across countries could possibly be explained by the factors outlined in Chapter 1. One possibility is subsumed under what they call "macro-structural" arguments, namely that the extent of volunteerism in the nonprofit sector can be explained by the attitude of a country's government toward social services and the voluntary sector. Thus one might expect to find less volunteering when governments carry out many services themselves (the "crowding out" hypothesis) and/or if they are hostile to the sector and impose restrictions on it. Their analysis of the data in 24 countries reveals that the first explanation is not supported by their data; indeed, high levels of government spending are associated with high levels of voluntary activity (e.g., Sweden, Finland, France). The "restrictiveness hypothesis" is also not supported.

A second set of "micro-structural" arguments proposes that volunteering is associated with a social climate that supports and encourages social connections. They test this notion by treating the size of the nonprofit sector in each country (as measured by Full Time Equivalent—FTE) as a proxy for societal support for the nonprofit concept. They find a good correlation between these measures and volunteerism.

Recruiting Volunteers

Recruiting volunteers is simply another marketing task and should proceed in a planned strategic way. Consistent with our discussions in earlier chapters, the challenge for each nonprofit marketer is to do the following:

- Determine the target *market segments* he or she is going to pursue.
- Determine the organization's own *positioning* vis-à-vis its competitors—which includes not volunteering.
- Craft a powerful marketing mix to implement the positioning against the target markets.

Positioning and Targeting

In seeking market segments that might be responsive to recruiting efforts, one place to begin is with data on characteristics associated with volunteering. Data from Goss's analysis of the DDB Needham data on volunteering between 1975 and 1998 reveal a number of factors—demographic, lifestyle, and attitudinal—that were positively (+) and negatively (–) associated with volunteering—or not associated at all (blank). These data are reported in Table 16-2.

The data from the 2005 Bureau of Labor Statistics study previously cited also indicate demographic differences. Clearly the choice of targets for each specific organization will depend on its own mission and what it knows about its geographic and social environment. Analysis of the characteristics of existing volunteers is also an excellent way to assess market potential. The next step, positioning, is a matter of positioning both the organization and the volunteering opportunity. Positioning the volunteer

TABLE 16-2 Correlates of Reported Volunteering by Age Group			
Factor	*Young Adults* (*<30 yrs.*)	*Middle-aged* (*30–59 yrs.*)	*Seniors* (*60+ yrs.*)
Year (1975–1998)	+ +	+ +	+ +
Employment status	+ +	+ +	+ +
Married			– –
Education		+ +	+ +
Children at home		+ +	
Female	–		+
Good health			
Live in county with high volunteering	+ +	+ +	+ +
Gave/attended dinner parties	+ +	+ +	+ +
Attended club meetings	+ +	+ +	+ +
Attended church	+ +	+ +	+ +
TV is primary entertainment	– –	– –	– –
Feel "hassled"	+		+ +
Financial worries			– –
See most people as honest		+	
Wish for the good old days		–	– –
Like to be thought of as a leader	+	+ +	+ +
Overall R^2	.141	.187	.175

+ + or – – Significant at .01 level.
+ or – Significant at .05 level.

Source: Kristin A. Goss, "Volunteering and the Long Civic Generation," *Nonprofit and Voluntary Sector Quarterly,* Vol. 28, No. 4 (December 1999), p. 409. Reprinted by permission of SAGE Publications, Inc.

opportunity requires more extensive analysis of the factors that are likely to cause someone to volunteer.

Developing a Recruitment Strategy

As we have said repeatedly, the conduct of any campaign must begin with an in-depth understanding of the potential target audience. This means understanding what is likely to make them act as the organization wishes and determining who is the organization's major competition. In most instances, competition is at one of four levels.

First, the organization may be competing against inertia. Certainly, Robert Putnam has argued in his book *Bowling Alone* that this is an increasing problem in the American culture.[14] A second level of competition is for the type of contribution the individual might make. Given that the person wishes to give something back to his or her society, this can take many forms. The person can donate, perform free services (as lawyers and doctors typically do), or volunteer for some organization. Third, given that the person wishes to give time for volunteering outside of work, he or she may decide among broad categories, such as fundraising for some charity, coaching a soccer team, or helping a political candidate. The final level of competition is among various enterprises in the same category—different charities, different soccer teams, or different political candidates.

The strategy for influencing segments would obviously differ. Competing with inertia is mostly a matter of touting the values of public service generally, while competing with donations and free services could be a matter of arguing that one need not choose—one can donate but also volunteer. These two levels could merit cooperative strategies among several nonprofit organizations and/or with associations such as The Independent Sector or the Points of Light Foundation.

Competing at the final two levels then becomes more "personal" to the specific nonprofit. Why should someone help in their category and why choose Charity A over Charity B?

A recruiting campaign needs to make decisions early on as to where it plans to focus its competitive energies. This may well come from formative research that looks at the most likely target audiences and what these audiences say is the real competitor or competitors for volunteer time. The next step is to then understand how to bring about the desired action—namely, volunteering for the marketer's organization. The approach we recommend is to use the consumer behavior model introduced in Chapter 4. There we pointed out that there are two concepts that should drive market analysis at this stage. First, it should be recognized that people who have never acted will become volunteers in stages and it is, therefore, important to (1) figure out what stage a particular segment is in at present and then (2) tailor a strategy to that stage.

As noted above, efforts to move audiences from Precontemplation to Contemplation might well be left to broader-based organizations. The challenge for most specific organizations is with the Contemplators. There our second consumer framework, the BCOS model, becomes a useful organizing framework.

From Contemplation to Action

Volunteering for many is a high-involvement action, and individuals will undoubtedly consider the *exchange* they think they will have to make. But also weighing on the decision will be the influence of others—both for and against—and the individual's sense of self-assurance, whether he or she thinks that one can actually make the volunteering experience happen—for example, finding the time and, say, obtaining the boss's approval. Let's consider each of these BCOS factors in turn.

Benefits There are a great many benefits that have been found to cross the minds of individuals considering volunteering. Okun and Schultz argue that motives should be looked upon as serving different functions.[15] They identify six primary functions or motives:

- Career—gaining career-related experience
- Enhancement—enhancing self-esteem
- Protective—reducing negative feelings
- Social—strengthening social relationships
- Understanding—learning more about the world
- Values—expressing important values like humanitarianism or concern for animals or the environment

These authors conducted a multivariate analysis of data collected from volunteers at two affiliates of Habitat for Humanity International in Phoenix. They found that, as a person aged, motives shifted. In young people, broadening one's horizon is important and one reports motives labeled as career, understanding, and making friends as more important. As one ages, career and understanding drop off while interest in making friends first drops off in middle age and then rebounds among seniors. Advancing age correlated with more interest in social outcomes whereas the study found no age effects on protective and values functions.

The Corporation for National and Community Service lists a number of benefits that they have found motivate volunteers. These include:

- Connect with your community.
- Conserve funds for charities, nonprofits, and faith-based and other community organizations by contributing your time.
- Share your skills and gain new ones.
- Develop self-esteem and self-confidence.
- Meet new people from all walks of life.
- Enhance your resume and make important networking contacts.
- Promote a worthwhile activity.
- Feel needed and valued.
- Experience something new.
- Serve your country.[16]

Costs   A study by Chinman and Wandersman[17] found that there has been less research on costs in the literature—perhaps a reflection of the absence of a marketing (or exchange) perspective. A surprising result of their review is that it was often the case that higher participation rates were associated with higher costs as perceived by the participant. This is undoubtedly due to the deeper involvement and perhaps greater participation in volunteering. However, the studies also showed that these higher costs were well exceeded by higher levels of perceived benefits—as expected from their continuing participation. These authors argue for careful attention to benefit/cost ratios, an approach consistent with exchange theory.

Others   A number of studies have shown that having a personal motivation to volunteer (i.e., a high benefit/cost ratio) is not enough to promote action; others can be a very important influence. First of all, a great many studies show that a prime prompter of action is being asked to volunteer by someone else. In a 1999 survey, the Independent Sector found that only 22.3 percent of people volunteer when not asked, whereas 89.5 percent volunteer when asked.[18] In a number of studies, a great many individuals indicate that they learned about volunteer opportunities from others or they simply joined with others in volunteering. The Independent Sector study found that friends were the most commonly mentioned person who recruited a volunteer (50 percent), followed by someone at a church or synagogue (32 percent), a family member or relative (19 percent), or someone at work (12 percent).

It is important to recognize that "others" can also act as a *deterrent* to volunteering. A wide range of anthropological studies have established the importance of group norms in guiding action. Certainly, a strong determinant of volunteering among some religious groups like the Quakers is the positive norms of group solidarity and mutual help found. At the same time, although the evidence is only anecdotal, it is very likely that volunteering is not "cool" among many specific subgroups of the population, especially "outsider" teenagers.

Self-Assurance Motivating individuals and getting their friends or coworkers to support this behavior is not enough to ensure action. Everyone can recount volunteering opportunities that seemed promising and that others supported but were never acted on. Organizations seeking volunteers must pay careful attention to removing all barriers that may cause people to feel that they just cannot make the volunteer experience happen and be successful. Barriers to action must be removed. A 2001 study of teenagers who did not volunteer made clear that many of them just did not know how to "make it happen."[19] Among the reasons mentioned were these:

Personal schedule too full	33.1 percent
I'm too young	19.6 percent
No transportation	14.8 percent
Didn't know how to become involved	13.2 percent
May not be able to honor the volunteer commitment	7.1 percent
Don't have the necessary skills	4.6 percent

Clearly, significant increases in volunteering among this population could be achieved by simply showing them how to fit it into busy schedules (e.g., as other role models have done), describing activities for all age groups, providing transportation or carpooling, being clear on the steps involved, showing that the organization will be flexible in case the volunteer's future circumstances change, and making clear that all volunteers will be carefully trained.

In this regard, one development that has significantly increased the ease of volunteering is the World Wide Web. The Web is important in three ways. First, it provides access to broad databases of volunteering opportunities. Second, it allows individuals to go to a potential organization's own web site and learn something about it and its volunteering opportunities. This is particularly valuable because many would-be volunteers may be more willing to explore an opportunity anonymously rather than risk the embarrassment or the potential "sales pressure" should they make a personal appearance.

The final contribution is using the Web to match organizations with individual interests. The following are some useful sites available in the summer of 2006:

United Kingdom: National Centre for Volunteering (www.volunteering.org.uk)
SERVEnet (www.servenet.org)
VolunteerMatch (www.volunteermatch.org)
U.S. Department for Housing and Urban Development (www.hud.gov/volunteering/index.cfm)
White House USA Freedom Corps (www.usafreedomcorps.gov)
United Nations Vounteers (www.onlinevolunteering.org)
Western Australia: Volunteer Western Australia (www.volunteer.org.au)

Canada: Volunteer Canada (www.volunteer.ca)
Volunteer Abroad (www.volunteerabroad.com)

Preparation/Action

Besides removing all of the barriers to possible action, organizations should design opportunities for potential volunteers to experiment with a new behavior. Many potential volunteers will have hesitancies about their own competence, will be unsure about the possible benefits and costs, and may even feel that they won't know anyone at the volunteer site. Thus giving them a trial experience may do much to get over remaining hurdles and prompt permanent action. Certainly this is a clear, consistent finding in the literature on the adoption of innovations: New products and practices that permit trial are adopted faster than those that do not have this option.[20]

Maintenance—Retaining Volunteers

As we have said earlier in this text, marketing is not simply an external activity. It applies wherever the organization has a target audience and a behavior it needs to influence to be successful. Present volunteers represent just such an important target and clearly merit a specific effort of internal marketing. This is necessary for three reasons. First, internal marketing will help make volunteers better, harder-working, more loyal, and more involved, thus making the organization more effective. Second, internal marketing will make it less likely that they will leave. Private sector marketers know very well it is much less costly to market to "present customers" than always going out to find new customers. Finally, satisfied volunteers are likely to be an organization's best source for future volunteers as well as positive word of mouth to the general community.

In considering how to approach target audiences in the Maintenance stage, a useful starting point is with some informal research—talking to present volunteers. Among the sources of dissatisfaction that can surface are the following:

1. Unreal expectations when volunteering. This is sometimes the recruit's own fault in that he or she has unrealistic fantasies about how exciting it would be to join the Peace Corps, participate in a political campaign, or become part of the "United Way team," or about how much time would be involved. But just as often the culprit is the nonprofit organization, which, in its zeal to get recruits, paints an excessively optimistic picture of the volunteer's time commitment, type of work, and probable influence.
2. Lack of appreciative feedback from clients and coworkers.
3. Lack of appropriate training and supervision.
4. Feelings of second-class status vis-à-vis full-time staff.
5. Excessive demands on time.
6. Lack of a sense of personal accomplishment.

Managing Volunteers

The use of volunteers is not an unmixed blessing for a nonprofit organization. The mix of volunteers and full-time staff can be a volatile one. There can be problems on both sides.

On the side of the volunteers, because they are donating their services to the nonprofit and are not paid by the organization, many have the attitude that (1) they don't really *work* for the organization and so shouldn't be *told* what to do, rather, they should be *asked* if they would be willing to do something; (2) they should have a great deal to say about the content and timetable for their assignments; and (3) they deserve continual appreciation for their generosity and commitment. Further, some individuals volunteer, not because they really want to work, but because they have been coerced into volunteering by an employer or peers or because they wish to add an item to their resume. One manager of a large volunteer force has developed what he calls his "rule of thirds." One-third of his volunteer force works avidly with very little direction and encouragement. One-third will work only with considerable motivation and are only effective with careful supervision. And one-third will not work at all under any circumstances and are best ignored (unless they are causing morale problems among those who do work).

On the organization side, there is considerable opportunity for friction to develop if the professional full-time staff views the volunteers as second-class workers. Among the opinions professionals have been known to offer are these:

1. Volunteers are dilettantes. They are not there for the long haul and so don't have to live with the consequences of their impulsive or lethargic performance.
2. Volunteers never really pay attention to their training and instruction because they are only part time and so commit tactical and ethical missteps that hurt the organization.
3. Volunteers often come from occupations in which they boss others and so cannot or will not take direction.
4. Volunteers are often well-to-do members of the leisure classes who (a) consider themselves better than the professional staff (the "Junior Leaguers") and (b) are unwilling to perform grubby tasks like licking envelopes or cleaning bedpans.

Susan J. Ellis, president of Energize, a Philadelphia nonprofit, takes issue with society's "unquestioning acceptance of any work performed by volunteers as self-evidently good. . . . True service—to be of service—is an attitude, not an employment status." Ms. Ellis is concerned that great reliance on volunteers and with providing them with "helping" opportunities can affect the nonprofit's mission. For example, it may be inclined to continue providing help to the poor, the hungry, and the unemployed in order to give volunteers meaningful work. This, she worries, diverts attention from correcting underlying problems that may be causing the need for help.[21]

The potential for conflict between volunteers and professional full-time employees is therefore considerable. The situation can be exacerbated if management does not take firm control of the situation. Partly, it is a matter of *attitude.* If management's attitude is dominated by feelings of gratitude that these individuals have so kindly volunteered, all is virtually lost. Management will be unwilling to ruffle the feathers of volunteers. This will only encourage the volunteers' tendencies toward undisciplined performance. At the same time, management will likely squelch the grumblings of the paid staff for fear that they will upset these needed volunteers. This will only cause further unrest and surreptitious insubordination among the staff. The result will be that management loses control of *both* full-time and volunteer staff.

The solution that more experienced programs have developed is simply to treat volunteers as much as possible as professional, full-time workers indistinguishable from paid staff. Among other things, authors such as Ken Nations[22] suggest using the following standards and managerial practices:

1. Assess the volunteers' skills and, as nearly as possible, match these skills to the tasks to be performed in the organization.
2. Set out job responsibilities clearly and in detail in advance.
3. Set specific performance goals and benchmarks.
4. Clearly inform the volunteers of these goals and of the fact that they are expected to achieve them.
5. Inform the volunteers that if they do not perform satisfactorily in their jobs, they will be let go or assigned elsewhere (the most difficult task).
6. Follow through on the standards of accountability, knocking heads, and dismissing volunteers until the word gets around that management is serious in its commitments (the most crucial task).

This straightforward, professional style of volunteer management may seem risky to the inexperienced manager. But both volunteer and professional staff respond very favorably to it. Most volunteers like to be taken seriously and challenged. They appreciate the opportunity to be well trained and well supervised. Those who do not are the one-third you do not want anyway. Full-time paid staff appreciate management's firmness and the fact that they, too, can treat the volunteer seriously, giving orders as necessary and reprimands as required. Performance standards for both groups improve enormously and the nonprofit's effectiveness, efficiency, and morale rise noticeably. Indeed, the organization's volunteer positions can be highly coveted.

A more fundamental challenge is outlined in the 2003 Urban Institute study: "The greatest challenges that charities and congregations face is an inability to dedicate staff resources to and adopt best practices in volunteer management."[23] The study notes that only about a third of charities adequately recognize the efforts of volunteers; less than half have adopted best practices in the field. Two out of five charities and two-thirds of congregations with social service outreach activities do not have a paid staff person working on volunteer coordination

Principles for managing volunteers are available in several sources, including private firms like Energize Inc (www.energizeinc.com) and nonprofits like Serviceleader.org (www.serviceleader.org). In the early 1990s, the Points of Light Foundation, a national organization dedicated to engaging more people effectively in volunteer community service, developed 11 principles of effective volunteer management. These are outlined in Exhibit 16-1.

A recent analysis by the Corporation for National and Community Service says that a major shortcoming of volunteer management is giving volunteers too little to do and too mundane tasks like making fundraising calls. Boomers, particularly, have the education and skill sets to do more. The United Way of Greater Cleveland treats volunteers as "partners and owners. They make real decisions and have a hand in where nearly $40 million goes." Returning Peace Corps volunteers are now being given chances to serve short-term assignments under the Peace Corps Encore program. The latter is particularly attractive to those with tough career prospects.[24]

EXHIBIT 16-1

ELEVEN CHARACTERISTICS OF EFFECTIVE VOLUNTEER MANAGEMENT

1. The mission and priorities are framed in terms of the problem or issue the organization is addressing, not its short-range institutional concerns.

2. There is a positive vision—clearly articulated, widely shared, and openly discussed throughout the organization—of the role of volunteers.

3. Volunteers are seen as valuable human resources that can directly contribute to achievement of the organization's mission, not primarily as a means to obtaining financial or other material resources.

4. Leaders at all levels—policy making, executive, and middle management—work in concert to encourage and facilitate high-impact volunteer involvement.

5. There is a clear local point of leadership for volunteering but the volunteer management function is well-integrated at all levels and in all parts of the organization.

6. Paid staff are respected and empowered to fully participate in planning, decision

making, and management related to volunteer involvement.

7. There is a conscious, active effort to reduce the boundaries and increase the teamwork between paid and volunteer staff.

8. Potential barriers to volunteer involvement—liability, confidentiality, location of the organization, hours of operation, and so on—are identified and dealt with forthrightly.

9. Success breeds success as stories of the contributions of volunteers—both historically and currently—are shared among both paid and volunteer staff.

10. There is an openness to the possibility for change, an eagerness to improve performance, and a conscious, organized effort to learn from and about volunteers' experiences in the organization.

11. There is a recognition of the value of involving, as volunteers, people from all segments of the community, including those the organization seeks to serve.

Source: The Points of Light Foundation, *Changing the Paradigm: The First Report,* 1992. Used with permission of The Points of Light Foundation.

BOARDS OF DIRECTORS AND THE MARKETING FUNCTION

Boards of directors are extremely important groups for nonprofit organizations. Their members serve a number of important functions, many of which have a direct impact on the marketing activities of the nonprofit. In return, marketing principles can be used to recruit future board members.

The Influence of Boards on Marketing

Dynamic boards serve many functions.[25] The most important function of boards of directors is *oversight.* By statute in most states, nonprofit boards have a fiduciary responsibility for ensuring that the organization and its staff members serve the purpose for which the nonprofit organization was founded and do so in an ethical fashion. Thus boards are important to marketers whenever the marketers consider new ventures:

Boards ultimately must decide whether new directions are legitimate undertakings. Suppose that a museum marketer is considering entering a joint venture with a private sector computer equipment maker to sell CD-ROMs containing the museum's collection, and the agreement calls for the museum to promote the CD-ROM at museum events even though the equipment maker keeps 80 percent of the profits on every sale. The board would be the one that decides whether such a venture was within the charter of the organization. The answers are seldom clear, and marketers must spend some of their time cultivating board members (i.e., marketing to them) so that the board sees such ventures as being in the nonprofit's long-term interest.[26]

The board will also keep a close eye on the tactics used by the marketing department, asking whether they meet the board's concept of ethical behavior. Many boards, for example, will veto lotteries as fundraising devices if these lotteries are likely to appeal excessively to low-income people. Others will look askance at excessive hyperbole used to promote the product. Hospital boards are particularly sensitive in the latter regard.

A second function that some, but not all, boards serve is direct *decision making*. This is most often the case in small organizations and organizations in their earliest stages of growth. The board serves as a "joint CEO" until the enterprise is firmly established and it can afford a well-qualified independent CEO. In such situations, of course, the marketing manager may find that he or she is constantly going to the board to get approval for specific actions, ad budgets, prices for products and services, donation objectives, and so on.

A third function of many boards is to *provide specific expertise*. Very often, board members are chosen because they are lawyers, politicians, accountants, physicians, or bankers with the express intention that such experts would be called upon to provide direct help to the nonprofit in their areas of special knowledge. Other board members who do not have direct expertise (e.g., general managers and CEOs) will be recruited because they will "volunteer" experts within their own organizations to be helpful. Thus in 1995, a board member, Philip Marineau, then CEO of Quaker Oats, helped Georgetown University's McDonough School of Business develop a position statement for itself and a plan to implement that positioning.

Although marketing help can come indirectly as in the Quaker Oats–Georgetown case, surprisingly few nonprofits make an effort to have marketing people serve directly on their boards. A study of 1,190 board members in 66 agencies in Rochester, New York,[27] found the following representation of skills:

Function	Percentage	Function	Percentage
Legal, financial	27	General management	5
Medical	13	Marketing and sales	4
Human service	13	Manufacturing	4
Homemakers, retirees	11	Human resources	3
Educators	10	Public relations	3
Government personnel	6	Other	6

Only 7 percent were either marketing or public relations professionals. Yet as we have indicated throughout this book, nonprofits could make great use of marketing managers, marketing researchers, advertisers, retailers, and other promotional specialists in designing and implementing their strategies.[28]

Of course, an important function of board members is to help out in *fundraising*. Most board members are not only expected to be major donors themselves but also to serve as fundraisers reaching out to their peers and members of their own businesses. Thus board members many times serve as marketers themselves. Yet it is often the case that few of them have any marketing training. Moreover, because the board members are often very powerful in their own organizations or in the community, they are often reluctant to take advice as to how they ought to approach their fundraising tasks. The approach to "training" such powerful fundraisers that seems to work best is to involve them in the fundraising planning process rather than just asking them to solicit at the end of the planning process. Such involvement very often gets them to understand what is needed to make the campaign be fully customer-centered. This exercise typically causes them to change their own views about how to approach potential donors.

Finally, boards of directors provide an important function as a *link to the environment.* Board members who are bankers, politicians, community activists, and educators can serve marketers well by helping them keep in touch with and, where necessary, influence key components of the nonprofit's marketing environment. Politicians are good at sensing changes in societal attitudes and preferences. Community activists can tell what energizes people the most. Bankers can be sources of demographic and economic trends. Educators can often conceptualize broad themes that can help guide the organization and its marketers.

Recruiting Board Members

For many organizations, securing board members is no problem at all. Inducing someone to be on the board of a church, a public television station, the YMCA, or the local museum of art is relatively simple because of the prestige that an invitation to join the board implies. The only holdout might be the prospect who suspects that the invitation to the board will soon be followed by a large donation request that the prospective member is not prepared to meet.

However, nonprofits would like to have effective board members and not have to spend time recruiting and retaining board members. This is one reason that the late 1990s and early twenty-first century has seen increasing attention paid to institutional branding (discussed in Chapter 7). Nonprofits have recognized that they face real direct competition for high-quality board members. Defining and maintaining an organization's brand has been found to be a powerful strategic and competitive tool. Shocks to well-established brands such as the United Way in the late 1980s and the Boy Scouts in the late 1990s have shown the need for careful cultivation and management of strong brands.

Some board members are easy to attract because they have a commitment to the "cause" of the nonprofit. They may have helped get it started. Or they may be seduced by a charismatic founder. They leap on board because they are believers.

For a large number of nonprofits, however, getting board members and the right *kind* of board members is a difficult task, especially if they wish members to serve many of the five functions outlined previously. It is here that the marketing principles enunciated in this book can be helpful. Probably the most important of these principles is that the best recruitment campaign is one that *starts with an understanding of the target audience's needs and wants.* Just what is it that motivates people to want to join boards of directors?

Candace Widmer proposes an Incentive-Barrier model of board member involvement[29] that parallels the benefit/cost exchange model in Chapter 4. She suggests that there are four kinds of incentives for participation in nonprofit boards:

- *Material incentives:* tangible rewards in goods, services, or money for oneself or one's group.
- *Social incentives:* intangible rewards following from associating with others, including friendship, status, and honors.
- *Development incentives:* intangible rewards that result from learning new skills or assuming civic responsibilities.
- *Ideological incentives:* intangible rewards that come from helping achieve something greater than oneself.

In her study of 98 members of boards of 10 human service agencies in Central New York State, Widmer found strong confirmation of this model as well as a number of implications for recruitment strategies. First of all, consistent with the BCOS model, she found that the *precipitant* for joining a nonprofit board was having a friend ask the person to join. Forty-three percent of the respondents first talked about volunteering with a present member of the board. A further 17 percent were asked by a staff member or the nonprofit's CEO. It is clear that most board members join *people,* not causes.

Among the reasons these 98 board members gave for joining were:

- Wanting to help the community. Almost one-half gave altruistic reasons (involving social and ideological incentives).
- Believing in the agency's mission (ideological incentives).
- Wanting to accomplish something (developmental incentives).
- Being obligated by their employer. Many were required to be involved by their job descriptions (material incentives).
- Wanting personal development. Many wanted to learn, to grow, and to use skills (developmental incentives).
- Repaying the agencies. Six board members came aboard because family members had benefited from the agency.

When asked about benefits directly, 15 percent mentioned employment benefits, 6 percent mentioned at least one social benefit, 50 percent mentioned learning, and 10 percent mentioned ideological considerations.

These findings offer a number of examples of incentives that might be used to recruit new board members. Marketers in a specific nonprofit organization might begin their own efforts by asking their own current board members to reveal the benefits that they get from participating. Such benefits can then be used as a solicitation platform for a new campaign. The real targets of such a campaign will not be current members but prospective members. This makes it obvious that the marketer must also understand how nonmembers perceive the costs or barriers to joining the board. One way to do this would be to have each current board member identify one or two people like themselves who might have been board members (an example of "snowball sampling" as described in Chapter 5). These prospects could then be asked to report on the positive and negative outcomes that they think might be associated with joining the board. These results, coupled with the real experience of current members, can then be used as the basis for a message strategy designed to recruit new members. Data on prospective new members and their perceptions can also be used to develop a clear segmentation strategy. The next step is to use current board members, staff, and the CEO to deliver the message about the benefits to those picked among the target audience. As we noted earlier, people join *people*, not causes.

Summary

A key resource that a nonprofit organization needs to cultivate is people. This includes staff, volunteers, and board members. Staff members must be convinced that in the modern world they need not "take a vow of poverty" in order to work at a nonprofit. On the other hand, staff recruited from the commercial sector will need help adjusting to the unique management environment of the nonprofit world.

Nonprofits are unique in needing volunteers to help them accomplish their basic goals. Recruiting volunteers involves knowing the target audiences. The nonprofit should also know how to retain volunteers. Studies of former volunteers and the satisfaction and dissatisfaction of present volunteers can be helpful in this regard. Problems that emerge may involve volunteers' expectations, training, supervision, and feedback.

Managing volunteers can also be a problem if the organization has not committed enough—or any—resources to the task and is not truly professional in its approach. Many volunteers work hard and effectively with little incentive or guidance. Some hardly work at all under any circumstances. Most, however, respond best to being treated as professionals. This means matching responsibilities to skills; setting clear, achievable goals; and then holding volunteers to achieving them.

Boards of directors serve a number of functions that can have an effect on marketers. They carry out oversight, make decisions in some organizations, provide specific expertise, raise funds, and serve as a link to the external environment. Marketing skills can be used to recruit members of boards. Research carried out to determine the incentives and barriers to their participation can be used to develop effective recruitment strategies.

Questions

1. A friend of the nonprofit organization's CEO would like to join the board. You suspect she just wants the prestige of the position. She is a moderate donor and has only limited skills to bring to the board. You want the board to be small and efficient. How would you respond?
2. You are worried about volunteer turnover at Habitat for Humanity "building projects" in your city. You plan to interview a sample of people who did not return. What would you ask them and why?
3. You are the marketing vice president at the American Heart Association. You are paid $75,000 because of your business background. You have just learned that a colleague from your old firm—who has a job a lot like yours—earns $125,000. How would you react and why?
4. Describe how you would create a value proposition to get the mayor of your city to join the board of charity devoted to helping the homeless.
5. How would you use the Internet to recruit volunteers to a charity of your choice?

Notes

1. Peter Frumkin, "Going Beyond Efficiency," *Nonprofit Quarterly,* Vol. 8, No. 2 (July 2001), p. 22.

2. Evan Hochberg, "How to Get an Extra $1-Billion from Business," *The Chronicle of Philanthropy,* October 12, 2006, pp. 35–36.

3. Noelle Barton, Maria Di Mento, and Alvin P. Sanoff, "Top Nonprofit Executives See Healthy Pay Raises," *The Chronicle of Philanthropy,* September 28, 2006.

4. Alan R. Andreasen, Ronald C. Goodstein, and Joan W. Wilson, "Transferring Marketing Knowledge to the Nonprofit Sector," *California Management Review,* Vol. 47, No. 4 (Summer 2005), pp. 46–67.

5. *Volunteer Management Capacity in America's Charities and Congregations: A Briefing Report* (Washington, DC: The Urban Institute, 2004).

6. Issue Brief: Youth Helping America: The Role of Social Institutions in Teen Volunteering, November 2005 at www.nationalservice.gov/pdf/05_1130_LSA_ YHA_SI_factsheet.pdf (retrieved October 23, 2006).

7. Alexis de Toqueville, *Democracy in America* (New York: Vintage, 1954).

8. John Boli, "The Ties that Bind: The Nonprofit Sector and the State in Sweden," in Kathleen D. McCarthy, Virginia A. Hodgkinson, Russy D. Sumariwalla, and Associates (Eds.), *The Nonprofit Sector in the Global Community* (San Francisco: Jossey-Bass Publisher, 1992), pp. 240–253.

9. Miklós Marschall, "The Nonprofit Sector in a Centrally Planned Economy," in Helmut K. Anheier and Wolfgang Seibel (Eds.), *The Third Sector: Comparative Studies of Nonprofit Organizations* (Berlin: Walter de Gruyter, 1990), pp. 277–291.

10. G. Hyden, *No Shortcuts to Progress: African Development Management in Perspective* (Berkeley, CA: University of California Press, 1983); Helmut K. Anheier, "Indigenous Voluntary Associations, Nonprofits, and Development in Africa," in W. Powell (Ed.), *The Nonprofit Sector: A Research Handbook* (New Haven, CT: Yale University Press, 1987), pp. 416–433.

11. Helmut K. Anheier, "Private Voluntary Organizations and the Third World: The Case of Africa," in Helmut K. Anheier and Wolfgang Seibel (Eds.), *The Third Sector: Comparative Studies of Nonprofit Organizations* (Berlin: Walter de Gruyter, 1990), pp. 361–376.

12. Anna Maria Thränhardt, "Changing Concepts of Voluntarism in Japan," in Kathleen D. McCarthy, Virginia A. Hodgkinson, Russy D. Sumariwalla, and Associates (Eds.), *The Nonprofit Sector in the Global Community* (San Francisco: Jossey-Bass Publisher, 1992), pp. 278–289. See also Anna Maria Thränhardt, "Traditional Neighborhood Associations in Industrial Society: The Case of Japan," in Helmut K. Anheier and Wolfgang Seibel (Eds.), *The Third Sector: Comparative Studies of Nonprofit Organizations* (Berlin: Walter de Gruyter, 1990), pp. 347–360; Ezra F. Vogel, *Japan Is Number One—Lessons for America* (Cambridge, MA: Harvard University Press, 1980), p. 203.

13. *The New Nonprofit Almanac in Brief* (Washington, DC: The Independent Sector, 2001).

14. Robert D. Putnam, *Bowling Alone* (New York: Simon & Schuster, 2000).

15. Morris A. Okun and Amy Schultz, "Age and Motives for Volunteering: Testing Hypotheses Derived From Socioemotional Selectivity Theory," *Psychology and Aging,* Vol. 18, No. 2 (2003), pp. 231–239. See also E. G. Clary, "The Motivations to Volunteer: Theoretical and Practical Considerations," *Current Directions in Psychological Science,* Vol. 8 (1999), pp. 156–159.

16. At www.nationalservice.org/for_individuals/ why/index.asp (retrieved November 8, 2006).

17. Matthew J. Chinman and Abraham Wandersman, "The Benefits and Costs of Volunteering in Community Organizations: Review and Practical Implications," *Nonprofit and Voluntary Sector Quarterly,* Vol. 28, No. 1 (March 1999), pp. 46–64.

18. Giving and Volunteering in the United States: Findings from a National Survey: 1999 edition (Independent Sector 2000).

19. Meg Sommerfeld, "More Than Half of Youths Plan to Volunteer," *The Chronicle of Philanthropy,* September 20, 2001, p. 46.

20. Everett M. Rogers, *Diffusion of Innovations,* 4th ed. (New York: The Free Press, 1995).

21. Susan J. Ellis, "Reverse Discrimination: Volunteers vs. Employers," *NonProfit Times,* October 1999, p. 16.

22. Ken Nations, "Managing Difficult Volunteers Requires Structure and Limits," *NonProfit Times,* February 1993, p. 36.

23. *Volunteer Management Capacity,* p. 4.

24. Daniel Kadleg, "The Right Way To Volunteer," *Time,* September 4, 2006.

25. Paul J. Jansen and Andrea R. Kilpatrick, "The Dynamic Nonprofit Board," *The McKinsey Quarterly,* No. 2 (2004), pp. 21–29.

26. William G. Bowen, "When a Business Leader Joins a Nonprofit Board," *Harvard Business Review,* September–October 1994, pp. 38–43; F. Warren McFarlan, "Working on Nonprofit Boards: Don't Assume the Shoe Fits," *Harvard Business Review,* November–December 1999, pp. 64–80; Nancy Axelrod, "Who's in Charge?" *NonProfit Times,* December 1994, p. 32.

27. Robert D. Herman, "Board Functions and Board–Staff Relations in Nonprofit Organizations: An Introduction," in Robert D. Herman and Jon Van Til (Eds.), *Nonprofit Boards of Directors* (New Brunswick, NJ: Transaction Publishers, 1989), pp. 1–7.

28. Eugene H. Fram, "Nonprofit Boards Would Profit with Marketers Aboard," *Marketing News,* April 29, 1991, p. 6.

29. Candace Widmer, "Why Board Members Participate," in Robert D. Herman and Jon Van Til (Eds.), *Nonprofit Boards of Directors* (New Brunswick, NJ: Transaction Publishers, 1989), pp. 8–23.

17 WORKING WITH THE PRIVATE SECTOR

BRANDING YOUR PANDA!

Consider the following marketing presentation to a major corporation like Mattel, Outback Steakhouse, or the Dodge division of Daimler LLC.

How would you like to have promotional space for 12 months in a place that is usually open every day of the week and where, nationally, 143 million people visit each year. These visits are usually family affairs—parents or grandparents and kids—lasting several hours. People are in an upbeat mood. They are there to see things and gain new facts and perspectives. They usually take lots of pictures and videos and your brand may be featured in the background of many of them. And, best of all, there will be opportunities for local tie-ins and it might cost you only in the six figures!

Of course, these places are the nation's public zoos. For companies that have kids as a major market, zoos are a natural. Mattel's Fisher-Price division provided a picnic area with a food stand and tables at the San Francisco Zoo, all with the brand logo. At the same location, Outback Steakhouse sponsored a bird-feeding exhibit and managed to put up 200 banners everywhere. Dodge sponsored a wild safari ride in a Dodge Durango for visitors to the Philadelphia Zoo. Celestial Seasonings gave out 40,000 samples of an iced tea bag product at the Dallas Zoo. And so on. The Louisville Zoo lists 35 past and current sponsors on their web site (www.louisvillezoo.org/support/sponsor/) including Loews, Kraft, Coca-Cola, Krispy-Kreme, Whole Foods, Ford, Barnes & Noble, Toyota, and Papa John's pizza. The Oakland Zoo even allows you to attach your brand to a specific animal.

While some zoos are concerned about sponsorships being viewed as "a corporate sellout," Fisher-Price's brand marketing director sees it as a win-win situation. "The goal is to help them. We want to do things that make sense for our brand that provide a 'wow' for their [the zoo's] guest. The brand's helping to expand or enhance [consumers'] experience at the zoo."

Source: Andrew Hampp, "Animal Attraction: Marketing at the Zoo," *Advertising Age,* October 30, 2006, p. 16. Reprinted by permission of *Advertising Age.*

One of the most important features of the nonprofit environment at the beginning of the twenty-first century is the growing importance of resources drawn from the corporate sector. Nonprofits have found themselves increasingly strapped for financial support from traditional sources such as private donations and government subsidies. They are also increasingly interested in developing better management approaches. They are challenged by articles in such places as the *Harvard Business Review* and the *Stanford Social Innovation Review* that describe "The Nonprofit Sector's $100 Billion Opportunity,"[1] and "Why We Need a More Efficient Social Capital Market."[2] These articles explicitly or implicitly raise serious questions about the social sector's competence. When private sector managers migrate to the nonprofit world, they often express frustration at what they find there.

For their part, corporations are recognizing that there are many direct benefits to their own bottom lines from working with nonprofits. As noted in Chapter 15, a substantial number of corporations have foundations and make direct contributions to nonprofit organizations and their operations. They contribute money, loan their executives and their facilities, and help build coalitions to achieve local, national, and international social objectives. Many corporate CEOs have taken a direct part in nonprofit operations, serving on boards or heading up fund drives. Industry-funded agencies such as the Advertising Council have long offered specific services to help nonprofit organizations and campaigns achieve maximum impact.

An increasing number of corporations and private sector marketing executives are looking for ways to become more closely involved in joint ventures that have a *direct* benefit to the corporation. At one time, Chrysler Corporation found that it was having difficulty getting upscale consumers into its showrooms to look at the latest models. Therefore, the company worked out an arrangement with Boston Symphony Hall to place three brand-new luxury Chryslers in the lobby of the concert hall for a Handel and Hayden concert. Upon entering, patrons received marketing brochures and upon leaving got videotapes. In return for this opportunity, Chrysler donated generously to the orchestra's annual campaign.[3]

Partnerships to generate sales—usually labeled *cause-related marketing*[4]—are not without criticism and risks for nonprofit organizations. Although the possibility of corporate help can be very seductive, nonprofits need to think very carefully before they risk hard-won reputations by teaming up with the wrong kind of partner or getting involved in an inappropriate—even scandalous—venture. Nonprofits need to worry about how other resource contributors—donors, foundations, volunteers, and staff—feel about cross-sector developments.

From society's point of view, corporate–nonprofit partnerships are often suspect. Naming rights have become big revenue sources for nonprofits. The public that once saw hospitals and clinics named in memory of loved ones now find that the Children's Hospitals in Los Angeles and Providence, Rhode Island, are named for Mattel and Hasbro. City-owned sports arenas everywhere now have corporate names like FedEx Field, Target Center, and 3Com Park. Lawrence M. Small, former Secretary (CEO) of the Smithsonian Institution, found his appointment controversial in part because of the management rigor he introduced but also for his efforts to bring in new corporate sponsors that many staff fear will dictate exhibition design and operations.[5]

There are many forms of private–nonprofit partnership. We begin by looking at one of the best-known types of partnership between the private sector and nonprofit marketing efforts: the work of members of the advertising community on nonprofit campaigns, most notably the efforts of the Advertising Council.

ADVERTISING AGENCY PARTNERSHIPS

Every major community has advertising agencies (and sometimes marketing research firms) that are willing to make contributions of their skills and services in the public interest. Nonprofit organizations recognize the commercial benefits agencies think about when they contribute their services:

- They believe that the nonprofit organization will be supported by important community executives among its other volunteers and boards and so a volunteer campaign will be a major opportunity to make business contacts.
- Goodwill can be obtained by such public-spiritedness.
- Agency executives and staff can achieve personal psychic benefits from working on important social issues rather than just "selling soap."
- Opportunities in the campaign for individual creativity, agency creativity, or both may be considerably greater than when a paying client is "calling the tune." The agency may see a chance to make a major public impression with a highly innovative campaign.
- The campaign presents an opportunity to give experience to junior staff people where a major client is not at risk.

Contributed advertising services—like volunteers—can be a mixed blessing for a nonprofit. First, if the donated campaign is costly, the agency may skimp on production values. If it assigns junior people, the execution may not be of the highest quality. Also, if the agency focuses too narrowly on the campaign as merely a chance to make a major creative impact, it may lose sight of the nonprofit organization's basic advertising goals. If the nonprofit managers are alert to these potential dangers, however, they can typically be avoided with timely interventions. Again, as with volunteers, it is up to the nonprofit to treat the donated relationship *as if* it were a professional, fully paid-for relationship rather than a "charity case" for which the nonprofit organization should be grateful (and thus non-interfering).

The Ad Council
Perhaps the best-known example of donated advertising is the work of the Ad Council. The council was founded in 1942 just four weeks after the Japanese bombing of Pearl Harbor. Its initial challenge was to promote war-related programs such as buying war bonds, planting victory gardens, and home canning of vegetables. Observers believe that the lives of thousands of American servicemen and servicewomen were saved by the campaign telling citizens that "Loose lips sink ships."

Over the years, the Ad Council has been deeply involved in American life, creating over 1,000 campaigns. It has developed advertising slogans that are now widely familiar:

- "Only you can prevent forest fires."
- "A mind is a terrible thing to waste."

- "Help take a bite out of crime."
- "Pollution: It's a crying shame."

The Ad Council has brought us such memorable characters as Rosie the Riveter, Smokey the Bear, McGruff the Crime Prevention Dog, and Vince and Larry the crash dummies. In the fall of 2006, it was responsible for 48 campaigns in three areas, community, education, and health and safety. Projects in the area of community listed on its web site (www.adcouncil.org) include such important topics as:

- Adoption
- Community Drug Prevention
- Energy Efficiency
- Environmental Giving
- Father Involvement
- Generous Nation
- Global Warming
- Hurricane Relief–Housing Discrimination
- Mentoring
- Oceans Awareness
- Predatory Lending
- Troop Support
- Youth Voter Participation
- Youth Volunteerism

The Council also endorses campaigns by other organizations:

- National Arbor Day Foundation
- Habitat for Humanity's Cars for Homes
- Vision Council of America
- Energy Efficiency 'Super Powers'
- Youth HIV/AIDS Awareness

Samples of recent Ad Council advertising is found in Figures 17-1 through 17-5.

The Ad Council operates through donations from industry and assessments from sponsors of its causes. Sponsors pay for material costs but receive creative and media support free. In 2006, the market value of donated media was approximately $1.7 billion, which would place the Council among the major advertising spenders in the country. The year 2005 saw it aggressively tackle new media, developing partnerships with 250 online publishers, networks, and digital media companies yielding 30 billion impressions in places like the home pages of Yahoo!, MSNBC, and AOL. Samples of audio, video, digital, and print materials can be seen on the Ad Council's Web site.

Critics have charged that public service announcements (PSAs, the Ad Council's primary tool) are not effective because they rely on volunteered time and space and often are shunted to remote time slots and unattractive billboard and magazine placements. Most critically, such voluntary ad placement significantly reduces the chance that the PSAs will be targeted to specific segments. To address this issue, the Ad Council has

It only takes one afternoon to change a kid's life.

Although your stomach may need more time to recover.

Your small efforts can have a big impact on the drug problem. There are easy things you can do, things you already love to do. Share a skill, a passion, a hobby one afternoon a month with kids in your community and you can make a big difference.

That's because kids who enjoy a regular, positive activity with an adult are less likely to begin using drugs or alcohol. Find out how you can be a coach, a mentor, a volunteer. No matter what it is, you have something to offer.

Log on to helpyourcommunity.org or call 877-KIDS-313 and be a positive influence on the kids in your community.

FIGURE 17-1   Anti-Drug Ad

Source: Advertising Council. Reproduced with permission.

sought to look more carefully at what works and what doesn't. Among the research findings about Ad Council campaigns reported on its 2006 web site are the following:[6]

- Applications for Big Brothers/Big Sisters mentors soared from 90,000 a year to 620,000 in nine months, a seven-fold increase in the number of inquiries to Big Brothers/Big Sisters agencies.
- Ready.gov received more than 18 million unique visitors within the first 10 months of the launch of the Department of Homeland Security's preparedness campaign.

FIGURE 17-2 Promoting Teacher Recruitment

Source: Advertising Council. Reproduced with permission.

- Sixty-eight percent of Americans say that they have personally stopped someone who had been drinking from driving. The old saying "One More for the Road," has been replaced with "Friends Don't Let Friends Drive Drunk."
- Safety belt usage is up from 14 percent to 79 percent since the Ad Council Safety Belt campaign launched in 1985—saving an estimated 85,000 lives, and $3.2 billion in costs to society.

The "It's Only Another Beer"
Black and Tan

8 oz. pilsner lager
8 oz. stout lager
1 frosty mug
1 icy road
1 pick-up truck
1 10-hour day
1 tired worker
A few rounds with the guys

Mix ingredients.
Add 1 totalled vehicle.

Never underestimate 'just a few.'
Buzzed driving is drunk driving.

AdCouncil.org

U.S. Department of Transportation

FIGURE 17-3   Promoting Responsible Drinking and Driving

Source: Advertising Council. Reproduced with permission.

- Since 1972, The United Negro College Fund campaign has helped the organization raise more than $2 billion with the help of the "A Mind Is a Terrible Thing to Waste" slogan.
- Six thousand children were paired with a mentor in just the first 18 months of the Ad Council mentoring campaign.

FIGURE 17-4 Promoting Energy Conservation

Source: Advertising Council. Reproduced with permission.

- Destruction of U.S. forests by wildfires has been reduced from 22 million acres to less than 8.4 million acres per year, since the Ad Council Forest Fire Prevention campaign began.
- The amount of total waste recycled increased 24.4 percent from 1995 to 2000, and 385.4 percent from the 1980s after the launch of the Environmental Defense campaign.

me is Tyler,
years I'll be an alcoholic.

I start drinking in middle school, just a bit earlier.
my parents won't start talking to me about it until
high school. And by then I'll already be in some trouble.
The thing is, my parents won't even see it coming.

START TALKING BEFORE THEY START DRINKING

Kids who drink before age 15 are 5 times more likely to have alcohol problems when they're adults.
To learn more, go to www.stopalcoholabuse.gov or call 1 800.729.6686

FIGURE 17-5   Attacking Teen Drinking

Source: Advertising Council. Reproduced with permission.

The evaluation of a specific campaign around gun safety is described in Exhibit 17-1. Partly because of concern about the lack of control over the placement of public service advertisements (PSAs), a small but increasing number of larger nonprofit organizations and major federal programs have begun to conduct paid advertising and promotion campaigns. One example of this is the national drug abuse campaign sponsored by the Office of National Drug Control Policy (www.mediacampaign.org/index.html). This campaign builds upon the work of many years of the Partnership for a Drug Free America (www.drugfreeamerica.org). A second important example is the national

EXHIBIT 17-1

SAFE GUN STORAGE CASE STUDY

Beginning in 1999, the Ad Council, in cooperation with the U.S. Department of Justice and the National Crime Prevention Council, began creating a public service campaign to "increase awareness around the safe storage of firearms." Although national violent crime statistics had dropped in the early 1990s, accidental deaths and injuries, particularly involving children, were still unacceptably high. The goals of this campaign were "to increase awareness about the danger of leaving unlocked, loaded guns in the home" and "to encourage Americans to store their firearms safely."

Advertising agency Foote, Cone, & Belding (FCB) worked pro bono on the strategy and creative design of the campaign. This issue posed several challenges for FCB and the Ad Council. First, they are focusing on a small target market (gun-owning parents with young children). Second, this market is probably already aware of the danger of improper storage. Third, many of these parents felt defensive when their right to own a gun was questioned.

In order to meet their objectives and overcome the obstacles, the team engaged in extensive research pulling from a variety of areas including public health organizations, the police, the gun industry, and academia. They also conducted qualitative research in-home with gun owners. The key finding of this research was the "protection paradox": People owned guns for protection, but those guns were a danger to those they were trying to protect.

The campaign consisted of child-like drawings with children voiceovers describing accidental gun violence. To test the creative work, they performed a qualitative test with gun-owning parents that confirmed the effectiveness. Additionally, a market research company conducted a quantitative copy test that showed better-than-average recall, understandability, likeability, and motivation.

The campaign was begun in June 2000 with the nationwide launch in September. Campaign materials were distributed to more than 25,000 TV, radio, and print outlets. To assess the effectiveness the Ad Council measured donated media support, survey results, public relations, and fulfillment results.

Donated Media Support. Over a two-year period (June 2000–June 2002), the campaign received nearly $62 million in donated media support, which is around the average for Ad Council campaigns.

Survey Results. Prior to the national launch, a tracking survey of gun-owning parents was launched making the benchmark June 2000. Post-wave surveys were then conducted in June 2001 (Post-wave I) and July 2002 (Post-wave II). Survey results showed modest shifts in awareness, attitudes, and behaviors. *Awareness*: Recall of the ads grew from 26 percent at Post-wave I to 31 percent at Post-wave II. *Attitudes*: A large number of respondents used the word "lock" in their definition of safe storage. However, in the pre-wave, only 34 percent of survey respondents included "storage in a gun cabinet or rack" in their "locked" definition of safe storage. By Post-wave II, that number was up to 58 percent. *Behavior*: Previous research has shown that most gun-owning

(*continued*)

EXHIBIT 17-1   (cont.)

parents report that their guns are stored in a place that is hard for children to access. In the Pre-wave 86 percent of respondents stated this, and by Post-wave II this increased to 91 percent. In Post-wave II, the number of parents reporting moving guns or locking them for the first time, increased from 6 to 12 percent.

Public Relations. The campaign also received news coverage with an estimated value of $957,000; therefore, based on circulation and impression figures of print and TV media, it is estimated the campaign reached 6 million people through local news.

Fulfillment Results. Finally, the campaign had a web site (www.unloadandlock. com) which, although not a focus of the campaign, received more than 150,000 hits over two years.

Source: This summary was prepared by Michelle Greene of Georgetown University from material at: www.adcouncil.org/default.aspx?id=315#Safe%20Gun%20Storage%20Campaign.

anti-tobacco campaign of the American Legacy Foundation, the prime beneficiary of hundreds of millions of dollars in the national U.S. tobacco litigation settlement (www.americanlegacy.org).

OTHER MARKETING ALLIANCES WITH THE PRIVATE SECTOR[7]

The dramatic growth in marketing alliances with business[8] can be traced to 1982 when Jerry C. Welsh, then chief of worldwide marketing for the American Express Company, agreed to make a five cent donation to the arts in San Francisco every time someone used an American Express card and two dollars every time American Express got a new member. In three months, the campaign raised $108,000. The approach gained national attention when American Express (AmEx) tried it out on a country-wide basis. In 1983, AmEx agreed to set aside one cent for every card transaction and one dollar for each new card issued during the last quarter of 1983 to support the renovation of Ellis Island and the Statue of Liberty. The program was a great success. American Express reported sales increases of 28 percent over the same period a year earlier with a total of $1.7 million eventually donated to the renovation project.[9]

The marketing alliances that have evolved since then take many forms.[10] They may be either contractual or relational (i.e., having or not having a fixed termination point). They are typically part of—but distinguishable from—the broader category "corporate social responsibility." The latter encompasses all of a corporation's responsibilities to society including its treatment of its employees and the environment, its accounting and disclosure practices, and its corporate ethics. The latter responsibilities often are described as minimizing the potential *negative* impact of a corporation on society whereas the marketing alliances we are discussing here are designed to have a positive impact (as is the goal of traditional corporate giving).

If one considers the first cause-related marketing venture by American Express in 1982 as the starting point of the recent intense interest in social marketing partnerships, it seems fair to conclude that most reported social alliances to date have been contractual alliances. The dominance of the contractual form may be changing as commercial organizations see the strategic potential of other kinds of social alliances and so develop longer-term, more open-ended relationships. One example of a longer-term alliance is the agreement signed between Coca-Cola and the Boys & Girls Clubs of America (BGCA) through which Coca-Cola agreed to invest $60 million and significant staff time over 10 years to help BCGA increase the number of young people participating in its programs (www.bcga.org). Such a relationship meets our criteria in that:

1. Coca-Cola was able to significantly increase its exposure to a prime market target (young people), improve staff morale through local community activities, and improve its corporate image.
2. BGCA received significant investment capital, volunteer assistance, and new promotional opportunities.
3. BGCA did not pay Coca-Cola for the services it rendered to BCGA.
4. The result is intended to be a significant increase in the number of at-risk young people involved in positive after-school activities.

Corporate–nonprofit alliances can sometimes be distinguished from traditional corporate philanthropy. When Digital Equipment Corporation, IBM, and Sony agree to contribute equipment to the National Center for Missing and Exploited Children to help it create and distribute posters depicting missing children, it was considered corporate philanthropy because reports indicated that none of the companies used its support for promotional purposes. The same is said to be true of ARCO's support of an educational program called ALIVE (Alternatives to Living in a Violent Environment). Although some might dispute it, ARCO claims the program is not designed to impress final consumers.[11] Many authors suggest the most important criterion for charitable donations from other marketing alliances is whether funding comes out of the firm's marketing budget or out of its regular charitable donations.[12]

Contractual and strategic alliances have proved to be very successful. For example, consider the ongoing Avon Breast Cancer Awareness Crusade, which was initiated in 1993 and is run through the Avon Foundation. Through 2005, Avon has raised and donated $400 million in 50 countries for medical research, access to services, screening, education, and support services. Avon, with other partners, carries out walks and runs and sells special merchandise (e.g., pins with the insignia of the pink breast cancer ribbon) through its 600,000 Avon agents worldwide. Thirty-nine countries now participate in Avon's annual Walk Around the World for Breast Cancer. These efforts have distributed millions of flyers on breast cancer detection.[13]

Gourville and Rangan[14] have suggested that corporate–nonprofit alliances be distinguished in terms of whether they produce first-order and second-order benefits. First-order benefits for the corporate partner would be sales and other forms of direct revenue while for the nonprofit organization it would be direct financial payments or the contribution of goods, services, and volunteers. Sales-related cause-marketing transactions are a common example in this category where a nonprofit gets a donation every time a customer of a corporation buys something.

Second-order benefits are not immediate but are anticipated in the future. For the corporation, a second-order benefit might include improvement in employee morale that leads to more sales enthusiasm or less workforce absenteeism. Another second-order benefit in the twenty-first century is the attractiveness of socially responsible firms to investors and investment firms like Fidelity and Calvert.[15] Another benefit from alliances may be the chance to partner with other businesses as when Blockbuster partners with Coca-Cola to produce a commercial for Boys & Girls Clubs of America to be shown in Blockbuster outlets.

Nonprofit second-order benefits may stem from brand enhancements from partnering with a prestigious corporation that influences future support from individuals and other corporations. Increased visibility for an obscure nonprofit may result as well as a shift in evaluation of its managerial competence. There may be learning of new marketing skills that can improve future effectiveness. The Independent Sector recently listed a number of second-order benefits:[16]

- Increased revenue
- Impact on mission
- Enhanced visibility of the cause or the nonprofit's message
- Access to new audiences
- Connections to the corporation's network of employees, suppliers, distributors, and other contacts
- Expertise in marketing, strategy development, and other corporate experience

One should note, however, that nonprofits may not be capturing as much of the first- and second-order benefits as they should. It has been suggested that nonprofit organizations may simply not charge enough to capture their share of the corporate payoff.[17]

A prominent and long running collaboration in history is that between the National Football League (NFL) and United Way of America. When it began back in 1973, United Way wanted to dramatically raise its profile and the NFL was eager to promote its players, who are hidden behind pads and helmets. The United Way-NFL campaign, featuring TV and radio ads primarily, has dramatically helped both organizations achieve their goals. The image shown in Figure 17-6 is reflective of the contributions that NFL players make off the field by working with United Way.

Corporate–Nonprofit Alliances

Berger, Cunningham, and Drumwright have suggested that cross-sector partnerships can vary on a number of dimensions:[18]

1. *Number of partners.* Some alliances are one-on-one but many involve multiple players.
2. *Length of commitment.* Some alliances are for a single event or promotion such as a race or some other fundraiser. The Boys & Girls Clubs of America partnership with Coca-Cola is, of course, a 10-year partnership as is the Clubs' series of 3-year partnerships with Procter & Gamble's Crest.
3. *Level of investment.*
4. *Few or many initiatives.*
5. *Brand-level or company-level collaboration.*
6. *Dedicated manager and dedicated marketing budget or none.*
7. *Fixed or variable donation amounts.*
8. *Opportunities for grassroots engagement of company employees and customers or not.*

Alliances may take a number of forms we shall consider next.[19]

FIGURE 17-6   Softening the NFL's Image

Source: Courtesy of the United Way of America.

Corporate Issue Promotion

This is the case where a corporation promotes some socially desirable behavior on its own without the involvement of any nonprofit—although the latter may benefit from it. A prime example is the Anheuser-Busch campaign promoting responsible drinking (www.beeresponsible.com) and the use of designated drivers (www.designateddriver.com). While the ads promote socially desirable behavior, they also remind consumers of the product brand name and cast the corporate product line in the image of one that is purchased by sensible, mature drinkers.

Liz Claiborne has ads calling attention to domestic violence (www.loveisnotabuse.com). Timberland attempts to combat racism with billboards in New York and Germany. Many years ago, Benetton produced shocking ads designed to energize consumers to care about AIDS[20] and a 96-page insert in major newspapers in late 1999 designed to protest the death sentence.[21]

There are also many examples of corporations simply marketing desirable social behaviors to their own employees. Take, for example, obesity. Corporations recognize that overweight employees are risking not only their own health and lives, but they also can cost the corporation in terms of lost work time and various health service costs. Minor approaches have been taken: Nextel built its parking lots a five-minute walk from its offices. A bigger investment is one by Microsoft that will pay up to 80 percent of the cost of a comprehensive clinic-based weight-loss program for employees. Microsoft also provides obese employees personal trainers, behavioral and nutrition counseling, support groups, and medical supervision. *Business Week* reports that since 2002, 2,152 Microsoft employees have lost 61,100 pounds![22]

Joint Issue Promotion

This is where a corporation, in cooperation with a nonprofit or government organization, pays for and/or designs a campaign to urge certain behaviors without expecting any immediate direct payback. Safeway helps fund and promote several causes. It provides $110 million worth of food and merchandise to local food banks. It has raised over $87.5 million for Easter Seals and the Muscular Dystrophy Association and, since 2000 given more than $130 milllion to support education and schools.

Sales-Related Promotions

This is where a corporation agrees to donate funds or equipment to a nonprofit or charitable organization in proportion to the number of sales or other customer transactions that are made. This type is typically what is meant by cause-related marketing, although the term has come to encompass other types of alliances. The American Express campaign was such an alliance. Until very recently, the campaign donated two cents of every cardholder purchase during a specific holiday period to its campaign "Charge against Hunger." It has donated millions of dollars over the years to Share Our Strength, a Washington, D.C., hunger organization, under this program.[23] Another common form of sales-related alliance are those developed by credit card issuers. These cards are used to attract new customers while the corporation saves costs by not offering as many card features as non-affinity cards. In 2001, MasterCard had 15,000 affinity and co-branded cards worldwide.[24]

Most Americans are familiar with Newman's Own, a company that takes sales-related alliances to the highest level, boasting "All profits for charity."[25] The company was started by actor Paul Newman and writer A. E. Hotchner in 1982 as something of a lark and had an initial investment of $20,000. The company's products are now available all over the world, furthering its approach to marketing as "Shameless exploitation in pursuit of the common good." Newman's Own along with Paul Newman himself have donated over $200 million in after-tax profits to thousands of charities in the United States and elsewhere.[26]

Campbell's Soup Company and a number of other corporations—especially supermarkets—have long had programs involving donations to schools based on product sales. For example, in 1999, Campbell collected 250 million labels which it converted into purchases of school equipment. General Mills has a similar program involving boxtops.[27]

Licensing and Co-branding

Historically, nonprofit organizations have from time to time licensed their logos to private sector marketers and reaped financial benefits, either a flat fee or a percentage of profits from sales of co-branded products. Universities are prime examples of this approach—for example, Georgetown sweatshirts are found in all corners of the planet. Where the licensing arrangement involves another well-known brand, these programs are sometimes referred to as co-branding. Many years ago, the American Cancer Society (ACS) developed a co-branding relationship with SmithKlineBeecham, the makers of NicoDerm, and the Florida Citrus Commission whereby both businesses could use the ACS logo on their products. The American Cancer Society justified these arrangements not so much for the licensing fees they would produce but because consumption of these products could help prevent cancer. The ACS's view was that if its logo would increase consumption, then the society's own mission would be advanced. For example, the slogan in the television ads for NicoDerm in 2002 was "Partners in helping you quit."

In other examples, Bristol-Myers Squibb has run full-page advertisements for Pravachol, a cholesterol-lowering drug that featured the name and logo of the American Heart Association. Similarly, Electrolux LLC negotiated an exclusive arrangement with the Asthma and Allergy Foundation to use its name and logo on the cartons in which its vacuum cleaners are packaged and in product literature.

Licensing can also work in the other direction. It is now common for nonprofit organizations like universities and some cultural institutions to have franchised restaurants and coffee shops on their premises. Perhaps the most unusual of these ventures was the decision of the Family Christian Center in Munster, Indiana, to put a Starbucks in its church lobby. Church officials said that the site does not generate a lot of revenue but "It tears down walls and the perception that church is stuffy and cold."[28]

Other Alliances

There are other forms that alliances take, some of which are described in other chapters. Lichtenstein, Drumwright, and Braig suggest that some volunteering projects by corporate employees are really alliances that can have human resources benefits and long-term sales payoffs. For example, many efforts to provide software and train users in poor countries in computer use not only makes employees of Cisco and HP feel good but these efforts can influence brand preferences and future sales.[29]

Volunteering alliances can also help in recruiting. Recently, Yahoo! volunteered its own programmers—including co-founder David Filo—to help charities improve their web sites. *Business Week* says: "Yahoo sees the contribution not just as philanthropy but as a tool in the red-hot tech talent wars."[30] Other organizations make volunteering an employee perk. An employee at a New England software company was thrilled that her company offers employees three days at full salary for volunteer work. She commented: "My previous company donated money to a few charities, but this makes me feel more personally useful."[31]

There are also alliances that have more political ends—designed to ingratiate a company with a local government—and sometimes the international community. In the early days of family planning social marketing programs in India, Unilever and Brooke Bond Tea Company both helped distribute condoms and other contraceptive products along with their soaps and teas.[32] Post, Preston, and Sachs suggest that such ventures are, in part, *a license to operate* in potentially hostile political environments.[33] In 2002, Marathon Oil wanted to expand natural gas operations off the coast of Equatorial Guinea. Marathon partnered with nonprofit organizations and the local government to attempt to stop the spread of malaria, pouring $12 million into the effort. In two years, the number of infected mosquitoes fell 95 percent and the number of infected children fell from 45 to 26 percent. Only 2 or 3 cases affected Marathon personnel compared to 20 to 30 in the past. Similar steps against malaria have been undertaken by BP in southern Mozambique.[34]

Perhaps the most impressive effort to attack malaria is the NetMark project in Sub-Saharan Africa. It is described by Bill Smith, Executive Vice President of the Academy for Educational Development, in Exhibit 17-2.

EXHIBIT 17-2

BILL SMITH OF THE ACADEMY FOR EDUCATIONAL DEVELOPMENT ON NETMARK: A CASE STUDY IN SUSTAINABLE MALARIA PREVENTION THROUGH PARTNERSHIP WITH BUSINESS

NetMark Accomplishments 2000–2005:

- More than US$18 million has been invested by private sector partners in developing the commercial ITN market in Africa.

- Nearly 15 million more people are protected from malaria by insecticide-treated bed nets (ITNs).

- More than 100 million people have been educated about malaria, the importance of ITNs, and how to use them effectively.

- More than 350,000 pregnant women and children under five have gotten discount vouchers for ITNs, of which 243,000 have been redeemed.

- Treated nets now cost from 30 to 75 percent less than untreated nets did in 2000 due to competition fostered by NetMark.

- NetMark has increased the supply of ITNs in eight African countries, with the number of ITN distributors increasing from 2 in 1999 to 29 in 2005.

NetMark is a unique cross-sector partnership created to fight malaria in sub-Saharan Africa where the disease kills more than 2 million people each year. It was initiated by the United States Agency for International Development (USAID) and developed under the management of the Academy for Educational Development (AED), a nonprofit human and social development organization.

NetMark's mandate is to increase demand for and expand the availability of insecticide-treated nets (ITNs), a simple but effective way to prevent the mosquito bites that cause malaria. To accomplish this task, AED has developed a market-based approach of shared risk and investment dubbed Full Market Impact™ (FMI™), based on the premise that as demand grows within a competitive market, consumers will benefit from improved quality, lower prices, and wider availability.

FMI™ provides an operational model that creates common ground between the private and public sectors. Partners from both sectors agree on common objectives while observing their respective roles across each of the five factors: supply, distribution, affordability, demand/appropriate use, and equity/sustainable markets.

NetMark's FMI™ model was intentionally designed to reflect the way businesses thought about the market, thus the model's convergence with the classic "4 Ps" of marketing: product, place, price, and promotion. In this way, FMI™ demonstrates how meeting the needs of the poor can translate into good business that promotes expansion into new market segments. AED believes that FMI™ challenges the way businesses think about market opportunity, taking a broader view of the role their products play and the consumer behaviors they influence, while addressing critical public health issues and serving the needs of the poor.

In its six years, the NetMark project has shown that international and African companies are willing to invest in producing, marketing, and distributing ITNs when working in partnership with the public sector.

Data from household surveys conducted by NetMark in 2004 show considerable gains since the baseline research in 2000 and the first country launch in late 2001. In all NetMark countries, awareness and use of nets and ITNs increased dramatically, and more nets are being treated or purchased pre-treated. For example, the percentage of households that owned a net or ITN in Nigeria rose from 12 percent in 2000 to 27 percent in 2004; in Senegal from 34 to 56 percent; and in Zambia from 27 to 50 percent. Moreover, NetMark's commercial sector consumers approach resulted in increased use among all socio-economic groups. Net coverage rates are increasing equitably, and vulnerable groups are being reached in both urban and rural areas.

By 2004, ITN sales by NetMark's formal partners neared the 2 million mark. While this represented only 62 percent of the ambitious projection total made by the various commercial partners for 2004, it represented a 132 percent increase over 2003 sales. Progress is being made in a sustainable manner, and the market appears to be poised for rapid growth now that supply issues are being addressed. Overall commercial sales in NetMark countries have reached 9 million based on reports from partners, and estimates of additional sales made by NetMark based on market research conducted in 2004.

This demonstrates the broad impact NetMark has had on growing the overall market.

Challenges still lie ahead. Public policy must continue to support ITNs and a role for the commercial sector; free and subsidized ITN programs must be fully targeted to the poorest and not totally undermine commercial investments; NetMark and partner marketing efforts must continue to build sustainable demand; and NetMark's commercial partners must expand their investment in ITNs to replace the support provided by NetMark. Under these conditions, the ITN market will continue to grow while serving the public health fight against malaria.

Many alliances take the form of web site promotions. Starbucks has a webpage where it discusses social responsibility issues and it has an online newsletter on similar topics. Hurricane Katrina prompted many corporations to use their Internet sites to reach out to hurricane victims. These included State Farm, Wal-Mart, and Wachovia.[35] A broader complex set of brand-building and social investment approaches is followed by McDonald's. It is well known for its Ronald McDonald houses and related charitable efforts. But it also participates in immunization programs for kids and provides mobile medical and dental clinics for underserved families.[36]

Another form of alliance is that of providing retailing help for nonprofit products. At one time, Timberland provided space in selected stores for City Year's fledgling attempts at marketing a line of branded apparel. UNICEF holiday cards are available at IKEA and Pier 1 stores. More recently, Hallmark agreed to distribute UNICEF cards year round—not just the winter holiday line. UNICEF cards have been more successful overseas than in the United States. Germany provides about one-quarter of gross revenues for UNICEF's card sales. Hallmark says that it will also contribute its design skills to the venture.[37]

Time magazine devoted a page of their "web shopping guide 2006" to gifts "for the humanitarian" with links to web sites where one can shop and support featured charities. The promotion featured Global Exchange, Ten Thousand Villages, and Novica. The latter helps distribute the works of 1,700 artists around the world who would not otherwise have access to such a large potential customer base.[38]

Results

The level of cross-sector social alliances is significant. With respect to cause-marketing only, a 2004 survey of leading Fortune 500 product manufacturers and national and regional retailers reported that *every one* of them engaged in cause-related marketing. Of these projects, 41 percent were multi-year and 95 percent involved a relationship at least five years old.[39] The IEG Sponsorship Report reports total expenditures for all kinds of sponsorships at an estimated $12.1 billion for 2005, up 8.8 percent from 2004.[40] International sponsorships in 2005 were estimated at $8.4 billion in Europe, $5.8 billion in the Pacific Rim, $2.5 billion in Central and South America, and $1.6 in other regions.

Because "sponsorships" include a great many ventures that are purely commercial—such as sponsoring NASCAR races or golf tournaments, one needs to focus on sponsorships of "causes," which amounted to $1.17 billion in 2005 and an estimated $1.34 billion in 2006 (a 14.5 percent growth).[41] A comparison of the growth in cause-marketing partnerships to that of corporate philanthropy in general[42] is instructive. Cause sponsorships amounted to $120 million in 1990 and corporate philanthropy was $7,690 million. By 2004, sponsorship of causes grew 823 percent, whereas corporate philanthropy grew only 56 percent. In the more recent period between 2002 and 2004, cause-related marketing grew 13 percent and corporate philanthropy actually declined.

Positive anecdotal results abound and several books have been published detailing both examples and suggestions about how to do alliances well. Among the more valuable are books by Adkins and by Pringle and Thompson, mostly with U.K. examples, and by Kotler and Lee and by Daw for recent U.S. examples.[43] The Cause Marketing Forum and IEG Sponsorship newsletters provide even more timely examples.

The effect on corporate customers and potential customers is undoubtedly a major driver of these alliances. The most frequently cited study in this regard is the 2004 "Cone/Roper Corporate Citizenship Study." Cone/Roper reported that 86 percent of the adults they surveyed reported that they would "switch from one brand to another that is about the same in price and quality if the other brand was associated with a cause." Further, 74 percent of the respondents said that a company's commitment to a social issue would be important to them in deciding which products and services they would recommend to other people.[44] Other studies reflect the same phenomenon. Interestingly, the studies also suggest that favorable corporate citizenship would also affect people's job choices as well as having a company located in their community.[45] An international study in 20 countries revealed that supporting a cause increases company awareness by respondents by 56 percent. Further, 43 percent believed that such firms sold good quality products and 53 percent said they would buy from them.[46] Another study showed that half of consumers studied in both the United States and the United Kingdom had switched brands or increased brand usage because of social involvements.[47]

It should be pointed out that many of these studies are potentially biased towards results favorable to partners in cause-marketing ventures. For example, if someone is asked "if all other things are equal, would you buy Brand X if it offered something more—something that is a socially valued feature?" the answer is highly likely to be "yes." The real test would be if the product or service cost more!

Obviously, there are similar benefits to nonprofit organizations from associations with well-known brands beyond the money they bring in. As we have noted, the partnerships can increase visibility and favorable perceptions, especially if the nonprofit is not well known.[48] It can bring in new knowledge and motivate nonprofit workers. Corporate executives may volunteer and serve on the board. And access to other resources—meeting space, contacts with civic leaders, and the like—can come from having the corporation be a co-sponsor of some venture.

Risks

It might seem that marketing alliances represent a classical win–win situation. The nonprofit marketer gets needed funds, assistance, and attention to an issue; the private sector marketer gets more sales, a better public image, improved employee morale, and, in many cases, better relations with distributors who participate in programs. There are, however, a number of potential pitfalls for both sides of the relationship.

Risks For Marketers

For many private sector marketers, there is a potential for significant negative publicity if the relationship is not the proper one and is not handled in an ethical manner. Consumers may be very cynical about actions that seem to be transparent attempts to win tolerance of unhealthy business practices. For example, despite its considerable investment in nonprofit causes such as the Bill of Rights commemorative promotion, Philip Morris has faced a great many criticisms of its actions as cynical. Many thought that, through the Bill of Rights program, Phillip Morris was simply trying to curry support for its efforts to hold back increased restrictions on smoking. Philip Morris's more recent attempts to say that it truly does not want teens to smoke—its "Think Don't Smoke" campaign—has also met with criticism. A study showed that the campaign not only made respondents think *more favorably* about the industry, the probability of a teen intending to smoke went up![49] Greenpeace criticized General Motors for its tree-planting program as "greenwashing" because the program tries to cover over the fact that GM has been "a leader in the lobby against fuel efficiency in cars, and that lack of fuel efficiency is one of the primary causes of the greenhouse effect."[50]

If the marketer is not fully candid with the public, especially about the amount being donated, its image may suffer. American Express is always very clear to say that it is involved in cause-related marketing at least in part because it hopes to increase sales, employee morale, and so forth. By contrast, Barnes & Noble, in a cause-related marketing project in Minneapolis, promoted "Operation Bookshelf" in which the public was invited to buy books for donation to children's programs. What the chain did not tell the public was that the company donated *nothing* to the children's program. In fact, it kept the profits on the book sales.[51]

If the partnership does not fit with the corporation's core product and service offerings, there can also be a backlash. It makes sense for Home Depot to partner with Habitat for Humanity International but probably would raise questions in the minds of consumers if it got involved in AIDS issues or the stem-cell research controversy. Ethos Water's effort to contribute funds from branded bottled water sales to aid water projects in Bangladesh, Ethiopia, and India is a good example of a seamless fit.[52] Scott Farrell of Golin/Harris says that when a partnership is not tied to a brand's core meaning, it's a problem: "When it's a bolt-on, it's almost the kiss of death."[53]

Also, problems can arise if the marketer is not candid with its partner nonprofit. Bad feelings and bad press can emerge. A good example is the experience of the Women in Community Service (WICS) program. According to WICS, a public relations firm, Fleishman–Hillard, contacted the agency and said that the retailer Limited Express had designated WICS as the recipient of a program it had devised. Under the program, people would bring in used jeans to Express, get a 25 percent discount on new jeans, and WICS would get the used jeans. Limited Express put flyers announcing the program in billing statements to 200,000 of its customers. What it neglected to do was ask WICS if it wanted to participate, which it did not, in part because it had no way to make use of the used jeans it was to be given. Subsequently, no jeans were given to WICS, and WICS claimed that Limited Express owed it $110,200 for the use of its name in a promotion that sold 3,800 pairs of jeans at $29. Lawyers then became the beneficiary of the fiasco. As Carole Cone of Cone Communications noted, "This was just a case of bad business. A good cause-related marketing project is . . . not something shoved down the throat of one party."[54]

Excessive righteousness on the part of a corporation can cause critics to lie in wait until the corporation shows its first flaw. In a 1994 editorial in *Advertising Age,* editor Rance Crain criticizes corporations like the Body Shop, saying "the common denominator of these kinds of companies is that they maintain a holier than thou attitude. But if they should stumble and show any evidence of not living up to their lofty preachings, their customers will hold them strictly accountable, more so than if they operated a more mundane—if less contentious—institution."[55]

In an age in which pressure groups can quickly mount protests—even boycotts— through the Internet, it is a brave corporation that becomes involved, even indirectly, in a controversial topic. Mattel produces a line called American Girl and gave $50,000 to Girls, Inc. for a program promoting math skills. But the nonprofit Pro-Life Action League said that Girls Inc. supports abortion rights and so it urged a boycott of Mattel products. American Girl spokesperson Julie Parks said: "We're a political ping-pong ball."[56] And Kraft faced a complaint at a stockholders meeting when it supported the 2006 Gay Games VII.[57]

Finally, the ultimate negative is simply that the nonprofit alliance does not really have any significant payoff. A recent article in the *Stanford Social Innovation Review* documents a number of cases where the payoff has been marginal or nil. The authors note that consumers may express a favorable attitude toward socially responsible firms but simply not act on these attitudes. They cite the experience of Starbucks as support. Sales levels of Starbucks' promotion of Fair Trade coffee have been "much lower than expected."[58]

Risks For Nonprofits

There are also a number of important risks to nonprofits' revenues and prestige from becoming involved in cross-sector marketing alliances. The private sector marketer may unduly restrict the nonprofit's operations because he or she wishes to "own" the charity venture. Many marketers feel they can benefit most if they are very closely identified with a specific cause, as the Body Shop is with the environment or 7-Eleven is with the Muscular Dystrophy Society. Marketers may seek an exclusive arrangement with the nonprofit that is not in the latter's interests. They may also simply put pressure on the nonprofit not to engage in other cross-sector marketing ventures or even certain kinds of fundraising that the marketer considers competitive.

The private sector marketer may attract unwanted negative publicity to the nonprofit from its actions in other domains. For example, in October 1993, Jenny Craig Inc. announced that it would give $10 for every new enrollment in its weight-loss programs to the Dallas-based Susan G. Komen Breast Cancer Foundation and would spend $7 million on advertising promoting breast cancer awareness. However, just before the program was announced, Jenny Craig was cited by the Federal Trade Commission for engaging in deceptive advertising practices by making unsubstantiated weight-loss claims. Although the Komen Foundation was aware of the pending charges when it entered the arrangement with Jenny Craig, it was hoping that the matter would be settled before the program was announced.[59]

Close identification with a major corporation may cause individual potential donors to believe that the nonprofit has less need for direct funding because it is "being taken care of" by the company. The Salvation Army is worried that a large donation from Joan Kroc may inhibit ordinary givers. Donors and other supporters may also be put off by what they see as the nonprofit's excessive commercialism. The introduction of corporate partnerships in public schools has led many parents and social critics to say that schools are feeding their kids to the corporate world and mainly teaching them to be good consumers. Many think this should not be a major (or any) undertaking of school systems even when they are significantly strapped for cash.

Then there is a danger that the nonprofit will lose credibility or integrity through its corporate joint venture. There is the potential of an organization being accused of "selling out" to corporate interests. This is particularly a potential problem for cultural organizations. We previously mentioned the problems of Lawrence Small at the Smithsonian Institution. More recently, the art critic of the *New York Times* lambasted the Los Angeles County Museum for its corporate alliance for an exhibition of King Tut artifacts. He lamented the case that most people accept the fact that the museum "has effectively sold its good name and gallery space to a for-profit company. . . . [A]t cultural institutions today, it seems to increasingly corrupt ethics and undermine bedrock goals like preserving collections and upholding the public interest."[60]

When new food labels were introduced in the United States in 1994, the makers of Quaker Oats Squares, Healthy Choice pasta sauce, Progresso Healthy Classic soups, and a home cholesterol test kit helped the American Heart Association distribute brochures explaining the labels. But two-thirds of the brochures comprised cents-off coupons for the sponsoring products.[61] Many felt that this venture compromised the Heart Association's independence as a voice advocating the best heart-healthy eating and exercising programs.

A dramatic example of co-branding gone wrong was the 1997 agreement between the American Medical Association (AMA) and Sunbeam, which permitted Sunbeam to put AMA's name on products ranging from blood pressure monitors to heating pads. This was an exclusive agreement whereby the American Medical Association name could not be used with rival products. AMA members raised a storm of protest over this agreement, fearing that the AMA name on these Sunbeam products would imply an endorsement and/or would signify that the products were superior to competitive products. The AMA abandoned the arrangement but paid Sunbeam $10 million to settle a breach-of-contract lawsuit.[62]

Frustration on the part of the nonprofit organization with its corporate alliance can emanate from several sources as detailed in a recent study of such alliances.[63] These include:

- Misundertandings—often at the start of an alliance—where, for example, each side had unrealistic expectations of the other party
- Misallocation of costs and benefits—especially when the nonprofit feels it is getting much less than its "fair share"
- Mismatches of power—for example, where the nonprofit receives very little recognition in corporate promotions of the alliance
- Mismatched partners—especially in management styles
- Misfortunes of time—without effort, alliances can get stale
- Mistrust—worry about the other's motives can lead to a lack of candor or, worse, efforts to weaken or undermine a partner

Developing a Sound Cause-Related Marketing Strategy

From the nonprofit marketer's standpoint, there are a number of steps to be followed if a cross-sector marketing alliance is to be successful:

1. Use board members and community supporters to identify potential partners. They also can often detect possible problems.
2. Select a partner with whom there is a mutuality of interest. Thus the Special Olympics should look to sporting goods companies as sponsors, hunger programs to supermarket chains, and alcohol abuse programs to the beer or liquor industries. It was natural for the National Center for Missing and Exploited Children to turn to Kodak to develop a photo identification system called KidCare ID that would assist police in cases of missing or abducted children.[64] Mutuality of interest has a number of advantages:
    - Both parties are likely to understand the nature of the social problem and the major solutions.
    - The public is likely to be less suspicious of the marketer's involvement. That is, they will not see it as the marketer doing a "cause-of-the-month."

- Corporations with mutual interest will be much more receptive to solicitations for joint ventures.

3. Screen out partners who may present a conflict of interest. Wallace and Mintz list four potential disqualifiers. A nonprofit should exclude partners:

   - Whose product/service conflicts with the nonprofit's mandate (e.g., Frito-Lay should not sponsor a fat reduction program).
   - Whose product is hazardous to health or the environment.
   - Who is under investigation for health, environment, or other violations.
   - Whose product and service claims, especially in the area of health, are unsubstantiated.[65]

4. Ensure that the proposed relationship meets the corporation's needs and wants (remember that this is a *marketing* task). The nonprofit marketer seeking a corporate partner should be imaginative in portraying how a cause-related marketing venture could meet corporate interests. For example, Second Harvest, a Chicago-based network of community food banks that feed the hungry, seeks out food company help noting how participation in Second Harvest food donations can meet some important bottom-line needs:

   - Solving excess inventory problems
   - Providing an opportunity for tax benefits
   - Distributing products in a visible manner that can substitute for media promotion
   - Deflecting charitable requests that would have gone to the retailers with which they are trying to build goodwill[66]

5. Develop a carefully designed, well-thought-through proposal before contacting the corporation. Include the following:

   - Show how the charitable organization is well run and its brand has zero blemishes.
   - Show how the corporation will benefit in terms of *its own* strategic and tactical interests.
   - Show how the corporation can add value to the project.
   - Specify the resource level required of both parties.
   - Describe how the project will be evaluated.[67]

   Note that it is not always necessary to have a proposal in writing to present. Kurt Aschermann, formerly of the Boys & Girls Clubs of America, believes strongly in "proposal-less" partnership building. He believes that it is critical to have a dialogue with the potential partner and mutually build a personal relationship as well as an organizational one.

6. Make sure that there is a clear specification of the roles that each partner is to play. Make sure that there is full communication so that no one is surprised, especially with unpleasant publicity. Again, Kurt Aschermann has been very careful to discuss with potential partners what he calls his "will do/won't do" list at the very outset of negotiations. Most importantly, this sets out what the nonprofit organization will *not* do for a partner. This has saved the organization from some awkward demands by partners with whom it really wants to work.

7. Insist on complete candor with the public. Nothing will sabotage a good cause-related marketing program faster than the public learning that while corporation X is donating 1 percent of sales to charity Y, there is a limit on total giving—and the limit is rather low! The Better Business Bureau keeps a close watch on such practices and points to dubious examples such as the pharmaceutical company that advertised that up to $400,000 would be donated to a health and education charity based on the amount of donations contributed by customers. In fact, the company guaranteed the $400,000 in advance (which was good in itself), but the amount was totally unrelated to what any consumers did.[68] The corporate partners must also agree to be totally candid about what they are putting into and what they are getting out of the arrangement. The public will respect organizations that acknowledge that a program helps their bottom line while benefiting a major social cause.

8. Make the relationship a long-term one. The nonprofit should beware of the corporation that jumps on an issue quickly, perhaps for a quick "image fix." The nonprofit may be hurt if it relies on a corporation with a short-term objective that bails out after a brief period—and plenty of publicity. A long-term orientation to the partnership also allows the partners to evolve into other projects as initial ventures serve their purpose.

9. Requests from the corporate partners should not be excessively restrictive so that the nonprofit's operating flexibility is unduly hampered. The nonprofit should, at minimum, agree not to involve competing organizations in the venture. Corporations like to dominate a charitable project or at least be dominant over direct competitors.

10. Evaluate the results honestly. This will be particularly important to the corporate partner which often must justify cross-sector ventures to stockholders. It is also very important for both sides to learn from each venture so as to improve future efforts. Careful research can often be the basis for attracting new partners in the future who, as is more and more common these days, want hard numbers about likely payouts. The appropriate evaluation depends on the project.

11. Make sure that the corporate gets significant praise for what it is doing. If nothing, corporations almost always are eager to be recognized as good community—and world—citizens. The United Way is particularly good at this (see Figure 17-7).

The Collaboration Continuum

In a 2000 book published by the Drucker Foundation,[69] James Austin of Harvard University summarized the experiences of a number of major social alliances including those between Timberland and City Year, Starbucks and CARE, and The Nature Conservancy and Georgia-Pacific. Austin discovered that these relationships tended to evolve through three stages:

- The *Philanthropic stage* where organizations get to know each other through the traditional process of seeking and gaining corporate donations. This stage often leads to strong personal connections.
- The *Transactional stage* where organizations move on to a specific partnership to exchange resources around a specific delineated activity. Much cause-related marketing is of this type.
- The *Integrative stage* where "the partners' missions, people, and activities begin to experience more collective action and organizational integration."

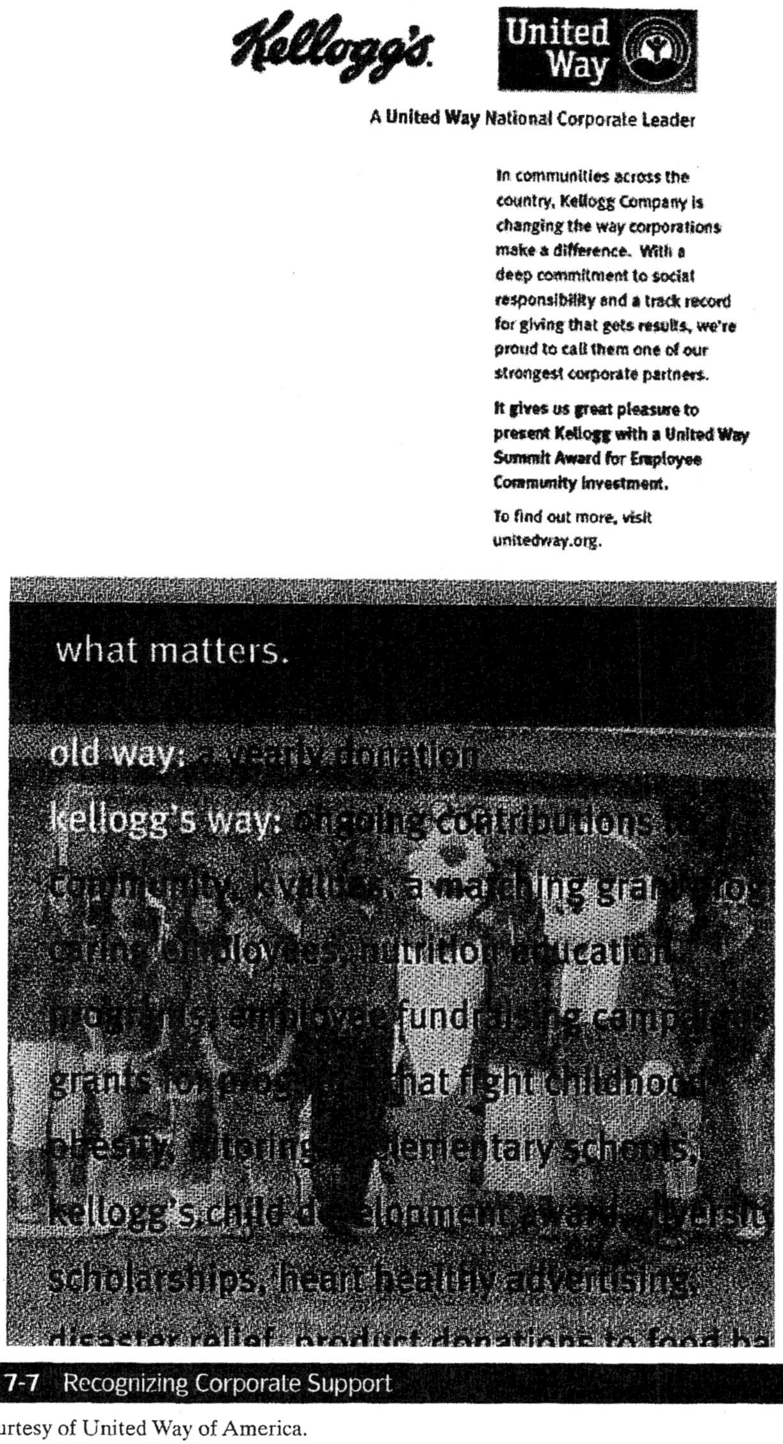

A United Way National Corporate Leader

In communities across the country, Kellogg Company is changing the way corporations make a difference. With a deep commitment to social responsibility and a track record for giving that gets results, we're proud to call them one of our strongest corporate partners.

It gives us great pleasure to present Kellogg with a United Way Summit Award for Employee Community Investment.

To find out more, visit unitedway.org.

what matters.

old way: a yearly donation

kellogg's way: ongoing contributions to community. values. a matching grant to caring employees. nutrition education programs. employee fundraising campaigns. grants for programs that fight childhood obesity. tutoring in elementary schools. kellogg's child development awards. diversity scholarships. heart healthy advertising. disaster relief. product donations to food ba

FIGURE 17-7   Recognizing Corporate Support

Source: Courtesy of United Way of America.

EXHIBIT 17-3

JAMES AUSTIN'S SEVEN C'S OF STRATEGIC COLLABORATION

CONNECTION with Purpose and People. Alliances are successful when key individuals connect personally and emotionally with the alliance's social purpose and with each other.

CLARITY of Purpose. Collaborators need to be clear—preferably in writing— about the purpose of joint undertakings.

CONGRUENCY of Mission, Strategy, and Values. The closer the alignment between the two organizations' missions, strategies, and values, the greater the potential gains from collaboration.

CREATION of Value. High-performance collaborations are about mobilizing and combining multiple resources and capabilities to generate benefits for both parties and social value for society.

COMMUNICATION between Partners. Even in the presence of good personal relations and emotional connections, strategic fit, and successful value creation, a partnership is without a solid foundation if it lacks an effective ongoing communication process.

CONTINUAL Learning. A partnership's evolution cannot be completely planned or entirely predicted and so partners should view alliances as learning laboratories and cultivate a discovery ethic that supports continual learning.

COMMITMENT to the Partnership. Sustainable alliances institutionalize their collaboration process. They weave incentives to collaborate into their individual systems and imbed them in organizational culture. As insurance against the exit of key individuals, they ensure continuity by empowering all levels of the organization.

Source: James Austin, *The Collaboration Challenge* (San Francisco: Jossey-Bass Publisher, 2000). Reprinted by permission of John Wiley & Sons, Inc.

Achieving the Integrative stage is where the two partners really appreciate that various kinds of continuing collaborations produce important values for both sides. Based on his extensive experience, Austin has developed the "Seven C's of Strategic Collaboration" to guide potential partners. These are outlined in Exhibit 17-3.

Portfolio Management

An important development in the twenty-first century with respect to corporate alliances is the growing number of nonprofits that are currently engaged in multiple simultaneous partnerships. For example, a count in 2005 showed the following number of corporate partners of major nonprofit organizations:[70]

Organization	Corporate Partners
Habitat for Humanity International	72
Boys & Girls Clubs of America	39
Easter Seals	23
Girl Scouts	27

A challenge for these nonprofits is both how to manage each relationship over time and how they should relate to each other. The latter can well be handled by the portfolio models as discussed in Chapter 3. Partnerships can be arrayed on three dimensions. First, following Austin, they can be considered philanthropic, transactional, or integrative. Second, they can be arrayed in terms of the particular resources they bring in: money, volunteers, and expertise (e.g., marketing skills). Third, they can be partitioned into those with high and low long-term potential. This yields the following matrix:

	Philanthropic *Low potential*	Philanthropic *High potential*	Transactional *Low potential*	Transactional *High potential*	Integrative *Low potential*	Integrative *High potential*
Brings money						
Brings people						
Brings expertise						

Finally, each potential venture could then be described (inside its cell) as to its present or potential scope, say large, medium, and small. Clearly, the nonprofit would want to:

1. Have ventures at all three stages of development. Ideally, one would like a large number of high-potential integrative partnerships of large size yielding resources in all three areas. However, these will be rare and will not necessarily last forever— for example, as corporate (and nonprofit) goals change. Thus the nonprofit needs to have other ventures in the transactional and philanthropic stages with high potential. These can be large or medium in scope and perhaps, on occasion, small if the potential seems huge (e.g., with a very close and obvious mission fit).
2. Have ventures yield resources of all three kinds. It is especially important to generate "expertise" resources. As we have said throughout this volume, the private sector has much to teach nonprofit managers, and partnerships are great vehicles for achieving this.
3. Minimize the number of low-potential partnerships at all stages and involving all resources. In the private sector, it is well-known that weak products and brands will have huge hidden costs because managers will be spending too much time on them, wasting funds and staff time that could be productively used elsewhere. The same is true with weak partnerships.
4. Consider organizing the partnership staff around these divisions. It takes a different kind of person and different systems and management styles to run philanthropic ventures than those that are transactional or integrative. Similarly, managing partnerships where the "currency" is people will be very different from those that are organized around money.

Nonprofits are grappling with these options. Kurt Aschermann, formerly of the Boys & Girls Clubs of America, describes his approach in Exhibit 17-4. This is an area in which we may expect considerable growth in the development of more sophisticated planning models over the next decade.

EXHIBIT 17-4

KURT ASCHERMANN OF BOYS & GIRLS CLUB OF AMERICA ON CAUSE PARTNERING

In the early '90's as Senior Vice President for Resource Development I realized, after approaching Reader's Digest for their annual 30K gift, that the corporate funding world was changing. Our usual contact, within the Chairman's office, referred us to the marketing and sales department in order to get our gift. After procrastinating, I did contact them and concluded they were looking for us to become more a partner with them in using the money to foster the understanding of Reader's Digest as a good corporate citizen. They were also asking us to be creative on reaching potential new customers. We stumbled around to provide what they were looking for and eventually presented an "awareness based" enhanced program.

Our new approach lead to the $30K annual gift growing to a five year, $1 million commitment. It seemed this new approach worked.

After discussions with a member of our board, Rick Goings, then CEO of Avon, we concluded we needed to formulate new strategies for reaching corporate donors with more than just a hand out. Our cause-related marketing strategy was the result, and we created new systems for doing business called Proposal-less fundraising.

In the mid-1990s we realized we were on to something and began to fine-tune the system. We asked our board for staff, which we recruited from the for-profit sector, and created a relationship marketing team. This team changed our language, and our way of operating again, and began to formulate a Strategic Philanthropy strategy (Roberto Goizueta, the late CEO of Coca-Cola, was the first to use that term to describe how Coke was approaching its charitable work). This strategy called for the implementation of systems for exploring the corporation's marketing and sales strategy as well as its consumer targeting methods, and was centered on convincing potential partners we cared about their business, as well as what they could do for us. A $60 million commitment from Coca-Cola as well as several $7 million commitments from the likes of J. C. Penney, GAP, and others resulted.

Finally, though we quickly gained a reputation as a charity that "got it," as we approached the twenty-first century, we realized the new business climate, including the explosion of the dot.com world, mandated us to be even more sophisticated in our relationships with corporate partners.

Much of our success, we believed, resulted from our using business practices in our dealings with corporations. We understood that CRM, the acronym for cause-related marketing in the nonprofit world, meant customer relationship (or relations) marketing in the for-profit world, and we understood our customers were the corporations. We took specific steps to re-invent ourselves to behave in new ways:

- We began to treat our corporate partners as their ad agency and promotions agency would, with teams of people working on the account.
- We responded at all costs and encouraged our partners to think creatively about their business and how their charity could enhance it, then moved quickly to implement their ideas.

- The Corporate Opportunities Group was born, the first (we believe) formal nonprofit, cross-functional team ever constructed exclusively to target and "land" big corporate accounts for a charity. The strength of the COG was coming from an agency-wide commitment by senior management to "loan" employees to the team where their performance on the team entered into their compensation package. The COG works and has already seen great success with Crest/P&G, the Sports Authority, Post Cereals, and Circuit City, who have all signed multi-year, multi-million dollar cross-promotion deals with the Boys and Girls Clubs of America.

Summary

In addition to cash donations and volunteer support, there are a great many other kinds of help that nonprofits need in order to carry out their objectives. More and more nonprofits are turning to business alliances for help to leverage their own limited resources.

Advertising agency partnerships have been one of the longest-running sources of business support for nonprofits. Agencies often wish to help nonprofits because of the business contacts the relationship brings and for the goodwill, the chance to be highly creative, and the chance to give experience to junior staff where a major client is not at risk. However, there are risks for the nonprofit if the ad agency skimps on production values or loses sight of the nonprofit's goals.

A rapidly growing form of business–nonprofit partnership is cause-related marketing. Cause-related marketing is an arrangement by which a corporation seeks to increase its own sales by contributing to the objectives of one or more nonprofit organizations. Started in 1982 by American Express, cause-related marketing is now estimated by some to be a $1.34 billion business. There are four main types of cause-related marketing: corporate issue promotion, joint issue promotion, sales-related fundraising, and licensing. Other types of alliances involve web support, volunteering, and business expertise.

There are first- and second-order benefits and risks for both marketers and nonprofits in alliances across sectors. Marketers can be accused of cynical attempts to cover up unhealthy business practices. A lack of candor can affect their corporate image or poison their relationship with the nonprofit. They can also be charged with excessive righteousness and/or exploitation. For the nonprofit, there are risks that total donations may be reduced. Corporate partners may overly restrict the nonprofit's actions. They may bring unwelcome "baggage," and the nonprofit may lose its own integrity in the wrong kind of partnership. Cultural institutions have particular challenges of "selling their soul" to the corporate world.

Steps involved in developing a sound cause-related marketing strategy require careful selection of corporate partners with mutual interests, possibly using board members' advice. Partners with conflicts of interest should be screened out. Solicitation of partnerships should follow the sound marketing principle of showing them how the partnership will meet corporate needs and wants. The partnership proposal should be set out in careful, precise terms. Ideally, the relationship should be long term and one of complete candor both with the public and between partners. Results should be evaluated honestly.

Questions

1. You are about to engage in a partnership with a corporation for a charity event. It is providing staff help and some products. Its corporate name will be displayed everywhere, including on all event souvenirs. How do you figure out what to charge the corporation?

2. You have a major soap company that wants to sponsor a campaign to encourage hand washing in the Sudan. But it wants to be the exclusive brand involved in the campaign. You have government funding for part of the campaign. Would you agree to the company's demand? Why?

3. When should a nonprofit organization abandon a partnership? Are there situations where it would suffer some damage if it did so?

4. Your corporate partner says that it is a better marketer than you. It has assigned one of its top junior staff members to your campaign. It insists on making most of the major decisions about advertising, community outreach, public relations, and lobbying. How would you react and why?

5. Would you recommend that a nonprofit organization take on as many partners as it can? Suppose the American Lung Association has 11 drug companies and several product and service marketers that want partnerships. Should it take them all? If not, what rules would you set?

Notes

1. Bill Bradley, Paul Jansen, and Les Silverman, "The Nonprofit Sector's $100 Billion Opportunity," *Harvard Business Review,* May 2003.

2. William Meehan, Derek Kilmer, and Maisie O'Flanagan, "Investing in Society: Why We Need a More Efficient Social Capital Market—And How to Get There," *Stanford Social Innovation Review,* Spring 2004, pp. 35–43.

3. Stephen H. Judson, "Maestro, Hand Me the Sales Brochure," *New York Times,* April 3, 1994.

4. Jocelyne Daw, *Cause Marketing for Nonprofits* (San Francisco: Jossey-Bass, 2006).

5. Jaqueline Trescott, "Smithsonian Benefactor Cancels $38 Million Gift," *Washington Post,* February 5, 2002, p. A1; Milo Beach, "Why I Think the Smithsonian Is Misguided," *Washington Post,* January 27, 2002, p. G1; Philip Kennicott, "Open Letter Berates Smithsonian's Small," *Washington Post,* January 7, 2002, p. C4.

6. www.adcouncil.org/default.aspx?id=68 (retrieved October 24, 2006).

7. Some of the material in this chapter is drawn from Alan R. Andreasen, "Cross-sector Marketing Alliances: Partnerships, Sponsorships and Cause-related Marketing," in Joseph Cordes and Eugene Steuerle (Eds.), *Nonprofits and Business: A New World of Innovation and Adaptation* (Washington, DC: The Urban Institute, forthcoming). See also Walter Wymer and Adrian Sargeant, "Insights from a Review of the Literature on Cause Marketing," *International Review on Public and Nonprofit Marketing,* Vol. 3, No 1 (June 2006), pp. 9–21.

8. Minette E. Drumwright, Peggy H. Cunningham, and Ida E. Berger, "Social Alliances: Company/Nonprofit Collaboration," Report #00-101 (Cambridge, MA: Marketing Science Institute, 2000).

9. "Charity Fund-Raising Is a Popular Marketing Tool," *Washington Post,* September 3, 1991, p. D2.

10. See also Frederick Long and Matthew Arnold, *The Power of Environmental Partnerships* (Orlando, FL: Harcourt and Company, 1995); Joseph Galaskiewicz and Michele Sinclair Colman, "Collaborations Between Corporations and Nonprofit Organizations in Richard Steinberg and Walter W. Powell, *The Nonprofit Sector: A Research Handbook,* 2nd Edition (New Haven, CT: Yale University

Press, forthcoming); Flo Frank and Anne Smith, *The Partnership Handbook* (Ottawa, ONT.: Minister of Public Works and Government Services Canada, 1997); Sherri Torjman, *Partnerships: The Good, The Bad and The Uncertain* (Ottawa, CA: Caledon Institute for Social Policy, June 1998).

11. Shari Caudron, "Fight Crime, Sell Products," *Industry Week*, November 7, 1994, p. 49.

12. P. Rajan Varadarajan and Anil Menon, "Cause-Related Marketing," *Journal of Marketing*, 52 (July 1986) p 59.

13. Alan R. Andreasen and Minette E. Drumwright, "Alliances and Ethics in Social Marketing," in Alan R. Andreasen (Ed.), *Ethics in Social Marketing* (Washington, DC: Georgetown University Press, 2001), pp. 95–124.

14. John T. Gourville and V. Kasturi Rangan, "Valuing the Cause Marketing Relationship," *California Management Review*, Vol. 47, No. 1 (Fall 2004), pp. 38–56.

15. Samuel R. Graves and Sandra A. Waddock, "Institutional Owners and Corporate Social Performance," *Academy of Management Journal*, Vol. 37, No. 4 (1994), pp. 1034–1046.

16. Cause Marketing Forum, "Why Are Nonprofits Turning to Cause Marketing?" 2004, www.Causemarketingforum.Com/Page.Asp?ID=82 (retrieved January 4, 2006).

17. Association of Fundraising Professionals, "Charities Not Charging Enough for Marketing, Sponsorship Deals," September 7, 2004, www.Afpnet.Org/Tier3_Cd.Cfm?Folder_Id=2345andcontent_Item_Id=1 7968 (retrieved January 1, 2006).

18. Ida E. Berger, Peggy H. Cunningham, and Minette E. Drumwright, "Social Alliances: Company/Nonprofit Collaboration," *California Management Review*, Vol. 47, No. 1 (2004), pp. 58–90.

19. An alternative list is provided in Philip Kotler and Nancy Lee, *Corporate Social Responsibility* (New York: John Wiley & Sons, 2005).

20. Ibid.

21. Bob Garfield, "The Colors of Exploitation: Benetton on Death Row," *Advertising Age*, January 17, 2000.

22. Michelle Conlin, "Micro, Less Soft," *Business Week*, November 27, 2006, p. 42.

23. Anthony Giorgianni, "Big Businesses Are Finding that Good Causes Are Good for Business," *The Hartford Courant*, November 25, 1994.

24. Henry K. Y. Fock, Ka-Shing Woo, and Michael K Hui, "The Impact of a Prestigious Partner on Affinity Card Marketing," *European Journal of Marketing*, Vol. 39, No. 1–2 (January 2005), pp. 33–53.

25. www.newmansown.com

26. Charles Champlin, "Hot, Sexy and (Almost) 70," *Los Angeles Times*, December 18, 1994.

27. Stephanie Thompson, "Pepsi Hits High Note with Schools," *Advertising Age*, October 9, 2000, p. 30.

28. Michelle McCalope, "Church Retailing," *Time*, 2001, p. 11.

29. Donald R. Lichtenstein, Minette E. Drumwright, Bridgette M. Braig, "The Effect of Corporate Social Responsibility on Customer Donations to Corporate-Supported Nonprofits," *Journal of Marketing*, Vol. 68, No. 4 (2004), pp. 16–32.

30. Jessi Hempel, "Geeks Bearing Gifts," *Business Week*, March 13, 2006, p. 13.

31. Amy Joyce, "Programs of Give vs. Take," *Washington Post*, November 6, 2005, p. F9.

32. P. D. Harvey, *Let Every Child Be Wanted: How Social Marketing Is Revolutionizing Contraceptive Use Around the World*, (Westport, CT: Auburn House, 1999).

33. J. E. Post, L. E. Preston, and S. Sachs, *Redefining the Corporation: Stakeholder Management and Organizational Wealth* (Stanford, CA: Stanford University Press, 2002).

34. Christine Gorman, "Marathon Fights Malaria," *Time*, September 2006, pp. A9–A11.

35. Nancy Coltun Webster, "Katrina Gives New Meaning to Web-led Crisis Response." *Advertising Age*, June 12, 2006, p. S-2.

36. www.rmhc.org/rmhc/index.html (retrieved November 7, 2006).

37. Stephanie Strom, "Deal Will Put UNICEF Cards in Hallmark Stores Year-Round," *New York Times*, November 6, 2005.

38. "For the Humanitarian," *Time*, November 13, 2006, p. 134.

39. Association of Fundraising Professionals, "U.S. Corporations Embracing Cause-Related

Marketing," 2004, www.Afpnet.Eor/Tier3_Print.Cfm?Folder_Id=2345andcontent_Item_Id=17188 (retrieved January 1, 2006).

40. IEG Sponsorship Report, 2005, "'06 Outlook: Sponsorship Growth Back to Double Digits," December 26, 2005, p. 1 www.Sponsorship.Com/Iegsr/2005/12/26/ (retrieved December 31, 2005); Association of Fundraising Professionals, "Nonprofit, Association Sponsorships Expected to Rise in 2005," AFP Resource Center Web site February 25, 2005, at www.Afpnet.Org/Tier3_Cd.Cfm? Folder_Id=2545andcontent_Item_Id=19950 (retrieved December 30, 2005).

41. Peter Panepento, "To Market, To Market," *The Chronicle of Philanthropy,* May 18, 2006, pp. 20–25.

42. The Giving USA estimates are based on what is reported as charitable giving on corporation financial statements. Thus there may be overlap between the estimates of corporate donations and estimates of cause alliances when the latter are reported as deserving of tax deductions.

43. Sue Adkins, *Cause Related Marketing: Who Cares Wins* (Oxford: Butterworth-Heinemann, 1999); Hamish Pringle and Marjorie Thompson, *Brand Spirit* (New York: John Wiley & Sons, Ltd., 1999); Philip Kotler and Nancy Lee, *Corporate Social Responsibility* (New York: John Wiley & Sons, 2005); Jocelyn Daw, *Cause Marketing for Nonprofits* (Hoboken, NJ: John Wiley & Sons, 2006).

44. *Cone Corporate Citizenship Study: Building Brand Trust* (Boston: Cone, 2004). See also Carol L. Cone, Mark A. Feldman, and Alison T. Dasilva, "Causes and Effects," *Harvard Business Review,* Vol. 81 (July 2003), pp. 95–101; R. W. J. Endacott, "Consumers and CRM: A National and Global Perspective," *Journal of Consumer Marketing,* Vol. 21, No. 3 (2004), pp. 183–189.

45. Golin Harris (2005), *Doing Well At Doing Good: The Trajectory of Corporate Citizenship in American Business* (2005), available at www.Golinharris.Com/Cap_Global_Social.Htm (retrieved December 31, 2005).

46. Cause Marketing Forum, "Cause Marketing's Power Shown in Medialab Study" (2004), www.Causemarketingforum.Com/Page.Asp?ID=192 (retrieved January 3, 2006).

47. Brand Benefits (2003/2004) at www.Bitc.Org.Uk/Resources/Research/Research_Publications/Brand_Benefits.Html (retrieved January 1, 2006).

48. B. A. Lafferty, and R. E. Goldsmith, "Cause-Brand Alliances: Does the Cause Help the Brand or Does the Brand Help the Cause?" *Journal of Business Research,* Vol. 58 (2005), pp. 423–429.

49. Matthew C. Farrelly, Cheryl G. Healton, Kevin C. Davis, Peter Messert, James C. Hersey, and M. Lyndon Haviland, "Getting to the Truth: Evaluating National Tobacco Countermarketing Efforts," *American Journal of Public Health,* Vol. 92, No. 6 (2002), pp. 901–907.

50. Jeffrey D. Zbar, "Wildlife Takes Center Stage as Cause-Related Marketing Becomes a $250 Million Show for Companies," *Advertising Age,* June 28, 1993, p. S-1.

51. Robert Franklin, "Help the Needy—and Maybe Merchants, Too," *Minneapolis Star Tribune,* December 24, 1993.

52. Rob Walker, "Big Gulp: How a Bottled Water Tries to Quench Consumers' Thirst to Do Good," *New York Times,* February 26, 2006, p. 16.

53. James Tenser, "The New Samaritans," *Advertising Age,* June 12, 2006, p. S-4.

54. Stephen W. Colford, "Jeans Giveaway Labeled a Poor Fit," *Hartford Courant,* November 25, 1994.

55. Rance Crain, "Social Marketing Misses the Mark," *Advertising Age,* September 26, 1994, p. 22.

56. "Controversy of the Week," *Business Week,* November 25, 2005.

57. Stephanie Thompson, "Kraft Stands Fast Behind Gay Games," *Advertising Age,* May 1, 2006, p. 8.

58. Timothy M. Devinney, Patrice Auger, Gianna Eckhardt, and Thomas Birtchnell," The Other CSR," *Stanford Social Innovation Review,* Fall 2006, pp. 30–37.

59. Anthony Giogianni, "Big Businesses Are Finding that Good Causes Are Good for Business," *Hartford Courant,* November 25, 1994.

60. Michael Kimmelman, "What Price Love?" *New York Times,* July 17, 2005, pp. AR1, 26.

61. Ibid.

62. Glenn Collins, "A.M.A. to Endorse Line of Products," *New York Times,* August 13, 1997, p. A1; Greg Johnson, "Officials Urge Limits on Use of Nonprofit Logos," *Los Angeles Times,* April 7, 1999, p. C1.

63. Berger, Cunningham, and Drumwright "Social Alliances."

64. Shari Caudron, "Fight Crime, Sell Products."

65. Gwynneth Wallace and James Mintz, "One Step at a Time," *Health Promotion in Canada,* Summer 1994, pp. 1–3.

66. Sir Geoffrey Mulcahy, "The Four Principles of Corporate Giving," *Financial Times,* October 25, 1993, p. 15.

67. Albert B. Crenshaw, "Looking a Gift Horse in the Mouth: Consumers Should Be Cautious About Business/Charity Fund-Raisers," *Washington Post,* September 1, 1991, p. H3.

68. Howard Schlossberg, "Common Sense, Research Should Guide Cause-Related Marketing Campaigns," *Marketing News,* December 18, 1989, p. 12.

69. Kevin P. Kearns, *Private Sector Strategies for Social Sector Success* (San Francisco: Jossey-Bass Publisher, 2000).

70. Andreasen, "Cross-sector Marketing Alliances."

ORGANIZING AND CONTROLLING MARKETING STRATEGIES

18 | ORGANIZING FOR IMPLEMENTATION

"WE'RE STUCK AND WE CAN'T SEEM TO GROW!"

Do nonprofit organizations have life cycles? A number of management theorists and consultants think they do. The April 6, 2006, *The Chronicle of Philanthropy* tells the story of the Shakespeare Theatre of New Jersey as just such an organization. Under artistic director Bonnie Monte, it had been quite successful for nine years, raising $7.5 million in a capital campaign and moving into a new building. But systems were not keeping up and there wasn't enough economic growth. A life cycle perspective suggested that the company had a case of "arrested development."

How does one update systems while maintaining creativity and vibrancy?

A major problem is often that the kind of leadership an organization needs at one stage is not always best for another. A new organization needs a charismatic, hard-charging motivator. Ideally, this would be someone who can inspire volunteers to help, donors to give generously, corporations to help out with partnerships, and new staff to take below-market salaries and work long hours because they believe in the leader's vision.

But with success, a different kind of person is often needed. An organization needs a boss who can fire early recruits because, despite their initial help and enthusiasm, they're not doing their job. Personalized donor solicitations have to give way to systems for donor tracking, long-term cultivation, and frequent recognition. New ventures needing new capital must have well thought out strategic plans. Potential corporate partners will want to see more "professional" management. It is a brave board that recognizes that, at this life cycle stage, it may be that the founder needs to step aside and perhaps assume a different role—say, board chair, "CEO Emeritus," or some other face-saving option. Lucky is the organization whose CEO understands his or her limitations and voluntarily moves on to a new nonprofit organization which is back at the infant stage of the organizational life cycle. Even luckier is the organization that has a CEO that sees the need for changed leadership and responds.

Conducting a life cycle analysis will show the CEO—like Bonnie Monte—that the current problems are not his or her fault. The problems are to be expected at the stage in which the organization finds itself. The challenge is to deal with the new realities. To her credit, Bonnie Monte hired two fundraisers so that the theatre's economic base could catch up with its artistic growth. Funds have doubled since.

Sometimes a problem is a mismatch between the board and the CEO because one is at one life cycle stage while the other is somewhere else. Several consultants describe a "bureaucratic" stage where organizations—often large ones—become calcified. If the board is populated by those who helped start the organization and made it grow, they may be in the bureaucratic stage and at odds with a CEO—typically a new one—who is frustrated by the lack of innovation and dynamism. Usually, one or the other has to change. For the organization's sake, one hopes it is the board.

Executive director Robin Prothro of a Maryland affiliate of the Susan G. Komen Breast Cancer Foundation had such a problem. As she saw it, the organization was at a point described as the "go-go stage." According to Prothro, they needed to integrate their fundraising efforts under the staff's control, but many on the board still wanted to run the organization's signature event—the Race for the Cure—themselves. Prothro won out and the board changed but "it was painful. We lost board members."

Source: Holly Hall, "Getting Over Growing Pains," *The Chronicle of Philanthropy,* April 6, 2006, pp. 41–44. Reprinted with permission of *The Chronicle of Philanthropy,* philanthropy.com.

As we have seen, a number of nonprofits are becoming large-scale organizations involved in a range of complex undertakings and more often are recruiting business-people and their concepts and tools to improve their performance. Nonprofit organizations must often manage significant numbers of partnerships with the private sector, large and fluid volunteer staffs and, in many cases, work through multiple channels. Many nonprofits, such as Habitat for Humanity, are undertaking significant international ventures.

Of course, the majority of nonprofit organizations are not large. Thus we begin by considering the challenges of organizations that are only beginning to think that marketing might comprise a useful set of concepts and tools that may help them achieve their missions more effectively.

INTRODUCING MARKETING—PUSHING OR PULLING?

When marketing is first proposed as a philosophy and set of techniques for improving an organization's performance, this introduction typically comes about in one of two ways. One pattern is for marketing to be *pushed* into the organization by one or more key individuals who have been exposed to its potential in outside seminars or in formal academic training. They may also be board members or people who come to the nonprofit from a commercial enterprise where marketing is a very powerful force. These potential change agents shuttle about the organization trying to convince others, most importantly CEOs, of the wisdom of their views. They frequently encounter considerable intraorganization resistance, which is often reflected in disparagement of the marketing function and frequent allusions to its nastier manifestations. Unless the change agents are very highly placed in the organization or are extremely convincing in their personal promotion campaigns, the introduction period is likely to be quite prolonged under a "push" scenario.

The other common pattern for the introductory period is for marketing to be *pulled* into the organization by environmental forces. This condition occurred in health care in the 1980s as market conditions increased the pressures on nonprofit hospitals to improve performance. Marketing came to be viewed as a potentially highly useful approach to such improvement. A similar pattern is apparent in organizations that "discover" social marketing. Pressures to introduce marketing are heightened if one or more direct competitors begin to use marketing or are rumored to be beginning soon. Marketing is likely to be introduced much faster under a "pull" scenario than if it is "pushed" into a sometimes reluctant institution.

In the growth phase following marketing's introduction, attempts are made to expand marketing's role and formalize its position in the organization. Typically, marketing is first formalized as a staff function *coordinating* programs and providing advice to others. Only later, as marketing proves its value and/or environmental pressures become more intense, is it often changed into a specific line function with its own staff and responsibilities for programs and specific volume results.

Even when marketing becomes a formal department during the growth phase, its role may be inconsequential. The mature phase can therefore be identified by the transition of marketing from being just another division or function to being a top-level management concern. In this phase, marketing philosophy has permeated much of the organization's planning. Marketing has relatively few detractors and virtually no effort is needed to market marketing itself. Concern has shifted to this issue: how to market *well*.

In this chapter, we first discuss where marketing should be positioned within the organization. We then turn to a discussion of how marketing activities should be structured and how a marketing orientation can be implemented before turning to the important challenges now facing the very largest nonprofits.

MARKETING'S POSITION IN THE ORGANIZATION

The positioning of marketing in an organization, and even what to call it, is not a trivial decision. In the 1970s and 1980s, when marketing was first being introduced in a serious way in the nonprofit field, marketing was often positioned either far down in the organization or in some advisory staff position. When a marketing person was first introduced at the American Cancer Society, the candidate was responsible for "market intelligence" and was positioned far down the organizational chart, reporting to the vice president of communications, who also supervised a vice president for public relations and advertising and a vice president for product production. This reflected both a lack of understanding of marketing across the organization and a lack of appreciation for the contributions that it might make to the organization's mission. After a number of years and considerable attention to demonstrating how strategic marketing works and promoting marketing successes, the chief marketing person became the vice president of strategic marketing and branding, reporting directly to the CEO.

Even today, there is much disagreement in many nonprofits about where marketing ought to fit. In our view, marketing should be at the very top of the organization. Depending on the organization's mission, it may be appropriate for the CEO to have strong marketing skills and a "marketing mindset." This follows our argument at the very start of this book that marketing is vital because its role is to influence behavior and its armamentarium of concepts and tools is—in the best organizations—focused in a laser-like fashion on this behavioral bottom line. As we noted in Chapter 3, nonprofits have a large number of constituencies that they need to influence, including clients, funders, regulators, commercial partners, and the media. Because influencing behaviors is critical to success, marketing must be central to the mission.

Many organizations have historically been dominated by skill sets other than marketing. A case in point is the Centers for Disease Control and Prevention. This organization is strongly influenced by medical scientists, epidemiologists, and others who historically thought marketing was too crass, too intrusive, too trivial for their main mission. However, beginning in the 1990s, the CDC slowly adopted social marketing as a prime paradigm and marketing thinking slowly seeped through the organization. Finally, in July 2006, the CDC created the National Center for Health Marketing within its Department of Health and Human Services (www.cdc.gov/healthmarketing/). It defines health marketing as "creating, communicating and delivering health information and interventions using target audience-centered and science-based strategies to protect and promote the health of diverse populations." It is, of course, the interventions that distinguish a marketing approach from more traditional "health communication."

If units like the CDC's National Health Center are to be most effective, however, the marketing function needs to have the resources and the control necessary to be successful—that is, to bring about the organizational impacts the nonprofit needs to prosper. This means that marketing must ultimately be a *line position* with significant budgets and direct authority to make designated behaviors happen. In early years, it may be prudent for marketers to adopt a staff role until such time as they prove their merit and ingratiate themselves with suspicious traditional staff.

The next question, then, is this: What should marketers control? This issue was still not resolved in 2006 in various organizations with which we have contact. Here are some marketing titles we have run across:

- Vice President of Strategic Marketing and Branding
- Senior Director of Line of Service Marketing
- Vice President of University Relations
- Director, Sales and Marketing
- Senior Vice President, Marketing and Communications
- Director, Relationships/Marketing Group
- National Director of Advancement
- Director of Development
- Vice President of Communications
- Manager, Brand Stewardship

It is clear from these titles that, in the very best organizations, the word "marketing" is sometimes not even in the job title. Further, it often comprises one or more of the following functions—but typically not all:

- Communications
- Development (which usually means fundraising)
- Membership (which can also include fundraising)
- Public affairs (which can mean public relations)
- Brand management
- Sales (which can include catalog and retail operations)

Most commonly, communications is in their work scope. This undoubtedly reflects higher management's view of marketing as "the message people." It also may be a tactical decision in some organizations to "hide" marketing behind nonthreatening nomenclature. It may also be that someone in a communications or development role has simply been told "you're now also the marketing person"! In any case, the simple choice of the title can cause one of several kinds of problems:

1. It may reflect an "image problem" where marketing is seen only as communications and so the organization misses its full potential.
2. Marketing may only be given control over communications or development and not have responsibility over other departments and functions that have major impacts on target audience behavior.
3. It may echo "turf wars" within the organization where other areas do not want to be subsumed under "marketing."

There are other challenges. In many organizations, a major decision will be what to do with fundraising, membership development, and public relations. Should they be part of marketing or parallel to it? Early on, most nonprofit organizations will keep these functions separate, arguing that they have different roles and require different expertise. However, as marketers prove that they can be impactful and management begins to perceive that all of these separate functions are really about influencing behavior, then marketing stands a chance to migrate higher in the organization chart with control over these other activities. Even where absorption does not happen, senior management ought to establish informal links to ensure that "marketing thinking" pervades these other areas.

One might ask this: What *should* marketing control (i.e., have responsibility for)? We would argue that, in the ideal organization, marketing would:

- Be *directly responsible* for functions and staff whose primary responsibility is to influence key target publics of the organization. This could mean responsibility for:
  - Communications—directed at many publics
  - Public relations—directed at influencing the media
  - Direct sales (catalogs, sales)
  - Volunteer recruitment
  - Membership recruitment
  - Fundraising

- Have an *advisory* role for functions that can *indirectly* impact target audiences (positively or negatively) or that have as their principal roles tasks more important than the marketing components of their portfolio. This could include:
  - Volunteer management
  - Human resources (negative staff interaction with a target audience can sabotage the best marketing campaigns)
  - Membership services
  - Information technology and web site management

These are not ironclad distinctions. Today, more and more organizations see their web site as a major marketing tool. Where the target audience is teenagers, the Web is perhaps the single most important tool for reaching and having an impact on this group.

Recruiting Great Marketers

Once marketing staff positions are defined, the next critical step is recruiting first-rate marketers to fill them. Fortunately, since the early 1990s the pool of talent available to nonprofit organizations encompasses a significant number of mainstream commercial marketing people. No longer are nonprofit marketers drawn from within the nonprofit world (e.g., former managers of fundraising, advertising, public relations, or direct mail divisions). They are—or should be—grounded in the principles set out in this volume.

Part of this shift in the human resource pool is attributable to the growing sophistication of nonprofit marketing and to its significant size and scope of operations. Commercial marketing managers who are thinking of a career move to the nonprofit sector know they are much more likely today to have the resources and supportive management that were not present even 20 years ago. However, there remain a number of barriers to attracting the best talent, some of which we have discussed in earlier chapters. An initial problem is salary.

The Salary Problem

One of the distinct problems managers have in attracting talented marketing people to the nonprofit world is the low salaries that are routinely paid to managers and staff. There are a number of reasons for this situation. First, decades ago, work in nonprofit organizations was "women's work," and job categories in all sectors in which women dominate have historically been underpaid.[1] Second, the culture of many nonprofit organizations is one of sacrifice in the face of daunting challenges. Members of an organization trying to do something about a dreadful social problem are not expected to reap private gain for doing so. Such a culture is common in organizations still in the "founder stage," during which they are dominated by dedicated leaders who will sacrifice for their cause and expect others to do so also.

Third, most donors to nonprofit organizations (and many staff people and members of boards of directors) expect that most of the organization's revenues will go to services for their target audiences. Staff members are not supposed to take money that should be going elsewhere. Fourth, as we have noted throughout this book, nonprofits often have very limited budgets and feel they cannot afford higher salaries. Finally, a great many of those men and women who choose nonprofit careers are *willing* to take lower salaries because they gain significant psychic income from what they do.

There are also external pressures to keep salaries low. Concerns about "extravagant" salaries have led to scandals in organizations such as the United Way of America. These scandals have prompted a subcommittee of the U.S. House of Representatives to consider a federal law to place a cap on salaries paid to nonprofit executives.

The consequence of all of these forces is that low salaries are often set for marketing positions and nonprofit organizations often cannot attract the kind of talent they need if they are to become truly effective. As Marianne Briscoe has said, "It can be difficult for . . . founders to understand that to move to higher levels of effectiveness people with experience and special skills must be brought into the organizations—people who know about computer systems, financial management and fund-raising for example."[2] She could easily have added marketing researchers, product managers, advertising copywriters, and so on to her list. To attract the first-rate MBA majoring in marketing who could easily earn $75,000 or more at Procter & Gamble or IBM, the ambitious nonprofit has to offer a lot more than what Briscoe calls "Peace Corps wages." Indeed, even though we have seen some improvement in the mindset of CEOs and boards around the salary issue in recent years, some nonprofit marketers have become so frustrated with the salary and perks in the nonprofit world that they have migrated back to the private sector. Jay Steenhuysen, director of philanthropic planning at Brown University, sees a "brain drain" among fundraisers as being a potentially very serious threat for nonprofits.[3]

The problem is even more serious overseas. Americans seeking to work in other countries find the wages there are even lower, unless they are able to work for a multinational nonprofit such as CARE or Childreach that provides cost-of-living adjustments to their expatriate workers.[4]

One promising solution may be pay-for-performance plans. Although it is much more difficult to define "performance" in the nonprofit environment than in the private sector, pressures to implement such plans have grown significantly in the last decade. Part of the reason is pressure from foundations and venture philanthropists to make nonprofit organizations more "managerial." Another reason is the pressure to appear more professionally managed for the media and watchdog groups.[5]

Two Cultures

In an earlier chapter we referenced a series of in-depth interviews of marketers who have moved from the commercial to the nonprofit sectors.[6] These interviews made clear that there is often a culture shock in moving over from the private sector. A number of interviewees expressed frustration with their new environment. In part this reflects contrasts in the two cultures described in Chapter 3. Where commercial marketers are accustomed to such tactics as segmenting markets and ignoring difficult-to-influence targets, to worrying about issues of efficiency and the acceptance of risks, this often runs counter to the norms and values of those brought up in social service cultures. Heated battles often ensue.

Interviewees also found differences in the "decision styles" across the sectors. In the private sector, they were accustomed to decisions being made relatively quickly by an executive with authority to take action. He or she would listen to the analysis and arguments raised by staff and/or consultants and make a decision. Once the decision was made, responsibility for performance was assigned and goals set, and the participants moved on to other issues and challenges. Marketers who did not perform well could reasonably be expected not to advance or even lose their jobs!

In nonprofit organizations, marketers report important, frustrating differences. First, the process takes much longer. Two reasons for this appear to be that decisions are often considered the responsibility of a group rather than an individual and there is a felt need to consult with every possible stakeholder who might be affected by the decision. A second problem is that there is a reluctance to take risks. If analysis shows some downside potential, nonprofit managers are often reluctant to move forward or, at best, will postpone the decision, hoping some new, conclusive insight will emerge. Finally, there is a frequent tendency not to assign blame for inadequate performance.

A possible explanation for these differences in style goes something like this:

1. Individuals in nonprofit organizations join up because they wish to avoid the judgmental rat race of the commercial world.
2. They accept reduced salaries in return for not only working on socially important problems but also having a "workstyle" that is much less stressful.
3. They do not want to be responsible for making coworkers' work life unpleasant.
4. They prefer decisions that leave everyone happy or at least not feeling neglected.
5. They consider it harsh and unpleasant to be too judgmental about poor performance.

It may be expected that, over time, this environment will shift more in the direction of the commercial model as more and more nonprofits pay attention to achieving high performance as recommended by students of the field like Letts, Ryan, and Grossman[7] and increasingly demanded by foundations, philanthropists, and nonprofit watchdogs.

MARKETING MARKETING

Andreasen in 2002 addressed the problem of advancing marketing practice in considering how social marketing might be spread further.[8] He suggested using the BCOS model to understand what might be going through the heads of potential adopters of marketing approaches and how these factors can be used to advance marketing. Each of the BCOS factors could be the following:

Benefits are significant:

- The target audience is guaranteed to play a major role in developing and implementing the planned program.
- All program elements will be focused on behavior change rather than settling for changes short of that goal (such as changes in awareness, liking, etc.).
- Influence attempts will be tailored to specific *segments* of the target audience, thus assuring efficient use of limited resources and tactics that are more effective because they "speak" to the specific interests, needs, and wants of distinct groups or individuals in the target audience.
- Through the application of the "4 Ps," influence attempts will always move beyond the promotion of the benefits of the desired behavior by paying attention to reducing the costs of the behavior and making it popular and easy.

Costs are coming down:

- Finding competent and experienced nonprofit marketers is becoming easier. For example, the social marketing listserver[9] now has over 1,500 participants in over 38 countries.
- Additional resources are coming online as more and more private sector marketers want to apply their professional skills to social problems (i.e., doing volunteer work that is more rewarding than painting a club room or ladling soup in a soup kitchen).

Others are increasing supportive:

- Marketing is increasingly widely adopted. For example, the American Marketing Association now offers an annual conference for nonprofit marketers. The conference attracted over 350 participants in its fourth year of existence.
- Examples of first-rate nonprofit marketing routinely appear in *Advertising Age, Business Week,* and *Marketing News.*

Self-assurance is growing—marketing is easier to do:

- There is a dramatically growing arsenal of written and electronic material available for someone to develop familiarity and skills in using marketing approaches. These materials can be mined for help in all stages of the design and implementation of marketing strategies. Among the web sites specifically helpful to those involved in marketing campaigns in the nonprofit sector are the following:

Science Panel on Interactive Communication and Health
   www.health.gov/scipich
American Communication Association (Links to many communications sites)
   www.uark.edu/~aca/acastudiescenter.html
University of Iowa Department of Communications Studies (Links to communications resources)
   www.uiowa.edu/~commstud/resources/
Purdue University (Health communications programs)
   www.sla.purdue.edu/healthcomm/Research.html
Centers for Disease Control and Prevention (Risk info)
   www.atsdr.cdc.gov/HEC/primer.html
Centers for Disease Control and Prevention (Health communication)
   www.cdc.gov/od/oc/hcomm
National Cancer Institute (Communications research)
   www.dccps.nci.nih.gov/communicationscenters
National Youth Anti-Drug Campaign
   www.mediacampaign.org
Health Canada's social marketing web site
   www.hc-sc.gc.ca/hppb/socialmarketing/
Social Marketing Manual, Ohio University
   oak.cats.ohiou.edu/~cm130791/social/social.htm
Tools of Change
   www.toolsofchange.org

Resources developed by Weinreich Communications, California
members.aol.com/weinreich/index.html
Communications Initiative (in Spanish)
www.commintit.com/la/
Proyecto Acción SIDA de Centroamerica
www.pasc.org
Centers for Disease Control and Prevention Spanish web site
www.cdc.gov/spanish/
National Social Marketing Strategy (UK)
www.nsms.org.uk/public/default.aspx

MANAGING MULTINATIONAL NONPROFITS

A growing phenomenon in the 1990s and early twenty-first century is for nonprofit organizations to locate in more than one country. Organizations such as CARE, the Red Cross, and the Salvation Army have had operations worldwide for many years. Many others, like the United Way, Goodwill, and Habitat for Humanity, are becoming similarly international. This raises a number of important organizational questions with respect to marketing operations. When a nonprofit decides to move internationally, there are a number of options:[10]

- *The Export Department.* In this form, the marketing operation is headquartered in a single country such as the United States and marketing experts go from country to country carrying out their programs as need dictates. The Academy for Educational Development, a major nonprofit consulting firm, adopts this approach.
- *The Multinational (or Multi-Local) Organization.* The organization has operations in a number of countries. Each country has its own local management and a considerable amount of autonomy. Coordination is managed at headquarters. CARE operates as a multinational.
- *The Global Organization.* This organization treats the world as one single market and develops universal strategies that apply everywhere. Local managers may adapt programs slightly to meet local needs. Habitat for Humanity's programs reflect this thinking.

The strongest debate is between multinational and global organizations.[11] Managers with a global point of view argue that barriers between countries have broken down greatly, that nonprofit problems are surprisingly similar in various countries, and that there can be great savings by developing a single basic strategy. They also argue that global programs offer consistency around the world that can increase awareness and effectiveness. Global strategies also mean that the nonprofit marketing organization can, over time, become extremely good at the few things that are its central global strategy.

Managers with a multinational orientation argue the opposite. They say that, although barriers have broken down between countries, this applies mainly to middle- and upper-class markets. Thus one might have a global strategy for certain kinds of direct mail fundraising directed at the middle classes. However, for programs targeting the lower classes, differences across countries are significant, especially when one considers differences in language and culture. Separate programs are needed for each country. Indeed, many argue that differences *within* countries merit treating local ethnic market segments as "mini-nations." Even for programs where cultural differences are of minimal importance, multinationalists argue that differences in rules and regulations across countries make local programs essential. They do not deny that much can be gained from standardizing across countries; however, they argue that too much is unique to each nation or to each subregion to have a single strategy that will fit every situation.[12]

The multinational form appears to dominate in the early twenty-first century. Tom Harris, chairman of the World Fund Raising Council, is quoted as saying, "Very few nonprofits operate effectively transnationally. Organizations like Save the Children have national organizations with perhaps an international secretariat: rarely will you find a Frenchman working permanently in the offices in another country." Harris attributes this pattern to the fact that "all nonprofit organizations throughout the world tend to be chauvinistic."[13] This observation suggests that, over time, as the nonprofit world itself becomes more global and chauvinism fades, we may see more globally centered organizations emerge as they have in the private sector.[14]

MULTI-SITE ORGANIZATIONS

Another challenge facing large nonprofit organizations is marketing through multiple sites in a single country. This is the case where organizations like the American Cancer Society or the Boys & Girls Clubs of America have individual chapters or clubs in different cities or, in some cases, several within a city. Habitat for Humanity International has operations in several countries as well as cities in the United States. The relationship between these individual units and the central "headquarters" is a crucial component of marketing planning and branding

There are two important dimensions here. First, a manager must ask this: Should local units be independent and to what degree? In the Boys & Girls Clubs of America, like many other nonprofits, each club is independently run with its own board of directors and its own set of activities. At the American Cancer Society, individual chapters are, in a sense, local offices of a central organization. In comparison to the private sector, the Boys & Girls Clubs of America is like General Motors or Ford with independent dealerships, whereas the American Cancer Society is like Macy's with every store beholden to central management. The challenges for each are different.

In the "local office" model, the major challenges are two. First, to what extent should marketing capability be built into the local operation and, second, what should be the relationship with "headquarters"? Pushing marketing capacity down the chain of command to the extent possible makes sense to many organizations in that it increases the pervasiveness and acceptance of marketing and it increases the probability that strategies will be more responsive to local idiosyncrasies. Clearly, some local operations will be too small to hire a marketing person. However, it should still be the case that the local CEO be given extensive indoctrination into the marketing mindset and a thorough appreciation of the need to be target audience-driven. This will make future coordination easier and will often produce insights from the local level that will improve country-wide performance.

An alternative that some larger organizations have adopted is to establish regional offices with marketing staff. These bring the marketing perspective closer to the field and help ensure local coordination and cooperation. In some cases, campaigns might properly be segmented on these very same regional bases.

The more difficult challenge is when there is local autonomy of some considerable degree either because it is given or because it is seized by powerful local factions. Autonomous local organizations can be very powerful. For example, in the United Way system, local operations in New York, Chicago, and Los Angeles annually have operating budgets in the hundreds of millions of dollars. As a consequence, they are likely to have strong CEOs, powerful local boards, and their own marketing staffs. This, of course, can make for much more potent and target audience-centered campaigns and programs at the local level. However, it also can lead to great fragmentation and a lack of coordination when *country-wide* strategies are put in place. This has proven especially troublesome when the organization attempts to mount a new national branding campaign as Volunteers of America has recently attempted.

One approach to this problem is for the central organization to consider its role to be a service arm meeting the needs of the "locals." The alternative route—the one more typically taken—is to seek to manage the organization nationally. The "secret" to coordinating such national efforts in an autonomous multi-site system is simply to apply the marketing principles we have been espousing throughout this book. This is another case where one has a target audience (the local enterprises) and a set of behaviors (say, getting "on board" with a nationwide branding and positioning effort) that needs to be influenced. Headquarters must be sensitive to local needs and wants and to demonstrate the ways in which the desired behavior (cooperation) will meet local interests. This is, of course, oftentimes easier said than done, especially when there is a history of friction and/or where strong personalities are involved. It also can be very troublesome when the national efforts are ineffective or counterproductive. It is not surprising to find large locals concluding that they can do it better.

Of course, friction between headquarters and the field will be especially high if there is any scandal or evidence of malfeasance at the central office. The relationship between autonomous chapters and headquarters is typically where the locals raise funds and submit regular fees (franchise fees in the private sector) to headquarters. Misuse of these funds, as with the United Way in the 1980s, can sunder ties with locals in ways that can take years to repair.

ORGANIZATIONAL DESIGN

As the marketing department in any one unit (e.g., national headquarters) grows in physical size, how it is organized internally becomes a critical question. This will affect not only how the department is run but what kinds of people should be employed. The options typically found in the private sector as design alternatives can be adapted to nonprofit marketing with limited rethinking. These alternatives are (1) functional organization, (2) offering-centered organization, (3) target audience-centered organization, and (4) mixed organization.

Functional Organization
Most growing nonprofit marketing units first take on the appearance of a functional organizational structure as shown in Figure 18-1A.

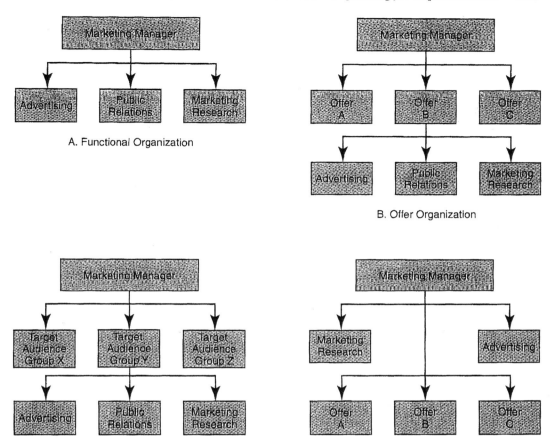

A. Functional Organization

B. Offer Organization

C. Target Audience Organization

D. Mixed Organization

FIGURE 18-1   Alternative Organizational Designs

As the marketing group absorbs once separate functions such as public relations, advertising, and marketing research, it is natural to keep them as separate functional units within marketing. Each function may initially be the responsibility of a single employee. As the marketing group grows, the functional units inevitably grow, and each function may well have its own manager.

The organization may choose to retain a functional structure for a long time. One obvious reason for this would be if the subunits never become larger than one or two persons. Even if they did, however, many in the private sector believe that keeping marketing people aligned with their functional specialties has advantages:

1. *Economies of scale.* A single public relations or advertising group can produce mass communications programs at much less cost or can develop more "clout" with significant outside agencies than can individual advertising or public relations people scattered throughout a complex nonprofit organization.

2. *Functional skill synergies.* Several advertising or public relations people working together in physical proximity will stimulate each other to produce much higher quality work.
3. *Professional affinities.* A functional organization is consistent with the natural affinities of those it hires. That is, other things being equal, advertising people will feel more comfortable with other advertising people, and public relations people with other public relations people. Even if they are initially located apart, they will gravitate toward each other. Therefore, why not put them together in the first place?

In mature organizations, functional structures are desirable under two conditions. First, the product and target audience mix should be relatively homogeneous. Second, the industry to be served should not be particularly dynamic. If the former is not the case, there is serious danger that functionally oriented specialists will ignore product or target audience groups that don't interest them. In rapidly changing markets, focusing on individual specialties and not on products or target audiences may lead functionally oriented departments to miss major changes in target audience behavior, competitor strategies, or both.

The functional approach also has other disadvantages:

1. Informal criteria for performance may become centered on what the *function* values and not on what is good for the nonprofit enterprise. Thus advertising people working with each other may tend to feel rewarded for "impressive" advertisements. Public relations people may pride themselves on industry awards for their brochures or public education campaigns. Peer accolades may take the place of market performance.
2. Coordination is more cumbersome. If the organization has several products or services, the general marketing manager will have to spend a lot of time running between functional specialists to ensure that campaigns complement each other, that work is done on time and in proper sequence, and so on.
3. Bottom-line responsibility is diffused. If a product or service is unsuccessful or if a major target audience group is stolen away by a competitor, functional specialists will blame "the other guy." If, for example, a new adult extension program in a hospital is a flop, the advertising people may blame the public relations people for not getting enough free TV time or news releases in local papers describing the program. For their part, the public relations people may blame the adult education staff for not being target audience-oriented enough in actually running the classes. No one person takes final responsibility for the disappointing performance.

Offering-Centered Organization

Many of the leading private sector marketers have turned their functional departments into product/service-centered organizations, as shown in Figure 18-1B. One person is put in charge of a specific product or service (or a set of relatively similar products and services) and is charged with making them a success. In the nonprofit world, there are offerings that involve neither products nor services but still seek socially desirable behaviors. For this reason, we have adopted the term "offer-centered" rather than the more traditional distinction. The virtue of the approach is that responsibility in this framework is inescapable. If the organization is large enough, each offer manager would manage his or her own advertising, public relations, and marketing research specialists.

In smaller organizations such as those one often encounters in the nonprofit sector, it may be necessary to adopt a mixed form of organization like that in Figure 18-1D, which attempts to capture at least the major features of the offer-centered design. In the mixed format, functional *staff* departments are established along with offer departments. Each offer manager then "buys" functional services (e.g., marketing research), coordinating their use and ensuring that the "purchased" service provider pays strict attention to market performance.

The offer-centered organization has a number of advantages:

1. Responsibility is clear. If behavioral objectives are not achieved, there is only one person to blame. If they are achieved, or if significant movement is made toward them, one person probably deserves most of the credit (and the rewards that go with it).
2. This single responsibility forces close attention to market dynamics, shifts in target audience tastes and preferences, and competitors' current and planned strategies and tactics. The offer management structure typically is much "faster on its feet" than the functional system.
3. General management skills are developed. Marketing proves to be a good training ground for future top managers. Since all offer managers have their own little enterprises to manage, they should become very good at overall strategic planning, budgeting, coordination, and personnel management—all skills that should quickly qualify them for higher-level management positions.
4. Small products or services and minor behavioral challenges are not neglected.
5. Intraorganizational competition is fostered. Hospital OB/GYN marketing programs could be set in competition with its programs for emergency or outpatient care or for adult education. This internal competitiveness in the private sector seems to keep marketers even more alert and aggressive than do other structural designs.

Despite these important advantages, the offer management system can have serious limitations. Some are inherent. Broad general management skills are necessary in this kind of system, but often the offer managers filling the ranks are young and not yet experienced enough to handle the complex managing job effectively. Further, an emphasis on offerings can mean relatively weak skill development in functional areas. Thus the offer manager may not be particularly strong in advertising or marketing research or public relations and will need to defer too much operational responsibility to functional specialists. Finally, the offer management structure may encourage top management to assign management roles to persons with deep knowledge of products, services, or behavioral offerings rather than marketing skills and target audience sensitivity. Thus an older nurse with a large family may be seen as the best person to head up the OB/GYN marketing program. The adult fitness program may be assigned to the hospital "fitness freak," while the outpatient program is assigned to the young woman who dropped out of medical school for a management career.

Clearly, the major disadvantage of the offer management approach is that the manager is not given direct line authority over his or her functional specialists. Thus offer managers need great persuasive skill to get staff functional specialists to do what is needed *when* it is needed. With other managers competing for the same staff specialists, there is a great chance that programs will be poorly coordinated. Further, where authority does not equal responsibility, offer managers will feel considerable frustration at being held accountable for things they cannot totally control.

If there is the danger of this frustration occurring, three steps must be taken. First, top management must back up the offer manager by according him or her an important role in the overall organization and by stressing to functional staff people that their job is to serve the offer managers and not to decide what should or should not get done. Second, offer managers should be chosen partly for their interpersonal and persuasive skills. Third, reward systems should explicitly make allowances for situational factors the offer manager cannot control.

The Target Audience-Centered Organization

If, as we have argued, successful marketing organizations should be target audience-centered, then it might reasonably be asked why this shouldn't apply to their marketing structures as well (see Figure 18-1C). Take the case of the YMCA, for example. The Y has many offerings—physical fitness programs, arts and crafts programs, educational programs, and so on. An offer management system would call for appointing a person to head each major program. Thus a physical fitness director would study people's needs and interests in physical fitness and would develop plans for expanding the offerings and attracting more users, as well as for pricing the programs competitively. This person would advise various local Y units on how to make their physical fitness programs stronger.

The Y also serves a variety of markets divided by sex (male, female) and age (teens, young adults, adults, senior citizens) and could organize itself around them. In a marketing system organized by target audience group, a person would be appointed to focus on each major market. Thus the market manager for teens would study teens' needs and develop programs that satisfy these needs while another person focuses on elderly women. These individuals would consult local Ys that are having trouble attracting teens or elderly women and propose new programs that might be offered.

IMPLEMENTING A TARGET AUDIENCE ORIENTATION

Establishing the marketing structure appropriate to a particular organization does not necessarily make the organization *target audience-oriented*. Nonetheless, it is crucial that the departments and key managers and staff everywhere in the institution—whether called marketers or not—have the proper philosophy. Inculcating this philosophy may be the marketing manager's most important task. This can be a challenge if the marketing manager has limited influence on how many in the organization think and behave toward target audiences and other publics. The marketing officer in a college, for example, cannot order professors to show a stronger interest in their students. A marketing vice president in a hospital cannot require nurses to smile and act promptly to meet patient needs or discharge clerks to be solicitous of patient anxieties. The marketing manager, instead, must work patiently to build up the right mindset. It is not possible for a nonmarket-oriented organization to be transformed into a fully responsive market-oriented organization overnight. Installing the marketing concept calls for major commitments and changes in the organization. As noted by Edward S. McKay, a long-time marketing consultant:

> It may require drastic and upsetting changes in organization. It usually demands new approaches to planning. It may set in motion a series of appraisals that will disclose surprising weaknesses in performance, distressing needs for modification of operating practices, and unexpected gaps, conflicts, or obsolescence in

basic policies. Without doubt, it will call for reorientation of business philosophy and for the reversal of some long-established attitudes. These changes will not be easy to implement. Objectives, obstacles, resistance, and deep-rooted habits will have to be overcome. Frequently, even difficult and painful restaffing programs are necessary before any real progress can be made in implementing the concept.[15]

Any attempt to reorient an organization requires a plan. The plan must be based on sound principles for producing organizational change. Achieving a target audience orientation calls for several measures, the sum of which will hopefully produce a market-oriented organization within three to five years. These measures are described next.

Top Management Support

An organization is not likely to develop a strong marketing orientation until its chief executive officer believes in it, understands it, wants it, and wins the support of other high-level executives for building this mindset. This was a major weakness in the study referenced earlier.[16] The CEO should be the organization's highest "marketing executive" and should create the climate for marketing by talking about it and agitating for it. Ideally, the CEO of a social service agency, for example, should frequently remind the head of fundraising, the telephone operators, billing agents, and others of the importance of being responsive to target audiences and their needs—obviously within limits. By setting the tone that the organization must be service minded and responsive, the CEO prepares the groundwork for introducing further changes later.

In-Company Marketing Training

An early task of any new marketing executive should be to develop a series of workshops to introduce marketing concepts and tools to various groups in the organization. These groups are likely to have antiquated or biased views of marketing and limited understanding of its potential benefits.

The first workshop should be presented to top corporate and divisional management. Their understanding and support are absolutely essential if marketing is to work in the organization. The workshop may take place at the organization's headquarters or at a retreat; it may consist of a highly professional presentation of concepts, cases, and marketing planning exercises. From there, further presentations can be made to the human resources, operations people, financial people, and others to increase their understanding of how marketing ideas can help them in their own jobs.

Better Employee Hiring Practices

Training can only go so far in inculcating the right attitudes in employees. If a hospital has grown accustomed to concentrating on the latest procedures and interventions instead of target audience care, it will be hard to change its attitudes and behavior. However, the hospital can gradually rectify the imbalance by taking advantage of turnover and hiring doctors, nurses, and frontline personnel who have a more patient-friendly point of view.

The first principle in developing a caring organization is to hire caring people. Some people are more naturally service minded than others, and this can be a significant criterion for hiring. Delta Airlines historically did much of its flight attendant recruiting from the deep South where there is a tradition of hospitality; it hires fewer attendants in large Northern cities because people from these cities tend to be less hospitable. Southwest's former CEO said that he only hired people who had great personalities, arguing that he can always train them in the specifics of their job but could not change who they were.

New employees should go through a training program that emphasizes the importance of creating target audience satisfaction. They can be taught how to handle complaining and even abusive target audiences without getting riled. Skills in listening and target audience problem solving would be part of the training.

Rewarding Market-Oriented Employees

One way for top management to convince everyone in the organization of the importance of target audience-oriented attitudes is to reward those who demonstrate these attitudes. The organization can make a point of citing employees who have done an outstanding job of serving target audiences. Many colleges have "best teacher" awards based on student voting. Some hospitals carry a picture in their employees' magazine showing the "nurse of the month" and describing how this person handled a difficult situation. By calling attention to examples of commendable target audience-oriented performance through internal marketing, it is hoped that other employees will be motivated to emulate this behavior.

TARGET AUDIENCE-DRIVEN ORGANIZATIONAL CHANGE: AN EXAMPLE

The American Cancer Society is the fifth-largest charity in the United States. In the 1980s, the American Cancer Society was extremely successful, dominating the field of cancer research and treatment. Gains in donations were double digit every year. However, pressure was building inside and outside the organization. Like many nonprofits, the American Cancer Society operated with a national office and regional and divisional affiliates. The latter collected funds and remitted 40 percent to the national office which, in turn, supplied services and support to local efforts.

By 1990, regional and local officials were criticizing the central operation. A member of the national board accused the organization of having "a sort of stuffy tradition, and a lot of sacred cows." The biggest complaint was that "national" was *not target audience-oriented*. The organization was demanding too much of its local affiliates and not giving them the kind of help they wanted and needed in return. As the executive vice president of the New Jersey division said, "The national office [would] develop what it wanted to and offer it to us, never really asking what we wanted." It was an excellent example of the kind of *organization-centered* operation we described in Chapter 2. The national American Cancer Society office was selling its offerings to its target audiences, the regions, and divisions, but not meeting the latter's needs and wants.

In the 1990s, competitive pressures were also rising dramatically from other charities that focused on specific cancers, such as breast, prostate, and so forth. Gains in donations fell to single digits. In response, two dramatic changes in the way the American Cancer

Society was organized and operated were initiated. First, it decided to focus its efforts. Rather than try to do everything, the organization decided to emphasize a relatively small number of target areas: eliminate tobacco use, promote early detection of breast cancer, promote school health programs, recruit new volunteers, and promote income development. The society also set specific "measures of success" for each area.

Second, it undertook a bottom-up organizational change process. It was clear that a new organizational structure was needed. However, the American Cancer Society's new CEO, John Seffrin, decided to let the employees and volunteers design the new organization rather than imposing a new order from the top down. This bottom-up approach involved a committee of 20 staff members and volunteers who met over the course of eight months and came up with solutions that were enthusiastically received by Seffrin and the board of directors. In the process, the American Cancer Society got the very best ideas from those on the firing line. Employees and volunteers got ownership of the process and the outcome. It was clear that any eventual downsizing and streamlining came from below, not above.

As a result of this change process, national departments such as the Prevention Department were given the task of becoming target audience-driven. They were given the responsibility of coming up with the materials and training programs that the divisions needed and liked. Under the new regime, the only way a department could grow would be if it showed that it was meeting its target audience's (division) needs.

The result of the process was increased focus and greatly heightened morale that set a course for the American Cancer Society into the next century. As the executive vice president of the Virginia Division noted, "If this fails—and I don't think it will—then we all fail together. It's not something that has been imposed upon us divisions, we bought into it from the very beginning."

Clearly, being target audience responsive applies as much to organizational change as it does to raising funds and changing final target audience behavior.

A description of how these changes have affected the American Cancer Society's marketing efforts is offered by the vice president for international marketing, Cynthia Currence, in Exhibit 18-1.

EXHIBIT 18-1

CYNTHIA CURRENCE, VICE PRESIDENT FOR INTERNATIONAL MARKETING ON THE AMERICAN CANCER SOCIETY'S MARKETING CHALLENGES

Internal marketing is essential to accomplishing goals at the American Cancer Society. The American Cancer Society is a large organization in terms of numbers of talented and passionate staff and volunteers. These very committed people address a highly complex cause that touches virtually all segments of the American population. If you know someone who has been cured of childhood leukemia, someone who has had a mammogram, someone who is taking Herceptin or Tamoxifen for breast cancer, someone who has stopped smoking, or

(continued)

EXHIBIT 18-1 (cont.)

someone who has received life-saving cancer information in the middle of the night, then you know someone who has been touched by the work of the American Cancer Society. There are numerous options for target audiences, strategies, and activities that would make progress in bringing cancer under control within the shortest amount of time. In order to achieve and maintain strategic focus for measurable outcomes, the organization must build and sustain consensus around the priority areas that will generate the greatest gains for the cause. Internal communications and marketing regarding rationale and accomplishments related to strategic directions help achieve this focus.

The organization's nationwide priorities are (a) providing high-quality and understandable information 24 hours a day/seven days a week, (b) funding research, (c) improving cancer patients' quality of life, and (d) increasing prevention and detection behaviors among appropriate populations. The American Cancer Society maintains a National Cancer Information Center that is available all day, every day to talk with people about cancer issues. This call center handles over 1.2 million "inbound" calls each year and there were over 24 million visitors to the cancer.org web site project for 2006. Twenty percent of the web traffic originates outside the United States. E-mail addresses are solicited as both a way to deliver information instantaneously to consumers and as a way to begin a longer-term dialogue and relationship with them. Special communities have been built online for special constituencies such as cancer survivors (Cancer Survivors' Network) and Relay For Life participants. Relay For Life is the Society's signature event and generates over $300 million per year with people from over 4,000 communities in the United States and 20 different countries involved.

Summary

When marketing is first introduced in a nonprofit organization, it is either *pushed* by one or more key individuals who have been exposed to it elsewhere or *pulled* by environmental forces that make marketing essential to survival and success. Marketing may begin as a staff function coordinating programs and providing advice. It may then move on to be a line function. Only when it is fully accepted as a top-level management function will marketing achieve its maximum effectiveness.

The twenty-first century brings new organizational challenges to large, complex nonprofits. They are often multinational and/or multi-site. Thus they must choose among structures that have either strong central control and consistent positioning and branding or allow local autonomy and the ability to effectively adopt global programs to meet local needs to a great extent.

The choice of initial projects can have an important effect on the acceptance of marketing. These projects should have high economic impact yet be relatively easy to implement. They should be completed in a short period of time and be given high visibility if successful.

Once marketing is well established, a critical question is what organizational structure is best. The major alternatives are a functional orientation, an offer management orientation, a target audience orientation, or some mixture. Although the specific form chosen should depend on the experience, market conditions, and mission of the organization, the target audience-centered form most explicitly incorporates the philosophy emphasized in this book. And even when the target audience-centered form is not chosen, it is essential that the organization adopt a target audience perspective. This can be accomplished by careful hiring and training, explicit top management support, and a reward structure that reinforces target audience-centered behavior.

Target audience-driven approaches can also ensure effective organizational change and training, especially for large nonprofits whose national offices have regional divisions as their target audiences.

Questions

1. You are eager to bring more staffers to your Red Cross regional office. At the moment you have 325 people, of which only 28 have business backgrounds. What characteristics would you look for in potential business candidates? What would you avoid?

2. You have just hired five marketing specialists for the Kennedy Center for the Performing Arts. You want to brief them before they start. What are the five most important things they need to appreciate about the differences between their old employers and their new one?

3. The marketing director for a new Philadelphia HIV/AIDS program decides to run a marketing program to get more African-Americans to undertake testing—especially those at risk. The first campaign features dozens of dramatic bus stop posters with a bold statement urging viewers to get tested and/or call a hotline number. Expenses exceed $40,000. Few calls are received after the campaign is launched and no appreciable change in testing appears to have taken place. Staffers who are jealous of the marketer's large budget urge you (as the CEO) to cut back on this activity. How would you respond?

4. The executive at your largest chapter—one whose practices are often emulated by executives at other chapters—has decided that she does not like the branding approach that you have devised and plans to develop her own, one she says will be more appropriate to her city and suburbs. How would you respond?

5. You believe that your Goodwill operation is insufficiently customer-oriented. How would you go about changing this?

Notes

1. Francine D. Blau and Marianne A. Ferber, "Occupations and Earnings of Women Workers," in Karen Shallcross Koziara, Michael H. Moskow, and Lecretia Dewey Tanner (Eds.), *Working Women: Past, Present and Future* (Washington, DC: The Bureau of National Affairs, Inc., 1987), pp. 37–68.

2. Marianne G. Briscoe, "The Politics of Cheap: Are Low Salaries Damaging Nonprofits?" *Nonprofit Times*, September 1994, p. 12.

3. Debra E. Blum and Domenica Marchetti, "Fund Raisers Find For-Profit Jobs Give Them Best of Both Worlds," *The Chronicle of Philanthropy*, November 16, 2000, p. 24.

4. Sonya Freeman Cohen, "Working in Europe: A Nonprofit Perspective," *Nonprofit Times*, February 1993, pp. 33–34.

5. Ludwig Theuvsen, "Doing Better While Doing Good: Motivational Aspects of Pay-for-Performance Effectiveness in Nonprofit Organizations," *Voluntas: International Journal of Voluntary and Nonprofit Organizations*, Vol. 15, No. 2 (June 2004), pp. 117–136.

6. Alan R. Andreasen, Ronald C. Goodstein, and Joan W. Wilson, "Transferring Marketing Knowledge to the Nonprofit Sector," *California Management Review,* Vol. 47, No. 4 (Summer 2005), pp. 46-67.

7. Christine W. Letts, William P. Ryan, and Allen Grossman, *High Performance Nonprofit Organizations* (New York: John Wiley & Sons, Inc., 1999).

8. A. R. Andreasen, "Marketing Social Marketing in the Social Change Marketplace," *Journal of Public Policy & Marketing,* Vol. 21, No. 1 (Spring 2002), pp. 3-13. See also A. R. Andreasen, "The Life Trajectory of Social Marketing: Some Implications," *Marketing Theory,* Vol. 3, No. 3 (2004), pp. 293–303.

9. listproc@listproc.georgetown.edu

10. George S. Yip, "Global Strategies . . . in a World of Nations," *Harvard Business Review,* Fall 1989, pp. 29-41.

11. Terry Clark, "International Marketing and National Character: A Review and Proposal for an Integrative Theory," *Journal of Marketing,* Vol. 54 (October 1990), pp. 66–79.

12. See also Dennis Young, Bonnie Koenig, Adil Najam, and Julie Fisher, "Strategy and Structure in Managing Global Associations," *Voluntas,* Vol. 18, No. 4 (December 1999), pp. 323–344.

13. Sonya Freeman Cohen, "Working in Europe."

14. Saeed Samind and Kendall Roth, "The Influence of Global Marketing Standardization Performance," *Journal of Marketing,* April 1992, pp. 1–17.

15. Edward S. McKay, *The Marketing Mystique* (New York: American Management Association, 1972), p. 22.

16. Andreasen, Goodstein, and Wilson, "Transferring Marketing Knowledge."

19

MARKETING EVALUATION, MONITORING, AND CONTROL

PILOTING YOUR NONPROFIT

KaBOOM! is a charity whose vision is for there to be a great place to play outdoors within walking distance of every child in America. Its major activity is getting community volunteers organized under a KaBOOM! manager to build playgrounds. The idea for KaBOOM came about in 1995 when two Washington, D.C., nonprofit workers, Darrell Hammond and Dawn Hutchinson, read about two children who suffocated while playing in an abandoned car. They started KaBOOM! to create safe playgrounds, and since 1995 the organization has built 5,000 playgrounds nationwide using donations from businesses and 200,000 volunteers, often provided by the business sponsors themselves. To keep up this pace, goals were set for the 26 KaBOOM! managers at 18 playgrounds a year to continue to meet the organization's goals.

But Kate Becker, a KaBOOM! vice president, became worried in 2005. What disturbed her was something she saw on her desktop computer. Fortunately for her, earlier in 2004, Darrel Hammond discovered a better way to provide tracking information for KaBOOM! staff. He was visiting the CEO of one of his biggest sponsors, Home Depot, and was impressed by the colorful graphics on the CEO's two computer screens. At that point, Hammond was accustomed to reviewing written reports on projects, turnover rates, and so on. But typically there was too much data not in very useful forms. Home Depot, it turned out, was using a new system called a "dashboard." Hammond decided that KaBOOM! should create its own dashboard. It was this dashboard that gave Kate Becker vivid graphics right on her desktop showing her how the organization was doing against key benchmarks. The top screen gave major tracking information on "vital signs," program efficiency, fundraising efficiency, and "build" efficiency. These top-line numbers then could yield underlying supporting data.

What she noticed was a red figure that highlighted the fact that turnover among KaBOOM! managers was increasing. Further, the building projects were being rushed—6 weeks instead of the more careful 10–12 weeks. So, Becker decided to cut the number of projects expected annually from each manager to 14 instead of 18. The impact was noticeable in that the dashboard soon showed that the average tenure of project managers grew from 16 to 22 months and the number of volunteer leaders recruited for projects grew 8 percent.

The dashboard has proven very valuable day-to-day management tool and critical to long-range planning. KaBOOM!'s next move is to share the dashboard information with selected donors.

Source: Debra K. Blum, "Checking the Dashboard," *The Chronicle of Philanthropy,* October 12, 2006, p. M-6.

Strategic planning in marketing is crucial in setting the nonprofit organization off in the proper direction, whether for multiple years of activities or for a specific campaign. But careful plans and detailed execution must include effective evaluation and control systems. Evaluations are essential because, as we noted in early chapters, nonprofit organizations have the peculiar characteristic that their funding (and volunteer support) is not provided—at least not in total—by the clients or other target audiences on which its offerings focus.

Control systems are equally critical. It is a planner's cliché that plans never work out! The marketing manager's objective is to learn as quickly as possible when they do not and adjust accordingly. But this takes effective control systems. In this chapter, we begin by distinguishing two types of control: strategic control and program control.

Strategic control focuses on larger issues and requires tracking changes in the broad environment, competitors' actions and plans, perceptions of the organization and its brand held by the general public, organization strengths and weaknesses, and broad trends in organization performance. *Program control* requires the development of systems for more or less continual monitoring of program performance for purposes of day-to-day fine-tuning of specific campaigns to correct for undesirable performance.

Control, however, is focused on whether the organization is going in the right direction and is on track. *Evaluation,* on the other hand, is concerned with final outcomes. Did the campaign actually work? Did it achieve its behavioral influence goals? What seemed to be the major drivers of success? What didn't work as planned? What of the organization itself? Can it boast that it is achieving its mission? What objectives are within reach? Should they abandon some? These are all questions requiring sound systems of evaluation.

As we shall note, control systems must focus in major part on the target audience as the touchstone for whether things are working. Target audiences may be several groups including potential clients, the media, legislators, volunteers, or businesses. But these target audiences are always the guideposts. Evaluation research, on the other hand, is focused more on the organization's major constituencies. Is the organization meeting the needs of its major sources of resources—donors, volunteers and staff, the board, granting agencies, and business partners—and those who may use or purchase its products and services? Is it meeting its obligations to society?

Throughout this chapter it should be remembered that not all evaluation research and control systems need be expensive or time-consuming. As we noted in Chapter 5, there are many techniques available for doing inexpensive *but good* marketing research. A good example was reported many years ago by Peter Drucker, the well-known management consultant and teacher. Drucker noted that he had been teaching for over 60 years. Once a year, he takes a few days to telephone a random sample of 50 or 60 students who graduated 10 years earlier. He asks, "Looking back, what did we contribute in this school? What is still important to you?" He follows this by asking "What should we do better? What should we stop doing?" He reports that "This feedback has been absolutely essential in those areas where I had some leadership responsibility."[1]

We begin with the more straightforward challenge of developing effective control systems at the campaign level.

MONITORING AND CONTROL OF CAMPAIGNS

When we described the process of developing campaign plans, we emphasized the need to use the target audience member as the touchstone for every element of the campaign. And we emphasized the need for *listening* at the outset, *pretesting* before going into the field, and *monitoring* to keep track of progress. Monitoring is critical to help campaign managers know such things as:

1. Is the campaign on schedule?
2. Are we reaching all of the target segments?
3. Are we having the desired impact on each segment?
4. What elements of the campaign are working well and which ones are not?
5. What's missing from the campaign?
6. Has the competitive or social environment changed in important ways that would recommend campaign changes?
7. How are our partners (if any) responding; is their participation likely to change?
8. What do other contributors—for example, volunteers or funders—think of the campaign and its progress?

Many surprises are likely to occur during any campaign's execution that will call for new responses or adjustments. Some things will work and some won't. Marketing monitoring and control systems are an intrinsic part of the campaign planning and implementation process since they permit such crucial and timely adjustments.

As indicated in Figure 19-1, the control process is in reality a cybernetic system that will ideally function not unlike a thermostat regulating a building's temperature. Management sets a goal (the desired temperature) and puts in place a device or system

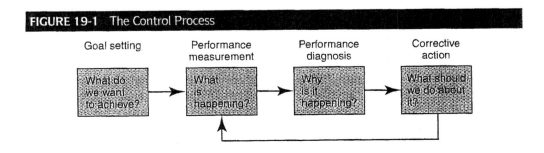

FIGURE 19-1 The Control Process

Goal setting — What do we want to achieve?

Performance measurement — What is happening?

Performance diagnosis — Why is it happening?

Corrective action — What should we do about it?

for detecting deviations from the goal (a thermometer) and ascertaining causes of the deviations (above or below ideal temperature because the space has warmed or cooled). The loop in the system is then closed by a device or subsystem that makes the necessary corrections (a trip-switch that restarts the furnace or turns on the air conditioning).

Control systems in nonprofit organizations, of course, can differ greatly in complexity, timeliness, and precision. For example, a library can simply monitor its total circulation and periodically smooth out irregularities or stimulate increased book use through radio ads, newspaper articles, web site promotions, or direct mail. Or it can look periodically at the circulation of each of its departments during different parts of the day or week and seek corrective actions that would boost lagging departments or increase patronage in particular departments during off-peak hours or days. At a more complex level, it could attempt to look not just at circulation but at *who* was taking out books, and develop program elements that would, say, bring the number of elderly or teenagers coming to the library up to goal levels.

Monitoring systems can also vary as to timeliness. The library can measure its performance daily, weekly, monthly, quarterly, or even annually. Users of web sites potentially can monitor the system moment by moment. Obviously, the faster an organization's environment changes and the more competitive the activity that takes place, the more frequently the system should be "read." Thus libraries can get by with relatively infrequent measures. Hospitals in major urban centers will want daily reports. Fundraisers in the midst of a telethon will want—and brag about—minute-by-minute totals.

Finally, it is important to remember that monitoring and evaluation are not the same thing. If the nonprofit organization relies heavily on grants from foundations or government funding, there is usually a requirement that a program be evaluated. Typically this is interpreted to mean "show us at the end of your campaign what you have achieved." This typically gets translated into a before-and-after evaluation protocol where baseline measures are taken before the program is started and then the same measures are taken at the end. Differences are then submitted as evidence that the program worked (or didn't) and that the money was well spent. Many naïve nonprofit managers think that this is adequate for monitoring purposes. But such a before-and-after approach means that the campaign had no control along the way—defects would not be discovered. And, of course, neither management nor the funder would ever really know how effective the program *could* have been if adjustments were made along the way.

Monitoring systems are designed to avoid these occurrences by providing managers with along-the-way measures that provide timely adjustments and maximize program cost-effectiveness.

A Caution

It is important to note the distinction between specific behaviors and broader social impact. The marketer's job is to influence specific behaviors. It is NOT to solve some social problem! To illustrate the point, assume that a multiyear program is designed to increase the number of immunizations of children under the age of two in Ghana. Such a program can be monitored by counting the number of children showing up for—and getting—the immunizations. From a marketer's standpoint, this will be the major benchmark for performance because the marketer's "job" is to bring about these desired behaviors. However, social critics or funders might ask (1) does an increase in child immunizations lead to better health and longer lives for the target children and (2) is it possible that immunizations would rise while general morbidity and mortality also rise? Is it possible that (1) the immunizations made the children healthier; (2) because they were healthier, parents send them out to work at a much younger age; and therefore (3) they are getting sick and dying more often—and at a younger age—from work-related causes? In the latter case, from the country's standpoint, the specific marketing campaign was a success but the *real* objective—what the society really sought (healthier children)—was not achieved; in fact, it was made worse.

It is *not* the marketer's responsibility to decide what the goal of a specific behavior-influence program should be. This is the responsibility of the program sponsor or the nonprofit organization's strategic planning committee. Ultimately, the marketer's task is to bring about the assigned behavior in an effective and efficient manner.[2] However, it is possible that the marketer could play a role in the setting of social goals and the choosing of behavioral objectives. If the marketer is properly target audience-focused and has carried out at least some audience research, he or she may be in a position to help funders decide what is feasible—given the funders' broader social goals. As the staffer in the program who will be most in touch with the target audience, as a program rolls out, the marketer ought from time to time ask whether the campaign is really likely to achieve the social change outcome everyone wants.[3]

Types of Monitoring Tools

A monitoring system like that described in Figure 19-1 is driven by an approach called *management by objectives*. Top management starts the process by developing aggregate goals for each program (or the entire enterprise) for the planning period (for example, number of people reached, messages delivered, trial behaviors taken, relationships created, and so on). These goals can then be assigned to individual managers or supervisors.

What are the monitoring indicia that might be used by management to check on the progress of their programs in reaching their goals? Given the marketing framework of this book, it is clear that the starting point must be (1) a clear specification of *behavioral* objectives—even if they are long run and (2) an explicit road map of how the organization proposes to get there. The monitoring process then is simply a set of tracking devices for measuring progress along the road. A thorough tracking process also has the advantage of allowing complex ex post facto analyses and modeling of cause-and-effect relationships that allow managers to confirm, revise, or abandon their mental models of what it takes to achieve the behavioral outcome in future campaigns.

While the monitoring system must emphasize behavioral outcomes and the steps necessary to achieve them, it is also critical to track marketing costs. Marketing managers must be tasked not only with achieving—or at least moving toward—key behavioral objectives, he or she must also be charged with doing so in a cost-effective manner. While we do not discuss this component here, it is important that marketing management be able to answer the following questions:

1. Are we over- or under-spending the budget allocated (or the one the manager asked for)?
2. Are all of the program elements cost effective—what are the benefit/cost ratios of various outlays? Was the big kickoff banquet worth it? Are we spending too much on web site development? Should we keep renting this equipment or buy it ourselves?

3. Is the budget adequate to the task? Is it excessive (few will conclude this!)?
4. Is the budget appropriately allocated—are we getting equivalent performance from a dollar spent in each program component?
5. How are our marketing staff members using the money entrusted to them—are some more wasteful than others?

We begin where all good nonprofit programs ought to end—with behavior.

Tracking Target Audience Behavior

The single most important kind of measure for any nonprofit should be a measure of *behavior*. In retail and catalog ventures, the behavior is captured in sales. In other cases, marketers might look at such behaviors as (1) membership applications, (2) votes, (3) volunteering, (4) donations, (5) attendance, (6) trash recycled, or (7) letters written to legislators. In social marketing cases, they might look at the number of people in the target audience who stopped smoking or immunized their children, the number of child abuse cases reported, or the number of missing children found. In each of these cases, the experienced marketer would like to develop a tracking system to measure success both at any point in time and over time.

Non-Behavioral Measures

Of course, behavioral impacts may take a long time to achieve (this is just one of the many profound differences in the nonprofit sector). In such cases, interim measures of progress will be important. It is critical for this task that the marketer have a good model of the behavioral determinants. In our own work, we rely extensively on the stage of change and the BCOS frameworks. Measures of knowledge, attitudes, and intentions of individuals toward the behavior (for example, reducing energy consumption) will indicate the size of the audiences at the various stages. Measures of the number of people who have formed perceptions of benefits and costs of proposed actions will give a sense of the size of the group in the Contemplation stage and other data will give a sense of untapped segmentation possibilities. These measures will also give valuable insights into what might need to be done to change these perceptions— for example, alerting management to the need to add new benefits.

It will also be useful to find out how many people are trying to change (in the Preparation/Action stage) and the number already doing the new behavior (in the Maintenance stage). Studies of those in these two stages should be designed to not only estimate the size of the groups but also to identify barriers that seem problematic for the first group and rewards that seem to be working for those in Maintenance. If upstream factors appear to be inhibiting behavior, it may be that new campaign elements will need to be introduced to address these challenges.

Simple bar charts tracking the number of people in major segments who are at each stage can be an excellent visual device on the dashboard for seeing progress and communicating it to those stakeholders inside and outside the organization.

Measuring Change

Monitoring involves the measurement of change where change is the primary goal. (Of course, some anti-drug or anti-violence campaigns want to keep people *not* changing— a more difficult measurement challenge.) To measure change, one must have the right instruments. Researchers who wish to monitor the performance of a target market over time can choose among four basic types of change measures:

1. *Retrospectively,* by asking a single sample of target audience members what they are thinking and doing now and what they thought and did at some past point in time.
2. *Cross-sectionally,* by comparing thoughts and behaviors of a single sample of target audience members presumed to be earlier or later in a process (e.g., comparing seat-belt attitudes of and use by 21- to 30-year-olds with that of 31- to 40-year-olds, or those never exposed to a particular campaign with those exposed for two, four, and six months).
3. *Cross-sectionally over time,* by asking about thoughts and behaviors of different samples at two points in time (e.g., as in traditional political polling).
4. *Longitudinally over time,* by taking thoughts and behavioral measures of the same panel of target audience members at different points over time. Various web-based data gathering systems like SurveyMonkey are very good for this.

The value of the last approach, panel studies, as compared to cross-sectional polls, is suggested in the following hypothetical but realistic example. Suppose AARP creates a detailed report on the impact of Internet health insurance fraud on the elderly as part of a campaign to get the U.S. Congress to pass a federal statute regulating insurers who are seeking target audience members over the Web. The report is filled with dramatic examples of elderly people who have been duped into unneeded expenditures. AARP distributes the report to Congressional offices and to the media. Further, suppose that a small survey of 100 Congressional staffers and several reporters was taken before and after the report was issued using *different* samples and that these samples showed that the proportion of individuals supporting the legislation rose from 40 to 50 percent. Understandably, AARP would be pleased with such results. But this pleasure is based on a belief that if one studied the *same* target audience members before and after the report (a panel study), the shifting of their positions over time would reveal whether it was a good or a not-so-good result—all the while yielding what would seem like overall growth from 40 to 50 percent.

As shown in the first example of good results, the AARP report added nicely to its present core of supporters. However, if the "not-so-good results" were found, the report would show that AARP alienated three-quarters of its supporters but attracted a third

TABLE 19-1 Hypothetical Panel Study Results

Before Report	Good Result After Report		Not-So-Good Result After Report		Total
	Support Legislation	*Oppose Legislation*	*Support Legislation*	*Oppose Legislation*	
Support legislation	40%	0%	10%	30%	40%
Oppose legislation	10%	19%	10%	19%	30%
No preference	0%	30%	30%	0%	30%
Total	50%	50%	50%	50%	100%

of those opposing the legislation and *all* those previously undecided. If it had access to the latter finding, AARP would realize it had to move fast to win back its original supporters while at the same time trying to hold on to the possibly fickle "undecideds" who have just switched over to supporting AARP. Learning this crucial information is *only* possible with panel data. Only panel data can show *who* changed. Such data would be absolutely crucial to an organization that wishes to move quickly and correctly in a volatile marketplace.

Panel data, however, have their problems. First, there is a serious danger that prior measures will influence later measures or interact with the intervention to foul up the results. In the previous example, people contacted before the AARP report may have been stimulated to pay more attention to the topic (and the report) and so the intervention would appear to be *more* effective than it really was. A second problem is dropouts. The previous example assumed that the panel stayed intact. But if some people drop out between waves and they are the ones indifferent to the topic, measures of those still in the panel will again overstate the effects.

The alternative, of course, is to use different cross-sections each time. One gives up the ability to understand who changed for (presumably) a more accurate measure of gross effects. This is the approach most commonly used in political tracking studies. The advantage there is that pollsters tend to take continuing polls and believe—with some justification—that any trends would eventually show up as they track knowledge and opinions about issues and candidates over time.[4]

Tracking Target Audience Satisfaction and Likely Repeat Behavior

Even when a significant number of target audience members are in the Maintenance stage, many marketing managers will want measures that indicate the likelihood of repeat transactions (i.e., regular recycling, repeated donations, recurring news stories in print or on TV, revisits to the symphony or museum, or continued participation in exercise programs). A key measure used in the commercial sector for this purpose is a measure of target audience satisfaction. Such measures should be considered as a major indicator of potential repeat behaviors. Satisfaction measures can be very helpful as control measures to track an ongoing campaign and in evaluative studies as well. They can be particularly useful in tracking satisfaction of volunteers or partners—such as businesses—in a campaign. In Cleveland, local hospitals at one time banded together to produce a twice-yearly target audience member attitude study. Patrick McTigue, President of Corbett Health Connect, noted that the research "has become a major quality-driving effort on the part of Cleveland's hospitals that are not doing well."[5]

Satisfaction is a function of what the individual expects and what he or she thinks the outcome was.[6] Conceptually a person can experience one of three states of satisfaction. If the results *exceed* the person's expectations, the person is highly satisfied—even delighted. If the results match the expectations, the person is just satisfied. If the results fall short of the expectations, the person is dissatisfied. Satisfaction may not be the ideal for some organizations. "Customer delight" has become a mantra for many commercial marketing managers and can well apply to volunteer or donor participation in nonprofit efforts.[7]

If there is a gap between expectations and outcomes—the diet didn't work, the volunteer task was boring, the "free gift" was tacky—some target audience members will try to *minimize* the felt dissonance by imagining that performance was really better than they first thought or by thinking that perhaps they set their expectations too high. Still other target audience members might have the opposite reaction—exaggerating the perceived performance gap because of their disappointment—and perhaps not plan to repeat their effort. The latter case will be more of a challenge for the marketer because these audience members are more prone to reduce or lose contact with the organization and/or complain to friends and coworkers.

Thus to understand satisfaction, we must also understand how people form their expectations. Expectations are formed to some extent on the basis of people's past experience with the same or similar situations, messages, and statements made by friends and associates. The marketer, therefore, needs to monitor both the performance of its offerings and also the expectations they raise. The marketer needs to be careful not to raise expectations too high as this is likely to create subsequent dissatisfaction. On the other hand, setting low expectations risks lowering the number of transactions by suggesting that the behavior only promises limited benefits.

Monitoring target audience member satisfaction can be extremely helpful to management, especially if "total quality" is a major part of a strategy—for example, in hospital or education settings or in various participation programs (stop smoking, dieting, exercise).

Complaint and Suggestion Systems

One possible approach to collecting satisfactions data for service businesses like hospitals, universities, soup kitchens, and work with the homeless is to establish complaint and suggestion systems. A responsive organization makes it easy for its participants to complain if they are disappointed in some ways with the service they have received or for business partners to protest if things are not working out to their satisfaction. Management will want complaints to surface on the theory that target audiences who are not given an opportunity to complain might reduce their relationship with the organization, spread negative word of mouth, or abandon it completely. Indeed, it has been found that dissatisfied target audience members are likely to tell 9 to 12 other target audience members, whereas satisfied target audience members speak to only 2 or 3.[8]

Voicing complaints has, by itself, a potentially salutary effect. The likelihood of negative effects will be reduced substantially if dissatisfied target audience members are encouraged to voice their complaints to the nonprofit. They are more likely to continue to volunteer or donate *even if* the nonprofit does not respond to the complaint to the complainer's satisfaction. Indeed, it has been found that the faster the marketer responds to a voiced complaint, the more likely it will lead to a favorable attitude on the part of the target audience member.

Target Audience Satisfaction Surveys as Evaluation and Monitoring Tools

A major problem with volunteered complaints, as noted in a 1977 Andreasen and Best study, is that they are unrepresentative of both the types of complaints and the types of complainers.[9] The study found that target audience members are more likely to volunteer complaints about problems in which high costs (economic, social, and psychological) are involved or by which they are seriously inconvenienced. Further, they are more likely to complain if they think the nonprofit organization is to blame and they themselves did not contribute to the problem. Finally, they are more likely to complain if the nature of the problem and its source are manifest—that is, if the existence of a problem is not really a matter of individual judgment. For these reasons, a nonprofit is more likely to receive complaints about issues involving large monetary and time costs on the part of clients. Problems involving broken items, delayed services, and discourteous employees are more likely to surface than problems in which, say, medical care is just a bit impersonal or in which the staff of an educational seminar seems underprepared and the seminar is not taught very well. Yet it is just these more minor kinds of unreported feelings of dissatisfaction that management would like to know about. The obviously bad features of any program usually quickly become apparent without much management research. The subtle things that can truly sink a basically good program or institution through poor word of mouth, lack of repeat behavior, and, perhaps worse still, just plain apathy are the very things that don't get volunteered by dissatisfied target audience members. People must be asked.

People must also be asked because not all of them will speak up. To voice a complaint, one must not only have a problem or a dissatisfaction, but one has to understand where and how to complain and have the skills to do so and the gumption to speak up. Not everyone has these qualities. Indeed, research has consistently shown that vocal complainers are much more likely to be socially upscale and have higher incomes and better educations. They are also likely to be relatively young. Yet many nonprofit programs, such as those in social work or those requiring long-term behavioral change, like stopping smoking or exercising regularly, have downscale audiences or the elderly as their primary targets. Hearing from these people is essential to program success, yet they may be the least likely to volunteer information about their dissatisfaction.

Finally, the voicing of complaints is sometimes inhibited by the institution itself. Unless the circumstances are right and the nonprofit marketer sets the right tone, people are relatively unlikely to complain about their church, their doctor, or even their lawyer or accountant. When patients perceived problems with their medical and dental care, they were significantly less likely to speak up about them. And when they did, Andreasen and Best found the medical and dental community much less responsive than other marketers in resolving their complaints. Only one in six of those who had a serious dissatisfaction felt bold enough to speak up about it and were lucky enough to have it handled satisfactorily.

The better, more responsive nonprofits supplement the devices described earlier with direct periodic surveys of target audience member satisfaction. They send questionnaires or make telephone calls to a random sample of past users to find out how much they like the service. Some organizations also survey clients of competitors or of marketers of unrelated products and services to identify potential market opportunities on which they might capitalize. Through direct surveys, they avoid the several biases of complaint monitoring systems.

Target audience member satisfaction can be measured in a number of ways that help campaign monitoring and final evaluations. Some of the options are discussed next.

Directly Reported Satisfaction   A volunteer manager can distribute a questionnaire to a representative sample of volunteers, asking them to state their satisfaction with the nonprofit as a whole and with specific aspects of the volunteer experience. The questionnaire would be distributed on a periodic basis either in person, in the mail, through the Internet, or through a telephone inquiry.

The questionnaire would contain questions of the following form:

Indicate how satisfied you are with _____ *on the following scale:*

1	2	3	4	5
Highly dissatisfied	Dissatisfied	Indifferent	Satisfied	Highly satisfied

Here, five values are used, although some scales use only three values and others use as many as eleven.

When the results are in, a histogram can be prepared showing the percentage of volunteers who fall into each group. Of course, volunteers within any group—such as the highly dissatisfied group—may have quite different intensities of dissatisfaction ranging from mild feelings of disappointment with the nonprofit to intense feelings of anger. Unfortunately, there is no way to make interpersonal comparisons of intensity and we can only rely on the self-reported feelings of the respondents.

If the histogram shows more answers skewed to the left, then the nonprofit volunteer program is in deep trouble. If the histogram is bell shaped, then it has the usual number of dissatisfied, indifferent, and satisfied volunteers. If the histogram shows more answers to the right, the nonprofit can be very satisfied that it is a responsive organization meeting its goal of delivering high satisfaction to the majority of its target audience members.[10] Finally, if the distribution is bimodal (i.e., two peaks), the organization may need to develop a second offering to meet the needs of the dissatisfied market while retaining the present offering to serve the satisfied group.

Derived Dissatisfaction   The second method of satisfaction measurement is based on the premise stated earlier that a particular volunteer's satisfaction is influenced by the perceived performance and his or her expectations. The individual is asked two questions about each component of the volunteer experience, for example:

The challenge involved in the volunteer experience:

a. How much was there?

(min)   1   2   3   4   5   6   7   (max)

b. How much did you expect?

(min)   1   2   3   4   5   6   7   (max)

Suppose the volunteer circles 2 for part (a) and 5 for part (b). We can then derive a "performance deficiency" score by subtracting the answer for part (a) from part (b), here 3. The greater the performance deficiency score, the greater the degree of dissatisfaction (or the smaller the degree of satisfaction).

This method provides more useful information than the previous method. By averaging the scores of all the respondents to part (a), the researcher learns the average perceived performance. The dispersion around the average shows how much agreement there is. If all volunteers see the volunteer experience as approximately 2 on a 7-point scale, this means the program is pretty bad. If volunteers hold widely differing perceptions of the program's actual quality, further analysis is needed of why the perceptions differ so much and what individual or group factors it might be related to.

It is also useful to average the scores of all the respondents to part (b). This reveals the average volunteer's view of how much quality is expected in the experience. The measure of dispersion shows how much spread there is in volunteer opinion about the desirable level of quality. This is, in effect, a good measure of how clear the institution's brand image is.

Problem Rates   A third approach is simply to ask respondents three major questions: (1) Have you engaged in some transaction with us in the last 12 months? (2) If yes, did you experience any problems with it? (3) If no problems are mentioned, was there any way in which it could have been better for you? There are several advantages to this approach. First, specific problems or deficiencies can be identified, including many that management may not have anticipated. These can then be the subject of immediate corrective action, especially if respondents indicate how serious a problem it was for them.

Second, respondents reporting problems can be asked about their subsequent actions, including whether they complained to the nonprofit, spoke with friends, or took other actions. This would yield data on how well the organization's complaint-generation system was working. Those who complained to the organization could also be asked how this process turned out so that management could monitor the effectiveness of its complaint-handling operation.

Doer–Ex-Doer–Non-Doer Analysis

A useful way to track performance both for evaluations and control is to compare three groups. First, there are those currently performing as your campaign or the nonprofit intended. They continue to volunteer; they are repeat donors; their corporation stays involved in a partnership. Then there are the "ex-doers"—those who used to do each of these things but dropped out, often recently. Finally, there are the target audience members who did not act in the first place but should have. The latter could be those solicited for a gift or for participation in a cause-related marketing program or a volunteer event who did not follow through.

Comparison of the three groups—or at least the first and second—can be very illuminating in showing the nonprofit organization what it is doing well and what it needs to change. Did ex-doers find their experience unsatisfying or, worse, annoying or unpleasant? Is the case with non-doers that they say that you are simply missing ingredients that they were looking for? Finally, a comparison between doers and non-doers can suggest where the organization might be at risk of losing doers if programs are only marginally satisfactory on dimensions that appear to have driven non-doers away.

Relation Between Target Audience Member Satisfaction and Other Goals of the Organization

Many people believe that the marketing concept calls upon an organization to *maximize* the satisfaction of its target audience members. This, however, is not realistic, and it would be better to interpret the marketing concept as saying that the organization should strive to create a high level of satisfaction in its various target audience members about recommended behaviors, though not necessarily the maximum level. The reasons are several.

First, target audience member satisfaction can always be increased by accepting additional cost. Thus a university might hire better faculty, build better facilities, and charge lower tuition to increase the satisfaction of its students. Obviously, however, a university faces a cost constraint in trying to maximize the satisfaction of this particular public.

Second, the organization has to satisfy many publics. Increasing the satisfaction of one public might reduce the satisfaction available to another public. The organization owes each of its publics some specific level of satisfaction. Ultimately, the organization must operate on the philosophy that it is trying to satisfy the needs of different groups at levels that are acceptable to these groups within the constraints of its total resources. This is why the organization must systematically measure the levels of satisfaction expected by its different constituent publics and the current amounts they are, in fact, receiving.

The organization hopes to derive a number of benefits as a result of creating high satisfaction in its publics. First, the staff of the organization will work with a better sense of purpose and pride. Second, the organization creates loyal publics and this reduces the costs of market turnover, for example, among donors or volunteers. Third, the loyal publics say good things to others about the organization, which attracts new target audience members without requiring as much direct effort on the part of the organization.

Determining Causation

The social sector has a problem rarely found in the commercial world. In the latter, corporation marketers know when behaviors happen and—usually—whether their campaign (new ads) led to the recorded outcome (increased market share). In nonprofit campaigns, this is often far from the case. That is, it is often very hard to determine if a campaign is effective for the following reasons:

1. Outcomes may take a long time to appear—for example, developing lifetime healthy eating habits
2. Outcomes may not have observable indicators—for example, not smoking or not doing drugs
3. Typically, many (friendly) competitors are seeking similar behavioral outcomes—for example, reducing unsafe sex practices in HIV/AIDS campaigns
4. Target audiences may be unaware of which marketer caused which behavior

Experimental designs or cross-sector comparisons can often minimize these challenges.

COMPREHENSIVE MONITORING SYSTEMS

In recent years, several general tracking systems have been developed for nonprofit organization senior managers and staffers. One of the approaches, championed by Robert Kaplan, is called the Balanced Scorecard (BSC). In his work with the private sector, Kaplan was frustrated by the dominance of financial performance measures in business and believed that they neither told the full story of performance nor indicated how the company was improving itself to compete better in the future.[11] Kaplan later adapted the BSC to nonprofits.[12] The Balanced Scorecard recommends diagnostics that continually track four measures:[13]

1. Financial performance—Is the organization generating increased revenues? What sources are growing? Are competitors more effective with funding sources?
2. Target audience perceptions—How is the organization seen by key constituencies (clients, donors, volunteers)? What features of the organization are most critical to each group?
3. Core competencies—What should the organization be especially good at, and how is it performing? How are employee skills? What is turnover? Do partnerships add value or not?
4. Innovation—Is the organization improving its ability to provide new offerings, to do things in new ways? Are staffers encouraged to be innovative, to think outside the box?

In the commercial sector, financial performance is central. Stockholders are the key constituency. But in nonprofit organizations, finances are mainly an enabler. Further, financial performance is not always linked to performance on the mission. Funding may be subject to other factors and factors beyond the organization's control, for example, government appropriations decisions or the stock market. Other kinds of resource contributors such as volunteers and corporate partners may be equally important resources. Balance among the multiple resources is critical. The ideal balance will vary by organization and—often—over time.

Another challenge for the application of this approach is recognized by Kaplan. Nonprofit organizations have decisions to make about *whose* needs and wants are going to drive the organization. For years, the United Way considered its charities to be its major "customer group." The charities had social problems they needed to address and United Way strove to fund their ability to tackle them. In the 1990s, United Way switched to a target donor focus. They argued that, if they did not generate adequate and growing donations, the charities could not perform. Then, in the twenty-first century, the new CEO Brian Gallagher switched the focus a third time, saying that United Ways were really community organizations and they ought to focus on divining, sometimes shaping, and then meeting the community's needs. Its new campaign around "What Matters" carries out this new strategy (see Figure 19-2).

The mission and vision of United Way of America in 2006 is now the following:

MISSION
To improve lives by mobilizing the caring power of communities.

VISION
We will build a stronger America by mobilizing our communities to improve people's lives.

TO DO THIS WE WILL:
- Energize and inspire people to make a difference
- Craft human care agendas within and across our communities
- Build coalitions around these agendas

FIGURE 19-2   Community Needs Strategy

Source: Courtesy of United Way of America.

- Increase investments in these agendas by expanding and diversifying our own development efforts and supporting those of others
- Measure, communicate, and learn from the impact of our efforts
- Reflect the diversity of the communities we serve[14]

Another global tracking system that has been adopted by many nonprofit organizations is "the Dashboard"[15] that we saw KaBoom! using in our vignette at the start of the chapter. Blackbaud, a commercial organization that markets software to nonprofit organizations, offers a Performance Dashboard system. Its web site uses an automobile metaphor to describe its Information Edge System as:

"A flexible solution that can create a custom performance dashboard for your organization to help you monitor:

- **Fuel**
  Easily monitor revenue sources from fundraising campaigns and other events so you know how much can be invested in your mission programs
- **Speed**
  Assess the performance of your people and programs so you continue your successes and eliminate nonproductive activities
- **Signals**
  Empower your staff with accurate, up-to-date accountability measures to manage, track and analyze key performance indicators, so everyone is pulling in the same direction to meet your goals
- **Warning Lights**
  Set up simple warning signs to let you know when you fall short or surpass predetermined performance benchmarks"[16]

The notion of the Dashboard is that it is like that in an automobile. It is always visible, and it provides real-time (or as close as possible) measures of how the system is doing. These real-time data allow organizations to potentially adjust campaigns on the fly or step back and assess overall performance against longer term goals. Setting up the Dashboard and deciding what should be measured is, of course, a critical challenge that deserves wide involvement of those to be affected. Discussions about these issues (as with Balanced Scorecard issues) can be an extremely important organization-building exercise itself. Organizational conflicts can often be resolved, misperceptions identified, and staffers and other key resource people can come to agreements about where the organization is going.

EVALUATION: PROBLEMS AND SUGGESTIONS

Because nonprofit organizations are—at base—supported by the public through tax dollars, donations, grants, subsidies, and the like, they are routinely challenged to prove their merit. Are they making society a better place? Are they making progress on key issues? What can they say about their work that justifies their continued existence? Inevitably, this means that there must be some kind of public evaluation of the organization and its work. The BSC and Dashboard approaches help address the organizational competence and performance issues. However, it is important to both internal and external constituencies that specific campaigns and projects (e.g., a new web site or a new patient information base) be formally evaluated once completed.

Evaluation studies for organizations are very difficult to do for a number of reasons. The simplest evaluation model is one that takes a set of baseline measures on key variables and then revisits them when the campaign or project is completed. At the organization level, the equivalent would be annual reviews. There are a number of problems that such a seemingly sensible approach can evidence:

1. Environmental measures may be incomplete. For example, a study of economic programs in India may neglect to track the level of environmental hardships or tribal feuding which may explain disappointing outcomes to a much greater degree than any program element.
2. Competition may be ignored. Nonprofit organizations often do not like to think that they have competitors except when it comes to funding. But a program failure may be as much attributable to a parallel program's innovative approach and success as to the nonprofit's own actions.
3. Change may be observed but, as noted above, its cause or causes are unclear or hidden.

Robert Hornik has long studied the evaluation of social programs, particularly focusing on their educational and communications components. In a recent essay,[17] he reviewed a number of attempts to measure the impacts of health interventions and noted a number of challenges to explanations:

1. Some effects may simply be the result of historical trends. Declines in smoking rates in developed cultures today may be less due to specific health education programs and other interventions than to sweeping changes in social norms.
2. Campaigns may have their effects not by directly influencing target audiences but in changing those social norms through increased media coverage the campaign generated. In effect, the influence of the "Other" factor in the BCOS model dominates the Beliefs and Cost components.
3. Institutional policy changes separate from program components may affect change. For example, increased cigarette taxes in California and no-smoking ordinances and building restrictions may be the real cause of smoking declines. These may or may not be traceable to the nonprofit marketing campaign.
4. In a similar sense, changes in institutions may liberate behaviors. Thus if the activity and publicity surrounding a campaign leads to the city building a park or making streets safer, poor kids will exercise more and be less often obese. The target audiences already knew the Benefits and Costs and recognized (but maybe temporarily ignored) what Others wanted them to do but simply lacked Self-assurance because institutions really did not make the desired behavior easy. The behavior then became easier although institutional change was not a direct objective of the nonprofit organization.
5. Interventions themselves may simply not have been "large enough"—for example, the target audiences may not have had enough exposure to campaign elements for them

to have a result. This would not mean that the approach was basically faulty, only that expenditure levels and persistence over the long-term were simply inadequate.

Hornik's reflections suggest a number of factors that need to be monitored, such as seasonal trends and changes in norms, policies, and institutional structures. Evaluations should also find ways to assess whether there is a scale problem. A number of programs have made use of experimental designs at the community level to provide some of these answers. Doubling the budget in one community and halving it in another can provide some evidence as to whether *scale* is an issue. Such experiments were common in the HealthCom projects that focused on child health in developing countries in the 1980s.[18] These interventions allowed for a conclusion by Hornik that the level of exposure to messages is perhaps the strongest explanation for why some programs worked in some provinces in some countries and not in other provinces in the same or other countries. It may not be *what* the campaign did, but *how much* it did!

A COMMENT ABOUT GOVERNANCE AND ETHICS

A growing phenomenon in the nonprofit sector is the amount of public monitoring of the ethical behavior of organizations in the field.[19] This is partly a result of the recent scandals in the sector, but it is also a result of more and more outside organizations and philanthropists demanding measures of performance beyond just effectiveness and efficiency. Formal regulation is exercised by the Exempt Organizations Division of the Internal Revenue Service. Outside the government, the Better Business Bureau's standards (found at its web site, www.give.org) provide ethical and operational guidelines that are perhaps the most extensive. The Better Business Bureau describes its approach as follows:

> The BBB Wise Giving Alliance Standards for Charity Accountability were developed to assist donors in making sound giving decisions and to foster public confidence in charitable organizations. The standards seek to encourage fair and honest solicitation practices, to promote ethical conduct by charitable organizations and to advance support of philanthropy.

The Alliance sets out a detailed list of 18 standards for both behavior and reporting by charities in the following areas:

- Governance and Oversight
- Measuring Effectiveness
- Finances
- Fundraising and Informational Materials

The last-mentioned is of most relevance to marketers. The BBB specifically urges the dissemination—including through web sites—of accurate, truthful, and candid information; full and clear annual reports; and information on any cause-marketing alliances and how they benefit the charity. It also recommends careful attention to privacy concerns that might arise and urges the availability of effective compliance systems.

There are a number of other watchdog groups with which the nonprofit marketer should be familiar. These include:

Guidestar (www.guidestar.org)
Charity Watch (www.charitywatch.org)
Charity Navigator (www.charitynavigator.org)

These groups and the popular press are especially senstive to malfeasance from excessive salaries to wasteful spending on campaigns. They also pay attention to special treatment given to organization staff (e.g., loans at low interest) or non-arms-length contracting to friends and relatives.

And, of course, some nonprofit specific sectors have their own challenges and watchdogs. The most obvious example is the political arena. Here there are specific watchdog groups that track campaign spending and the truthfulness of political marketing. Among the sites involved are the following:

- Center for Public Integrity
- Judicial Watch
- Black Box Voting
- Citizens For Legitimate Government
- Free Speech in the USA
- FAIR—Fairness & Accuracy in Reporting
- Institute for Public Accuracy

Other sites tracking and evaluating on approaches through the media include:[20]

- Accuracy in Media—Conservative watchdog group for fairness, balance, and accuracy in news reporting.
- Adbusters—Foundation with the goal of changing the way society and the mass media interact.
- Alternative Media Watch—Media group showcasing underreported news stories and issues.
- American Journalism Review—National magazine covering all aspects of print, television, radio, and online media.
- Center for Media and Public Affairs—Nonpartisan, nonprofit research organization in Washington, D.C., conducting scientific studies of the news and entertainment media.
- Columbia Journalism Review—Publication serving as a watchdog of the press in all its forms.
- Fairness & Accuracy In Reporting (FAIR)—National media watchdog group advocating independence and criticism in journalism.
- Global Media Monitoring Project—A twice-a-decade study of the media's news coverage to be undertaken worldwide with the aim of documenting the participation and portrayal of men and women in the world's news media.
- Independent Press Councils (IPC)—Containing details of press councils that have successfully adapted the idea of self-regulation to their own cultural and political context, to facilitate the exchange of views and information, and to promote and support self-regulation.

- Media Monitors Network (MMN)—Nonprofit, non-partial, and non-political platform for serious media contributors and observers.
- Media Research Center—Conservative group founded to bring political balance to the news media and responsibility to the entertainment media.
- Media Talk—Wisconsin Public Radio show looking at current issues inside network television, cable, newspapers, magazines, the Internet, and radio. Hosted by Dave Berkman. Audio archives link included.
- Media Transparency—Watchdog organization tracing funding sources of many media and political organizations.
- Media Watch—Organization focusing on media literacy and the challenging of stereotypes commonly found in the media.
- Media Watch (ABC TV)—A leading forum for Australian media analysis. Summary, news, bungled stories, and viewable episodes of the weekly program, plus archive of previous coverage.
- MediaChannel.org—Nonprofit site dedicated to the political, social, and cultural impacts of the media.
- Morality in Media—Established in 1962 by Father Morton A. Hill, S.J. (1917–1985), to combat obscenity and to uphold decency standards in the media. MIM maintains the National Obscenity Law Center, a clearinghouse of legal materials on obscenity law.
- National Institute on Media and the Family—Providing research and education on the media's effect on families and children.
- On the Media—Site representing weekly, one-hour National Public Radio program devoted to media criticism and analysis.
- The Pew Research Center for the People & the Press—Independent opinion research group studying attitudes toward the press, politics and public policy issues.
- PR Watch—Investigative reporting on the practices of public relations and public affairs industry, from the Center for Media and Democracy.
- Project Censored—Locating stories about significant issues of which the public should be aware, but is not, for one reason or another.
- Stats—Weblog and articles highlight abuses of science and statistics regarding policy issues.
- Tyndall Report—Monitoring the American television networks' weekday nightly newscasts.

Some of these sites are unbiased and objective. However, observers should recognize and make allowances for the political biases of some of the sources.

Summary

Nonprofit managers must have in place carefully designed measurement systems in order to track organizational performance and make appropriate adjustments. There are two broad categories of control systems. Strategic control systems monitor the organization's environment, competitors, publics, strengths and weaknesses, and performance. Tactical control systems monitor day-to-day performance for the purposes of fine-tuning current marketing efforts. New comprehensive approaches such as the "Dashboard" and the Balanced Scorecard are now more commonly used.

Two types of tactical control systems are those that measure organization influence on behavior and those that measure target audience member satisfaction. Tracking of behavior requires formal monitoring systems. Panel studies are useful vehicles for accomplishing this. However, nonprofit organizations face major challenges in tracking many behavioral outcomes and linking them to organizational marketing.

Target audience member satisfaction should also be a major objective of all nonprofits. Complaint tracking systems provide one way of assessing this satisfaction over time. However, complaint measures are typically biased both as to the types of complaints and persons affected. Periodic direct surveys of target audience members do not suffer from these biases. They can measure satisfaction directly as simple ratings, indirectly as derived dissatisfaction, or as problems. Studies of problems can be particularly helpful if they also track performance of the organization's complaint-handling activities.

External evaluation is a growing concern for nonprofits in the twenty-first century. As the result of recent scandals involving charitable organizations, many media watchdogs and citizens groups are asking whether nonprofits are meeting their social responsibilities. One outgrowth of this increased scrutiny has been the rise of codes of ethical conduct. The Better Business Bureau has produced an extensive code that can serve as a model for many nonprofit organizations.

Questions

1. Your nonprofit provides support to nonprofit organzations in South Korea that help migrants from North Korea adjust, find homes, and find work. You worry that the Patriot Act may cause you to be targeted for prosecution for indirectly—or even directly—supporting "axis of evil" regimes. What mechanisms would you put in place to minimize your risk?

2. Your Girl Scout region has 348 troops spread throughout a three-state area. You want to set up a Dashboard system to track indicators that are important to both the regional office and to individual troop leaders. What components would you include?

3. You are conferring with your administrative assistant and notice on her screen an e-mail message to the person who is the supplier of cleaning and maintenance services to your three-state facilities. Since this is not an area of her responsibility, you ask what this is about. She says that it is a personal e-mail because the recipient is her cousin. This troubles you. What are the ethical issues here and what should you do next?

4. You run a soup kitchen and think that having some "client satisfaction" data would be very helpful in indicating which offerings are valuable and which are not. However, you recognize that many of your clients have low literacy skills and sometimes mental problems. In addition, you suspect that many will simply tell you that everything is great because they fear losing a service they might someday need. How would you proceed?

5. As the manager of the performing arts center in Des Moines, you would like to learn more about customer satisfaction that would someday allow you to segment audiences. What data would you collect and how? To what use would you put it?

Notes

1. Peter F. Drucker, "The Nonprofit Bottom Line," *NonProfit Times,* February 1994, pp. 44–45. See also Kevin P. Kearns, "The Strategic Management of Accountability in Nonprofit Organizations. An Analytical Framework," *Public Administration Review,* March/April 1994, pp. 185–192.

2. It is, of course, a personal ethical decision for the nonprofit marketing professional as to whether he or she wishes to use his or her

skills to bring about behaviors with questionable social outcomes. Marketing is a powerful set of tools. The nonprofit marketer must be careful to use them for good ends.

3. Alan R. Andreasen (Ed.), *Ethics in Social Marketing* (Washington, DC: Georgetown University Press, 2001).

4. Vicki G. Morwitz and Carol Pluzinski, "Do Polls Reflect Opinions or Do Opinions Reflect Polls? The Impact of Political Polling on Voters' Expectations, Preferences, and Behavior," *Journal of Consumer Research,* Vol. 23 (June 1996), pp. 53–67.

5. Kim Cleland, "Patient Power Over Hospitals Grows," *Advertising Age,* October 24, 1994, p. 46.

6. See Ralph E. Anderson, "Target Audience Member Dissatisfaction: The Effect of Disconfirmed Expectancy on Perceived Product Performance," *Journal of Marketing Research,* February 1973, pp. 38–44.

7. Timothy L. Keiningham and Terry Vavra, *The Customer Delight Principle: Exceeding Customers' Expectations for Bottom-Line Success* (New York: McGraw-Hill, 2001); Rakash Seth and Kirti Set, *Creating Customer Delight: The How and Why of Customer Relationship Management* (Thousand Oaks, CA: Sage Publications, 2005).

8. Technical Advisory Research Program (TARP), *Target Audience Member Complaint Handling in America: Final Report* (Washington, DC: U.S. Department of Health, Education and Welfare, 1979).

9. See Alan R. Andreasen and Arthur Best, "Target Audience Members Complain— Does Business Respond?" *Harvard Business Review,* July–August 1977, pp. 93–101.

10. It is, however, not uncommon for the typical pattern of responses to be more positive than negative or indifferent (the "yea saying" bias).

11. Robert S. Kaplan and David P. Norton, *Alignment: Using the Balanced Scorecard to Create Corporate Synergies* (Boston: Harvard Business School Publishing Corporation, 2006).

12. Robert S. Kaplan, *United Way of Southeastern New England* (Boston: Harvard Business School Case, 1997).

13. Paul R. Niven, *Balanced Scorecard Diagnostics: Maintaining Maximum Performance* (Hoboken, NJ: John Wiley & Sons Publishers, 2005).

14. http://national.unitedway.org/about/ missvis.cfm (retrieved October 26, 2006).

15. Debra E. Blum, "Checking the Dashboard," *The Chronicle of Philanthropy,* October 12, 2006, p. M-6.

16. www.blackbaud.com/products/intelligence/ dashboards.aspx (retrieved October 26, 2006).

17. Robert Hornik, "Introduction: Public Health Communication: Making Sense of Contradictory Evidence," in Robert Hornik (Ed.), *Public Health Communication: Evidence for Behavior Change* (Mahwah, NJ: Lawrence Erlbaum Associates, 2002), pp. 1–19.

18. Robert C. Hornik, Judith McDivitt, Susan Zimmicki, P. Stanley Yoder, Eduardo Contreras-Budge, Jeffrey McDowell, and Mark Rasmuson, "Communication in Support of Child Survival: Evidence and Explanations from Eight Countries," in Robert Hornik (Ed.), *Public Health Communication: Evidence for Behavior Change* (Mahwah, NJ: Lawrence Erlbaum Associates, 2002), pp. 197–217.

19. Robert O. Bothwell, "Trends in Self-Regulation and Transparency of Nonprofits in the U.S.," *The International Journal of Not-for-Profit Law,* Vol. 2, No. 3 (March 1900); Joel L. Fleishman, "Public Trust in Not-for-Profit Organizations and the Need for Regulatory Reform," in Charles Clotfelter and Thomas Ehrlich (Eds.), *Philanthropy and the Nonprofit Sector in a Changing America* (Bloomington: Indiana University Press, 1999); Regina E. Hertzlinger, "Can Public Trust in Nonprofits and Governments Be Restored?" *Harvard Business Review,* Vol. 74, No. 2 (March–April 1996), pp. 97–107.

20. http://dmoz.org/News/Media/Watchdogs/ (retrieved December 11, 2006).

Index